Social Welfare Policy for a Sustainable Future

Social Welfare Policy for a Sustainable Future

The U.S. in Global Context

Katherine S. van Wormer

University of Northern Iowa

Rosemary J. Link

Simpson College

Los Angeles | London | New Delhi
Singapore | Washington DC | Boston

Los Angeles | London | New Delhi
Singapore | Washington DC | Boston

FOR INFORMATION:

SAGE Publications, Inc.
2455 Teller Road
Thousand Oaks, California 91320
E-mail: order@sagepub.com

SAGE Publications Ltd.
1 Oliver's Yard
55 City Road
London EC1Y 1SP
United Kingdom

SAGE Publications India Pvt. Ltd.
B 1/I 1 Mohan Cooperative Industrial Area
Mathura Road, New Delhi 110 044
India

SAGE Publications Asia-Pacific Pte. Ltd.
3 Church Street
#10-04 Samsung Hub
Singapore 049483

Printed in the United States of America

A catalog record of this book is available from the Library of Congress.

ISBN: 978-1-4522-4031-2

This book is printed on acid-free paper.

Acquisitions Editor: Kassie Graves
Editorial Assistant: Carrie Montoya
Associate Digital Content Editor: Lucy Berbeo
Production Editor: Melanie Birdsall
Copy Editor: Grace Kluck
Typesetter: C&M Digitals (P) Ltd.
Proofreader: Ellen Brink
Cover Designer: Michael Dubowe
Marketing Manager: Shari Countryman

15 16 17 18 19 10 9 8 7 6 5 4 3 2 1

Brief Contents

Detailed Contents

Preface

Vision of the Text

Sustainability is an inspiring concept. It conjures up all sorts of images and even a color, which would have to be green—the color of nature, fresh and bountiful. As a season, it would be spring. When applied to social work, we have *green social work*, a new term introduced in the title of a recent environmentally based book by Lena Dominelli (2012).

Appropriately, therefore, the publishers of this book have chosen for its cover a globe tinged in various shades—from chartreuse and emerald to a deep forest green.

Young people everywhere have a burgeoning interest in sustainability. Today, colleges and universities across the United States, Canada, and the United Kingdom are at the forefront of the green movement. An environmental sustainability focus is seen in university building design, the sponsorship of interdisciplinary ecological research, the introduction of energy-saving initiatives, expanded curricular offerings to promote ecological awareness, and the training of a new generation of environmental leaders.

Sustainability is a highly versatile concept. Not only does it relate to the preservation of natural resources for future generations, but it also refers to policies necessary to meet the needs of the people at the present time. When applied to the social welfare system, the notion of sustainability links the social, economic, and environmental dimensions of human existence and leads us toward social justice considerations. As the profession that aims to enhance people's well-being and work toward social equality, social work has a vital role to play in the promotion of environmental rights and economic justice.

In common with other social work textbooks on social policy, our aim is to describe contemporary U.S. social welfare policies that impact social work practice and to analyze the success of such policies in meeting the needs of all the people. Following the basic values and ethics of social work, we consider areas in need of substantive change and strategies for effecting such change. A second, but not secondary, purpose in writing this text is to do something that no other book does at present—to examine U.S. social policy within the context of sustainability. Toward this end, we will show how caring for people is inextricably linked to caring for our natural habitat, and we will explore ways in which social welfare provisions maintain human life and livelihood. As we examine the delivery of health and mental health care services, we will remind ourselves to ask "To what extent are current policies sustainable or unsustainable?"

To get at the answers, a global perspective is essential. In this way, solutions that seem impractical or even impossible can be shown to be doable and cost-effective. An experiment in one part of the world can thus be emulated elsewhere if it works or rejected if turns out to be a failure. Never before has information concerning social and scientific discoveries traveled so fast, and never before have so many nations relied on communication of their findings through a common language—English—with instant translation possible across multiple languages through universally available computer programs.

Nations are interlinked today not only by means of instant communication but also by an ever-increasing flow of goods and investments. Virtually no part of the world today is immune from transnational economic forces, and international corporations along with the world banks often determine not only monetary policies in a given country but the shape of social welfare policies as well. Investment in capitalist enterprises is generally favored over investment in the people. International forces, in short, need to be understood as a part of our critical analysis of social welfare policies and in our shaping of proposals for change.

Consistent with a global perspective, our analysis of social policy is informed by an awareness that such policy is not shaped in a vacuum but reflects a nation's cultural ethos. A comparative approach helps explain why an approach that is feasible and productive in one country may not even be considered elsewhere. Still, cultural beliefs change over time, so a historical view can provide us with hope that intransigent attitudes may not be so intransigent after all.

A basic assumption of this book is that the first step toward impacting social policy is to learn the forces that sustain them and the barriers that have to be overcome to successfully advocate for change. Three key factors—cultural ideologies, economics, and political constraints—are viewed as integral to shaping and maintaining particular social welfare provisions. To provide some basic understanding of how the system works is an underlying goal of writing this text.

To achieve this mission, *Social Welfare Policy for a Sustainable Future* is divided into two major sections. Part I explores social policies within a theoretical and historical context. The U.S. social welfare system is discussed in terms of its structure and function. Chapters on environmental sustainability, social and economic globalization, poverty and inequality, and issues related to minority groups are included in this section.

Part II looks at the specific policies themselves, policies that are designed to meet human needs and/or for social control, such as child welfare policy, health care offerings, mental health policy, and care for older adults. Separate chapters are devoted to human rights and policy analysis and practice. Information on the social work profession and roles for social workers is infused throughout all the chapters.

Consistency With Council on Social Work Education Requirements

Given its international focus, this book helps fulfill the Council on Social Work Education (CSWE) requirement for students to achieve a global awareness in their studies. The countries chosen for a close focus are countries in which the authors have lived and worked: These are the United Kingdom and Norway. Boxed readings from writers on South Korea, Nicaragua, Zambia, and Ghana provide detailed information on those countries as well. The following statement is included in the 2015 CSWE Educational and Policy Accreditation Standards (2015) for undergraduate and graduate programming:

> The purpose of the social work profession is to promote human and community well-being. Guided by a person-in-environment framework, a global perspective, respect for human diversity, and knowledge based on scientific inquiry, the purpose of social work is actualized through its quest for social and economic justice, the prevention of conditions that limit human rights, the elimination of poverty, and the enhancement of the quality of life for all persons, locally and globally. (p. 1)

Social Welfare Policy for a Sustainable Future aids social work departments in meeting these goals by providing the policy analysis and international content in one source. Previously, a supplemental text would have to be used if such content was to be provided in the social welfare policy course. Now, there is a textbook that presents the basic facts on social welfare policy and policy analysis in the United States while placing the policies (e.g., health care provisions) within a global context.

This text also uniquely

- provides a sustainability focus (environmental and economic sustainability) in a textbook to be used for the core social work curriculum;
- evaluates government policies in terms of sustainable and unsustainable aspects;
- contains a focus on economic globalization and the conflict between corporate interests and policies designed to meet the needs of all the people;
- includes a chapter on the impact of human activities on the natural environment and forces of the natural environment on human life;
- incorporates biological content in a policy book through attention paid to health/mental health care as well as to human needs pertaining to access to clean air, water, and uncontaminated soil;
- draws parallels between the importance of cultural diversity in human life and biodiversity in plant and animal life;
- is informed by concepts not ordinarily found in other U.S. policy books, such as social exclusion, anti-oppressive policy analysis, harm reduction, restorative justice, and sustainability ethic; and
- includes personal narratives to bring home the human side of facts presented in relevant and meaningful ways.

The Book's Audience

Our book is designed for the generalist portion of the social work curriculum. This encompasses the junior and senior policy classes for undergraduate students and the first year, or foundation course, for graduate students who did not major in social work as undergraduates. To meet the needs and interests of this audience, we have made every effort to write in a readable, user-friendly style, and to emphasize memorable events in the evolution of social welfare and social work up to and including modern times.

The Sustainability Theme

Missing from the social work literature, as stated in the descriptions above, is a social work policy text that offers an international perspective in conjunction with a presentation of the basics of U.S. social welfare policy—the history, sociological aspects, and a focus on policies pertaining to dependent populations—persons in poverty, children, and the frail elderly. The most exciting piece of this book, in our opinion, however, is the choice of sustainability as the organizing theme.

The selection of this theme for the text is consistent with Nancy Mary's (2008) proposal for the development of a new paradigm of sustainable practice for social work. The focus of this model is on prevention, community development, and a recognition "that the natural environment is an integral part and the foundation of our world and must be sustained as a living and sacred part of our global social welfare" (p. 25).

The Learning Design

Included in this book are brief, dynamic boxed readings that make the subject matter come alive for the student. Some will be biographies, such as of social work pioneers Jane Addams, Katherine Kendall, and Sattareh Farman Farmaian. Others will be writings of social workers who have practiced abroad or who have successfully lobbied for the passage of a piece of legislation or who have confronted some aspect of injustice in the system.

At the end of each chapter we have included critical thinking, or thought questions, to help enhance the reading and direct the analysis of the content. To highlight the reading, we have selected from our personal files (and other sources) two or three photographs to include with each chapter.

A Note to Students

It is our hope that if you are a social work major, this book will give you an appreciation for a different and more activist side of social work than what you have seen before in your other classes (which likely focused on direct practice). And for students of all majors, we hope what you learn here will inspire you to want to become politically active, if you are not so already, and to advocate for the kinds of policies that will improve social conditions and thereby enhance social policy development.

A Note to the Instructor

A comprehensive instructor's manual with essay and multiple-choice exam questions, creative exercises, references to films, and other relevant resources is provided at study.sagepub.com/vanwormer. Additionally, PowerPoint® slides are available for lecture use.

Information on the Core Competencies

As an organizing framework, sustainability corresponds nicely with the requirements of the CSWE's (2015) most recent Educational Policy and Accreditation Standards. These standards require that students in accredited programs receive an education that prepares them for an understanding of how policies are formulated in order to engage in advocacy for the implementation of policies. For this text, in a separate format provided by SAGE Publications we have provided a breakdown by chapter and section of the placement of content related to the competencies as mandated by CSWE.

References

Council on Social Work Education. (2015). *Educational policy and accreditation standards*. Alexandria, VA: Author.

Dominelli, L. (2012). *Green social work*. Cambridge, England: Polity Press.

Mary, N. L. (2008). *Social work in a sustainable world*. Chicago, IL: Lyceum.

Acknowledgments

I (Katherine van Wormer) wish to acknowledge Kassie Graves, senior acquisitions editor, for her support and patience through this lengthy process, Peter Labella, developmental editor, for his helpful guidance and suggestions and many thanks to Melanie Birdsall for an outstanding job on the production. From this end, I'd like to thank my graduate assistant Whitni Warnke, whose proofreading and suggestions about the wording were very helpful. Finally, I owe a debt of thanks to my husband, Robert van Wormer, and son, Rupert van Wormer, for their photographic contributions.

SAGE gratefully acknowledges the contributions of the following contributors:

Stephanie Warnecke Adams, Eastern Kentucky University

Yolanda Meade Byrd, Winston Salem State University

Michel Coconis, Wright State University

K. Abel Knochel, Augsburg College

Shannon D. Mathews, Winston Salem State University

David J. Pate, Jr., University of Wisconsin-Milwaukee

Jacky Thomas, Eastern Kentucky University

*This book is dedicated to people
of courage across the world who are often
overlooked when accolades are given: environmental
activists; conscientious objectors everywhere; families
of murder victims who speak out against the death penalty;
survivors of sexual violence who take a public stand against
the treatment of victims; gay, lesbian, and transgender people
and their allies who advocate for justice; and above all, the people
who see themselves not as citizens of a particular nation or commonwealth
but, rather, as citizens of the world. There has been no time of greater
need for us to grasp the sense of being global citizens than now.*

PART I

FOUNDATIONS OF SOCIAL WELFARE POLICY

Social work scholar Bruce Jansson has aptly described the United States as a "reluctant social welfare state," by which he means reluctant to provide social services. The American welfare state seems even more reluctant today than it was when Jansson first used the term (in his book title) in 1992. What does this mean for our society? What can—and should—we do about it? In Part I of this book, we will look at the foundations of social welfare policy, exploring the realms of sociology, religion, history, environmental science, and economics in our search for answers. And we would have to include politics as well.

Our present-day social welfare system does not exist in a vacuum, of course. It has both global and temporal implications. In light of this, we will be looking at the U.S. social welfare system in a global context throughout the book. In addition, we will be looking at social policy through a sustainability perspective. Simply put, we need to form policies that not only address present-day problems but also act responsibly for future generations.

We draw on these concepts in Chapter 1. Following a brief introduction, this first chapter presents the basic concepts and definitions that we will need go forward. What are the major models and typologies used by social scientists to explain the functions of the social welfare system? What are the roles of leading economic theories and politics in shaping social welfare provisions? How can sustainability as a model, and as a concept, guide our understandings?

A study of conceptualizations and ideology alone is not enough, however, to get the whole picture. To really understand how major policy developments arise and fall, we need to study our history, from colonial times to the present day. We will focus on the key paradigm shifts and turning points that have formed the development of social welfare policy. In this look at the historical underpinnings of social welfare policy, we will touch on the evolution of sustainability concepts and movements as well.

Chapter 3, "Purpose and Structure of Social Welfare Policy," explores influential teachings from the major religions of the world to show the moral and cultural imperatives for religious bodies and other social organizations to meet the needs of the poor and the sick. We will examine the notion of *American exceptionalism* through the lens of the social welfare system and through the inequities in the distribution of resources. Following a consideration of values and ideology, we describe the workings of the most basic of the social welfare programs—for example, Medicare and Social Security—from a sustainability perspective.

Environmental sustainability within the context of social welfare policy is the subject of Chapter 4. The aim of this chapter is to expand social work's person-environment conceptualization with its focus on interactionism to encompass the interconnectedness of various life forms and the natural environment. From an economic, as well as environmental perspective, we examine the impact of corporate agriculture on meeting people's needs and look at the state of farming today. Implications for the social work profession are examined.

That economic sustainability is inextricably linked with environmental sustainability is a basic assumption of this book. It is also linked to oppression in its many forms. This comes through in Chapter 5, which explores poverty and inequality in U.S. society, and in Chapter 6, which documents the unjust treatment and oppression of minority groups.

Reference

Jansson, B. (2012). *The reluctant welfare state* (7th ed.). Belmont, CA: Brooks/Cole.

Social Work and Social Policy

A Sustainability Framework

I pledge allegiance to the earth, and to all life that it nourishes, all growing things, all species of animals, and all races of people. I promise to protect all life on our planet, to live in harmony with nature, and to share our resources justly, So that all people can live with dignity, in good health, and in peace.

—The Montessori Pledge

Definitions and Standards

Let's begin with the most basic questions—What is social policy, and why should we study it? And what does social policy have to do with social work anyway? For the time being we will define social policy as "the activities and principles of a society that . . . includes plans and programs in education, health care, crime and corrections, economic security, and social welfare" (Barker, 2014, p. 399).

Social workers require knowledge of social policy, number one, to fulfill their roles as social work professionals. According to the National Association of Social Workers (NASW; 2008) code of ethics, a major mission of social work is to "engage in social and political action" to help people meet their basic needs (2008, Standard 6.04a). Social workers additionally are urged to "promote policies that safeguard the rights of and confirm equity and social justice for all people" (Standard 6.04c).

In addition to the ethical considerations, there is also a practical side to the study of social policy. Learning about social welfare policy is every bit as practical for social workers, in fact, as is the knowledge acquired in the direct practice classes. Just as the skills courses teach students the basic counseling skills and prepare students to engage in crisis intervention, the policy part of the social work curriculum helps prepare students to have an impact on the field of social work practice at the macro-level. To this end, the social worker might work with local legislators on a specific piece of legislation, for example, to raise the standards for home health care workers or nursing home employees or, conversely, to organize people to oppose discriminatory measures such as the passage of anti-immigrant legislation. Policy practice might include studying community needs and applying for a state-funded grant to get those needs met.

The first step on the path toward effecting social action is to learn everything you can about the shaping of social policy, including developing a familiarity with the basic, most relevant concepts. The concepts and definitions introduced in this chapter provide a foundation for understanding the content of later chapters.

Yet as the opening epigraph of this chapter suggests, we live in an ecosystem, wherein, ideally, our national priorities take into consideration the rest of the planet's inhabitants. Our interconnectedness and responsibility for taking care of the earth's resources reflect the major theme of this book—sustainability.

Source: ©istockphoto.com/lynngrae.

The Iowa Prairie. One of the most diverse ecosystems in the world is found in what remains of the Midwest Prairie.

Sustainability is the notion that humans must live in harmony with one another and with other species while preserving our natural resources for future generations. The notion of sustainability is used to study economic and cultural as well as environmental practices. Across the span of human history, the impetus for sustainability has never been more front and center than it is today.

As the world grows forever smaller, unsustainable practices in one part of the world have a major impact globally. By the same token, we can learn from sustainable practices and policies. Consider the following news headlines that reveal our global interconnectedness:

- *New York Times*: "W.H.O. Chief Calls Ebola Outbreak 'Crisis for International Peace'" (Bruce, 2014)
- *Wall Street Journal*: "U.S. Stocks Weighed Down by China" (Dieterich, 2014)
- *Reuters*: "European Shares End Higher on Upbeat U.S. Company Results" (Prakash, 2014)
- *USA Today*: "Stocks Tumble on Renewed Bank Fears in Europe" (Shell, 2014)
- *New York Times*: "Borrowed Time on Disappearing Land: Rising Seas" (Harris, 2014)
- *Yorkshire Post*: "Agri-Science Finds Green Solutions to Global Hunger" (White, 2014)

As the preceding headlines show, our concern in this book on social policy is with economic and social as well as environmental sustainability. Given the reality of global interconnectedness of many of the social problems of the world, globalization is a major concern of this text as well. Let's take a closer look at sustainability and globalization and their implications for social welfare policy.

Sustainability

The concept of sustainability—meeting the needs of the present generation without compromising the ability of future generations to meet their needs (Brundtland, 1987)—has a long history. It has been central to agriculture, where the benefits of conservation of the natural resources are most obvious. The notion of sustainability is applied today to economic and social as well as to ecological components of society. A sustainability ethos alerts us to the future impact of present wasteful practices.

Consistent with the pervasive and dominant ideologies of laissez-faire politics, such practices include the continuing deforestation; mass production of farm animals; chemical pollution of the water, soil, and air; and economic mortgaging of our children's future. As citizens of the world, our increasing awareness of scarcity, of the fact that the earth's resources are not infinite, heightens our focus on sustainability. The ravages of perpetual war, refugee crises, and the impact of climate change associated with extreme natural disasters all alert us to the need for massive systemic change.

The now classic UN Brundtland Report, "Our Common Future," highlighted three fundamental components to sustainable development: environmental protection, economic growth, and social equity. According to the Brundtland (1987) United Nations document,

> As a system approaches ecological limits, inequalities sharpen. Thus when a watershed deteriorates, poor farmers suffer more because they cannot afford the same anti-erosion measures as richer farmers. When urban air quality deteriorates, the poor, in their more vulnerable areas, suffer more health damage than the rich, who usually live in more pristine neighborhoods. When mineral resources become depleted, late-comers to the industrialization process lose the benefits of low-cost supplies. Globally, wealthier nations are better placed financially and technologically to cope with the effects of possible climatic change. Hence, our inability to promote the common interest in sustainable development is often a product of the relative neglect of economic and social justice within and amongst nations. (chap. 2, Points 25, 26)

These words resonate today, and they make a good fit with the social justice and ecosystems emphases of social work. Accordingly, the sustainability concept is useful for practice at both micro- and macro-levels. Sustainability, like social work, requires thinking that is sensitive to the interactions among ecosystems, economics, and social and human development (Healy, 2008).

Social work programs today increasingly are offering courses in sustainable development or with a sustainability focus. For the 2010 CSWE (Council on Social Work Education) annual conference in Portland, Oregon, sustainability in social work was chosen as the basic theme. A major emphasis at the conference was on promotion of sustainability throughout the social work curriculum.

On the university campus, a surge in interest in sustainability is evidenced in a scanning of college catalogs. This interest ranges from architectural design to cafeteria food that is purchased from local organic farms and is reflected in a variety of course offerings. The substance of the curriculum parallels a heightened interest today in the future of our planet as well as ethical issues such as the purchase of products for sale to students that come from Latin American sweatshops. Warren Wilson College in North Carolina, for example, views itself as a living laboratory for sustainable practices; a sustainability focus, in fact, is infused throughout the entire curriculum. More examples from this sustainability movement on college campuses are provided in Chapter 4.

A major goal of the CSWE (2008) educational policy was to prepare students to "provide leadership in promoting sustainable changes in service delivery and practice to improve the quality of social services" (Educational Policy 2.1.9). To achieve such sustainability, Nancy Mary (2008) called for major shifts in our economic system, for a significant reduction in military spending matched by an increase in spending to better meet the needs of the people.

Table 1.1, developed by Smith-Osborne, Welch, and Salehin (2013), provides an interdisciplinary model for viewing sustainability principles. Note that the biodiversity, so central to environmental health is matched by social diversity in the community. Note also the emphasis on conservation and balance throughout the different systems.

Table 1.1 Comparison of Disciplinary Perspectives on Sustainability

Environmental	Economic	Engineering	Social
Biodiversity	Decentralization of production	Innovation in all aspects/levels of human/nature interaction	Diversity at micro-, meso-, and macro-levels of interaction
Natural cycling of energy sources, natural resources	Development of long-term systemic efficiencies	Emphasis on renewable energy sources	Transgenerational care for social and natural environments
Waste products reused in ecosystem	Development of renewable materials, waste reduction	Redesigning materials and production techniques toward renewal, waste, elimination	Development of attitudes, behavior, and values toward environment and desirable future
Balance between consumption and limitations of natural resources	Balance between supply and demand	Balance between energy input and output	Balance between material, social, and spiritual well-being

Source: Smith-Osborne, A., Welch, J., and Salehin, M. (2013, November 1). *A Place for Social Work in Interdisciplinary Global Sustainability.* Presentation at the Council on Social Work Education (CSWE) 59th Annual Program Meeting. Dallas, Texas. Printed with permission of Alexa Smith-Osborne.

In the following pages of this book, we will be concerned with three basic themes of sustainability: the natural environment (including food cultivation), the economic system (meeting basic needs through equitable social welfare policies), and the state of the social health of the people. These three elements are intertwined. In a flourishing ecosystem, the stress on short-term economic goals does not take precedence over considerations of environmental and social health. The priorities of a society are reflected in the social policies that prevail.

Social Policy From a Sustainability Perspective

One way to institute social justice in society and to lessen the extent of social inequality is through the shaping of progressive government programs or policies. Policies are generally thought of as written rules for organizations, small or large, to follow in addressing certain situations. Policy provides a road map that members of an organization, government, or city officials follow. One thinks, for example, of university admission standards and of immigration policy. But often, policies arise from tradition and do not exist in writing. Policy is thus closely intertwined with practice—that is, as long as the practice is followed (Graham, Swift, & Delaney, 2002).

Jansson (2012) defines policy as a goal-driven "collective strategy that addresses social problems" (p. 10). However, there are many collective strategies that address social problems that are not policies, such as a movement for civil rights or even a mass riot. Conversely, some policies are not collectively formulated, may not address problems, and may even cause problems.

And so we turn again to *The Social Work Dictionary* (Barker, 2014) for clarification. Barker distinguishes *policy* as that which guides an organization or government for action from *social policy*, which guides the whole society and relates to customs and values. Our interpretation of this difference in types of policies is that social policy is the macro term: You would not say "agency social policy"; you would say "agency policy," but you can have local or national policy as well. *Social policy* is defined by Barker in full as

> the activities and principles of a society that guide the way it intervenes in and regulates relationships among individuals, groups, communities, and social institutions. These principles and activities are the result of the society's values and customs and largely determine the distribution of resources and level of well-being of its people. Thus, social policy includes plans and programs in education, health care, crime and corrections, economic security, and social welfare made by governments, voluntary organizations, and the people in general. It also includes social perspectives that result in society's rewards and constraints. (p. 399)

Combining these two definitions—the social action, goal-directed focus of Jansson (2012) with the apolitical definition provided by the social work dictionary—we can view social policy within the context of social work as a standard to guide the process toward a progressive goal such as the alleviation of poverty. Two stages of the social policy process that are the most significant are policy analysis and policy implementation.

In social work, *policy practice* is practice concerned with policy changes in large systems. Ideally, this involves a series of orderly steps in the formulation and implementation of programs to solve social problems. Policy practice has its origins in the settlement house movement of the late 1800s. Participants in this movement, the most famous of which was Jane Addams, argued for making social change and policy reform central to the new profession of social work (Herrick, 2008). A broad array of economic and social policies affect social welfare, ranging from tax policy to educational policy (Herrick, 2008). Such policies can be gauged in terms of their effectiveness in meeting their goals. Interestingly, as we will see later in the history chapter, the earliest social workers in the Progressive Era were working toward the same kind of social reform policies that concern the social work profession today. The common ground is shaping a world in which all people get their basic needs met, working toward the principles of equality and social justice. The desired policies are those geared toward maintaining sustainability to promote health and human life.

Globalization

A concept closely related to sustainability is globalization. *Globalization,* as defined by Chapin (2011), "refers to the international economic, political, and social integration of the world's nations" (p. 134). In general usage, the term often simply refers to an interconnectedness of persons worldwide. It is useful to distinguish among communication, economic, and cultural aspects of globalization. Indeed, this is a term with a number of meanings depending on the context in which it is used and the ideological viewpoint represented.

Globalization has both positive and negative connotations. From a positive perspective, one marvels at the technological revolution and the wealth of information at one's fingertips. From the more commonly articulated negative viewpoint, we might consider the masses of desperate and powerless workers pitted against one another, competing globally in a no-win, perpetual "race to the bottom." Sweatshop wages and working conditions in the Global South are mirrored in industrialized nations through the experiences of many workers who earn below a living wage and through the ever-increasing gap in income levels between the top and the bottom.

The current globalization of the economy requires that social workers broaden their horizons and view many domestic social justice issues within a global framework (Polack, 2004). The fact that this concept is making great inroads in the social work literature is evidenced in a search of *Social Work Abstracts.* There are 193 abstracts listed as of May 2014, which is more than double the increase from nine years before. Significantly, the references tend to be very positive, related to social work intervention, or negative, related to economic policies and ideology.

The notion that the world is growing palpably smaller is a universal theme in socioeconomic literature. The impact of this commercial "flattening" of the world is seen not only in the blurring of trade and political barriers but also in the nature of crime, the passage and enforcement of transnational laws, the creation of economic refugees, and the victimization of women (Friedman, 2005; Stiglitz, 2007). Feminist theory recognizes that economic factors stemming from global competition play a part in the international exploitation of women's labor and the trade in girls' and women's bodies. The ubiquity of organized crime, terrorism, drug abuse, and the sex trade industry graphically illustrates the interconnectedness of nations in this regard.

The world banks—The International Monetary Fund (IMF), the World Bank, and the World Trade Organization (WTO)—are powerful institutions that help globalize free market capitalism through lending billions of dollars to industrializing nations under conditions that are almost draconian. Nobel Prize winner Joseph Stiglitz, former president of the World Bank, has revealed, based on firsthand knowledge and internal documents from his organization, that the policies of these international banking institutions were geared to benefit a small class of capitalists at the expense of the masses of the people. These lending institutions required that the nations that received the big loans open their doors to transnational corporations; they also must agree to export certain agricultural products and other natural resources. One of the worst aspects, from a social work perspective, is the requirement that the nations raise capital for business and pay back the loans by drastically reducing their social welfare programs. These World Bank mandates are euphemistically called *structural adjustment programs.*

The backdrop for any discussion of issues, such as economic recession or mass poverty, must include an analysis of the workings of the amazingly powerful and well-coordinated web that the multinational corporations and financial institutions have spun across the world. Political, military, and ideological powers have all come together in the service of global capitalism. And through global competition, it seems that the same forces are operating everywhere, creating great opportunities for some and horrendous suffering for those who are left without resources.

There are many excellent books to explain the workings of the global markets and how the world's wealth rests in the hands of a few. Facts contained in books such as the following are fueling a new economic awareness as they highlight the ever-increasing gap between the top 1% and the rest of the population: *The Rich and the Rest of Us: A Poverty Manifesto* by Tavis Smiley and Cornel West (2012); *The Price of Inequality: How Today's Divided Society Endangers Our Future* by Joseph Stiglitz (2013); *Capital in the 21st Century* by Thomas Piketty (2014); and *Pity the Billionaire: The Hard-Times Swindle and the Unlikely Comeback of the Right* by Thomas Frank (2012). From a social welfare standpoint, we recommend *Globalization, Social Justice, and the Helping Professions* edited by William Roth and Katharine Briar-Lawson (2011). Finally, from the top of the *New York Times* best-seller list, we recommend *A Fighting Chance* by Elizabeth Warren (2014).

Some knowledge of the dynamics of global markets is essential to discern some of the special challenges faced by welfare states and human services professionals. Such knowledge, as indicated by Roth and Roth (2011) is needed not only to recognize possibility but also to recognize the limitations of local action.

Lawson (2011) argues that globalization is not inherently problematic; new institutions must be invented and have the possibility of being invented through the use of our global imaginations and collaboration to confront the pervasive threats from transnational corporations. The key to such change, first of all, is increasing one's understanding of globalization processes and structures and how power can be acquired through the spread of knowledge and the tools of mass communication.

International Social Work Practice

Many professions today—for example, health care, business, and law—must come to grips with the consequences of economic and cultural globalization. This includes human migration, natural disasters, economic crises, war, human rights abuses, poverty, and contagious disease. Many schools of social work are emphasizing the relevance of world perspectives for everyday social work practice. An increasingly important aspect of international social work is the recognition that global issues and information are no longer a separate part of social work but influence the everyday interactions of social workers with their clients (Elliott & Segal, 2008). See Box 1.1 in which a social worker reflects on the eye-opening experience he had as a graduate student on a volunteer work trip in Nicaragua.

Source: Published with permission of Brandon Luke.

Brandon Luke Displays Art Work of Nicaraguan Child. Social work students volunteering to work with children of Nicaragua.

BOX 1.1 SOCIAL WORK FIELD VISIT TO NICARAGUA

Brandon Luke, MSW, Director of Social Services, Salvation Army's Quad Cities

I would have to say the major turning point in my life was my summer trip to Nicaragua. This trip was the first time in a long time that I had been out of the state, let alone the country! This amazing trip really turned out to be a real life changing event for me.

I had seen pictures of Nicaragua before I went on the trip and heard stories. Now I know where the saying "words just can't describe it" comes from. The intense heat, prostitution of teens, the smell of burning waste, and the constant noise of city chaos cannot be shown in pictures or stories.

It was overwhelming for me to experience what is known as a Third World country. I had never seen homes with no roof, children eating from the city dump and families who sell their children into prostitution to put food on the table. This was a whole new level of poverty that I had never seen in

(Continued)

(Continued)

my life. I believe that by taking this trip I have gained a whole new level of gratefulness.

We first visited a cotton mill that was run by the local residents. This cotton mill is important, because it provided fair wages to all residents working at the facility (unlike the local sweat shops nearby). The site was still under construction, so we all assisted with transporting gravel to the new cotton mill area and spreading it level once there. We then toured the facility and learned about all of the different products that are offered.

Once done at the cotton mill, we went to a local dump so that we could see how desperate many of the residents who live in Nicaragua really are. You could see trucks backing up and crowds of people and farm animals hoping to find something good. Many of the children walked through the dump without shoes on, and the smell was unbearable.

Next, we visited an orphanage that seemed to serve mostly single teen mothers. Many of these women had nowhere else to go, and they all really appreciated the orphanage for providing the services offered. We learned that many of the women living at the facility were victims of trafficking, or prostitution. While visiting the orphanage we helped by providing games and activities for the children, painting some of their buildings, and cleaning their tables. It was a very rewarding experience to spend time with the children and too see how important social services are—especially in a country with virtually no government support.

Last, we visited a community clinic. It was amazing to see the long line of clients requesting services and how many had walked miles hoping to receive services. Of course, not all of the clients could receive services, so they would come back day after day until they could be helped. The clinic grew many of their own herbal supplements, which proved to be extremely cost-effective, especially when there is virtually no operational budget. The clinic was run by doctors visiting on mission trips from all different countries.

We also did a good amount of sightseeing in Managua and Granada. This included zip-lining through the jungle canopy, climbing mountains, kayaking, and tasting the local cuisine. It was an amazing experience and left me with a new appreciation for how fortunate we are here in the United States.

Before going on this trip I never knew what the real difference was between wants and needs. I would think that I had to have a new video game, or I had to have that new iPod. After this experience, I learned that there is a great deal of difference between the two. Now I can see that there are so many things in our lives that we don't need; we just convince ourselves due to our materialistic lifestyles. I can now see my faults, and I believe that by being able to do this I can live a much more fulfilling life.

Source: Printed with permission of Brandon Luke.

Lynn Healy (2008) delineates four major dimensions of international social work practice. These are domestic practice and advocacy involving populations from foreign lands (e.g., refugees), professional exchanges and research on successfully used innovations from overseas, employment or volunteer work abroad, and international policy formulation and development through international organizations. Relevant to social policy, Healy states that globalization can be seen in the extent to which social welfare policies adopted in one country affect other countries. In some cases, the impetus for the homogenization comes from a regional association, such as the European Union, or a world banking establishment such as the IMF. More generally, forces of global economic competition and global markets support conservative trends toward reduced social welfare programming.

Worldview Versus World View

For creative, well-informed policymaking on the local or global level, a multi-cultural worldview is paramount. The term *worldview* denotes a perspective as in "the European versus the American worldview" (related to gun ownership, for example). *World view*, on the other hand, is the goal to obtain a vision that gets beyond ethnocentrism, a vision that is truly global in scope. In an earlier book by van Wormer (1997), *Social Welfare: A World View*, for example, the major objective was to critically examine social welfare issues from an international perspective. The comparative approach was chosen as the best way to reveal the uniqueness of the U.S. ideology regarding human needs and structural attempts to address those needs. In this book as well, we will view the shaping of social welfare policy within the context of North American value dimensions and within the context of universal values. The United Nations' (1948) Universal Declaration on Human Rights will serve as the guide to internationally agreed-upon values by members of "the human family" (Appendix A, this volume). The world view adopted in this book will make available to us a breadth of vision for considering policy proposals. Often a solution to a problem in one part of the world that seems to work, such as the restorative justice model, is adopted elsewhere, and it may become a legally sanctioned approach in the second country as well. This brings us to a discussion of social welfare and the social welfare state.

The Welfare State in the Face of Challenges

The word *welfare* comes from Middle English "well fare." According to *The Shorter Oxford English Dictionary* (2007), the term refers to well-being or happiness. An alternative meaning is an organized provision for the "basic (esp. physical and economic) well-being of needy members of a community; financial support for this." Being on welfare refers to "receiving financial assistance from the state for basic living needs" (p. 604).

When we think of social welfare, we are thinking more of a nation's system of programs and benefits to help people meet their basic needs. This concept can apply to almost any such arrangement offered by any country or state. There is no implied judgment. The term *welfare state* involves a judgment, however, because this is a level of achievement to which many nations presumably would aspire. "The bottom line," as Kennett (2004) suggests, "should be the guarantee of basic income protection to those resident in the society" (p. 128). This term is commonly used by social scientists from the Global North as a label for democratic nations that provide a safety net for people in need. Japan, as Kennett indicates, is the only non-Western society to be generally referred to as a social welfare state. However, others such as South Korea and the municipality of Hong Kong should also qualify.

According to *The Social Work Dictionary*, the definition of *welfare state* is "a nation or society that considers itself responsible for meeting the basic educational, health care, economic, and social security needs of its people" (Barker, 2014, p. 454). A definition that is highly useful and nonjudgmental.

Karger and Stoesz (2013) bring our attention to a troubling aspect of the structure of the social welfare state in the United States, the features of which militate against a major expansion of government, and in fact, have resulted in a retrenchment of public, nonprofit services. The number of human service corporations—for-profit firms providing social welfare through the marketplace—has risen substantially. Karger and Stoesz refer to the fragmented system that has arisen over the last several decades as a "mixed welfare economy" (p. 2). The burden of paying for record budget deficits related to excessive government spending has fallen on the middle and working classes and exacerbated the growing inequality. Today, the top-earning 20% of Americans received just under 60% of all income generated in the United States. This is the highest income gap between the rich and the poor ever recorded (Domhoff, 2013). Welfare state supporters decry the increasing income inequalities (the wealth inequality is even more striking) and see the steady flow of attacks on government programs by the society's elites, and the politicians who represent them, as a new form of class warfare.

A great deal of media attention has been paid recently to the publication (translation from the French) of Thomas Piketty's (2014) *Capital in the 21st Century*. Through the use of a plethora of charts and graphs and a scholarly review of history, Piketty documents the growth of inequality over the last three decades. Unless capitalism is regulated, he argues, the nation's wealth is likely to become even more concentrated in the hands of a few. A nation's economic growth, Piketty further suggests, is impaired when the rate of return on wealth (investments) is greater than the growth of the economic system as a whole. Critics such as Krugman (2014) attribute the success of Piketty's book to the way that it successfully demolishes the America-as-a-meritocracy myth or the belief held by conservatives that people achieve success on their own merits and that the system is just. In truth, this rise in inequality is a major threat to the welfare state.

"Au Revoir, Welfare State" is the title of a recent article in *Time* magazine that focuses on this "age of austerity" in Europe as in the United States (Schuman, 2011). In France, according to the article,

The welfare state—that political-economic concoction of extensive social spending, state protection and regulated capitalism—aids every French man, woman and child from the day of their birth to the time of their death. Family subsidies pay mothers to stay home to care for children or hire a nanny instead. Visits to the doctor are almost always free. (p. 2)

New austerity measures, however, are being introduced throughout much of Europe: in France where the retirement age was raised, in the United Kingdom where university tuition was increased, in Spain where bonuses for the birth of a child were eliminated, and in Italy where increases were made in health care fees (Schuman, 2011). The welfare state, in short, is under considerable threat as a series of economic crises creates a situation ripe for exploitation by external forces.

Naomi Klein's (2007) *The Shock Doctrine* convincingly establishes a connection between the occurrence of cataclysmic events such as terrorist attacks and natural disasters and the institutionalization of neoconservative initiated policy change. Following the mass destruction of New Orleans by Hurricane Katrina, the way was paved for free market proponents to work toward the closing of Charity Hospital, considered one of the best teaching hospitals in the country, and to shut down the whole public school system in favor of charter school developments. Public housing, similarly, was not allowed to come back.

The major crisis today, one that affects virtually every country, is economic indebtedness in connection with the growth of national deficits. This situation renders the individual nations at the mercy of the world lending institutions to mandate drastic reductions in social welfare spending. Today, the center of power, as Michael Reisch (2011), indicates, has shifted from the state to the big banks and the corporate sector. Human service organizations therefore must struggle to continue to serve the public in the midst of the "ongoing ideological attacks, the contraction of state-funded services, and the spread of regressive modes of taxation [which] have undermined public confidence in the state's potential to create effective services" (p. 2). In the neoliberal or free market, corporate-controlled society, social workers are at risk of becoming professionally marginalized. In their advocacy for people in need, their voices are effectively silenced.

The social work tradition is a proud one. The profession is rooted in two major developments that took place in the Progressive Era. First and most famously, the settlement house movement, founded by Jane Addams, engaged in such activities as promoting factory legislation, adequate wages and limited working hours, better housing, community sanitation, and employment services. This grassroots community organization is often contrasted with the Charity Organization Society movement (Haynes & Mickelson, 2010), which promoted the provision of direct services and social casework. The seeming polarization of these two approaches to helping the poor largely reflects the dual vision of the profession that is with us still. Yet as most social workers would agree, each aspect of the helping process—political advocacy and the provision of direct services—is as essential as the other.

According to the first and most basic of the ethical standards as spelled out in the NASW (2008) Code of Ethics, social workers' primary responsibility is to promote the well-being of clients (p. 7). In relation to social services delivery, this obligation encompasses activities that promote clients' access to social services, maximize their rights, and reduce obstacles to services (DuBois & Miley, 2010). Within social service agencies, social justice work entails working at the agency level to develop client-centered practices and the education of colleagues about social justice principles. With respect to social policy, social workers advocate changes or, in today's global economy, fight to maintain funding for the social services we currently have.

It is for a good reason that social work is known as the "policy-based profession." This phrase comes from a book title, *The Policy-Based Profession*, by Popple and Leighninger (2010). Note the use of the word *the* rather than *a* in Popple and Leighninger's book title. Although the legal profession is clearly policy based—at least when lawyers get involved in politics—when it comes to the helping professions, such as clinical psychology, family therapy, and mental health counseling, social work is the one for which policy issues hold the most resonance. Social work is unique in that it is the primary profession that works within the social welfare system, and it got its start, not in private therapy chambers but in the inner-urban community and settlement houses of Chicago. Social workers have been working with politicians from the earliest days of the profession, and the tradition of political advocacy is well with us still, even in the harshest of economic times. In fact, the very value of the social work degree relates to this political activity, to a large extent. NASW, both nationally and through local chapters, engages in lobbying to ensure the saliency of the social work profession and to improve social policy development to protect vulnerable people, for example, people with physical and mental disabilities. "Why does social work matter?" asks social worker Marianne Mallon (2012).

> It is the only profession whose mission is improving the well-being of individuals, families, and communities with a concurrent commitment to social justice and a respected code of ethics guiding its members to consider the environmental conditions that contribute to private and public problems in living. (p. 4)

Consider the following headlines from recent issues of the NASW newsletter—*NASW News*:

- "NASW Joins White House to Help Reduce Gun Violence" (Pace, 2013, p. 1)
- "NASW Staff, Members Join Marriage Equality Rally" (Pace, 2013, p. 6)
- "Briefing Focuses on Rights of Parents with Disabilities" (2013, p. 5)
- "Social Workers Protest NYPD's Stop-and-Frisk" (2014, p. 6)

It is not for nothing that social work is called a social justice and human rights profession. Social workers are social welfare advocates; only through knowledge of the system can they be effective advocates for their clients. And only through such knowledge of the system can they know why substantive change does not come easily, or may not even come at all.

Challenges to Social Welfare:
Power, Exploitation, and Unintended Consequences

THINKING SUSTAINABLY

The end of the Cold War in the early 1990s, with the collapse of the Soviet Union, was widely viewed as the triumph of capitalism over Communism. In the past 25 years however, the gap between the very wealthiest and the rest of the citizens in the United States has only widened. According to a 2013 study published by the Pew Research Center, current income inequality has not been this pronounced since 1928—the eve of the Great Depression.

The ever-increasing gap in economic inequality is considered to be unsustainable for a democratic society. The "American Dream" seems to have shifted to the desire for instant wealth. How might that desire be at odds with long-term, sustainable economic health for society as a whole? Does the great wealth accumulated by the super-rich truly "trickle down" to the middle and lower classes—and if not, what are the reasons for that, as well as the arguments for maintaining the status quo?

Power

To learn about social policy, we need to study power, how it is acquired and how it is used, often in conjunction with privilege—the privilege of being a member of the majority group within a certain category (privilege is discussed in some depth in Chapter 6). The classic definition of power to the sociologist is that provided by Max Weber (1920/1947): "*Power* is the probability that one actor within a social relationship will be in a position to carry out his own will despite resistance" (p. 152). Note the focus on relationship here; however, Weber also referred to the same power dynamics in the plural. Some people, he argued, desire power for economic reasons, but others like to have power for its own sake. We can take this definition one step further to infer that situations involving extreme power imbalances and the threat of negative consequences are associated with a sense of powerlessness on the part of the parties who are dominated by others. Consider the subordination of women, for example, in a patriarchal family or within the family system. Such subordination is associated with low self-esteem, anxiety, and dependency in many cases.

Power is not merely an attribute of individuals and groups but a function of control over resources. When power imbalances become extreme, exploitation of the weak by the strong is likely. Economic dominance by the strong over the weak is especially pronounced internationally. The privileged nations of the Global North are in a position to extort resources from debt-ridden nations in the Global South. Dominelli (2002) warns that the new economic ideology is guiding the planet into increasingly dangerous terrain of a predatory form of capitalism "which greedily ingests those who do not subscribe to its tenets" (p. 3).

Economic Exploitation

When historians look back on the present age, they are apt to single out the global economic crisis as a key defining event of the era. The reason is that so many other crises coalesce around economic shortfalls—for example, record budget deficits, conflict over spending priorities, and battles over depletion of natural resources. The political ramifications are grave, as conservatives and liberals propose conflicting solutions to the problem. In the United States, the proposed solutions focus on reducing government spending on social services, health care, and education. Social welfare programs that were once considered sacrosanct are now on the chopping block.

Practitioners in all of the helping professions are greatly affected by the budget cuts. Yet the need for mental health professionals and social welfare workers is greater than ever (Malia, 2012). Social workers increasingly are seeing clients who are suffering from the negative effects of a strained economy, including mass unemployment.

In his recent book, *Pity the Billionaire*, Thomas Frank (2012) marvels that for the first time in history, after a crash of capitalism, the public response has been to ask for more of the very thing that got us into trouble in the first place—a greater reliance on the free market to make things right. Frank's explanation is this: "The reborn Right has succeeded because of its idealism, not in spite of it" (p. 12). He addressed a similar issue in his earlier best seller, *What's the Matter With Kansas?* In that book, Frank (2004) sought answers for the paradox in which blue collar workers were voting with Wall Street business interests and against their own interests. The common bond between them was a kind of anti-intellectualism. This was a part of a "30-year backlash" against a supposedly liberal establishment. Right-wing politicians, moreover, attracted many low- to middle-income voters by railing against such side issues as same-sex marriage and abortion.

The Tea Party movement and Occupy Wall Street are two opposing mass movements related to the economy. The Tea Party movement channeled the people's anger to express disdain for government regulation and to trump the virtues of freedom. A countermovement, Occupy Wall Street, has also been successful in galvanizing the public, although

Source: Photo by Robert van Wormer.

Occupy Seattle. Protesters from the Occupy Wall Street movement carry signs outside a bank building.

a different public at that. Hundreds of "occupy" movements across the country have given voice to members of the silent majority—the 99%—who resent the deep economic inequality that pervades society. Much of the protest is directed at corporate interests that are redefining the goals of education, financing political campaigns, and threatening the planet. The "occupy" movements have spread the message far and wide that it will take massive mobilization to change the policies and institutions that create this inequality. Social workers, social work faculty, and students have been active participants in this movement.

Not only are people exploited for the sake of the capitalist system, but also the physical environment is exploited for the sake of immediate profits. Throughout the world, the destruction of vast areas of forest, the pollution of the air and already scarce fresh water sources are among the consequences of shameless prioritizing of economic development over sustainable development. Bringing about environmental justice and alleviation of the other injustices related to exploitation requires a placing of global priorities ahead of national or corporate interests.

In the United States, corporate power has grown exponentially over the past several decades. As a result of mergers, the major corporations in the United States increase their political clout to the extent that the government is controlled by the corporation rather than the other way around (Roth, 2011). Corporate strategies that have proven successful include: extensive payments to political campaigns, lobbying for lower tax rates at state and federal levels, employing skilled tax attorneys, writing the tax codes to their advantage, playing one state off against another for additional benefits, and controlling the media through advertisements. Nations in the Global South are thus even more vulnerable to the impacts of the transnational corporate power.

Unintended Consequences

Ameliorating conditions brought about by exploitation is no easy task. Policy is instituted based on certain expectations about outcome. Will poverty be alleviated? Will children get a better education? These are typical questions asked about a specific course of action. Ideally, to validate a course of action, pilot studies will be conducted by unaffiliated research teams and only after careful experimentation will nationwide policy changes be implemented. We will see that without this close scrutiny (and sometimes, even with it) the unintended consequences of a policy may be worse than the original problem. The war on drugs is a case in point—and some believe that the war on terror will prove to be as well. "First, do no harm" is a cautionary slogan for the medical and helping professions that we would do well to keep in mind.

Writing from a historical perspective in *That's Not What We Meant to Do: Reform and Its Unintended Consequences in Twentieth-Century America*, Gillon (2002) details some of the scientific and government spending follies of the last century. Among the examples he provides are, first from science, the use of antibiotics that helped spread and strengthen the bacteria they were intended to conquer, and the widespread planting of kudzu, the Japanese vine that promised to stem soil erosion yet swallowed whole forests in the United States South. Secondly, from a business standpoint, Gillon asks us to consider the introduction of the office computer that was expected to create a paperless office but has actually used more paper, not less. Finally, Gillon provides case studies of public welfare allotments, which he claims had a negative impact on work incentive; deinstitutionalization of mentally ill patients, many of whom ended up homeless or in prison; the abolition of affirmative action for college admission in California, which led to a decrease in admissions of non-Asian minorities into some state universities; immigration policies producing an influx of unskilled workers and their relatives; and campaign finance reform, which because of loopholes has increased the contaminating influence of corporate money on lawmakers.

What are the reasons for such fallacies? Gillon (2002) lists miscalculation due to poor planning, drastic changes based on media-generated moral indignation, a political culture hostile to state power, and just plain human error for the negative outcomes that plague society.

The global implications for the sustainability of our planet are often bound by such miscalculations (see Dominelli, 2012). The use of chemical pesticides and herbicides to combat certain pests can affect other animal and plant populations in a vastly more dangerous way. Negative effects are also being experienced in terms of human health, water pollution, and the natural selection of insects strong enough to have resistance to the chemicals used in pesticides. Use of pesticides to protect crops from insects illustrates how natural selection can operate to achieve the opposite result of what was intended. Because only the strongest of the insects survive to breed, ultimately a resistant strand of insects is produced. Parallel effects are seen in the use of antibiotics that eventually lose their power.

Attempts to control weeds have led to a serious decline in populations of monarch butterflies and bees due to the destruction of their food supply. Ironically, relatively new pesticides that had been welcomed as an environmental plus because they were thought to be less harmful to other wildlife than earlier versions seem to have produced a global decline in honeybees and bumblebees. The spray itself is thought to lead to disease in the bee populations.

Many of the examples of poorly thought-out environmental policies, such as a loosening of restrictions on pollution controls, are more a result of misplaced priorities rather than of well-intentioned policies or solutions that backfired. We are talking of the placing of short-term economic interests above public health concerns. Climate change, according to an extensive report from the British medical journal *The Lancet*, could be the biggest global health threat of the 21st century ("Managing the Health Effects of Climate Change," 2009). When we use fossil energies, such as coal, oil, or gas, we burn carbon, thus adding carbon dioxide into the atmosphere—about 20 billion tons per year worldwide. The indirect effects of climate change on water, food security, and extreme climatic events are likely to have a catastrophic impact on global health (Chapter 4). This is just one of many of the trends today affecting the social welfare worldwide. How, then, can the field of social work help define policies that will actually help people while at the same time sustain our world? Let's consider this question.

Social Welfare Policy and Social Work

At a time when social services are being downsized and even eliminated, involvement in the policymaking process is essential. The kind of policymaking we will be dealing with here is, of course, the shaping of policies to benefit *all* the people as opposed to the conservative notion that policies favoring the global corporations will produce a healthy economy that will benefit the masses. Other basic themes that are evident throughout the pages of this book are the following:

- The global exchange of information concerning successful strategies is an essential mission of social work.
- In accordance with the dictum "knowledge is power," the starting point for progressive policy development is an understanding of the dynamics of corporate control of politics and of the media.
- Powerful groups in the society play an important role in determining how differences are defined and which differences matter.
- Injustice and oppression are normal but not inevitable outcomes of power imbalances.
- Recognition of group differences and advocacy for ethnic-sensitive and gender-sensitive policies are essential to meeting the needs of vulnerable populations.
- The person-environment focus of social work must stress the importance of the natural as well as social environment.
- Environmental challenges are inextricably linked to social and economic inequalities.
- Just as biodiversity is important to healthy plant life so cultural diversity is enriching to social and political life.
- "What goes around comes around"; the promotion of unsustainable practices hurts the policymakers as well as marginalized populations in the long run.
- Social injustice and perceived differences in race, class, gender, sexual orientation, and so on, are linked.
- Reality is rarely dichotomous but more often exists on a continuum; similarly, there is no longer a clear division between the foreign and the domestic.
- A critical perspective and the ability to draw on what we call "our social work imagination" are essential to our quest for social policies that are economically and environmentally sustainable.
- Finally, social work matters.

Social work is founded upon an imperative to create social well-being through ethical responsibility, appreciation of diversity, and a regard for human rights. These principles resonate with the core themes of sustainability. Well-being, in a social work context, involves the coordination of social, economic, and environmental aspects of a community to enhance the quality of life (Smith-Osborne et al., 2013). Thinking sustainably draws on our intellectual resources, interdisciplinary knowledge, and challenges our social work imagination.

The need for collaborative communication is enhanced today through technological advances that bring all peoples of the world ever closer together and which bring social work trends and innovations from one part of the world to the doorstep of other parts of the world. For example, consider the rapid spread of knowledge concerning treatments for disease and other ailments.

From a negative standpoint, literature from the social sciences typically points to the impact of global competition on employment conditions and social welfare benefits. The standardization of policies in the global age is such that the harried service worker in rich nations may more closely identify with an average worker in a poor region of the world than with the bankers and CEOs in his or her own country. Social workers, according to an article in *NASW News* on recession fallout, may find themselves under heightened stress today as they navigate through new methods and try to adapt their programs to mandated changes (Malai, 2012). Trends toward managed care restrictions and privatization and consolidation for greater efficiency are universal trends.

Social workers are challenged as they see more clients today who have fallen on hard times through no fault of their own. Advocacy is the cornerstone of the social work profession, and Malai (2012) recommends that social workers raise their voices to keep programs and welfare aid from being cut even further. Because social work is the profession most closely linked with social welfare and with working with marginalized populations such as immigrants, the unemployed, and families who are homeless, a global perspective on personal troubles is paramount.

Source: Photo by Robert van Wormer.

Protest Against Racism. Social workers and social work educators were among the protesters in Bowling Green, Kentucky, following the acquittal of George Zimmerman, neighborhood guard, for the shooting of 17-year-old Trayvon Martin.

A pro-worker and union-rights protest in Madison, Wisconsin.

There are essential skills, as well as habits of heart and mind, that animate the profession of social work. Let's consider a few of them as an introduction.

Empowerment

Empowerment is a concept closely associated with the feminist movement and conscious-raising experiences for women. But the focus also has deep roots in social work practice and traditions. A multilevel construct that is applicable to individuals as well as to groups and community organizations, empowerment is both a process and an outcome. To facilitate empowerment, social workers integrate strategies at the personal level, helping clients draw on their strengths and inner resources when dealing with crisis situations. Parallel interventions are applied within the interpersonal and political realms.

Celebration of human diversity, the maintaining of a critical perspective, and promotion of social justice are all themes of empowerment and of social work practice generally. To counteract conditions of powerlessness, empowerment-based practice is widely used with vulnerable populations such as women and other minority groups (Parsons, 2008). Empowerment-oriented social workers typically rely on a strengths-based approach to help clients tap into their underlying strengths.

The strengths perspective, as Kirst-Ashman and Hull (2008) note, assumes that power resides in people and that social workers should do their best to promote empowerment by avoiding paternalistic behavior, refusing to label clients, and trusting clients to make appropriate decisions. A presumption of health over pathology and an emphasis on self-actualization and personal growth are key tenets of strengths-based approaches (see Saleebey, 2013).

Just as empowerment concepts have enriched feminist theory, so has feminist theory enriched empowerment practice theory, especially insofar as women's issues are concerned. The feminist and empowerment perspectives both view power and powerlessness—related to race, gender, and class—as central to the experiences of women in poverty and women of color. Empowerment theory views individual problems as arising not from personal deficits but from the failure of society to meet the needs of all the people (Gutiérrez & Lewis, 1999).

Some feminist social workers subscribe to a *feminist empowerment* approach. Central to this approach is the view that humans are unique, multifaceted beings with the potential to make a contribution to their communities (Kelley, 2011). This contribution can be made quietly or through the raising of public consciousness and networking, for example, through membership in self-help groups or specialized organizations.

From a positive standpoint, power can be a liberating force. Gaining a sense of personal power can be a first step in assuming personal responsibility for change and moving individuals and groups away from a sense of fatalism and in the direction of positive social action. Political empowerment can occur through activities such as lobbying politicians and mass media campaigns. Issues relevant to women in the throes of political and personal oppression include activities such as lobbying for victims'/survivors' rights, working toward legislative changes to protect single mothers on welfare from losing their benefits, and working to enhance affirmative action programs to increase the female-to-male ratio in male-dominated fields of employment.

Empowering practice begins by acknowledging that structural injustices have prevented many individuals and groups from receiving the treatment and resources to which they are entitled (van Wormer, Kaplan, & Juby, 2012). Empowerment practice, as Gutiérrez and Lewis (1999) suggest, requires social workers to be agents of change, to help people gain or regain power in their lives, and to work toward social justice at the societal level.

British, Canadian, and Australian schools of social work generally prefer the concept *anti-oppressive* in place of empowerment. Payne (2014) likens anti-oppressive practice to an empowerment approach because of its attention to power differentials in worker/client relationships and the need to help clients gain control of their lives. Workers, as Payne suggests, can avoid oppressing (and thereby empower) clients through partnership, client choice, and seeking to create changes in the agency and in wider systems that adversely affect clients.

The Social Work Imagination

Implicit in the development of strategies to maximize a people's sense of empowerment, as represented in the examples above, are the types of opportunities that social workers have to draw on their own fertile imaginations to help people emerge from an impasse. Whether working in an impoverished community or with an individual who is chronically unemployed, the challenges to the social worker are many. And because every situation is different, there is no distinct path to follow. Resourcefulness, then, is a key ingredient of effective social work practice.

Social work imagination is defined here as a suspension of disbelief in clients' capabilities, a kind of faith that if they work at it, even the most disreputable or downtrodden of clients can find some meaning in life. Such imagination challenges all our creative resources to discover, in collaboration with the client, what countless others may have overlooked, some obvious solution to a problem, perhaps, or some new way around a difficulty.

Social work as a profession, then, is sustained by an idealism as old as humankind, as members of the profession continue to advocate for the poor, the sick, and the oppressed. Some journals in the field devoted specifically to human rights and poverty issues are *Afillia: Journal of Women and Social Work*, *International Social Work*, *Journal of Gay/Lesbian Social Services*, *Journal of Multicultural Social Work*, *Journal of Ethnic and Cultural Diversity in Social Work*, and *Journal of Progressive Social Work*.

The quest for our social work imagination reaches back to the world of our inheritance, to our foremothers devoting their lives to community volunteer work and forward to a burgeoning new age of ecological awareness. By ecological awareness, we mean a sense of the synthesis, connectedness of things, in the face of pending environmental crises. Perhaps, in our wrestling with the twin realities of economic uncertainty and rapid climate change, we can recapture some of the courage and resourcefulness that has gone into making the field of social work what it is today.

Thinking Critically

Critical thinking concentrates on the process of reasoning and at times questions what others take for granted (Gambrill & Gibbs, 2009). In their workbook, *Critical Thinking for Helping Professionals*, Gambrill and Gibbs have devised numerous exercises that instructors can use to generate discussion and help students discover fallacies that range from claims in advertisements to studies of the effectiveness of certain treatment interventions. Critical thinking, in short, focuses on questioning beliefs and assumptions and not taking claims of facts at face value.

In their best-selling book, *Academically Adrift: Limited Learning on College Campuses*, sociologists Arum and Roksa (2011) researched the educational progress of over 2,000 undergraduates at 24 institutions. They found that almost half of college students showed no significant gains in critical thinking and complex reasoning skills after 4 years of college. Citing these findings, an editorial in *USA Today* by Lionel Beehner (2012) states the following:

> Today's college students are experts at pantomiming their classmates and professors. They can cram for tests and summarize books with gusto. But they are not learning to think critically. That involves more than just good memorization or math skills, but also a healthy skepticism and intuition to understanding the world around them. (p. A11)

In today's world, the emphasis is on efficiency, accountability, and the attainment of measurable and tangible skills. Critical thinking involves playing with ideas, lengthy debate of the issues, and activities that are enhanced by extensive reading and listening and that require much contemplation. But today's students are under considerable economic stress and time constraints as they are often forced to work at mindless jobs to meet the tuition costs at their universities. In terms of their career goals, they know that a tight job market puts a premium on the acquisition of marketable skills and obtaining degrees in applied rather than abstract fields of study. Faculty pressures parallel the pressures that the students are under. The values of efficiency and accountability dictate the way lectures are organized and delivered. The heavy use of student evaluations to determine the retention and promotion of faculty in turn encourages a teaching style that relies on the presentation of bulleted facts, use of PowerPoint® presentations, and handing out guidelines before the midterms and finals to enable students to do well on tests with a minimum amount of time spent mastering the material. The use of multiple-choice exams is efficient in terms of grading; the focus tends to be on factual content rather than critical analysis. The end result is that instead of poring over intellectually stimulating articles and books and questioning the basic theoretical hypotheses and arguments, faculty and students focus their efforts on achieving tangible goals to meet the contemporary demands of a highly competitive society.

Critical thinking is not about maintaining the status quo; it is about questioning. Some conservative groups, apparently, oppose the teaching of critical thinking concepts. The 2012 platform of the Texas Republican Party, for example, contains a number of provisions that caused concern among Texas academics. The relevant platform as cited by the *Inside Higher Ed* ("Texas GOP vs. Critical Thinking," 2012) website states, "We oppose the teaching of Higher Order Thinking Skills (HOTS) (values clarification), critical thinking skills and similar programs that are simply a relabeling of Outcome-Based Education (OBE) (mastery learning), which focus on behavior modification and have the purpose of challenging the student's fixed beliefs and undermining parental authority" (p. 1). Challenging fixed beliefs is integral to education, the literal meaning of which is "to lead out" (*Shorter Oxford English Dictionary*, 2007).

Feminist educator bell hooks (1994) articulates Freieran premises in terms of "teaching/learning to transgress" and critical thinking as "the primary element allowing the possibility of change" (p. 202). In the context of policy development, social justice can be pursued by means of constant critical scrutiny of existing social structures and knowledge about how power differentials and oppression characterize the experiences of various groups. The kind of critical thinking called for, as Gutiérrez and Lewis (1999) indicate, is not mere factual knowledge concerning specific group characteristics, such as familiarity with certain Indian tribal customs, for example. No, the goal of what Gutiérrez and Lewis refer to as "affective learning" embodies awareness of one's own prejudices and beliefs and of how one's worldview affects one's attitudes and behavior. Once we recognize how much our biases and presumptions (such as prioritizing occupational success over relationships) are culturally derived and relative, only then can we come to appreciate a worldview that is different from our own. And in knowing another culture, we can gain a sense of perspective about our own.

The goal of critical thinking is a generalized goal; it can be defined as the ability to put phenomena (whether problematic or just customary) in perspective. This goal is as applicable to the members of minority groups themselves (and realize that we are all members of various diverse categories) as to members of the mainstream population. To think critically, we need to be able to see parts of the whole—practitioners urge clients to partialize or break down problems into manageable parts. But we also must never lose sight of the whole (that is, the cultural rhythm or pattern) itself. In this way, thinking critically ties in with an outlook that is both global in scope and focused on issues of sustainability.

Adopting a Global and Sustainability Lens

To understand U.S. social policy, we need to discover in what ways it is different or unique. We need therefore to look across borders to view a range of approaches to global problems with which we are collectively concerned—poverty alleviation, mass immigration, depletion of natural resources, oppression of minority groups, crime control, and meeting the needs of the very young and the very old. With this broad, international perspective, we can discover what is doable and what is not as we begin to grasp the uniqueness of any one country's approach.

Consciousness of our global connectedness is a good example of macro-level critical thinking, the kind of thinking that is so crucial for our ultimate survival. Nancy Mary (2008) describes this ethos as a new paradigm of thinking—a holistic, systemic shift in approach, which entailed a move from modernism to sustainability. Such thinking incorporates all life forms, cooperation rather than individualism, and an understanding of the interactionism among physical, mental, and spiritual worlds. We may apply such critical scrutiny to national policies concerning family planning restrictions at home and abroad, for example, in light of an awareness of estimated population increases worldwide.

In some parts of the world, including a few places in the United States, students of social work are uniting with members of grassroots organizations to work among the poorest and most needy groups of society. Today in Chile, for example, and throughout Latin America, schools of social work are training their students in a collectivist consciousness and learning through the practice of dialog rather than a lecture format. The goal is individual and collective growth; the means is education designed to engage all participants in the process of personal and political transformation in their work with populations that are different from themselves.

Summary and Conclusion

Like most introductory textbook chapters, Chapter 1 deals broadly with issues of concepts, definitions, and theoretical assumptions. Concepts defined in this chapter are the rudiments of planning for social change, concepts such as *globalization, sustainability, welfare state, empowerment, critical thinking,* and *policy analysis.* The purpose of this chapter was to provide the reader with the theoretical tools needed for a genuinely historical and comparative understanding of U.S. social welfare policy. We also wanted to link the notion of sustainability to sound economic principles and to the need to preserve the physical environment for future generations.

To fulfill the social work profession's social justice mission for the 21st century, social workers need to be prepared to analyze current policies in terms of their global and regional origins and ramifications. Unlike social scientists and many other policy analysts, social workers often see firsthand the unintended consequences of social policies. By becoming politicized and organized, social workers can have a voice, albeit indirectly, in shaping policy. Cultural competence and empowerment counseling skills alone will not shape policy to reduce oppression. Confidence as well as competence is required, and the development of confidence comes with acquiring the tools needed to affect policy and achieve success.

The major threat to social work today, and this is true worldwide, does not come from within, it comes from the outside. It is the thrust toward privatization associated with subcontracting services; declassification of job requirements; the threat of agency layoffs; and a reduction in pay, benefits, and job security. The political war on welfare combined with a decline in skilled employment is also an assault on the profession most closely associated with social welfare. Meeting this challenge and still surviving as an established and respected profession will require tapping into the reservoir of our social work imagination (collectively and individually, historically and contemporarily) to salvage our integrity and our truth. For planning intervention strategies, practitioners will need to draw on their critical thinking skills to examine the relevant social welfare policies and the ideological bases on which they are shaped. These are topics for Chapter 2 under the section on privatization.

Critical Thinking Questions

1. Examine Table 1.1 and consider the importance of biodiversity in the environment (farming, for example). How does the concept of biodiversity relate to cultural diversity as it exists in social life?

2. Discuss the difference between *worldview* and *world view*. How do these concepts relate to the learning experience described by the student who did volunteer work in Nicaragua in Box 1.1?

3. Why have certain groups of people been more vulnerable to poverty, employment problems, and social exclusion than other groups in society? What are some of the forces that have sustained this?

4. The ever-increasing gap in economic inequality is considered to be unsustainable for a democratic society. In what ways is this inequality unsustainable?

5 How do you think social workers can draw on their imaginations and resourcefulness when working in the community to encourage community bonding? Draw on the concept of the social work imagination.

6. How does consciousness of our global connectedness relate to critical thinking at the macro-level?

7. Give examples of ethical dilemmas when the client's and social worker's cultural values come into conflict? How can such a dilemma be resolved?

8. Find illustrations from current news sources that show a prioritizing of economic development over sustainable development. How do the illustrations relate to economic concepts as discussed in this chapter?

9. What are some strategies, as suggested in this chapter, which the power elites of society use to manipulate working-class people to vote with them on economic issues?

10. Compare and contrast strategies and aims of the Tea Party movement with the Occupy Wall Street movement. How are these movements different in their approaches to effecting change?

11. What are some of the major challenges facing the social work profession related to the global market economy?

12. How is a general understanding of social policy initiatives crucial to members of the social work profession?

References

Arum, R., & Roksa, J. (2011). *Academically adrift: Limited learning on college campuses*. Chicago, IL: University of Chicago Press.

Barker, R. (2014). *The social work dictionary* (6th ed.). Washington, DC: National Association of Social Workers Press.

Beehner, L. (2012, May 10). Forget résumé padding: Stress critical thinking. *USA Today*, p. 11A.

Briefing focuses on rights of parents with disabilities. (2013). *NASW News*, p. 5.

Bruce, N. C. (2014, October 14). W.H.O. chief calls "crisis for international peace." *New York Times*. Retrieved from www.nytimes.com

Brundtland, G. H. (1987). United Nations document: Report of the World Commission On Our Common Future. New York, NY: United Nations.

Chapin, R. (2011). *Social policy for effective practice: A strengths approach* (2nd ed.). New York, NY: Routledge.

Council on Social Work Education. (2008). *Educational policy and accreditation standards*. Alexandria, VA: Author.

Dieterich, C. (2014, September 22). U.S. stocks weighed down by China. *Wall Street Journal*. Retrieved from http://online.wsj.com

Domhoff, G. W. (2013). *Who rules America? The triumph of the corporate rich*. New York, NY: McGraw-Hill.

Dominelli, L. (2002). *Anti-oppressive social work theory and practice*. Hampshire, England: Palgrave.

Dominelli, L. (2012). *Green social work*. Cambridge, England: Polity Press.

Dubois, B., & Miley, K. K. (2010). *Social work: An empowering profession* (7th ed.). Boston, MA: Allyn & Bacon.

Elliott, D., & Segal, U. (2008). International social work. In B. W. White (Ed.), *Comprehensive handbook of social work and social welfare: The profession of social work* (pp. 343–376). Hoboken, NJ: Wiley.

Frank, T. (2004). *What's the matter with Kansas? How conservatives won the heart of America*. New York, NY: Metropolitan Books.

Frank, T. (2012). *Pity the billionaire: The hard-times swindle and the unlikely comeback of the right*. New York, NY: Metropolitan Books.

Friedman, T. (2005). *The world is flat: A brief history of the 21st century.* New York, NY: Farrar, Straus & Giroux.

Gambrill, E., & Gibbs, I. (2009). *Critical thinking for helping professionals: A skill-based workbook* (3rd ed.). New York, NY: Oxford University Press.

Gillon, S. (2002). *That's not what we meant to do: Reform and its unintended consequences in twentieth-century America.* New York, NY: W. W. Norton

Graham, J., Swift, K., & Delaney, R. (2002). *Canadian social policy: An introduction* (Rev. ed.). Boston, MA: Prentice Hall.

Gutiérrez, L. M., & Lewis, E. A. (1999). Preface. In L. M. Gutiérrez & E. A. Lewis (Eds.), *Empowering women of color* (pp. xi–xix). New York, NY: Columbia University Press.

Harris, G. (2014, March 29). Borrowed time on disappearing land: Facing rising seas. *New York Times,* p. A1.

Haynes, K. S., & Mickelson, J. S. (2010). *Affecting social change: Social workers in the political arena* (7th ed.). Boston, MA: Prentice Hall

Healy, L. (2008). *International social work: Professional action in an interdependent world* (2nd ed.). New York, NY: Oxford University Press.

Herrick, J. (2008). Social policy: Overview. In T. Mizrahi & L. E. Davis (Eds.), *Encyclopedia of social work* (Vol. 2, pp. 61–66). New York, NY: Oxford University Press.

hooks, b. (1994). *Teaching to transgress: Education as the practice of freedom.* New York, NY: Routledge.

Jansson, B. S. (2012). *Becoming an effective policy advocate: From policy practice to social justice* (6th ed.). Belmont, CA: Cengage.

Johnson, C. (2003). *Blowback: The costs and consequences of American empire.* Berkley, CA: Owl Books.

Karger, H. J., & Stoesz D. (2013). *American social welfare policy: A pluralist approach.* Boston, MA: Pearson.

Kelley, P. (2011). Narrative theory and social work treatment. In F. Turner (Ed.), *Social work treatment: Interlocking theoretical approaches* (pp. 315–326). New York, NY: Free Press.

Kennett, P. (2004*). A handbook of comparative social policy.* Northampton, MA: Edward Elgar.

Kirst-Ashman, K., & Hull, G. (2008). *Generalist practice with organizations and communities* (5th ed.). Belmont, CA: Brooks/Cole.

Klein, N. (2007). *The shock doctrine: The rise of disaster capitalism.* New York, NY: Picador.

Krugman, P. (2014, April 28). The Piketty panic. *New York Times,* p. A19.

Lawson, H. A. (2011). Collaborative, democratic professionalism aimed at mobilizing citizens to address globalization's challenges and opportunities. In W. Roth, & K. Briar-Lawson (Eds.), *Globalization, social justice, and the helping professions* (pp. 39–67). Albany: State University of New York Press.

Malai, R. (2012, February). Social workers face new challenges. *NASW News, 57*(2), p. 4.

Mallon, M. (2012, March/April). Editor's note. *Social Work Today, 12*(2), p. 4.

Managing the health effects of climate change. (2009, May 13). *The Lancet.* Retrieved from www.thelancet.com/climate-change

Mary, N. (2008). *Social work in a sustainable world.* Chicago, IL: Lyceum.

National Association of Social Workers. (2008). *Code of ethics.* Washington, DC: Author.

Pace, P. R. (2013, March 8). NASW joins White House to help reduce gun violence. *NASW News,* p. 1.

Pace, P. R. (2013, May). NASW staff, members join marriage equality rally. *NASW News,* p. 6.

Parsons, R. (2008). Empowerment practice. In T. Mizrahi & L. E. Davis (Eds.), *Encyclopedia of social work* (20th ed., pp. 123–126). New York, NY: Oxford University Press.

Payne, M. (2014). *Modern social work theory* (4th ed.). Chicago, IL: Lyceum.

Piketty, T. (2014). *Capital in the 21st century*. Cambridge, MA: President and Fellows of Harvard College.

Polack, R. J. (2004). New challenges for social work in the 21st century. *Social Work, 49*, 281–290.

Popple, P., & Leighninger, L. (2010). *The policy-based profession: An introduction to social welfare policy analysis for social workers* (5th ed.). Boston, MA: Prentice-Hall.

Prakash, A. (2014, April 17). European shares end higher on upbeat U.S. company results. Retrieved from www.uk.reuters.com

Reisch, M. (2011, June 10). *Being a radical social worker in reactionary times*. Keynote address at the Washington, DC: 25th Anniversary Conference of the Social Welfare Action Alliance, Washington, DC.

Roth, W. (2011). Economics, transnational corporations, and social justice. In W. Roth & K. Briar-Lawson (Eds.), *Globalization, social justice, and the helping professions* (pp. 71–88). Albany: State University of New York Press.

Roth, W., & Briar-Lawson, K. (Eds.). (2011). *Globalization, social justice, and the helping professions*. Albany: State University of New York Press.

Roth, W., & Roth, W. (2011). Contextualizing the helping professions. In W. Roth & K. Briar-Lawson (Eds.), *Globalization, social justice, and the helping professions* (pp. 25–38). Albany: State University of New York Press.

Saleebey, D. (Ed.). (2013). *Introduction: power to the people. The strengths perspective in social work practice* (6th ed., pp. 1–23). Boston, MA: Pearson.

Schuman, M. (2011, November 28). Au revoir, welfare state. *Time*, pp. 1–6.

Shell, A. (2014, July 10). Stocks tumble on renewed bank fears in Europe. *USA Today*. Retrieved from www.usatoday.com

Shorter Oxford English Dictionary (11th ed.). (2007). Oxford, England: Oxford University Press.

Smith-Osborne, A., Welch, J., & Salehin, M. (2013, November 1). *A place for social work in interdisciplinary global sustainability*. Presentation at the Council on Social Work Education 59th Annual Program Meeting, Dallas, TX.

Social workers protest NYPD's stop-and-frisk. (2014, January). *NASW News*, p. 11.

Stiglitz, J. (2007). *Making globalization work*. New York, NY: W. W. Norton.

Texas GOP vs. critical thinking. (2012, June 29). *Inside Higher Ed*. Retrieved from www.inside highered.com

United Nations. (1948). *Universal declaration of human rights*, Resolution 217A (III). New York, NY: United Nations.

van Wormer, K. (1997). *Social welfare: A world view*. Chicago, IL: Nelson-Hall.

van Wormer, K., Kaplan, L., & Juby, C. (2012). *Confronting oppression, restoring justice: From policy analysis to social action*. Alexandria, VA: Council on Social Work Education.

Weber, M. (1947). *The theory of social and economic organization*. New York, NY: Oxford University Press. (Original work published 1920)

White, J. (2014, May 6). Agri-science finds green solutions to global hunger. *Yorkshire Post*. Retrieved from www.yorkshirepost.co.uk

2

Historical Foundations of Social Welfare Policy

We cannot escape history.

—Abraham Lincoln (1862)

History is much more than the accumulation of dates and facts. It also provides an understanding of social forces and how they come together in a particular time and place to bring about social change. In the United States, history from the standpoint of social policy is the story of progressive change and conservative backlash. It is also the story of traditional policies that are no longer acceptable to the masses or important to interest groups who allow them to expire or be rescinded. Change agents such as social workers need a familiarity with this history to know both the possibilities as well as the stumbling blocks, even as they recognize the uniqueness and intransigence of American ideology. This ideology is informed by a belief in individual liberty that paradoxically serves to support the liberation of minority groups but also their oppression. By the same token, it also serves to support both financial individual success and personal failure. Looming through the whole history of America, from the early colonial settlements to today's corporate-controlled society, is a faith in individual responsibility for one's own and one's family's well-being and a belief in the personal freedom to pursue one's dreams.

Nevertheless, each age has its own unique character reflected in the politics of the time. Just as ideology—the temper of the age—shapes history, so history has a strong effect on ideology. We will see how much so as we move forward in this chapter, as we examine all the shifts in value orientations, dominant perspectives, and voting patterns concerning how people at the margins should be treated and how social deviants should be tolerated or punished.

Some of our basic value orientations can be traced back to Europe in medieval times. This is where we will then start.

Feudalism set the tone for a class system in which most of the people were serfs who worked the land. Over time, new technologies threatened this system as each advance produced a crisis, often related to a reduced need for labor. Government policies were enacted to either remove the people from the land or require them to stay on the land, depending on the needs of the landowners. With the arrival of the Industrial Revolution, which came in the 1700s in Britain, the whole social structure was transformed; people flocked to work in the cities, and the government was forced to pass to new measures of social control.

U.S. history began in colonial days with collective rebellion and the writing of a Constitution that laid down principles as a cornerstone for social policies, many of which are still honored in the present day. States' rights related to the ownership of slaves became a major issue that resulted in the Civil War. And out of the wreckage of the Civil War, came federal laws to protect the former slaves. This marked the birth of the present public welfare system, inadequate and disorganized though it was.

Meanwhile, industrial advances transformed the landscape and the working life through urbanization and the exploitation of workers and children. Social work, the profession, is rooted in these developments as part of a societal response to the suffering of the masses. This period became known as the Progressive Era. World War I, however, effectively put an end to the thrust toward reform, and capitalism enjoyed a brief resurgence bolstered by an ideology that the wealth concentrated at the top would eventually trickle down to the social classes below. Then the banks failed; the Great Depression got under way, and the national belief system was shattered. The government introduced universal work programs and social work moved to center stage under the New Deal. World War II ushered in a new conservative era along with prosperity. The ideology shifted with the Civil Rights Movement in the 1960s and back again in the 1980s with the birth of neoliberalism, which wasn't liberal at all. This is American social welfare history in a nutshell.

Our viewpoint in telling the history of social policy is not to tell the history of the national leaders and policymakers but, like Howard Zinn (2003), to tell the history from the ground up, with attention to the impact of the social welfare of the ordinary people. In so doing, we hope to refrain from mythology. In the words of Zinn:

> The history of any country, presented as the history of a family, conceals fierce conflict of interest (sometimes exploding, most often repressed) between conquerors and conquered, masters and slaves, capitalists and workers, dominators and dominated in race and sex. And in a world of conflict, a world of victims and executioners, it is the job of thinking people, as Albert Camus suggested, not to be on the side of the executioners. (p. 10)

Feudalism and the Rise of Capitalism

Before the Norman Conquest in 1066, England was a rural land, a tribal society lacking in social organization. All this changed rapidly with the Norman invasion. The Normans, who spoke French, were descended from the Norsemen, or Vikings from Normandy, France, who established the tradition of serfdom, built castles, and redistributed land titles on a feudal basis to their followers (Dolgoff & Feldstein, 2012). It is important to note that the language we speak today with its abundance of French words, along with the English class system of nobility and privilege, are rooted in this foreign invasion.

Just like conquest, technology is a major catalyst for change; it affects productivity and the need for labor. Take the invention of the oxen-drawn plow: The plow put more land into production faster, which had an effect on the social institution of serfdom. Peasants no longer needed to till the land were displaced from their land as the owners enclosed their fields with hedges and filled them with sheep and other livestock. The buying and selling of land that ensued reinforced the removal of peasants from their homes and opened the door to capitalism. Jansson (2012) pinpoints the historic development of the use of paper money, coins, and precious metals as mediums of exchange. In a money economy, the dictates of the market began to determine the price of goods. So there you have it—the beginning of capitalism in England in the Middle Ages.

A major terror in this period of history was the plague. When the Black Death struck in 1348, a frantic populace went after minority groups with a vengeance—slaughtering Jews, Muslims, lepers, persons with disabilities, homosexuals, and women. Over the next 300 years, Jews and Muslims were scapegoated mercilessly and hundreds of thousands of women (e.g., older beggars) were accused of witchcraft and killed (Aberth, 2005; Day, 2009). The attack on beggars effectively released the public from its obligation to provide charity to the poor. Returning to the pestilence, the crisis led to a labor shortage.

To keep workers from getting the upper hand in a time when their bargaining power had increased, a special law was passed called the Statute of Laborers in 1349 (Kirst-Ashman, 2010). Begging was outlawed, except for those thought to be deserving—the poor and physically disabled. Peasants were now required to stay on the land and work as needed. This was a significant development, a distinction between persons who could expect to receive aid from the church and those who were deemed undeserving. Whereas England had a brutal policy of forcing peasants off the land when the landowners so wished and back on the land when their employers wished to restrict their mobility, in Sweden, the society's rulers transferred the land to peasant ownership (Bryson, 1992). These historical differences between the two countries remain fundamental to understanding the more positive attitudes of Swedish people toward government and the welfare state in the present day.

Although the Industrial Revolution was not to get under way until much later, the climate that produced the scientific discoveries was rooted in the crisis related to the loss of population during the devastation of the Black Death (Aberth, 2005). The decline in the number of workers spurred labor-saving inventions and paved the way for a more scientific outlook yet to come.

To sum up thus far, population shifts and new discoveries and technologies are inextricably linked, each having a bearing on the other. The tendency is for lawmakers to control the wealth and to have sufficient power to write laws to control the masses for their own benefit. We have not yet touched on religion and ideology, forces without the consideration of which social welfare history cannot even begin to be understood.

European countries were united under one religion and a pope in Rome who assumed awesome political as well as religious powers. This state of affairs might have continued indefinitely had it not been for Martin Luther's historic act of defiance. In 1517, in a state of agitation over corruption in the church, Luther nailed a list of Rome's abuses in his "95 Theses" to a church door in Germany. This simple act of rebellion was pivotal for both Europe and America in many ways. Out of one man's break with Rome came the Protestant reformation, a reform movement that can be considered by far the most important event for the growth of mercantilism, capitalism, and ultimately for social welfare itself (Day, 2009; Erikson, 1966).

Among the important influences of Luther's teachings was his introduction of the notion of vocation as a calling to do God's work in all things—whether as a member of the clergy or as a teacher, farmer, or laborer. This notion of a calling ultimately revolutionized the social system; it gave a meaning to work, which went beyond the work itself. As Dolgoff and Feldstein (2012) indicate, Luther's teachings improved the morale of laborers giving them a sense of duty in a long day's toil.

A second major change relevant to social welfare was the abolition of monasteries and convents. These social institutions had served the needy—including paupers, widows, and orphans—for centuries. In the future, the state would have to find a way to assume these functions.

The American Experience:
"Exceptionalism" and Its Discontents

While the rudiments of a modern social welfare system were being shaped in Britain, on the western side of the Atlantic Ocean, the religious dissenters set sail to unknown territory in hopes of setting up a religiously monolithic society. As one would expect, the settlers, being English, carried much of British culture and traditions over on the boat with them, and a sense of cultural superiority prevailed. Except for the Quakers, the early American settlers replicated the brutal policies of the European explorers in their dealings with the native inhabitants. Although they at first relied on friendly natives to help them through the severe winters, they soon took over the land they wanted, killing or enslaving the inhabitants (Zinn, 2003). The diseases the Europeans spread eventually wiped out much of the indigenous population.

Whereas the townships took responsibility for those thought to be the deserving poor, vagrants and those who harbored them were subject to prosecution. By 1636, as Phyllis Day (2012) notes, the colony of Massachusetts was placing the poor to work, and sometime later, towns were required to supply basic necessities to the needy. A carryover from the British poor laws, investigations were conducted to determine people's worthiness to receive poor relief. Later, there were even residency requirements. Day further brings our attention to developments in the use of institutions as social policies of social control. First there were almshouses and then workhouses, then houses of correction and penal institutions. People who showed signs of mental illness were often whipped to get the devils out of them and some were confined in mental asylums. From the 1600s through the early 1980s, two trends relevant to social policy can be identified: the first was the trend toward reliance on state rather than local authority; the second was the trend toward institutionalization as the answer to every social problem.

The American Revolution, which lasted seven years, was unlike European revolutions that followed in that it was about economic grievances and the desire for independence to make decisions concerning commerce and politics. It was not an overthrow of the government by a large class of landless peasants and therefore in its victory did not bring about any dramatic changes in the nation's social structure (Jansson, 2012). The significance of the revolution for the study of policy was that it ushered in an era of limited government in which the federal government's responsibility for social welfare was severely limited, and the framers of the Constitution followed suit. Slavery was not outlawed; there was no guarantee of the right to work or of humane care of the poor or even of free public education. In contrast, as Jansson indicates, the French Constitution did all of these things. However, the amendment process does give the United States Constitution some flexibility to evolve with changing circumstances (Jimenez, 2010). The first ten amendments, known as the Bill of Rights, provide for due process in a court of law and rights of the individual, but they do not provide for universal welfare protections.

The Protestant Ethic and American Exceptionalism

The German scholar, Max Weber in *The Protestant Ethic and the Spirit of Capitalism* (1905/1930) compared work productivity levels in Protestant and Catholic regions of Germany, and elsewhere, as evidence for his theory correlating Protestantism and capitalism. Protestantism emphasized the autonomy of the individual and repudiated dependence on the church, priesthood, and ritual, according to Weber. The qualities of self-discipline, hard work, and communal service were viewed as likely signs of salvation. Martin Luther's belief in work as a "calling" gave Protestantism a uniquely practical bent. John Calvin, who was Luther's counterpart in France, and later Switzerland, provided the first great systematic formulation of the Reformation faith. Taking Luther's argument one step further, Calvin introduced the notion of predestination into the Protestant vocabulary (Erikson, 1966). Predestination is the doctrine of God's election or choice of souls to salvation or damnation. The interpretation of predestination, carried by way of England and Scotland (through the preaching of John Knox) to America, was that those predestined to salvation could be identified in this life through the evidence of their wealth.

With its emphasis on individual achievement, frugality, and opportunity, the creed of Calvinism has very much affected the American character, even long after the direct religious connection was lost. For instance, the 18th-century inventor and atheist, Benjamin Franklin, espoused the principles of the Protestant work ethic in his often-cited sayings such as "early to bed, early to rise makes a man healthy, wealthy, and wise"; "the early bird catches the worm"; "time is money"; and "a penny saved is a penny earned."

American uniqueness, its exceptionalism, as social commentator Sarah Vowell (2008) states, is reflected today in the U.S. readiness to launch into "preemptive war in the name of spreading democracy in the Middle East" (p. 5). Her highly readable book on the Puritans, *The Wordy Shipmates* convincingly argues that it was not the pilgrims who arrived on the Mayflower who had such a lasting impact on America, in terms of values and belief systems, but rather the hundreds who arrived ten years later in 1630 with John Winthrop as one of the founders of the Massachusetts Bay Colony. His vision of the colony was eloquently expressed in his famous "City-Upon-a-Hill" speech. "We shall be as a City upon a Hill; The eyes of all people are upon us," he proclaimed (cited by Vowell, p. 69). In these words, we can trace the roots of American exceptionalism, as Vowell suggests. Winthrop's words themselves have been cited on important occasions by Presidents John Kennedy and Ronald Reagan, former Vice President Al Gore, and Supreme Justice Sandra Day O'Connor among others.

Eventually, the American colonies, with their different denominations, settled on a separation of state and church as a logical prevention of conflict. This is not to say, however, that the religious fervor of the early 1600s did not leave its mark.

Slavery and Indian Removal

The counterpart of the North American belief in salvation for the elect few (those who were "saved") is the sense of superiority over persons of other religions and cultures who did not worship the Christian God. In this, the Protestant religioeconomic creed fed a darker, less salutary force—the institution of slavery. With much land to be cultivated, there was a serious labor shortage. In the latter part of the 17th century, the settlers modeled the Europeans in Brazil and the Caribbean by establishing slavery in many of their colonies. One century later, between one-half and two-thirds of white immigrants were indentured servants who were bonded to their masters (Jansson, 2012). The mistreatment of these servants began, as it did with slaves, on the voyage over to America; the death toll was great as many died of starvation after the food ran out, and the spread of disease on the overcrowded ships was rampant (Zinn, 2003).

Indentured servants were also subject to abuse and exploitation. In fact, they could be bought and sold like slaves. They were contracted to work for five to seven years in exchange for passage to the New World; the masters had no incentive to maintain their health as their bondage was only temporary. After they completed their terms, they usually became tenant farmers and worked at low wages for landowners (Jansson, 2012). Unlike black slaves, however, they did get their freedom eventually, and their children were born free.

Before the Civil War, there were half a million free persons of African descent in the United States (and 4 million slaves); half of the freed slaves were in the South (Day, 2009). The free persons of color engaged in a considerable amount of charity work through churches and relief associations. In New Orleans, many of the free black males worked in highly skilled trades. Free blacks dominated such skilled trades as carpentry, masonry, and barrel making, and male slaves were highly skilled in these and other trades, such as bricklaying, painting, blacksmithing, shoemaking, and baking (Louisiana State Museum, 2012). Several free black and slave women plied their trade as seamstresses.

Slavery in North America operated in the absence of legal or cultural restraints; the slaves first and foremost were property. We should mention that in some parts of southern Louisiana and Latin America, the institution of slavery existed in a somewhat more benevolent form, softened under the teachings and traditions of Catholicism (see Gates, 2011; Mills, 2013) The paradox of slavery for the Catholics was that the slaves were both people and property. With regard to the Protestant ethic, the paradox was that the hard work in the service of wealth was performed by slaves while their carefree masters reaped all the benefits, presumably in the afterlife too. A third related paradox, noted by historian Kenneth Clark (1969) is that slavery was, in every sense of its being, contrary to Christian teaching.

And yet . . . scripture was quoted even by some Catholic priests whose religious orders owned slaves to condone the practice of slavery. A single religious text, as we know, can be used to serve diametrically opposed interests, both to condone slavery and to oppose it, as theologian Karen Armstrong (2008) indicates. And the same was true with racial segregation when it was institutionalized under law in the South.

Let us consider some relevant passages from the Bible. The 1611 King James Version of the Bible states, "Servants, obey in all things your masters according to the flesh: not with eye service as men pleasers, but in singleness of heart, fearing God" (Colossians 3:22). Later versions translated the word *servants* as *slaves* to better reflect the meaning of the term. The Old Testament, similarly, accepted slavery as a part of the social system in general, despite the celebration of Moses's leading the Hebrews out of slavery. The white slave owners cited the verses that supported their position, and the black slave preachers emphasized the Hebrews' escape into the promised land. This strategy of looking to religious doctrine for sanction for morally questionable practices has persisted to the present day and is not unique to Christianity (see Chapter 3).

American Indians received a different form of treatment—removal. In his *People's History*, Howard Zinn (2003) discusses in detail the policies under President Andrew Jackson that led to the forced removal of American Indians from the Southeast United States to western territories starting in 1830. The forces that led to what later would be known as the "Trail of Tears" did not come from the poor white farmers who were their neighbors but from the forces of industrialization and commerce, the growth of the populations and the rise in the values of the land. The removal of the Cherokees, who were the last tribe to be relocated, took place in the winter of 1838. Thousands died of the cold, disease, and hunger along the route to Oklahoma.

The Civil War and Its Aftermath

One of the great tragedies of American history was the death and destruction associated with the Civil War. It ended in the deaths of around 600,000 men, many of whom died from infectious diseases. Although it wound up as a war against slavery and tends to be remembered for freeing the slaves, the real issue, according to Day (2012), went beyond slavery—this was states' rights. This same issue has come up again and again when there is disagreement between federal laws and laws of the states, often as before, in the southern states.

Slavery was an emotional issue and captivated the consciousness of many, North and South. The power of the nationwide abolitionist movement should not be ignored, therefore, in providing the rationale for this horrific war. The abolitionist movement, according to Piven (2008), had multiple and intertwined roots and was sparked by the egalitarian ethos of the era. Moreover, the church denominations of the North played a central role. One small denomination that was especially influential was that of the Quakers. As the number of union sympathizers grew in the South, many Quaker families felt forced to move to the North. Their role was paradoxical in arousing sentiments for a war, in that the Friends, or Quakers, were pacifists and opposed to all wars. The conflict was movingly portrayed in the 1956 movie *Friendly Persuasion*.

Economic factors preventing compromise over the slave question were significant too. The plantation economy of the South was based on the sale of cotton nationally and internationally. The cotton trade, as we know, depended on slave labor "as cogs in the profit-making machine" (Piven, 2008, p. 112). As farmers in the Midwest, many of whom were immigrants, became a real force in agriculture, they feared competition from the slave labor in the South just as southern planters feared competition from the family farmers in the North.

The fact is, slavery was not sustainable and would have eventually died out, as new technologies reduced the need for the labor and as a nation sought workers who were educated and highly skilled. Most important, the buying and selling of humans, as if they were cattle, was not morally sustainable in a world that increasingly was concerned with individual rights. In any case, after the Civil War settled the matter by destroying the economy of the South to the extent that it would not recover for nearly 100 years, the nation did abolish slavery forever. Little thought was given, however, to the welfare of the former slaves or of the society in which they would live. The period of Reconstruction was brief, and not much was reconstructed. Ultimately, the southern system of feudal labor with black people divested of all political rights, would be restored and last until well into the 20th century (Piven, 2008). In the meantime, thousands of ex-slaves took to the roads, wandering aimlessly from county to county. It is safe to say that more families were broken up during the first year of freedom than by any year of slavery. Many others, however, stayed on the land and worked for their former owners as sharecroppers.

There are people alive today who grew up in this Jim Crow system. In *The Maid Narratives* (van Wormer, Jackson, & Sudduth, 2012), Mamie Johnson, who was born in 1922 in rural Mississippi,

Source: ©istockphoto.com/ConstanceMcGuire.

Picking Cotton in the Old Days. A system of feudalism sprang up following the Reconstruction Era in the South.

describes how her whole family—children included—barely eked out a living working sunup to sundown picking cotton:

> Now when these black people would live in them [small houses, sometimes ex-slave cabins], and I'm going to tell you, you can catch onto what I'm saying. These black people were living on this land for these sharecroppers. Well, you see, they lived there and they worked there. And when they worked there, you was supposed to be working on behalf of these landowners. They was supposed to be giving you half and he taking half. Well, you see, they never would let you have no book to see what they was giving you. See what I mean? Now, you know that was crooked, don't you? They was supposed to be sharecropping! When you raised that stuff [cotton] and he gets ready to sell it up with you, he was supposed to . . . have this book and pull it up and show you how much money he gone let you have and what you owe, and how much he got for this cotton. But he never would pull out no book!
>
> "So, Mr. Gullich, we want you to settle up, we need some clothes for our kids for Christmas and we want to know when you going settle up." We might say this to him, and then he'd say, "Well, I hadn't ever sold the cotton yet because it wasn't five cents and it wasn't the right price." Well, the workers would wait and wait. And I can remember one time, my daddy went up to the place to talk and get a settlement on their crop. But Mr. Gullich would tell him how much and the others how much they owed. "Next year," he'd say, "you'll do better. You'll do a little better next year." (pp. 79–80)

While the South remained largely agricultural for a long time, sweeping industrial activity resumed in the North following the Civil War. Americans, unlike the English who introduced the world to capitalism, took to capitalism with a passion unknown even in England (Jansson, 2012). Most Americans were small capitalists in their ownership of farms and investments in crops and commodities, such as pieces of clothing, which they exported to Europe. The American Industrial Revolution got under way much later than its British counterpart; it was based on coal, iron, and eventually electricity. To work in the mines and factories, immigrants flocked into the country to join the six million people who had come to America between 1820 and 1860 (Day, 2012). We will discuss the social welfare implications of all these developments shortly.

Nineteenth-Century Social Policies: The Church and the State

Because there were numerous religious sects in America to establish peace, the separation of church and state was a necessary response by the government to an otherwise volatile situation. The flourishing of so many dynamic sects and churches led to competition in providing help for the people in times of need, as well as for converts. Protestants established orphanages, reform schools, and mental hospitals. Quakers spent their time and resources helping southern slaves to escape before abolition while Catholic church groups devoted much attention to African Americans and American Indians, with a special focus on needy children (Day, 2009). The Ursuline Sisters played a major role in the settlement of New Orleans. Brought to New Orleans in 1727 from France, the nuns operated a hospital, established the nation's first orphanage, and founded a school for girls of European parentage, but they also helped educate under-privileged girls from all races (Arrigo, 2008).

Outdoor relief is a term used to refer to welfare aid provided to people in their own homes. *Indoor relief*, which was more common in the North where the work ethic was especially pronounced, forced the poor to move into almshouses and poorhouses (Jimenez, 2010). Poor persons, mostly women and children, were kept in local establishments where they were required to work, for example, spinning cotton, weaving, and shoemaking. Conditions generally were unsanitary and diseases spread rapidly. Because these places were unsustainable in solving the problems of the day, as well as a drain on city finances, the concept of indoor relief was abandoned in the early 20th century.

A major principle of poor relief borrowed from the British was the distinction between the deserving poor and the undeserving poor. Mentally ill persons were housed in poorhouses and later in insane asylums and prisons. When Dorothea Dix was invited to teach Sunday school at a women's prison in Boston, she was shocked to find mentally ill women locked in cages in appalling conditions (Colman, 2007). That was in 1841. Over the next few years, she conducted research into conditions facing persons with mental illness and traveled across the states visiting hundreds of institutions. Through a program of lobbying state legislatures and the United States Congress, she created the first generation of American mental asylums. When Dix tried to solve the problem at the federal level, however, and even though the bill to buy land to construct mental hospitals passed both houses of Congress, President Pierce vetoed the bill (Leighninger, 2012). This veto was significant because it was based on the argument that the states, not the federal government, should provide social welfare services (Dolgoff & Feldstein, 2012). By this act, a precedent was set that would be followed for the next 75 years.

The Reconstruction period was also a time of some welfare progress. Even before the Civil War was over, the needs of the people—civilians and war veterans—were great. Following the war, the needs of the former slaves were probably the most neglected needs of all the people. In 1865, the federal government established the Freedmen's Bureau as part of the War Department (Jansson, 2012). Goals of this bureau were to prevent civil disorder and provide temporary relief, help to reunite families that had been broken by slavery and to provide education, employment, and health care for the newly freed slaves. The Freedmen's Bureau failed to achieve its lofty goals for a number of reasons. For one thing, its position in the War Department ensured that its functions would only be temporary. Second, virtually no funding was provided to the new agency; it was assumed that philanthropy would be provided by Northern sympathizers to help the freed slaves. Although its work ended abruptly, the Freedmen's Bureau established an important precedent in its offering of comprehensive relief at the federal level during a national emergency.

Industrialization and Social Darwinism

The Industrial Revolution that swept England in the mid-1700s, arrived in the United States almost a century later and transformed the American landscape from a primarily agricultural nation to one primarily producing manufactured goods by 1900.

People, including the continuing influx of immigrants from Europe, flocked to the cities. Children worked alongside their parents in the factories under conditions that were life threatening.

The prevailing ideology of the era (the late 1800s) was social Darwinism. Social Darwinism applied the concept of survival of the fittest as a goal rather than a mere observation; it is generally considered a perversion of the evolutionary theory of Charles Darwin. Carried to extremes, this meant that because competition strengthens the species, subsidizing the poor would weaken the gene pool and therefore the society. Social Darwinism used pseudoscientific explanations to rationalize increasing socio-economic competition (Reisch, 2014). Laissez-faire economics made a good fit with this philosophy.

In Europe, in contrast, the seeds were being sown for programs that were universal in nature to provide social insurance for all. In Germany, an economic depression occurred that threatened the German government under the leadership of Chancellor Otto von Bismarck (a ruler who despised the teachings of the socialists). Bismarck introduced social legislation in hopes of undermining the campaign of the socialists (Otto von Bismarck, 2012). The social insurance scheme that was adopted provided old-age insurance and a form of socialized medicine. In 1884, accident insurance was made compulsory (Encyclopaedia Britannica, 1993). These benefits were to be financed through contributions by both employers and employees. A decade or so later, Austria, Sweden, and the Netherlands adopted similar programs.

Merging with the force of social Darwinism was the practice of Christian charity. When the same economic depression that affected Europe struck in the 1870s, and large numbers of people were thrown out of work, churches and private citizens set up soup kitchens and distributed fuel and clothing to the poor. Charity organization societies and settlement houses were established to provide formal, but voluntary, services to people in need. These early forms of social services emerged during the Progressive Era.

The Progressive Era (1900 to World War I)

Society's dominant ideology—whether the prevailing explanation for poverty is personal troubles or public issues or somewhere in-between—is reflected in the priorities of social work and its methods of treatment. Social work emerged during the Progressive Era, and during that time, as the name implies, the focus was on social reform. It was during this era that social work became synonymous with social welfare itself. As a reaction to the heartlessness that had characterized the preceding period, progressives campaigned against the ruthless practices of big business and advocated strong government regulation for the public good. There was even a Progressive Party, which was actively supported by the nation's most respected social workers, women reformers, and many intellectuals. As a result of pressure from this political party and the burgeoning socialists, impressive government reforms were enacted. Laws were passed to increase workers' rights, and many states established minimum wage and maximum working hours legislation. Poverty-stricken widows were granted mothers' pension (Day, 2012).

Social scientists and national leaders alike emphasized social, economic, and political factors that had to be taken into account in understanding social problems.

Concomitant with the reform-minded ethos of the Progressive Era was a growing conviction that individuals had the inherent capacity to achieve positive change through drawing on their own resources and on resources in their surroundings. The environment, therefore, was seen as both the cause and the healing agent of social problems.

The person-in-environment conceptual model that came to characterize social work is thus rooted in the profession's early history. Central to this history is the study of the evolution of two organizational movements that assumed the major share of responsibility for social welfare during the rapidly expanding Industrial Era: charity organization societies and settlement houses.

Charity Organization Societies

Patterned after the London Charity Organizations Society (COS), the development of COS in 1877 in Buffalo, New York, was implemented by an Episcopal minister, who was an Englishman by birth. COS's began as an effort to coordinate relief giving by operating community-wide registration bureaus to provide direct relief and education for the poor and needy. Friendly visitors had the task of investigating the circumstances that surrounded the applicants' needs and to attend to the "moral deficits" of poor families, as well as attend to their economic needs (Leighninger, 2012). The COS movement was built on the social Darwinistic principles that viewed the poor as being in need due to their own shortcomings. The public, according to Leighninger, viewed the COS as a kind of crusade to save the city from the evils of poverty. The success of the movement was evidenced in the fact that within 20 years virtually every large city in the country had a Charity Organization Society. Why, though, were the charity societies so successful?

Blau and Abramovitz (2010) point to the economic turmoil of the times, which would have boosted incentives to find better methods of ending pauperism. Trattner (1999) attributes the success of the COS movement to the organization's compatibility with the values of the day—emphasis on trust in science, belief in progress, and the belief that the poor needed moral supervision to help them combat such vices as intemperance, indolence, and improvidence. The "friendly visitors" were entrusted to investigate appeals for assistance, distinguish between the worthy and unworthy poor, and above all, provide the needy with the proper amount of moral exhortation (Trattner, 1999). COS workers (volunteers in the early days) were to become forerunners of today's social workers, and their methods (record keeping and counseling) anticipated social casework. To summarize, the COS emphasis was on outdoor (non-institutional) relief; the principles of Calvin, the work ethic, and social Darwinism guided their work. Not surprisingly, COS workers believed the source of poverty was located in the individual. Over time, however, as they gained experience with human suffering, the COS workers came to identify, to some extent, with their charges and then joined social action efforts to produce much needed change.

By the early 1900s, COS workers became increasingly aware that the abysmal urban conditions so rampant during this time could not simply be attributed to faulty character (van Wormer & Besthorn, 2011). Gradually, COS leaders began to acknowledge weaknesses in the friendly visiting model. In its place arose the belief that poverty was a function of environmental circumstances.

The Settlement House Movement

The second organizational movement that assumed a major share of responsibility for social welfare in the late 19th and early 20th centuries was the settlement house. Beginning in the late 1800s in England, the settlement house movement, such as that of the COS, was a response to the urban, industrial conditions of the times. Following a visit to Toynbee Hall in London in 1889, Jane Addams returned to Chicago to found with her associate and close friend, Ellen Starr, the American counterpart to Toynbee Hall at Hull House. Unlike the COS, however, settlements were expressly devoted to reforming society to reduce the hardships to the people, especially to the arriving immigrant populations from southern Europe. Following a theme of the liberal Progressive Era, the leaders of this movement believed that poverty could be eliminated. These leaders saw themselves as social reformers, rather than dispensers of charity. But they were also educators who focused on socializing new arrivals to the neighborhood in the norms of middle-class American society (Berg-Weger, 2013). With their goal to bridge the gap between classes and their emphasis on prevention rather than treatment, these workers lived in the same neighborhood as those with whom they worked. Together, they all participated in the life of the community and worked to improve the social conditions as well as to raise the cultural standards. Finding the lack of sanitation, absence of playgrounds for the children, lack of child care, and exploitation of workers unacceptable, the settlement workers became politicized and pursued social reform through legislation and social policy change (van Wormer & Besthorn, 2011). Within the walls of the settlements, the leaders provided a day nursery for working mothers, health clinics, and classes in dance, drama, art, and sewing. Even though women were not allowed to vote at the time, due to these reformers' advocacy and their universal respect by the public and political connections, they were able to bring about changes in child labor laws, in women's labor laws, and in the institutional care of persons with mental disabilities. The establishment of child welfare services and juvenile courts were other accomplishments that sprang out of this movement.

The Philosophical Basis of Social Work

The dualism that is evident in social work today between a focus on individual contributions to one's plight and an awareness of structural barriers to success is reminiscent of the dualism between the Charity Organization Societies and the settlement house movement. This early history of social work was pivotal to its developing conceptualizations of person and environment and of its linking the two into a person-in-environment conceptualization. The works and writings of their leaders, especially Mary Richmond and Jane Addams, established the parameters for social work's ongoing dual concern for both constructs (van Wormer & Besthorn, 2011).

Richmond's legacy is in the professionalization of social work. She embraced the use of social scientific research as a foundation for social casework, thus establishing a scientific foundation for social work practice (Leighninger, 2012) According to Lorenz (1994), the first school of social work was founded in Amsterdam in 1896 and owed its existence to philanthropy and the international settlement movement. Americans generally credit New York with having the first school of social work. Following calls for formal training, the New York Summer School of Applied Philanthropy in New York City was opened in 1898, a forerunner to the now prestigious Columbia School of Social Work. The foundation for the University of Chicago School of Social Service Administration was laid shortly after.

Parallel developments took place in England and Germany. The term *social work* was used for the first time in Germany (*Sozial Arbeid*) and was adopted by leaders of the American settlement movement (Lorenz, 1994). This term was consistent with the profession's historical origins. In Norway and Sweden, a specialized term is used for qualified social workers—*socionomer*—in addition to the broader term. In the United States, because social work is such a general term, sometimes it gets used incorrectly for nonprofessional workers, for example, child welfare workers or welfare workers.

By 1915, more than 300 settlement houses had been established, and most cities in the United States had at least one settlement house (Karger & Stoesz, 2013). At that time, there were 10 settlements that specifically served African Americans and at least a few more that reported having a mixed clientele (Leighninger, 2012).

As we reflect on the legacy of early social work practice before it was even called social work, we can trace many of the approaches and concerns of today in the philosophy and intervention of the pioneers. The empowerment perspective, central to social work practice today, was evidenced in the settlement house's reliance on this approach to help clients help themselves and to develop their self-efficacy. This perspective can also be traced back to the early workers' attempts to work through mayors and other political representatives to obtain the power to effect social change.

Ecosystems concepts, also central to social work theory today, can be said to have originated in the strong emphasis placed by the Hull House leaders on effecting improvements in the physical environment of the surrounding area. As Anastas (2012b) points out in a lead editorial in *NASW News*, social work's concern today with environmental justice and the need to combat environmental racism harks back to the Progressive Era when Jane Addams and Frances Perkins and others fought to improve neighborhood sanitation and workplace safety for all. In her recent visit to India, Anastas observed inspiring practices by social workers in setting up shelters for social services and working with patients' families to provide care for their mentally ill relatives.

Read Box 2.1, "Lessons From Hull House." This essay was written by social worker Laura Gale upon learning of the closing of the social services office at the Hull House that had served needy clients for 120 years. The closing of the agency marks the end of an era, according to an article in *NASW News* (Malai, 2012).

BOX 2.1 LESSONS FROM HULL HOUSE

Laura Gale, LCSW

My staff member knocks tentatively on my half-open office door, and I invite her in. I notice immediately the wide eyes and how she is twisting a strand of long brown hair around her finger.

"Is it true?" She asks.

"Will I lose my job? What about my clients? Sergio can't go without his medication, and Nancy just started with the behavioral aide it took us four months to line up. What would happen to them?"

I settle back in my chair. I've had this conversation before. Despite my best efforts to maintain an environment of safety for both my clients and my staff, rumors once again emerged. News stories of county and state budget cuts make their way into lunchtime conversations. Fears arise, and conversations like the one I am about to have must take place.

I have been fortunate. My organization has not had to shut down programs, pulling through each year by reducing costs and managing staff reductions through attrition rather than layoffs. We are the exception rather than the rule. Even established, respected institutions are having to make hard economic choices regarding which services to continue to offer and which to abandon to keep their doors open, as the recent closing and subsequent filing for bankruptcy of the Hull House Association in Chicago illustrates.

Founded by Jane Addams in 1889, Hull House provided social services to residents of Chicago for 122 years. In recent years, the agency focused services in the areas of foster care, domestic violence, and job training. At the time of closure, it employed more than 300 workers, and served over 60,000 clients in 50 programs at 40 sites throughout Chicago (Jane Addams Hull House Association, n.d.).

While rumors about mismanagement of funds began to circulate and fingers began to point regarding the agency's over-reliance on government funds, there is another lesson to be learned from this tragedy. The social work profession has forgotten about its role in advocating for social justice at the policy level.

It has been reported that 85% of Hull House funding came from various federal, state, and local grants and contracts, whereas only 10% came from unrestricted private donations. As a result, when government money dried up, the agency's revenues decreased by almost half, from a high of $40 million in the 1990s to $23 million (Wisniewski, 2012). The management of Hull House is being criticized for not diversifying its funding streams more effectively, and for not putting more emphasis on private donations.

But is reliance on unrestricted private funds and foundation grants any more reliable in tough economic times? Would Hull House have realistically been able to raise an additional $17 million to cover existing programs? Perhaps, but individuals and foundations are also struggling with limited funds. What is available is being stretched over the increased need for services that a poor economy stimulates, resulting in difficult dilemmas about who should receive services. When economic times become difficult and government money seems to be unavailable, it is easy to throw up our hands and blame the now struggling nonprofit for not seeing that the good times would end. Perhaps an additional approach would be to put pressure on local, state, and federal governments to increase commitment to social welfare programs in times of economic challenge.

When Jane Addams began her work at Hull House, she was an active fundraiser for her organization. However, she also involved herself heavily in the areas of political and social reform. She sat on the Chicago Board of Education, was a founding member of the American Civil Liberties Union (ACLU), and was a charter member of the National Association for the Advancement of Colored People (NAACP). She also campaigned heavily for Theodore Roosevelt and the Progressive Party, contributing to the eventual passage of the Social Security Act and the foundation for many of our government welfare programs today ("Women in History," n.d.).

Jane Addams understood the vital role that government funding needed to play in the provision of social services and was committed to engaging in policy advocacy work toward this end. It has been the habit of the social work field to shy away from macro practice in times of political conservatism and to focus heavily on micro work, waiting passively for the political and economic times to change before becoming involved in policy work once again. However, it is exactly in times of greatest economic and political challenge that social workers need to grab the public's attention and work to focus our political systems on the needs of our most disadvantaged citizens.

Through involvement in political campaigns, social workers can help ensure that progressive candidates who share our values of social justice and equality are voted into office. We can use the many easily accessible media outlets available today to educate the public about how the provision and funding of quality social services positively affects all of society. We can become aware of the policies that are being proposed in Congress every day that affect our clients, both positively and negatively, and work to ensure the passage of those that support our clients' best interests, including those that appropriate funds to important social issues.

(Continued)

(Continued)

So, perhaps the greatest lesson from the closure of Hull House is that the field of social work needs to recommit itself to macro-policy work. Yes, private money and the diversification of funding will always play a vital role in the sustainability of social service agencies, as will the sophisticated and skillful management of boards of directors and nonprofit administrators. However, without government commitment to adequate and timely payments to nonprofits, long-term sustainability will be difficult to achieve for many organizations. It is time to recommit to the work that Jane Addams so clearly understood—that social work is not just about meeting individual client needs; it is also about creating changes within systems that will have a radical impact on the quantity and quality of services our clients receive.

References

Jane Addams Hull House Association (n.d.). Who we serve. Retrieved from http://hull house.org/aboutus/whoweserve.html

Wisniewski, M. (2012, January 19). Chicago Hull House closing for lack of funds. Retrieved from www.reuters.com/article/2012/01/19/us-hullhouse-closing-idUS TRE80I2IQ20120119

Women in history. (n.d.). In *Jane Addams biography*. Retrieved from http://www.lkwdpl .org/wihohio/adda-jan.htm

Laura Gale, LCSW, is an adjunct lecturer for the University of Southern California School of Social Work Virtual Academic Center. She has 20 years of experience in the areas of nonprofit administration, clinical supervision, and social welfare policy.

Source: The New Social Worker, Spring 2012, *19*(2), pp. 18–19. All rights reserved. Reprinted with permission of Linda Grobman, Publisher/Editor.

The Backlash Against Social Reform

When World War I, which was billed as the war to end all wars, broke out, the liberal fervor for social reform came to an abrupt end. The mood of American culture after World War I, between 1917 and 1930, was much different from what it had been before (Trattner, 1999). Although western European nations had expanded social welfare provisons at this time, similar attempts in the U.S. failed. Americans generally lacked class consciousness and class-based political parties, for one reason (Reisch, 2014). States-rights sentiment was strong, for another. The end result was that the reform spirit of the prewar days was gone, largely replaced by growing self-absorption and scientific managerialism in the arena of public interest. Business ideologues endeavored to create a new popular faith in American capitalism and in the "American way" (Reisch, 2014; van Wormer & Besthorn, 2011). COS techniques were refined to provide a "social diagnosis" as the scientific basis for intervention (Karger & Stoesz, 2013). The emerging field of social work was shaped by a belief in the necessity to ground one's methods in science. This necessity had been driven home in 1915, according to Karger and Stoesz, by Abraham Flexner, a renowned authority on medical education. Social work was not a profession, Flexner had indicated, because it did not have autonomy and its own body of scientifically derived knowledge. Flexner's criticism was to have a decisive impact on social work for the following decades. Leaders turned to Freudian teachings for the body of knowledge that seemed to be lacking. This swing toward individualism was consistent with the ideology of the times. Progressive ideas seemed to have vanished, and activists were accused of being Communists (Karger & Stoesz, 2013). The leaders of the settlement house movement now were considered suspect due to their feminism and pacifism during the First World War (Kemp & Brandwien, 2010).

By the 1920s, social casework that was directed toward changing individuals to help them adjust to society grew rapidly in the family served agencies. These agencies were often run by men; increasingly, Freudian theory, which was now the dominant theoretical perspective, was clearly incompatible with feminist ideals (Kemp & Brandwein, 2010). Social workers now mainly worked for private agencies doing group work within settlement houses and the YMCA/YWCA (Leighninger, 2012). Only a short time before this, the first wave of feminism had made its mark after years of organized effort to win the vote for women (see Box 2.2). But now activist women found themselves repressed, given the dominant conservative ethos of the day.

Racism and Anti-Immigrant Legislation

Following Reconstruction in the South and perhaps related to economic recession, Jim Crow laws were passed to keep the races separate. This happened in state after state in the late 1880s. The paradox was the close intimacy in which the races were bound, especially white housewives and their maids who managed household affairs together and often formed close attachments. And yet they never socialized as equals (van Wormer et al., 2012). The races in the North were more fully separate, generally living in separate neighborhoods and attending separate schools. Racism was thus rampant in the United States during the years following World War I.

Other races also suffered from restrictive legislation, some direct and some indirect. "The yellow peril" was a phrase aimed at Chinese immigrants. The Chinese exclusion act was passed in 1882 to ban the immigration of ethnically Chinese people and to deny the right to citizenship to those already here (Cottle, 2012). Chinese men had been brought to America in large numbers to build the transcontinental railroad (Jimenez, 2010). They were not allowed to bring women with them and not allowed to marry whites. Many states banned interracial marriage in general.

BOX 2.2   JANE ADDAMS AND ALICE PAUL

Jane Addams, the mother of social work.

Jane Addams (1860–1935)

She had no children, but for those of us who are social workers, Jane Addams was the mother of us all. The social action focus, empathy for people in poverty, campaigning for human rights—these priorities of social work had their origins in the work and teachings of this remarkable woman. Unlike the "friendly visitors" before her, Addams came to realize, in her work with immigrants and the poor, that poverty stems not from character defects but from social conditions that need to be changed. From the vantage point of the Chicago Hull House, the most famous settlement house of her day, Addams addressed such issues as political corruption, child labor, urban sanitation, women's suffrage, and race relations. "We don't expect to change human nature," she said, "we people of peace, but we do expect human behavior."

By the turn of the century, Jane Addams was the most famous woman in America. By the culmination of her career in 1931, she was awarded the Nobel Peace Prize for her international work following the destruction in Europe in World War I. But during a major part of her life, she was neither honored nor beloved.

A Quaker by upbringing, she opposed war and military engagements her whole life. Because of her staunch pacifism during World War I—a position that branded her a subversive and radical for the rest of her life—Addams rapidly fell out of favor. Just as she had been universally acclaimed prior to the war, Addams experienced a fall from grace unparalleled among public figures in U.S. history (Knight, 2010). She was hounded by the FBI. She was even given the dubious honor of a life membership in the Daughters of the American Revolution and then subsequently was expelled.

Some historians and scholars present Addams as a woman who never knew love. Mary Rozet Smith, however, was her companion for most of her life

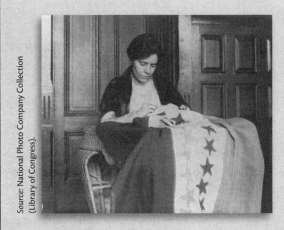

Source: National Photo Company Collection (Library of Congress).

Alice Paul sewing suffrage flag, 1922.

(Knight, 2010). During her day, unmarried women often paired off and developed intimate relationships; no questions would have been asked.

"If you are different from others, you need to act on that difference if society is to advance" (cited in Knight, p. 107): This statement by Jane Addams succinctly sums up her life. Her award of the Nobel Peace Prize at the age of 71 was a proud moment for social workers, Quakers, and women the world over. The story of Jane Addams is one that can inspire us all.

Alice Paul (1885–1977)

Alice Paul was known to Jane Addams from the women's suffrage movement. Like Addams, she was brought up in a Quaker family. Facts about the life of Alice Paul are well known due to the popularity of the 2004 movie, *Iron Jawed Angels* starring Hilary Swank as Alice Paul. In the movie we learn of her activities as a suffragist organizer of mass demonstrations and the civil disobedience and punishment she endured to help pass the 19th amendment for women's right to vote. (The romantic subplot was a sheer fabrication, however.)

What is less well known about Alice Paul is that she was one of the first graduates of the New York School of Applied Philanthropy and spent her early career working in both settlement houses and Charity Organization Societies. We have Hawranick, Doris, and Daugherty (2008) to thank for their article in *Affilia: Journal of Women and Social Work,* which fills a significant gap in the social work literature concerning Alice Paul's social work connections. Their article begins dramatically, with a spectacular march. Organized by Alice Paul, the parade of over 8,000 women was one of the most memorable mass demonstrations in history. This event took place in 1913 in Washington, D.C., on the day before Woodrow Wilson's inauguration as president. The president's gathering was unusually small because of this extraordinary women's parade that filled the streets. The parade of women dressed in costumed marching units and college women in their academic regalia was accompanied by 26 floats and six

(Continued)

(Continued)

bands. Immigrant women were dressed in their native costumes (Hawranick et al., 2008; Stevens & O'Hare, 1995). One reason the parade is remembered is that spectators began fighting and caused a riot. Hundreds ended up in the hospital. Washington had never seen anything the likes of this. And this militancy in America was just getting under way.

What had led Alice Paul and other suffragist leaders to this moment of carefully planned direct action? These women who represented the first wave of feminism had come to their prime in the Progressive Era, and they had been schooled in organizing social policy reform through the settlement house movement (Hawranick et al., 2008; Stevens & O'Hare, 1995). They had seen their advocacy for public health reform bear fruit, and they had seen their limitations as women in a male-dominated society. To secure more progressive social policy changes, women needed to have the vote. The birth of the women's suffrage movement, therefore, was in the settlement houses in the United States and England. Paul herself had practiced social work and learned of the extreme militant activism, hunger strikes, and passive resistance of the English suffragists (Hawranick et al., 2008). She was arrested, jailed, and tortured by forced feeding. And she brought all of these strategies of resistance back to the United States.

It was Woodrow Wilson himself who granted women the right to vote in 1920. After ratification by the states, many of the suffragists, such as Jane Addams, went no further in demanding women's rights. Alice Paul, however, graduated from law school and devoted the rest of her life to securing passage of an Equal Rights Amendment (ERA) to the Constitution. The ERA wasn't passed by Congress until 1972, but it was never ratified by the states.

As one of the most prominent and influential social workers of all time, Alice Paul deserves appropriate recognition by the social work profession. Her contribution fails to be acknowledged by the most recent edition of the NASW (National Association of Social Workers) *Encyclopedia of Social Work* or to my knowledge by any of the leading textbooks on social welfare policy. However, she was acknowledged in the Hawranick et al. (2008) article (which brought her social work training to my attention), and she is acknowledged here.

References

Hawranick, S., Doris, J., & Daugherty, R. (2008). Alice Paul: Activist, advocate, and one of ours. *Affilia: Journal of Women and Social Work, 23*(2), 190–196.

Knight, L. (2010). *Jane Addams: Spirit in action.* New York, NY: W. W. Norton.

Stevens, D., & O'Hare, C. (1995). *Jailed for freedom: American women win the vote.* Troutdale, OR: New Sage Press.

Legislation that discriminated against minority groups indirectly is particularly evident in the antidrug laws. This has been a theme throughout American history, to the present day. The drugs that are associated with a particular racial group in a particular time in history are apt to carry excessively harsh penalties.

When cocaine was widely used by middle- and upper-class whites, it was legal. After the turn of the 20th century, however, cocaine became identified with the urban underworld, and Southern blacks (Abadinsky, 2011). Fear of the effects of cocaine intensified until official regulation was inevitable.

The culmination of the fear of addiction and the association of the use of narcotics with the lower classes and foreigners culminated in the Harrison Act, which became law in 1914. The Harrison Act severely restricted the amount of opioids or cocaine in any remedy sold without a prescription (Maisto, Galizio, & Connors, 2011). It is important to note that this legislation related to the payment of taxes; enforcement was through the Treasury Department. Nevertheless, with the passage of this legislation, the criminalization process began in earnest (Robinson & Scherlen, 2014). Marijuana at this time was associated with Mexicans. In the early 20th century, in the United States, when anti-immigrant sentiment grew (associated with a wave of emigration to the American Southwest following the Mexican Revolution of 1910), rumors began to spread that Mexicans were distributing the "killer weed" to American schoolchildren (Schlosser, 1994). The drug was also associated with jazz musicians in New Orleans. Between 1914 and 1931, 29 states outlawed marijuana. The Marijuana Tax Act of 1937 essentially criminalized the possession of marijuana throughout the United States.

One technological development that turned society upside down and became a major threat to social stability was the distillation of alcohol. With the introduction of alcohol that was much stronger than wine or beer, tavern life thrived, and so did drunkenness in men. Protestant women organized to rescue family life and to outlaw strong liquor. Many of the suffragists were also active in the American temperance movement. The movement got more extreme over time and took on a decidedly anti-immigrant flavor. Instead of the target being liquor, the focus turned on the sorts of people who were the most prone to heavy drinking—the thousands upon thousands of immigrants to the United States from countries with their own drinking practices (Abadinsky, 2011). Large numbers of German immigrants consumed a tremendous amount of beer. Many Irish immigrants also brought their drinking habits with them. Unlike the Germans, the Irish were more tolerant of a pattern of regular intoxication.

The anti-immigrant and anti-Catholic nativism in the United States combined to give the temperance movement a new and fierce momentum. This fervor led to the passage of the 18th Amendment to the Constitution and established national Prohibition in 1919 (to begin in 1920). It was rescinded in 1933 during the Great Depression.

Welfare Policies During the Progressive Era

Herrick (2012) summarizes key social policies of an era in which the belief in social reform was strong. There was much advocacy, but a major stumbling block was the belief that it was unconstitutional for the state or federal governments to make laws providing protections for people, for example, limiting working hours to 10 hours daily. Special laws were passed, however, on behalf of women workers. This policy had a negative effect by limiting women's opportunities and confining them to certain kinds of work.

Somewhat more progress was made in the housing area where low cost housing was constructed; this established an important precedent for later New Deal subsidization of housing. Some progress was also made in child welfare, thanks to the efforts of Jane Addams and other settlement house workers. In 1912, a children's bureau was created to investigate conditions for children. Lobbyists were unsuccessful in their efforts to end child labor, given the general belief that business could not be regulated in any way. It took until 1930 before the states created some form of child protection laws.

A major development came after 1911 when mothers' or widows' pensions became available to prevent the children of widows from having to go to an orphanage. Widows were encouraged to give up their full-time jobs and stay home to care for their children. Divorced women were often denied the pensions and seen as unworthy to receive the aid in most states, as were the mothers of children born out of wedlock.

State intervention was readily accepted in one regard; this was insurance for workers' compensation. Businesses supported such laws, perhaps in fear of lawsuits for negligence toward the worker. Businesses and the general public, however, did not accept the idea of health insurance or of unemployment compensation. It would take a major crisis before Americans would question free market capitalism and accept having the government play a stronger role in human affairs. Such a crisis came with the Great Depression.

The Mid-20th Century: The Great Depression, the New Deal, and Beyond

The "Roaring '20s" ended with the uproar of the stock market crash of 1929. A trickle-down economic policy had seemed to be working with a mass market in consumer spending and plenty of work to go around. But after the crash, the banks were forced to close temporarily, and unemployment reached a high of 24%. The times were ripe for a complete paradigm shift as faith was broken in corporate control and capitalism.

Social workers, who now were doing group work and individual psychotherapy, gradually began to shift from a focus on curing individual defects back to an appreciation of the economic and social conditions that needed to be changed. Freudian ideas, as Leighninger (2012) indicates, were less salient.

In the midst of demonstrations, strikes, riots, and general national panic, the Democrats won the election and Franklin Roosevelt assumed the presidency in 1933. Major challenges to the Democrats came from radical political organizations such as that of the Communists and Huey Long of Louisiana with his *Share the Wealth* movement.

These challenges helped catapult Roosevelt into immediate corrective action. Much of what he got accomplished was in the first 100 days.

The Civilian Conservation Corps put people back to work immediately. At its peak, it employed 500,000 young people. They lived in camps, planted millions of trees, built tens of thousands of miles of roads, and gave help to people threatened by floods (Zinn, 2008). The Works Progress Administration (WPA) got started in 1934. Many public facilities that are still standing were built during this period. The WPA staffed clinics, preserved historic records, and even put writers to work interviewing ex-slaves to record their stories for posterity (van Wormer et al., 2012). All together, by the time it closed, the WPA employed 8.5 million Americans and changed the nature of the relationship between the national government and the states (Taylor, 2009).

Three professional social workers played active roles in shaping the New Deal legislation. These were Harry Hopkins, who headed the Emergency Relief Program; Jane Hoey, who headed the public assistance component; and Frances Perkins, the secretary of Labor (Jimenez, 2010; Leighninger, 2012). Hopkins, of Grinnell, Iowa, who had a strong background in child welfare, recruited professionally trained social workers to fill key positions. Hoey followed suit and stressed the hiring of qualified social workers in child welfare offices across the United States (Leighninger, 2012). Perkins was instrumental, along with Hopkins, in designing the Federal Emergency Relief Administration in 1933 and later the Social Security Act (Jimenez, 2010). During her career in politics she helped change the 58-hour work week for women to 48 hours, fought for a minimum wage law and unemployment benefits, and helped draft the National Labor Relations Act and the Fair Labor Standards Act.

Perkins's biography is interesting. When she came to the White House, she brought with her a background of firsthand social work experience working at the Hull House. She also had conducted research while a graduate student of economics and political science at Columbia University on industrial conditions and advocated for a shorter work week for women. *The Woman Behind the New Deal: The Life of Frances Perkins*, by Downey (2009), describes facts about Perkins's personal life. Here was a woman with deep family problems, including a husband with psychiatric problems, an estranged daughter, and a secret lesbian relationship, who was still able to rise to the occasion again and again to assume leadership positions as an advocate for progressive causes. As a member of the Roosevelt administration, through all his terms of office, Frances Perkins became one of the most influential women of the 20th century. In her role as secretary of Labor, she saw to it that talented, activist women were appointed to influential posts in the new government (Reisch & Andrews, 2002). In this way, many of the radical ideas of the Progressive Era got woven into the basic fabric of U.S. society under the New Deal.

The centerpiece of the New Deal was the Social Security Act, which was passed in 1935. Its most important component at that time was Old Age Assistance (now part of Supplemental Security Income), and unemployment compensation (Reisch, 2014). In addition, this act provided for retirement benefits, maternal and child welfare grants, aid to the blind, and Aid to Dependent Children (ADC). To help protect children and ensure that their parents could care for them, the ADC was established through funding from the states. Because the ADC was administered by the states, huge disparities arose regarding the disadvantages of blacks under the Jim Crow policies of the South. To understand the limitations of the Roosevelt administration's policies, it is important to understand that the passage of the new legislation depended on support from powerful Southern Democrats. No civil rights legislation could have been passed at this time, under the circumstances. And as Michael Reisch (2014) indicates, provisions in the Social Security Act bear the imprint of the southern congressmen in one important regard. This was the omission of farmworkers and domestic servants—both occupations dominated by African Americans—from coverage. The effect of the discrimination was that the social safety net that was developed benefited white, male industrial workers but not women or racial minorities.

The Social Security program and others of the New Deal will be described more fully in Chapter 3. For now, the important point is that these New Deal policies marked a reliance on the federal government to help alleviate suffering during the Great Depression. This reliance on the federal government was a complete reversal of previous policy that had basically left it up to people to fend for themselves or rely on private charity in times of need. This change never would have come about, as Frances Fox Piven (2008) explains, had it not been for the threat of mass social unrest and the power of well-organized groups representing the interests of poor people. Only during such a period of severe national crisis would the old ways be seen as not working and new ways be tried.

President Roosevelt delivered what has become known as the *Four Freedoms Speech* in his 1941 State of the Union address. His focus was on the right for everyone in the world to enjoy universal rights. These were freedom of speech and expression, freedom of every person to worship God in one's own way, freedom from want, and freedom from fear. No longer, as historians Alterman and Mattson (2012) suggest, would freedom be defined simply as protection from abusive powers of the government. These are positive freedoms. Roosevelt went even further in his 1944 State of the Union address and included the right of every worker to earn an adequate living, the right for every family to have a decent home, the right to protection from economic fears, and the right to a good education. To place these developments in chronological context with other events in social welfare and social work history, see Table 2.1.

World War II and the 1950s

World War II energized the American economy in a way the New Deal could not; it was actually the arms build up for involvement in the war that ended the Depression (Blau & Abramovitz, 2010). As with all wars, it also ushered in a conservative era that was a major setback for women. Following the war, America boomed while Europe faltered and was slowly recovering. The climate of opinion remained very conservative in the United States; segregation persisted in the South, and social work values were not always maintained by social workers.

Table 2.1 Later Milestones in Social Welfare and Social Work History

1750–1850: The Industrial Revolution occurs.
1769: The steam engine is invented and migration to cities for factory work occurs.
1776: Adam Smith publishes *The Wealth of Nations*, which promotes ideas of competition and the free market as beneficial for society.
1776: The Declaration of Independence by American colonies is adopted by the Continental Congress.
1788: The Constitution is ratified by the states and joined by the Bill of Rights, which was ratified several years later.
1800: London's population reaches one million.
1834: The New Poor Law imposes restrictions on the poor who are sent to workhouses; the principle of less eligibility is introduced.
1838: Dickens's *Oliver Twist* is published and helps promote a call for reform.
1838–1839: The forced march of the Cherokees occurs.
1845–1855: The Irish potato famine kills nearly 1 million while another million emigrate.
1848: Marx and Engels's *Communist Manifesto* is published: socialist ideas spread.
1859: Darwin's *Origins of Species* is published; later social Darwinists interpret this theory to justify reduction in help for the poor.
1860: Over 27,000 miles of railroad track are built through federal funding.
1861–1865: The U.S. Civil War occurs.
1863: President Lincoln passes the Emancipation Proclamation, freeing all slaves in the Confederate Territories.
1865: The 13th Amendment to the Constitution is implemented, abolishing slavery.
1865–1872: The Freedmen's Bureau provides relief for newly freed slaves.
1865–1900: Rapid U.S. industrialization occurs.
1869: The Charity Organization Society is established in England.
1877: America's first Charity Organization Society begins.
1880–1914: Twenty-one million immigrants arrive.
1881: The germ theory of disease is generally accepted.
1884: Toynbee Hall, the first settlement house, is established in London.

(Continued)

Table 2.1 (Continued)

1889: Hull House is opened.
1895: The first social worker (called a hospital almoner), Mary Stewart, was hired to work in a hospital in London.
1896: The first school of social work was founded in the Netherlands and, shortly after, in London.
1898: The first U.S. school for social workers was established; it later became the Columbia University School of Social Work.
1899: The first juvenile court in Chicago opens.
1919–1933: Prohibition begins.
1920: The 19th Amendment grants suffrage to women.
1929: The Great Depression begins with the crash of the stock market.
1933: The New Deal proclaimed by Franklin Roosevelt begins; social workers play an active role in planning and instituting massive work and welfare programming.
1935: The U.S. Social Security Act is passed.
1935: Alcoholics Anonymous is founded.
1942: The Beveridge Report in Britain recommends a comprehensive social welfare package.
1946: The National Health Service is established, and it is still going strong today.
1955: The National Association of Social Workers (NASW) is created through a merger of existing organizations.
1964: The Great Society programs and food stamp program begins. The Civil Rights Act is passed under the presidency of Lyndon Johnson.
1965: Medicare and Medicaid are added to the Social Security Act.
1965–1975: The War in Vietnam depletes the budget for the War on Poverty and leads to heavy casualties.
1969: The Stonewall Inn riot initiates the gay rights movement.
1970: The Clean Air Act directs the states to reduce emissions of hazardous air pollutants; it is strengthened in 1990 with a greater enforcement by the EPA.
1972: The Supplemental Security Income Program is enacted.
1972: The Clean Water Act is passed to set water quality standards.
1980: President Ronald Reagan ushers in a return to free market economics and the lowering of percentage paid in taxes by high-income earners.
1980: The American Psychiatric Association adds post-traumatic stress disorder to its manual of mental disorders.

1992–2000: Democrat Bill Clinton is elected; he works to change welfare as we know it and signs into law the Temporary Act for Needy Families.

2000–2008: The election of George W. Bush occurs. He cuts taxes, further downsizes the social welfare system, and invades Iraq; the toll taken by the war on U.S. troops reinforces the social work profession's concern with trauma as war-wounded soldiers return.

2008–2013: The election of the first African American president, Barack Obama, who was elected to two terms, occurs; he signs into law the health care reform bill—the Affordable Care Act—and repeals the military's discriminatory "Don't ask, don't tell" law.

There was much criticism of the behavior of professionals in Germany under Hitler, for their accommodation of the Nazi regime in crimes against humanity (see Kunstreich, 2003). In Australia, social workers participated in the forced removal of mixed-race children from Aboriginal mothers into orphanages or white homes. The goal was total assimilation of the Aboriginal people. In all, over 100,000 children were taken from their families in this way until the policy was discontinued in the 1960s. The survivors are known collectively as "the stolen generation" (see the Australian government's website at www.Australia.gov.au.) The popular 2002 Australian film, *Rabbit Proof Fence,* tells the true story of the children's escape from an institution, all the way home. Federal assimilation policies were also practiced in North America during this time; children were forcibly removed from the reservations (reserves in Canada) and placed in boarding schools where they were not allowed to communicate in their tribal languages (Blau & Abramowitz 2010). Years later, many stories of child abuse, including sexual abuse, came to light and received widespread media attention. In 1978, the U.S. Congress enacted the Indian Child Welfare Act to protect American Indians by giving tribal jurisdiction over Native American children who have been removed by the state for reasons of child maltreatment. The Canadian government has made major strides as well, and has turned over funding for child welfare services to the tribes. The particular measures taken vary by province. Amnesty International, however, has pointed to a fiscal imbalance in funding provided for Indigenous services and for services for the rest of the child population (Assembly of First Nations, 2006).

Racist and classist social policies were also carried out by the states. Social Darwinism, the corrupted version of Darwin's theory of survival of the fittest, still had an influence on medical practices in the form of mass sterilization campaigns against people who were considered likely to breed defective offspring during the 1940s and even after World War II, in North Carolina. In an editorial in the *NASW News*, NASW president Jeane Anastas (2012a) decries the fact that state-employed social workers in North Carolina made the decision that women would undergo forced sterilization procedures. The women were generally poor and African American and often in the care of the state. These practices have only fairly recently come to light, as victims have unsuccessfully requested compensation. "History lives on," Anastas concludes, "often uncomfortably, but if we are able to reflect honestly on it we can bend the curve toward human rights" (p. 3).

The Cold War against the Soviet Union, which was reinforced by extensive propaganda in the media, produced a kind of panic in the United States. The paranoia was later termed the Red Scare. From the late 1940s through the 1950s and even into the early 1960s, free speech was stymied; school children were led in endless drills to prepare for the expected Russian invasion. Very little opposition was voiced in the universities, the pulpits, or anywhere.

When Senator Joseph McCarthy conducted televised hearings of prominent national figures, including Hollywood actors and producers who were accused of being Communists or Communist sympathizers, fear was aroused in the minds of the onlookers. Workers in certain professions, such as teachers and professors, had to sign loyalty oaths to the government of the United States. The period would later be known as the McCarthy era. Before the repression came to an end, thousands of teachers, social workers, journalists, artists, and government workers would lose their jobs. Joe McCarthy later extended his witch hunt into the heart of Congress and was exposed for claims that were fabrications.

Gays and lesbians were especially vulnerable to accusations of being spies for the Soviet Union. This was not only due to the intolerance of the period but also due to the belief that homosexuals led secret lives, and they therefore could be blackmailed and forced to act as spies for the Soviet Union. When the Civil Rights Movement got its start in 1955 with the Montgomery, Alabama, bus boycott, rumors started that the movement was infiltrated by Communists.

To read the stories of women social workers who played key roles in history, read Box 2.3.

BOX 2.3   IRENA SENDLER, KATHERINE KENDALL, AND SATTAREH FARMAN FARMAIAN

Founded as a field of strong women (most of whom remained unmarried by choice) and gentlemen who stood alongside them, social work stands uniquely among the professions as woman centered. In this field, the pioneers are women; the doers and shakers of the past are women. We will see this in the lives and contributions of these four remarkable women, all of whom strived to help alleviate the suffering of their fellow human beings and showed courage in trying times at great personal risk—none more so than the rescuer of Jewish children, Irena Sendler.

Irena Sendler (1910–2008)

Many American social workers were not familiar with the rescue work that heroine Irena Sendler, a young Polish social worker, did during the Nazi occupation of Poland. When the Columbia Broadcasting Company (CBS) presented a well-publicized, made-for-TV movie in 2009, her story became widely known.

We learn from a *New York Times* story, that Sendler, who had connections from her work in Warsaw, was able to rescue around 2,500 Jewish children by slipping them out of the ghetto where they were trapped with their families and taking them to the homes of sympathizers outside the ghetto (Jones, 2008). Her work was done through an organization called Zegota, which was formed and financed by the Polish Government in Exile (in London). Sendler had to persuade the parents to give up their small children, which many of them refused to do. Once outside the walls of the ghetto, collaborators (known as couriers) would take the infants and children to temporary housing. The children acquired new names and awaited fake baptismal certificates. In 1943, Sendler was caught and tortured. She was able to escape only because her organization bribed a guard, who let her go. In the final years of the war, Sendler continued working for Zegota, and she returned to helping children and families as a social worker after the war. Her story would not have come to light had it not been for a group of schoolgirls from Kansas who wrote a play about Sendler and later formed a friendship with her. The media covered the story, which was eventually made into a documentary and later a made-for-TV movie.

Katherine Kendall (1910–2010)

"A mark of greatness," writes Kendall (1989), "is breadth of vision." She said this in an article she wrote in praise of three extraordinary social work leaders of the 1930s—Alice Salomon of Germany, Eileen Younghusband of the United Kingdom, and Edith Abbott of the United States—who had a deep commitment to international concerns. Katherine Kendall herself, who was born in Scotland and moved to Chicago with her family after World War I, possessed a breadth of vision that many who knew her would consider to be a mark of greatness. She made a major contribution to the development of social work nationally, but it is her practice in the international arena for which she will chiefly be remembered. "It is fair to say," as stated by Julia Watkins (2010), "that international social work would not be what it is, or where it is today, without Katherine Kendall" (p. 167).

She was inspired to seek a career in social reform upon reading Upton Sinclair's (1906/2001) muckraking novel, *The Jungle*, which exposed the plight of immigrant workers in Chicago's meatpacking industry. She discovered that social work was the best field for social advocacy for which she was awarded a master's degree in 1939 (Healy, 2008). Her goal to fight against injustice led her to work for the American Red Cross during World War II and in the international service department of the U.S. Children's Bureau (Malamud, 2011).

(Continued)

(Continued)

Katherine Kendall, Pioneer of International Social Work. Kendall continued to be active at functions given by the Council on Social Work Education (CSWE) until shortly before her death.

After working for the United States Children's Bureau in international service, she went to work for the newly formed United Nations (UN). The impact she had from her position as a researcher on the state of social work worldwide turned out to be enormous. After receiving the results of her survey on social work training worldwide, the UN passed a resolution calling for the professionalization of social workers through higher education. Her influence on the UN, therefore, extended far beyond her few years employment there.

After leaving the UN, Kendall helped form the Council on Social Work Education (CSWE), an organization that she helped influence for many decades. Some of her most profound and rewarding work was produced when she became the first full-time secretary general of the International Association of the Schools of Social Work (IASSW), an organization that was responsible for university curriculum and placement of social workers in program work around the world (Obituary, 2010). It was under Kendall's leadership that the IASSW expanded from what was essentially a European organization into a global organization (Healy, 2008). Setting up family planning projects through schools of social work in Asia and Africa was a major accomplishment of Kendall's social development work. Kendall encountered significant opposition from Latin America. In Singapore, when she delivered a speech that criticized the government for its restrictive policies, she was harshly criticized by the nation's press. After her retirement from the IASSW, Kendall continued to share her wisdom as an honorary president (Healy, 2008).

The authors each individually had the pleasure of knowing Katherine Kendall through attendance at conferences at the CSWE. She was as warm and lovable a person as you would want to meet. A fascinating fact about her life is that when she officially retired, she kept working and remained active as a writer of biographies of social work pioneers and social work organizations. She continued to be actively involved in international conferences until she reached her mid-90s, if not later. In 2005, she endowed an institute for international education for CSWE, now called the Katherine Kendall Institute for Social Work Education (Watkins, 2010).

In her description of the early visionaries of the profession is a message for today. "In embracing the necessity to join social reform with individual help," she wrote, "(the visionaries) long ago settled the question of whether social work should be equally concerned with therapeutic action and social action" (Kendall, 1989, p. 30). Kendall's concern was always with these two dimensions—the personal and the political.

Kendall saw herself as a world citizen and spoke out against the tendency of the most powerful country in the world to use its wealth and influence for destructive ends (Healy, 2008). Her hope for social work was that it would remain humanizing and continue to attract students who are committed to professional values and to improving programs in order to help people.

Sattareh Farman Farmaian (1921–2012)

Because Sattareh Farman Farmaian published her autobiography detailing her life from early childhood to her middle years when she was exiled to the United States, it is easy to feel that we know her. I discovered her book, *Daughter of Persia: A Woman's Journey From Her Father's Harem Through the Islamic Revolution* in the 1990s shortly after it came out. All I was looking for was a bit of escapism, and I was curious about what it would be like to grow up in a harem. The last thing I expected was to be reading the autobiography of "the mother of social work in Iran." But about halfway through the book, I found myself reading about a woman who had the opportunity to venture to the United States to attend college during World War II and while there to get a bachelor's degree in sociology at the University of Southern California, and then to go on to get a master's degree in social work. The education she got on her field placement there, she describes as follows:

> Whereas in my country help came to the needy only through alms, for the first time I saw how social workers developed ways to address the problems that made people needy: well-regulated orphanages, licensed homes for the aged, the disabled and the mentally ill. There were thousands of family service agencies, hospital clinics, and training programs in which social workers not only assisted human beings in emergencies but tried to give them ways of dealing themselves with broken families, sickness, physical disability, mental illness, old age, relocation, unemployment,

(Continued)

(Continued)

alcoholism, and other problems—always with the goal of helping them to rely not on benefactors and protectors, but on themselves. (p. 167)

What she was seeking in her social work studies was the knowledge that she needed to take back with her to Iran "to fight Iran's human miseries" (Farman Farmaian, 1992, p. 167), and this knowledge was about systems of child welfare, social work advocacy, and care for the poor. Her ambitions were extraordinary. Alice Lieberman (2010) puts this young woman's goals in perspective, "Here was Satti [her nickname], determined to bring a profession that did not exist to not only her entire country but also into a tribal culture, where getting assistance from outside one's own family was unheard of" (p. 202).

Several things had to happen first before Farman Farmaian could fulfill her mission. Practicing social work in the United States, she had to acquire a vast knowledge about social welfare programming and the shaping of social legislation (Saleh, 2008). And she did. And she needed the present government in Iran to be overthrown and one in which her family had influence to be installed. And that happened too.

Inspired by her dedicated mentors at USC School of Social Work, teachers who engaged in a constant fight for social reform and "who had the gift of making us feel we had been chosen, like physicians, to heal all the ills of society," Farman Farmaian returned to her home country to pursue her mission. From 1954 to 1958 Farman Farmaian worked for the United Nations in Baghdad, Iraq, as a social welfare consultant. Through this position, she was able to set up social welfare programs all over the country (Lieberman, 2010).

Then, blessed by high family connections that extended to the royal palace, Farman Farmaian was authorized (with a limited stipend) in 1953 to start a graduate training school—the Tehran School of Social Work. The social work literature, which had been written for an American audience, was entirely unsuitable for use in a nonindustrialized nation. Since there was not even a Persian word for social worker, the term *madadkar* was invented, meaning "one who helps." According to Farman Farmaian (1992, p. 212), the education for a madadkar was comprehensive:

I was requiring them to study numerous subjects: planning a family's diet, hygiene, first aid, human physical development and reproduction, family finances, and social and individual psychology. (There were no courses in psychotherapy, a subject of exceedingly limited use to social workers in the developing nations of the world, whose inhabitants are mainly concerned with surviving from one day to the next). (p. 168)

In their field placements, the students, women from middle-class back-grounds and men from working-class backgrounds, encountered a wretchedness they had never dreamed existed. Visiting insane asylums and orphanages, they found the inhabitants literally groveling in filth. Together, with a host of vol-unteers, the social work students physically cleaned (shoveling out excrement) the premises as a first step in providing care. Family planning was another area of intensive organizing activity. Soon, over time, the students' integrity and unselfish devotion to social work enhanced the reputation of the school and a BSW program was established. The number of applications soared and the school was accorded university status in 1961.

Although under the Shah or king (Reza Pahlavi), Iran was a country in which free speech was unknown and the extreme social problems could not be publicly documented, when governmental pressures became too much, the school was protected by the active support and influence of the Shah's Westernized wife, Queen Farah.

Social work educator Charles S. Prigmore (1990), who visited Iran during this pioneering period, provided an outsider's view of what social workers were able to accomplish. He was impressed with the modernization and efficient bureau-cratization of Iran. An elaborate health and welfare network delivered a variety of needed services to the people. There were over 2,500 family planning clinics. A trip to the welfare office in one of the large cities indicated that 34 social workers served the city, and a shortage of trained social workers continued to be a primary problem.

In events that culminated in the revolution of 1979, however, religious fun-damentalists destroyed everything that smacked of a secular culture. Ordered to return to covering themselves from head to toe with a black garment called the *chador*, women were driven from their jobs at factories, and offices were segregated by sex. Farman Farmaian found herself arrested for establishing birth control clinics. With the forced closing of the school of social work, the "daughter of Persia" fled at great personal risk to the United States. It would be years and years before social work would be established again.

In a personal interview with Satti, Lieberman (2010) asked her what was happening to social work in modern Iran. "The Tehran School of Social Work is no more," she said (p. 210). When the revolution came, she further stated, all universities were closed. When they finally reopened, social work education was housed in the social science department. The name *madadkar* is still used as the professional term, and social workers are still working with the poor.

Both Farman Farmaian and Prigmore, in their earlier writings, agreed that the hope of the future lies in the women of Iran. While the laws are against

(Continued)

(Continued)

them, the legacy of strength, strong family roles, and the experience of a period of liberation unite them.

References and Further Reading

Farman Farmaian, S. (1992). *Daughter of Persia: A woman's journey from her father's harem through the Islamic revolution*. New York: Crown.

Healy, L. (2008). Katherine A. Kendall (USA), honorary president since 1978. *Social Work and Society International Online Journal, 6*(1). Retrieved from www.socwork.net/sws/articles/view/109/398

Malamud, M. (2011, February). Kendall "had exciting, important role" in profession. *NASW News, 6*(2), p. 7.

Saleh, M. F. (2008). Sattareh Farman Farmaian: Iranian social work pioneer. *Affilia: Journal of Women and Social Work, 23*(4), 397–402.

Obituary: Katherine Anne Tuach Kendall. (2010, December 22). *Washington Post*. Retrieved from www.washingtonpost.com

Watkins, J. (2010). Katherine A. Kendall: The founder of international social work. In A. Lieberman (Ed.), *Women in social work who have changed the world* (pp. 167–181). Chicago, IL: Lyceum.

The New Frontier and the Great Society

While conservatism lingered on through much of the 1960s, the election in 1960 of John F. Kennedy ushered in a spirit of idealism and reform. His "New Frontier" promised new approaches to social problems such as poverty and discrimination, as well as new goals such as space travel and other technological advances. Many young people were passionate in their support of Kennedy, which, thanks to his regular presence at televised press conferences, only grew stronger over time. The general public was fascinated as well with the glamour of the whole Kennedy (extended) family that was regularly played up in the popular magazines of the day—*Look* and *Life*.

Continuing the pattern of social policies established during the New Deal, President Kennedy evoked memories of Franklin Roosevelt in his references to the hunger and deprivation he had seen (Reisch, 2012). Kennedy proposed legislation to aid both the working poor and recipients of welfare aid. Legislation was also passed to raise the federal level of funding to the states for social services.

The Civil Rights Movement, largely under the leadership of Martin Luther King, Jr., was gaining strength throughout the 1960s, as the nonviolent protest movement grew in size and visibility. Much of the momentum for the movement came from the power of the folk music and protest music of the day. Songs such as "We Shall Overcome," "Blowin' in the Wind," and "We Shall Not Be Moved" were heard repeatedly by integrated groups whose songs, if not heard on the street corner, were heard on the radio and TV. The moral force of the Gandhian strategies of pacifist resistance stirred the nation—and the horror of images such as fire hoses and police dogs set on nonviolent protestors had the same effect.

The Kennedy administration, which had moved cautiously on the integration front due to the fear of splitting the Democratic Party (which was still very strong in the South), finally started moving more forcefully. Under the attorney general, Robert F. Kennedy, numerous lawsuits were filed attacking the constitutionality of many of the laws preventing integration. The administration sent federal troops to southern states to enforce integration laws.

Kennedy's death by assassination in 1963 brought a southerner, Lyndon B. Johnson to the White House. Ironically, Johnson's commitment to integration in particular, and social justice in general, was clearly greater than Kennedy's, and there was a new impetus to outlaw segregation and enforce the voting laws. Johnson took up the civil rights legislation that had languished in Congress under Kennedy and used his intimate knowledge of Congress as well the bully pulpit of the presidency to ram the bill through both houses. The passage of the Civil Rights Act in 1964 was a major triumph.

Johnson's concept of the Great Society was closely linked to the civil rights agenda (Reisch, 2012). Crucial to the goals of the Great Society was the eradication of inequality, not only in terms of race but also wealth. Johnson launched his "War on Poverty" in 1964, passing legislation to boost employment and to develop programs such as the Job Corps and VISTA (Volunteers in Service to America), a kind of domestic Peace Corps, which started under the Kennedy administration.

The social protest that had helped the Civil Rights Movement achieve some lasting change also helped spawn other protest movements. Starting slowly, but building up steam as the Civil Rights Movement came to a crescendo, the antiwar movement started to raise serious doubts about the U.S. involvement in Vietnam. Johnson, advised that Vietnam was a crucial domino in the Communists' desire to impose their system throughout the world, escalated the war starting late 1964. Johnson repeated the optimistic words of the military men who advised them that the will of the Vietnamese would break in the face of our massive military might. But as the years passed and little or no progress was made as television viewers watched news programs bring the horrors of war into their living rooms each night, opposition to the war mounted. In addition to what seemed like senseless killing to many, the war also drained resources that otherwise would have been spent on domestic programs; the increased spending on the military budget led to inflation, and Johnson's popularity plummeted to the extent that he, in essence, fled from office in 1968. Protests continued under President Nixon, and the war sputtered to a conclusion, with the withdrawal of all U.S. troops coming in 1973.

The feminist movement, which had been dormant since the New Deal, emerged out of the activism of the male-dominant peace movement, borrowing the spirit of the Civil Rights Movement. The feminist mantra "the personal is political" linked women's individual problems to the structure of patriarchy (Kemp & Brandwein, 2010). Thanks to the grassroots feminist movement that reemerged in the 1970s, awareness of women's needs and issues became paramount once again. Women's problems were depathologized and then politicized. The National Organization for Women was founded in 1966 and worked within the system through legislation and litigation. As Kemp and Brandwein indicate, the impact on the social work profession was belated, but it did come. By the mid-1970s, academic journals showed the influence of feminist ideas in the focus of articles, for example, the emphasis on gendered violence, but not until the 1980s did the content turn to more in-depth analyses of women's oppression in society.

Out of the consciousness-raising of the protest movement of the 1960s, other minority groups also felt moved to organize for the passage of protective legislation. Persons with disabilities successfully worked to ensure building accessibility and nondiscrimination in hiring. The so-called gay liberation movement got started in 1969. Older adults lobbied extensively for the passage of legislation to protect their rights. Throughout the Western world, similar campaigns for civil rights took place, most dramatically in Northern Ireland, where the Catholics had been relegated to second-class citizens for years, and in South Africa, where the blacks had been violently suppressed.

The Backlash: Late 20th Century and the Modern Era

A backlash against liberal ideology that is usually traced to the election of Ronald Reagan in 1980 had a profound effect on social policy and on the basic foundation of the welfare state. A great deal of wealth poured into conservative policy institutes to promote the conservative agenda. These "think tanks"—for example, the American Enterprise Institute, the Cato Institute, and the Heritage Foundation—conduct research and release their findings to politicians and the general public (Stoesz, 2012). The method behind the strategy was that if you can change the public's belief systems, the politicians will follow and vice versa. Historian Michael Kazin (2014) explains the turn that history took leading to the rise of the Tea Party extremism:

> Like the Left in the early twentieth century, conservatives built an impressive set of institutions to develop and disseminate their ideas. Their . . . lobbying firms, talk radio programs, and popular periodicals have trained and financed two generations of writers and organizers. . . . Conservatives have marshaled such media outlets like Fox News and the editorial pages of *The Wall Street Journal* to their cause. (p. SR4)

Ronald Reagan successfully lowered the tax rate to 38% on earned income and much lower on unearned income. So instead of the richest Americans paying 70% or more of the highest proportion of their income to the treasury as they did in the 1960s and 1970s (it was even higher, 90%, under President Dwight Eisenhower in the 1950s), the tax bite became a lot less. The philosophy behind the tax cuts was that if more wealth were accumulated at the top, it would trickle down to the middle and working classes.

Other policies that began with the Reagan administration, and were reinforced by Republicans and Democrats alike in the future, were the deregulation of the banking industry, amendments to the Social Security Act, advancing the age for benefits, a focus on privatization of services, transferring of federal programs to the states, and enforcing work requirements for welfare recipients. Another legacy of the Reagan presidency was its influence on the Democratic Party, as Stoesz (2012) suggests. For example, the replacement of Aid to Families of Dependent Children with Temporary Assistance for Needy Families (TANF), a block grant that was devolved to the states under the Clinton administration, effectively ended long-term welfare programs for many poor families.

President Clinton's attempts to redress issues such as health care, discrimination against gays and lesbians in the military, and family health and well-being were mostly stymied by a Republican-controlled Congress. Occasionally, Clinton moved to the right, such as in his willingness to sign the 1996 Personal Responsibility and Work Opportunity Reconciliation Act into law. This bill was designed to move more people (mainly single mothers) off the welfare rolls into work and is perhaps the most controversial of his accomplishments (see the section on Temporary Assistance to Needy Families in Chapter 5). On the positive side, during the Clinton years, the country enjoyed high employment and a strong economy that seemed to maintain the president's high popularity despite the personal sexual scandals that led to impeachment hearings (DiNitto, 2011). Clinton bequeathed to George W. Bush a nation that no longer carried a national debt.

Elected in 2000 in a highly contested election George W. Bush followed in Reagan's footsteps, advocating for increased privatization of the social welfare system and devolution of funding for social welfare programs in the states. Central to this approach is a belief in "trickle-down" economics, which posits that increased prosperity of the rich will filter down the entire social structure. Apart from leaving a national debt in the trillions, Bush's most memorable accomplishments were the extensive tax cuts that he got Congress to pass while at the same time conducting a costly war on terrorism.

In 2009, when Barack Obama assumed the presidency, much attention was focused on the fact that he was the first African American president. Unfortunately, as the national leader he inherited a huge national debt and wars on two fronts—Iraq and Afghanistan. Then the Great Recession, which had actually begun at the end of 2007, struck (DiNitto, 2011). The recession grew out of the failure of the banks, a failure related to the making of increasingly high-risk loans to poorly qualified borrowers at interest rates that, in many cases, ballooned over time. Unable to make their payments, homeowners lost their houses, and homes all across the United States were foreclosed. This, in turn, caused property values to fall, which forced more people to abandon their homes.

The Obama administration had promised "change we can believe in" but was hampered by entrenched Republican opposition. Using the strategy of railing against the government for the need to reduce the national debt, conservatives were able to transfer the blame from their own party to the Democrats and from the expanded tax cuts that benefited the rich to a focus on costly middle-class social insurance programs, primarily Medicare and Social Security. Conservatives, as DiNitto (2011) indicates, rallied against Obama's attempts to stabilize the economic situation, although he was able to pass some important legislation early in his term to boost the national economy and rescue two American carmakers in addition to the big banks. His passage of the Affordable Care Act, or "Obamacare," greatly expanded health care options and undoubtedly will be his best-known legacy and one with important implications for social work practice.

Trends in Social Work Today

Social work began as a religiously oriented movement through the generosity of wealthy donors who believed in the cause. It emerged as a secular profession that holds a focus on multiculturalism and values critical to all clients, especially those who are members of oppressed groups (Jimenez, 2010). Yet many of the same issues that concerned the field at the beginning are with us still. Whether social work should focus on the individual or society—*case versus cause*—is the major question that concerns the field.

It is worth looking at the NASW code of ethics and examining how this issue is handled if not resolved (see the code online at http://www.socialworkers.org/pubs/code/code.asp). The purpose of the code is to identify primary social work values (see Chapter 3), provide broad ethical standards through which to hold the profession accountable to the public, and spell out the standards by which the profession may judge its members' conduct. At a glance, the reader can see that much of the weight is devoted to social workers' ethical responsibilities to their clients, colleagues, and practice settings, but not to the neglect of responsibilities to the broader society. As stated in Standard 6, social workers are expected also to engage in social and political action. The NASW, as we saw in Chapter 1 and as a review of any issue of *NASW News* will show, is an activist organization. The profession regularly writes legal briefs in cases to go before the Supreme Court on issues concerning human rights violations and maltreatment of minority groups. The profession also endorses politicians for Congress and the presidency based on factors related to social work values and ethics. Returning to the issue of case versus cause, it is clear that the question is not one of either/or. Social workers must attend to both the individual and the society and the interaction between them.

The majority of social work students today want to pursue careers in direct practice—working with children in need of assistance, counseling family members, and working at substance abuse and mental health agencies. According to Reardon (2012), the choice to work with individuals is a practical matter related to the job market as there are fewer opportunities in community organizing, and such jobs as there are do not pay very well. A second factor gearing students toward the clinical direction is the need, in many states, to pass a licensing exam. The focus with such exams is largely on assessment and direct practice of individual clients. The specialization of master's programs reflects this interest. Statistics provided by the CSWE (2011) show that around 20 times as many master's level students are enrolled in a direct practice as in a community organization concentration.

When Specht and Courtney (1994) claimed controversially that social work had drifted away from social justice, and that the field is no longer concerned with the plight of the poor and the homeless, it was almost another Flexner moment—a time when social work educators would take a good hard look at the field and echo the criticism. Theirs was a message that continues to resonate with social workers worldwide.

The profession of social work is shaped by the politics of any given time. It is not surprising, therefore, given the conservative temper of the times and the funding resources geared more toward the treatment than the prevention end of the problem-solving spectrum, that the social work education focus is more on case than on cause. "Just follow the money and look at the decline in funding of programs that support advocacy," says social work educator Frederick Reamer (quoted in Reardon, 2012, p. 22).

From a Canadian perspective, Bob Mullaly (2006) sees the social work vision as leaning toward a conventional as opposed to a progressive view. His concern is with a shift in the Canadian Association of Social Work (CASW) Code of Ethics, a retreat to an earlier time when the concern was more with helping people to cope with oppressive social structures than with working toward social change. And instead of the widely accepted anti-oppressive focus toward diversity, the new code (under the ethical guidelines) speaks of acknowledging diversity, which implies tolerance rather than appreciation.

Nancy Mary (2008) expresses a similar concern with the U.S. social work code of ethics, in that it is more narrowly focused than European codes, which are more centered on human rights. She contrasts the important roles social workers played in fighting oppression in the 1930s and 1960s with what she defines as the "narrow focus on individuals and families and their treatment" found in modern social work (p. 159). Mary's vision is strikingly broad. We must, she argues, connect the fate of the family with the fate of the earth. Despite her criticism of U.S. social work for its shortsightedness, Mary is optimistic in her hope for a sustainable future.

We too are hopeful; we do not think social work has abandoned its mission. The person-in-environment focus keeps our eyes on people and their environments in constant interaction. Interventions to solve social problems are geared toward both the person and the environment. The environment may be a high-crime neighborhood, or it may be a social structure such as a school in which bullying is pronounced. The introduction of the ecosystems concept marks a major theoretical advance in social work knowledge and education. The extent to which social work has changed is not a case of values or vision; it is, as political scientists Pierson and Hacker (2010) contend, that the ecosystem of politics has changed, a politics guided by high-paying interest groups.

Our social work imagination shows signs of being as strong as ever before, as evidenced in the international connectedness emphasized in our professional organizations; the continuing social activism in movements such as the Social Welfare Action Alliance; and the wealth of literature on diverse topics such as environmental social work, ethics and values in social work, international social work, and empowerment and anti-oppressive practice. These works represent not only a wealth of knowledge but an innovation of the richest sort.

Sometimes we have to draw on our imaginations to serve clients and follow policies that are more bureaucratic than helpful; sometimes we have to use our imaginations to get around policy that is cumbersome. And we have to draw on our powers of critical thinking to detect latent functions of policy that makes no sense on the surface yet persists with a vengeance. To work toward social change, it is important to know not only the possibilities but also the limits.

So far we have looked at the tendency to dichotomize the field into case versus cause, or micro– versus macro–social work, and strategies to attract or appease funding sources. We have argued that practitioners work within the parameters of policy and that individually or collectively they can work toward policy improvement or

change (see Chapter 10). Social work education, following the accreditation requirements from CSWE, tries to strike a balance across levels of focus through building
competencies in students that encompass individual counseling skills, advocacy for
social justice, and the fundamentals of empirical research. Now let us look briefly at
the theoretical framework that best incorporates micro- and macro-fields of practice,
case versus cause issues, and concepts that link the person with the environment—the
ecosystems perspective.

An Ecosystems Framework for Sustainability Practice

Ecosystems principles are merely that—principles—rather than a full-blown
explanatory theory. It is best viewed, like so-called systems theory, as an outlook, or
perspective, for exploring how the individual parts work together to form a whole.
Systems theory emerged in the 1940s and 1950s in the biological and social sciences,
but it did not really enter the social work vocabulary until the late 1960s and 1970s, and
then it was embraced wholeheartedly (Payne, 2014). Family systems theory as conceptualized by Murray Bowen (1978) was highly influential not only in the field of social
work but also in substance abuse treatment. Individuals within the family system were
viewed as played roles that were mutually complimentary for the survival of the family
unit. Emphasis was put on the types of boundaries that existed between individuals in
the family and between the family and the outside world. Bowen's concern was more
with the impact of poor family communication on the individual, and substance abuse
treatment theorists were more concerned with the impact of the alcohol or other drug
on an individual or family. Either way, the effect was interactive. Group therapists
borrowed these concepts in their understanding of the group process and how individual members influence and are influenced by group dynamics.

Systems theory requires us to think about the social and personal elements in any
social situation and at the same time see how those elements interact with one another
to integrate as a whole (Payne, 2014). The influence of systems concepts on social
work, whether from sociology or family theorists, marked a major advance in social
work theory, which became more sociological than psychological in its understanding
of human behavior.

This perspective was expanded by Germain and Gitterman's (1980) introduction of their life model or ecological formulation. The person and his or her environment were seen as interdependent. Germain and Gittleman's life model of social
work practice reformulated systems theory, emphasizing the importance of stressful
life transitions on people's ability to adapt to circumstances. The life model sees
people as constantly adapting in an interchange with many different aspects of their
environments (Payne, 2014).

The ecosystems approach combined systems theory with ecological principles.
From this perspective, every system is simultaneously a whole with its own distinctive
qualities, a part of a larger system, and a container of smaller systems. Coates (2003)
broadened the lens of ecological theory to relate to the natural environment and issues
of social injustice in our exploitation of the earth's resources. Drawing on the systems
concept of boundaries, he argues that the earth is a closed system and that the resources
are finite. His focus is on sustainable development in a global context.

Nancy Mary's (2008) contribution of a sustainable social work model for the study of social institutions is a welcome addition to social work theory that takes us into new realms of investigation. She, like other ecological theorists, is concerned with risks to the environment through overpopulation and overuse of harmful chemicals in agriculture, transportation, and warfare.

Besthorn and McMillen (2002) have expanded social work's ecosystems model to take us into the spiritual realm. Spirituality, which had earlier received almost no attention by proponents of ecosystems, has today received the recognition it deserves as a part of the deep ecology movement. Deep ecology looks to the realm of nature for insight and sees all life—human and nonhuman—as one in the universe (van Wormer & Besthorn, 2011). Mary (2008) is optimistic that social work with sustainability as its focus will be able to deal with spirituality as well as science and environmental and economic issues as well as politics.

THINKING SUSTAINABLY

Social work has been in the forefront of applying biologically based concepts of ecology as a metaphor to discuss the relationship between people and their environment. What are the basic concepts of ecosystems as a model, and how does it relate to sustainability?

Consider discrete units such as individuals, family, community, and wider culture: How might they interact to provide a balanced appreciation of each?

Global Social Work Settings

We have been focusing primarily on the United States in our chronicling of this history of the development of social work in the context of national political paradigm shifts. Let us now venture to learn of social work practice in other countries. To represent geographical and cultural diversity, we have selected the nations of Ghana and the United Kingdom. Our emphasis is on challenges facing professional social workers in each of these countries.

BOX 2.4 SOCIAL WORK PRACTICE IN GHANA: HISTORY AND RECENT TRENDS

Augustina Naami

In precolonial Ghana, social problems were mostly addressed within the traditional system. Families provide for their members due to Ghanaians' belief in the extended family system. Ghanaians believe that anything that affects

(Continued)

(Continued)

a family member affects everyone in the family. Hence, family members do everything to help preserve their families. The family system provided for the socioeconomic and psychological well-being of its members. Elder siblings, for example, provided for their younger ones, as well as their parents; aunties and uncles provided for their needy nieces and nephews; and grandparents provided for their grandchildren. Social issues, like homelessness, were addressed by living in intergenerational family homes. The family institution also provided counseling for members. These practices are still performed in most communities in Ghana despite the breakdown in the family system. Apt and Blavo (1997) note that along with the traditional system of addressing social problems in the precolonial era was the assistance religious organizations offered to the poor. The institutions integrated the gospel with charity for the poor. Most religious organizations continue to provide charity, as well as counseling for the poor.

Social welfare systems in Ghana, as well as the social work profession, began with the colonial administration by the British (Wicker, 1958). The colonial administration created the first social welfare policy, the Colonial Development and Welfare Act, in 1940 (Wicker, 1958). Other structures were later created including the Department of Social Welfare and Housing (1948), which later became, and still is, the Department of Social Welfare and Community Development (Mwansa & Kreitzer, 2012).

Social workers who worked within these structures were trained in Britain (Mwansa & Kreitzer, 2012) instead of through the colonial administration's facilities to help Ghanaians effectively address their social problems. The first social work institution—the School of Social Work—was established in 1946 and offered a certificate course in social work (Apt & Blavo, 1997). Mwansa and Kreitzer (2012) argue that the British social welfare structures established in Ghana used the remedial approach to address social issues rather than preventive and structural change approaches, which could also address the root causes of social problems. In other words, the colonial social welfare policies failed to provide a holistic approach to addressing social issues in Ghana. For example, Mwansa and Kreitzer emphasize that with the British welfare system, "attention was given to physical and mental health rehabilitation, with special attention to homeless children, disabled people, women and migrants" (p. 399).

These authors claim that the social work profession continues to use the colonial remedial approach to addressing social problems. The major social work programs—the University of Ghana Department of Social Work; the Department of Sociology and Social Work at the Kwame Nkrumah University of Science and Technology; and the School of Social Work, established in colonial Ghana—provide training based on curriculum that is more Western centered rather than focusing on the Ghanaian context.

However, community development initiatives, which according to Abloh and Ameyan (1997) were developed by indigenous Ghanaians with financial support from the colonial government, became essential in the socioeconomic development of the country in the 1950s. The program, which provides services such as adult literacy, self-help village programs, and vocational training for girls and persons with disabilities, is presently experiencing a cut in government funding (Kreitzer et al., 2009). Therefore, currently, there is a proliferation of nongovernmental organizations in Ghana, practicing at both micro- and macro-levels, and many social workers work in this setting. These organizations "fill in the gaps where government funded, traditional community structures historically provided services" (Kreitzer et al., 2009, p. 149). However, social workers practice in other settings, including hospitals, prisons, community development, marriage and family settings, schools, and child welfare services.

The social work profession, though relatively old, struggles to gain recognition in the Ghanaian society compared with other professions. Many Ghanaians do not know much about the profession and what social workers do. Social workers used to be seen as welfare officers, liaising between the government and the vulnerable population. I remember that after college (from 1997), I unknowingly practiced social work for 4 years. I worked with a nongovernmental organization taking persons with disabilities from the streets, giving them formal education and vocational training, and helping them to establish their own businesses. My undergraduate degree was in economics because I thought I could not do any work that required working outside of an office. However, my passion for advocating for the human rights of persons with disabilities grew while in college, and that was what led me to work in the nonprofit sector.

After 4 years of working in an environment that teaches persons with disabilities how to become self-sufficient, I was awarded a scholarship to pursue a master's degree, outside of the country, to integrate the practical skills that I had obtained with the appropriate knowledge and theory needed to better help the vulnerable population. That was how I was mentored into the social work profession. After completing my master's degree program, I returned to Ghana and worked with another nonprofit organization for 3 years, building the capacity of women with disabilities to advocate for their human rights as well as their socioeconomic and political development. I contacted the president of the Ghana Association of Social Workers (GASOW), where I lived, but for the whole period that I stayed in Ghana (2004–2007) the group never met.

(Continued)

(Continued)

Undoubtedly, the social work profession in Ghana is currently emerging, as we see many social workers practice in other settings besides the traditional setting. However, a lot more needs to be done to change Ghanaians' perceptions about the profession and to gain recognition in Ghanaian society. The GASOW could do a lot more to showcase the profession. For example, it can organize conferences, publish newsletters and a journal, as well as publicize the profession through print and electronic media and other avenues.

References

Abloh, F., & Ameyan, S. (1997). Ghana. In H. Campfens (Ed.), *Community development around the world: practice, theory, research, and training*. Toronto, Canada: University of Toronto Press.

Apt, A. A., & Blavo, E. Q. (1997). Ghana. In T. D. S. Mayadas, T. D. Watts, & D. Elliott (Eds.), *The international handbook on social work theory*. Westport, CT: Greenwood Press

Kreitzer, L., Abukari, Z., Antonio, P., Mensah, J., & Afram, A. (2009). Social work in Ghana: A participatory action research project looking at culturally appropriate training and practice. *Social Work Education, 28*(2), 145–164.

Mwansa, L. K., & Kreitzer, L. (2012). Social work in Africa. In K. Lyons, T. Hokenstad, M. Pawar, N. Huegler, & N. Hall (Eds.), *The SAGE handbook of international social work* (pp. 393–406). London, England: Sage.

Wicker, E. R. (1958). Colonial development and welfare, 1929–1957: The evolution of a policy. *Social and Development Studies, 7*(4), 170–192.

Source: Published with permission of Augustina Naami.

BOX 2.5   SOCIAL WORK IN THE UNITED KINGDOM

Katherine van Wormer

Unlike Scandinavia, with its high value on social equality and labor interests represented within the government, instead of peripheral to it, Britain is a two- or three-tier society. Angry attacks by one group against the other and national strikes by workers are characteristic. Social work is not immune to such strife and, as in the United States, reflects the shifts and moods of national politics. The social work profession in Britain, according to Dominelli (2009), is full of contradictions. Social work is much appreciated when it supports people and receives a positive press in times of disaster. At other times, such as when a child in care is murdered, social workers are in the headlines for bearing responsibility. Internally, "disputes about what constitutes good practice make social work a troubled and troubling profession" (pp. 2–3). Because it depends on the state for a definition of its boundaries, it is constantly being restructured and emerging in different forms. Still, its core tasks of caring for people and regulating their behavior—its care and control functions—remain.

History of Social Work in the United Kingdom

Much of British history of course relates to American history, since American culture is derived from the original colonies that belonged to Britain. The early settlements, as mentioned at the beginning of this chapter, carried with them the principles of the 1601 Poor Law that provided some aid for the poor who were deemed worthy of such aid. This poor law, and others, remained until the Poor Law of 1834 was passed to reflect the fact that Britain was no longer a largely agricultural society and the expense of serving the poor had mounted. The Industrial Revolution had advanced the British economy but brought much suffering to the common people, especially to children forced to labor up to 12 hours daily in factories. The misery is immortalized in the reform novels of Charles Dickens. The Poor Law of 1834 was passed not long after the British business classes got the vote and took dominance away from the landed aristocrats (Garfinkel, Rainwater, & Smeeding, 2010). At this time, outdoor relief (or assistance in the form of money, food, clothing, or goods without the requirement that the recipient enter an institution) was abolished for the able-bodied poor, and people without work were required to enter the workhouse as a test of need. According to the principle of *less eligibility*, the value of the aid given to the poor had to be lower than the wages of the poorest worker. This policy effectively kept the level of aid very low and therefore unappealing to the public (Jimenez, 2010). The Poor Law of 1834 was an advance in that it involved centralization of responsibility for poor relief, but the conditions were very harsh.

It took the devastation of World War II to create a climate conducive to major policy advances. It was then that the social welfare state was created on European soil. Social work was a part of this scheme and experienced rapid growth. According to Payne and Shardlow (2002), the European varieties were more comprehensive than the more individualistic form in the United States, the ambiguous role of state welfare in the developing countries, and the forms of social development in Africa.

The solidarity in Britain from fighting the Nazis paved the way for social welfare reforms. The government commissioned reports during the war, the

(Continued)

(Continued)

most influential of which was the report of economist William Beveridge. The Beveridge report proposed the creation of a universalistic welfare state that would shield the British population against major modern economic and social risks. Following the model, right after the war the government set up the acclaimed National Health Service, which granted health care to all British people (Béland, 2010).

Lavalette (2011), the author of *Radical Social Work Today*, provides a description of the educational climate that developed in the late 1960s when the young generation became radicalized ahead of their faculty and rebelled against the heavy emphasis on the psychological and medical knowledge in their programs. The students were influenced by Marxist and feminist writings. Eventually, the curriculum changed to a more radical approach to the material.

The election of Margaret Thatcher as Prime Minister and leader of the Conservative party was a major turning point in British welfare history that paralleled the changes that took place in the United States in 1980 with the election of Ronald Reagan. The two rulers grew very close as each one worked to launch a coherent free market ideological campaign in their respective countries (Béland, 2010). Their fights against the growth of the welfare state legitimized cutbacks, privatization, and a focus on individual responsibility. Lavalette (2011) calls this turning point of the first Thatcher government "a ruling class offensive against trade unionism, local 'socialism' within councils, state-provided welfare and poor people" (p. 6). Social work was under attack as the cause of welfare dependency and political correctness (a negative term in Britain). Even through these times and the conservative decades that followed, the British social work profession has maintained its commitment to anti-oppressive practice and social advocacy.

Social Work Education

Starting in 2003, degree-level professional qualifications included a course in general studies followed by education and training for various specialized fields within social work (Dominelli, 2009). Scotland, for example, introduced a 360-credit qualification that social workers who are lead practitioners and managers in children's services must attain in the future. Social work competencies in England are monitored by specialized bodies that spell out their requirements to carry out key roles such as assessment, practicing values and ethics, and evaluation. Universities incorporate the trainings in their coursework.

Trevithick's (2012) textbook, a popular practice handbook for British students that is used worldwide, is very informative concerning the treatment modalities that are used. *Social work*, as Trevithick states, is a protected title in the United Kingdom that can be used to refer only to social workers who are qualified and who hold a social work qualification recognized by the General Social Care Council. *Social care workers*, in contrast, provide practical help to people in need. Trevithick, as most British social work educators today, does not use the word *client* but, rather, *service user,* which is considered the preferred term. To prepare to work with service user, students study the British Association of Social Workers' (BASW) code of ethics, which emphasizes social justice. Advocacy is taught to prepare students to seek to change social structures that perpetuate inequality and injustice. This is more difficult, as Trevithick informs us, as a shift has taken place in recent years in social work role expectations: from notions of "care and cure" toward a focus on control. For specialists in youth work, the antisocial behavior of youths is now called "youth offending" and has been reconceptualized and criminalized (p. 41).

As a member of the European Union, the United Kingdom stands to benefit from the establishment of the Bologna Accords of 1999. The declaration created a process designed to make academic degree standards compatible all over Europe and allows for free exchanges of students from member nations (Hokenstad, 2008).

Challenges

Compared with the United States, the United Kingdom has a lower crime rate, lower rates of illness, and somewhat higher rates of equality (George, 2010). The fact that the United Kingdom has universal health care is a major benefit to all its residents and to recipients of social welfare benefits. Yet, as Dominelli (2009) indicates, the universality of the program is undermined by the tacking on of user fees for service. Prescription drug charges and dental fees are examples, as are means-tested charges for residential care for older adults. Dominelli argues for an alternative vision to one offered by neoliberal politics in "a culture of individual self-sufficiency" (p. 160).

In recent years, declassification of jobs that formerly were filled only by qualified social workers has occurred, allowing for the appropriation of social services activities by other professionals and nonprofessionals. For example, risk assessments in child abuse cases can now be done by child psychologists, and mental health work has been opened to professionals without social work degrees (Dominelli, 2009). Similar changes are happening in elder care as well.

A scanning of *Community Care* online (www.communitycare.co.uk), a social work news network, is revealing. Articles point to the large numbers of social

(Continued)

(Continued)

work "vacancies" in all parts of the United Kingdom; except for Northern Ireland, positions have not been filled. We also learn of expanding caseloads. It is clear that the profession does better under a Labour than a Conservative government, but it is also clear that even under Labour, the autonomy of the profession is threatened. One news report states that pay cuts that had been instituted by the previous administration of Southampton Council would now be reversed as a result of a recent Labour victory (McGregor, 2012). There is information also about proposed declassification of social work jobs. The following excerpt is from a news item titled "Councils Urged to Replace Social Workers with Non-Qualified Staff" (Samuel, 2012):

> The biggest potential area of saving was from "changing the mix of staff grades and skills that councils employ" to carry out assessments, by replacing social workers and occupational therapists with social work or OT assistants or other staff without professional qualifications." (p. 1)

The risk to social workers is a lack of job security. Yet due to the shortage of qualified social workers in the United Kingdom, as mentioned above, the United Kingdom has recruited overseas to fill the ranks. Many have been from the United States. In a recent exchange on the Social Work Network Group, a listserv of professional social workers, the topic of social work in the United Kingdom was discussed. Generally, the respondents commented that they believed the status of social workers to be lower than in the United States. However, they also remarked that being American was an advantage when connecting with the families. Generally, the respondents seem happy in their work and in the opportunity to travel. Here are some samples:

> R. W.: What I find in the United Kingdom is you are not permitted to practice psychotherapy; you cannot refer to yourself as a therapist. The psychologists do not perceive master's level social workers as qualified to provide therapy. I now practice as a holistic health counselor.

> R. L. (A British respondent): Regrettably, clinical social work is a lost art in many of England's social work outlets. However, your skill set would be welcomed in child and adolescent and mental health settings.

> S. S.: I am in a child protection team in Cornwall. It does seem that social workers here have a lot less respect than stateside. However, I am constantly able to use my being American as a way to connect. The weather and food are generally lousy, but I wouldn't trade this experience for anything!

Summary and Conclusion

History often emerges only in retrospect. As we look across the sweep of this history of social welfare and of the profession most closely aligned to it, we can see the patterns in the seeming meaninglessness of events. And drawing on our knowledge of the past, we can make certain predictions about the future. We can also see progression over time, albeit in a spiraling fashion of shifting paradigms. And we can see two overriding themes. From an optimistic standpoint, we can conclude that whenever privilege and power conspire to lead the nation into a downward spiral, the people eventually rise up. They lead and the politicians follow. Taking a more cautious stance, we can predict that policies that are deemed to be unsustainable, at least for the nation as a whole, will eventually give way to policies that are better designed to meet people's needs.

Consider the progressive reforms and sense of national optimism of these periods: 1900 to 1916, the New Deal of the 1930s, the civil rights struggle of the 1960s, the legislative advances that widened opportunities for women, minorities, people with disabilities, and gays and lesbians of the 1970s. Social work was in its prime during each of these eras of progressive social change.

The opposite occurs as well, sometimes in reaction to the social advances for human rights: Resentments arise against progressive programs of all sorts—for example, antipoverty programs and affirmative action initiatives. Conservative ideology is reinforced by media hype over illicit drug use, immigration problems, and the expense of universal social insurance programs (e.g., Social Security). Politicians can play into the backlash and thereby promote it. During wartime, democracy suffers, paranoia spreads, and the people under military threat are apt to repress dissent. An unpopular war, however, can have the opposite effect and mobilize people into acts of resistance.

Consider the rise of Jim Crow laws in the post-Reconstruction South, the war hysteria and anti-immigrant fervor during World War I, and the McCarthy witch hunts that followed World War II. The social work profession was forced to keep a low profile during the attacks from the Right. These policies and practices eventually were seen as counterproductive, so they did not endure.

Sometimes, though, policies that were shown to be a dismal failure earlier; for example, providing free range to banks and business corporations in conjunction with trickle-down ideology as precipitated the Great Depression (McNeese, 2010), or continuing to invest vast resources and lives in an unwinnable war such as Vietnam, are tried once more in the absence of learning from history.

So the pendulum swings back and forth. Today, the intransigence of the radical Right, along with the consolidation of power as income and wealth that have concentrated at the top, leaves us with a nation strongly divided, politically and economically.

The short history of the first wave of social work in Iran illustrates the spirit of social work, imagination, and the universality of that spirit, if not always of the specific content. The integration of social work with community development was possible due to a complex but favorable government response as well as to the political pull, personal charisma, and dedication of a remarkable woman. This same history also underscores the political vulnerability of schools of social work to political and social repression forces, especially when they are directed against women and ethnic minorities (in this case, the attacks were against women and "Zionists").

Looking back over the history of social work, we can see the roots of the two-pronged approach to helping people in the contributions of our two foremothers (that is, favoring interventions that focus on the individual or working toward social/political change). We find the same spirit in the stories of social work in the United Kingdom and Ghana as well. The uniqueness of social work as a helping profession is that students are prepared to do work at both micro- and macro-levels, and NASW, in its code of ethics, includes standards for both. In our overview of the history of social work, we can conclude that it is a proud history—the story of strong women and gentle men in many ways ahead of their time who worked for social reform or to help individuals in distress. The economic challenges are great. Nevertheless, the spirit of the foremothers of social workers lives among us now, critical and indomitable.

Critical Thinking Questions

1. Which two technologies from early history do you consider to have had the greatest impact on society?

2. Can you think of two or three new technologies that have appeared in the early 21st century with relevance for social welfare? Discuss the impact they have had on our society.

3. How might America be different today had not Martin Luther transformed church history?

4. What were some of the functions of slavery for the South? How might life in the United States be different today had the South been allowed to secede from the union?

5. What is the similarity in Paul Ryan's expressed views and those of social Darwinism, according to Robert Reich or your own analysis?

6. Which principles from the British poor laws carried over to America are still with us today?

7. Review the roles that social workers played in setting up the New Deal. What would it take for the profession to play a similar role today?

8. A number of portraits of women pioneers of social work are presented in this chapter. Reviewing these portraits, which one in your opinion best represents the essence of social work policy practice?

9. What are the basic concepts of ecosystems as a model, and how does it relate to sustainability?

10. Note the parallels between the history of social work in the United Kingdom and that in the United States. What are some differences?

References

Abadinsky, H. (2011). *Drugs: An introduction* (7th ed.). Belmont, CA: Cengage.

Aberth, J. (2005). *The black death: The great mortality of 1348–1350.* Hampshire, England: Palgrave Macmillan.

Alterman, E., & Mattson, K. (2012). *The cause: The fight for American liberalism from Franklin Roosevelt to Barack Obama.* New York, NY: Penguin.

Anastas, J. (2012a, February). Eugenics: We can learn from history. *NASW News, 57*(3), p. 3.

Anastas, J. (2012b, April). Social work month goes global. *NASW News, 57*(4), p. 3.

Armstrong, K. (2008). *The Bible: A biography.* New York, NY: Grove/Atlantic.

Arrigo, J. (2008). *Plantations and historic homes of New Orleans.* Minneapolis, MN: Voyageur Press.

Assembly of First Nations. (2006). *Leadership action plan on First Nations child welfare.* Retrieved from www.turtleisland.org/healing/afncf.pdf

Béland, D. (2010). *What is social policy? Understanding the welfare state.* Cambridge, England: Polity Press.

Berg-Weger, M. (2013). *Social work and social welfare: An invitation* (2nd ed.). New York, NY: Routledge.

Besthorn, F., & McMillen, D. P. (2002). The oppression of women and nature: Ecofeminism as a framework for an expanded ecological social work. *Families in Society, 83*(3), 221–233.

Blau, J., & Abramowitz, M. (2010). *The dynamics of social welfare policy.* New York, NY: Oxford University Press.

Bowen, M. (1978). *Family therapy in clinical practice.* Northdale, NJ: Jason Aronson.

Bryson, L. (1992). *Welfare and the state: Who benefits?* New York, NY: St. Martin's Press.

Clark, K. (1969). *Civilization.* New York, NY: Harper & Row.

Coates, J. (2003). *Ecology and social work: Towards a new paradigm.* Halifax, Nova Scotia: Fernwood.

Colman, P. (2007). *Breaking the chains: The crusade of Dorothea Lynde Dix.* Lincoln, NE: iUniverse Press.

Cottle, M. (2012, February 20). Race baiting: All the rage. *Newsweek,* p. 5.

Council on Social Work Education. (2011). *2010 statistics on social work education in the United States.* Alexander, VA: Author.

Day, P. (2009). *New history of social welfare* (6th ed.). Boston, MA: Allyn & Bacon.

Day, P. J. (2012). Social policy from Colonial times to the Civil War. In J. Midgley & M. Livermore (Eds.), *The handbook of social policy* (2nd ed., pp. 103–113). Thousand Oaks, CA: Sage.

DiNitto, D. M. (2011). *Social welfare: Politics and public policy.* Boston, MA: Allyn & Bacon.

Dolgoff, R., & Feldstein, D. (2012). *Understanding social welfare: A search for social justice* (9th ed.). Boston, MA: Prentice Hall.

Dominelli, L. (2009). *Introducing social work.* Cambridge, England: Polity Press.

Downey, K. (2009). *The woman behind the New Deal: The life of Frances Perkins, FDR's secretary of labor and his moral conscience.* New York, NY: Nan A. Talese.

Encyclopaedia Britannica. (1993). Social welfare. *The New Encyclopaedia Britannica, 27,* 372–392. Chicago: University of Chicago Press.

Erikson, K. (1966). *Wayward Puritans: A study in the sociology of deviance.* New York, NY: Wiley.

Garfinkel, I., Rainwater, L., & Smeeding, T. (2010). *Wealth and welfare states: Is America a laggard or leader?* New York, NY: Oxford University Press.

Gates, H. L., Jr. (2011). *Black in Latin America*. New York: New York University Press.

George, S. (2010). *Whose crisis, whose future? Toward greener, fairer, richer world*. Cambridge, England: Polity Press.

Germain, C., & Gitterman, A. (1980). *Life model of social work practice*. New York, NY: Columbia University Press.

Herrick, J. M. (2012). Social policy and the Progressive Era. In J. Midgley & M. Livermore (Eds.), *The handbook of social policy* (2nd ed., pp. 116–132). Thousand Oaks, CA: Sage.

Hokenstad, T. (2008). International social work education. In T. Mizrahi & L. E. Davis (Eds.), *Encyclopedia of social work* (Vol. 2, pp. 488–491). New York, NY: Oxford University Press.

Jansson, B. S. (2012). *Becoming an effective policy advocate: From policy practice to social justice* (6th ed.). Belmont, CA: Cengage.

Jimenez, J. (2010). *Social policy and social change: Toward the creation of social and economic justice*. Thousand Oaks, CA: Sage.

Jones, M. (2008, December 28). The smuggler: Irena. *New York Times Magazine*, p. MM46.

Karger, H. J., & Stoesz D. (2013). *American social welfare policy: A pluralist approach*. Boston, MA: Pearson.

Kazin, M. (2014, Spring). The fall and rise of the U.S. populist left. *Dissent*. Retrieved from http://www.dissentmagazine.org/article/the-fall-and-rise-of-the-u-s-populist-left

Kemp, S. P., & Brandwein, R. (2010). Feminisms and social work in the United States: An intertwined history. *Affilia, 25*, 341–364.

Kendall, K. (1989). Women at the helm: Three extraordinary leaders. *Affilia, 4*(1), 23–32.

Kirst-Ashman, K. (2010). *Introduction to social work and social welfare: Critical thinking perspectives* (4th ed.). Belmont, CA: Cengage.

Knight, L. (2010). *Jane Addams: Spirit in action*. New York, NY: W. W. Norton

Kunstreich, T. (2003). Social welfare in Nazi Germany: Selection and exclusion. *Journal of Progressive Human Services, 14*(2), 23–52.

Lavalette, M. (2011). *Radical social work today*. Bristol, England: Policy Press.

Lieberman, A. (2010). Sattareh Farman Farmaian: Bringing social work education. In A. Lieberman (Ed.), *Women social workers who have changed the world* (pp. 158–210). Chicago, IL: Lyceum.

Leighninger, L. (2012). The history of social work and social welfare. In C. N. Dulmus & K. M. Sowers (Eds.), *The profession of social work: Guided by history and led by evidence* (pp. 1–34). Hoboken, NJ: Wiley.

Lincoln, A. (1863). Annual message to Congress, December 1, 1862. In M. Cook & C. G. Leland, *The Continental Monthly, 3*(1), 126.

Lorenz, W. (1994). *Social work in a changing Europe*. London, England: Routledge.

Louisiana State Museum. (2012). *The Cabildo: Antebellum Louisiana*. Retrieved from www.crt.state.la.us/louisiana-state-museum/online-exhibits/the-cabildo/antebellum-louisiana-urban-life/

Maisto, S., Galizio, M., & Connors, G. (2011). *Drug use and abuse* (6th ed.). Belmont, CA: Cengage.

Malai, R. (2012, April). Remembering Hull House. *NASW News, 57*(4), pp. 1, 6.

Mary, N. (2008). *Social work in a sustainable world*. Chicago, IL: Lyceum.

McGregor, K. (2012, August 21). Council proposes to reverse social worker pay cuts. *Community Care*. Retrieved from www.communitycare.co.uk/2012/08/21/council-proposes-to-reverse-social-worker-pay-cuts-by-april-2014/

McNeese, T. (2010). *Discovery U.S. history: The Great Depression 1929–1938*. New York, NY: Chelsea House.

Mills, G. B. (2013). *The forgotten people: Cane river's creoles of color*. Baton Rouge, LA: LSU Press.

Mullaly, B. (2006). Forward to the past: The 2005 CASW code of ethics. *Canadian Social Work Review, 23*(1–2), 145–150.

Otto von Bismarck. (2012). In *Encyclopaedia Britannica*. Retrieved from www.britannica.com .proxy.lib.uni.edu/EBchecked/topic/66989/Otto-von-Bismarck

Payne, M. (2014). *Modern social work theory* (4th ed.). Chicago, IL: Lyceum.

Payne, M., & Shardlow, S. (2002). *Social work in the British Isles*. London, England: Jessica Kingsley.

Pierson, P., & Hacker, J. (2010). *Winner-take-all-politics: How Washington made the rich richer and turned its back on the middle class*. New York, NY: Simon & Schuster.

Piven, F. F. (2008). *Challenging authority: How ordinary people change America*. Lanham, MD: Rowman & Littlefield.

Prigmore, C. (1990). Social welfare in Iran. In D. Elliott, N. Mayadas, & T. Watts (Eds.), *The world of social welfare: Social welfare and services in a international context* (pp. 171–182). Springfield, IL: Charles C Thomas.

Reardon, C. (2012, March/April). "Case" and "cause" in social work education: A balancing act. *Social Work Today, 12*(2), 20–23.

Reisch, M. (2012). Social policy and the Great Society. In J. Midgley & M. Livermore (Eds.), *The handbook of social policy* (2nd ed., pp. 151–168). Thousand Oaks, CA: Sage.

Reisch, M. (2014). U.S. social policy and social welfare: A historical overview. In M. Reisch (Ed.), *Social policy and social justice* (pp. 43–100). Thousand Oaks, CA: Sage.

Reisch, M., & Andrews, J. (2002). *The road not taken: A history of radical social work in the United States*. London, England: Routledge.

Robinson, M. B., & Scherlen, R. G. (2014). *Lies, damned lies, and drug war statistics*. Albany, NY: State University of New York Press.

Samuel, M. (2012, August 23). Councils urged to replace social workers with non-qualified staff. *Community Care*. Retrieved from www.communitycare.co.uk/2012/08/22/councils-urged-to-replace-social-workers-with-non-qualified-staff/

Schlosser, E. (1994, August). Reefer madness. *Atlantic Monthly, 274*(2), 45–59.

Sinclair, U. (1906/2001). *The jungle*. Mineola, NY: Dover Thrift Books.

Specht, M., & Courtney, M. E. (1994). *Unfaithful angels: How social work abandoned its mission*. Toronto, Canada. Maxwell Macmillan Canada.

Stoesz, D. (2012). Social policy: Reagan and beyond. In J. Midgley & M. Livermore (Eds.), *The handbook of social policy* (2nd ed., pp. 169–178). Thousand Oaks, CA: Sage.

Taylor, N. (2009). *American-made: The enduring legacy of the WPA: When FDR put the nation to work*. New York, NY: Bantam.

Trattner, W. A. (1999). *From poor law to welfare state: A history of social welfare in America* (6th ed.). New York, NY: Free Press.

Trevithick, P. (2012). *Social work skills and knowledge: A practice handbook*. Berkshire, England: Open University Press.

van Wormer, K., & Besthorn, F. H. (2011). *Human behavior and the social environment, macro level*. New York, NY: Oxford University Press.

van Wormer, K., Jackson, D. W., & Sudduth, C. (2012). *The maid narratives: Black domestics and white families in the Jim Crow South*. Baton Rouge: Louisiana State University Press.

Vowell, S. (2008). *The wordy shipmates*. New York, NY: Riverhead Books.

Weber, M. (1905/1930). *The Protestant ethic and the spirit of capitalism*. Translated by Talcott Parsons. London, England: Unwin Hyman.

Zinn, H. (2003). *A people's history of the United States*. New York, NY: HarperCollins.

Zinn, H. (2008, April 7). Beyond the New Deal. *The Nation*. Retrieved from www.thenation.com

Purpose and Structure of Social Welfare Policy

Should any political party attempt to abolish social security, unemployment insurance, and eliminate labor laws and farm programs, you would not hear of that party again in our political history. There is a tiny splinter group, of course, that believes you can do these things. Among them are Texas oil millionaires and an occasional politician or business man from other areas. Their number is negligible and they are stupid.

—Dwight D. Eisenhower, Presidential Papers (1954)

During the 2012 national election campaign, the welfare system was very much in the news. When President Obama passed on some of the responsibility for writing guidelines for welfare eligibility to the states, Republican candidates seized on the opportunity to create an ad in order to capitalize on white fears of black power. According to a Mitt Romney TV ad, "Since 1996, welfare recipients were required to work on July 12, President Obama quietly ended the work requirement, gutting welfare reform. . . . Mitt Romney's plan for a stronger middle class will put work back in welfare" (Delaney, 2012).

The image of a black president reducing work requirements for welfare recipients who are thought to be mostly black played into a stereotype of welfare recipients that has persisted for as long as these programs have been in place. In 1971, for example, country western singer Johnny Cash, a Nixon admirer, was asked by the president to sing the popular song "Welfare Cadillac," written by Guy Drake (2007/1970). This song stereotyped poor white and black people; the singer brags that he doesn't work but and lives in a shack with 10 kids and that his wife is shopping for a new Cadillac with the welfare money they get. Cash's refusal to honor the president's request was widely publicized in the media at the time. Ronald Reagan picked up on this stereotype during his presidency and feminized it. On his campaign he made up a story about a "welfare queen" who cheated the system and drove a Cadillac. He was playing on the racial and social fears of white voters and stressed his opposition to busing, affirmative action, and welfare aid (Jansson, 2012). Even before Nixon, Lyndon Johnson had correctly anticipated the backlash against the progressive programs he worked to enact into law. "The blue collar worker," he said in his memoirs, "felt that the Democratic Party had traded his welfare for the welfare of the black man" (Black, 2007, p. 520). It was thus no surprise when the Romney-Ryan ticket of the 2012 election chose to make work requirements for welfare recipients—and false claims about President Obama's easing up on these recipients—a focal point of their campaign.

Social welfare policies are not created in a vacuum but are embedded in the social fabric of the society of which they are a part. Our first task in this chapter, then, consistent with the world view of this book, is to present an overview of the teachings about care for others—especially the poor and the sick—from the world's major religions. Next, we focus on how these religious principles became ingrained in American values—values we will spell out as they relate to social welfare. Then we consider the social functions of welfare and consider questions of sustainability. We contrast the aims of socialist models at one end of the economic spectrum and capitalist models at the other. In this way, we move from the abstract teachings about social welfare to their practical implications.

The Religious Underpinnings of Social Welfare

The religious traditions in a given country are important in shaping social welfare policy. These traditions and belief systems linger with us still; they are decisive in determining the general response to people in need as well as to people who are different—the LGBT community, for example. All the religions discussed here have significant differences between the most orthodox and most liberal groups within each religion, but our concern in this section is with the basic traditions related to caring for the poor and needy. A second, though not secondary, concern is with caring for the earth and the sense of a sacredness in nature.

We begin with an overview of the world's major religions by the Tibetan Buddhist Dalai Lama (2001) who offers the following insight: "Though we may find differences in philosophical views and rites, the essential message of all religion is very much the same: They all advocate love, compassion, and forgiveness" (pp. 8–9).

Karen Armstrong (2011), in her study of altruism in religion, agrees. Drawing on research from neuroscience, she argues that through evolution our brains have become wired for the capacity to feel empathy for others. This empathy is expressed in the teachings of all the major religions.

Hinduism

Indian civilization is very old. Based on a belief in spiritual oneness, Hinduism has a 4,000-year history that began with Aryan invaders. Central to the Hindu faith is the caste system, in which poverty was not a condition for personal blame in the present life. Rather, people were placed in poverty to atone for past lives or to prepare for future ones. Accordingly, caste and poverty—fortune in life—are viewed as inevitable. Still, nonviolence and giving charity to beggars are basic principles for living under Hinduism (Moses, 2002). The practicing Hindu believes in nonviolence, linked to the belief of the inherent worth of all people. In this way, there is a focus on helping people in the local environment while reaching out to wider social systems, even globally.

Hindu principles emphasize *dharma*—a set of obligations linked to family, society, occupation, and the wider realm or universe. Canda and Furman (2010) differentiate traditional Hinduism, which is more other worldly, from the more action-oriented Gandhian Hinduism, influenced by Mahatma Gandhi. Gandhian principles, upheld by many in India, highlight the importance of a spiritually explicit, compassionate approach to social action that can guide social workers in community organizing work. Many environmentalists draw their inspiration from the life of Gandhi (Jain, 2011).

What in Hindu beliefs are relevant to sustainability? Under Hinduism, simple living is a model for the development of sustainable economies. Millions of Hindus recite mantras daily from sacred texts, such as the *Upanishads*, an ancient collection of teachings on the reverence for all life, human and nonhuman. The *Upanishads* explain the interconnection of five basic elements—space, air, fire, water, and earth, which are respected through material simplicity (Jain, 2011). Reciting the mantras, Hindus revere their rivers, mountains, trees, animals, and the earth. This value reduces violence by encouraging people to perform their work, to live simply and to limit environmental damage insofar as is possible (Canda & Furman, 2010). Dharma—often translated as "duty"—can be interpreted to include a responsibility to care for the earth (Jain, 2011). According to Narayanan (2003), however, the ecological messages are not necessarily seen as injunctions to be followed. The same could be said of the texts of other religions as well.

Buddhism

Like Hinduism, Buddhism originated in India, yet this religion has consistently denied the religious status of caste. Buddhism was founded in the sixth and fifth centuries BCE by Siddhartha Gautama, later known as the Buddha. As early as 300 BCE, hospitals and shelters for both people and animals were endowed by Prince Asoka of India following his conversion to Buddhism. In the first century CE, Buddhism entered China and through its priest exhorted China's rulers to care for the poor, and poverty was redefined as a holy state (Day, 2009). A meager system of welfare developed, providing only food and shelter. In times of natural disaster, according to Day (2009), the Chinese government's relief policy enabled the poor to buy food from its granaries, or if they could not pay, they could receive free grain. Additionally, the poor were taken from ravaged areas and resettled on new lands.

In *Twelve Steps to a Compassionate Life*, Karen Armstrong (2011) discusses compassion, or Karuna, in Buddhism, which is defined as a determination to liberate others from their grief. The Buddha's crucial insight was that to live morally was to live for others; one must strive to alleviate the suffering of other people. He taught that we should make an effort to extend our benevolence to the farthest reaches of the earth.

British environmentalist Patrick Curry (2011) states that ecologically speaking Buddhism has a lot to offer. He even asks if there is a green Buddhism. Respect for nonhuman as well as human life is strong in Buddhist teachings. In this religion, direct action rather than faith is what counts. This fact is exemplified by (a) the monks in Thailand who have worked tirelessly campaigning against deforestation and (b) the work of the current Dalai Lama.

Judaism

A most significant cultural source for the values of the Western world has been the Judeo-Christian heritage. Emerging out of a desert existence, the sense of Judaic community was strong; hospitality was provided to the stranger. The Bible explains this in the following passages:

> You shall give to him [your poor brother] freely, and your heart shall not be grudging when you give to him, because for this the Lord your God will bless you in all your work and in all that you undertake. (Deuteronomy 15:10, King James Version)

> Love ye therefore the strangers for ye were strangers in the land of Egypt. (Deuteronomy 10:19, King James Version)

The Talmud is the second great collection of Jewish scripture after the Torah, the first five books of the Bible. The Talmud consists of interpretations of the Torah for its application to new circumstances. Charity, justice, and loving kindness—these are the basic precepts of Judaism. To honor the poor is to honor God. These concepts, which form the basis for altruism, were codified in the Talmud after the Babylonian captivity around 600 BCE (Day, 2009). Social welfare, according to Dolgoff and Feldstein (2012), became institutionalized in two important aspects: expected behavior and providing for the poor without demeaning them. In Talmudic times, for example, there was a community charity box devised in such a way that when people put their hands into it others would not know whether they were giving or taking money.

Among the social welfare practices developed by the Jews were hospitable reception of strangers; education of orphans; redemption of lawbreakers; endowment of marriages; visitation of the ill and infirm; burial of the dead; consolation of the bereaved; and care of widows, slaves, divorcees, and the aged (Leighninger, 2012). Since the late 1800s in the United States, numerous Jewish-sponsored human service organizations resettled refugees and provided professional services and community centers (Canda & Furman, 2010).

The Old Testament in Genesis 1:24 and 2:15 describes the bounty of the earth—the animals that God put on earth and his placing of Adam in the Garden of Eden. This passage, as Curry (2011) suggests, places humans in the role of stewards of the land.

Christianity

The ideals of Christianity are a blending of all that had gone before—Jewish teachings and later Greek and Roman influences. Christianity is a religion based on Jesus Christ. What is known to us about the historical life of Jesus is contained in the four gospels of the New Testament and in the writings of Flavius Josephus, a Jewish-Roman historian who lived to about 100 CE. Because of Jesus's remarkably zealous followers—chief among them, Paul—the teachings of Jesus were spread across the ancient world and immortalized in scripture.

Jesus taught that every person would someday be judged by God. And what was the basis for this judgment? The standard was not to be the individual's belief in certain creeds but rather his or her compassion for others (Armstrong, 2011). In words that may be highly familiar to the reader, Jesus is quoted as saying,

> When saw we thee a stranger, and took thee in? Or naked and clothed thee? Or when saw we thee sick, or in prison, and came unto thee? And the King shall answer and say unto them, Verily I say unto you, inasmuch as ye have done it unto one of the least of these my brethren, ye have done it unto me. (Matthew 25:38–40, King James Version)

The development of Christianity held profound implications for social welfare (Dolgoff & Feldstein, 2012). Charity, near sanctification of the poor, and the denigration of conspicuous consumption or materialism were the central themes. Until the Protestant reformation, in fact, these themes were fundamental to Western social welfare practice.

After the death of Jesus, Paul stressed the importance of individual responsibility in his writings: "If any would not work, neither should he eat" (2 Thessalonians 3:10, King James Version). The early Christian church, and the generations that followed, took seriously the command of Jesus, a revolutionary, to carry out the expression of love and compassion. The poor, slaves, widows, orphans, and those persecuted for their Christian beliefs were aided. Women were actively engaged in charitable works from the very start (Day, 2009). By the fourth century, Christianity was legalized by the Roman emperor Constantine. Christians donated funds openly; they built hospitals for the sick and established a network of charitable activities. Monasteries often served as all-purpose but primitive, social service agencies for the needy. Later, saints renounced material goods and family ties and led lives of poverty.

Regarding what Curry (2011) calls the ecological ethic, the Christian message has been interpreted differently by different commentators. Jesus did give a blessing to "the lilies of the field" and noted how much God cares for the sparrows, yet some critics say since the Old Testament states that God told early man to "subdue the earth," humans have the right to do anything to the earth that they want (Curry, 2011, p. 33). Positive interpretations of God's wishes, however, most strikingly were provided by St. Francis who had a spiritual love for God's creatures and Pope Benedict XVI who has called wanton destruction of the environment a new sin. Today, within the Protestant evangelical movement there is a strong faction of activists working to help the poor and protect the environment; the predominant belief—according to Marcia Pally (2011), author of *The New Evangelicals*—is that the mission of Christianity is to promote social and environmental justice. The message of the new evangelicals implies a principle of sustainability; our duty is to protect and preserve the earth.

According to a recent national survey conducted by the Pew Research Center (2012), 73% of Americans consider themselves actively Christian. Almost 20% are unaffiliated—of whom almost 6% are atheist or agnostic. Of the Christians, 48% are Protestant, 22% Catholic, 1% orthodox, and 2% Mormon.

Confucianism

More a moral philosophy than a religion, Confucianism, which developed around 500 BCE, is based on the teachings of the philosopher Confucius. These teachings have been highly influential in China and South Korea. No specific welfare programs are attached to Confucianism, but the focus on moral behavior for individuals includes a duty to be helpful to others (Chapin, 2014). Self-sacrifice is expected in order to help others. The concentric circles of compassion are integral to this belief system; compassion is taught in the family because through family we learn to live with other people (Armstrong, 2011).

Central to Confucianism is a focus on care for the environment; followers are enjoined not to waste grain or to catch more fish and turtles that can be eaten (Moses, 2002). The Confucianism teachings of respect, harmony, and reciprocity can be extended from human relations and applied to the whole of creation.

Islam

Founded by the prophet Muhammad—who died in 632 CE—Islam is the youngest and in some ways the most simple and direct of the world's great religions. The focus of this religion is on the worshiping of the one true God—Allah. The meaning of Islam is submission to God. Islam is the dominant religion today in large parts of Asia and North Africa, the Middle East, Pakistan, Malaysia, and Indonesia. Islam's salient feature is its devotion to the Koran. Unlike the Bible, the Koran (Qur'an) was produced in a limited time period, and it is a homogenous whole (Armstrong, 2011). The verses that deal with forgiveness and kindness are far more numerous than those dealing with the conduct of battle. Muslims are instructed to show compassion and to give a regular proportion of their income to the poor (Armstrong, 2011). Piety was seen as disbursing wealth among one's kin, orphans, beggars, and also in freeing the slaves (Koran 2:177). Central to Islam, as Canda and Furman (2010) inform us, is a strong social justice value. Muhammad advocated social reforms on behalf of women, children, and disadvantaged groups.

In 650 CE, the followers of the prophet Mohammed were told they had an obligation to help poor people and that paying a *zakat*, or "purification" tax, to care for the

Source: Photo by Robert van Wormer.

Islamic Center. This mosque was built in Bowling Green, Kentucky, for the Bosnian refugees who settled there. Today, a diverse population of people from Pakistan, Egypt, and Iraq worship there.

poor was one of the obligatory duties of Islam (Chapin, 2014). This duty, to give alms to the poorer class, alternated from being voluntary to mandatory to being voluntary once again. Benevolence toward the needy is the prime social responsibility of a Muslim. By the 12th century, Islamic hospitals were magnificently built and equipped, and the Islamic universities were the centers of scholarship and culture (Day, 2009).

In his article on Islamic environmentalism, Richard Foltz (2003) states that the only thing one should take into account when trying to understand the Islamic perspective on ecology is the *Koran* and for Sunni Muslims, the *Hadith*. And as Foltz argues, such environmentally friendly sources as these instruct Muslims to look toward nature, where orderliness and fertility abound.

Native American Indigenous Religions

These diverse tribal groups had their own rites and rituals, but many common themes can be identified. Their helping approaches were communal and holistic; the importance of caring for one's neighbor was emphasized (Chapin, 2014). In fact, sharing was vital to the survival of the tribe. The basic social structure of the typical tribe reflected a basic approach when using the tribe's resources. Chapin provides an example from a Puritan document that described arrangements made by tribal leaders to care for widows and very old people.

Values of environmentalism are the strongest in the American Indian belief systems as compared to all other religious groups. The natural world is regarded as a source of inspiration (Canda & Furman, 2010). Native religious healing traditions centered on a shaman as healer who emphasized the curative power of nature and the fact that there is much we can learn from nature. Moses (2002) quotes a Sioux saying that God is the father and the earth, the mother. The symbols, stories, and ceremonies represent elements from the natural world. The Medicine Wheel is used as a teaching device to indicate the cyclical rhythms of life. Some tribal members want the rituals and beliefs as knowledge to be kept to themselves and not co-opted by outside groups; others feel the need to share these wise teachings in order to change the course of industrialism that is destroying the earth (Canda & Furman, 2010).

As we move into a discussion of the U.S. social welfare system, we can take note of the universal themes that permeate these early religious belief systems: themes of altruism, care for the less fortunate, and appreciation for the bounty of the earth. Early religious writings condone the giving of charity to the less fortunate and see this act as a blessing to the one who gives and the one who receives. Nancy Mary (2008) outlines four dimensions of sustainability that must be attained to ensure the continuation of all life on the planet: human survival, biodiversity, equity, and life quality. These sustainable values, Mary suggests, are at the root of all major religions and found in our code of ethics. At the personal level, ecosystems theory advocates social justice and looks toward a viable match between human needs and available resources.

The Practical Application of Values

The qualities that define these cultural religious traditions continue to influence social welfare to this day (Chapin, 2014). Of course there are contradictions—greed (national or personal) often trumps need, and materialism competes with spiritual values for pre-eminence. In many ways, the present condition of the United States reflects the challenge of putting religious ideals into practice in an advanced capitalist society. Let's consider some of these challenges.

Socialism

The ideas of Karl Marx—with his radical economic determinism—have had considerable impact on social welfare policy, especially in Europe. Following the Second World War, labor-dominated governments in Europe implemented sweeping social reforms. Today, strong unionization and socialist party political affiliations are characteristic of many European members of the social work profession. U.S. social welfare and social work, in contrast, were stymied at crucial historic periods by a strict capitalist political economy.

Proponents of socialism argue that the fundamental nature of capitalism is detrimental to advancing the public good because the primary motive is profit. Such a system, from this perspective, can only lead to greater inequality (Karger & Stoesz, 2013). Democratic socialists, such as Senator Bernie Sanders of Vermont, are strong believers in democracy. (To read his historic filibuster to Congress on corporate greed, see Sanders, 2011.) They advocate for change to take place through the electoral process, not by means of a violent revolution. They do want to see the eradication of the oppressive economic and political structures in society (Day, 2009). The problems pertaining to social welfare are seen as arising in a structural, not an individual, context.

Workers of the World Unite. This protest was held in Dublin, Ireland, as part of the Occupy movement.

The term socialism had negative connotations in the United States, except during its heyday prior to World War I—in the Progressive Era. Today, Democrats, such as President Obama, are sometimes wrongly accused of being socialists or European in their thinking. Recently, for example, Republican Mitt Romney, in his candidacy for the presidency, accused his chief opponent of the latter. "If you follow the president," he stated on the Consumer and Business Channel (CNBC) television network, "we're going to be more like Europe, more like a European social welfare state. If instead we take my course, we're going to look more like America, if you will, creating more opportunity for more people" (Cox, 2012). Earlier in the campaign, President Obama was criticized for his alliance with community organizers in inner-city Chicago and the radicalism associated with this kind of work.

The community-organizing tradition is strong in social work. During the 1970s—reacting against the social control aspect of the social welfare system—radical views rose to prominence (Payne, 2014) and influenced social work. Community organization, which stresses systemic, collective action and an emphasis on client advocacy and empowerment, has its roots in formulations from Europe and countries undergoing rapid socioeconomic change. In its history of advocacy for the poor and in its public service, the U.S. social work profession was influenced not only by the Judeo-Christian tradition but also by the economic views of Marxism. This influence is more apparent in Latin American and European and Canadian social work, however. Unlike a liberal approach, which accepts the social system, the structural school seeks transformation

(Mullaly, 2007). Socialist and structural approaches favor government-run social services over those run by the private sector and are consistent with the ideology of an institutionally or universally oriented society.

The Care Versus Cure Continuum

Whether it is more sustainable for society to seek to *prevent and eliminate* social problems—for example, homelessness, poverty, and unemployment—or to *invest in treatment* for people who really need the help is the question that plagues all modern societies. This is the care versus cure consideration, and it represents a classic dichotomy. Of course, no society exclusively focuses on prevention or cure, but we can imagine a continuum on which to place societies with which we are generally familiar. At one end of the continuum would be the care-oriented or *institutional approach* to social services. At the other end would be the *residual approach*. Wilensky and Lebeaux (1958) coined these terms, which have been widely used in social work textbooks ever since. The *institutional approach* provides universal benefits or guarantees a minimum income, support for having and raising children, free health care, and care for older adults who are no longer able to care for themselves. Such services are considered a right under this configuration. The *residual approach* separates people into the deserving and undeserving. In social welfare, this kind of thinking leads to the kinds of programs in which eligibility is based on proving a need for services, with strict guidelines for applying for services and with a finite time period built in. Programs are judged to be successful on the basis of reducing the welfare rolls, rather than reducing the numbers of people who live in poverty. The residual approach is also known as the safety net approach. The fact that many clearly fall through the cracks suggests that this metaphor is misleading at best.

In a residually oriented society, a stigma is attached to receiving welfare aid. As Zastrow (2009) suggests, the causes of welfare clients' difficulties are often seen as rooted in their own malfunctioning—the people themselves are blamed for problems perceived as stemming from their own inadequacies. Only when unemployment becomes so high overall (e.g., the Great Depression) do we begin to reduce the stigma and move from a residual position to an institutional one. Under conditions of mass economic crisis, then, the system rather than the individual receives the blame. Victim blaming is a natural human tendency by which we distance ourselves from others' misfortunes as it keeps us from empathizing and then feeling bad. We like to believe the world is just and that good things happen to good people (Ryan, 1976; Zastrow, 2009).

Where does the United States fall on this continuum? One source people look at is the United Nations Human Development Index (United Nations Development Programme, 2014). The UN rankings, however, are based on education and economics where the United States in the year of the study ranks fifth. Given the high rate of poverty in the United States, this high ranking seems undeservedly high. The flaw in the UN ranking system is its failure to consider key factors that speak to a country's ability to deal with social welfare issues such as infant mortality rates, long life span, health care, and social security, among others—which would provide a more complete picture of a sustainable society. In fact, according to Human Development

Reports (United Nations Development Programme, 2012), plans are now under way to develop a more people-oriented human development index that will involve an assessment of sustainability that reflects matters of intergenerational equity and global justice. At the time of this writing, however, a sustainable human development index has not materialized.

A tool that already speaks more to these social issues is Save the Children's Mothers' Index Ratings (Save the Children, 2012). This ranking includes items such as maternal and infant mortality rates, paid maternity leave, health care for new mothers, preschool opportunities, and gender equality measures. African nations were at the bottom; the Scandinavian countries, starting with Norway and Iceland, at the top; Canada at 19; and the United States at 25. These rankings provide some measure of documentation to bolster our case that Scandinavian societies are institutionally based with government-funded welfare programming and the North American countries more residually based, in that most universal services are absent. Social welfare policies that allow for a disproportionately high infant mortality rate and maternal death rate in relation to comparably rich nations are not sustainable policies because they do not meet the needs of present and future generations.

American value orientations, especially individualism and its corollary, independence—from which springs the notion of American "exceptionalism" that we discussed in Chapter 2—are a partial explanation for our "reluctant social welfare system" (Jansson, 2012). To put our more residually based system—and the fundamental values that lead us to them—in some global context, let's first examine an institutionally based system considered by international standards to be the best in the world.

THINKING SUSTAINABLY

The care versus cure dichotomy is a crucial tension in the search for sustainable social welfare policies. Religious undertones have always helped inform American attitudes on everything from free speech and the necessity for war to social welfare even as corporate values have also exerted a major influence, especially in in recent times. How do fundamental religious values influence the care versus cure dichotomy? How about corporate values? Are these fundamentally either/or value systems, or is there a common ground between them?

Norwegian Social Welfare System

This discussion is informed by my personal experience working as an alcoholism counselor for 2 years in Norway, follow-up visits, and an interview with a Norwegian social worker.

Practically every year Norway is first on the United Nations Human Development Index and most other rankings of social welfare systems. For a start, Norway has a number of advantages:

- A cold, but relatively mild, climate for the high latitude that extends above the Arctic Circle; nights are long in winter, but the temperature is rarely very far below freezing
- Abundance of seafood and forests
- Access to vast resources of oil in the North Sea
- A relatively homogeneous population

On the negative side,

- The growing season is very short and the terrain mountainous, so travel is difficult and most of the produce has to be imported
- The language is not well known outside the country, so for the sake of travel, Norwegians have to learn a second language—English
- The geographical location is remote from Central Europe

Cultural Context

The singular most striking cultural characteristic of the Norwegians is the belief in equality—that no one should act as if he or she is better than anybody else. The word for equality and sameness is the same word; there are no rigid class divisions or distinctions.

Children are taught from an early age not to brag and to be cooperative rather than competitive. This tradition is known as *Jantelov* (the law of Jante), "a tendency toward self-effacement and modesty familiar to most Norwegians" (Bjornen & Ravna, 2011, p. 13). As stated by one Norwegian university exchange student at Berkeley,

> The U.S. has a very liberalistic economy. Everyone looks up to the rich and there is no *Jantelov* like back home. But there is also a lot more homeless people here; it seems like there is no support system when things go wrong. (quoted in Bjornen & Ravna, p. 13)

Norway, first and foremost, is a child-oriented society. This is evidenced in customs and in the law. The National Constitution Day—May 17th—is a huge celebration. Instead of military pageantry, the major event consists of parades of children with their teachers in every town, all dressed in their national costumes. All corporal punishment of children is against the law and has been for some

Source: ©iStockphoto.com/Nanisimova.

Norwegian Parade of Children, Oslo, May 17. Constitution Day in Norway is celebrated by a parade of children dressed in traditional costumes who march with their teachers.

time. The child welfare system is formidable in Norway to the extent that social workers *sosionomer* are often seen as a threatening force associated with the removal of
children from their homes.

Skivenes and Skramstad (2013), in their extensive research on a large sample of
English, American, and Norwegian child welfare workers, found that the Norwegians
stood apart from the others in that services were designed to be preventive rather than
waiting until harm had come to the child. The threshold for intervention, according to
these researchers, is low. There is much concern about the welfare of children, for
example, when their parents separate. Mental health counseling is offered free of
charge for family problems. Here is what the *New in Norway* (2013) bulletin says about
protecting children during that time:

> Family counseling offices mediate in connection with separation or the break-
> down of relationships. All married couples with joint children under the age of
> 16 must undergo mediation when they separate. Cohabiting parents who end
> their relationship, must also seek mediation. This is compulsory in Norway.
>
> The purpose of mediation is to help families to agree on parental responsibilities
> and the children's situation in the time ahead, where the children are to live and
> how much time they will spend with the parent they do not live with. (p. 61)

Norwegians are nature lovers; many town dwellers also have houses in the coun-
tryside where they go cross-country skiing. Children learn to ski not long after they
learn to walk. Snow is seen as a blessing and used in many ways to enhance the movement of people. Daily exercise is considered a cultural norm—skiing, walking, and
biking—and the Norwegian diet is a healthy one. According to an article in the *Chicago
Tribune*, they are the slimmest people in Europe (though less so than 30 years ago)
(Hundley, 2007). Economic and environmental sustainability are key values. The government has funneled profits into a fund, now worth over $750 billion, as an invest-
ment for future generations (Mohsin, 2013).

Criminal Justice System

Consider the following American newspaper headline: "Norway: Rich Man Fined
$109,000 for Drunk Driving" (2009, p. A5). We read that in amazement. But digging
deeper, we learn that Norwegian courts set traffic fines based on income and personal
wealth. The man being fined had wealth in the millions, so he had to pay a substantial
fine so the pain would equal that of someone with far fewer resources. Thus, the punishment considers not only the crime but the individual committing the crime, with
the ultimate goal of an egalitarian criminal justice system.

If Russian novelist Dostoevsky (1882/2004) was right—that the degree of civilization in a society can be judged by entering its prisons—then Norway would do very
well on this measure alone. The guiding philosophy of the correctional system, according to Pratt (2008a), is to approximate life outside prison as much as possible. Prisons,
therefore, are small; there are many open as well as closed prisons. Even in the closed
prisons, family privacy time is encouraged, and family members can stay there, usually

at monthly intervals. In both kinds of prisons, prisoners receive an allowance; some with short sentences to serve continue with their previous employment.

Pratt (2008a) describes the Bastøy Prison in Norway as "the shining jewel in the Scandinavian open prison system" (p. 123). On the picturesque island where this prison is located, 100 men live in chalet-type facilities where they work in the agricultural or building trades and freely use knives and saws to build things. Their families can stay on the weekends with them in guest houses. A closed prison—Halden—is described in *Time* magazine as "the world's most humane prison" because even though the prison is inside walls, the focus is on transforming lives rather than punishment (p. 14). Prisoners, who are called "pupils," are taught by the officers (half of whom are women) social skills and a sense of family (Adams, 2010). They have access to modern amenities and jogging trails. The recidivism rate is extremely low by international standards. The maximum sentence that convicts serve is 21 years.

Social Welfare Benefits

Norwegian welfare state provides "cradle to grave" care. This includes free health care, education, child care, and job training, in addition to generous unemployment and sick leave benefits. Wages are high, and most workers belong to unions. Taxes are high—around 50% of earnings—but there are no payroll taxes or insurance costs for health care. Pratt (2008a) describes the political structure as built on social democratic values and a cross between the free market and state socialism. It is believed that the best way to prevent crime is through meeting everyone's needs.

The fact that Norway has managed to stay out of the European Union has allowed this country to maintain its high standard of social welfare offerings as compared to Sweden and Denmark. Sweden, for example, has privatized its pension system, which is now tied to global economic markets. Unlike other European nations, Norway has not suffered an economic crisis and unlike other energy rich countries, the government invests rather than spends much of its oil money (Thomas, 2009).

Health care services are considered among the best in the world and are available to everyone. Older Norwegians seeking to escape the dark northern winters can retire to government-run geriatric communities in sunny Spain (Hundley, 2007). Maternity leave is for 1 full year at 80% of full pay. Out of this year, the father is expected to take 10 weeks (Norwegian Labour and Welfare Services, 2012). Child benefits are around $160 tax free dollars per month per child up to age 18. Single parents get paid double the amount for one extra child. Taxes go as high as 50%, but there are deductions—for example, for living in the Arctic region. An extra bonus is given by the government in the form of holiday pay for workers to enable them to travel for their vacations. Paid vacations are for 25 working days per year. An extra week is added after age 60. One in three people work in the public sector; artists, for example, receive living grants (in 2007 they were paid $35,000 per year) (Pratt, 2008b).

Norway is not experiencing the aging crisis seen throughout the industrialized world—the increase in numbers of very old residents is matched by a serious decline in fertility levels. The average number of children per family is still just under two. Norwegians continue to retire in their 60s because they can afford to do so; many

Americans, in contrast are working longer out of financial necessity (Wacker & Roberto, 2011). The government in Norway subsidizes home modifications to encourage living at home. And yet, a much higher percentage of Norwegians over the age of 65 live in assisted-living housing and institutions (11.8%) than in other European countries (around 5–6%) or the United States (4.2%). Wacker and Roberto (2011) attribute this to the strong tradition of government support for caretaking and free nursing home care.

Research by sociologists Reisel and Brekke (2010) comparing higher education dropout rates between minority groups in the United States and Norway found a significant difference. Whereas American minority students have a lower graduation rate compared with nonminority students, in Norway there is no such difference. This is true even though minority students in Norway are also economically disadvantaged. The researchers attribute the difference to the greater stress in Norway on economic and social equality.

Although the Labour Party is one of the strongest parties in the parliamentary system, a right wing party (the Progress Party) increasingly has gained in popularity over the past two decades as more immigrants—many of them refugees from Africa and the Middle East—have moved to Norway. Pratt (2008b) sees a backlash brewing in this regard, which is a threat to the generous social welfare system. Another threat to this Nordic social welfare state, as foreseen by Pratt, is the increase in consumerism and materialism. A nation of such tremendous wealth is at risk of losing its egalitarian values as individuals build luxurious second homes in the country in place of the traditional Spartan huts.

American Exceptionalism and the Corporation

We spoke briefly in Chapter 2 about some of the key components of the American beliefs, commonly identified as American *exceptionalism*: work ethic, moralism, equal opportunity, mobility, competition, individualism, independence, family, and materialism. Central to these value orientations is the belief that through hard work individuals will prosper. Equality of opportunity is the goal. Moralism and the work ethic are intertwined and related to the Protestant ethic as defined by Max Weber. The moralism is a legacy from a Puritan past and is reflected in extremely high incarceration rates and widespread acceptance of the death penalty. Together these orientations are consistent with the making of a society that works in terms of national prosperity.

The concept of *exceptionalism* is sometimes used by foreign commentators to denote America's sense of its own superiority. Recently, Vladimir Putin (2013) wrote in a *New York Times* editorial that he expressed disagreement with American exceptionalism. "It is extremely dangerous," he wrote, "to encourage people to see themselves as exceptional, whatever the motive." Putin was referring to both a specific situation—President Obama's threat to conduct missile strikes against Syria—and to U.S. ideology in general.

Let us now look at one of the unique key features of American exceptionalism—individualism. It is a quality that cuts both ways. Individualism—in materialist terms—can be taken to the extreme as being rapacious greed and consumerism. These traits are incongruent with the norms that make sustainability possible—sacrifice for the public good, cooperation, and economic justice. Tim Wise (2010), however, speaks of *illuminated individualism* that "tries to recognize this truth that we are made up of many identities, and that these matter" (p. 157). Jimenez and colleagues (2014), similarly, indicate that in the form of a belief in individual rights and personal freedom, individualism is not necessarily negative and can have a beneficial effect on the welfare system. On the other hand, "believing in the individual locus of control and in the moral value of hard work and material goods puts at jeopardy those who are unemployed or marginally employed in low paying jobs" (p. 77). Jimenez et al. further indicate that there is a punishing aspect to work ethic, which is expected to lead to success and social mobility. When this does not happen—as is the case for many social work clients—they are judged as morally inadequate. Perhaps we should conclude that it is not the qualities themselves that are at fault but the degree to which they are upheld without the humanizing quality of compassion. In her recent speech at the Democratic National Convention, former Harvard law professor and candidate for the Massachusetts Senate, Elizabeth Warren (2012) described her values. In doing so, she turned to religion and discussed her teaching of Sunday school at a Methodist church:

> One of my favorite passages of scripture is: "Inasmuch as ye have done it unto one of the least of these my brethren, ye have done it unto me." Matthew 25:40. The passage teaches about God in each of us, that we are bound to each other and called to act. Not to sit, not to wait, but to act—all of us together. (p. 3)

Warren went on to talk about a calling. "We are called to restore opportunity for every American," (p. 3) she said. The concept of *the calling* is rooted in the teachings of Martin Luther, as we discussed in Chapter 2. This notion is linked to the Protestant work ethic, so we are talking about historical values that are recognized as central to American exceptionalism (Jimenez et al., 2014).

What about values of freedom and democracy? As the nation was on the brink of war, President Franklin Roosevelt (1941) gave a powerful speech. He spoke of the importance of equality of opportunity for youth and ending privileges for the few. Then he identified four freedoms that he viewed as essential for a democratic world. "The four freedoms" are freedom of speech and expression, freedom to worship God as one wishes, freedom from want, and freedom from fear.

These too are American values, and they closely relate to the shaping of social policy. Both Roosevelt and Warren emphasized equality of opportunity. Their vision was of a society characterized by a sense of fair play and social mobility.

Social mobility, as we know, is on the decline today in the United States over previous historical eras, and now the United States has become less mobile than comparable nations. This fact is revealed in several large empirically based studies, according to the *New York Times* (Paple, 2012). For example, a study by Swedish economists found that 42% of American men raised in the bottom fifth of incomes stay there as adults. That shows a level of persistent disadvantage much higher than in Denmark (25%) and Britain (30%)—a country famous for its class constraints. Paple speculates that the depth of U.S. poverty compared to that in these other countries may account for restricted American mobility.

We are now ready to suggest that something besides American values is holding the United States back from instituting policies congruent with sustainable economics. Why cannot the U.S. government ensure that every child born in America has a decent standard of living and, as enshrined in the Declaration of Independence (1776), the "certain unalienable rights," among them "life, liberty, and the pursuit of happiness"?

Economic Justice and the Rise of the Corporation

Economic justice, according to Craig Mosher (2009), is one of the pillars of sustainability. Economic justice involves equity or fairness. In a sustainable society, the people have to have faith in the system; they have to believe they and their children have the opportunity to achieve some success. But an increasing sense that the game is, in effect, rigged, has undermined that confidence. As wealth is concentrated in an ever smaller number of hands and as our electoral system itself seems to be bought and paid for by huge corporate interests, our questioning of the values that have led us here is inevitable. Speaking of the 2012 presidential election, environmentalist Gar Smith (2012) argues,

> In the United States, money doesn't just talk—it dictates. How can we hope to make progress on the path to sustainability when the road is blocked by barricades of bullion backed by battalions of billionaires? How do we break through the political gridlock?

The earth's richest 1,000 individuals now control as much wealth as the poorest 2.5 billion people on the planet. This super elite uses its vast wealth to control the media, influence politicians, and bend laws to its favor. In the United States, the wealthy dominate our government: 47% of U.S. representatives are millionaires as are 67% of U.S. senators. The Center for Responsive Politics reports congressional wealth has increased 11% between 2009 and 2011.

Not only is our economy out of balance with nature; our economy is also out of balance with the practical limits of physical and fiscal reality. As the Occupy Wall Street movement has indelibly framed it, we are now a society divided not only by haves and have-nots but also a nation—and a world—divided into the 99% and the 1% (p. 1).

So in the belief that something bigger than American values is responsible for the course that the social welfare system has taken and is taking today, we turn our attention to capitalism and the power of the corporation.

Let us start with a little history. The satirical Canadian film *The Corporation*, which has introduced many viewers to the little-known history of the corporation, was based on the book with the same title by Canadian law professor Joel Bakan (2005). From these sources we learn that the modern corporation grew out of the industrial age in England and was all about productivity—how much coal could be mined per man-hour and how many products could be produced in a certain time period. The framers of the American Constitution believed that the interests of the public welfare were paramount, not the interests of business. In the later 19th century, there was a legal turning point for the corporation, however. This came in the form of a Supreme Court decision that seemingly granted corporations the full rights of citizens of the United States.

The Supreme Court decision in question involved an interpretation of the equal rights laws originally added to the Constitution in the 14th Amendment to protect newly freed slaves. This amendment was interpreted to apply to corporations as well, to grant them the rights of a person—for example, freedom of speech. This decision took place in 1886. Before that time, corporations were severely restricted to keep them from gaining too much power or wealth (Hartmann, 2010). And after that time, the corporation was on its way to operate with impunity, but it took a long time before the situation became what it is today. In the words of Bakan (2005),

> Over the last 150 years, the corporation has risen from relative obscurity to become the world's dominant economic institution. Today, corporations govern our lives. They determine what we will eat, what we watch, what we wear, where we work, and what we do. We are inescapably surrounded by their culture, iconography, and ideology. (p. 5)

The following news headlines are revealing:

Seattle Times: "AP Investigation: Monsanto Seed Biz Role Revealed" (Leonard, 2009)

Time: "Big Tobacco's New Targets" (Kluger, 2009)

USA Today: "Body Scanner Makers Doubled Lobbying Cash over Five Years" (Schouten, 2010)

Time: "How Supermarkets Turn Shoppers into Hoarders" (Lindstrom, 2011)

Psychiatric Times: "The NRA versus the Doctors: A Psychiatrist's Take on an Explosive Issue" (Kweskin, 2011)

To understand how groups, such as the National Rifle Association (NRA) mentioned above, accrued such influence on keeping gun control laws at bay and how the manufacturers of body scan equipment got Congress to pass legislation supporting their use at airports, we need to consider the political aspect. Political scientists Hacker and Pierson (2011) attribute the unprecedented rise in corporate control over legislation, as well as the accumulation of capital by the super rich, to the role of political action committees (PACs). It is through the financial power of the PACs that decisions are made regarding which candidates should run for office, who should win the election, and who should stay in office. According to Hacker and Pierson, the whole political ecosystem has been transformed as politicians have become increasingly dependent on special interest lobbying groups for the financing of their political campaigns. Senators, such as John McCain, and many members of the public have argued vehemently for campaign finance reform. Then, in 2010 the U.S. Supreme Court ruled in favor of Citizens United, stating that corporations had the same rights as citizens to freedom of speech and therefore the government could not prohibit them from spending unlimited amounts of capital for political purposes. The PACs were then on the road to becoming super PACs, and the election of 2012 was to be the most expensive election in U.S. history.

Virtually all legislators today are beholden to special interest groups—to corporations such as pharmaceutical companies, hospitals, insurance companies, and weapons manufacturers. When the health care reform act was finally signed into law by President Obama, as Hacker and Pierson remind us, it was built on concessions to key industry players—the hospitals and drug companies. Otherwise Obama could not have gotten it passed through Congress.

Recently, the Global Commission on Elections, Democracy, and Security (2012), headed by former UN secretary general Kofi Annan and comprising former world leaders and Nobel Prize winners, has condemned the role of financing in electoral campaigns internationally. The United States is singled out as a flagrant example of questionable practices. U.S. campaign finance rules, which have allowed wealthy individuals to pour millions of dollars into the 2012 presidential election, have shaken public confidence in the political process, according to the report. The commission blamed the situation on a series of court decisions, in particular the controversial Citizens United ruling, which has "undermined political equality, weakened transparency of the electoral process, and shaken citizen confidence in America's political institutions and elections," according to the report by the Global Commission (2012, p. 34). Canada, in contrast, is praised for the balance its courts have managed to strike between safeguarding individual speech and protecting the overall integrity of the electoral process.

Contemporary Capitalism and the Tax System

Taxation in a capitalist system represents a thorny problem. Implicit in socialism is the belief that the nation's wealth should be shared so that all citizens can have their needs met. The optimal welfare state, the one that progressives would most like, would promote benefits as a right of citizenship, benefits that would be funded by a tax structure that derives its revenues largely from the rich (Karger & Stoesz, 2013). To a large extent, this is the program that the United States had under the New Deal and through the prosperous 1950s, during which time the very rich paid tax rates of 90% on their earnings. In subsequent years, the rates were lowered to 74%, which was the situation when Ronald Reagan came into power. Influenced by the conservative Heritage Foundation, he cut tax rates on the income of the rich from 74% to 38% (Hartmann, 2011). This move reduced the tax revenues and led to a substantial federal debt. During the Clinton administration, a cap was placed on domestic spending (Karger & Stoesz, 2013). The final tax adjustment took place under George W. Bush, who reduced the upper limit to 35% and cut the taxes on unearned income—interest on savings and stock dividends—to a mere 15%. The super rich are likely to pay taxes at the 15% rate as their money comes from their investments. If their investments are in real estate, however, they may not pay any taxes at all because of deductions.

One positive development that has been a tremendous help to working-class people is the earned income tax credit (EITC). The idea, which was to provide a strong incentive for people to work, actually came from conservatives to return the taxes paid to people whose income was below a certain level. It was passed into law by President Ford and then expanded by later presidents. The EITC lifts more children out of poverty than any other federal program (Linn, 2012).

Generally, capitalism in a residually oriented society passes legislation geared toward the welfare of the rich and the corporations. The ever-increasing access that business coalitions and industry lobbyists have to the political process further promotes winner-take-all policies. In *Winner-Take-All Politics: How Washington Made the Rich Richer—and Turned Its Back on the Middle Class*, Hacker and Pierson (2011) argue that from the erosion of job security to the rising toll of home foreclosures, winner-take-all has become the defining feature of American economic life. Their research revealed that between 1979 and 2005, the wealthiest one-tenth percent of the U.S. population received over 20% of all after-tax gains compared with the 13.5% enjoyed by the bottom 60% of the population. Hacker and Pierson state that there is no precedent for such a "mind-boggling" difference in all the years before the late 1970s (p. 3). Nor is there any parallel in the advanced industrialized world.

The flaws in free market capitalism, as Karger and Stoesz (2013) indicate, reached fruition in the 2007 global economic crisis when the U.S. housing market crashed. The deregulation of the banking industry, which began under President Clinton, led to far more liberal lending policies. This new ability to get credit led many Americans to make high-risk investments and to buy houses that were beyond their means. The economic crisis was worsened by huge tax cuts for the rich under the George W. Bush administration and a rapidly increasing national debt related to vast expenditures incurred through the fighting of two wars simultaneously in the Middle East. Deficits to finance wars are unsustainable because they pose a burden on future generations to pay for the damage. Today, according to military historian Andrew Bacevich (2010) author of *Washington Rules: America's Path to Permanent War*, the United States spends nearly as much on military power as every other country in the world combined. Politicians from both political parties fear loss of votes through any serious reduction in the defense budget, and the weapons industry is one of the largest of the lobbying groups in Washington.

What is the impact of these neoliberal capitalist policies on social work? Social workers are strongly influenced by the dictates of capitalism and by the growing inequality in today's society. Work demands become even higher with fewer resources and fewer workers doing more work. With *efficiency* and *economy* as watchwords, our government has turned over to the corporate world control of institutions that were once solidly in the public domain (Bakan, 2005). This includes social services as well as water and power utilities, health care, and prisons. These developments that have taken place in recent history are important to our study of social policy.

The Trend Toward Privatization

The increasing reliance on private health, educational, and social institutions to provide services is not merely national but international in scope. Proponents of privatization focus on cost savings and efficiency in the services offered; workers in this system generally receive less pay than workers in the state system and fewer benefits. In situations where public and private services are in competition, a two-tier system may develop as people with more money select services in the private sector, leaving the poor to the public programs. Eventually, those programs become stigmatized and their funding is reduced. Three arenas in which the thrust for privatization is having a significant impact are the growth of charter schools, private prisons, and nursing homes.

Before we consider specific examples of privatized services, we need an understanding of what is behind these trends. There is no better explanation than that offered by Si Kahn and Elizabeth Minnich (2005) in their book, aptly titled, *The Fox in the Henhouse: How Privatization Threatens Democracy*. Focusing on the schools, prisons, and the military, the authors forcefully argue that privatization is one of the most important political and economic developments of our time, a development that has crept up on us slowly and that now affects every social institution in the United States. Instead of serving the public good, privatization paves the way for powerful corporations to replace government authority with a private profit culture. This means that the basic programs in which Americans can take pride—mass education, Social Security, Medicare, public utilities, the post office—are all under attack. As Kahn and Minnich convincingly argue, the privatization agenda is not just something that happens here and there but is rather a deliberately calculated agenda to undermine public institutions. The scheme works like this: reduce the funding from the targeted services. Once agencies and services have been deprived of necessary funding, the ability to provide service suffers, and consumers become angry. With this "proof" that the government is inefficient, introduce a private sector "solution," and, above all, control the media to control the message. We need to keep this scheme as depicted by Kahn and Minnich in mind as we hear the case made for ever more reliance on private markets to solve the nation's problems.

Readers with an interest in preserving public education will want to take a look at Diane Ravitch's (2013) *Reign of Error: The Hoax of the Privatization Movement and the Danger to America's Public Schools*. Over and over, as Ravitch states, the message is sent out that our schools are failing; our teachers are incompetent; and our children are unable to compete on a global scale. At the same time, the funding is cut; the teachers are forced to teach to the demands of standardized testing; and they are underpaid and demonized. But the truth, as Ravitch argues, is that our schools are doing the best job they can under the circumstances, and she effectively demolishes the myth that the charter schools are far exceeding regular public schools. To improve the state of public education, she advocates for ending poverty, for comprehensive social services, for neighborhood schools, and for universal high-quality preschools. Privatization, she says, leads to social stratification, segregation, and demoralized teachers.

One of the most important sections of Ravitch's book relates directly to the unprecedented success of the privatization movement. This is the role of a little known organization called the American Legislative Exchange Council (ALEC), which is financed by major corporations to promote free market principles. ALEC's task is to write model legislation that can be used by state legislatures in the forms of bills they can pass in conservative states. The "stand your ground" laws that give individuals the right to use deadly force if they feel threatened (and were cited in the infamous Trayvon Martin killing in Florida), were widely adopted, for example. Generally, ALEC favors for-profit schools; the elimination of unions, tenure, and seniority; and laws restricting women's reproductive choices.

Consider these trends in relation to what has happened in the public school system in Chicago. Teachers went on strike in opposition to the mayor's plans to replace as many public schools as possible with publicly funded but privately operated charter schools (Rich, 2012). Teachers at these schools are rarely unionized and are paid $15,000 to $30,000 less than their counterparts at traditional district schools. Today, there are 96 of these schools in Chicago. Meanwhile, public school officials have closed 50 schools, most in the inner city; this has placed children in danger as many of them must walk across gang-infested areas to and from their new schools. Other neighborhood schools are left to operate with overcrowding and diminished budgets (Fitzpatrick, 2013). Now the district has quietly issued a call for new charter schools as a way to solve the crisis.

The trend toward privatization is felt across many professions. For-profit hospital chains are a major American industry. CEOs (chief executive officers) of the top health corporations, in fact, are among the highest-paid CEOs in the United States, if not the world. For-profit prisons and juvenile correctional facilities are springing up, and virtually every state prison system contracts out for services such as health care and food service. The majority of nursing homes (two-thirds) are operated for profit with public-funds (through Medicare and Medicaid programs) accounting for the majority of their revenue. Official reports from state and federal inspectors show a high rate of health-related

Source: ©iStockphoto.com/jcenteno89.

Trayvon Martin Protests Held in Over 100 U.S. Cities. Protests took place all over the United States when Martin's killer, an off-duty security guard, was found not guilty at his trial.

deficiencies in nursing homes, most related to understaffing; the highest number of violations is in the private, for-profit facilities (Pear, 2008).

The distinction between nonprofit private agencies, those from the business sector that seek to maximize income and reduce expenditures in order to make a profit, and their for-profit counterparts is increasingly blurred. Nonprofit agencies reap tremendous tax funding as well as public relations advantages. Predictions are that in light of current economic trends the expansion of public-private partnerships will only continue (Dolgoff & Feldstein, 2012). The unprecedented level of federal debt, the secular drift toward private enterprise as a way of life, and the growing recognition of the role of the private sector in social service delivery, enhance the attractiveness of this option. However, government intervention is as necessary as ever, perhaps even more necessary, to protect individuals from uncertainties inherent in a market-based economy.

Corporations get rich by keeping labor costs low by avoiding rehiring, substituting temporary for full-time workers, increasing productivity, and shifting employment abroad. As a consequence, unemployment rises and the income of full-time workers declines. The impact on the social welfare system and on the profession of social work is considerable. In fact, British social worker Donna Dustin (2008) wrote of this impact in *The McDonaldization of Social Work*. Just as with the business model that has brought such profits to McDonald's fast food restaurants, the same managerial application of efficiency, calculability, predictability, and control is transforming the social work profession. The author questions whether the relabeling of service users as customers or consumers and the focus on productivity contributes to empowering practice.

Generally, social workers work for nonprofit agencies, whether in the private or public sector, such as in child welfare at the Department of Health and Human Services. In the interest of cost-effectiveness, however, much of the direct service work is subcontracted out to private agencies that rely on part-time workers. Some social workers are employed by for-profit, private agencies. In these organizations, the neediest clients are likely to be screened out and referred elsewhere. Such agencies increase their profits through heavy marketing of their services, more efficient use of personnel, and reliance on part-time workers and volunteers.

The vast corporatization of America has in many ways taken traditional values such as competition and individualism to such extremes that we find our lives out of sync with the democratic system that we have been raised to revere. We need to look beyond basic values and recognize the politico-economic forces that impact social welfare policy today. In upcoming chapters, we will consider specific programs and how both traditional values and economic realities inform them.

Summary and Conclusion

We began the chapter by looking at the major religions and their teachings, which have contributed to our notion of social welfare. Common themes include the prohibition of the selfish pursuit of riches and the importance of taking care of others who are in need. We turned then to look at how these values play out in the real world, looking at the *care versus cure* continuum and contrasted the Norwegian and American experience. We looked at traditional American values—individualism, independence, and competition but also equal opportunity and democratic values—such as the four freedoms articulated by President Franklin Roosevelt. These values seem to be fairly consistent with a sustainable and universal social welfare system, except perhaps when taken to extremes.

The rise of Corporate America, and the subsequent turn to privatization has had an enormous effect on many institutions, including many of our social welfare programs. Well-financed think tanks conduct research, the findings of which are disseminated through the media, and they exert political influence through PACs. Reflecting the interests of big business and business leaders, multinational corporations play a major role in determining who the policymakers are and the direction that the policies will take. Small government, means-tested programs, privatization of social services, and low tax rates—these are among the policies supported. Major policy issues such as the control and distribution of society's wealth and citizens' rights to health, education, and shelter are bound up in the shift from public to private responsibility for social welfare.

We shift gears now in the following chapter to focus our attention on the concept of sustainability with a special emphasis on the natural environment as a social policy issue.

Critical Thinking Questions

1. How were people who received welfare money ridiculed and stigmatized in the 1960s? From your own experience, do these attitudes persist today?

2. What is the major theme that is threaded throughout all major religious beliefs? Which one do you consider the most closely related to social welfare values of generous care for the needy? Why?

3. Discuss the concept of "blaming the victim." How does it relate to attitudes toward poor people, if at all?

4. Consider Elizabeth Warren's biblical quote at the Democratic National Convention of 2012. How does this quote relate to some of the modern political trends?

5. What is *American exceptionalism*? How is our welfare system unique compared to that of other industrialized nations?

6. How do you feel about the argument that American values are out of sync with the dominant conservative views regarding welfare benefits?

7. Discuss how corporations were able to obtain such enormous power in our society? What is their role related to the shaping of social policy?

8. Research a recent development related to a pending crisis and proposals to rely on private markets as a way to solve the problem. How does this development relate to the models developed by ALEC or a similar right-wing organization?

9. Explain how a program that becomes means-tested changes character. Why would conservatives want to make a universal program—such as Social Security—available to only people who are below a certain income level?

10. How is the social welfare system in Norway consistent with the nation's values? What especially stands out for you in the description of social welfare in that country?

References

Adams, W. L. (2010, May 10). Halden: A look inside the world's most humane prison. *Time*, p. 14.

Armstrong, K. (2011). *Twelve steps to a compassionate life*. New York, NY: Anchor Books.

Bacevich, A. (2010). *Washington rules: America's path to permanent war*. New York, NY: Metropolitan Books.

Bakan, J. (2005). *The corporation: The pathological pursuit of profit and power*. New York, NY: Free Press.

Bjornen, M., & Ravna, S. (2011, Fall/Winter). School days. *News of Norway*, p. 13.

Black, C. (2007). *Richard M. Nixon: A life in full*. Toronto, Canada: McClelland & Stewart.

Canda, E. R., & Furman, L. D. (2010). *Spiritual diversity in social work practice: The heart of helping* (2nd ed.). New York, NY: Oxford University Press.

Chapin, R. (2014). *Social policy for effective practice: A strengths approach* (3rd ed.). Boston, MA: McGraw-Hill.

Cox, J. (2012, January 11). Romney moves ahead, rails against "social welfare state." *Consumer News and Business Channel*. Retrieved from www.cnbc.com

Curry, P. (2011). *Ecological ethics: An introduction* (2nd ed.). Cambridge, UK: Polity Press.

Dalai Lama. (2001). *An open heart: Practicing compassion in everyday life*. New York, NY: Little, Brown.

Day, P. (2009). *New history of social welfare* (6th ed.). Boston, MA: Allyn & Bacon.

Declaration of Independence. (1776, July 4). Government archives. Retrieved from www.archives.gov/exhibits/charters/declaration.html

Delaney, A. (2012, August 20). Mitt Romney welfare ad repeats false claim. Huffington Post. Retrieved from www.huffingtonpost.com

Dolgoff, R., & Feldstein, D. (2012). *Understanding social welfare: A search for social justice* (9th ed.). Boston, MA: Prentice Hall.

Dostoevsky, T. (2004). *House of the dead* (C. Garner, Trans.). New York, NY: Dover Thrift Editions. (Original work published 1882)

Drake, G. (2007/1970). *Welfare Cadillac*. Composed in 1970. Retrieved from www.cowboylyrics.com/tabs/drake-guy/welfare-cadillac-6468.html

Dustin, D. (2008). *The McDonaldization of social work*. Franham, England: Ashgate.

Eisenhower, D. (1954). Presidential papers. In B. Burrough (2009), *The big rich: The rise and fall of the greatest Texas oil fortunes* (pp. 221–222). London, England: Penguin.

Fitzpatrick, L. (September 15, 2013). Despite closings and budget cuts, CPS calls for new charter schools. *Chicago Sun-Times*. Retrieved from www.suntimes.com

Foltz, R. C. (2003). *Islamic environmentalism in theory and practice. In worldviews, religion and the environment: A global anthology* (pp. 358–365). London, England: Thomson-Wadsworth.

Global Commission on Elections, Democracy, and Security. (2012). *Deepening democracy: A strategy for improving the integrity of elections worldwide*. Retrieved from www.idea.int/elections/global-commission-2012/

Hacker, J., & Pierson, P. (2011). *Winner-take-all politics: How Washington made the rich richer— and turned its back on the middle class*. New York, NY: Simon & Schuster.

Hartmann, T. (2010). *Unequal protection: How corporations became "people"—and how you can fight back*. San Francisco, CA: Berrett-Koehler.

Hartmann, T. (2011). *Rebooting the American dream: Eleven ways to rebuild our country*. San Francisco, CA: Berrett-Koehler.

Hundley, T. (2007, November 11). From pool of cash, good fortune flows. *Chicago Tribune.* Retrieved from www.chicagotribune.com

Jain, P. (2011, April 10). 10 Hindu environmental teachings. *Huffington Post.* Retrieved from www.huffingtonpost.com

Jansson, B. S. (2012). *The reluctant welfare state: Past, present, and future* (7th ed.). Belmont, CA: Brooks/Cole.

Jimenez, J., Mayers Pasztor, E., & Chambers, R. M (with Pearlman, C.). (2014). *Social policy and social change: Toward the creation of social and economic justice* (2nd ed.). Thousand Oaks, CA: Sage.

Kahn, S., & Minnich, E. (2005). *The fox in the henhouse: How privatization threatens democracy.* San Francisco, CA: Berrett-Koehler.

Karger, H. J., & Stoesz, D. (2013). *American social welfare policy: A pluralist approach* (Brief ed.). Boston, MA: Pearson.

Kluger, J. (2009, July 27). Big tobacco's new targets. *Time*, pp. 50–51.

Kweskin, S. (2011, April 5). The NRA versus the doctors: A psychiatrist's take on an explosive issue. *Psychiatric Times.* Retrieved from www.psychiatrictimes.com

Leighninger, L. (2012). The history of social work and social welfare. In C. N. Dulmus & K. M. Sowers (Eds.), *The profession of social work: Guided by history and led by evidence* (pp. 1–34). Hoboken, NJ: Wiley.

Leonard, C. (2009, December 14). AP Investigation: Monsanto seed biz role revealed. *Seattle Times.* Retrieved from www.seattletimes.com

Lindstrom, M. (2011, November 7). How supermarkets turn shoppers into hoarders. *Time*, p. 58.

Linn, J. G. (2012, February 13). Earned income tax credit: A boost for Iowa families. *Des Moines Register,* p. 9A.

Mary, N. (2008). *Social work in a sustainable world.* Chicago, IL: Lyceum.

Mohsin, S. (2013, July 23). Norwegians promised more oil-funded welfare as vote nears. Bloomberg Business Week. Retrieved from www.bloomberg.com

Moses, J. (2002). *Oneness: Great principles shared by all religions* (Rev. and expanded ed.). New York, NY: Ballantine Books.

Mosher, C. (2009, May). *A new paradigm for sustainability and social justice.* Paper presented at the meeting of the International Eco-Conference: Building Bridges Crossing Boundaries, Calgary, Alberta, Canada.

Mullaly, B. (2007). *The new structural social work: Ideology, theory, practice.* New York, NY: Oxford University Press.

Narayanan, V. (2003). Water, wood and wisdom. Ecological perspectives from the Hindu traditions. In R. C. Foltz (Ed.), *Worldviews, religion and the environment: A global anthology* (pp. 130–143). London, England: Thomson/Wadsworth.

New in Norway. (2013). The Norwegian Directorate of Integration and Diversity. Retrieved from www.nyinorge.no/Documents/Ny%20i%20Norge%202013%20-%20pdf/New%20 in%20Norway_2013.pdf

Norway: Rich man fined $109,000 for drunk driving. (2009, May 13). *Waterloo/Cedar Falls,* p. A5.

Norwegian Labour and Welfare Services. (2012). *Family benefits.* Oslo: Ministry of Children, Equality and Social Inclusion. Retrieved from www.regjeringen.no/en/dep/bld/topics/ family-policies/family-policy.html?id=670514

Pally, M. (2011). *The new evangelicals: Expanding the vision of the common good.* Grand Rapids, MI: Eerdmans.

Paple, J. (2012, January 5). Harder for Americans to rise from lower rungs. *New York Times,* p. A1.

Payne, M. (2014). *Modern social work theory* (4th ed.). Chicago, IL: Lyceum.

Pear, R. (2008, September 30). Violations reported in 94% of nursing homes. *New York Times,* p. A20.

Pew Research Center. (2012, October 9). "Nones" on the rise: One-in-five adults have no religious affiliation. Pew Forum on Religion and Public Life. Retrieved from www.pewforum.org/2012/10/09/nones-on-the-rise/

Pratt, J. (2008a). Scandinavian exceptionalism in an era of penal excess: Part I. *British Journal of Criminology, 48*(2), 119–137.

Pratt, J. (2008b). Scandinavian exceptionalism in an era of penal excess: Part II. *British Journal of Criminology, 48*(3), 275–292.

Putin, V. (2013, September 12). A plea for caution from Russia. *New York Times*, p. A 31.

Ravitch, D. (2013). *Reign of error: The hoax of the privatization movement and the danger to America's public schools.* New York, NY: Alfred A. Knopf.

Reisel, L., & Brekke, I. (2010). Minority dropout in higher education: A comparison of the United States and Norway using competing risk event history analysis. *European Sociological Review, 26*(6), 601–712.

Rich, M. (2012, September 13). Push to add charter schools hangs over strike. *New York Times*, p. A22.

Roosevelt, F. D. (1941, January 6). [Speech before the 77th Congress of the United States.] Retrieved from www.americanrhetoric.com/speeches/fdrthefourfreedoms.htm

Ryan, W. (1976). *Blaming the victim* (Rev. ed.). New York, NY: Vintage Books.

Sanders, B. (2011). *The speech: A historic filibuster on corporate greed and the decline of our middle class.* New York, NY: Nation Books.

Save the Children. (2012). *Mothers' index ratings.* Retrieved from www.savethechildren.org

Schouten, F. (2010, November 22). Body scanner makers doubled lobbying cash over five years. *USA Today*. Retrieved from www.usatoday.com

Skivenes, M., & Skramstad, H. (2013). The emotional dimension in risk assessment: A cross-country study of the perceptions of child welfare workers in England, Norway and California. *British Journal of Social Work.* doi:10.1093/bjsw/bct177

Smith, G. (2012, September 9). Politics and plutocrats: A parade of inequality. *Earth Island Journal.* Retrieved from www.earthisland.org

Thomas, L. (2009, May 14). Thriving Norway provides an economics lesson. *New York Times*, pp. A1, A4.

United Nations Development Programme, Human Development Reports. (2012, June 20). Going beyond GDP, UNDP proposes human development measure of sustainability. Retrieved from www.undp.org/content/undp/en/home/presscenter/pressreleases/2012/06/20/oing-beyond-gdp-undp-proposes-human-development-measure-of-sustainability/

United Nations Development Programme, Human Development Reports. (2014). *Human development index—2013 rankings.* Retrieved from http://hdr.undp.org/en/content/table-1-human-development-index-and-its-components

Wacker, R., & Roberto, K. A. (2011). *Aging social policies: An international perspective.* Thousand Oaks, CA: Sage.

Warren, E. (2012, September 5). [Transcript: Elizabeth Warren's Democratic Convention Speech.] Retrieved from www.abcnews.co.com

Wilensky, H., & Lebeaux, C. N. (1958). *Structural and ideological roots of public expenditures.* New York, NY: Praeger.

Wise, T. (2010). *Colorblind: The rise of post-racial politics and the retreat of racial equality.* San Francisco, CA: City Lights Books.

Zastrow, C. (2009). *Introduction to social work and social welfare: Empowering people* (10th ed.). Belmont, CA: Brooks/Cole.

4

Environmental Sustainability and the Social Work Profession

But ask now the beasts, and they shall teach thee;
And the fowls of the air, and they shall tell thee;
Or speak to the earth, and it shall teach thee.

—Job 12:7–8, King James Version

Social workers have opportunities to expand into new arenas by addressing environmental issues and practicing green social work within a redistributive framework that operates locally and globally.

—Lena Dominelli, *Green Social Work* (2012, p. 9)

The standard definition of sustainability focuses on the meeting of present needs while preserving resources for future generations. In other words, the focus is on two dimensions of time—the present and the future. As defined in the *Social Work Dictionary, sustainable development* is "the international goal of achieving more permanent economic well-being within the existing physical environment. An economy is sustainable only when it uses but does not deplete its resources or ruin its environment for immediate economic gain" (Barker, 2014, p. 421). The emphasis in sustainability, in fact, is always on the future. If you can take yourself out of a consumerist mind-set to an environmental one, the obvious question is, what will happen next? But focusing only on the present and the future isn't quite enough. This brings us to a three-pronged approach to sustainability—the meeting of present needs with a focus on addressing the harms done by previous generations while simultaneously maintaining a future orientation.

One of the purposes of this chapter is to help you begin the process of expanding social work's person-environment construct to include nature as well as neighborhood, global as well as local considerations, and environmental as well as social justice. As will become readily apparent, the goals of sustainability are entirely consistent with professional values promoting social justice and human well-being. In light of emerging global ecological crises—pollution, floods, drought, famine, and so on—much of them human-generated, the policy implications are profound.

We will briefly review historical concerns by scientists and leading social workers regarding the health consequences of unsustainable practices and provide an overview of environmental challenges that affect us all. We will see how these challenges are intertwined with social and economic inequalities and examine the role that social work can play in promoting ecological awareness and advocacy for policies to promote clean and safe living conditions. Finally, we will examine some innovative strategies of sustainability that simultaneously address problems of poverty and inequality.

A Brief Eco History

Humans have been changing the planet ever since the dawn of civilization. Agricultural developments—the clearing and cultivation of forest land for the planting of crops—followed much later by the impact on waterways and population growth associated with the Industrial Revolution altered the ecosystem drastically. The predominant paradigm of industrialization was that the forces of nature could be subdued or controlled; this was regarded as progress. Systems theorist Gregory Bateson (1972) summarized this destructive belief in the following terms: "It's us against the environment" (p. 500). Overpopulation was a special concern for Bateson because the eradication of diseases without limiting the birth rate would inevitably lead to an imbalance between demand and availability of resources.

Awareness of nature as something more than an infinite resource for human exploitation has been in the public consciousness ever since the publication of Rachel Carson's (1962) groundbreaking book, *Silent Spring* (McKinnon, 2012). This book documented the decline in songbird populations as a result of the use of pesticides and insecticides. Her focus on unintended consequences led to revolutionary changes in the laws affecting air, land, and water. Carson's work captured the interest of broad audiences at a time when more and more citizens seemed to be sensing that nature itself was under attack and that defending it required a more radical way of thinking. Her passionate exposé was instrumental in launching the environmental movement. This new environmentalism shifted the meaning of the term environment away from social contexts and toward nature.

Even before this time, however, because of social work's concern with the elimination of poverty and the well-being of children, organizations such as the Charity

Organization Society and the settlement houses were concerned about unclean conditions in their clients' immediate surroundings (McKinnon, 2012). Jane Addams's work as sanitation inspector and her establishment of parks and recreation centers in Chicago is well known. We saw in Chapter 2 how the social work profession's shift from a structural to a psychological focus was a setback to the development of a holistic biopsychosocial model for social work practice.

The paradigm shift related to the Great Depression brought in new economic government policies, and social workers quickly retreated to their political roots and assumed leadership in the creation of economically innovative programs. Interactionist concepts about the reciprocity of relationships began to replace too-simplistic notions of cause and effect. The transition away from a psychological determinism did not happen overnight, but new ways of conceptualizing the relationship between personal and environmental dimensions of practice began to take shape and emergent ideas from general systems theory began to seep into the social work literature. The early writing of Carel Germain (1968) used *systems concepts* to demonstrate how people's roles are interconnected and reciprocal. Building on systems theory, social work theorists, such as Germain (1978, 1991), constructed a substantial body of theory known as the ecological approach or the *person-environment* formulation. As time passed, the notion that the person and environment were in constant and dynamic interaction entered the mainstream of social work education and theory, and the value of an ecological model of human behavior became recognized. This model underscored social work's commitment to the person-environment configuration for practice with individuals and families, and the adoption of ecological principles was helpful for engagement with communities in political advocacy. Ecosystems theorists then took Germain's conceptual formulation one step further and combined ecology with systems concepts to put the consideration of the physical environment at the forefront of the discourse (van Wormer & Besthorn, 2011). The focus was not so much on individual adaptation to the environment (generally the social/cultural milieu in Germain's formulation) as it was on the impact of the physical surroundings on the individual.

Ecosystems concepts were consistent with teachings of the environmental movement that grew stronger from the 1980s into the 1990s. There were the radical activist groups such as Earth First and Greenpeace, mainstream organizations such as the Sierra Club that lobbied to preserve biodiversity, and the publications of environmental scientists on the biological impact of human activities on the atmosphere. The message stemming from all of these groups was that the earth and its resources are finite and that human overconsumption and overproduction must stop. Environmental awareness was taught in school systems across the globe, the importance of recycling, composting, and so on, and children began enlightening their parents. Environmental science became a popular concentration or major at the university level, and media reports carried and continue to carry the information forward.

Today, increasing attention is paid to humanitarian crises, often related to extreme weather events. These are mostly sudden in their impacts such as hurricanes, tornadoes, and tsunamis. Other natural disasters have evolved over time, such as desertification and severe drought, and are related either directly or indirectly to destructive human activities and the overconsumption of natural resources. The implications for social work of such catastrophic events are clear. In affected areas, social workers and other helping professionals are consumed with attempts to alleviate human suffering and to meet people's immediate survival needs. At the macro-level, social workers, individually and collectively, advocate for progressive environmental policies to ensure that people have access to clean air and water and secure housing.

The Planet in Crisis: The Scope of Environmental Loss and Damage

In every country of the world, the sources of life's basic necessities are threatened, depleted, or polluted at alarming and possibly irreversible rates (Hoff & McNutt, 2009). We are talking about human-created damage to the planet and to all that dwell therein—the flora, fauna, soil, water we drink, and air we breathe. We are talking about unsustainable development in which economic progress is valued at the expense of social development.

The Unintended Consequences of "Growth"

In calculating a nation's economic performance, the gross domestic product (GDP) takes into account economic activity and profits but not loss of topsoil, water reservoirs, or forests involved in reaping the profits. This is a result of the world's fixation on growth that ignores a rapid and largely irreversible depletion of natural resources that will seriously harm future generations (Raab, 2012). Paradoxically, the greater the loss, the greater the growth. This is no small matter; countries with solid GDP measures qualify for extensive loans from international banks to finance more "growth" as resources are being steadily exhausted. When an expansion does occur, it is an expansion of desert land, population, and pollution to the atmosphere. To provide a more accurate measurement, the United Nations has introduced a yardstick that goes beyond the GDP aimed at encouraging sustainability. This is the Inclusive Wealth Index. Despite registering GDP growth, China, the United States, South Africa, and Brazil were shown on this new index to have significantly depleted their natural capital bases since 1990, which included fossil fuels, forests, and fisheries. It is hoped that use of this new indicator will focus greater attention on the value of the ecosystem in relation to the wealth of nations.

In truth, the health of the planet is deteriorating at a rapid pace. High levels of carbon dioxide emissions coming from the consumer-driven economies of the Global North and increasingly from the Global South in combination with agricultural-based herbicides, pesticides, and other pollutants released into the ocean in one part of the world are transported to distant parts of the planet with predictable and unpredictable results (Besthorn, 2008). Not too long ago economic growth was hailed as the way to improve people's lives, both within nations and internationally, as it was thought the benefits would trickle down through the classes. Better circumstances for the few were created but often at the expense of the many. Economic development, as we noted above, is often the reverse of social development. Pressure from international monetary lending sources to increase the capital available for business investment has mandated the sacrifice of health, nutritional, and other programs for people.

A second myth is the equally optimistic belief that a green revolution, through the wonder of fertilizers and pesticides, could feed the world. The problem is that after a few years of treating (or mistreating) the soil with toxic chemicals, the increased yields taper off, and soil erosion and water pollution hinder further food production.

Today, due to agricultural and industrial pollution and evaporation, which scientists relate to global warming, at least a billion people lack access to clean water. The clearing of forestland is proceeding at a rate of over 5 million hectares a year (Brown, 2012). One hectare is roughly two-and-a-half acres. Deforestation on a massive scale has happened in Brazil, Indonesia, and western Canada and is associated with a decline in rainfall. Since more water is stored in the plants of the earth than its lakes, the loss of plants means a serious decline in the amount of water vapor released into the atmosphere. The clearing of forests is also associated with soil erosion as well as flooding and mudslides as mud flows down to the riverbanks. Replanting, if it is done at all, usually involves only one or two tree species. Because they are all of the same age and size, the new plants often fail even to regenerate and the biodiversity of the region is lost permanently. In Europe, the forests are threatened by air pollution, often from industrial fumes hundreds of miles away. Everywhere land is being lost through urban sprawl and industrialization. Population migrations into cities result from recent agricultural trends pushing small farmers off the land, along with other economic pressures and ethnic tensions.

As most environmentalists are painfully aware, human activities—for example, burning fossil fuels, polluting the land and waterways, and bulldozing forests—now

Source: ©iStockphoto.com/Sara Winter.

Biodiversity in Nature. Biodiversity is essential to the preservation of a healthy ecosystem.

match or even surpass natural processes as agents of change. The first comprehensive study of this issue by the world's scientists, the Global Biodiversity Assessment, estimated in a UN report that more than 30,000 plant and animal species now face possible extinction (Connor, 2006). Since 1810 nearly three times as many bird and animal species have disappeared as in the previous two centuries. This report decries the loss of genes, habitats, and ecosystems. We are losing something else as well—beauty. The scenic beauty of our land, notes Zastrow (2010), is being spoiled by a variety of human activities: among them deforestation, strip mining of coal, oil drilling, highway construction, and parking lots. Hoff and McNutt (2009) point to the "devastation of aesthetic values" in the despoliation of nature, which directly affects individual and community welfare (p. 297).

Human activities are transforming the global environment in ways that are only beginning to be realized. People in richer, highly industrialized countries, with only one quarter of the world's population, consume most of the world's energies. Most of the gases and chemicals emitted into the atmosphere are from these countries. Yet people in the rest of the world, where three fourths of the population reside, are also contributing to resource depletion.

Numerous rural communities, including Native American reservations, are fighting plans to site solid waste disposal facilities in their communities (Hoff & McNutt, 2009). Communities do not want this waste, yet it has to go somewhere. A more serious problem is the need to dispose of radioactive waste material. Zastrow (2010) discusses this problem in the United States; there is no safe way of getting rid of this material. These wastes are particularly hazardous because they remain radioactive for around 300,000 years.

War and Environmental Accidents

Sometimes the despoiling of the environment is intentional. A clear example is the string of the tragic events in Kuwait, 1991, when Saddam Hussein of Iraq ordered his military forces to set six hundred oil wells in Kuwait on fire during the Gulf War. Skies were blackened for months and the quality of human and lower-level animal life suffered greatly thereafter.

Social work scholars Schmitz, Matyók, James, and Sloan (2012) bring our attention to the environmental and social destruction caused by war. The 10 poorest countries in the world, they point out, have been ravaged by war, drought, and poverty. They have been plagued by battles over resources. The authors illustrate the interconnection of these issues with the example of Somalia. Somalia has experienced the violence of war, poverty, drought, and environmental destruction. When governments invest their resources in weaponry instead of development of resources for the people, sustainable development suffers. In the United States, while almost 50% of the tax dollar is spent on past and present military, only a fraction (6%) of the tax dollar is spent on environmental and physical resources, including agriculture (War Resisters League, 2012).

Then there are the environmental accidents. The Exxon oil spill in 1989 in Valdez, Alaska, resulted in the death of millions of birds, animals, fish, and plants. Although many critics focus on capitalism as a primary culprit, the Communist approach to rapid industrialization also has contributed to ecological crises. The nuclear power plant explosion in Chernobyl, Ukraine, placed the lives of tens of thousands of persons in Eastern and Western Europe in extreme jeopardy. The 2010 Deepwater Horizon BP (Beyond Petroleum) disaster claimed the lives of 11 workers and released more than 4.1 million barrels of crude oil over 87 days into the Gulf whose $3 billion fishing industry provides one-third of all seafood consumed in the United States (Fisk, 2012). This oil spill killed animal life, made a mess of sand beaches, and accelerated the loss of Louisiana's delicate marshlands, which were already rapidly disappearing before the largest oil spill in U.S. history.

The nuclear explosion at Fukoshima, Japan, in 2011 is described by Dominelli (2012), author of the groundbreaking *Green Social Work*, as a multiple hazard situation that confirmed the fears of many people who were already opposed to this form of energy production. When an earthquake reached a magnitude of Point 9 on the Richter scale and a subsequent tsunami breached the protective seawall and flooded the area in which the nuclear plant resided, dangerous radiation leakages took place. Three reactors experienced a full meltdown; people were removed from the area, which was now uninhabitable, and food grown in its environs was banned from sale. It is too early to know the long-term health consequences from Fukoshima, but we all know of the much publicized birth defects and deaths by cancer that have alerted the rest of the world to the dangers of nuclear energy and to the interconnectedness of environmental problems.

Climate Change

With our massive burning of fossil fuels, we are overloading the atmosphere with carbon dioxide, which pushes the earth's temperature to ever higher levels. According to Lester Brown (2011), the president of the Earth Policy Institute, this process generates more frequent and dramatic climatic events, including crop-withering heat waves, intense droughts, severe floods, and destructive storms.

Said to be the official word on climate change from the world's top climate scientists, the final summary report (United Nations, 2014) underscores three major facts about climate change: it's human-made and already having dangerous impacts across the globe; if the world community acts now, warming can still be kept below the politically agreed upon "safe" limit of 2 degrees Celsius; the ability to secure a safe climate future is not only possible but also economically viable.

July 2012 was the hottest month in U.S. history. With oppressive heat waves, devastating droughts, ravaging wildfires, and hard-hitting rainstorms, the summer of 2012 was record-breaking. Scientists agree these events underscore the reality of climate change. Even with cooler-than-average temperatures in Alaska and Northern Europe, the Northern Hemisphere observed its all-time warmest summer on record (National Ocean and Atmospheric Administration [NOAA], 2012). And even with below-average temperatures across much of Southern South America and Northern and Eastern Australia, the Southern Hemisphere observed its 10th warmest winter on record. These regions experienced extreme drought.

Given what we know about the ability of greenhouse gases to warm the earth's surface, it is reasonable to expect that as concentrations of greenhouse gases in the atmosphere rise above acceptable levels, the earth's surface will become increasingly warm (NOAA, 2012). The majority of scientists attribute the global warming we are experiencing today to the enormous growth in the use of fossil fuels and the associated rise in carbon emissions to the point where they exceed the earth's capacity to absorb them.

The polar ice cap is melting at an unprecedented rate. If Greenland's ice sheet melts, as it seems to be doing, this would inundate the rice-growing deltas of Asia, due to the rising level of the oceans (Brown, 2011). Shrinking polar ice sheets, from an economic standpoint, are a prelude to falling coastal real estate values. The consequences will be far more than economic, however. People from the poorest regions of the world will face increased flooding as sea levels rise; whole island nations may be underwater. An international report from the Norwegian Polar Institute (2009) projects a global warming of at least several degrees Fahrenheit overall and a much higher warming in the Arctic by the end of this century, assuming the implementation of some greenhouse gas reduction measures. From 1979 to 2009, sea ice in the Arctic shrank more than 40%. Such a dramatic warming does bring new opportunities (opening up northern waterways for shipping and the extraction of oil). At the same time, if the process continues, the lives of people in certain latitudes will be seriously affected. Above the Arctic Circle, indigenous populations that engage in hunting and rely on travel routes to herd animals will find their lifestyles threatened. Further south, hundreds of millions of people in low-lying coastal areas may lose their homes due to rising sea levels, and whole nations—for example, Bangladesh, and parts of Vietnam and Holland, may even be at risk of extinction. Additionally, according to the report, millions of people may be affected if freshwater availability decreases due to changes in snow and glacier reservoirs or flooding of groundwater reservoirs. An update on polar ice levels from the National Snow and Ice Data Center (2012) indicates the greatest loss of ice on record and a reduction in the quantity of ice since 1979, which has now reached 49% of its original size.

Climate change could be the biggest global health threat of the 21st century. This is according to a report from the British medical journal—*The Lancet* (Costello et al., 2009). The report based its predictions on a 2- to 6-degree warming over the next century but focusing on the average, a 4-degree rise. The health consequences—the indirect effects of climate change on water, food security, and extreme climatic events—are expected to be severe. People's health, according to the report, will be impacted through changing patterns of disease, water and food insecurity, vulnerable shelter and human settlements, extreme climatic events, and population migration.

Consider what happened in Eastern Africa, where in 2011, severe drought conditions left 8 million people in need of food aid—including 1.2 million Kenyans (see NOAA, 2011). The rising cost of food due to the death of livestock also played a role in the food shortage. The United Nations, which conducted an assessment, expected more people and livestock to perish due to the lack of food and potable water. The dry conditions also prompted migrations from the country into urban areas or outside the country. Over 10,000 Kenyans migrated eastward into Uganda, while as many Somalis migrated into Kenya.

The Lancet (Costello et al., 2009) spells out the following physical health risks of the earth's steadily rising temperatures:

- The spread of diseases such as dengue fever and malaria, once confined to warmer areas, will move north and become more widespread as a result of increased temperatures.
- Deaths directly from the heat itself will occur, similar to what happened in Europe in 2003 when more than 70,000 people died.
- Deaths from starvation will occur as crop yields decline, leading to greater food insecurity in a world where 800 million already go to bed hungry every night.
- Water shortages will lead to more gastroenteritis and malnutrition, among other health problems.
- Extreme climactic events such as flash flooding due to changing rainfall patterns and melting ice sheets, will threaten people's livelihoods and health; severe cyclones and hurricanes will also take more lives.
- More people living in cities will lead to a shortage of housing, which will lead to slums and in turn lead to inadequate sanitation systems and increased vulnerability to extreme weather events.

Climate change is now a fact of life on this planet and a threat to all life—human and nonhuman. Written by a team of over 300 scientific experts, the National Climate Assessment (2014) was recently released by the White House. Due to the rapid melting of glaciers and frozen ground in the northern latitudes, the oceans are rising, and storms are whittling away at fragile coastlines as entire communities in Alaska, for example, are fleeing inland. The report, which received a great deal of media attention, singles out the three most significant threats from climate change in the United States. These are the rising sea levels along the coasts, droughts and fires in the Southwest, and extreme precipitation in the form of torrential rains. Concerning rising sea levels, the government report concurred with warnings issued earlier in the year by the United Nations Intergovernmental Panel on Climate Change (IPCC), which said that sea levels could rise by as much as 3 feet globally by the end of the century if emissions continue at the present pace.

The last installment of the UN's (2014) Fifth Assessment Report, builds on a series of earlier IPCC reports that have been released over the last 12 months and which have detailed the scientific, impacts and solutions for climate change. This report takes us into the economic realm and issues the starkest warning yet on the impact of global warming. Heat waves and drought already have devastated crops and killed tens of thousands of people, according to the expert panel.

These warnings are nothing new. Reports such as that issued by The Worldwatch Institute's (2009) *State of the World 2009: Into a Warming World* urged a drastic reduction in carbon emissions to avoid catastrophic disruption to the world's climate. Success toward this end will require mass public support internationally; we must institute new ways of living that are environmentally sustainable. Failure to reduce greenhouse emissions poses a major threat to society with food shortages and the flooding of low-lying cities and entire island nations. Indirect consequences will be violent international conflicts accompanied by a world refugee crisis. The cumulative risks of climate change are so profound, according to the recent report, that they could reverse all progress in the fight against global poverty and hunger if greenhouse emissions continue at the present pace. And yet, as Gillis (2014) indicates, energy companies continue to spend billions each year to locate more coal and petroleum reserves. With help from government subsidies, utilities and oil companies continue to build coal-fired power plants and refineries. Fortunately, today there is a much greater consciousness of the need for urgent action and a move in the direction of a new paradigm. And if the world community acts now, as the UN (2014) assures us, global warming can still be kept below the politically agreed upon "safe" limit of 3.6 degrees Fahrenheit. The ability to secure a healthy climate future is not only possible but also economically feasible. Fortified by such United Nations summits and the grassroots energy surrounding these international events, environmentalists are leading the way toward a reappraisal of the traditional focus on short-term growth, "progress," and "modernization" as ends in themselves.

The starting point for a paradigm shift may be to replace a focus on the costs of inaction with a focus on the benefits of action. "Better Growth, Better Climate" produced by the Global Commission on the Economy and Climate (2014) is timely in this regard. The commission seeks the solution to global inequality and low productivity in structural reform of urban and farm management and energy markets. Cities are where the world population growth is likely to occur in the future, so it is important to manage urbanization carefully. Sustainable urban planning means to reduce urban sprawl and encourage population density. When cities spread outward, government expenses are high in terms of the provision of more extensive systems of roads, sewers, and highway congestion. The report recommends good public transportation for the people. As commuters would switch from cars to light rail and bicycles, greenhouse gas emissions would be considerably reduced. The report also calls for drastic changes in agricultural subsidies away from fertilizers and toward more sustainable practices to ensure long-term preservation of the natural resources.

Similarly, Naomi Klein (2014) in her bestselling *This Changes Everything* looks to a new form of sustainable capitalism to replace what she terms the "disaster capitalism" (p. 51) that is favored today by political leaders of the Global North. "Our economic system and planetary system are now at war," she asserts (p. 21). Targeted in her book for their role in the pending climate crisis are the fossil fuel extracting corporations, car companies, shipping industry, the airlines, and the U.S. military which "is by some accounts, the largest single consumer of petroleum in the world" (p. 113). Klein's basic thesis is that the climate crisis will lead to a new politics that will transform economic priorities for the benefit of all the people. Hence the title of her book— "This Changes Everything." Among the solutions that she spells out are the following: policies promoting high-density cities; cheap public transit, including clean light rail; the building of affordable, energy efficient housing; safe bike lanes, and low-energy forms of agriculture.

How the global market will respond to the ever-expanding world population is a major question for future planning. Emphasis on preservation of our limited natural resources is at the heart of the sustainability ethos. Let us now examine the global challenges in this regard.

Food, Water, and Population Growth

Lester Brown (2012) in his recent book, *Full Planet, Empty Plates,* cites three reasons the world can expect food shortages and hunger. A primary reason is population growth. In 1960, the world population was 3 billion. By 2011, it had risen to 7 billion. The rate of increase is now nearly 80 million people each year. Soon the demand, as Brown indicates, will exceed the sustainable yield.

The second reason concerns changes in eating habits; people moved from eating largely vegetables to eating more grain-intensive livestock and poultry products. Brown (2012) calls this "moving up the food chain" (p. 15). Today, with incomes rising fast in emerging economies, there are at least 3 billion people moving up the food chain, most are in China. Because grain is also used as fuel for cars, much grain is siphoned off for ethanol.

The third major reason is the loss of fertile land to drought. Among the countries where water tables are falling and aquifers are being depleted are the big three grain producers—China, India, and the United States. In Northwestern China and Central Africa, huge new dust bowls are forming. Soil erosion is a related problem. Brown (2012) estimates that around 30% of the world's cropland is losing productive topsoil.

Managing Our Waters

By choosing to concentrate its swelling population along the coasts, humanity is locating the ecological damage of its activities precisely where the world's most productive ecosystems are concentrated. The lakes, rivers, and oceans are overfished, badly polluted, and poorly managed. A chief concern is the destructively effective harvesting technology practiced by fishing fleets from Japan and the United States. Because of the lack of enforceable international environmental agreements, four fifths of the world's ocean fisheries are being fished at or above capacity; at this rate the fishing industry is headed for collapse (Brown, 2011).

Pollution from coastal populations, offshore oil and gas production, and agricultural runoffs affect the aquatic food chain as toxic compounds are commonly found in coastal organisms. Oil and even hypodermic needles washed up along beaches are familiar images, thanks to extensive press coverage of these disturbing events. The use of pesticides by the world's farmers spreads pollution in creeks, streams, lakes, and ground water. Acid rain is an additional source of contamination formed from emissions of cars, trucks, and industrial plants that combine with rain as it falls back upon the land and water. This is a major problem in China as well as in other rapidly industrializing nations.

Equally alarming in its immediate impact is the fact that vast underground reserves of water deposited over thousands of years are being seriously and rapidly depleted. More and more cities and farms overdraw aquifers to keep expanding economies afloat and to quench the thirst of growing populations (Jackson & Keeney, 2010). One quarter of the water that irrigates, powers, and bathes the United States is taken from an ancient network of these underground aquifers.

In urban areas throughout the world, waste disposal has become a major problem. The soil and the drinking water are contaminated with human waste. We see this in parts of Latin America where serious communicable diseases are on the rise. In China, rapid industrialization has led to the use of rivers as chemical dumps, and sanitation systems in many areas are under extreme stress (George, 2010). Some rivers have dried up through overuse of the water, and many former residents of the area have become environmental refugees.

As we discussed in the section on global warming, exceptional droughts have contributed to this water crisis, and strategies are desperately needed to make fresh water widely available and to build and maintain sewers for the growing populations in poor regions of the world.

Overpopulation and Scarcity

Population growth and food insecurity are closely linked. The poorest regions of the world are those that are expected to experience the sharpest rise in population. Estimates are that Pakistan, Nigeria, Congo, Bangladesh, Uganda, India, and Ethiopia will be responsible for much of the world's projected increase in population (Dominelli, 2012). Famine is a regular occurrence in Ethiopia where the population doubled from 1984 to 2009, far faster than any rise in agricultural production. The famine, which was exacerbated by warfare, claimed over 1 million lives. Humanitarian responses were inadequate and focused on short-term needs while encouraging dependency. Dominelli (2012) argues for a set-aside relief fund based on taxes on citizens of the world to be used for disasters such as famine. She also makes the point that long-term solutions should be found to develop the necessary infrastructures to ensure an adequate standard of living for all. Existing food systems need to be transformed through community development into more environmentally friendly and socially just ones.

The best long-run solution for overpopulation is prevention, and the best form of prevention is control of the birth rate through family planning. A recently reported project in St. Louis conducted by Peipert, Madden, Allsworth, and Secura (2012) tracked more than 9,000 women, many of whom were poor and uninsured. The women were given a choice of various contraceptive methods that were free of charge—from birth control pills to implants. The results were striking: The rate of teen pregnancy was considerably reduced to a rate that was one fifth of the national rate. The abortion rate was reduced to well below the general St. Louis rate and well below the national rate. The research shows that the Affordable Care Act, which provides free contraceptives, should cut way down on the number of unplanned pregnancies.

These findings provide further evidence of what we already know about the effectiveness of family planning services worldwide. Granting girls and women access to modern contraceptives and sex education has been shown to reduce the number of abortions (United Nations, 2010). This is crucial to saving the lives of women, because in many parts of the world, so many women die in childbirth or due to pregnancy-related conditions. Where restrictive abortion laws make it difficult to obtain a safe abortion, women who have an unwanted pregnancy tend to turn to unsafe abortions. According to the UN report (2010), unsafe abortions claim the lives of approximately 68,000 women each year. It is estimated that there are about 19 million to 20 million abortions done annually by individuals without the requisite skills; 97% of these take place in the Global South. In the interest of saving lives, the UN recommends that abortions under safe medical conditions be available at family planning clinics so that women will have a choice about their futures.

Unfortunately, because of the abortion controversy in the United States, restrictions on funding family planning have been applied. Under conservative presidencies starting with Ronald Reagan, a global gag order was enacted to prohibit nongovernmental family planning groups from receiving U.S. funds for family planning services, if the countries provided abortions (Sullivan, 2009). The end result was a serious decline in contraceptive use, an increase in unwanted births, in deaths of women for pregnancy-related conditions, and in rates of HIV/AIDS contraction.

All family planning programs, as Costello et al. (2009) indicate, require political commitment, and clear management and supervision. Beyond these basic requirements, it is clear that success in family planning depends on dismantling the barriers to contraception. This means providing mobile services as well as public clinics, commercial outlets, and cooperation of the local media. Equally important, to Costello et al., is the removal of conservative (attitudinal) barriers, combined with the education of lawyers, health care providers, and religious leaders about the importance of reproductive health.

The Importance of Empowering Women

In many countries, such as Mexico, the United States, Canada, and southern Europe, family size has shrunk to maintenance levels of four or less, while elsewhere—usually where men make the decisions—the birth rate continues to be high. In these same countries, where boys are greatly favored over girls, the male-female ratios have become lopsided. The *World's Women Report* (United Nations, 2010) provides the following facts:

- There are approximately 57 million more men than women in the world. In 2010, some regions have an obvious "shortage" of men, others of women.
- Europe is home to many more women than men. In contrast, some of the most populous countries have a "shortage" of women.
- China has a ratio of 108 men per 100 women; India, 107; Pakistan, 106; and Bangladesh, 102 (United Nations, 2010, pp. 2–3).

As we mentioned earlier in the chapter, it is important that women be empowered throughout the world so that they can make healthy choices for themselves and society regarding family size. Drawing on demographic data, Engelman (2012) reports that the single most important factor in preventing food shortage is in population control. Because 40% of pregnancies in the Global South are unintended, as Engelman states, family planning is the key to a sustainable future. Girls' education and empowerment will go a long way to help women seek control of their own lives.

At the landmark women's conference in Beijing in 1995, a Platform for Action was passed and endorsed by governments. This platform stressed that women's role in sustainable development is hampered by unequal access to land, financial resources, and agricultural information and technologies and lack of involvement in political activities. All these barriers continue to exist years after the Platform for Action was written (UN, 2010). To overcome the problems humans have created, we need the participation of everyone.

Modern Agriculture and the Loss of Biodiversity

Poet and environmentalist Wendell Berry (1977), in his classic work on agriculture, *The Unsettling of America*, states that if we regard plants as machines, we wind up with huge monocultures (corn and soybeans), and if the soil is regarded as a machine, then its life—its involvement in living systems and cycles—must perforce be ignored. If, like the strip miners and the "agribusiness" interest groups, we look to the earth's resources for fuel or extractable energy, we can do nothing but destroy it. And ultimately, what we turn against turns against us.

Soil is the source of life. Food chains are the living channels that conduct energy upward; death and decay return it to the soil. Soils depleted of their storage, or of the organic matter that anchors it, wash away faster than they form. This is erosion.

Soil erosion exceeds soil formation on one-third of the world's cropland, draining the land of its fertility. As documented by Lester Brown (2011), president of the Earth Policy Institute, forests are shrinking by 13 million acres per year, as we cut trees for lumber and paper and clear the land for agriculture. Because of population growth and industrialization demands in the Global South, the increasing burning of coal as the primary energy source is causing crop and forest damage in scores of countries (Dominelli, 2012).

The Importance of Biodiversity

The term *biodiversity* refers to the variability among living organisms that maintains each organism's health. Shahid Naeem (2009), a professor of ecology at Columbia University, has participated in extensive research of combinations of plant species. Results revealed that the greater the plant diversity, the greater the retention of nutrients and resistance to invasive species and to disease. Other experimental research that Naeem cites consistently shows that in all forms of life, including marine life in the oceans, declining biodiversity is generally associated with reduced ecosystem functioning. Almost all aspects of human well-being, whether we are talking about human health, education, or economic structure, trace back to biodiversity for their foundations.

We are losing biodiversity of plant and animal life at an unprecedented rate and a thousand times faster today than in the millions of years previously. Ecologist Patrick Curry (2011) fears that soon we will reach a tipping point if present levels persist. From 1970 to 2003 alone, there was a 31% decline in terrestrial biodiversity. At the present rate of extinction, according to Curry, 12% of bird species and 25% of mammal species are likely to disappear by 2030. They will disappear along with "the wild places" in the world as the population expands (p. 17).

The destruction of the forests in the Amazon region in Brazil is taking a devastating toll on the ecosystem in Central America. This region is home to amazing levels of diversity and a variety of plant and animal species not found in any other part of the world. In fact, as Brown (2012) indicates, the deforestation of the region is having an impact on the climate of the entire world. The incentive for the removal of the rain forest is the search for new land for soybean production. The forests here and in other regions in the Global South are being cleared to grow soybeans to feed beef cattle, not people, and for export, not for local consumption. Fortunately, due to the environmental impacts experienced most directly in a loss of rainfall and international pressure, the Brazilian government has taken steps to restrict the clearing of the land. As world demands for food rise, however, the economic pressures to plant more soybeans may become intense.

Contemporary Farming

Wendell Berry (1993) describes our treatment of the land as *land abuse*. Any form of land abuse—a clear-cut forest, a strip mine, an overplowed or overgrazed field—is a dire threat to the earth's ecosystem, he suggests. Land abuse goes back to early American history. To force some life out of the depleted soil, farmers today use an incredible amount of chemicals, many of them highly toxic, which seep into the rural waterways, drinking water, soil, and air. Industrial agriculture, as Wes Jackson (2009), the founder of The Land Institute in Salina, Kansas, indicates, is a threat to biodiversity of the earth. The economic reality has overtaken the ecological reality, as Jackson

Source: ©iStockphoto.com/David Sucsy.

Cornfield in Illinois. Monocultural farming, such as shown here, is harmful to the soil and requires heavy use of pesticides and herbicides for continual planting.

further states, and nutrients and water are being lost by present methods. Crops must be rotated and planted on land that has been grazed. Monoculture farming (which means producing a single crop continually to maximize yield while minimizing labor) produces a situation in which the row crops are particularly vulnerable to invasive pests or to a change in weather conditions (Korten, 2009). This is just one of the problems stemming from the loss of biodiversity. It is crucial for ecosystems to contain more than a handful of species. Bees are needed to pollinate the plants; trees are needed to store carbon and promote precipitation.

In their chapter in the book, *A Watershed Year: Anatomy of the Iowa Floods of 2008*, Laura Jackson and Dennis Keeney (2010) describe a time before the coming of the Europeans to the Midwest in the mid-1800s when the prairie soil protected the land from flooding, when the rich Iowa soil, filled with a dense and deep underground network of plant roots, was able to absorb the raindrops. Today, 98% of the tall grass once present in the Northern Plains is gone, so the contribution of the bountiful root system is gone as well. But prairie soil can be cultivated through land use change. Apart from prairie research centers, this kind of traditional planting persists in scattered plots of land cultivated by the Old Order Amish people. The Amish treat the soil with special care, plant only perennial crops, and rely on work horses to till the land instead of soil-compressing tractors. There is much we can learn from the Amish people (Weil, 2011).

At the personal level, many small farmers are unable to obtain the financing necessary to make farming a profitable enterprise. In rural areas, when the family farms fail, so do the local hardware store, the farm equipment store, the local school, and the café. For the farm family, the connection to the land is often a legacy from parent or grandparents, a family heritage that links family members to the wider community.

The biggest beneficiaries of modern agricultural policies are not the large growers, but the distributors of chemicals, such as pesticides, and the food processing industry. These giant corporations do well even when a farm recession is under way; thanks to heavy lobbying groups, they receive heavy government subsidies.

The Corporate Role in Farm Production

A good starting point for this discussion is a viewing of the 2008 film, *Food, Inc.* narrated by environmental scientist Michael Pollan. Based on the book of the same title by Peter Pringle (2003), the film traces our evolution from an agrarian nation to one of monocrop farming. Health and safety of the animals produced, of the workers on the assembly lines, and of the consumers actually eating the food are not major considerations of companies focused on productivity and profits. The film devotes much attention to the strategies of Monsanto, a company famous for the producing of Agent Orange, which destroyed so many lives in Vietnam and which plays a dominant role in genetic engineering of crops today.

Monsanto's bioengineered soybeans command over 90% of the U.S. market, and genetically altered corn is up to 80% of corn. These crops are designed to be unaffected by the weed killer Roundup, which is also produced by Monsanto. This company hauls other farmers into court if some of its pollen blows onto the farmers' land and intermingles with the farmers' seeds (Arndt, 2010). Farmers who buy the genetically modified seeds do so

Source: Published with permission of the Des Moines Catholic Worker photo archives.

Protest Against Monsanto, Winner of World Food Prize, Des Moines, Iowa. Surveys show that worldwide, Monsanto is the least liked corporation. Critics protest their genetically modified seeds and corporate farming practices.

on the promise of higher yields. They must sign a contract that dictates how and when the crop is grown. Saving seeds is forbidden; in fact, Monsanto has sued farmers for doing this (Karger & Stoesz, 2013). Why do farmers put up with this and the ever-increasing prices? The reason is that the genetic modifications mean that farmers don't have to till the fields, and they can cultivate more land. And since the modified plants can withstand exposure to the chemicals, farmers can use the weed killer after the crops have come up (Whoriskey, 2009).

An interesting recent development is that Roundup, which for years has helped farmers increase profits, is losing its effectiveness and forcing growers to use more chemicals to control the weeds, according to a report from *Bloomberg Business Week* (Kaskey, 2011). Monsanto had insisted until recently that the chemical wouldn't create resistant weeds. These are the weed killers that the crops are engineered to tolerate. The greater the chemical use, the greater the contamination of the soil and waterways, and this overuse has real public health implications.

The process of resistance is familiar to us in the creation of superbugs. This originates in corporate farming as well. To increase production, factory farms make liberal use of antibiotics given to cattle, hogs, and poultry, not just to treat illnesses but also to prevent the spread of disease when large populations are kept in confined spaces and even to promote faster growth (Greider, 2012). Because these drugs are often the same as those used to treat people, the bacteria become drug resistant. Farms spread the bacteria as animals excrete the germs, which get in the soil and water. The problems many hospitals are having with staph infections can be traced to the presence of drug-resistant bacteria that originate from factory farms.

Recently, the Centers for Disease Control, in a significant move, confirmed a link between routine use of antibiotics in livestock and growing bacterial resistance killing 23,000 people a year. The link has been suspected for years but Congress, beholden to the drug and livestock industries, has blocked efforts by the Food and Drug Administration to scale back their use (Lochhead, 2013).

There is much concern today among proponents of sustainable agriculture about plans that are currently under way by the agricultural corporations to stem world hunger through the use of chemically-intensive agriculture, a process that brings a higher yield per acre than traditional farming. In Tanzania, for example, the seed company, AgriSol, has announced plans to develop an 800,000 acre farm. AgriSol is due to reap enormous profits from this enterprise (Guebert, 2012). Until recently, Iowa State University School of Agriculture was involved. But in response to a barrage of international criticism, the university decided to back out. The criticism raised objections to two particularly problematic aspects of the deal: that the government of Tanzania was to pay less than $1.00 an acre to lease the land and the planned displacement of over 160,000 Africans. Not surprisingly, this arrangement is considered in some quarters as a form of colonialism.

The United States has been equipping farmers in India with billions of dollars' worth of chemical fertilizers and pesticides. In the Punjab region, thousands of farmers were plunged into debt as their jobs were lost through the use of the modernized methods of farming with machine technology. Between 1988 and 2006, there were 1,400 cases of farmer suicides. Many drank pesticides or hanged themselves in their fields (Reznicek, 2012). These are among the unintended consequences of supplanting traditional practices with those that are alien to the culture.

Frances Lappé (2013), the author of *Ecomind,* urges us to shift from fearmongering about pending world starvation that only the big corporations can solve through their new technologies to an ecological perspective. Referring to the farmer suicides in the Punjab region, Lappé is heartened to find in the same state that over 5,000 women are farming organically and carefully preserving and sharing their seeds. Through their cooperative, the women have built conservation trenches, and there is now an abundance of food in the region.

A new advocacy and public health movement is urgently needed to bring together governments, international agencies, nongovernmental organizations, mental health professionals, and academics from all disciplines to thoroughly research food shortage situations and means of alleviation.

The Promise of Social Work

Everything is connected: the future to the past, the parts to the whole, the biological to the social, the inner to the outer (body, mind, etc.), personal to political, the local to the global. This is what the ecosystems perspective of social work teaches. The promise of social work lies in our grasping the essence of this awareness of interconnectedness, this almost spiritual sense of relatedness and being. To fulfill its promise, social work also needs to call attention to the international crisis related to sustainability that we all must face.

Social work has only just begun to fulfill its mission and address the issue of sustainability and how it impacts professional values, theories, and practice. In his groundbreaking book, *Ecology and Social Work: Toward a New Paradigm*, Canadian social work educator John Coates (2004) criticized the profession for its failure to give serious consideration to the consequences of environmental devastation. Still, the fact that his book was written at all was significant. And we should not neglect to mention the groundbreaking contribution of Hoff and McNutt's (1994) book, *The Global Environmental Crisis: Implications for Social Welfare and Social Work*, which was published in Britain.

Coates's (2004) vision was of a shift from a focus on modernization to sustainability, from an anti-collectivist paradigm to a community-focused one. Following Coates, Mary (2008) believes that if social work is to remain viable, it must become a force for systemic change toward the creation of a socially just and sustainable community. We must avail ourselves, she argues, of new paradigm thinking about the global economy, work, energy resources, and "the commoditization of our biological, physical, and social goods" (p. 21). Craig Mosher (2009), in his presentation at a social work education conference centered around the theme of sustainability, similarly challenged social work to develop a new paradigm of practice, one that is more holistic and committed to long-term sustainability of both ecosystems and social systems. Let's consider some ways that a contemporary vision of social work can help create a better world.

Expanding Environmental Awareness

Dominelli (2012), in *Green Social Work*, emphasizes the necessity for social workers to understand the science behind climate change, engage in debates about the topic, draw upon the knowledge developed by physical scientists, work to spread energy awareness to consumers, and contribute to policymaking on environmental concerns. "Is Social Work a Green Profession?"—this is the title of a recent article by Terry Shaw (2012). Based on her survey of a cross section of almost 400 members of the National Association of Social Workers (NASW), Shaw concludes that much more needs to be done before this question can be answered in the affirmative. Social workers in her survey emerged as no more, or less, environmentally knowledgeable or friendly than the general population. The message to social work education is clear: Much more emphasis needs to be placed on the environmental component of the person-environment model taught in the social work curriculum, and the environment must stress the importance of the physical as well as the social environment. Despite the developing body of social work literature concerned with ecological issues, the profession, according to Shaw, has not fully embraced the need to incorporate these issues into social work education or practice.

Social work can expand on ecological awareness by using several basic strategies: first, involvement in educational and publicity campaigns, such as organizing "teach-ins" with charismatic speakers who can excite students and community members on key issues related to globalization and climate change, engaging in and supporting organic farming, working to help clean local streams and creeks, and infusing the university curriculum with sustainability content.

Second, student and faculty involvement in political action for policy development at the state and local levels is educational and may bring about real social change. Lobbying legislators can best be done through the state NASW organizations.

At the local level, social workers can work to establish community gardens and support farmers' markets and the movement to provide healthy school lunches with plenty of fruits and vegetables to children. And when city councils introduce proposals to bring into the community corporations known for their questionable and environmentally damaging practices, social workers can help organize opposition to such proposals. When exploitation of the people does take place and an accident happens, such as in the mining disaster in Chile, social workers can join others in holding the corporation accountable. As a profession with the knowledge and skills for engaging in holistic and empowerment-based practice, social work is ideally suited to provide leadership in working toward environmental and economic sustainability. The profession is also one that is closely attuned to issues involving race and class. We discuss issues related to environmental classism and racism in Chapter 6. Suffice it to say for the moment that the impact of pollution falls most heavily upon the poor and minorities, not only in the United States but also in the industrializing nations of the world. The privilege of having access to clean air, water, and uncontaminated soil is an advantage that dominant groups everywhere typically have preserved for themselves.

The injustice in disparate access to a clean and healthful environment is increasingly viewed as a moral issue by religious groups, such as the National Council of Churches (2012). Happily, many of these religious groups are playing active roles in the environmental movement. This includes Muslims and Jews as well as Christians. They and others, whether believers or not, often find a spiritual presence in nature.

Acknowledging a Spiritual Dimension

Ecological destruction and the threats of global climate change are increasingly seen as moral issues, as social work educator Craig Mosher (2010) indicates, partly because religious groups have identified this work as caring for God's creation. In addition, people are realizing that their own society and economic system is damaging the planet, so they feel a moral responsibility to solve the problem. Some see a moral imperative to redistribute wealth and develop a moderate lifestyle based on the value of sufficiency rather than material greed. The values of consumerism (spend, spend, spend) and the values of the major religions of the world, as discussed in Chapter 3, are strongly in conflict.

At the UN summit on climate change in Copenhagen, the presence of religious groups was strongly felt (Winter, 2009). At a time when political leaders were struggling to get their nations to make a strong commitment to protection of the environment, here were numerous preachers, rabbis, ministers, and other faith-based leaders bringing a spiritual presence to the conference. Representatives from the National Council on Churches, which represents over 45 million congregation members in the United States, Nobel Peace Prize winner Desmond Tutu from South Africa, and representatives from various evangelical associations all attended the conference and strongly advocated 1 international agreements to restrict ecological destruction.

America's religious communities have shed their long-standing suspicion of the environmental cause (Winter, 2009). Many have rallied behind the belief that we are called upon to protect God's creation, including human and all other life. This belief cuts across all religions, with authentic green movements springing up in Muslim, Jewish, and Catholic communities, among many others.

THINKING SUSTAINABLY

In Chapter 3, we talked about the various religious traditions that have informed social welfare policy. Discuss various ways religions and spiritually oriented people have turned to nature to find peace and solace. What are the basic qualities that are inherent in most world religions that seem explicitly connected to living sustainably? Can you think of other qualities central to most world religions that are antithetical to sustainability? What are some of the religious groups doing to further care for the environment?

Valuing Cultural Diversity

Philosophically we can look toward Native American and feminist sources for the concepts and values needed to enrich an expanded ecological model of social welfare. American Indian tribes valued their natural resources and did not waste them. They saw themselves as one with the earth and its creatures (Coyhis & Simonelli, 2008). Ecofeminists, similarly, see the earth as mother and deplore aspects of the modern male ethic—stressing disconnectedness, hierarchy, and power over others (Curry, 2011). This notion of oneness with the universe is congruent also with the Darwinian notion of the interrelatedness of species in a "web of life." Thus, science and religion are joined in an appreciation for the genius of nature. Mosher (2010) points to an additional linkage of science and spirituality in the teachings of Eastern mystics in their descriptions of reality and by high-energy physicists who express a sense of mystery in their descriptions of particles in the nucleus of the atom. Common to both is a sense of awe and mystery.

A celebration with a close connection to the bounty of the earth and the harvest is the African American Kwanzaa. Such ceremonies and rituals, as are represented in the Kwanzaa holiday celebration, play an important role in providing meaning and purpose in life, bringing the generations together, enhancing a collective sense of peace and harmony, as well as connecting to the sacred (Canda & Furman, 2010). Kwanzaa is a Swahili word that means "first fruits." From December 26 to January 1, the African American celebration of Kwanzaa occurs. It is a celebration based on African traditions when the ancestors gathered together to celebrate the harvesting of the first crops. In Bowling Green, Kentucky, social workers and church leaders are actively involved in the annual celebration that generally takes place at a local Baptist church near downtown (see van Wormer & Besthorn, 2011).

Human beings evolved to thrive in natural environments, as Andrew Weil (2011), author of *Spontaneous Happiness* suggests. Our brains are simply not suited for a sedentary indoor life. Weil believes that many of us in the modern-day world suffer from depression as a result of nature deficit, eating processed food, and being deluged with information overload. He singles out the Old Order Amish for having a lifestyle that is more consistent with meeting our needs as human beings. He should have also looked to Norway.

Norwegians, a highly secular people, often turn to nature for solace and mental health. As described by Fred Besthorn, the land and landscapes in Norway, some of the most beautiful in the world, are understood as having deep spiritual/existential meaning and significance (in van Wormer & Besthorn, 2011). Much like indigenous groups around the world, many Norwegians share a wide-ranging belief that the land is a sacred place. Natural environments are a spiritual sanctuary. For this reason, everyone has the right to free and open entry onto both public and private lands. Every worker has the right to access a window with an outside view at his or her work station. Every prison inmate has a similar right in Norway not to be shut off from nature, even in confinement.

Social Welfare Policy Considerations

We have spoken about the link between spiritual and religious values that call upon us to treasure the bounty and mysteries of nature. We have also seen how through religious organizations as well as through the social work profession, individual environmentalists are working toward social change. Let's now turn to potential policy changes that can reverse some of the damage that has been done and point the way to a more harmonious future.

Hoff and McNutt (2009) identify the following social welfare policy areas, which are major concerns to social workers: national health policy, which so often lacks a public health focus; the need for housing policies to protect disadvantaged social groups from substandard living conditions and exposure to toxic wastes; and the lack of adequate and reliable public transit. Social workers advocate for: legislation to support urban gardening and ecological education for community members; projects to support greater energy efficiency; promotion of research for the reduction of harmful waste and safe forms of waste disposal; and investment in resources to address the developmental needs of girls and women as an approach to population control.

Hoff and McNutt (2009) call for expanded government funding for research to develop sustainable techniques of production of food, energy, low-impact housing, and transportation. Moreover, they favor a tax policy that provides incentives for the restoration of environmental resources and a strengthening of regulatory agencies. These recommendations are consistent with the core social work values of social justice and service and with the NASW (2012) policy statement on environmental justice. These recommendations are also consistent with social work's solution-focused emphasis in helping people change.

Seeking Solutions

In the face of imminent ecological collapse and the social disintegration that accompanies it, we often become so engrossed in negative thinking that the problems seem overwhelming and unsolvable. Nordhaus and Shellenberger (2007), authors of *Break Through: From the Death of Environmentalism to the Politics of Possibility* warn us against such a mind-set, which is destructive to the environmental movement. They direct our attention to the verbs that are most commonly associated with environmentalism and conservation. These are negative words such as *stop, restrict, reverse, prevent, regulate,* and *constrain.* All of them direct our thinking to stopping the bad, not creating the good. Only in seeking a "politics of possibility" can we find an avenue for hope.

Fortunately, there is increasing awareness today of the need to find ways to promote environmental sustainability that simultaneously increases social equality and meets economic needs. In this section, we first look briefly at green job creation for a green economy, then examine the growth of sustainable economic practices in farming, and then discuss a variety of successful developments taking place on college campuses.

Green Jobs

The creation of green jobs is seen as a promising avenue to help people adopt clean technologies while improving local economies. The American Reconstruction and Reinvestment Act offers billions of dollars to initiatives to improve energy efficiency; a substantial portion of the funding is set aside for green job training as a pathway out of poverty (*Recovery Act*, 2009). The United States took a major step toward building a national high-speed rail network when the Obama administration awarded 8 billion dollars in grants for rail building projects with the promise of creating tens of thousands of new jobs (Clayton, 2012).

There are many green jobs as we will see in the following sections on organic farming and rail construction. In his book, *Our Choice: A Plan to Solve the Climate Crisis,* Al Gore (2009) discusses the possibility of moving America forward environmentally through solar, geothermal, and wind power developments. The job growth in these areas will be extensive.

The construction of green schools and even whole green towns are not totally out of the realm of reality. Many new schools being built are following environmentally progressive principles as in the small town of Richardsville, Kentucky, which is among 78 schools named as green ribbon schools by the U.S. Department of Education (Mason, 2012). This building, a net-zero building, is the first in the nation to generate more energy than it uses. Children learn a lot in this farm community about energy conservation and sustainability. Elsewhere, such as in Madison, Wisconsin, there is a focus on simply having children walk or ride bikes to school. This trend, however, contradicts the national movement toward school consolidation, which means fewer children are within walking distance from the school (van Wormer & Besthorn, 2011).

How about whole green towns? This possibility became a reality when 95% of Greenburg, Kansas, was blown away in a tornado. Thanks to grassroots organizing and inspirational leadership by environmentalists, town members agreed to rebuild following green design for public buildings (Environmental Protection Agency, 2011). The town also voted to reduce energy use considerably. Financial support came rolling in from environmental consultants and from the Environmental Protection Agency (EPA). Today, Greenburg has become a model of sustainable development on the prairie. And even cities such as Houston, Texas, that are not starting from scratch are "going green" in terms of overhauling energy codes for business and adding a bike sharing program and 20 miles of light rail track ("Greening Houston," 2012, p. 29).

Natural Systems Farming

Prairie ecologist Wes Jackson (2009) leads us to look to nature to find the answers "to questions we haven't even asked." Speaking before an audience at the University of Northern Iowa, he further stated, "Natural systems are information rich. We must begin to think like a prairie, like a forest." Jackson proposes that we adopt a different kind of economics, one that is focused on long-term enrichment, and on resilience rather than growth. Jackson recommends that we engage in a sustainable agricultural system in the following ways:

- Supporting soil conservation and working toward the restoration of the soil and the protection of water resources
- Moving away from the planting of annual crops
- The planting of perennial crops, which will grow deep roots to protect the soil from runoff
- Reducing the use of chemicals and decreasing fossil fuel dependence to prevent pollution of the streams and rivers and help reduce greenhouse gases

An ultimate goal of Jackson's Land Institute is to show the world how to develop ample food supplies to end hunger. The growth of natural systems and organic farming is an exciting development that has the potential to attract a younger generation of farmers and revitalize rural communities.

Cuba, according to a report from the United Nations Environment Programme (UNEP) (2011a) is a model for sustainable agriculture. While ensuring national food security under a trade embargo, Cuba's transition to organic agriculture came out of necessity. Yet this development has had a positive impact on people's livelihoods by guaranteeing a steady income for a significant proportion of the population. Moreover, according to UNEP, the lack of pesticides for agricultural production is likely to have a positive long-term impact on Cubans' well-being, since such chemicals are often associated with various negative health implications such as certain forms of cancer. Unfortunately, the recent economic opening of the country to foreign investment could boost Cuba's potential for increasing renewable energies, but it is also leading to increased chemical fertilizer and fossil fuel use—weakening Cuba's sustainability (King, 2012).

Organic farming is coming into prominence today in the United States, as a visit to any general grocery store will show. The movement started out of concern for the environment but also a desire for good-tasting and healthy food. Because there is a growing demand for organically grown food, many people who did not grow up on farms are buying land and learning how to farm without chemical fertilizers or pesticides.

According to the following UNEP (2011a) report:

Food crops produced in excess of these quotas could be freely sold at farmers markets, thereby providing a price incentive for farmers to effectively use new organic technologies such as biofertilisers, earthworms, compost and the integration of grazing animals. Farmers also revived traditional techniques such as intercropping and manuring in order to increase production yields. (p. 1)

In Waverly, Iowa, social work educator Tammy Faux, who teaches at Wartburg College, and her husband, Rob, raise a variety of wildflowers on their 5-plus acre organic farm. They also grow organic vegetables without the use of pesticides or herbicides. She describes their mission in a local news article:

We believe in the importance of being good stewards of our environment and good citizens of our community. We strive to work in harmony with nature to produce good-tasting foods (using no pesticides, herbicides or chemical fertilizers) to support the health of our neighbors and our local economy. (Golden, 2007, pp. 1–2)

It's a mission Tammy takes into the classroom. "How we get our food and where we get it from is a social issue," she said, noting that much of the produce consumed in the United States travels at least 1,500 miles and is often imported.

If you consume locally produced food, you cut down on the use of fossil fuels that were used to transport it. You cut down on the times it has to change hands. And if it's local, it probably tastes better, because it was picked when it was ripe, whereas the produce you often get in grocery stores ripen on the truck. (Golden, 2007, pp. 1–2)

Mass Transportation

Travel by train is a family-friendly way to cover long distances and see the scenery. For an aging population, the availability of reliable and flexible rail travel within cities and cross-country is essential to prevent social isolation. Access to city transit is crucial for the urban poor in facilitating job seeking and access to stores and farmers' markets to buy reasonably priced healthy food and merchandise. On the environmental side, transportation policies have an important role to play given that our current transportation systems consume a huge amount of fossil fuels and account for nearly a quarter of energy-related carbon dioxide emissions (UNEP, 2011b). The building of a high-speed rail system across the United States would go far to relieve America's dependence on oil.

All across Europe and Canada and in many Asian countries, the major cities have elaborate networks of trolleys that workers conveniently use to commute to work. In Western Europe, where you can set your watches by the train, travel by rail is a popular way to sightsee and visit other countries; today England and France are even connected through a tunnel ("the chunnel"). Japan and China have thousands of miles of smooth-riding rails that reach speeds of around 200 miles per hour (Tuttle, 2009). The United States, in contrast, where spending has largely focused on interstate highway projects, has nothing comparable.

Source: Photo by Robert van Wormer.

Ready to Board Amtrak. In some parts of the United States, travel by train is still possible for a pleasant and scenic trip across the country.

Nevertheless, some positive developments are taking place in U.S. cities in the form of light rail and streetcars. Light rail is expensive because it runs on its own lines, but it is faster and goes longer distances than streetcars that run with the streets. Portland, Oregon, is the leader of light rail in the United States and has been compared to Freiburg, Germany, with its similar emphasis on recycling, sustainability, biking, and public transit ("Is Oregon's Metropolis a Leader?" 2010). Many ride bicycles to work, made easy by extensive bicycle lanes; others travel to work by light rail. Billions of dollars have been invested in this system, which serves over 100,000 passengers each weekday. A surge in property values has resulted in housing within walking distance of the rail lines.

Many city planners are convinced that resurrecting streetcars or trolleys is good for the local economy and attractive to young professionals who wish to return to urban living (Associated Press, 2013). Thirty cities are currently building streetcar systems or have already done so, including Salt Lake City, Los Angeles, and Kansas City. These streetcars bring a sense of community to neighborhoods as residents get to know one another as they walk back and forth to the stops.

Another development with environmental benefits is the expanding use of freight trains to carry merchandise instead of hauling it on trucks. Simply getting the large trucks off the road is a major improvement in driving safety. Environmental studies show a significant reduction in air pollution. Estimates are that if just 10% of long-distance freight that is currently moving by truck were to be moved instead by diesel trains, the resulting carbon emission reduction would be the equivalent of taking 2 million cars off the road (Association of American Railroads, 2012). On average, trains are four times more fuel efficient than trucks. Since a single freight train can carry the load of several hundred trucks, trains reduce highway gridlock, lower greenhouse gas emissions, and reduce pollution. Through the use of greener and cleaner technologies and more efficient operating practices, the trains are steadily improving and becoming much more widely used.

Summary and Conclusion

To the extent that the aim of social policy is to enhance social well-being, we can gauge its success or failure in terms of its sustainability. Sustainability is a concept that relates to time: How long can we keep doing what we are doing to the earth, in the way that we are doing it? How long can we continue to pollute the land and still have healthy soil? How long can we continue to expand the world's population in light of the diminishing food supply? We face a momentous choice, whether to continue doing what we are doing or to seek global solutions to problems that are no longer confined to any one country or part of the world.

The gravest threat to our social welfare—habitat destruction—is a problem about which one thing is certain: Countries of the world cannot go on doing what they are doing now. Environmentally, the world is interconnected; industrial fumes in one part of the earth travel over to pollute another part. With regard to contamination of the air, forests and water, there are no national boundaries. As we have seen in this chapter, economic development and social development are not synonymous and very often gross business profits take place at the expense of natural resources. Governmental and world monetary policies that are penny wise and pound foolish have helped create some massive problems, including the depletion of fossil fuels, industrial air pollution, the introduction of dangerous chemicals into our water through overzealous use of pesticides, overpopulation in the poorest regions of the world due to inadequate attention to family planning, overfishing, and shrinking of arable land due to overdevelopment.

That all the environmental problems that we have discussed in this chapter are interconnected is a major theme of sustainability. For example, we have seen how global warming affects agricultural conditions through droughts in some regions and flooding in others, how agricultural chemicals brings about toxicity of the soil and water, how overpopulation increases the scarcity of available land and water while leading to the increase in pollution-generating vehicles, which adds to the air pollution that in turn is associated with global warming. Deforestation, which is connected to agriculture, is also a recognized factor in climate change and global warming. The end result of climate change is food shortage in the midst of continued population growth in the poorest regions of the world.

The negative impacts of environmental crises—overpopulation; overconsumption; pollution of the air, water, and soil; global warming—on individuals and communities are challenging the social work profession to address these issues educationally and to respond to them through political action. The person-environment perspective, central to social work, necessarily includes attention to the physical or natural environment. As we have seen in this chapter, the inextricable links among ecological damage, poverty, and risk to human health are considerable. Yet there are qualities that we can nurture—both individually and as part of the social work profession—that can help stem these crises, and even turn them around.

Although the social work profession was slow to adopt an ecosystems-sustainability model, the impact of climate change and worldwide attention to the human ramifications of a string of natural disasters has put the environment, sustainable economics, and well-being in the spotlight.

As we move on to the next chapter on poverty and inequality, keep in mind the interconnectedness of economics and environmental sustainability. The time of making a distinction between economy and ecology is over. Any ecological disaster is an economic disaster and vice versa. The world's military spending and preparation for war are destructive for both realms—the environment and the economy. Replacing competition with creative and peaceful interdependence and mobilizing the world's nations toward global solutions are the challenges facing our species today. We need to do as Nancy Mary (2008) advises—combine science with spirituality and move from a dominator model to a partnership model. The social welfare professions, in coming to conceptualize the person-in-the-physical (as well as social) environment, have an important role to play in promoting human survival.

Critical Thinking Questions

1. "It's us against the environment" (Bateson, 1972). Does this statement have any meaning for you? Think of ways we try to subdue nature.

2. How does environmental awareness go back to the early days of social work?

3. Think back to when you became environmentally aware. Were you encouraged to recycle paper, for example, or to respect the earth in other ways?

4. What is the difference between economic and social development? How do they overlap?

5. What is the impact of deforestation on weather patterns on this planet?

6. Visit the War Resisters League website and examine where the tax money goes. What does this say about our values?

7. Do you think cultural diversity is important, and how does it parallel an emphasis on biodiversity?

8. Consider the impact of the melting of the polar ice cap. Are there some advantages to this development?

9. Discuss the connection between climate change and food shortage. Wh some reasons for expected shortages and famine in some countries in the f

10. How is the education of girls crucial to ending famine?

11. Discuss the impact of monocultural farming on natural resources. What is the impact on family farmers today?

12. How do Amish people follow traditional practices? What can we learn from them?

13. Do research on the history of Monsanto. What is this corporation's role today in seed production?

14. Discuss various ways religious and spiritually oriented people have turned to nature to find peace and solace. What are some of the religious groups doing to further care for the environment?

15. List solutions to the environmental crisis. Which solutions are important for long-term sustainability?

16. Describe the circular history of streetcars and micro-rail in our cities. What is the importance of recent developments?

17. What is your university doing to promote sustainability?

References

Arndt, M. (2010, January 11). *Monsanto v. Food, Inc. over how to feed the world.* Retrieved from www.businessweek.com

Associated Press. (2013, November 13). Once nearly extinct, streetcar gets new life in U.S. *Waterloo-Cedar Falls Courier*, p. C5.

Association of American Railroads. (2012, June). The environmental benefits of moving freight by rail. Retrieved from www.aar.org

Barker, R. (2014). *The social work dictionary* (6th ed.). Washington, DC: NASW Press.

Bateson, G. (1972). *Steps to an ecology of mind: Collected essays in anthropology, psychiatry, evolution, and epistemology.* Chicago, IL: University of Chicago Press.

Berry, W. (1977). *The unsettling of America: Culture and agriculture.* San Francisco, CA: Sierra Club Books.

Berry, W. (1993, March/April). Decolonizing rural America. *Audubon, 95*(3), 100–105.

Besthorn, F. H. (2008). Environment and social work practice. In T. Mizrahi & L. E. Davis (Eds.), *Encyclopedia of social work* (20th ed., Vol. 2, pp. 132–136). New York, NY: Oxford University Press.

Brown, L. (2011). *World on edge: How to prevent environmental and economic collapse.* London, England: W. W. Norton.

Brown, L. (2012). *Full planet, empty plates: The new geopolitics of food scarcity.* London, England: W. W. Norton.

Canda, E. R., & Furman, L. (2010). *Spiritual diversity in social work practice: The heart of helping.* New York, NY: Oxford University Press.

Carson, R. (1962). *Silent spring.* New York, NY: Houghton Mifflin.

Clayton, M. (2012, August 21). Obama plan for high-speed rail, after a hitting a bump, moves forward. *Christian Science Monitor.* Retrieved from csmonitor.com

Coates, J. (2004). *Ecology and social work: Toward a new paradigm.* Halifax, Nova Scotia: Fernwood.

Connor, S. (2006, July 20). Earth faces catastrophic loss of species. *The Independent.* Retrieved from www.independent.co.uk

Costello, A., Abbas, M., Allen, A., Ball, S., Bell, S., & Bellamy, R. (2009). Managing the health effects of climate change. *The Lancet, 373*(9676), 1693–1733.

Coyhis, D., & Simonelli, R. (2008). The Native American healing experience. *Substance Use and Misuse, 43,* 1927–1949.

Curry, P. (2011). *Ecological ethics: An introduction* (2nd ed.). Cambridge, England: Polity Press.

Dominelli, L. (2012). *Green social work: From environmental crises to environmental justice.* Cambridge, England: Polity Press.

Engelman, R. (2012). Population indicators. *The Berkshire Encyclopedia of sustainability: measurements, indicators, and research methods in sustainability* (pp. 282–286). Berkshire, UK: Berkshire.

Environmental Protection Agency. (2011, April 5). Collaboration and partnerships: Rebuilding Greenburg, Kansas. Retrieved from www.epa.gov

Fisk, L. (2012, February 23). BP spill victims still feel economic impact as trial nears. *Bloomberg Business Week.* Retrieved from www.businessweek.com

George, S. (2010). *Whose crisis, whose future: Towards a greener, fairer, richer world.* Cambridge, England: Polity Press.

Germain, C. B. (1968). Social study: Past and future. *Social Casework, 49*(7), 403–409.

Germain, C. B. (1978). General-systems theory and ego psychology: An ecological perspective. *Social Service Review, 52*(4), 535–550.

Germain, C. B. (1991). *Human behavior in the social environment: An ecological view.* New York, NY: Columbia University Press.

Gillis, J. (2014, November 3). U.N. panel issues its starkest warning yet on global warming. *New York Times International,* p. A6.

Global Commission on the Economy and Climate. (2014, September). Better growth, better climate: A new pathway for economic policy. Retrieved from www.newclimateeconomy .report

Golden, K. (2007). Faux real: Couple plants seeds in classroom, at home. *Wartburg Magazine Online, 23*(3), 1–2. Retrieved from www.wartburg.edu/magazine/fall07/fauxgarden.html

Gore, A. (2009). *Our choice: A plan to solve the climate crisis.* New York, NY: Puffin Books.

Greening Houston: Changing the plans. (2012, July 14). *The Economist,* 29.

Greider, K. (2012, October). Battling superbugs. *AARP Bulletin, 53*(8), 18–20.

Guebert, A. (2012, January 8). Tanzania ag deal sullies ISU's good name. *Waterloo-Cedar Falls Courier,* p. D3.

Hoff, M. D., & McNutt, J. G. (Eds.). (1994). *The global environmental crisis: Implications for social welfare and social work.* Aldershot, England: Avebury.

Hoff, M. D., & McNutt, J. G. (2009). Social policy and the physical environment. In J. Midgley and M. Livermore (Eds.), *The handbook of social policy* (pp. 296–311). Thousand Oaks, CA: Sage.

Is Oregon's metropolis a leader among American cities or just strange? (2010, April 17). *The Economist,* pp. 32–34.

Jackson, L., & D. Keeney (Eds.). (2010). Perennial farming systems that resist flooding. In C. Mutel (Ed.), *A watershed year of the Iowa floods of 2008* (pp. 215–226). Iowa City: University of Iowa Press.

Jackson, W. (2009, April 20). *Events leading to 50 year farm bill.* Speech presented at the Center for Energy and Environmental Education. Cedar Falls, IA.

Karger, H. J., & Stoesz, D. (2013). *American social welfare policy: A pluralist approach.* Boston, MA: Pearson.

Kaskey, J. (2011, September 12–18). The superweed strikes back. *Bloomberg Business Week,* pp. 21–22.

King, M. D. (2012). *Cuban sustainability: The effects of economic isolation on agriculture and energy.* Paper presented for the National Political Science Association, Portland, OR.

Klein, N. (2014). *This changes everything: Capitalism versus climate.* New York, NY: Simon & Schuster.

Korten, D. C. (2009). *Agenda for a new economy: From phantom wealth to real wealth.* San Francisco, CA: Berrett-Koehler.

Lappé, F. M. (2013). *Ecomind: Changing the way we think to create the world we want.* New York, NY: Nation Books.

Lochhead, C. (2013, September 16). Report links antibiotics at farms to human deaths. *San Francisco Gate.* Retrieved from www.sfgate.com/health

Mary, N. (2008). *Social work in a sustainable world.* Chicago, IL: Lyceum Books.

Mason, C. (2012, December 23). "Net-zero" school pays off. *Daily News,* pp. 1A, 5A.

McKinnon, J. (2012). Social work and changing environments. In K. Lyons, T. Hokenstad, M. Pawar, N. Huegler, & N. Hall (Eds.), *The SAGE handbook of international social work* (pp. 265–278). Thousand Oaks, CA: Sage.

Mosher, C. (2009, May). *A new paradigm for sustainability and social justice.* Paper presented at the meeting of the International Eco-Conference: Building Bridges Crossing Boundaries, Calgary, Alberta, Canada.

Mosher, C. (2010). A wholistic paradigm for sustainability: Are social workers experts or partners? *Critical Social Work, 11*(3), 102–121.

Naeem, S. (2009, May–June). Lessons from the reverse engineering of nature: The importance of biodiversity and the true significance of the human species. *Miller-McCune Magazine,* 56–71.

National Association of Social Workers. (2012). Environmental policy. NASW, *Social work speaks: NASW policy statements 2012–2014,* pp. 123–128. Washington, DC: NASW Press.

National Climate Assessment. (2014). *Climate change impacts in the United States.* Retrieved from www.nca2014.globalchange.gov

National Council of Churches. (2012). *Unequal exposures: Toxic chemicals in communities of color.* Retrieved from www.louisvillecharter.org/downloads/ejchemicals.pdf

National Ocean and Atmospheric Administration. (2011, April). *State of the climate global hazards.* U.S. Department of Commerce. Retrieved from www.ncdc.noaa.gov

National Ocean and Atmospheric Administration. (2012, September, 24). *Study finds that ocean acidification is accelerated in nutrient-rich areas.* U.S. Department of Commerce. Retrieved from www.noaanews.noaa.gov/stories2012/20120924_oceanacidification.html

National Snow and Ice Data Center. (2012, October 1). *Poles apart: A record-breaking summer and winter.* Retrieved from http://nsidc.org/arcticseaicenews/2012/10/poles-apart-a-record-breaking-summer-and-winter/

Nordhaus, T., & Shellenberger, M. (2007). *Break through: From the death of environmentalism to the politics of possibility.* New York, NY: Houghton Mifflin.

Norwegian Polar Institute. (2009, December 14). *Melting snow and ice: A call for action.* Centre for Ice, Climate and Ecosystems. Retrieved from www.regjeringen.no

Peipert, J., Madden, T., Allsworth, J., & Secura, C. (2012). Preventing unintended pregnancies by providing no-cost contraception. *Obstetrics and Gynecology, 120*(6), 1291–1297.

Pringle, P. (2003). *Food, Inc.: Mendel to Monsanto—the promise of the biotech harvest.* New York, NY: Simon & Schuster.

Raab, A. K. (2012, June 17). *UNU-IHDP and UNEP launch sustainability index that looks beyond GDP*. International Human Dimensions Programme. Retrieved from www.eurekalert.org/pub_releases/2012-06/ihdp-uau061312.php

Recovery act: Pathways out of poverty. (2009, June 23). U.S. Department of Labor. Retrieved from www.07.grants.gov

Reznicek, J. (2012, June). Occupy the world food prize. *Via Pacis, 36*(2), 9.

Schmitz, C., Matyók, T., James, C., & Sloan, L. M. (2012). The relationship between social work and environmental sustainability: Implications for interdisciplinary practice. *International Journal of Social Welfare, 21*, 276–286.

Shaw, T. (2012). Is social work a green profession? An examination of environmental beliefs. *Journal of Social Work, 13*(1), 3–29.

Sullivan, A. (2009, January 23). Obama repeals the abortion gag rule, very quietly. *Time*. Retrieved from www.time.com

Tuttle, B. (2009, May 11). *The fastest trains on the track*. Budget Travel. Retrieved from www.budgettravel.com/feature/090511_speedytrains,6779/

United Nations. (2010). *The world's women 2010: Statistics and trends*. Department of Economic and Social Affairs. Retrieved from http://unstats.un.org/unsd/demographic/products/Worldswomen/WW2010pub.htm

United Nations. (2014, November 1). *Climate change 2014: Synthesis report*. International Panel on Climate Change fifth assessment. Retrieved from www.ipcc.ch/pdf/assessment-report/ar5/syr/SYR_AR5_SPM.pdf

United Nations Environment Programme. (2011a). Green economy: Organic agriculture in Cuba. Retrieved from www.unep.org/greeneconomy/SuccessStories/OrganicAgricultureinCuba/tabid/29890/Default.aspx

United Nations Environment Programme. (2011b). Transport: Investing in energy resource efficiency. Retrieved from www.unep.org/greeneconomy/Portals/88/documents/ger/GER_10_Transport.pdf

van Wormer, K., & Besthorn, F. H. (2011). *Human behavior and the social environment, macro level*. New York, NY: Oxford University Press.

War Resisters League. (2012). Where your income tax money really goes. Retrieved from www.warresisters.org

Weil, A. (2011). *Spontaneous happiness*. New York, NY: Little, Brown.

Whoriskey, P. (2009, November 29). Monsanto's dominance draws antitrust inquiry. *Washington Post*. Retrieved from www.washingtonpost.com

Winter, B. (2009, December 6). Religious groups active in climate debate. *USA Today*. Retrieved from www.usatoday.com

Worldwatch Institute. (2009). *State of the world 2009: Into a warming world*. Retrieved from http://www.worldwatch.org/node/5982

Zastrow, C. (2010). *Introduction to social work and social welfare* (10th ed.). Belmont, CA: Cengage.

5

Poverty and Inequality

Suzanne McDevitt

Inequality—that feeling of a few doing very well, while so many slip further behind—that is the defining challenge of our time.

—Bill de Blasio, Mayor elect, New York City (2013)

Some people continue to defend trickle-down theories, which assume that economic growth, encouraged by a free market, will inevitably succeed in bringing about greater justice and inclusiveness in the world. This opinion, which has never been confirmed by the facts, expresses a crude and naive trust in the goodness of those wielding economic power and in the sacralized workings of the prevailing economic system. Meanwhile, the excluded are still waiting.

—Pope Francis, *Evangelii Gaudium* (2013, p. 46)

The provision of food is indeed a central issue in general social ethics since so much in human life does depend on the ability to find enough to eat. In particular, the freedom that people enjoy to lead a decent life, including freedom from hunger, from avoidable morbidity, from premature mortality is quite centrally connected with the provision of food and related necessities. Also, the compulsion to acquire enough food may force vulnerable people to do things which they resent doing and may make them accept lives with little freedom. The role of food in fostering freedom can be an extremely important one.

—Amartya Sen, *Food and Freedom* (1987)

Poverty and Inequality in the 21st Century

Nearly everyone in the United States understands poverty as a lack of monetary resources. But the meaning attached to it, the status ascribed to it and how it is defined is less simple. Rising inequality has received extensive media attention since the recession. Many Americans have asked themselves and their society "How did we get here?" This chapter seeks to answer at least part of that question. It focuses on causes, impacts, and remedies for poverty.

Why are social workers interested in poverty? Since the beginning of the profession, poverty has been a focus. Social workers began to understand the structural problems of minority status, poor living standards, the human capital aspects of poverty, and the contribution of poor education to persistent poverty. Throughout its development as a profession, social work has been concerned about the effects of poverty as an issue of social justice and as it produces additional stress on the families that the profession works with in every area of service across the life span.

The preamble of the National Association of Social Workers (NASW; 2008) Code of Ethics states,

> The primary mission of the social work profession is to enhance human well-being and help meet the basic human needs of all people, with particular attention to the needs and empowerment of people who are vulnerable, oppressed, and living in poverty. A historic and defining feature of social work is the profession's focus on individual wellbeing in a social context and the wellbeing of society. Fundamental to social work is attention to the environmental forces that create, contribute to, and address problems in living.

Though most social workers do not work in basic needs agencies, the historic recognition of the importance of the environment that the client lives in and interacts daily with continues to be important.

Defining and Measuring Poverty

The term poverty is one of those that most people think they recognize, though if they are asked they cannot always readily define. Many people of the older generation, the writer's grandmother, for example, used to say, ominously, "I'm going to end up in the poorhouse." The threat of the poorhouse, the place where someone goes when they have no assets and no one to take care of them, loomed over generations of Americans. The old poorhouse has long been gone but the fear of impoverishment is as prevalent as ever. In most instances, the poorhouse has morphed into a nursing home.

Poverty does not have simple definitions, and the psychological impacts of the fear of becoming poor may be as damaging as poverty itself. It is both a quantitative measure and a state of mind.

In effect, poverty has to do with concepts of scarcity and abundance. Americans become more aware of poverty in times such as the Great Depression and the Great Recession, when people who had attained a more prosperous status begin to fall back. Both of these economic calamities happened after a time of steady wage erosion, while, at the same time, the assets of the top 20% of the population were growing.

As Mark Rank (2013) notes, in the *Encyclopedia of Social Work*, "Poverty has been a subject of concern since the early days of social work" (p. 1). When we attempt to discuss poverty and inequality, we first might think of wages or income. Rank quotes Adam Smith who, in *The Wealth of Nations* (1776), declared poverty to be "a lack of those necessities that "the custom of the country renders it indecent for creditable people, even of the lowest order, to be without" (p. 2)—or as Michael Harrington (1962) put it in the 1960s, not necessarily the stark reality of near starvation that still lingers in some developing countries but "existing at levels just below that necessary for human dignity" (p. 9). Thus, definitions of poverty in relationship to standard of living have been remarkably constant over time.

Monetary Thresholds

Poverty definitions may focus on absolute amounts of money, as in the definition devised by the U.S. Department of Agriculture economist Molly Orshansky (1963) and adopted by the United States or may be relative in nature, such as the ratio to median wage rate adopted in a number of European countries and the European Union.

In 1963, Orshansky wrote a discussion paper devising two systems of poverty thresholds. Both systems used food plans developed by the Department of Agriculture.[1] She used both the economy (now called the thrifty plan) and the slightly higher low-cost plan to develop budgets that would indicate different levels of economic opportunity among demographic groups of families with children. She calculated that if the cost of food is about 30% of a family's budget, then the poverty threshold could be established at three times the rate of that market basket.

Her article describing the poverty thresholds appeared in the *Social Security Bulletin* in July of 1963 (Orshansky, 1963). Six months later, in January 1964, President Johnson declared the War on Poverty and the 1964 Report of the Council of Economic Advisors included a chapter on poverty that referred to Orshansky's thresholds (Fisher, 1992).

The measure developed by Orshansky was adopted and continues to be used as the official poverty level. As Ruggles (1990) noted, Orshansky (1963) used the lowest possible budget so that it could not be challenged for its generosity, much as Benjamin Rowntree (1910) had at the beginning of the 20th century. At the time, the amount was the equivalent of about half of the median after-tax income of a four-person, two-child family (Citro & Michel, 1995, p. 138). By the late 1990s the poverty line had fallen to less than a third of household income (Glennerster, 2002), but during the 2000s wages stagnated and then fell during and after the recession. The ironic result was that the

---

1. The Thrifty Food Budget has the lowest cost of four food budgets developed and refined since 1894 by the U.S. Department of Agriculture Food and Nutrition Service. The Thrifty Food Budget was established as the standard for the maximum benefit in the 1964 Food Stamp Bill. The Thrifty Food Budget "represented a minimal cost diet (based on up to date dietary recommendations, food composition data, food habits, and food price information)" (Carlson, Lino, Juan, Hanson, & Basiotis, 2007). It has been revised several times, most recently in 2006.

poverty line is now a larger proportion of median household income than it was during the 1990s.

In recent years, the Census Bureau has, in addition to continuing to report information using the Orshansky (1963) definitions, also developed and begun to report on poverty using alternative measures. Following a review of the last 15 years of research on the poverty measure, a Supplemental Measure, which includes more aspects of income and deductions than the standard, will be reported along with the standard measure. Table 5.1 describes the differences between the two models.

The number of people in poverty appears to be higher using the Supplemental Poverty Measure (SPM) than the official measure. In 2012, 47 million people were poor using the official definition, but 49.7 million people were poor using the SPM (Short, 2012, p. 5).

The Supplemental Poverty Measure uses a formula that adds the value of benefits and subtracts the expenses, as in Table 5.2.

Table 5.1   Poverty Measure Concepts: Official and Supplemental

	Official Poverty Measure	**Supplemental Poverty Measure**
Measurement Units	Families and Unrelated Individuals	All related individuals who live at the same address, including any co-resident unrelated children who are cared for by the family (such as foster children) and any cohabiters and their relatives
Poverty Threshold	Three times the cost of a minimum food diet in 1963	The 33rd percentile of expenditures on food, clothing, shelter and utilities (FCSU) of consumer units with exactly two children multiplied by 1.2
Threshold Adjustments	Vary by family size, composition, and age of householder	Geographic adjustments for differences in housing costs by tenure, family size, and composition.
Updating Thresholds	Consumer Price Index: all items	Five-year moving average of expenditures on FCSU
Resource Measure	Gross income before tax cash income	Sum of cash income, plus noncash benefits that families can use to meet their FCSU needs, minus taxes (or plus tax credits), minus work expenses, minus out-of-pocket medical expenses, and child support paid to another household

Source: Short (2012).

Table 5.2	Resources Included in Calculation of Supplemental Poverty Measure

Plus:	Minus:
Supplemental Nutrition Assistance (SNAP)	Taxes (plus credits such as the Earned Income Tax Credit [EITC])
National School Lunch Program	
Supplementary Nutrition Program for Women, Infants and Children (WIC)	Expenses Related to Work
	Child Care Expenses
Housing Subsidies	Medical Out-of-Pocket Expenses
Low-Income Home Energy Assistance (LIHEAP)	Child Support Paid

Source: Short (2012).

Food Security

Another way of looking at poverty is to evaluate food security. Since food is such a basic need, the relationship between poverty and having enough to eat is a significant one.

Nord (2010) found that from 2000 to 2007 median food spending by low- and middle-income U.S. households grew more slowly than food prices over the same time period. Food spending by middle- and low-income households actually declined after adjusting for inflation. "The deterioration in food security was greatest for households with incomes in the 20th to 40th percentile, for which the prevalence of very low food security increased by about 50 percent" (Nord, 2010, p. iii). The decline in food spending occurred at the same time that spending on housing rose. In the lowest quintile, the decline accompanied an overall decline in spending. American families were already stressed before the beginning of the Great Recession.

Measuring Food Insecurity

Since 1995, the Current Population Survey has administered the Food Security Supplement every December. The supplement is used to develop the food security reports issued annually by the Economic Research Service, Department of Agriculture. *Food Security* is defined as,

> Access by all people at all times to enough food for an active, healthy life. Food security includes at a minimum: (1) the ready availability of nutritionally adequate and safe foods, and (2) an assured ability to acquire acceptable foods in socially acceptable ways (e.g., without resorting to emergency food supplies, scavenging, stealing, or other coping strategies).

Food insecurity is defined as "limited or uncertain availability of nutritionally adequate and safe foods or limited or uncertain ability to acquire acceptable foods in socially acceptable ways" (Bickel, Nord, Price, Hamilton, & Cook, 2000). *Very low food security* is characterized by times, during the year, when the food intake of household members is reduced and their normal eating patterns are disrupted because the household lacks money and other resources for food.

Over 94% of those suffering from very low food security

- [Reported] they could not afford to eat balanced meals (94%)
- Reported having worried that their food would run out before they got money to buy more (99%)
- Reported that the food they bought just did not last and they did not have money to get more (97%)
- Reported that an adult had cut the size of meals, or scaled meals, because there was not enough money for food (96%)
- Reported that they had eaten less than they felt they should because there was not enough money for food (95%) (Coleman-Jensen, Nord, & Singh, 2013, p. 5)

Nationally, food insecurity (very low food security is a subcategory of food insecurity), increased 29.2% from an average of 11.3% in 1996 to 1998 to an average of 14.6% in 2008 to 2010,[2] and only declined by one tenth of 1% in 2010 to 2012, although the recession was over in June, 2009. This represents approximately 48.9 million individuals in the United States. The rate of very low food security, which affects approximately 17,179,000 individuals, actually rose (Coleman-Jensen et al., 2013, p. 6).

While the rate of food insecurity declined .2%, from 2008 to 2010 to 2010 to 2012, very low food security increased. Nationally, the rate of very low food security increased 51.3%, from 3.7% in 1996 to 1998, to 5.6% in 2008 to 2010 and increased an additional one-tenth percent from 2010 to 2012. Table 5.3 demonstrates the decline of food security and increases in food insecurity since 1998.

The majority of the increase in food insecurity occurred in the very low food security statistic and it continued to increase after the end of the recession. Table 5.3 shows both the increase in food insecurity and the growth in the percentage of very low food security.

Figure 5.1 shows the prevalence of trends in food insecurity over the last 18 years.

Food assistance has moved from being used primarily by the low-income, non-working population to being a mainstay of the low-income working population. Rank and Hirschl, quoted in Rank (2004), writing before the onset of the Great Recession, found, based on longitudinal analysis of data from the Panel Study of Income Dynamics, that "by age 65, 64.2% of the population has received an in-kind program, such as food stamps, at least once in their life (Table 4.5 in Rank, 2004, p. 103).[3]

---

2. Data are averaged for greater reliability.

3. The Panel Study of Income Dynamics is a nationally representative, longitudinal sample of households and families interviewed annually since 1968. "The measure of welfare use in Table 4.5 is constructed from a series of questions asked by the PSID interviewers about whether the household has received any cash or in-kind public assistance programs at some time in the previous year. . . . In-kind programs include Food Stamps and Medicaid" (Rank, 2004, p. 262).

	Food Insecurity Percentage	**Low Food Security Percentage**	**Households That Are Food Secure**
Table 5.3 Percentage of Households by Degree of Food Security, 1996 to 2012			
Average 1996–1998	11.3	7.6	88.7
Average 2003–2005	11.4	7.6	88.6
Average 2006–2008	12.2	8.2	87.8
Average 2008–2010	14.6	9	85.4
Average 2010–2012	14.5	8.8	85.5

Source: Coleman-Jensen, Nord, & Singh (2013). Data are averaged for greater reliability by the author.

Figure 5.1   Trends in Prevalence Rates of Food Insecurity and Very Low Food Security in U.S. Households, 1995–2012

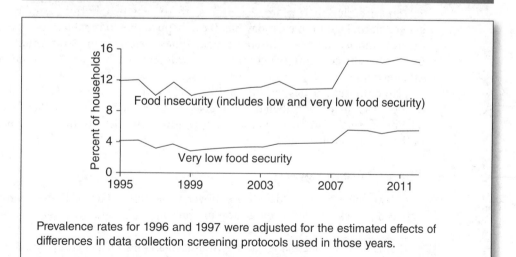

Source: Calculated by ERS based on Current Population Survey Food Security Supplement data.

Shaefer and Wu (2011), using the Survey of Income and Program Participation (SIPP),[4] found that low-educated women (those with a high school diploma or less) between the ages of 22 and 55 who entered employment from 1990 to 1994 and from 2001 to 2005 experienced an increase in unemployment insurance eligibility but not in unemployment benefit receipt during periods of unemployment. They found that "receipt of food stamp benefits is far more common than either unemployment insurance or cash welfare" (p. 222).

Thus, in the Great Recession, food assistance emerged as a critical part of the safety net, and the only one that expanded based on need.

Global Measures: Relative Poverty and Social Exclusion

While the United States relies on a dollar definition based on actual expenses, which may be described as an absolute measure, the European Union definition uses a more relative measure, a ratio of median income. While it varies among EU members, it is a ratio of 40% to 70% of median income (European Anti-Poverty Network, 2013). The EU definition, generally referred to as social exclusion, is broader than money, thus

> people are said to be living in poverty if their income and resources are so inadequate as to preclude them from having a standard of living considered acceptable in the society in which they live. Because of their poverty they may experience multiple disadvantages through unemployment, low income, poor housing, inadequate healthcare and barriers to lifelong learning, culture, sport and recreation. They are often excluded and marginalized from participating in activities (economic, social and cultural) that are the norm for other people and their access to fundamental rights may be restricted. (Council of the European Union, 2004, p. 9)

Social exclusion is a broader process that keeps people from employment and general participation in everyday life. It can happen due to monetary poverty but also due to minority status and disability: sometimes even by being stranded in a rural or poor inner city community with no transportation to enable participation in jobs and other activities.

Note the similarities to both Smith (1776) and Harrington (1962) in the phrase "standard of living considered acceptable in the society in which they live." Thus, whether poverty is defined in absolute or relative terms, it must be seen in the context of the society one lives in.

The Culture of Poverty

Over the years the debate on poverty has often focused on the difference between a lack of work—or a lack of training to obtain work—and a so-called

---

4. The Survey of Income and Program Participation (SIPP) is administered by the Bureau of the Census. The SIPP provides a nationally representative sample, developed through clustering addresses within cities and counties. It surveys respondents on demographics, income sources, public assistance program participation, household and family structure, jobs, and work history (Shaefer & Wu, 2011, p. 210).

Source: Photo by Brandon Luke.

Absolute Poverty in Nicaragua. Children search through rubbish heaps for food and useful items.

culture of poverty, where the poor have caused their own problems by their own poor judgment.

Recent research has addressed, at least to some extent, the "culture of poverty" and found it related to the stress of being poor. In *Scarcity*, Mullainathan and Shafir (2013) found in experiments in both New Jersey and India that the stress of poverty greatly impacts the judgment of the poor. In interviews with shoppers at a New Jersey mall, participants were asked their incomes and were classified (unbeknown to them) as rich or poor. Then they were asked what they would do if their car broke down and needed a $150 repair: take out a loan, pay in full, or just postpone. On this task both rich and poor participants exhibited similar scores on willpower and intelligence tests. Then the test was repeated but this time the price was $1,500. With the raise in price, the intelligence and willpower scores of the poor declined sharply.

Since the enactment of the Personal Responsibility and Work Opportunity Act of 1996 (popularly known as welfare reform) there has been an increased focus on low-wage workers. This growing emphasis gained ground during the Great Recession, which began, according to the National Bureau of Economic Research (NBER, 2010) in December 2007 and reached its lowest point in June of 2009. In the early months of the recession, the winter and spring of 2008, the U.S. economy lost 800,000 jobs per month. The problem persisted until April 2009 (Greenstone & Looney, 2011), although every month 125,000 new workers entered the job market. Even for those workers who quickly regained employment, the jobs they were able to find paid, on average, 17% less than their previous positions. Even at this writing, in the fall of 2013, annual GDP remains depressed. The percentage of the population with a job in August 2013 reached the lowest level since 1978.

During the recession, long-term unemployment (that is over 26 weeks) rose to a level higher than at any time in the last six decades and remains an ongoing concern. In August 2013 nearly two fifths (37.9%) of the 11.3 million people who were looking for work had been looking for 27 weeks or more. At the beginning of the recession there were about seven jobseekers for every open job. In August 2013, the ratio had declined to 3 jobseekers for every available job (Stone, 2013).

In 1959, prior to the War on Poverty, 22.4% of the population lived below the poverty line. By the early 1970s, the poverty rate had fallen to about half that amount: 11.1% in 1973. By 1983 it had risen to 15% and has never returned to the 1973 level. In 2000, at the end of the Clinton administration, it again dipped to 11.3%, then rose to 12.4% and then increased sharply during the 2007 recession to 15%, where it currently remains (Gabe, 2013).

How many people, over a lifetime, experience poverty? Once a year, the Census Bureau issues a report that states the proportion of the population whose income is below the poverty rate. However, this only partially describes the actual number of people who over their lifetimes have experienced poverty. Rank and Hirschl (1999) found that between the ages of 18 and 75, 58% of Americans will experience at least one year with income below the poverty level and 75% will have at least one year of income below 150% of the poverty line. In addition, two-thirds of Americans will rely on a means-tested program such as SNAP (Supplemental Nutrition Food Assistance Program) between the ages of 20 and 65 (Rank & Hirschl, 2002).

> Yet, for most Americans poverty only lasts a year or two before their income recovers, at least to a certain extent. Sendoval, Rank, and Hirschl (2009) found that during the 1990's, the risk of acute poverty (spells of a year or two living in poverty) increased especially for white males as a whole and nonwhite males in their 30s, 40s, and 50s, while chronic poverty (spells of over 5 years out of 10) declined (p. 731). Thus, according to Sendoval et al. the American life course is increasingly characterized by periodic spells of economic turmoil. . . . If anything, it may have intensified given the continuing patterns of job insecurity, erosion of social protection programs, levels of financial debt, and wage stagnation during the 2000s. (p. 734)

Growing Inequality

Since the mid-1980s economists have realized that after 3 decades of the income distribution remaining stable, suddenly inequality began to rise (Krugman, 1992). Though some economists had been writing about income inequality for decades, suddenly in the spring of 2014, in the words of Stephen Colbert, Thomas Piketty's new book, *Capital in the Twenty-First Century*, "blew the lid off inequality" (Gasperak, 2014). Piketty's contribution is extensive data analysis of both income taxes and wealth across both developed and developing countries. He demonstrates that concentrations of capital by the top 20% allows those at the top level an increased ability to make even more money. Through data analysis that covers over a century, he shows that while income inequality diminished dramatically post World War II, it was mainly the result of the "shocks of the Great Depression and World War II" (Piketty, 2014, p. 15).

Until the mid-1970s all groups experienced growth in income at the same rate; since 1980, income inequality has increased significantly, "especially in the United States, where the concentration of income in the first decade of the twenty-first century regained, indeed slightly exceeded, the level attained in the second decade of the last century" (Piketty, 2014, p. 15). Income inequality in the United States has returned to levels not seen since before the Great Depression, and "inherited wealth comes close to being as decisive at the beginning of the 21st century as it was in the age of Balzac's *Pere Goriot*" (p. 22).

Piketty's (2014) work also demonstrates that the more wealth one has to begin with the more likely one is to gain even more wealth. The more surplus income, the easier it is to invest and grow part of that income. Thus, such tendencies, over time, contribute to greater concentrations of wealth, as has been seen since the 1980s. How does this happen? Piketty (2014) states plainly, "The resurgence of inequality after 1980 is due largely to the political shifts of the past several decades, especially in regards to taxation and finance" (Piketty, 2014, p. 20).

Stated simply, unchecked great wealth creates even greater concentrations of wealth in the hands of the wealthy. Progressive taxation systems and investment in training and education promote the growth of a more equal society, which in the long run, benefits society as a whole.

Source: Photo by Rupert van Wormer.

Immigrant Laborers Doing Yard Work. These Mexican laborers in Seattle experience many barriers in their pursuit of the American dream.

Piketty does not discuss the role of unions, but certainly collective bargaining in the U.S. resulted in steady increases in wages and benefits and helped to promote more equality and a higher standard of living for its members.

The lessons are relatively simple. Regulation and reform of the tax code to produce a more progressive system and greater support for public education and training will result in more wealth for average Americans, which will result in less inequality.

Factors That Differentiate the
Great Depression From the Great Recession

There are two major differences between the 1930s Depression and the most recent Great Recession. One is the general availability of credit, through credit cards, to consumers. Early in the recession, in 2008, the average borrower carried $9,887 in charges. By 2012, according to Traub and Ruetschlin, the average carried was down to $7,145. However, 40% of households report using credit cards for basic living expenses. The availability of credit cards in the 2007 recession contributed to the ability of households to cover shortfalls and maintain their ability to stay current on expenses and basic needs such as food and rent. The only credit available during the 1930's Depression was generally from local grocers (and butchers such as the writer of this chapter's grandfather) who would allow families to run an account.

Second is the vast array of major social insurance and safety net programs that protect, at least to some extent, people in the throes of poverty. Social insurance programs such as Social Security have provided the ability to keep older adults and persons with disabilities participating in the economy as consumers, while unemployment insurance has helped to maintain the consumer behavior of working Americans while they looked for work.

Income maintenance programs are social welfare programs designed to prevent or combat poverty through contributions to the income of individuals or families. Included in this category are the seeming opposites: social insurance programs and public assistance. The former is a universal-style program in which people receive benefits as legal entitlement based on their own contributions. The latter, the public welfare dimension, is financed out of general tax revenues. Public assistance is not universally available but rather means tested. Let's take a look at some of the key income maintenance programs that are designed to help mitigate the effects of poverty and to help level the playing field for American citizens.

Social Insurance Programs

Major social insurance programs include Social Security, Medicare, and unemployment insurance. Social insurance operates much like any other type of insurance; people pay against future risk. Social insurance programs are government programs to protect citizens from the full consequences of the risks and situations (such as unemployment) to which they are vulnerable (see Barker, 2014, p. 398).

Social insurance programs are financed at a level about four times higher than public welfare. Older adults are the principal beneficiaries of U.S. social insurance programs.

Social Security

Old Age, Survivors, and Disability Insurance (OASDI), popularly referred to as Social Security, was created by the 1935 Social Security Act and later amendments. Administered by the Social Security Administration, Social Security is primarily financed through payroll taxes, Federal Insurance Contributions Act (FICA) (Social Security Administration, 2014a). Payroll taxes are paid by employees and matched equally by employers. There are three separate programs; old age benefits (this is what is commonly referred to as Social Security), disability benefits, survivors benefits, and a death benefit.

The original Social Security Act provided only retirement benefits and only to the worker (Social Security Administration, 2014a). The 1939 amendments added benefits to spouses, minor children of the worker, and survivors. These benefits are paid to the family in the event of the worker's premature death. As of 1975, automatic increases based on the annual Cost of Living Adjustment (COLA) were added every January. Since 1990, the payroll tax rates have been 12.4% for Social Security and 2.9% for Medicare (Social Security, 2013). For 2015, the maximum taxable earnings amount for Social Security (OASDI) taxes is $118,500. There is no limitation on taxable earnings for Medicare's hospital insurance taxes. The current FICA tax rate applicable to each employee and employer is 6.2% for OASDI (temporarily reduced to 4.2% in 2012 for employees as part of the American Recovery and Reinvestment Act, popularly called the stimulus bill). Medicare is an additional 1.45%. The self-employed pay double these rates on a voluntary basis, since they pay both the employee and employer share.

Retirement benefits from this program are provided to fully insured workers age 66 or older. Dependent spouses over 62 and dependent children under age 18 (19 if enrolled full time in an elementary or secondary program) are also covered. The minimum retirement age for full old-age Social Security benefits ranges from age 65, beginning with people born in 1938 or earlier, to age 67 for people born after 1959 (Social Security, 2014c).

Disability Benefits

The disability program was added by amendment in 1954, though cash benefits were not paid until 1965. Initially it was restricted to workers ages 50 to 65 (the prime ages for disabling conditions) but was gradually widened to include dependents and disabled workers of any age.

Financial Concerns

A major concern in recent years has been the financial soundness of the social insurance programs. A putative crisis was fueled by the economic recession that started in 2007 and resulted in a high rate of job loss, an unprecedented concern by right-wing politicians over the federal deficit, demographic changes (a dropping birth rate plus an increase in life expectancy), and a commonly voiced yet unverified concern that providing any financial aid to laid-off workers would act as a disincentive to motivate them to seek work and increase an unhealthy dependency (Wallace, 2010).

Table 5.4 Social Security Fact Sheet

In 2013, almost 58 million Americans will receive $816 billion in Social Security benefits.

June 2013 Beneficiary Data			
Retired workers	37 million	$47.4 billion	$1,269 average monthly benefit
Dependents	2.9 million	$1.8 billion	
Disabled workers	8.9 million	$10 billion	$1,129 average monthly benefit
Dependents	2.1 million	$69 billion	
Survivors	6.2 million	$6.6 billion	$1,221 average monthly benefit

Social Security is the major source of income for most of the elderly:

- Nearly 9 out of 10 individuals age 65 and older receive Social Security benefits.
- Social Security benefits represent about 39% of the income of the elderly.
- Among elderly Social Security beneficiaries, 53% of married couples and 74% of unmarried persons receive 50% or more of their income from Social Security.
- Among elderly Social Security beneficiaries, 23% of married couples and about 46% of unmarried persons rely on Social Security for 90% or more of their income.

Social Security provides more than just retirement benefits:

- Retired workers and their dependents account for 74% of total benefits paid.
- Disabled workers and their dependents account for 16% of total benefits paid.
- About 90% of workers ages 21 to 64 in 2012 who have enough time paid (calculated in quarters of a year) into the Social Security system and their families have protection in the event of a long-term disability.
- Just over one in four of today's 20-year-olds will become disabled before reaching age 67.
- Sixty-nine percent of the private sector workforce has no long-term disability insurance.
- Survivors of deceased workers account for about 10% of total benefits paid.
- About one in eight of today's 20-year-olds will die before reaching age 67.
- About 96% of persons ages 20 to 49 who worked in covered employment in 2012 have survivor's insurance protection for their young children and the surviving spouse caring for the children.

An estimated 163 million workers are covered under Social Security:

- Fifty-one percent of the workforce has no private pension coverage.
- Thirty-four percent of the workforce has no savings set aside specifically for retirement.

In 1940, the life expectancy of a 65-year-old was almost 14 years; today it is more than 20 years:

- By 2033, the number of older Americans will increase from today's 45.1 million to 77.4 million. There are currently 2.8 workers for each Social Security beneficiary. By 2033, there will be 2.1 workers for each beneficiary.

Source: Social Security Administration (2013, June).

A counterargument is that unemployment benefits help keep families out of poverty, provide time for a person to seriously look for suitable work, and boost the economy by increasing consumption.

The Social Security Trust Fund will need adjustments to be maintained; the simplest way to ensure solvency is to remove the cap on Social Security taxes. As of 2014, payroll taxes are collected on incomes up to $117,000. By removing the cap and collecting payroll taxes on all earned income, the funding concerns can be alleviated.

Once the baby boom generation has passed on, the current funding issues should resolve and the system should replenish itself. Because it prevents large numbers of older Americans from living in dire poverty and because they or their family members have paid for this protection during their working years, this is a program worth saving.

Social Security has come under attack by conservative legislators in the U.S. House of Representatives. Initiatives during the George W. Bush administration to privatize the system were not popular and did not pass in Congress. An initiative that found some support across party lines was to recalculate inflation so the amount paid out to recipients did not increase to the extent that it currently does. Yet, as former Secretary of Labor Robert Reich (2013) informs us, this decrease in income would be disastrous for many low-income elders who depend on Social Security as their major source of income. Employed in low-wage jobs during their working years, these adults were not able to save toward retirement. Even Social Security's current inflation adjustment understates the true impact of inflation on older adults due to the fact that they spend 20% to 40% of their incomes on health care on average, and health care costs have been rising faster than inflation.

In fact, as Burk (2011) indicates, Social Security does not contribute to either the national debt or the yearly deficit. It is run outside the federal budget and has historically maintained a surplus.

The revenue problem stems from demographics—the imbalance in the population due to the "baby boom," which took place following World War II when the men returned home from the war and started families. Due to the increased life expectancy today of Americans, the bulge in the now aging population from this birth cohort, and a decline in the numbers of younger workers paying into the system, taxes need to be increased or the money diverted from elsewhere to compensate for the shortfall. But, according to Reich (2013),

> Social Security isn't in serious trouble. The Social Security trust fund is flush for at least two decades. If we want to ensure it's there beyond that, there's an easy fix—just lift the ceiling on income subject to Social Security taxes, which is now $113,700. (p. 1)

Proposed Reforms

Responding to the dramatic economic downturn of the Great Recession, Americans increased pre-retirement withdrawals from their 401ks (Argento, Bryant, & Sabelhaus, 2013) and the percentage of people applying for Social Security at age 62 increased dramatically, reversing a decadelong decline in early retirements (Rutledge, Coe, & Wong, 2012). Responding to these trends Senator Tom Harkin (D-Iowa) introduced the Strengthening Social Security Act of 2013, proposing a 15% increase to benefits over a 10 year period, improving the Cost of Living Adjustment (COLA) to include medical costs, and removing the cap on the payroll tax over the course of 10 years to stabilize the trust fund.

Social Security Disability Insurance (SSDI)

Social Security Disability Insurance (SSDI) is a federally funded social insurance program introduced in 1954. It is granted to a worker who has paid into Social Security and become blind or disabled and is no longer able to work. The monthly disability benefit amount is based on the Social Security earnings record of the insured worker and the length of time worked.

Significantly, the number of workers receiving SSDI increased from 2.9 million in 1980 to 8.8 million in 2012. Dire projections have been made about this social insurance program (Daly, Lucking, & Schwabish, 2013), and it was the subject of a negative Planet Money report on *This American Life* (Joffe-Walt, C., 2013). While the Planet Money report was widely cited, the *Columbia Journalism Review* found that it was poorly researched and lacked context (Lieberman, T., 2013). It appears that SSDI has expanded in relationship to demographic trends and changes in other benefit programs. According to Pattison & Waldron (2013), 94% of the growth in the program is explained by three factors: population growth, growth in the proportion of women insured for disability, and movement of the baby boom generation into disability prone ages (ages 50 to 65).

In addition, Guo and Burton (2012) found that increases in disability applications and awarded benefits were a result of changes in workers' compensation programs in the 1990s that restricted eligibility and lower benefits.

Medicare

Federal health insurance for the aged, Medicare was incorporated into law in 1965 and Old Age, Survivors, and Disability Insurance (OASDI) became Old Age, Survivors, Disability, and Health Insurance (OASDHI). Medicare consists of two separate but coordinated programs: part A is hospital insurance and part B is supplementary medical insurance of which beneficiaries are charged a monthly premium. Part D (prescription drug coverage) is voluntary and the costs are paid for by the monthly premiums of enrollees and Medicare. Unlike Part B, in which you are automatically enrolled and must opt out if you do not want it, with Part D you have to opt in by filling out a form and enrolling in an approved plan (Social Security, 2014c). Unlike Social Security, Medicare spending does contribute to the national deficit. The reason is that former president George W. Bush added a benefit—the unfunded prescription drug program that was a bonanza for the pharmaceutical companies, because of a prohibition against government negotiation for drug prices (Burk, 2011).

Hospital insurance helps pay for inpatient hospital care, inpatient care in a skilled nursing facility, home health care, and hospice care. Coverage is limited to 90 days in a hospital and to 100 days in a skilled nursing facility.

In 1983, a system of diagnostic-related groups (DRGs) was established by the federal government. Under this cost-saving measure, Medicare's reimbursement rates to hospitals were set according to illness category. This reimbursement plan has resulted in intensified discharge planning to reduce hospital stays. This has resulted in the growth of home health care services and other changes far beyond Medicare patients.

Unemployment Insurance

At the time of the enactment of the 1935 Social Security Act, the provision for unemployment benefits was considered the major program. Overseen by the federal Department of Labor, every state administers its own unemployment benefit program. Unemployment insurance provides benefits to workers who have lost their jobs through no fault of their own. This program is available through federal and state cooperation. The weekly benefit amount for which the unemployed are eligible, along with the number of weeks of eligibility for payment (usually for up to 26 weeks), varies from state to state. In most states, the formula is designed to compensate for a fraction of the usual weekly wage, normally about 50%, subject to specified dollar maximums. Generally, extensions are granted during periods of economic recession. Eligibility requirements in most states are that the worker must have worked a certain number of weeks in covered employment, must be able to work, available for work, and be free from disqualifications.

The unemployment benefit program is fraught with difficulties (Reich, 2012). Jobless Americans today typically use up their benefits while they are still unable to find suitable work. The unemployment system was designed when workers were temporarily laid off until the economy rebounded, and they were hired back. Many of the states have steadily tightened eligibility requirements. At the height of the recession, only 40 percent of unemployed people qualified for unemployment benefits (Reich, 2012). People who have been fired from their jobs for cause, for example, do not qualify. Additionally, restrictions against students receiving benefits hinders recipients in long-term preparation for career change (Karger and Stoesz, 2013). Due to the very temporary nature of the coverage, when the unemployment rate is high, as it is today, only a fraction of unemployed workers are receiving benefits. In addition, the administrative systems in some states were antiquated at the time the Great Recession and prevented some potential recipients from receiving benefits (U.S. Government Accountability Office, 2013).

An article in *Bloomberg Business Week* puts these benefits in global perspective. In Norway, where unemployment is a mere 3.3%, laid-off or fired workers keep 72% of their annual pay in combined unemployment pay and state benefits (Scott, 2010). This compares to 28% on average in the U.S., and the time frame is far different. Germany pays one-third of the salaries of workers whose hours and wages are slashed by companies and provides job training. In Japan, with almost 5% unemployment, the government gives former workers 45% of their work pay the first year.

Workers' Compensation

Workers' compensation was the earliest U.S. social insurance program. It covers workers hurt on the job. Developed during the Progressive Era, as a response to devastating industrial accidents that not infrequently resulted in death and maiming of workers, it replaced a system in which the only recourse available to a worker was suing the employer. Between 1909 and 1920, 43 states enacted workers' compensation laws (Trattner, 1999). All 50 states and the District of Columbia participate.

Workers' compensation provides an automatic non–means-tested benefit to 90% of the workforce (Terrell, 2008). The approach is no-fault, in other words it does not matter how the injury occurred.

States administer the programs, and therefore benefits and conditions vary state by state. For example, in some states psychiatric and substance abuse conditions are covered; in others, they are not.

In most states, employers purchase workers' compensation coverage. In some instances the rates are affected by the number of claims, leading to safety campaigns to minimize on the job injuries.

Benefits cover medical expenses and supplies, temporary disability payments, permanent disability payments, treatment to cure and relieve the effects of the injury, replacement of wages lost, and funeral and dependency benefits in cases where a worker dies due to an occupational injury or disease (Clayton, 2003). The replacement of lost wages varies by state and type of disability: temporary or permanent. For temporary disability, payments average two-thirds of pretax wages, a level viewed as fair without providing a disincentive to returning to work (Terrell, 2008), though the rates varied substantially. In 2008, the highest weekly benefit was $1,133 in Iowa, and the lowest was $351 in Mississippi.

In the modern era, workers' compensation is part of a complex system of vocational rehabilitation, Social Security Disability, and other programs. Perhaps as the disability rights movement has developed, the attitude toward disability has shifted from a view of disability as a permanent condition to an increased emphasis on helping a person with disabilities return to the workforce. Recent analysis has focused on the impact of workers' compensation cases on SSDI. For example, Guo and Burton (2012) found that when workers' compensation benefits declined and eligibility rules tightened in the 1990s, the SSDI application rate increased.

Veterans Benefits

Veterans benefits is the oldest benefit program in the history of the United States, dating back to 1776, when the Continental Congress granted the states authority to provide Revolutionary War veterans half pay for life "in cases of loss of limb or other serious disability" ("History of Veterans," 2012). This burden was later assumed by the federal government. Throughout the 19th century, pensions were paid for veterans of armed conflicts, for varying lengths of time, to disabled veterans, widows, and dependents. The federal government established soldiers' homes and hospitals, as did some states.

Following World War I, rehabilitative services were added, and in 1924, a bonus to World War I veterans based on length and location of service was authorized, payable in 20 years. This led, during the Great Depression, to the bonus march of veterans requesting early payment of the bonuses.

The so-called GI Bill, or the Servicemen's Readjustment Act, enacted in 1944, provided 4 years of education and training, federally guaranteed housing, farm and business loans with no down payment, and unemployment compensation. It also established veterans hiring preference where federal funds are spent.

In the last 20 years waiting for disability claims to be decided has been a continuing issue. Problems grew apparent under the leadership of Veterans Affairs (VA) secretary Eric Shinseki and developed a new urgency in 2014, when it was revealed that some VA hospitals had developed secret waiting lists to conceal long wait times for appointments, resulting in Secretary Shinseki's resignation and the firing of some VA hospital directors (Lichtblau, 2014).

Veterans' health care benefits are open to any veteran who was discharged or released under conditions other than a dishonorable discharge (Department of Veteran's Affairs, 2010). This widened the availability for such benefits and aggravated already long wait times. Other benefits include disability compensation for an injury or illness incurred or aggravated during active military service based on a disability ranking from 10% to 100%; pensions to low-income veterans who are permanently or totally disabled or over the age of 65; education and training benefits based on the length of active-duty service (full benefits require 36 months), including tuition and fees, books and supplies, and housing allowances. Full benefits are transferrable to family members with the approval of the Department of Defense. There is also a work-study benefit. Home loans are available to eligible service members, veterans, and unmarried surviving spouses to buy, renovate, refinance, or install a solar heating or cooling system or other energy efficient improvements (Department of Veteran's Affairs, 2010). Life insurance and burial and memorial benefits are also available as well as health care benefits for the spouse and dependents of disabled veterans.

In addition to the Veterans Afffairs hospitals and related services, a system of Vet Centers has been established nationwide to aid veterans in readjustment following after discharge. Located in storefront offices they provide a

> continuum of care including readjustment counselling, community education, outreach to special populations brokering of services with communities and the Department of Veterans Affairs. They provide individual counselling, group counselling, marital and family counselling, medical referrals, assistance in applying for VA benefits, employment counseling, drug and alcohol assessments, sexual trauma counseling and referral and bereavement counselling for eligible family members. Vet Centers serve both veterans and active duty families. ("Serving Those Who Need," 2014)

An executive order of the Obama administration launched a major homelessness initiative to have every homeless veteran housed by 2015.

Attacks on Social Insurance Programs

Social insurance programs, which are designed to provide replacement income for when a worker is retired, unemployed, or disabled, are enormously popular with the general public. Older adults rely on Social Security, for example, for a significant part of their income. It is especially important for low-income people, as it may be their only source of retirement income. Most Americans feel entitled to Social Security since they or their spouses paid into this insurance program for a number of years. Still, political conservatives and libertarians argue that Social Security socializes a portion of the national income, discourages savings, and causes retired people to become dependent on the government (Allen, 2013). One strategy is for conservative politicians to plant the suggestion through constant repetition that the government will go bankrupt as the baby boom population retires and to continually stress that something has to be done. A second strategy is to alter the perception of a program by renaming it so that it takes on negative connotations. So it is with the term *entitlement*.

First applied to government benefits by President Reagan, the term was placed in quotes to imply that the recipients might not really be entitled to receive their benefits; this usage was quickly picked up the business press (Hertzberg, 2013). Over time the term *entitlement* was no longer used in quotes, but the pejorative aspect to the way the word was uttered prevailed. Thus in the 2012 presidential election campaign, Republican candidate Mitt Romney attributed his difficulties in garnering votes to the 47% of Americans who believe they are "entitled to health care, to food, to housing, to you name it" who would not vote for him. According to Hertzberg, he was denigrating the Social Security programs along with the people who depend on them (p. 23). However, compared to means-tested programs, such as TANF that provide benefits to those with very low or no income, social insurance benefits are highly regarded by the general public. As discussed above, the concerns with the soundness of Social Security financing are overstated, perhaps for political reasons.

Public Assistance Programs

Sometimes called *welfare* by the general public, programs restricted to the income eligible in which applicants must undergo a "means test" are highly stigmatized. Instead of being financed by the employee through his or her job, support for the public assistance comes out of general tax revenues.

Examples of means-tested programs are Temporary Assistance to Needy Families (TANF), Supplemental Nutrition Assistance Program (SNAP) formerly called Food Stamps, supplemental security income (SSI), Medicaid, the Earned Income Tax Credit, and housing assistance. These programs in contrast to social insurance programs are all based on need rather than entitlement. An important fact to note about means-tested programs is that when they are available only to people below a certain income and not available to others, resentment builds up, and the programs are stigmatized. Over time they are underfunded.

Temporary Assistance to Needy Families (TANF)

In the summer before the 1996 election, President Clinton signed into law the Personal Responsibility and Work Opportunity Responsibility Act of 1996 and repealed the open-ended welfare program, Aid to Families of Dependent Children (AFDC). The new program is now called the Temporary Assistance for Needy Families (TANF). This legislation (generally known as *welfare reform*) was designed by Clinton to end "welfare as we know it" and it did just that (Vobejda, 1996, p. A01). According to Vobejda, labor unions, religious groups, and organizations representing women, minorities, and immigrants, all of whom are key Democratic constituencies, expressed outrage over Clinton's decision to support the bill. Those within the Christian Right were fervent supporters of welfare reform because of its focus on behavioral reform and consistency with the Protestant work ethic (Martin, 2012). This philosophy—that taking care of small children is not work—and that only paid work counts reflects, as Seccombe (2011) argues, the low value that society places on caring for children. As a result of this attitude, about half of women with infants under a year old are employed. In the Scandinavian countries, in contrast, the values put a premium on the mother and father taking at least a year's leave from work to take care of infants, each parent in turn.

Providing the states with grants to be spent on time-limited cash assistance, TANF generally limits a family's lifetime cash welfare benefits to a maximum of 5 years and permits states to impose a wide range of other requirements as well—in particular, those related to employment. Block-granting TANF resulted in funds being diverted to fund day care, foster care and other eligible activities. TANF, which like AFDC, was designed to support mothers with children (the original target group as nonworking widows whose husbands' work histories had not qualified for Social Security), did not expand during the Great Recession, and eligibility in many states has become more restrictive.

The nation's largest public assistance program, TANF is the most stigmatized of the public assistance program. Tim Wise (2010) attributes this fact to racism. This was especially a factor in the 1970s, he says, as conservative politicians increasingly sought to scapegoat welfare efforts for everything from taxes to crime to family dissolution. In the belief that the types of people who need government aid are apt to use illicit drugs, legislators in at least 10 states are considering bills that would require adults on various types of public assistance to submit to drug testing. The results from Florida's experimentation revealed that few recipients failed the test and that this policy was expensive to the state. The punitive nature of these attacks on welfare recipients is obvious (Alvarez, 2012).

Significantly, the family aid program started in 1935 as a method of keeping mothers at home. Mothers were being supported to care for their children: in effect, paid for child care activities. Today, with middle-class mothers working with a fiercely renewed work ethic, a major objective of the program is to compel other single mothers, without a private means of support, to work or to train for work.

Meanwhile, intellectual rationales for reductions in welfare spending came with the publication of Murray's *Losing Ground* (1984). Since the antipoverty programs of the 1960s, according to Murray's argument, failed to reduce poverty, promoted dependency, and did not support the work ethic, they were actually harmful. This ideology was reflected in the Family Support Act of 1988.

Work expense and child care may be provided for up to 12 months after a family leaves the AFDC rolls because of employment. States have adopted a variety of approaches from workfare to job training and education programs, but most states have chosen an approach that focuses on readiness to work and work search efforts. Supporters point to the desire to end the dependency and stigma of the program. Detractors argue that welfare is punitive and reduces the number of well-paying jobs.

The myths about TANF are persistent. The facts to refute such myths are as follows:

- Ninety percent of TANF children live with their single mothers; the average family has fewer than two children.
- Before assistance was time limited, over half of the recipients received help for only 1 year, and 70% left after 2 years.
- Thirty-five percent of recipients are non-Hispanic white, 35% African American, and 23% Hispanic; the rest are Asian and American Indian.
- In 2008, 26% of TANF recipients were employed.

Medicaid (Title 19)

Title XIX of the Social Security Act is a jointly funded cooperative venture between the federal and state governments to assist states in the provision of adequate medical care to the poor. Known as Medicaid, this program became law in 1965. Because each state administers its own program, specific policies vary from state to state.

To be eligible for federal funds, states are required to provide coverage for individuals who receive federally assisted income maintenance payments such as TANF or SSI. Pregnant women without resources are generally required to be provided with services also.

The Personal Responsibility and Work Opportunity Reconciliation Act of 1996 (or *welfare reform*) made restrictive changes regarding eligibility for SSI coverage that affected the Medicaid program. For example, legal resident aliens and other qualified aliens who now entered the United States were ineligible for Medicaid for 5 years. This decision still stands under the 2010 Affordable Care Act (ACA), which was passed by Congress amid great difficulty and compromise between political factions. This act (often called Obamacare) includes a number of provisions that will expand access to subsidized health insurance coverage to the nonelderly population, including many immigrants. Major provisions of the ACA include

- the expansion of Medicaid up to 133 percent of the federal poverty level,
- new state-based health insurance exchanges combined with insurance market reforms,
- premium subsidies for individuals with incomes below 400% of the federal poverty level (FPL) and cost-sharing subsidies for individuals with incomes below 250% FPL, and
- an individual requirement to obtain health insurance coverage (U.S. Department of Health and Human Services, 2012, p. 1).

Beginning in 2014, the ACA expands Medicaid eligibility to include all individuals under age 65 in families with income below 133% of the federal poverty level. A state's Medicaid program must offer medical assistance for certain basic services to most categorically needy populations. These services as listed by the Social Security Administration (2011) generally include

- inpatient hospital services;
- outpatient hospital services;
- pregnancy-related services, including prenatal care and 60 days postpartum pregnancy-related services;
- vaccines for children;
- physician services;
- nursing facility services for persons ages 21 or older;
- family planning services and supplies;
- rural health clinic services;
- home health care for persons eligible for skilled nursing services;
- laboratory and X-ray services;
- pediatric and family nurse practitioner services;
- nurse-midwife services;
- federally qualified health center (FQHC) services and ambulatory services of an FQHC that would be available in other settings; and
- early and periodic screening, diagnostic, and treatment (EPSDT) services for children under age 21. (pp. 58–59)

Because individuals are not required to be parents of eligible children under the new law, the greatest increase in future enrollment is expected to be from adults under age 65. In most years since its inception, Medicaid has had very rapid growth in expenditures. This rapid growth has been due primarily to the increase in the older adult population, the revised federal mandates, the impact of the economic recession, and the expanded coverage and use of services.

Much of the expense of Medicaid is related to long-term care. Medicaid paid for nearly 41% of the total cost of nursing facility care in 2008 (Social Security Administration, 2011).

The government's report on Medicaid provision also mentions the role of managed care. Instead of a traditional fee-for-service system, the health maintenance organizations and other prepaid health plans will provide a set of services for a predetermined periodic payment for each person enrolled.

SNAP (Food Stamps)

The federal government provides 16 food assistance programs. Among them are the School Lunch and School Breakfast Programs, Summer Food Programs (to replace school lunch in the summer); the Women, Infants, and Children (WIC) program; and others, but the largest is the SNAP program.

Initiated on a pilot basis in 1961, the food stamp program, providing a monthly amount of coupons, was formally established by the Food Stamp Act of 1964 with 22 states participating. For years, food stamp coupons were purchased by participants, the amount varying according to household income. Poor families, however, had problems accumulating the cash to exchange for stamps. Then, in 1977, the method of procuring stamps was changed so that food stamps were sent directly to the needy.

In 2008, the food stamp program was renamed the Supplemental Nutrition Assistance Program (SNAP) to better reflect the needs of the clients, including a focus on nutrition and an increase in benefit amounts (U.S. Department of Agriculture, 2012). As of 2012, a four-person household with little to no income can receive a maximum of $668 per month in food stamps. Households with income receive the difference between the amount of a nutritionally adequate diet and 30% of their income after allowable deductions. Medical expenses, for instance, may be deducted for aged and disabled persons. Participating households receive monthly benefit allotments in the form of electronic debit cards (also known as EBT, or electronic benefit transfer).

SNAP benefits are limited to the purchase of food items for use at home as well as seeds and plants to produce food. Unlike TANF, the food stamp program is not a cash supplement but rather an in-kind benefit. The receipt of food stamps boosts a poor family's standard of living substantially. Benefits are entirely federally funded. Who is eligible? Eligibility of a household is determined by its assets, income, and size. People who receive TANF and/or SSI payments automatically qualify to receive food stamps.

Objections to the program focus on the restrictions in purchasing; that is, only food or seeds may be purchased—no prepared food or health and hygiene products. Nevertheless, the food stamp program has notable strengths: During the Great Recession it served many more people than did unemployment benefits. It helps the poor meet basic nutritional needs and is uniform in its allocation across the states. Additionally, this arrangement helps guarantee that children, even children of addicted or spendthrift parents, receive food.

Supplemental Security Income

The Supplemental Security Income (SSI) is a federal public assistance means-tested program that provides income support to persons age 65 or older, blind or disabled adults, and blind or disabled children (Social Security Administration, 2014c). In May, 2014, 8,414,000 individuals received SSI with an average benefit of $536. The program was authorized in 1972 and transferred the responsibility of state programs for the blind, aged, and disabled to the federal government. The definition of disability is the same as for SSDI: "the inability to engage in substantial gainful activity based on a medically determinable impairment that is expected to last at least 12 months or result in death" (Social Security Administration, 2014b). Blindness is also considered a disability.

The process of determination for children is similar to that for adults, but the standard is stricter; the recipient must have "marked and severe functional limitations," which means that the child's impairment must meet, medically equal, or be functionally equal to the listings (Social Security Administration, 2014b).

Housing Assistance

Enacted in 1937, the U.S. Housing Act was passed to help the poor get adequate housing. Similar to food stamps and Medicaid, housing assistance is an in-kind program to ensure the purchase of services. Several public programs assist in the purchase or rental of housing for low-income families. The Section 8 rental assistance program is currently the best-known housing support for low-income families. Often assistance is provided in the form of public housing, usually government-owned projects.

Both federal and state governments offer a wide array of housing programs, from financing and help for low- and moderate-income families and individuals, including help with down payment and closing costs for first-time buyers, to foreclosure prevention and renovation and repair funds. Built in the 1930s and 1940s, large urban public housing communities continue to be a significant, though inadequate, source of affordable housing for income eligible families, disabled individuals, and seniors. However, the shortage of affordable housing is a major problem in the United States today. In 2010, 4.9 million low-income families received federal housing support, 1.2 million for traditional public housing units, 2 million for tenant-oriented assistance (Section 8), and 1.1 million for subsidies to developers (Seefeldt, Abner, Bolinger, Xu, & Graham, 2012). This was a 26% decline since 2005, due in part to the HOPE IV program, which provides funding to transform public housing communities to mixed-housing developments, resulting in a decrease in total units available to low-income families.

Rising home prices and rents during the 2000s and the economic dislocations of the Great Recession dramatically increased the number of homeless, including homeless families (Sard, 2009). Only one in four eligible low-income households receives federal housing assistance because of program limitations (Schott & Finch, 2010). TANF benefits, which have not kept pace with inflation, cover a smaller share of housing costs over time and are leaving many families without permanent housing, if not homeless. Yearslong waiting lists for Section 8 vouchers have long been a feature of urban life for low-income families. These conditions were accentuated with the onset of the 2007 recession. For example, from July to November 2008, New York City saw a 40% increase in admissions to homeless shelters. Unfortunately, though the recession is over, the number of homeless continues to rise (Homelessness Research Institute, 2013).

Housing and health care are closely linked. Karen Seccombe (2011) in her book on welfare recipients, aptly titled *So You Think I Drive a Cadillac?* describes in graphic terms the plight of minimum-wage workers and women on public assistance who can't afford even a modest two-bedroom unit. Often they have to grapple with child care expenses as well. Seccombe describes poor children whose health and safety are at risk due to their substandard housing: "Exposure to rodents, crowding, and cold can wreak havoc on a family's health and well-being," as she indicates (p. 100). Many children each year are hospitalized because of asthma attacks caused by such exposure to rodents and roaches. There are also safety issues related to living in high-crime neighborhoods and the dangers of children being left unattended for long hours while their parents work.

Earned Income Tax Credit

The Earned Income Tax Credit (EITC) was first enacted in 1975 to offset the burden of payroll taxes for low-income working people with children. It is a federal tax credit for low- and moderate-income people. Twenty-five states also offer some form of this benefit.

In 2013 the EITC provided benefits to families with an income below about $37,900 to $51,000, depending on the number of dependents (Lewis & Beverly, 2008). It is administered by the Internal Revenue Service. In 2011, the most recent data available, 28 million working families and individuals received benefits with an average benefit of $2,905 (Center for Budget and Policy Priorities, 2014).

The intent of the benefit is to reward and encourage work. It has three levels: the phase-in range, the plateau range, and the phase-out range. When family income is low, the benefit increases as family income increases until it reaches a maximum benefit. Benefits begin to phase out once income reaches a significantly higher level. Thus, in 2014 a married couple with two children received a maximum benefit at $13,430 of earnings (the benefit amount would be $5,460). They will continue to receive the maximum benefit until their income reaches $23,260. At that point the benefit begins to decline until their income reaches $49,186, when they are no longer eligible for the benefit (Tax Policy Center, 2014). The credit is refundable. The maximum credit varies by the number of children and whether the caregiver is single or married. The maximum credit was $496 in 2014 for childless families and $6,143 for families with three or more children. The IRS reported that more than three fourths of eligible families claimed the EITC in 2005, which is significantly higher than SNAP enrollment.

The intent of the program is to reward and encourage work and in that regard seems to have been successful. Studies have shown that families use tax refunds to catch up on bills and purchase necessities (Mendenhall et al., 2012; Romich & Weisner, 2000). Mendenhall et al., interviewing 194 black, Latino, and white parents found that 57% reported that they planned to allocate a considerable portion of their refund to savings, and 39% were "estimated to accomplish their goal." Findings also suggested that the EITC provided backup funds to meet emergencies, debt, and bills, thus aiding in household stability. EITC also increases employment among single mothers.

There has been some criticism of misrepresentation of income resulting in a higher error rate. However, 70% of EITC claims are filed through commercial tax preparers, and the IRS believe most errors originate with these preparers. The IRS then required preparers to pass a competency test, which was blocked by a federal court when the preparers sued.

The Center for Budget and Policy Priorities (2014) states that simplification of EITC eligibility rules would likely reduce errors.

THINKING SUSTAINABLY

The general public's views on poverty and inequality, and resulting social welfare policy, have tended to change over time. With the ever-expanding role of the corporation in American life, the corporate view of welfare policy has tended to take hold: that these "entitlement" programs are basically free handouts given from those who work and produce to those who are lazy takers. Consider the following specific programs in light of the corporate view of welfare policy:

Social Security

Medicare

Unemployment Insurance

Food Stamps

Are these programs necessary, in your view? Briefly consider broad changes you might make to make them more fair, sustainable, and/or effective.

Contemporary Responses to Poverty in America

Seemingly spontaneous, in the second week of September 2011, squatter camps began to appear in numerous American cities—the Occupy movement had begun. Although the movements in New York City and Washington, DC, were carefully planned, at least as to date (Milkman, Luce, & Lewis, 2013), the initial gatherings gave rise to encampments all over the country in large cities, such as Seattle, and smaller, such as Lancaster and Erie, PA. It brought attention to the 99% who do not own most of the assets, "the creep of austerity and the continued anguish of the global middle class in the developed world after the Great Recession" (Thompson, 2011, p. 1). By October the movement had spread to Europe, Japan, and other global urban centers.

Though the Occupy movement was time limited by weather and displacement by city police, the movement shifted the debate at a time when conservative political movements were focusing on debt reduction and ignoring job development. It provided a reminder that the economy was not serving the middle class. Although the recession formally ended in 2009, the unemployment rate continued to be higher than before the recession.

By June 2013, as reported by the Economic Policy Institute (Shierholz, 2013), 734,000 public sector jobs (government jobs) had also been cut due to a combination of state government cutbacks and the federal sequester. As of November 2013, the labor force participation rate, or the proportion of the working-age labor force with jobs, sank to 62.8% from its high of 66.4% in January 2007. Also, disturbingly, the median wage was declining. In some parts of the country, workers are organizing to resist this state of affairs. After nationwide protests by fast-food workers, raising the minimum wage has become a front-page issue (Greenhouse, 2013).

Just as a declining economy increases the unemployment rate, a decrease in the number of people participating in the economy is a major factor weakening the economy as consumer spending is thereby reduced. This, in turn, reduces hiring and causes job layoffs. Speaking of the postrecession situation, Heidi Shierholz (2013) stated, "We need 8.0 million jobs to get back to the pre-recession unemployment rate, and at the average rate of growth of the last 12 months, that won't happen for another five years" (p. 1).

According to Stiglitz (2012), the major problem with the economy during the 2000s was not the housing bubble. "For a while the housing market obscured the underlying weakness in the economy, but as the economy moved from a focus on manufacturing to a focus on services wage rates declined" (p. 2). Even before the recession, for example, the lack of living-wage jobs has resulted in a decline in marriage for lower income Americans.

As Stiglitz (2012) noted in *Vanity Fair* "[prior to the 2007 recession] Incomes for most working Americans still hadn't returned to their level prior to the previous recession. The American standard of living was sustained only by rising debt" (p. 2). Growing inequality results in shrinking opportunity. Caused in part by a focus on tax cuts for upper brackets, more and more wealth has become concentrated in the top 1% of the population. The expanding income gap therefore continues to grow.

Since April 2009, as part of the American Recovery and Reinvestment Act (the stimulus passed in the early days of the Obama program to short-circuit the recession) participants in the Supplemental Nutrition Assistance Program (SNAP, until 2008 known as food stamps) had received a 13.6% benefit increase (Andrews & Smallwood, 2012). On average, this brought a $46 dollar increase to an average household. In the 4 and a half years since the enactment of the Recovery Act, food prices have continued to rise. Nord (2013) found that "from 2009 to 2011 . . . the food security of SNAP households worsened as inflation reduced the buying power of the ARRA SNAP benefit increase by about half" (p. 1). Despite the increase in food prices, the SNAP increase was cancelled as of November 1, 2013. The Food Bank for New York City found that even before the November 1 cut, three quarters of the food stamp recipients using city pantries and soup kitchens reported that their benefits lasted only through the first 3 weeks of the month (Hunger's New Normal, 2013).

The November 1, 2013, cut, in effect, reduced SNAP benefits below the levels of 2007, in terms of purchasing power. By November 10, accounts in the media were already describing the increased stress on SNAP recipient food budgets and the strain on the food bank/food pantry systems.

In addition, extended unemployment benefits were also cut on January 1, 2014. Aside from the pain and deprivation of recipients, the economy was also projected to suffer cuts in GDP. The Recovery Act had provided some immediate benefits to the economically devastated, but a second stimulus program became politically infeasible after large gains made by Republicans in the 2010 election.

Yet at the same time, Senator Tom Harkin of Iowa, introduced the Strengthening Social Security Act of 2013, described earlier, which proposes an expansion to the Social Security program that would alter the formula by which benefits are calculated, boosting benefits for all beneficiaries by $70 per month (targeted to those in the low- to middle-range of the income distribution), changing the cost-of-living adjustments to ensure that benefits better reflect expenses, and phasing out the cap on taxable income (now at $117, 000) to begin to collect taxes on all income.

Summary and Conclusion

This chapter on poverty and inequality began with a statement by Bill de Blasio, the newly elected mayor of New York City. Elected as a progressive Democrat following the long tenure of technocrat Michael Bloomberg, de Blasio captured the imagination of voters who had fallen further and further behind others in a volatile economy. He was elected only 4 days after the last provision of the American Recovery and Reinvestment Act of 2009 had expired. On election night he stated, "Inequality—that feeling of a few doing very well, while so many slip further behind—that is the defining challenge of our time."

In a nutshell, this statement effectively captures the essence of our discussion of poverty and inequality. In the United States, a nation of vast wealth and resources, there is enough in the way of money and food to go around. Yet, as we have seen, in the tax structure, the allocation of unemployment benefits, and the expansion of low-wage, service-oriented jobs and decline in living-wage employment, the society creates a situation ripe for increasing the gap between the rich, super-rich, and the poor. While education is often touted as a way to move forward, it was also under attack as state legislatures reduced support for state universities, and because tuition has risen, many students graduate owing significant amounts of student loans. The Obama administration did support an income-based repayment program to ease the burden of newly graduated students and has introduced other initiatives to make higher education more affordable and to ensure that it leads to eventual employment.

The Occupy movement was successful in informing the public about a lopsided economy that drastically needed to change for the benefit of all people. It is clear that the solutions to the current economic problems lie in the policy arena, such as represented in the proposal by Senator Harkin. The United States would benefit from less focus on the debt and a greater focus on rebuilding infrastructure and putting people back to work, in both the private and public sectors. The remedies that were applied by the Roosevelt administration to help bring the United States out of the 1930s depression, which were based on increased government spending even at the expense of incurring government debt in the short term, can once again work to heal the economy.

Critical Thinking Questions

1. Should the poverty level be viewed as absolute or as relative to correctly reflect the individual's sense of impoverishment?

2. What is the standard of living "necessary for human dignity" in the United States?

3. Should the minimum wage be raised? In arguing your points, state the basic argument's, pro and con.

4. What separates the Great Depression from the Great Recession?

5. Is the national debt really a challenge to U.S. policymaking? Why is it said to be so?

6. What is the meaning of social exclusion, and what is its relationship to poverty?

7. Is it a problem that a small proportion of people have a majority of the wealth in the United States?

8. How can the United States go about providing more living-wage jobs?

9. Should the United States adopt the Supplemental Poverty Measure? What are the advantages and disadvantages?

10. Discuss ways in which the stress that people experience when they lack monetary resources might result in bad decisions for the long-term. Do you personally know of any instances where this has occurred?

11. Why is the EITC more popular than SNAP?

12. Are food pantries a good way to help hungry people? Why or why not?

13. Discuss the proposition that Americans pay Social Security taxes on all their income, not just the proportion below a certain set amount ($117,000 as of 2014). What does this say about the issue of sustained inequality?

References

Allen, T. (2013). *Dangerous convictions: What's really wrong with the U.S. Congress.* New York, NY: Oxford University Press.

Alvarez, L. (2012, April 18). No savings are found from welfare drug tests. *New York Times,* p. A14.

Andrews, M., & Smallwood, D. (2012). *What's behind the rise in SNAP participation?* Amber Waves, Economic Research Service. Retrieved from www.ers.usda.gov/amber-waves/2012-march/what's-behind-the-rise-in-snap-participation.aspx#.VFCOT75Ny0s

Argento, R., Bryant, V., & Sabelhaus, J. (2013). *Early withdrawals from retirement accounts during the Great Recession.* Retrieved from www.federalreserve.gov/pubs/feds/2013/201322/201322abs.html

Barker, R. (2014). *Social work dictionary* (6th ed.). Washington, DC: NASW Press.

Bickel, G., Nord, M., Price, C., Hamilton W., & Cook J. (2000). *Guide to measuring household food security.* Retrieved from www.fns.usda.gov/guide-measuring-household-food-security-revised-2000

Burk, M. (2011, Fall). Rips in the safety net. *Ms.,* 44–45.

Carlson, A., Lino, M., Juan, W., Hanson, K., & Basiotis, P. (2007, April). *Thrifty food plan, 2006* (CNPP-19). Washington, DC. U.S. Department of Agriculture, Center for Nutrition Policy and Promotion.

Center for Budget and Policy Priorities. (2014, January 30). Policy basics: The earned income tax credit. Retrieved from cbpp.org

Citro, C., & Michel, R. (1995). *Measuring poverty: A new approach.* Washington, DC: National Academies Press.

Clayton, A. (2003). Workers' compensation: A background for Social Security professionals. *Social Security Bulletin, 65,* 7–15.

Coleman-Jensen, A., Nord M., & Singh, A. (2013, September 15). Household food security in the United States in 2012 (ERR-155). Washington, DC: U.S. Department of Agriculture, Economic Research Service.

Council of the European Union. (2004, March 4). *Joint report by the Commission and the Council on social inclusion.* Retrieved from http://ec.europa.eu/employment_social/soc-prot/soc-incl/final_joint_inclusion_report_2003 en.pdf

Daly, M., Lucking, B., & Schwabish, J. (2013, June 24). The future of Social Security disability index. Federal Reserve Bank of San Francisco. Retrieved from www.frbsf.org

de Blasio, B. (2013, November 6). De Blasio's victory speech. *New York Times,* p. 1.

Department of Veterans Affairs. (2010). *Federal benefits for veterans.* Washington, DC: Author.

European Anti-Poverty Network. (2013). *Poverty and inequality in the European Union.* Retrieved from www.poverty.org.uk/summary/eapn.shtml

Fisher, G. (1992). *The development and history of the U.S. poverty thresholds a brief overview.* Retrieved from http://aspe.hhs.gov/poverty/papers/hptgssiv.htm

Gabe, Thomas. (2013). *Poverty in the United States: 2012, Congressional Research Office 7–5700.* Retrieved from www.fas.org/sgp/crs/misc/RL33069.pdf

Gasperak, E. (Producer). (2014, June 2). Thomas Piketty. In J. Stewart, T. Purcell, & S. Colbert (Executive Producers). *The Colbert report* [TV series episode]. Los Angeles, CA: Comedy Central.

Glennerster, H. (2002, March). United States poverty studies and poverty measurement: The past 25 years. *Social Service Review,* 83–107.

Greenhouse, S. (2013, November 29). On register's other side, little to spend. *New York Times,* p. B1.

Greenstone, M., & Looney, A. (2011). *Have earnings actually declined?* Retrieved from www .hamiltonproject.org/files/downloads_and_links/02_jobs_earnings.pdf

Guo, X., & Burton, J. (2012). The growth in applications for Social Security disability insurance: A spillover effect from workers' compensation. *Social Security Bulletin, 72*(3), 69–88.

Harrington, Michael. (1962). *The other America: Poverty in the United States.* New York, NY: Macmillan.

Hertzberg, H. (2013, April 8). Sense of entitlement. *The New Yorker, 89*(8), 23–24.

History of veterans benefits. (2012). *Congressional Digest.* Retrieved from www.congressional-digest.com

Homelessness Research Institute. (2013). *The state of homelessness in America, 2013.* Retrieved from http://b.3cdn.net/naeh/bb34a7e4cd84ee985c_3vm6r7cjh.pdf

Hunger's New Normal. (2013). *Redefining emergency in post-recession New York City.* New York: Food Bank for New York. Retrieved from www.help.foodbanknyc.org

Joffe-Walt, C. (2013). Unfit for work, the startling rise in disability in America [Audio podcast]. *This American Life.* National Public Radio. Retrieved from www.thisamericanlife.org/radio-archives/episode/490/trends-with-benefits

Karger, H. J., & Stoesz, D. (2013). *American social welfare policy: A pluralist approach* (Brief ed.). Boston, MA: Pearson.

Krugman, P. (1992, Fall). The rich, the right and the facts: Deconstructing the income distribution debate. *American Prospect.* Retrieved from http://prospect.org/article/rich-right-and-facts-deconstructing-inequality-debate

Lewis, M., & Beverly, S. (2013). Earned income tax credit. Retrieved from http://socialwork.oxfordre.com.proxy-edinboro.klnpa.org/view/10.1093/acrefore/9780199975839.001.0001/acrefore-9780199975839-e-116?rskey=emtRnw&result=1

Lichtblau, E. (2014, June 15). V.A. punished critics on staff, doctors assert. *New York Times,* p. A1.

Lieberman, T. (2013). Disability, Social Security and the missing context. *Columbia Journalism Review*. Retrieved from www.cjr.org/united_states_project/disability_social_security_and .php?page=all#sthash.sp915EXn.dpuf

Martin, M. E. (2012). Philosophical and religious influences on social welfare policy in the United States. *Journal of Social Work, 12*, 51–64.

Mendenhall, R., Edin, K., Crowley, S., Sykes, J., Tach, L., Kriz, K., . . . the Congressional Budget Office and NBER. (2012). The role of earned income tax credit in the budgets of low-income households. *Social Service Review, 85*, 367–400.

Milkman, R., Luce, S., & Lewis, P. (2013). The genie's out of the bottle: Insiders' perspectives on Occupy Wall Street. *Sociological Quarterly, 54*(2), 194–198.

Mullainathan, S., & Shafir, E. (2013). *Scarcity why having too little means so much*. New York, NY: Times Books.

Murray, C. (1984). *Losing ground: American social policy*. New York, NY: Basic Books.

National Association of Social Workers. (2008). Code of ethics. Retrieved from www.social-workers.org/pubs/code/default.asp

National Bureau of Economic Research. (2010). US business cycle expansions and contractions. Retrieved from www.nber.org/cycles.html

Nord, M. (2010, October). Food spending declined and food insecurity increased for middle-income and low-income households from 2000 to 2007 (EIB–61). Washington, DC. U.S. Dept. of Agriculture, Economic Research Service.

Nord, M. (2013, August). *Effects of the decline in the real value of SNAP benefits from 2009 to 2011* (Report No. 151). Washington, DC. U.S. Department of Agriculture, Economic Research Service.

Orshansky, M. (1963). Children of the poor. *Social Security Bulletin, 26*(7), 3–13.

Pattison, D., & Waldron, H. (2013). *Disability shocks near retirement age*. Retrieved from www .ssa.gov/policy/docs/ssb/v73n4/v73n4p25.pdf

Piketty, T. (2014). *Capital in the twenty-first century* [Audio recording]. Cambridge, MA: Harvard University Press.

Pope Francis. (2013). *Evanelii gaudium (The joy of the gospel): Apostolic exhortation to the bishops, clergy, consecrated persons, and the lay faithful*. Rome, Italy: Vatican Press.

Rank, M. (2004). *One nation, underprivileged: Why American poverty affects us all*. New York, NY: Oxford University Press.

Rank, M. (2013). Poverty. *Encyclopedia of social work*. Retrieved from http://socialwork .oxfordre.com/view/10.1093/acrefore/9780199975839.001.0001/acrefore-9780199975839-e-297?rskey=1nqC8V&result=1

Rank, M., & Hirschl, T. (1999). Estimating the proportion of Americans ever experiencing poverty during their elderly years. *Journals of Gerontology, 54B*(4), S184–194.

Rank, M., & Hirschl, T. (2002). Welfare use as a life course event: Toward a new understanding of the U.S. safety net. *Social Work, 47*(3), 237–248.

Reich, R. (2012). *Beyond outrage: Expanded edition: What has gone wrong with our economy and our democracy, and how to fix it*. New York, NY: Random House.

Reich, R. (2013, April 4). Chained CPI for Social Security could hurt seniors. *Christian Science Monitor*. Retrieved from www.csmonitor.com/Business

Romich, J., & Weisner, T. (2000). How families view and use the EITC. *National Tax Journal, 53*, 1245–1266.

Rowntree Seebohm, B. (1910). *Poverty: A study of town life*. London, England: MacMillian.

Ruggles, P. (1990). *Drawing the line: Alternative poverty measures and their implications for public policy*. Washington, DC: Brookings Institution Press.

Rutledge, M., Coe, N., & Wong, K. (2012). *Who claimed Social Security early due to the Great Recession?* Center for Retirement Research, Boston College. Retrieved from http://crr.bc .edu/briefs/who-claimed-social-security-early-due-to-the-great-recession/

Sard, B. (2009, January 8). *Number of homeless families climbing due to recession.* Center for Budget and Policy Priorities. Retrieved from www.cbpp.org/cms/index.cfm?fa=view&id=2228

Schott, L., & Finch, I. (2010, October 14). TANF benefits are low and have not kept pace with inflation. Center on Budget and Policy Priorities. Retrieved from www.cbpp.org

Scott, M. (2010, May 10). The best places to lose your job. *Bloomberg Business Week*, p. 14.

Seccombe, K. (2011). *"So you think I drive a Cadillac?": Welfare recipients' perspectives on the system and its reform* (3rd ed.). Boston, MA: Allyn & Bacon.

Seefeldt, K., Abner, G., Bolinger, J., Xu, L., & Graham, J. (2012). *At risk: America's poor during and after the Great Recession.* School of Public and Environmental Affairs, Indiana University. Retrieved from www.indiana.edu/~spea/pubs/white_paper_at_risk.pdf

Sen, A. (1987). *Food and freedom.* Retrieved from http://library.cgiar.org/bitstream/handle/10947/556/craw3.pdf?sequence.pdf

Shaefer, H., & Wu, L. (2011). Unemployment insurance and low-educated, single, working mothers before and after welfare reform, *Social Service Review, 85*(2), 205–228.

Shierholz, H. (2013, November 8). Labor force participation falls to lowest point of the recovery. Economic Policy Institute. Retrieved from www.epi.org/publication/labor-force-participation-drops-lowest-point/

Short, K. (2012). *The supplemental poverty measure: 2012.* Retrieved from www.census.gov/prod/2013pubs/p60-247.pdf

Smith, A. (1776/1904). *An inquiry into the nature and causes of the wealth of nations.* Library of Economics and Liberty. Retrieved from www.econlib.org/library/Smith/smWN.html

Social Security Administration. (2011). Fast facts and figures about Social Security, 2011. Retrieved from www.ssa.gov/policy/docs/chartbooks/fast_facts/2011/fast_facts11.html

Social Security Administration. (2013, June). Social Security: Basic facts. Retrieved from www.socialsecurity.gov

Social Security Administration. (2014a). FAQs. Retrieved from www.socialsecurity.gov/history/hfaq.html

Social Security Administration. (2014b). Overview and background. www.ssa.gov/policy/docs/chartbooks/disability_trends/overview.html

Social Security Administration. (2014c, November 23). 2012 Social Security tax rate and maximum taxable earnings. Retrieved from www.ssa.gov/planners/maxtax.htm

Stiglitz, J. E. (2012, January). The book of jobs. *Vanity Fair.* Retrieved from www.vanityfair.com/politics/2012/01/stiglitz-depression-201201

Stone, C. (2013, September 6). Statement by Chad Stone, chief economist, on the August employment report. Retrieved from www.cbpp.org/cms/?fa=view&id=4008

Tax Policy Center. (2014). *Taxation and the family. A citizens guide for the 2012 election and beyond.* Washington, DC: Urban Institute and Brookings Institution, Tax Policy Center.

Terrell, P. (2008). Workers' compensation. *Encyclopedia of Social Work.* New York, NY: Oxford University Press.

Thompson, D. (2011, October 15). Occupy the world: The "99 Percent" movement goes global. *Atlantic.* Retrieved from www.theatlantic.com/business/archive/2011/10/occupy-the-world-the-99-percent-movement-goes-global/246757/

Trattner, W. (1999). *From poor law to welfare state: A history of social welfare* (6th ed.). New York, NY: Free Press.

Traub, A., & Ruetschlin, C. (2012). *The plastic safety net: Findings from the 2012 national survey of credit card debt of low and middle income households.* Retrieved from www.demos.org/sites/default/files/publications/PlasticSafetyNet-Demos.pdf

U.S. Department of Agriculture. (2012, April). *Building a healthy America: A profile of the supplemental nutrition assistance program.* Food and Nutrition Service. Retrieved from www.fns.usda.gov

U.S. Department of Agriculture. (2013). *Food distribution history and backgrounds.* Retrieved from www.fns.usda.gov/fdd/fdd-history-and-background

U.S. Department of Health and Human Services. (2012, April). *The Affordable Care Act: Coverage implications.* Office of the Assistant Secretary for Planning and Evaluation. Retrieved from www.aspe.hhs.gov

U.S. Government Accountability Office. (2013, Sept 11). *Unemployment insurance information technology: States face challenges in modernization* (GAO-13–859T). Retrieved from www .gao.gov/assets/660/657735.pdf

Vet Centers. (2014). Serving those who need. Retrieved from www.vetcenter.va.gov

Vobejda, B. (1996, August 23). Clinton signs welfare bill amid division. *Washington Post,* p. A01.

Wallace, C. (2010, July 9). The great debate: So unemployment benefits boost the economy. *Daily Finance.* Retrieved from www.dailyfinance.com

Wise, T. (2010). *Colorblind: The rise of post-racial politics and the retreat of racial equality.* San Francisco, CA: City Lights Books.

6

Minority Groups and the Impact of Oppression

[Prison] relieves us of the responsibility of seriously engaging with the problems of our society, especially those produced by racism and, increasingly, global capitalism.

—Angela Davis, *Are Prisons Obsolete?* (2003)

We cannot be sustainable unless we engage the disparities that historically have been created around intentional public policies.

—Robin Morris Collin (2011)

As we saw in Chapter 5, the consequences of poverty are enduring; they affect everything from educational opportunity and incarceration rates to health and mental health measures. The impact of race is strongly correlated with poverty levels and with health problems. For example, infant mortality is more than twice as high among African Americans as among non-Hispanic whites (Centers for Disease Control and Prevention, 2013).

In *Colorblind*, Tim Wise (2010), a popular antiracist speaker on college campuses, reveals how institutionalized racism is ingrained in American social policies as it has been since the days of slavery. It is true that there are paradigm shifts, moments in history when one or another of the formerly subordinate groups rises to a position of greater acceptability, often in conjunction with the passage of protective legislation providing full civil rights. But then, inevitably, the pendulum swings back often during a time of economic decline, and a backlash ensues. This is one of the major themes of this chapter—an examination of ideologies and policies, of those that protect and those that oppress.

A second major theme is the impact of institutionalized oppression on minority groups. We will talk about oppression in the economic system, in health care, and in the justice system. Rather than focusing on each minority group and the challenges peculiar to each group, we will examine the nature of oppression itself and the way it impacts all minorities. From here we move to a discussion of related concepts—social exclusion, privilege, and intersectionality.

Oppression

Oppression, as defined by the *Social Work Dictionary* is

> the social act of placing severe restrictions on an individual, group, or institution. Typically, a government or political organization that is in power places these restrictions formally or covertly on oppressed groups so that they may be exploited and less able to compete with other social groups. The oppressed individual or group is devalued, exploited, and deprived of privileges by the individual or group who has more power. (Barker, 2014, p. 303)

Some of the words used in this definition—*power, exploited, deprived, privileges*—are key variables related to oppression. Oppression can be viewed as an institutionalized system of power that encompasses a web of cultural practices that serve to exploit and deprive some groups in order to privilege other groups. This brings us to a consideration of a key question: Does prejudice in society lead to discriminatory legislation and practices? Or does the passage of oppressive laws directed against a minority group create a situation that engenders prejudice? We do know of situations in which people turned against minority groups—for example, American Indians, former slaves in the U.S. South, and various immigrant groups—and politicians responded accordingly. But we also know that the passage of discriminatory legislation has a strong influence on the social acceptability of a certain group. Consider the following historical situations: white South African children growing up under conditions of apartheid in which all black servants had to leave the town at nightfall, the passage and enforcement of Jim Crow laws in the U.S. South, and the segregation of school children in Northern Ireland on the basis of religious denomination. Studies demonstrate that when discrimination is mandated in the law, prejudice against the targeted minority groups, including hate crimes, increases. For a recent illustration, we can look to Alabama. In 2011, the state legislature passed HB 56, which allowed for background checks on anyone suspected of being an undocumented immigrant. The negative response against not only Mexicans but other dark-skinned people was immediate: over 6,000 calls reporting personal attacks were made to a Latino hotline (National Immigration Law Center, 2012). Reports ranged from police harassment, white shoppers telling dark-skinned shoppers to go back to Mexico, and the bullying of Latino children in the schools.

Even though the particular conditions and manifestations of oppression may vary, there are common elements pertaining to all oppressions:

- Vested interests by dominant groups to maintain and enhance their access to valued resources.
- Economic exploitation of marginalized groups.
- Representatives of dominant groups control media messages.
- The spread of ideologies holding members of the subordinate groups responsible for their own misfortunes or victimization. Moreover, these ideologies are built on and reinforce the latent forces of racism, sexism, ageism, ethnocentrism, ableism, heterosexism, classism, and sectarianism in the society (Appleby, Colon, & Hamilton, 2011).

Privilege

To Canadian social work educator, Bob Mullaly (2009), privilege is not something we take; it is given to us by society "if we possess the characteristics that society values, such as being male, white, heterosexual, affluent, and non-disabled" (p. 287). From Mullaly's chapter on privilege, we have filtered out the following striking characteristics of privilege:

- It is an unearned not an earned advantage.
- It is invisible to the people who possess the benefits.
- It is not an individual trait but a group characteristic.
- It increases people's power because it makes for more opportunities, advantages, and the status attached to them.
- It is maintained through various avoidance mechanisms such as denial, belief that members of this social circle are the good guys, refusal to hear about the oppression of others, and victim blaming.

Mullaly (2009) provides a wealth of examples of the advantages that people have in the various categories of privilege on the basis of class, traditional family, race, and age. For young and middle-age privilege, for example, he lists the following:

I do not have to endure people yelling at me because they assume I cannot hear.

I can be assured that people will not infantilize me by talking "baby talk" to me.

I am assured that other people will not try to make decisions for me, often, without consultation.

I am not likely to be viewed as a burden on society and draining society's resources (p. 308).

Being a U.S. citizen within the United States is definitely a privilege because it entitles the worker to vote, apply for college freely, and to not fear deportation if arrested. There is even privilege attached to being a citizen of the most powerful nation in the world when one travels abroad. American embassies look out for U.S. citizens in many instances. But, probably of even more importance, because the English language has become the international language, Americans can often rely on their native language when engaged in Internet use, foreign commerce, or travel abroad, whereas people from other countries, such as Norway, the Czech Republic, and Turkey would do well to rely on English as a means of communication when traveling outside of their own borders.

White Privilege

Mullaly (2009) provides an extensive list of situations in which white privilege is apparent. Among his most striking examples are the following:

- I can go shopping alone most of the time, pretty well assured that I will not be followed or harassed.
- I can, if I wish, arrange to be in the company of people of my own race most of the time.
- I can be pretty sure of renting or purchasing housing in an area that I can afford and in which I would want to live.
- I am never asked to speak for all the people of my racial group.
- I can do well in a challenging situation without being called a credit to my race.
- I can take a job . . . without having co-workers on the job suspect that I got it because of my race.

We can add to this the privilege that most northern whites and some northern blacks have of speaking Standard English, which is the brand of American English favored by TV and radio news stations. Paralleling the norms for standard American speech patterns in the U.S., there is also the preference for certain physical attributes that conform to contemporary standards of desirability.

The possession of white privilege is largely unrecognized by whites but very obvious to those who do not have it. In this regard, there is a huge racial divide. In the recent case of the not guilty verdict reached in the killing of black teenager Trayvon Martin by the neighborhood watch coordinator, George Zimmerman. Zimmerman had profiled Martin as a likely criminal and was stalking him when apparently a fight broke out between the two of them. Because of African Americans' awareness of inequities in the criminal justice system and of the historic role of racial profiling of young black males, opinion polls following the verdict revealed sharp racial differences. In a *Washington Post*–ABC News poll, 86% of African Americans stated they disapproved of the verdict, with most of them strongly disapproving as compared to only 31% of whites. A slight majority of whites even stated they thought that blacks received equal treatment in the criminal justice system (compared to only 14% of blacks) (Cohen & Balz, 2013).

Cultural standards of beauty, across racial and ethnic lines, often seem to reflect a preference for lighter skin. A fascinating recent documentary, *Dark Girls* (Duke & Channsin, 2013), highlights such discriminatory patterns in South Asia and even in some countries in Africa. The documentary reveals the business angle in the encouragement of women to spend large sums of money on skin-bleaching creams, while paradoxically, white women risk skin cancer by going to tanning booths to darken their skin. The preference seems to be an olive skin color rather than an absence of all pigment.

These skin-lightening and skin-darkening products and technologies are multi-million dollar businesses, but the big money is in cosmetic surgery. Many black women, as bell hooks (1992) notes, pursue white ideals of beauty and body build: straightening their hair and relying on body modification techniques. In parts of Asia, the situation is more extreme. In South Korea, for example, one in five South Korean women have had some form of aesthetic cosmetic surgery. This compares to around one in 20 in the United States (Stone, 2013). A powerful Korean consumer culture coupled with discrimination in employment against women who do not meet a certain standard of beauty has led to an equation of beauty with professional and economic success. The most common surgeries are eyelid operations to give Koreans the Western crease, or "double eyelid," and reshaping of the nose for a less flat look. We might consider then that young Asian women who achieve the modern standard of beauty in their countries are privileged in the competition for high-paying jobs.

Heterosexual Privilege

Heterosexual privilege is probably one of least thought about (by heterosexuals) and most pervasive of all types of privilege. Even more so than other forms of social attributes, this one tends to be taken for granted by majority groups.

Heterosexuals have the advantage of never having to explain their sexual orientation or of having their sexual practices assumed to be immoral based on who they are partnered with. Heterosexuals do not have to fear violence if they walk down the street arm in arm with their partners. Heterosexual teens do not have to deal with constant bullying and harassment based on their sexual identity, and they always have teachers and probably their parents as role models and social supports. In church, members of the majority orientation are not made to feel that their associations and relationships are immoral. Gays and lesbians cannot count on any of these advantages.

The pathologization of gays, lesbians, and transgender people has a long history in the United States. It was only as late as 1973, in response to heavy criticism, that the American Psychiatric Association (APA) retracted its notion of homosexuality as a mental disorder. In the fifth edition of the *Diagnostic and Statistical Manual of Mental Disorders* (American Psychiatric Association, 2013), again, in response to criticism, gender identity disorder was renamed gender dysphoria. This condition, which is said to occur when a person's identity as a male or female is not the same as the person's biological sex, is still viewed as a mental health disorder. This is a slight improvement in that it is now viewed as a temporary disorder rather than a permanent condition.

Life-threatening violence against known gays and lesbians is a reality worldwide. Recent headlines demonstrate this:

"No Place for Gays in Yemen" (Almosawa, 2013)

"Russian Anti-Gay Law Prompts Rise in Homophobic Violence" (Luhn, 2013)

"Two More Anti-Gay Attacks Are Reported in Manhattan" (Goodman, 2013)

"Uganda Anti-Gay Law Led to Tenfold Rise in Attacks on LGBTI People, Report Says" (Bowcott, 2014)

In the United States, despite remarkable legal advances in recent years, there is still much violence directed against people who are perceived as homosexual. Out of the 6,216 hate crimes reported by the Uniform Crime Reports, 20.8% were attributed to sexual orientation (Federal Bureau of Investigation, 2013).

The privilege of the right to marry for gays and lesbians has received a great deal of media attention within and outside the LGBT (lesbian, gay, bisexual, transgender) movement with the passage of marriage laws in some European countries and challenges to the Defense of Marriage Act (DOMA) passed by Congress in 1996 declaring that marriage was between a man and a woman (van Wormer, Kaplan, & Juby, 2012). Marriage is a right that has been taken for granted by dominant groups of men and women in society, but we should remember that not so long ago, many states in the United States had enforceable laws on their books that prohibited marriages between races. It was not until the height of the Civil Rights Movement, that the U.S. Supreme

Source: Photo by Robert van Wormer.

Homophobia Taught to Children at an Early Age. These children are learning homophobia at an early age. The protest took place at a memorial service for a young gay murder victim in Waterloo, Iowa.

Source: ©iStockphoto.com/Mari.

An Advocacy Group in Many Communities: PFLAG. Members of PFLAG (Parents, Families, and Friends of Lesbians and Gays) offer an excellent resource for social workers to refer family members of gays and lesbians dealing with coming-out issues.

Court (1967) ruled in *Loving v. Virginia* that these laws are unconstitutional. And it was not until 2013 that the ban on same-sex marriage by the federal government was lifted (Graff, 2013).

Male Privilege

In the 19th century, American women were viewed as defective based on their differences from men; women who resisted their subordinate roles in society were labeled by Freud as *castrating women*, a term that was widely used through the 1950s. Women, in general, were seen as irrational and as having inherent intellectual, emotional, and mental deficits. Arguments in opposition to women's right to vote claimed they were too temperamental, too emotional, and too frail and that they would even become disabled if allowed to vote (Baynton, 2009).

Male privilege is often taken for granted by men who may be amazed when it is pointed out. Mullaly (2009) provides the following illustrations of situations in which he, as a man, is privileged:

- I can dominate a conversation without being seen as dominating.
- I am praised for spending time with my children and for cooking and doing household chores.

- I am not expected to change my name when I get married.
- I can walk alone in public without fear of being harassed or sexually violated.
- I never worry about being paid less than my female counterparts.
- I don't have to choose between having a career or having a family. (p. 303)

A later section on oppression in the economic systems provides statistics that reveal more about the impact of male privilege.

Intersectionality

Intersectionality is the term used in oppression theory to address the experiences of people who are subjected to multiple forms of oppression and domination. Patricia Hill Collins (2010), explains how through this multidimensional lens, we can understand how membership in one minority group, such as female gender, combines with other key social characteristics and statuses related to oppression, such as race or ethnicity, to produce a synergistic or multiplying effect. This effect is probably stronger than even the sum of the separate categories of difference. National origin, culture, religion, caste or class, age, gender identity and sexual expression, (dis)ability, and/or having the status of ex-convict are other categories that in combination can subject people to heightened levels of discrimination.

Thinking back to past racial oppression in the hills of Kentucky, bell hooks (2009) reflects on the dualism of race and class:

> I was a little girl in a segregated world when I first learned that there were white people who saw black people as less than animals. Sitting on the porch, my siblings and I would watch white folks bring home their servants, the maids and cooks who toiled to make their lives comfortable. These black servants were always relegated to the back seat. Next to the white drivers in the front would be the dog and in the back seat the black worker. Just seeing this taught me much about the interconnectedness of race and class. (pp. 148–149)

To learn about race-class dynamics from the women of the Great Migration's point of view, see *The Maid Narratives* (van Wormer, Jackson, & Sudduth, 2012).

Tim Wise (2010) debunks the liberal dogma that we can separate the forces of racism from the forces of classism and claim that colorblind policies will overcome racial inequality through treating everyone the same. Moreover, by not considering the intersections of our multiple roles and identities, we can easily fall into arguments of comparison about whose oppression is worse. The end result of dichotomizing categories of difference is that oppression can then be blamed on just one group (e.g. working-class white men) rather than considering power relations within society as a whole.

We can also look to experimental research to gauge the degree of discrimination inflicted upon individuals who occupy two categories of difference simultaneously. Sociologist Devah Pager (2003) tested the concept of intersectionality in labor market research. She sent out pairs of white applicants (100) and otherwise identical black applicants (250), where one member of each matched pair had a criminal record (see also Pager, Western, & Bonikowski, 2009). Pager and her colleagues found that employers strongly discriminated against the black applicants and especially against those with supposed criminal records. They were even more likely to make job offers to whites with criminal records than to African Americans with clean records. This research provides evidence that the effect of race can be magnified by additional factors such as criminal history. Now we move from a focus on instances of discrimination to a consideration of the psychological impact of oppression.

Systemic Examples of Oppression

Oppression in the Economic System

According to the report, *The State of Women in America*, authored by Chu and Posner (2013), women now make up almost half of all workers in the United States. In 1969, they were only one-third of the workforce. And 2012 was a watershed year for women in terms of getting elected to public office, which brought their numbers up to 18% of the total seats in Congress. And yet, substantial inequalities remain.

We learn further from the report by Chu and Posner (2013) that although an increasing number of women are either the sole breadwinners for their family or they share the role with their partners, women are paid only 77 cents for every dollar a man makes. The pay gap is even larger for women of color. On average, African American women make 64 cents for every dollar that white men make.

One tangible aspect of privilege is the ability to obtain employment. See Figures 6.1 and 6.2 for the racial and ethnic breakdown of earnings and unemployment rates. Figure 6.1 also shows the disparity in earnings by gender. The female-to-male earnings ratio varied by race and ethnicity: White women earned 81.4% as much as their male counterparts, compared with black (89.6%), Hispanic (89.5%), and Asian women (78.5%) (Bureau of Labor Statistics, 2013). The differences among the men are interesting as well, with Latino men well below other racial and ethnic groups, and Asian men doing the best of all.

The success of U.S. Asians' earning levels is striking as indicated in Figure 6.1. We need to take into account, as Wise (2010) points out, that Asians and Asian-Americans in the U.S. are far better educated than Americans as a whole. He cites research that shows comparisons of Asian and white Americans at the same educational level, which indicate that whites earn from 14% to 28% more. Therefore, he concludes, we cannot dismiss the reality of white privilege with regard to Asians.

Disparities in the Health Care System

In his review of the research on the diagnosis and treatment of heart and stroke conditions, cancer, HIV/AIDS, and mental health, Robert Keefe (2010) found that to date, only a handful of several hundred studies find no racial and ethnic differences in health care. When statistically controlling for various factors including socioeconomic status, disparities by race and ethnicity in health care continue to emerge. For example, as Keefe indicates, the research shows that even after controlling for variations in

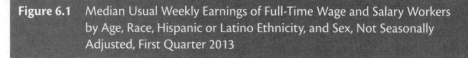

Figure 6.1   Median Usual Weekly Earnings of Full-Time Wage and Salary Workers by Age, Race, Hispanic or Latino Ethnicity, and Sex, Not Seasonally Adjusted, First Quarter 2013

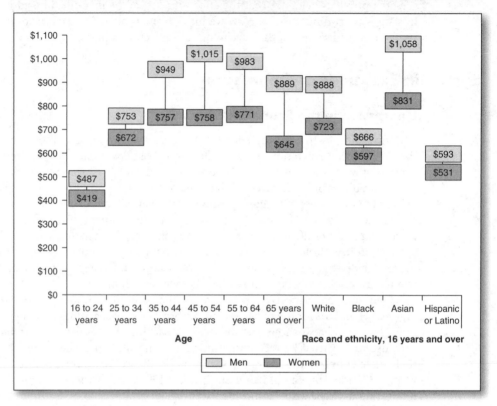

Source: Bureau of Labor Statistics (2013).

insurance status and income, African Americans, relative to whites and in some cases Hispanics, are less likely to receive appropriate cardiac medication. African Americans are also shown to receive cardiac bypass surgery significantly less often than whites. This fact helps to explain the greater mortality among African American patients. White Americans were also significantly more likely than Mexican Americans to have received appropriate medication.

Based on their history of economic exploitation and even of being the objects of medical experimentation, Dominiguez (2010) found that African Americans are significantly less likely than non-Hispanic whites to trust their medical providers to do what is best for them. This distrust is especially pronounced in patients receiving their care in health centers, outpatient clinics, or emergency departments, and they are less satisfied with the services they do receive.

Delgado (2007) discusses the widely reported phenomenon that recently arrived Mexicans are healthier on practically all health indexes compared with Mexican

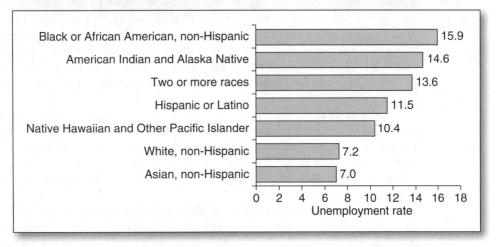

Figure 6.2   Unemployment Rate by Race and Hispanic or Latino Ethnicity, 2011 Annual Averages

	Unemployment rate
Black or African American, non-Hispanic	15.9
American Indian and Alaska Native	14.6
Two or more races	13.6
Hispanic or Latino	11.5
Native Hawaiian and Other Pacific Islander	10.4
White, non-Hispanic	7.2
Asian, non-Hispanic	7.0

Source: Bureau of Labor Statistics (2012).

Source: Photo by Robert van Wormer.

Latina Woman Addresses Crowd in Protest Against Wells Fargo Bank, Seattle. This was part of a nationwide protest against discriminatory lending practices by this bank. The bank later was fined $175 million by the civil rights branch of the Department of Justice for discrimination of minority groups.

Americans; the longer they live in the United States, the less healthy they become (this finding is not true for Cubans and Puerto Ricans). Factors singled out in the literature are a rise in eating disorders and substance use in general among second-generation Mexicans and barriers to health care including public health services for Latinos, inability to pay for treatment, and lack of transportation to medical clinics. Lack of health insurance is a major factor in preventing Latinos from receiving preventive and adequate health care. Undocumented workers are excluded from coverage under the Affordable Care Act, and although payroll taxes are removed from their paychecks for Medicare, they are not eligible to receive health care under this program, which covers adults over age 65 (National Immigration Law Center, 2013).

Similarly, Ramos, Jurkowski, Gonzalez, and Lawrence (2010) found through interviews with Latina women a close correlation between the high rate of poverty in Latino families and their inability to access health care treatment. Difficulties ranged from the unavailability of physicians or clinics, to lack of transportation, inability to afford treatment, lack of child care, and not feeling comfortable at family planning clinics.

One serious cultural barrier to mental health treatment is the stigma that pertains to mental health problems in many cultures. This may involve seeing individuals with psychological problems as bringing shame to their family, destroying the family's reputation, or even as a result of sin in a former life.

Related to health disparities is the disparity in access to a clean and uncontaminated environment. This disparity is reflected regionally as well as worldwide.

Environmental Oppression

When we examine the state of the physical environment in which people live, we come face-to-face with the reality of oppression. Economic and racial oppression are revealed in answer to a simple question: Who enjoys the bounties of nature with access to scenic views and clean air and water, and who lives in flood zones or near contaminated soil or polluting factories?

The global crisis caused by climate change, environmental degradation, and food and water insecurity has created fertile ground for global inequalities. These global inequalities are seen at the micro-level as well, within individual nations. This is where a concept we will call *environmental classism* comes into prominence.

Environmental classism comes into play when poor and marginalized people are pushed into the undesirable sections of town. We see it, likewise, when wealthy developers come from outside of the community and build factories for corporate profit that threaten the health of local people. A good example is provided by Schmitz, Matyók, James, and Sloan (2012), who describe what has happened with coastal development in some areas, where water has been pumped out of the aquifers, damaging the residents' water supply for the benefit of rich landlords and tourists.

Jerome Ringo (2010) has witnessed the effect of environmental destruction in Appalachia as well as in "the hood" in Washington, DC. Ringo, in his keynote speech at the Council on Social Work Education's (CSWE) landmark conference on sustainability, described his journey from an employee of a polluting petrochemical company to an environmental activist and researcher. The company Ringo worked for was situated near a poor, black neighborhood in southern Louisiana that later became known as "cancer alley." This place got its name from the high cancer rate caused by exposure to industrial toxins by residents of the area. Ringo traveled across the U.S. conducting investigations of corporate pollution. "I realized," he said, "it was not an issue of color, but an issue of poverty."

Collin (2010), on the other hand, stresses the racial factor. The best predictor of the location of hazardous waste sites is, as Collin suggests, the race of the community. Researchers, such as Rogge (2008), refer to this phenomenon as *environmental racism*. The population of neighborhoods in which hazardous waste sites are located has been found to be 56% people of color, notes Rogge. Not only are African Americans over-represented in such neighborhoods but also Latinos and Asian Americans. Rogge calls on social workers who work in low-income communities to learn how to recognize the signs of health problems caused by exposure to toxic substances, to educate parents on this subject, and to work in the political realm to effect policy change.

In actuality, classism and racism are inextricably linked. As a case in point, we can consider what happened in the natural disaster in New Orleans caused by Hurricane Katrina. The storm, as Dominelli (2012) indicates, exposed the risk factors of margin-alized residents (those without cars) and the protective factors for members of privi-leged groups. The latter not only had the means to leave town; their homes were more often on higher ground and substantially insured. Poor African Americans living in the Ninth Ward, where poverty, race, and class intersected, suffered the most damage during the storm. Even years afterward, the homes in this neighborhood have not been restored.

In Canada, First Nations leaders have engaged, for some time, in a struggle to preserve their ancestral homelands against the poisoning of their land by the extraction of tar sands. And in 2012, environmental activists organized in resistance against the construction of KXL South, built to pump up to over half a million barrels of toxic tar sands to be refined in Houston and Port Arthur, Texas (Nuss, 2013). The communities near the sites of these refineries, which are already heavily polluted, are mostly low-income communities of color—Latino in Houston and African American in Port Arthur. Already children living in the affected area in Houston are 56% more likely to get leukemia than those living 10 or more miles away. Asthma attacks and skin rashes are daily realities for residents.

Oppression in the Criminal Justice System

Blacks, who are 14% of the population, make up 37% of the prison population, including 42% of death row inmates (Norris, 2013). African American males are six times more likely to be incarcerated than white males and 2.5 times more likely than Hispanic males (Bureau of Justice Statistics, 2012). If present rates continue, one in three blacks and one in six Hispanic males can expect to spend some time in prison.

The prisons are heavily populated by minorities as a result of mandatory mini-mum drug sentencing passed as federal law in the 1980s and then modeled by the states. These laws were passed as part of the 1986 and 1988 Anti-Drug Abuse Acts, which established harsh mandatory minimum-sentencing guidelines targeting crack cocaine, a drug that had become associated in the public mind with inner-city crime.

The American War on Drugs Has Led to the Incarceration of Many. Around one in three black men can expect to spend some time in jail or prison.

In response to a politically motivated mass media campaign, which frightened the general public, Congress passed federal laws establishing punishment for possession and dealing of crack cocaine that was 100 times as high as the possession and dealing of the more expensive powdered form of cocaine. This calculation was based on the fact that the punishment for possession of 5 grams of crack cocaine was the same as that for possession of 500 grams of powdered cocaine. One result of the strict enforcement of antidrug laws was that the number of black women incarcerated for drug offenses increased 828% between 1986 and 1991 (Bush-Baskette, 2010). This increase was more than three times that of white women. Only recently were the 100 to 1 sentencing laws, which were widely recognized as racist and unfair, reduced through federal law to a still lopsided 18 to 1 ratio.

In *The New Jim Crow: Mass Incarceration in the Age of Colorblindness,* civil rights attorney Michelle Alexander (2010) provides compelling documentation for her contention that today's drug war is the new Jim Crow. An extraordinary percentage of black men in the United States are legally barred in many states from voting, public housing, jury duty, and many jobs as a result of their felony convictions. Some states are passing laws to force welfare recipients to pass drug tests before receiving benefits. Once a person is labeled as an ex-convict, the old forms of discrimination are suddenly legal. Today, discrimination is done through a different language and labels which appear to be colorblind but are racist in their connotations. In some major cities, Alexander reports, 80% of young African American men have criminal records and are subject to legalized discrimination, not because they are black but because they have a label that now substitutes for race. In fact, as she further points out, there are more black men behind bars or under the watch of the criminal justice system than there were enslaved in 1850.

When Angela Davis (2013) was delivering her keynote speech at the University of Northern Iowa, she was asked by a student in the audience about the school-to-prison pipeline. This was in reference to the criminalization of children today and especially of African American children, who are turned over to law enforcement when they get into trouble at school for offenses that would have been handled informally in the past. Some of them end up in juvenile institutions. Public schools today, according to Davis (2013), replicate the prison culture of discipline and punishment for breaking the rules. Thus, she says, we have a school-to-prison pipeline, which seems to prepare children in trouble at school for life in a correctional institution later on. The link between school and imprisonment is reinforced as well because the resources that could be devoted to education are devoured by the prison industrial complex. The prison industry is highly profitable, as Davis argues, with a stake in the continuing expansion of prisons and imprisonment.

Before we move on to a discussion of progressive, anti-oppressive policies in the United States and abroad—and the responses they engender—consult Table 6.1 for an abbreviated list of racist, sexist, and ethnocentric policies and events through U.S. history.

Table 6.1 A Shameful Past: Legacy of Discrimination in the United States

1838	Forced removal of 18,000 Cherokees from their land to west of the Mississippi River
1876–1964	Jim Crow laws enacted that mandated segregation in all public facilities in Southern states; laws overruled by the Civil Rights Act of 1964
1882–1930	More than 1,200 blacks were lynched in the South
1883	U.S. Supreme Court upholds state bans on interracial marriage; repealed in 1967
1896	The Supreme Court in *Plessy v. Ferguson* rules that state laws requiring segregation of the races is within the bounds of the Constitution as long as equal separate accommodations are available
1914	Harrison Act outlaws nonmedical use of opium, a drug associated with Chinese immigrants; Southwestern states passed laws against marijuana associated with Mexicans
1919–1933	Prohibition laws against alcohol sales are passed; alcohol use was associated with Catholic immigrants entering the United States
1924	The Ku Klux Klan claims 4.5 million members
1933	20 lynchings officially recorded during the worst year of the Depression
1942	U.S. government places around 110,000 Japanese Americans in relocation camps
1952	Homosexuality declared a mental disorder by the American Psychiatric Association; removed in 1973
1953	President Eisenhower fires all federal employees seen as guilty of "sexual perversion"
1960s	Indigenous children removed from their homes and placed in non-Native homes in Canada, Australia, and the United States

(Continued)

Table 6.1 (Continued)

1965–1970	Due to inhumane farm worker conditions, Mexican American labor organizer César Chávez leads a boycott of grapes
1969	Memorable police raid on a gay bar, the Stonewall Inn, in New York
1982	Equal Rights Amendment to provide equality for women falls three states short of ratification
1986	The Supreme Court rules that states can continue to outlaw homosexual acts between consenting adults; decision reversed in 2003
1986	Anti-Drug Abuse Act passed by Congress providing harsh sentences for possession and distribution of crack cocaine, which leads to mass imprisonment of blacks; law modified in 2010
1993	President Clinton announces a Don't Ask, Don't Tell policy for gays in the military
1996	Defense of Marriage Act signed into law by President Clinton stating that marriage was only between a man and a woman; overturned in 2013
2000	Supreme Court rules that Boy Scouts of America has the right to exclude members based on their sexual orientation
2008	Postville raid at an Iowa meat-packing plant results in the arrest of 300 undocumented immigrants; many are imprisoned and later deported
2010	Supreme Court removes restrictions on corporation campaign financing through *Citizens United v. Federal Election Commission,* which is a boon to the election of right-wing candidates
2013	Supreme Court overturns Voting Rights Act of 1965, which opens the door to states' use of voter-ID laws effectively restricting voting by poor and minority citizens

Source: van Wormer, Jackson, & Sudduth, C. (2012); Zinn, H. (2005).

Progress and Backlash

We have seen how oppression is kept in place by institutionalized ideologies and the propagation of doctrines that legitimize inequality and injustice. But such ideologies and doctrines are social constructions, which are often exchanged for non-oppressive alternatives. Sometimes, as it is said, the people lead and the leaders follow. Let's look at some of the recent moves toward a more progressive society and the backlashes that have followed them.

Progressive Policies

Women's Rights

The first feminist movement was born in 1848 at the Seneca Falls Convention when women demanded the right to vote. Its suffrage emphasis culminated when the 19th Amendment to the Constitution was ratified in 1919. The second feminist movement began in the late 1960s. It was bolstered by the Equal Pay Act of 1963, which required equal pay for equal work, and Title VII of the Civil Rights Act of 1964, which applied to wages as well as hiring and promotions. Even though sex was only added to the act by a sarcastic Congressman in hopes of derailing the bill's passage, and this addition was little noticed at the time, the Civil Rights Act was destined to be a boon to the legal challenges of sex discrimination.

The publication of Betty Friedan's (1963) *The Feminine Mystique* and Simone de Beauvoir's (1970) *The Second Sex* did much to raise the consciousness of educated women concerning their subordinate plight. Fortified by the example of the Civil Rights Movement, a number of varieties of feminism evolved in the 1970s and 1980s, with much overlap between them—for example, liberal feminism, radical feminism, black feminism (womanism), postmodernism, and so on. This period is known as the second wave of feminism. Emerging in the 1980s and 1990s, the third wave of the women's movement challenged the idea that poor women, women of color, and lesbians share the same problems as white middle-class women or similarly located poor men, men of color, or gay men (Price & Sokoloff, 2004, p. 3). Women at this time made enormous strides in pursuing higher education and taking their place beside men in professions, especially law and medicine.

Affirmative Action

Out of the groundswell of public opinion that took shape in the 1960s, other progressive policies were enacted, one of the most controversial being affirmative action. A term first introduced by President Kennedy, *affirmative action* refers to programs designed for the purpose of alleviating prejudice through encouraging equal status contact among people who are different. The focus on equal status contact is a key component in the alleviation of prejudice. A relationship between master or mistress and servant may be close, even intimate, but it is likely to be prejudicial as well. A relationship among equals, in contrast, helps dissolve feelings of superiority by one person over another.

A second key aspect of affirmative action is compensation for persons who have suffered from societal discrimination. In contrast to colorblind policies, which strive to overlook differences and treat everyone the same, these policies take a proactive stance in seeking to increase diversity in the educational and professional communities.

Through affirmative action policies, members of historically deprived groups, including women, have made significant strides in gaining access to privileges that might otherwise not have been available to them. As often happens when progress is made, a backlash ensues. And so it is with affirmative action. Opponents of affirmative action argue that minorities are hurt more than helped by policies that lower the standards for their admission or hiring and that such policies only arouse resentment by white or Anglo males and that such preferential policies undermine the principles of equal opportunity and fair play.

Persuaded by such logic, some states have retreated from their previous efforts toward educational integration, and efforts toward affirmative action are on the wane. "Just treat everyone alike," is commonly said. But such colorblindness may not be a practical option. Given the substantial decline in African American and Hispanic (although huge increase in Asian) enrollments at the top universities in California, today colorblindness means effective exclusion of many members of these minority groups from positions of influence, wealth, and power. Still, many conservatives and some liberals continue to profess a belief in colorblindness, arguing that society has an obligation to guarantee every citizen the opportunity to compete as equals (Wise, 2010). Other liberals, in contrast, contend that the equal opportunity focus perpetuates inequalities because we are indeed not all equal. In *Colorblind: The Rise of Post Racial Politics and the Retreat of Racial Equity*, Tim Wise (2010) contends that colorblindness can perpetuate and even deepen systemic racism. If university admissions counselors and employers, for example, fail to consider the way that applicants of color have been impacted by the opportunity structure as under a merit system, they are more apt to perceive these applicants as less qualified than their white counterparts and to reject their applications. In the interests of social justice, as Wise (2010) argues, we must continue to seek institutional remedies for the cultural sources of oppression in order to compensate for them.

LGBT Rights

The movement for LGBT rights got its impetus in 1969 when the police raided Stonewall, a gay bar, and the gay patrons fought back. Following heavy publicity, a new movement for human and civil rights was born. The level of formal, as well as informal, oppression, as documented earlier in this chapter, has continued to the present time. But almost overnight, in the summer of 2013, there was great cause for celebration among gays and lesbians and their allies. In a somewhat surprising decision, the conservative Supreme Court declared that the federal government must recognize *all* state-sanctioned marriages, including same-sex marriages (Graff, 2013). In other words, the Defense of Marriage Act was struck down. The significance of this ruling cannot be exaggerated. Now, for the first time, married gay and lesbian couples had access to their partner's Social Security benefits, the right to file their income taxes jointly for a lower rate, and much improved inheritance rights.

The state of same-sex marriage in America is constantly evolving as state laws are being upheld or struck down. The total number of states in which same-sex marriage is legal has risen, as of 2014, to 32. In one month, barriers to gay marriage fell in Arizona, Alaska, and Wyoming following a series of federal court actions declaring that the marriage ban laws were unconstitutional (Schwartz, 2014). The next month, a federal court ruled the other way and upheld the ban laws in four other states. This conflict among the federal appeals court paves the way for a return to the Supreme

Court so the nation's highest court can settle whether gay and lesbian couples have a fundamental right to marry under the U.S. Constitution or whether states can ban gay marriage (Eckholm, 2014). Meanwhile, surveys show that hostility to gay rights has declined significantly since the beginning of this century, with over half of Americans now favoring legal marriage rights for same-sex couples (Graff, 2013). Still, this leaves a sizable minority of the population in disapproval of gays and lesbians having these rights of citizenship, and their opposition is strong.

In summary, we have been describing in this section some key policy advances that have opened the doors to more equitable treatment for members of minority groups who have suffered societal discrimination. Along with protective legislation have come greater opportunities for people in the United States to take pride in their social identities and to pursue the "American dream." At the same time, there has been substantial resentment by members of the historically dominant class, rich and poor alike, who have experienced in some cases a certain loss in status. This brings us to a discussion of backlash.

Backlash Against Minority Group Advancement

Backlash occurs when people who have privilege in society in one context feel threatened that they have lost, or will lose, some aspect of their privilege—economically, socially, in employment, education, and so on—and they lash out against those they believe are the source of their frustration and resentment. Similar to victim blaming, people attach blame to those who they view as undeserving of any legal remedies for the plights that led to the passage of favorable or protective legislation in the first place. Let's take a look at some examples of this phenomenon, with a special emphasis on the reaction to the women's movement and its offshoots.

Anti-Immigrant Backlash

Mass immigration is taking place worldwide, in part due to economic globalization, which is displacing many workers, even as jobs are created for others. Transnational labor flows are taking place as many economies become dependent on a steady supply of cheap labor. Sometimes the migrants are driven out of their own countries due to free trade agreements that drive people off the land. The small farmers in Mexico, for example, can no longer compete with American farmers who ship large quantities of cheap produce to Mexico. So one of the unintended consequences of the North American Free Trade Agreement (NAFTA) was that it drove huge numbers of Mexicans north across the border. When the economic recession hit in 2008, the presence of these new immigrants was resented. Mexicans were accused of taking jobs away from "real" Americans, and state legislatures passed strict immigration policies (Ayón & Becerra, 2013).

Deportations under the Obama administration proceeded rapidly. By Obama's second term as president, approximately 1.2 million undocumented immigrants had been deported (Romero & Williams, 2013). Pending deportation, many immigrants are confined in privately operated detention centers. Private corporations are making huge profits in holding these immigrants; these companies build and administer the facilities in Britain and Australia as well as the United States. With little government or legal oversight, abuse and neglect of the inmates is common.

To better gauge the personal impact of U.S. anti-immigrant policies, Ayón and Becerra (2013) conducted focus groups involving 52 first-generation Mexican residents of Arizona. The participants reported experiencing discrimination at institutional and individual levels; this included insults due to their limited English proficiency and racial profiling. There were problems in the schools with teachers who announced that "they [the immigration authorities] are going to kick all Mexicans out of the country" (p. 213). And the children have become afraid of the police who are checking for documentation. A major finding that emerged from this research was that after the passage of the discriminatory laws by Arizona, people have become rude, even refusing to speak Spanish when they used to do so.

In Australia, anti-immigrant sentiment is reflected in the elections of more conservative governments with leaders who promise to restrict immigration. A nation paradoxically built by immigrants, Australia faces fresh challenges in dealing with new arrivals. An influx of migrants from India has been met with hostility and a spate of violent attacks on Indian students who have come to study in training programs. With a promise to use the navy to deport the boat people to remote Pacific Islands, the Conservative Party won the election in a landslide victory.

Australia is not the only government to be overturned due to the perceived immigration crisis. Norway recently elected a conservative prime minister and gave a strong showing to the far-right Progress Party, which has campaigned against immigration for years. According to Nilsen (2013), writing in *The Guardian*, the new government advocates tax cuts, deregulation, and a substantial reduction in public spending on welfare. And a recent article in the *New York Times* notes that the surge in right-wing populism is rapidly spreading from Denmark to France to all across Eastern Europe and is an outgrowth of an anti-immigration backlash.

The Antifeminist Backlash Against American Women

The publication of Susan Faludi's (1991) landmark *Backlash: The Undeclared War Against American Women* did much to raise women's consciousness concerning an antifeminist backlash against advances associated with the women's movement. Faludi provided extensive documentation to show the media reports linking purported problems in the American family with women's advances in the workplace stemmed from antifeminist propaganda pumped out by conservative research think tanks.

Thanks to the 2010 Citizens United decision, the Supreme Court gave corporations much of the same rights to political speech as individuals have, including anonymity, a torrent of corporate money is being funneled to push a far-right conservative agenda (Bai, 2012). Women's reproductive rights, immigrants' human rights, and social welfare programs are areas that have been especially hard hit.

Among the proposals that have been highlighted in the news are funding cuts to low-income preschool programs including Head Start; family planning services; and services for older adults living at home, including Meals on Wheels ("The War on Women," 2011). The term *entitlement programs*, as discussed in Chapter 5, has become a negative label originally used by Ronald Reagan and immediately picked up by the business community, and politicians and pundits of all political stripes are considering serious reforms affecting all these social insurance programs on which women in poverty increasingly are dependent upon (see Hertzberg, 2013).

The antifeminist backlash can be seen more clearly in the sharply increased rate of incarcerated women, especially poor and minority, throughout the 1990s—despite a significant decline in violent offenses committed by women. Today's women's prisons are now modeled off the medium security prisons designed for violent men, and the hiring of men as administrators and correctional officers in women's prisons has become the norm. Sexual abuse scandals involving women inmates and male officers have become commonplace (Amnesty International, 2011b).

The war on drugs has been characterized as a war on women of color. This claim, which is voiced by Bloom and Chesney-Lind (2007), is based on the increasing numbers of impoverished minority women serving lengthy sentences for involvement in drug-related offenses. This situation, in conjunction with the media's showcasing of isolated episodes of girls' and the right-wing war on women's reproductive freedom, can be viewed as a counterreaction to women's successes in other areas of social life.

The right to equality is also used against women in child custody situations. In a reversal of the traditional custom, women are no longer given preference in parenting arrangements. The rulings against women here, as in many of these legal situations, are that women are equal now, and as equals they can no longer expect special consideration. The media have both reflected and promoted this shift in perspective.

In recent years a fathers' rights movement has influenced family law with damaging consequences for many women and children and indirectly putting many battered women at risk of abuse (DeKeseredy, 2011). This is because judges increasingly are awarding the custody of children in contested cases to the fathers or responding to fathers' requests for joint custody in the affirmative. In either situation, the relationship between the former partners is unduly prolonged, as is the mother's dependency on the father for the right to visitation with the child.

Backlash Against Women in Health Care

Attacks on women's reproductive choices have been loud and clear; these have taken the form of restrictive legislative proposals and demands for funding cuts of women's health services that reflect a general climate of conservatism that swept across the United States in the second half of the Obama administration. Many have come about as a result of the tea party movement with attacks on liberal policies related to women's reproductive health and welfare aid for families living in poverty.

Planned Parenthood, which provides family planning services (abortion accounts for only about 3% of Planned Parenthood's activities), has been singled out for the brunt of the attacks (Chu & Posner, 2013). Despite the value of these services, state legislatures across the United States cut the funding for Planned Parenthood and other women-centered health care providers. Because so many women lack access to publicly funded contraceptive services, and because a smaller number are desperate for personal reasons to have an abortion, the closing down of these centers is predicted to have devastating results. Some states have even started mandating ultrasounds for women seeking an abortion in an effort to interfere with a woman's choice (Guttmacher Institute, 2013).

To put these restrictions in context, consider that although the United States spends more than any other country on health care, according to a report from the Center for American Progress, the United States has the highest first-day death rate for infants in the industrialized world (Chu & Posner, 2013). In addition, women in the United States have a higher risk of dying of pregnancy-related complications than those in 49 other countries, including Kuwait, Bulgaria, and South Korea (Amnesty International, 2011a). The Center for American Progress, however, applauds provisions in the Affordable Care Act that are geared toward providing women with the prenatal and maternity care that they need (Chu & Posner, 2013).

The Global Dimensions of Backlash Against Women

Over most of the course of human rights history, issues of gender have largely been ignored. Much of the reason lay in the philosophy of cultural relativism, the belief that we must respect cultural tradition, even those that seem abhorrent to us because of our own cultural conditioning. This reluctance of social scientists, including feminists, to appear ethnocentric, to judge other people according to principles of Western society, is understandable. But this reluctance has meant that until relatively recently, abuses such as family murders for adultery ("honor killings") and mutilation of girls' genital organs were not investigated and rarely, if ever, mentioned in literature. And it was believed that it was up to the women in the individual countries to bring about the changes they desired without outside interference.

Paralleling women's awakening to human rights issues and an awareness that women in some countries are much more empowered than are members of their gender elsewhere, a strong vigilance is evident to keep women "in their place." The fear in certain quarters across the globe is that if women's consciousness is raised, they will demand their rights. A counterreaction, therefore, has taken place, a backlash by entrenched forces with a vested interest in the status quo. This backlash is especially pronounced in regions of the world where religious fundamentalism has been used to threaten women and suppress them.

In a time when women's rights are threatened on the home front, major sources of protection from foreign aid sources are drying up. And for political reasons, family planning services have suffered severe funding declines in recent years, even in countries with scarce resources and where overpopulation is a major concern. Conservatives in the U.S. Congress have targeted international family planning funding out of the fear that abortion services might be offered. Paradoxically, the prevention of unwanted pregnancy is the best way to reduce the numbers of abortions, many of which now are performed under unsafe conditions. We also know from U.S. Agency for International Development (AID) data collected from seven countries that for every dollar invested in family planning and reproductive health care, there are significant savings in education, immunization, water and sanitation, maternal health, and malaria (Lasher, 2013). In Bolivia, for example, $9.00 is saved for every dollar invested.

In India, the practice of dowry (or a gift from the bride's family to the groom and his family) is implicated in over 8,000 deaths of young women every year. The problem arises when the bride's family does not fulfill what is believed to be the obligation of paying the dowry. Many more women are maimed through bride burnings and other attempts to inflict pain. This practice is forbidden in law and vehemently protested by feminists and other activists but still it persists.

The global economy makes women vulnerable to victimization in yet another way. Girls and young women from Eastern Europe, for example, who face economic hardship at home, can easily be enticed to relocate with the promise of lucrative employment abroad. They are then ripe for sexual exploitation, including being tricked into sex trafficking and/or economic enslavement.

At the same time that female vulnerability is increasing in some ways, the women's movement is effecting changes for women worldwide. And much attention is being paid in the international media and by nongovernmental organizations (NGOs) to the plight of the world's women. The adoption of a human rights framework is increasingly relevant today, given the realities of globalization and the enhancement of organizing efforts through modern technologies.

"Human rights are women's rights" became the motto of the international movement to protect women from abuse. In 1995, women from Austria to Zambia linked up at the United Nations Fourth World Conference on Women. The historic conference was held at Huaira and Beijing, China. Whereas at previous women's conferences, feminists from the Westernized nations were reluctant to join their sisters to criticize abusive traditions from other parts of the world for fear of being accused of lacking cultural sensitivity, this time women's voices were united on behalf of the many who are unable to speak. At this historic conference, the debate on health and reproductive rights was led primarily by delegates from the non-Western world.

Inspired by this international gathering of women who demanded an end to the abuses inflicted upon them, Amnesty International took up the call and listed trafficking in women along with torture, slavery, and jailing "prisoners of conscience" as serious violations. In its annual reports, Amnesty International continues to outline the mechanism by which hundreds of women a year are smuggled, imprisoned, exploited, raped continuously, blackmailed, and physically and sexually abused, and documents attempts made to combat these human rights violations.

Today, feminists and other social activists—in collaboration with indigenous women or women who have become refugees from violence—increasingly look to international law. The focus on human rights is, by definition, international—the belief in higher laws that transcend national laws. This broadening of focus is a legacy of the Nuremburg Trials that followed World War II when Nazi leaders were judged by a world body (albeit one organized by the victors) for crimes against humanity. Even more significant as a legacy and a model was the United Nations Declaration of Human Rights that was adopted in 1948 (see Chapter 12). Today, attention increasingly is drawn to this document (reprinted in Appendix A), which included women as an at-risk population whose rights need to be protected. Feminist groups today are networking globally around issues of injustice, violence, structural inequality, and women's right to resist fundamentalist religious movements that deprive them of human rights. Because Canada was a signatory (unlike the United States) to the entire UN Declaration, human rights activists in that country can turn to international law as a valuable tool for advocacy for social and economic justice within the era of globalization. Their counterparts in the United States are relatively limited in this regard.

THINKING SUSTAINABLY

The many gains women made in terms of the recognition of their equal rights in the 20th century have been threatened by an antifeminist backlash, which reveals itself in many ways here in the United States: the attack on abortion rights, the prevalence of domestic violence and rape, and the failure of women to be equally paid and represented in the work world. This backlash is similar to the one that has occurred since the enactment of the Civil Rights and Voting Rights Acts—legislation thought to be a first step in ending our struggles with racism. Fifty years on, racism and sexism are far more prominent in public discourse than thought possible.

Consider your own feelings on feminism and discrimination of minorities in general. How is the oppression of groups affecting the ability to achieve a sustainable society? Do you observe the backlash mentioned above in your own life? What direction do you envision for society in your own country over the next 50 years?

Work of UN Women

In July 2010, the United Nations General Assembly created UN Women, the United Nations Entity for Gender Equality and the Empowerment of Women. The task facing this organization is enormous. According to a fact sheet provided on the UN Women's (2013) website, these are some of the global problems facing girls and women:

- More than 64 million girls worldwide are child brides, with 46% of women aged 20 to 24 in South Asia and 41% in West and Central Africa reporting that they married before the age of 18.
- Approximately 140 million girls and women in the world have suffered female genital mutilation or cutting.
- Trafficking ensnares millions of women and girls in modern-day slavery with an estimated 4.5 million forced into sexual exploitation at the present time.
- Rape has been a rampant tactic in modern wars. Conservative estimates suggest that 20,000 to 50,000 women were raped during the 1992 to 1995 war in Bosnia and Herzegovina, while approximately 250,000 to 500,000 women and girls were targeted in the 1994 Rwandan genocide.

To help prevent such violence and enable women to become self-supporting, UN Women manages a trust fund, which provides grants to promote legal remedies to protect women from violence. In addition, this trust fund supports sustainable enterprises to help feed the population through farming.

To help protect the rights and well-being of these vulnerable women from across the world, initiatives financed by grants from UN Women (2012) conduct networking and educational campaigns. In Morocco, for example, the initiative works directly with single mothers and girls who have endured physical and sexual victimization to support their social reintegration through education, training, and employment opportunities. The program works through NGOs to conduct community-wide advocacy campaigns. Major goals are to improve legal protection for these vulnerable girls and women and to reduce the social stigma they experience in the community. In Iraq, the UN Trust Fund project works directly with the Ministry of Health to ensure that all health care providers are trained to detect and treat survivors of gender-based violence.

Positive Developments in International Law

An important but belated development in recent years was the recognition of rape of the enemy's women—a common occurrence during and after a war—as a war crime. The International War Crimes Tribunal in The Hague took a revolutionary step when three Bosnian soldiers were convicted of rape and sexual enslavement as crimes against humanity. The judgment followed years of lobbying by women's rights groups. Thanks to women's rights activists who have actively been involved in the establishment of the relatively new International Criminal Court (ICC), the ICC prosecutor has appointed a special advisor on women's crimes to ensure that the rights of women survivors are represented (International Law Observer, 2008).

Freedom from domestic assault is a major goal of the 1980 Convention on the Elimination of All Forms of Discrimination against Women. This important document has the support of all industrialized nations except for the United States as the U.S. Senate has never ratified it. The city of San Francisco did pass a model version for the city, and this has been influential in helping preserve programs for girls and women in the face of statewide budget cuts (Andronici, 2009). Such human rights laws provide a valuable theoretical and practical base for assisting in social change.

In Central America, several countries are working in collaboration with the UN Human Rights Office to integrate a Model Protocol into their legal systems to guide investigations and prosecutions launched in the wake of gender-based murders of women in Latin America (UN Women, 2014). This action by the Latin American countries, including El Salvador and Mexico, marks a turning point for taking a stronger stand against *femicide*, or gender-related killings, a leading cause of death for women in some countries. Both El Salvador and Mexico, as a result of advocacy by UN Women, enacted legal reforms that defined femicide as a criminal offense as well as measures to prevent and punish it. This example of reliance on international law to link partner violence with human rights violations has important implications worldwide for women who are subjected to behaviors that could be described as torture, including captivity. If the United States were to reclassify partner violence as a human rights violation, recognized as such by international organizations such as the United Nations, this move would aid in promoting international standards of humanity and equality.

Culturally Competent Social Work Practice

Cultural competence entails recognition of society's prejudices—ethnocentrism, sexism, classism, heterosexism, and racism—and of our own possession of many of these traits. To fully appreciate cultural differences, self-awareness is a must. Social workers must recognize the influence of their own culture, family, and peers on how they think and act.

The CSWE (2008) in its curriculum standards shifted from an emphasis on a study of cultural traits of specific cultural groups to an emphasis on oppression in social institutions. The incorporation of theories of oppression in the social work curriculum entails a shift in focus from race to racism, sex to sexism, ethnicity to ethnocentrism, and from oppressed to oppressor. The significance of this shift in the standards for the CSWE is that now the focus is structural instead of individual and general rather than specific. In its most recent formulation, CSWE (2015) uses the term *diversity and difference* as a major competency for social work education. To engage in social work practice, practitioners require an understanding of the essence of difference. They need to know that, as a consequence of difference, a person's life experiences may include oppression, poverty, marginalization, and alienation as well as privilege and access to power. Again the emphasis by CSWE is more on external forces than on inculcating knowledge about particular cultural traits and norms.

Still, in the interests of empowerment, in working with members of a diverse population, an effective social worker will make continuous efforts to learn about the client's culture—the norms, vocabulary, symbols, and strengths. In so doing, one avoids the colorblind and genderblind notions of many North American human service workers who refute the significance of color, culture, and gender as important categories of personal and group identity in the society. Delgado (2007) brings our attention to the "cultural blindness" that is so often evidenced on the intake forms used by mental health agencies (p. 130). Basing the definition of family on the nuclear family, for example, is culturally biased and often irrelevant to the Latino family. Many of the official forms, moreover, include questions that are problem- rather than strengths-oriented. When some of the foreign-reared Latino clients, for example, describe the herbal remedies that many of them use, they are apt to be criticized for what may be viewed by staff as ignorant practices.

By recognizing that significant differences do exist between people of different ethnic backgrounds, professionals are recognizing a person's wholeness and individuality. To tell a lesbian or gay person "just stay in the closet and you'll be all right" is to deny that person an important part of himself or herself. To tell an African American "we're all the same under the skin" is to deny the importance of race in society and pride in one's racial identity. Multicultural social work education exposes students to divergent thinking as they are forced to examine assumptions that were formerly taken for granted.

Earlier in this book (in Chapter 4), we discussed the necessity for biodiversity in nature, for the health of the ecosystem, and for the enrichment of plant and animal life. Similar advantages pertain to the cultural diversity in community life, which relies on the spread of knowledge and customs, such as food preparation, cross-culturally. In recognition of the fact that religion and spirituality are forms of diversity from which clients can draw strengths, National Association of Social Workers (NASW) has launched a special resource to provide social workers and educators greater insight into the religious viewpoints of the clients they serve. This resource is in conjunction with CSWE's Religion and Spirituality Work Group, an organization that includes social work and social services associations of Catholics, Jews, Mormons, and Muslims (Pace, 2012a).

Appreciation of a person's diverse racial or ethnic identity is a core competency that is encouraged in social work education and practice (Pace, 2012b). As social justice advocates, social workers must have an awareness of such experiences and a knowledge of the impact of the legacy of the past in order to address the long-term human costs of oppression. Even while the social worker is seeking evidence of strengths and resilience in a client or cultural group, he or she should be cognizant of the possibility of historical trauma. Historical trauma is considered to be a major factor, for example, in the high Native American mortality rates from alcohol-related conditions, including suicide and homicide and in the fatalism evidenced in some of the most impoverished regions of Appalachia (see Brave Heart, 2007; Messer, 2007; van Wormer & Besthorn, 2011).

For the social-worker-as-sustainability-advocate, an awareness of privilege as well as the impact of historical trauma is an important starting point. For those in a position of privilege, the social worker can take on the role of ally. For those who are members of social groups with a history of oppression, the opportunity is theirs to join with others, including clients, in solidarity.

The CSWE (2013) has issued guidelines for graduate programs of social work that have a trauma-informed concentration. Social work educators are urged to take into account disproportionate exposure to trauma on the basis of culture, race, and national origin, and to "incorporate an understanding of the influence of historical trauma on various cultures into assessment activities" (p. 15). We discuss trauma-informed care related to mental health treatment in Chapter 9.

Summary and Conclusion

This chapter was written with the belief that a sustainable society is one that is inclusive and anti-oppressive and that actively draws on the diverse talents and culture of its entire people. Diversity, as history shows, is as essential to social and economic development as biodiversity is to the natural environment.

The organization of this chapter was inspired by a shift in focus in CSWE's curriculum standards from education into cultural characteristics of a given national group, or tribe, to a focus on societal practices that perpetuate oppression. Such an orientation is more political and radical than a mere review of cultural characteristics of selected minority groups and in many ways is more consistent with a sustainability focus. Current trends related to economic globalization and political backlash compel us to address issues of oppression.

The ethic of sustainability requires us to confront disparities that exist whether because of the uniqueness of history or because of a seemingly natural tendency of those who "have" to not want to share with the "have-nots." This control may be curbed by progressive tax policies, antidiscrimination laws, and government programs, such as public education and universal health care. At the same time, some laws and policies are punitive and cause disproportionate harm to feared or disfavored minority groups.

A sustainability ethic requires a close examination of a nation's laws and policies, and the starting point of such an inquiry is a consideration of oppression and of its counterpart—privilege. Consistent with a sustainability ethic, this chapter presented an overview of types of oppression and mechanisms by which privilege sustains an oppressive status quo. We explored some of the most basic forms of privilege, the possession of which is most often taken for granted, though clearly apparent to non-privileged groups. White, heterosexual, and male privilege were the examples highlighted.

Our exploration of the nature of oppression took us into a look at oppression and disparities built into the economic system, health care options, environmental practices, and the criminal justice system. We presented a list in tabular form of laws that were designed to control the masses, including minority groups, in various ways, and then we learned how through organized opposition by the affected minority groups and their allies many of these oppressive laws were overturned or rewritten. But we saw also that although many of the most hurtful policies and practices have been altered and outlawed, the legacy of racism, sexism, and ethnocentrism endures.

A political backlash is in evidence today against the very groups that formerly received a boost through antidiscriminatory and affirmative action policies. The antifeminist and anti-immigrant legislation can be seen in this regard and also as part of a broader conservative movement. Once, we had a war on poverty; today, we have a war on drugs.

Social work as a profession, as we saw in Chapter 2 on historical foundations, is strongly affected by paradigm shifts in ideology. Under conservative administrations, social workers are impacted through a lessening of demand for their services, and they suffer vicariously when their clients' needs cannot be met. Until the dawning of a new progressive era, social workers will have to do their best to work toward making the unsustainable sustainable. And if the past is any guide, this is what they will continue to do.

Critical Thinking Questions

1. Discuss arguments in favor of being color- and genderblind. What are the arguments against this approach?

2. Can you come up with several elements common to all forms of oppression?

3. Review the facts pertaining to the well-publicized trial of George Zimmerman and his killing of Trayvon Martin. Why was the situation so troubling, and what were the differing responses to the verdict?

4. List the privileges that you have. Do you have the same privilege in every context or social group? Discuss the meaning of this concept to you.

5. Discuss the concept of privilege. How does it relate to youth and middle age?

6. What are some of the statements that Mullaly included in his list for white privilege? To this list add others of your own.

7. What are some examples of the use of body modification related to racial characteristics and dominant standards of beauty? Go beyond those provided in the text and discuss the significance of these physical alterations.

8. This chapter discussed male privilege. Do you think there is such a thing as female privilege?

9. What is intersectionality? What did Pager's experimental research related to job applications show about intersectionality?

10. How do environmental racism and environmental classism relate to the concept of intersectionality?

11. Study Figures 6.1 and 6.2. What do they say about employment by gender? How about race and ethnicity? Are there any surprises?

12. Provide several illustrations of impoverished groups affected by industrial pollution. What do you think could be done to alleviate this situation?

13. Discuss the claim that the war on drugs is a war on minority groups. Why are today's drug wars seen as the new Jim Crow?

14. Review Table 6.1. Which do you think are the three most startling decisions or events? Explain the reason for your choices.

15. Which of the progressive policies described do you find the most significant?

16. What is the importance of the Supreme Court decisions related to same-sex marriage?

17. Discuss the concept of backlash. How does it relate to the perceived immigration crisis?

18. Can you name three ways in which women have been affected by the antifeminist backlash?

19. How do the stresses of economic globalization relate to attacks on women worldwide?

20. How can the UN Fourth World Conference on Women be considered a turning point?

21. What is the significance of international law in protecting the rights of marginalized groups?

References

Alexander, M. (2010). *The new Jim Crow: Incarceration in the age of colorblindness*. New York, NY: New Press.

Almosawa, S. (2013, August 16). *No place for gays in Yemen*. Rome, Italy: Inter Press Service News Agency. Retrieved from www. ipsnews.net

American Psychiatric Association. (2013). *Diagnostic and statistical manual of mental disorders, text revision* (5th ed., DSM-5). Washington, DC: Author.

Amnesty International. (2011a). *Maternal health in the U.S.* Retrieved from www.amnesty.org

Amnesty International. (2011b). *Rape and sexual violence: Human rights law and standards in the international criminal court*. New York, NY: Amnesty International. Retrieved from www.amnesty.org

Andronici, J. (2009, Winter). A women's bill of rights. *Ms.*, 12–13.

Appleby, G. A., Colon, E., & Hamilton, J. (2011). *Diversity, oppression, and social functioning: Person-in-environment assessment and social functioning* (3rd ed.). Boston, MA: Pearson Allyn & Bacon.

Associated Press. (2013, November 14). Hawaii: Same-sex marriage becomes law. *New York Times*, p. A24.

Ayón, C., & Becerra, D. (2013). Mexican immigration families under siege: The impact of anti-immigrant policies, discrimination, and the economic crisis. *Advances in Social Work*, *14*(1), 206–228.

Bai, M. (2012, July 22). How much has Citizens United changed the political game? *New York Times*, p. MM14.

Barker, R. (2014). *The social work dictionary* (6th ed.). Washington, DC: NASW Press.

Baynton, D. C. (2009). Disability and the justification of inequality in American history. In P. Rothenberg (Ed.), *Race, class, and gender in the United States* (8th ed., pp. 92–102). New York, NY: Worth.

Bloom, B., & Chesney-Lind, M. (2007). Women in prison. In R. Muraskin (Ed.), *It's a crime: Women and justice* (pp. 542–563). Upper Saddle River, NJ: Prentice Hall.

Bowcott, O. (2014, May 12). Uganda anti-gay law led to tenfold rise in attacks on LGBTI people, report says. *The Guardian* [UK]. Retrieved from www.theguardian.com

Brave Heart, M. Y. (2007). The impact of historical trauma: The example of the Native community. In M. Bussey & J. B. Wise (Eds.), *Trauma transformed: An empowerment response* (pp. 176–193). New York, NY: Columbia University Press.

Bureau of Justice Statistics. (December, 2012). *Prisoners in 2011*. Washington, DC: Author.

Bureau of Labor Statistics. (2012, September 5). *Racial and ethnic characteristics of the U.S. labor force*. Retrieved from www.bls.gov/opub/ted/2012/ted_20120905.htm

Bureau of Labor Statistics. (2013, September 27). *Median weekly earnings by age, sex, race, and Hispanic or Latino ethnicity, first quarter*. Retrieved from www.bls.gov/opub/ted/2013/ted_20130419.htm

Bush-Baskette, S. (2010). *Misguided justice: The war on drugs and the incarceration of black women*. Bloomington, IN: iUniverse.

Centers for Disease Control and Prevention. (2013). Infant mortality statistics from the 2009 period linked birth/infant death data set (Table A). *National Vital Statistics Reports*. www.cdc.gov/nchs/data/nvsr/nvsr61/nvsr61_08.pdf

Chu, A., & Posner, C. (2013, September). *The state of women in America: A 50-state analysis of how women are faring across the nation*. Center for American Progress. Retrieved from www.americanprogress

Cohen, J., & Balz, D. (2013, July 22). Zimmerman verdict poll: Stark reaction by race. *Washington Post*. Retrieved from www.washingtonpost.com

Collin, R. M. (2010, October 16). *Carl A. Scott memorial lecture: Sustainability*. Lecture at the Council on Social Work Education Annual Conference, Portland, OR.

Collin, R. M. (2011, November 17). *Sustainability and environmental justice*. Keynote speech at the Global Institute of Sustainability, Tempe, AZ.

Collins, P. H. (2010). The New Politics of Community. *American Sociological Review*, *75*(1), 7–30.

Council on Social Work Education. (2008). *Educational policy and accreditation*. Standard 2.1.4. Alexandria, VA: Author.

Council on Social Work Education. (2013). *Guidelines for advanced social work practice in trauma*. Alexandria, VA: Author.

Council on Social Work Education. (2015). *Educational policy and accreditation*. Alexandria, VA: Author.

Davis, A. (2003). *Are prisons obsolete?* New York, NY: Seven Stories Press.

Davis, A. (2013, November 8). *Organizing for social change and human rights.* Keynote presentation at The 15th Annual Cedar Valley Conference on Human Rights, Cedar Falls, IA.

de Beauvoir, S. (1970). *The second sex.* New York, NY: Bantam Books.

DeKeseredy, W. S. (2011). *Violence against women: Myths, facts, controversies.* Toronto, Canada: University of Toronto Press.

Delgado, M. (2007). *Social work with Latinos: A cultural assets paradigm.* Oxford, England: Oxford University Press.

Dominelli, L. (2012). *Green social work: From environmental crises to environmental justice.* Cambridge, England: Polity Press.

Dominguez, T. P. (2010). Adverse birth outcomes in African American women: The social context of persistent reproductive disadvantage. *Social Work in Public Health, 26*(1), 3–16. doi:10.1080/10911350902986880

Duke, B., & Channsin, B. (2013). *Dark girls* [Motion picture]. USA: Duke Media & Urban Winter Entertainment.

Eckholm, E. (2014). Federal judge strikes down Michigan's ban on same-sex marriage. *New York Times*, p. A11.

Faludi, S. (1991). *Backlash: The undeclared war against American women.* New York, NY: Random House.

Federal Bureau of Investigation. (2013). *2012 hate crime statistics.* U.S. Department of Justice: Uniform Crime Reports. Retrieved from www.fbi.gov

Friedan, B. (1963). *The feminine mystique.* New York, NY: W. W. Norton

Goodman, J. D. (2013, May 22). Two more anti-gay attacks are reported in Manhattan. *New York Times*, p. A24.

Graff, E. J. (2013, September 27). What's next for the gay-rights movement? *Daily Beast (Newsweek).* Retrieved from www.thedailybeast.com

Guttmacher Institute. (2013). *Requirements for ultrasound.* Retrieved from www.guttmacher .org/statecenter/spibs/spib_RFU.pdf

Hertzberg, H. (2013, April 8). Sense of entitlement. *New Yorker*, 23–24.

hooks, b. (1992). *Black looks: Race and representation.* Cambridge, MA: South End Press.

hooks, b. (2009). *Belonging: A culture of place.* New York, NY: Routledge.

International Law Observer. (2008, December 5). *The ICC prosecutor's appointment of a special advisor on women's crimes.* Retrieved from http://internationallawobserver.eu

Keefe, R. (2010). Health disparities: A primer for public health social workers. *Social Work in Public Health, 25*(3–4), 237–257.

Lasher, C. (2013, June 9). *Under pressure: International family planning faces cuts from sequestration and budget-slashing mania.* Population Action. Retrieved from https://supreme.justia .com/cases/federal/us/388/1/case.html

Loving v. Virginia. 388 U.S. 1. (1967, June 12). Retrieved from https://supreme.justia.com/cases/ federal/us/388/1/case.html

Luhn, A. (2013, September 1). Russian anti-gay law prompts rise in homophobic violence. *The Guardian* [UK]. Retrieved from www.theguardian.com/world

Messer, D. R. (2007). *Ablaze in Appalachia: A social approach to a forgotten culture.* United States: BookSurge.

Mullaly, B. (2009). *Challenging oppression and confronting privilege* (2nd ed.). New York, NY: Oxford University Press.

National Immigration Law Center. (2012, August). *Racial profiling after HB 56.* Retrieved from www.nilc.org

National Immigration Law Center. (2013, March). *Immigrants and the Affordable Care Act.* Retrieved from www.nilc.org

Nilsen, A. (2013, September 10). Norway's disturbing lurch to the right. *The Guardian.* Retrieved from www.theguardian.com

Norris, M. (2013, August 26). Race in America, 50 years after the dream. *Time,* 93–94.

Nuss, E. (2013, September 21). Life at the end of the line: Drawing the line on tar sands in Houston's east end. Tar Sands Blockade. Retrieved from www.tarsandsblockade.org/endoftheline/

Pace, P. R. (2012a, February). NASW joins religion, spirituality work group. *NASW News, 57*(2), 11.

Pace, P. R. (2012b, February). Toolkit can help convey importance of social work. *NASW News, 57*(2), 1, 7.

Pager, D. (2003). The mark of a criminal record. *American Journal of Sociology, 108*(5), 937–975.

Pager, D., Western, B., & Bonikowski, B. (2009). Discrimination in a low-wage labor market: A field experiment. *American Sociological Review, 74,* 777–799.

Price, B. R., & Sokoloff, N. J. (2004). Introduction to Part I: Theories and facts about women offenders. In B. R. Price & N. J. Sokoloff (Eds.), *The criminal justice system and women: Offenders, victims, and workers* (3rd ed., pp. 1–10). New York, NY: McGraw-Hill.

Ramos, B. M., Jurkowski, J., Gonzalez, B. A., & Lawrence, C. (2010). Latina women: Health and healthcare disparities. *Social Work in Public Health, 25*(3–4), 258–271.

Ringo, J. (2010, October 15). The new color of green: A collective voice towards change. *Special plenary.* Council on Social Work Education, Annual Conference, Portland, Oregon.

Rogge, M. (2008). Environmental justice. In National Association of Social Workers *Encyclopedia of social work* (pp. 136–139). New York, NY: Oxford University Press.

Romero, S., & Williams, M. R. (2013, Spring). The impact of immigration legislation on Latino families: Implications for social work. *Advances in Social Work, 14*(1), 224–246.

Schmitz, C., Matyók, T., James, C., & Sloan, L. M. (2012). The relationship between social work and environmental sustainability: Implications for interdisciplinary practice. International *Journal of Social Welfare, 22,* 76–286.

Schwartz, D. (2014, October 17). Courts knock down gay marriage bans in Arizona, Alaska, Wyoming. *Reuters.* Retrieved from www.reuters.com

Stone, Z. (2013, May 24). The K-pop plastic surgery obsession. *Atlantic.* Retrieved from www.theatlantic.com

UN Women. (2012). *Annual report 2012–2013.* New York, NY: United Nations. Retrieved from www.unwomen.org

UN Women. (2013). *Facts and figures: Ending violence against women.* New York, NY: UN Women. Retrieved from http://comms-authoring.unwomen.org/en/what-we-do/ending-violence-against-women/facts-and-figures

UN Women. (2014, September 10). *Model protocol: Ending impunity for femicide across Latin America.* Retrieved from http://comms-authoring.unwomen.org/en/news/stories/2014/9/model-protocol-on-femicide-launched

van Wormer, K., & Besthorn, F. (2011). *Human behavior and the social environment, macro level.* New York, NY: Oxford University Press.

van Wormer, K., Jackson, D. W., & Sudduth, C. (2012). *The maid narratives: Black domestics and White families in the Jim Crow South.* Baton Rouge: Louisiana State University Press.

van Wormer, K., Kaplan, L., & Juby, C. (2012). *Confronting oppression, restoring justice: From policy analysis to social action* (2nd ed.). Alexandria, VA: Council on Social Work Education.

The war on women [Editorial]. (2011, February 26). *New York Times,* p. A18.

Wise, T. (2010). *Colorblind: The rise of post racial politics and the retreat of racial equity.* San Francisco, CA: City Lights Books.

Zinn, H. (2005). *A people's history of the United States 1492 to present.* New York, NY: Harper Perennial.

PART II

POLICIES
TO MEET
HUMAN NEEDS

The second half of the book takes us into the arena of policy practice. Sustainability continues to be a major theme as we examine the ability of social welfare policies to meet the needs of all the people. This section of *Social Welfare Policy for a Sustainable Future* contains six chapters, the first four of which are concerned with policies to meet the needs of vulnerable populations—children, older adults, people with health and mental health disabilities. The concluding chapters provide an in-depth coverage of human rights conventions and policy analysis as a stepping stone to shaping social welfare policy.

Chapter 7, "Child Welfare," the first chapter of Part II, draws on the United Nations Convention on the Rights of the Child. This convention serves as an organizing framework for the discussion of issues pertaining to the treatment and protection of children. Topics covered include child maltreatment worldwide, gun violence, child poverty, and inadequate health care.

Sustainable health care policies is the subject of Chapter 8. The history and development of U.S. health care policy leads into a close examination of both the Affordable Care Act, in terms of both its accomplishments and shortcomings. Following a discussion of disability policy, we explore global concerns and initiatives.

Chapter 9, "Mental Health Care Policy," examines political, economic, and social aspects of mental health treatment. Special topics addressed in this chapter are homelessness, trauma related to war, and substances abuse services. A discussion of trauma-informed care concludes the chapter.

Written by gerontology expert Christina Erickson, Chapter 10, "Sustainable Policy for Older Adults," provides a global perspective on care for older populations as well as information concerning the Older Americans Act, elder abuse, hospice care, and other issues.

Human rights is the topic of Chapter 11. The Universal Declaration Human Rights is the focal point. Following a discussion of its history and significance in today's world, we consider the implications of human rights for the social work profession. The book ends on a positive note with Chapter 12, "Sustainability Policy Analysis and Policy Practice." The discussion takes the reader from policy analysis (with a focus on sustainability) to direct social work practice. Harm reduction and restorative justice are presented as approaches consistent with the principles of a sustainability ethic.

7

Child Welfare

This global partnership will be guided in its work by the CRC (Convention on the Rights of the Child), that luminous document that enshrines the rights of every child without exception to a life of dignity and self-fulfillment.

—Nelson Mandela (2000)
In memory, July 18, 1918, to December 5, 2013

Inequality is the biggest economic issue of our time.

—Pope Francis (November 27, 2013)

Children are our most precious legacy for the future, yet many of them experience immense challenges in the 21st century. In the United States—the most resourced nation in the world—nearly one in five children live in poverty. Globally, the United Nations International Children's Emergency Fund (UNICEF) State of the World's Children research (2011) reports that 50% of adolescents who live in the Global South are unable to attend secondary school, while millions live without adequate health provision (United Nations Children's Fund, 2011).

The work of the United Nations and most recently the Global Agenda offers renewed attention to children's concerns. Pope Francis has also brought the economic imbalance of the world into focus with his recognition that democracy and capitalism are not synonymous. In candid language, Pope Francis calls attention to the wealth of the few and the dangers of excluding so many from well-being, including children. The economist Emmanuel Sasz confirms that "one fifth of Americans receive food stamps, 50% of children born to single mothers live in poverty" (27 November, 2013, reported in www.theguardian.com.uk ["Pope Francis Understands Economics Better Than Most"]). There is much data generated by the Children's Defense Fund to confirm that when adults are unemployed and struggling, children bear the brunt in terms of food and housing insecurity (Children's Defense Fund, 2014).

Social work plays a pivotal role in evaluating and helping to create policies that are making a difference in the standards of child welfare throughout the world. One example of macro-level policy is the Global Agenda that stands to replace the Millennium Goals for 2015. (See Box 11.3, Chapter 11.) The agenda is the result of the International Federation of Social Workers (IFSW) collaboration with the International Association of Schools of Social Work (IASSW) and the International Council on Social Welfare (ICSW).The Global Agenda is generated in the context of the progress made in implementing the central international policy instrument for children.

This central policy framework for child well-being is the Convention on the Rights of the Child (CRC). The CRC was voted into law by the United Nations in 1989 and is now accepted by most countries of the world. Its 54 articles and seven clusters of focused legislation provide a template for action that guides many agencies and has advanced the agenda for children everywhere, rich and poor.

The Convention on the Rights of the Child

There have been many areas of progress in relation to children's welfare in the last 100 years. Eglantine Jebb (1929) first drafted legislation in England to take children out of mines, to promote literacy, and to generate a global charter for their education and welfare. Eventually, her work evolved into a policy statement on the Rights of the Child, championed at the newly formed United Nations by Eleanor Roosevelt in 1948. At the 40th anniversary of the declaration in 1989, the United Nations passed the full CRC.

The CRC binds those countries that sign and ratify it to accede to international law regarding child welfare. The United Nations itself acts as an oversight committee, and countries are required to report to the UN Committee on the Rights of the Child regarding the status of child welfare and the implementation of the specific guidelines.

So widely recognized was the need for such a document that the CRC quickly became the most broadly and rapidly ratified human rights treaty in history. Virtually every country—and even some nonstate entities—has signed and ratified the document.

Among the exceptions are Somalia, for lack of established government, and the United States for complex reasons to be discussed in this chapter.

The convention came into effect in 1990, followed later by two optional protocols:

i. Optional Protocol to the Convention on the Rights of the Child on the sale of children, child prostitution, and child pornography (United Nations, May 2000, entry into force January 18, 2002).

ii. Optional Protocol to the Convention on the Rights of the Child on the involvement of children in armed conflict (United Nations, May 2000, entry into force February 12, 2002) (United Nations, 2000).

Given the rate of the spread of technology and access to children of all ages through unprotected portals, it may also be time for a third protocol. At a presentation to the Executive Women International dinner in Des Moines, 2012, Officer Justin

Keller discussed the need for greater public awareness of child prostitution and "virtual" pornography (Keller, 2012). In a chilling demonstration of Internet pornography, Keller spoke of the strengthening of international cooperation, the importance of policy instruments, and the lack of understanding of "new" crimes and the increase in child trafficking that has occurred with the spread of imagery through the Internet, worldwide. Many aspects of conventions and protocols designed by the United Nations address such examples of issues that cross borders and are truly global in reach and therefore beyond the province of distinct nation states.

The CRC in Practice

There is little in the CRC that any reasonable person would find objectionable, yet implementing the CRC has proven to be thorny. The policy implications of the convention make so much sense that it is easy to understand the frustrations of officials and the greater public at the abuses that still occur. Part of the difficulty lies in the deeply seated roles of parents, communities, and culture in the matter of raising children. Parents feel that "they know best," but sometimes their approach is not in the best interests of the child. A prime example is when discipline and physical punishment are confused. Professionals in the school system in Mona, Jamaica, have published a book for children, using language that speaks directly to them (Jamaica Coalition on the Rights of the Child, 1995). The brightly illustrated text says that children should respect the discipline of their families, but sometimes adults punish in ways that hurt them and they should know that they are protected by rights. The rights are explained in clear, accessible terms for discussion in schools.

Another area of difficulty in traditional approaches to children lies in attitudes toward work and labor, and these difficulties will be discussed in the following pages. Despite these difficulties, history shows a gathering awareness of the potential impact of the CRC, especially for policy translated into practice for child welfare work. In this context, policy to practice includes the intentional translation of a policy into the framework, mission, and practice of an organization.

Finally, we need to confront another important element, which is to put a complex legislative document such as the CRC—and many others—into comprehensible terms that clearly and concisely point the way to create policy that is effective. There are ways that social workers can and should approach these complex documents to lead to policy action.

Systems Theory

Social workers find that systems theory has offered a perspective on practice that reminds us to think more expansively yet at the same time more effectively about child welfare. Four levels of interventions constitute a fully rounded approach:

1. *Micro-level* interventions that are related to children's day-to-day lives, to the details of their healthy development, and to their secure environment and trustworthy adult caregivers;

2. *Mezzo-level* interventions that relate to cultural and community surroundings that reinforce identity and safety;

3. *Macro-level* interventions that relate to larger national and international forces affecting children, including trafficking, migration, disaster, poverty, and war; and

4. *The Gaia-level* of global interdependence that recognizes that we are all interdependent in our daily lives, including our access to natural resources, clean water, nutritious food, clothes, minerals, coffee, teak, and tea.

Applying these four levels to our approach to the CRC ensures that we consider all of the opportunities and challenging aspects of children's lives, from local to global perspectives. For example, many children leave their families (the microenvironment), cross borders, join new communities of immigrants (mezzo-level), and become workers in clothing factories and involved in the manufacturing of a variety of goods destined for other countries (macro-level of global markets). They may well be patients suffering from elusive and borderless diseases such as severe acute respiratory syndrome (SARS), West Nile virus, measles, tuberculosis, Ebola, and malaria and will be vulnerable to the exploitation of adults. Polio, to name another example, was thought to have been virtually eradicated in the 20th century, only to reappear during the devastation of the civil war in Syria in 2014. Children and their caregivers benefit from the knowledge provided by organizations such as the United Nations and the World Health Organization, which constantly monitor disease outbreaks, such as polio and malaria (Gaia level of interdependence).

Partializing Complex Legislation

In addition to utilizing systems theory, another crucial skill in the arsenal of social workers throughout the world is the ability to partialize: to break down something complex (in this case, a complex piece of legislation) into something manageable, understandable, and practical. The Affordable Care Act (ACA) in the United States, for example, can be broken down into areas of insurer compliance, finance, patient protections (such as against preexisting conditions), and global cooperation for general good.

The political rhetoric surrounding the U.S. presidential campaign in 2012 is an interesting example of how badly the skill of partialization is needed for the majority of citizens. The "simplified" version of Obama's push for what became the ACA was one word: *Obamacare*. In a sense that oversimplification did more to obscure the program than it did to simplify it. However, if the ACA is not viewed as a political document but instead broken into manageable policy elements, it will facilitate the law being incorporated into policy for everyday life—even as the implications for implementation and funding (for example, funding for Medicaid), continue to be complex. Where the policy proves too complex, it will be reviewed through democratic processes. Meanwhile, the ACA is now a primary avenue for children to be covered by health insurance.

The CRC in Practice

Using the skill of partializing, the CRC can be broken into seven clusters that help create a road map toward practical implementation. The *first* is startling in its significance and simplicity: definition; *second*, the guiding principles; *third*, civil rights; *fourth*, family environment and care; *fifth*, health and welfare; *sixth*, education, leisure, and culture; and *seventh*, special protection, including measures of implementation. Let us examine the CRC in this way.

First Cluster of Articles: Definition

This first cluster is a direct statement and explanation of the definition of a child: anyone under the age of 18. In India, children may be betrothed from an early age, but the country is now recognizing 18 as the age of consent. In the United States, there are arguments in several individual states that children who have committed serious and violent crimes should be considered adults at 17, and the whole controversy has slowed the United States in fully ratifying the convention. In 2005, the Supreme Court of the United States took the following step:

> Bowing in part to world opinion, the U.S. Supreme Court abolished the juvenile death penalty in a ruling that immediately sparked controversy over whether the justices should listen to the views of foreign countries when interpreting the U.S. Constitution. (Waldmeir, 2005, p. 10)

There is still debate concerning the rights of individual states to decide when a child should be tried as a minor; however, the death penalty is no longer allowed in the United States for anyone under 18.

Despite slow progress in some places, this special status of childhood has resulted in a wide array of protections in policy and action to ensure children's access to education, safe environments, and health services across the world. For example, the city of Postoia in Northern Italy designated itself a "child-friendly city" with pedestrian-only streets, street art, education for adults about child development, and child nurseries that encourage fathers as well as mothers to participate in a variety of activities with their children. The United Nations is identifying child-friendly cities as a potentially powerful tool in addressing the nurturing and safe environments that children need in order to thrive. Similarly, in India near the city of Mysore, the Odanadi organization has designed a safe house with the help of children's ideas. The safe house and surrounding community shelter children recovering from being trafficked (www.odanadi.org). The staff members at Odanadi draw on the tenets of the CRC for their agency policy and practice. According to the website, American School Health Association (ASHA) for Education (2007), this organization runs a relentless campaign to rescue girls, most of them minors, from traffickers in India. Hundreds have been rescued and rehabilitated so far. The government of Karnataka is actively supporting this effort.

Second Cluster of Articles: Guiding Principles

Following the definition of childhood, guiding principles are laid out in the second cluster. These guiding principles are perhaps best articulated by Nelson Mandela at a speech in Johannesburg, in May 2000. "This global partnership will be guided in its work by the CRC, that luminous document that enshrines the rights of every child without exception to a life of dignity and self-fulfillment" (Mandela, 2000, p. 1). This includes the right to survival and to a healthy and safe development.

Southside Family Nurturing Center (SSFNC) is a "star" agency according to the Minnesota Children's Defense Fund. The center works with families to promote positive and peaceful parenting and safe environments for children. The families are referred by social workers in public roles as local county child protection workers. Second to school social work positions, child protection is a significant employer for the social work profession. Frequently offices of child protection are pressured by levels of referral and caught up in acutely difficult decisions whether to maintain a child in a troubled home or remove them to foster care. The public is a harsh audience, ready to blame professionals for leaving a child too long who is physically and emotionally harmed by a family member but also often criticizing social workers for removing children. The key tension for social workers is tolerating risk so that children are not removed from the family, culture, affection, and community that they know to a system that in itself can be damaging. An agency such as SSFNC assists in tolerating risk by supporting parents and children together, with day programs for

Source: ©iStockphoto.com/Kali9.

Young artists at work.

toddlers, preschool programs, parent evenings, family meals, and days when only Spanish is spoken (www.ssfnc.org).

In terms of social policy, the focus is often on parents, but it is also on agency workers and teachers. The professionals need to be sure-footed in their own knowledge and actions in their personal lives before they can be effective in their policy practice. The value of international policy perspectives lies in the reality that we see other countries addressing physical discipline and winning with more peaceful approaches, especially through their child advocates and offices of the ombudsman (Morten Wenstob, 2011).

As mentioned above, child protection is one of the largest areas of employment, next to school social work, in North America and Europe. Typically, child protection social workers are public employees, organized in teams and dispatched according to the nature of referral, from another professional such as a teacher or police officer, from relatives and neighbors, from community members and from the children themselves. In the United Kingdom there is a geographic patch system that dates back to the Seebohm Report, a 1970s research report that put the well-being of children in the hands of social workers according to their geographic area. It was an unrealistic attempt to ask social workers to be responsible for every child on their "patch" especially in economically deprived areas of large cities. In the United States it is well known that child protection workers are overworked and undervalued, and this reality reflects a society that is ambivalent about allocating adequate resources to families and children experiencing poverty.

How do social workers value the cultural and nurturing context of a child's home, while simultaneously balancing his or her chances of being physically harmed by a relative, boyfriend, or extended family member? The tolerance of risk and the family strengths perspective is controversial, but social workers have the benefit of research to build frameworks and ways of assessing risk and protective and strength factors to guide their interventions (Saleebey, 1992). This debate continues and the idea of the collective responsibility of a community for its children may be the only truly effective intervention. There is a small town in Slovenia, Postojna, where adults with histories of drug dependence and child abuse come together to work with seniors in their community. They eat together, tell stories together, and walk together in the interests of the whole community. This author (Link, 2004) heard one child talking about his experience of being part of this intergenerational project: "It used to feel as though my family only walked in the rain, it was always a struggle, but since being part of this group I feel safe and dry." At the family center at Fulford, Bristol, in England, families are encouraged to build networks and to let others know when they are exhausted and frustrated by their circumstances.

Children and Gun Deaths

At the opposite end of the development spectrum we have institutional groups that are sanctioned by society (in the United States, the National Rifle Association) despite preventing safe development and child welfare. In America, the Children's Defense Fund has identified which states are the worst for child death from handguns (California, Texas, and Florida), and their data reveal that over 3,000 children were killed by handguns in 2005 (Children's Defense Fund, 2008). Similarly, Gary Younge (2012) has identified America's "Deadly Devotion" to guns in his research:

- 31,025 handgun deaths in 2011
- 90 guns for every 100 Americans
- 85 shootings per day
- Concealed weapon legislation passed in several states
- 0 protections for children
- $300 million budget held by the National Rifle Association (NRA)
- 20 states in 2011 with Stand Your Ground laws

Furthermore, Younge (2012) notes the lack of progress in controlling gun sales even though numerous polls of the general public report support for such action. A fact of key significance, as this reporter indicates, is that of the four individuals identified by the NRA as obstacles to the cause of protecting gun rights, two are women and three are people of color—namely President Obama; Secretary of State Hillary Rodham Clinton; Eric Holder (African American Attorney General); and Sonia Sotomayor (Latina Supreme Court judge). The opposition tends to be aging white men.

Similarly aware of the impact on child welfare of the prevalence of public acts of violence, the researcher James Garbarino chronicled the devastating presence of guns in children's lives with his interviews of boys in prison (*Lost Boys*, 1999). The case histories are tough reading, with children witnessing and later perpetrating violence that scars their lives forever. The key principle of the CRC is the child's best interests, which includes policies that promote education and safety to grow in a nonviolent environment.

Source: ©iStockphoto.com/Kali9.

Education to join the U.S. gun culture begins early.

Third Cluster of Articles: Civil Rights

As indicated above, it is a child's right to not be sentenced to death for violent crime. It is also a child's right to be treated fairly and without physical harm. Physical discipline has been the subject of discussion among the Children's Ombudsman association of the European Union: "Striking a human being is prohibited in European society and children are, after all, human beings" (European Network of Ombudsman for Children, 2005). Children do not have the right to vote, but in many places they are asking for the right to be heard.

Children and Corporal Punishment

A key tension throughout the world involves the right of parents to discipline their children in their own way—which may include corporal (physical) punishment. Many, if not most, parents would resist having their choice of control taken away. But global norms are evolving. Since 2000 it has been illegal to strike a child in Sweden; for many years it has been illegal for teachers to beat or strike a child in school in Norway, Iceland, Australia, New Zealand, and the 27 countries (as of 2013) of the European Union; but it remains legal in the United States. Child protection is a great challenge as parents worldwide find it difficult to distinguish between physical punishment and discipline.

At the Shelter for Teens in Celje in Slovenia, a poster of the Convention on the Rights of the Child is the first thing you see upon entering. When visited by U.S. students, the staff explained their policies and their role modeling of conflict mediation. A visiting student asked if they actually used the CRC; the staff member's response was "of course, all the time." The workers at the center often have to mediate between parents and their children in order to gain some space for the work of reconciliation without physical retribution.

In Box 7.1 some of the reasons why it is so difficult to change cultural perceptions of physical punishment are identified. The content of Box 7.1 was generated by a group of students at Simpson College, Iowa, ages ranging from 20 to 38, including a student who is a parent and one who is a veteran.

BOX 7.1 CORPORAL PUNISHMENT: COLLEGE STUDENTS OFFER THEIR VIEWS

Reasons for supporting physical punishment

Parents know what works.

Parents know best.

Too much government involvement is not good for families.

Lack of solid research and prediction that "spanking" has a bad effect.

(Continued)

(Continued)

It demonstrates consequences.

It protects children, for example, from running across the road.

Reasons for rejecting physical punishment

Teachers can crack down on domestic child abuse if the law says it is wrong to hit a person, and therefore wrong to hit a child.

Is the parent rational when they hit?

When to hit and not to hit is hard to decide in the "heat of the moment."

Who has authority to punish?

There is a precedent of violence—if I hit a child, what message does it give him or her on the playground when he or she feels provoked?

There may be negative consequences.

Students contributing to a lively discussion, quoted with their permission:

Connor Black, Misty Boucher, Heather Eime, Austin Hennings, Jake Leonard, Steven Murtha, Zac Sjoberg, Erika Staska, Sarah Swisher, Dre Thomas, Cody Waddell, Stacey Williams, Taylor Van de Kroll, and Kat Vampola.

The research done by Taylor, Manganello, and Lee (2010) is persuasive in connecting children's risk for later aggressive behavior with physical punishment. In their analysis of longitudinal data from a large-scale study of parent's discipline of children in 20 large U.S. cities, these researchers found that kids who were spanked often at age 3 were twice as likely as those who were not spanked to develop aggressive behaviors such as getting into fights, destroying things, or being mean to others at age 5. The significance of this study in comparison with others that obtained similar results is that the researchers were able to control for confounding variables such as maternal substance use, major depression, severe stress, and demographic features. Although this study does not prove that the physical punishment of small children causes aggression, it does reveal a significant link that remains when other possible explanations are excluded. These empirically based research findings are widely cited in the academic literature on childhood development and in media reports on physical punishment of children.

Although public and media attention is most often focused on the micro-level, or family level, there is also the prevalence of violence in institutions such as schools and juvenile

Source: ©iStockphoto.com/laartist.

Assault of another adult is against the law, but an assault on a child is often considered discipline.

detention centers. It is shocking to the students who contributed to the information provided in Box 7.1 that the Department of Education released data in 2012 confirming that, "according to conservative reporting 223,190 students were the victims of institutionalized violence at least once in the 2006 to 2007 school year, of which over 20,000 sought medical attention" (Office for Civil Rights at the U.S. Department of Education, 2010).

Although many countries have outlawed physical punishment in schools, there are still many examples of a breakdown in discipline and the use of violent punishment administered by teachers. In part, the use of physical punishment also reflects a country's larger systems, including gun violence and lack of policy and public voice to curb virtual and actual demonstrations of aggression.

Physical punishment of children can be considered a form of child abuse (Scott & Ward, 2007). The cases that come to the attention of the child welfare and criminal justice authorities are of the most severe variety, often correlated with alcohol and drug abuse and other family violence. Box 7.2 provides the latest statistics available on official reports of cases of child abuse and neglect in the United States.

BOX 7.2 CHILD MALTREATMENT IN THE UNITED STATES, 2013

Facts at a Glance

The following data are retrieved from the Administration for Children and Families (ACF). ACF is a division of the Department of Health & Human Services. Reports are submitted voluntarily by the states based on substantiated cases of neglect and abuse.

Of the Total Number of Reported Cases of Maltreatment

78% suffered neglect,

18.3% experienced physical abuse,

9.3% experienced sexual abuse,

Male victims constituted 48.7% of the total, and

53.5% of the perpetrators were female.

(Continued)

(Continued)

Racial/Ethnic Breakdown

44% white

21.8% Hispanic

21% African American

1.2% Native American

.8% Asian

4.1% of multiple race

Child Fatalities

1,640 children died in 2012; of these 70% were under 3.

69.9% involved situations of neglect.

38.3% were white.

31.9% were African American.

15.3% were Hispanic.

80% involved one or both parents.

8.5% had received services within the past 5 years.

Source: U.S. Department of Health and Human Services (2013).

Note: In evaluating the racial/ethnic backgrounds of the victims, one should consider that in the under-5 age group, the majority of children are minorities.

Fourth Cluster of Articles: Family Environment and Care

Central to the welfare of children is the protection of their rights within the family. Several key rights are spelled out in this cluster. Children are to be guaranteed the right to be protected physically and provided shelter; the right to be consulted when families separate or divorce; the right to know about their birth families and cultural identities; and the right not to be abandoned, sold, or trafficked.

Additional rights include access to immunizations (to be discussed in the section on health) and the right not to be exploited or used by adults—such as in everyday adult situations. An example of this is when immigrant clients bring their children to serve as translators. This role reversal places undue responsibility and stress, particularly on the very young child, and is a violation of care (Segal, 2012).

Adoption is the most prevalent way that children lose their birth families and cultural identities. International adoptions surged in the 1990s in the United States. Rotabi describes this "quiet migration," which often begins when the biological parents are impoverished and are tempted to give their children up for money (Rotabi, 2012). Child theft has increased in Central America, and the history of adoptions clearly demonstrates transfer of interest from one country to another, according to economic and political situations. After the fall of the Romanian dictator Ceausescu, there was a surge in international adoptions; similarly, after the tension between North and South Korea many children were adopted into U.S. families. The Hague Convention on International Adoptions is an expansion of children's rights to protect their own identities and families and is impacting the practices of every agency that assists in the processing of adoptions.

The right of children to be physically protected continues to be controversial. The traditions of physical punishment were discussed earlier in this chapter and have prompted new policies in agencies involved with children. Another key example of the need for protection continues to be access to guns and weapons. In the United States, for example, research demonstrates that when families are involved in gun violence, children are often at the dangerous end. The Children's Defense Fund has asked us to note the number of laws that control the use of car seats for infants in the United States (no baby should be facing forward in the front seat; place babies in the rear seat until a certain age, height, weight, etc.). They note the number of laws protecting children from guns: zero (Children's Defense Fund, 2008).

A third aspect of family environment involves separation and divorce. The divorce rates vary internationally from culture to culture with the highest rates in the Western Hemisphere and the lowest in smaller, homogenous communities, such as Japan. See Table 7.1.

As divorce rates vary widely throughout the world, so do the repercussions for children in terms of their housing, schooling, sibling relationships, and feelings of security versus loss. In Slovenia, the family centers established during the 1990s are required to meet with children of parents planning to divorce. Children are given separate advocates for their needs, and the country supports the ombudsman movement

Table 7.1   Divorce Rates in Selected Countries

The following are divorce rates in selected countries:

- In 2010, divorce rates increased by 5% over 2009 in England and Wales.
- Thirty percent of marriages end in divorce in Italy.
- In China, the state-run post office began offering couples a service where love letters they wrote to each other at the time would be sent 7 years later.
- Forty-eight percent of parents split by their children's 16th birthday in England.
- Russia had the highest divorce rate in the world in 2008.

Source: unstats.un.org/unsd/demographic.

in Europe to encourage parents to think of the developmental needs of their children, not just at the point the divorce is happening.

Another aspect of family environment is the focus on the child's need to be protected from being abandoned or trafficked. It is an extreme situation when children either leave home due to abuse and conflict or are sold for profit by "family" members. In 2013, the state of Minnesota revealed shocking evidence that active groups of child traffickers were coming into the state from Chicago and the internal "sea port" of Duluth (Leinen, 2013). Laws surrounding prostitution and trafficking are a complex mix of local and international statutes, and there is much work to do to tackle the human misery involved.

Fifth Cluster of Articles: Health and Welfare

One key source of research indicating child health and welfare is the UNICEF report titled "State of the World's Children." A major concern is the absolute poverty of many children in the Global South, with "almost half the children unable to attend school" in developing countries and millions without access to immunizations and basic health care (United Nations Children's Fund, 2011).

Poverty and the Health of Children

One of the most significant factors in the health and welfare of children is the income level of their parent(s). Unlike countries of the European Union that have widespread antipoverty measures (such as children's allowances), recognition that the roots of poverty are structural has not taken hold in the United States. The dominating theme that continues in the first decade of the 21st century is economic independence and opportunity for the individual: opportunity to be both rich and poor. It is very clear what the message is concerning the current legislation: This policy is a "tough but fair solution to dependency" (Department of Health Services, 1997). As stated in a brochure from the Minnesota Family Investment Program, "The intent of MFIP is to help you find work as soon as possible. Most families can only stay on MFIP for 60 months. So it is important that you act quickly to become self-sufficient" (DHS, 1997). The emphasis is on promoting individual responsibility and curtailing the negative behaviors of the assumed majority of people in poverty.

Fast-forward from the harsh policies of the 1990s in relation to "welfare reform" in the United States to 2015, and it seems as though social work is losing ground in its professional role of advocacy for the poor. In the state of

Source: ©iStockphoto.com/EricVega.

Many children grow up in poverty in rural Appalachia.

Florida, drug tests were introduced to prevent people from receiving assistance who did not "deserve" it due to their drug addictions. The implication was that people in poverty are more likely to exploit the system and be addicted to drugs than those in higher socioeconomic categories. The law was "ushered in amid promises that it would save taxpayers money and deter drug users" according to an article in the *New York Times* (Alvarez, 2012, p. A14). Actually, follow-up research showed that few of the welfare recipients were using illicit drugs, and there was no direct savings to the state, as people continued to apply for benefits. Several other states, unfortunately, are following Florida's lead to institute punitive policies against mothers and others receiving welfare aid.

In many countries of the Western world, including Europe and the United States, in recent years, the national rates of poverty rose as unemployment increased and the economic depression of 2008 gained hold for more than 4 years. For example, the U.S. Federal Income Guidelines below tell the story. The recent economic crisis, according to Appelbaum (2012), left the median American family in 2010 with no more wealth than in the early 1990s. The crash in housing prices accounted for a major loss in the wealth of the nation's families.

Although wealthier families have more assets to endure downturns in the economy, they too are affected. It is always the poorest groups who suffer the most, however, without any cushion or reserves when they run out of essentials. In an interview for the *Observer*, United Kingdom, the former Children's Minister, Sarah Teather (Helm, 2012) spoke out against the proposed 500-pound weekly cap on family benefits as "deeply socially divisive." This policy, she said, will have devastating effects on many families who are forced to be uprooted from their homes. This policy is a denigration of those who cannot find work and based on an unfair demonization of the poor. According to the *Observer*,

> Teather believes the effects may only sink in when children from "nice middle-class families who send their kids to the local primary school come home and say 'my friend has just disappeared.' I think then it might hit home and they might realise a whole set of children have disappeared from the class." (Helm, 2012)

When families are under strain, it means that relationships are also stressed. Following reports from emergency rooms and social workers that child abuse is on the rise during recessions, Dr. Rachel Berger studied 422 American children "mostly from lower-income families, known to face greater risks for being abused" (Tanner, 2011). The study found a 65% increase specifically in "abusive head trauma" and tracked the rates of poverty in the counties where the children lived. Unemployment rates in the 74 counties where the children lived had risen significantly and the proportion of children on Medicaid also increased, although it was high before. As stated in the article,

> Combine the stress of raising a young child with wage cuts or lost jobs and you get a "sort of toxic brew in terms of thinking about possible physical violence," said Mark Rank, a social welfare professor at Washington University, St. Louis. (Tanner, 2011)

The Effects of Budget Cutbacks

At times, it seems that Lyndon Johnson's War on Poverty has turned cruelly into a war on the impoverished. Cries for "smaller government" and "lower taxes" have led to significant cuts in budgets for care agencies. Take the SSFNC in Minneapolis, for example. This agency plays a crucial role in helping families learn constructive alternatives to physical discipline and provides valuable support in their efforts to find work and improve their socioeconomic circumstances. Although being recognized as a "gold star" agency by the Children's Defense Fund, the funding for SSFNC has been cut by a third, particularly in its public funding by Hennepin County Child Protective Services. Politicizing those in poverty—assuming that people who do not work are lazy or "takers"—seemed to gain momentum in the negative ad campaigns during the 2012 election and continues in some parts of the media, with scant attention to the consequences of harsh family policy for children. Handler (1995) notes, "To frame welfare reform policy in terms of moving recipients from welfare to the paid labor force is to fail to define the problem" (p. 6). When the blame is laid on those in poverty, questions do not have to be addressed concerning who those in poverty are, and why and what their needs are. Back in 1995, Handler made utterly clear warnings: "If welfare officials get too tough on mothers, state and local governments will have to pick up the pieces—more impoverishment, more need for health care, more broken homes, more children in foster care" (p. 8). This was prescient: From 2012 to 2013 in Minneapolis, the United States, London, the United Kingdom, and many inner cities in the Western world saw increasing homelessness and fragility of family life for children in poverty.

At the same time, the resources enjoyed by able-bodied middle-class homemakers has been untouched; they continue to receive "fiscal welfare" in terms of tax deductions for their dependents and their mortgages, without social stigma. Similarly to Teather in 2012, Handler (1995) suggested that "welfare policy is not addressed to the poor—it is addressed to the employed and wealthy. It is an affirmation of majoritarian values through the creation of deviants. . . . The poor are held hostage to make sure the rest of us behave" (p. 7). One illustration of this idea is that the able-bodied middle class who stay at home to raise their children or who are self-employed continue to receive "fiscal welfare" in terms of tax deductions for their dependents and their mortgages, without social stigma. However, for children there is no choice in terms of social status and enough attention has not been paid to the consequences of the harsher elements of welfare reform, including time limits, caps, sanctions, lack of support for parental education, and lack of affordable housing, on young lives. These early years of life are a period of great vulnerability. Without adequate nutrition and nurturing, many children will suffer delayed or stunted growth, impaired intellectual development, unresponsiveness, and low resistance to infection.

At a speech at the Council on Social Education Annual Program Meeting, Tiong Tan (2012) lamented that the gap between income levels of the richest and poorest families in China and Singapore, the "Genie Index," is widening but not to the extent it exists in the United States (Tan, 2012). While the United States has one of the most productive economies in the world, the gap between rich and poor is the widest in the world. When considering the issue of young mothers in poverty, there is a complex mixture of relative values and moral confusion. For example, it is well documented in relation to child poverty that it is economically hazardous for parents, mostly women,

Table 7.2   2014 Poverty Guidelines

One Version of the [U.S.] Federal Poverty Measure

The following figures are the 2014 Health and Human Services (HHS) poverty guidelines issued by the federal government. They indicate how much an individual or family could earn in 2014 in order to qualify for certain social service benefits such as food stamps. Many states require that the applicants be below the poverty level.

2014 Poverty Guidelines for the 48 Contiguous States and the District of Columbia	
Persons in Family/Household	**Poverty Guideline**
For families/households with more than 8 persons, add $4,060 for each additional person.	
1	$11,670
2	$15,730
3	$19,790
4	$23,850
5	$27,910
6	$31,970
7	$36,030
8	$40,090

Source: U.S. Department of Health and Human Services (2014).

to raise children under 5 years of age alone. Being a lone parent is hazardous because if parents stay at home to care for their children themselves, they have no access to income, or if employed, they are likely to be in part-time or low-income work.

In countries of the European Union, such as Sweden, Norway, and Italy, the emphasis on social policy is progressive, focusing on child allowance, family services, day care provision, and the overall well-being of the child. This is in marked contrast to the outlook in the United States.

To learn about a society that provides a progressive social welfare model for meeting the needs of families and children now and in the future (planning for sustainability), read Box 7.3. As you read this overview of the social services in South Korea, a nation to which the United States is closely linked in several ways—militarily, economically, and educationally—consider the cultural context, homogeneity of the population, and the economic situation.

BOX 7.3 WELFARE SYSTEM IN SOUTH KOREA: FAMILY POLICIES

Hyejoon Park, MSW, EdM

In order to improve the well-being and welfare of South Koreans, the Ministry of Health and Welfare was established in 1948. The department has been developing social policies and services to improve the quality of life, to assist in national development, as well as to protect people from social risks. The core policies and relevant services are the following: *social health policies* through reforming national pension, national health insurance fund, and enhancing the quality life for people with disabilities; *family policies* through reconstructing child care services, fostering children and youth health systems, and long-term care insurance for the elderly; *public health policies* by establishing a health care safety net, increasing health care benefits and food safety management; and *welfare policies* by fostering the health care industry and creating work in welfare services (see Ministry of Health & Welfare, 2013a).

Family Policies: Childbirth Promotion Policy

The low birth rate in South Korea has been a serious issue since 2005. In 2005, the fertility rate was around 1.08. The Korean government has begun to consider it a nationwide systematic problem along with the aging population and enacted the *Framework Act on Fertility and Population Policy* in the same year. The policy covers three areas, creating a childbirth and child care friendly environment, laying the groundwork for improving living standards in an aged society, and securing the growth engine and enhancing policies (see Ministry of Health & Welfare, 2013b). In fact, South Korea has the lowest birth rate of the rest of members of the Organisation for Economic Co-operation and Development (OECD) (World Health Organization, 2011).

The major areas that the policy emphasizes are balance of work and family commitments, alleviating the burden of marriage, childbirth, and child care, and creating a safe environment to raise children. The detailed services for the areas are as follows: First, implementing a *parental leave system,* as well as *reducing working hours* for parents during the child care period. This will enable working parents to raise their children and decrease the likelihood of career interruption. Second, enhancing *in-company child care facilities* will secure a high-quality workforce. Third, reducing financial burden by offering benefits such as *housing loan support, tax incentives for families with multiple children*, and expanding the *eligibility for child care support* and *raising child care allowance,* will encourage marriages and childbirth (Ministry of Health & Welfare, 2013c). In regard to parental leave, working women are allowed to have 90 days (more than 45 days immediately after a birth) for maternity leave. They are also allowed a certain number of paid days of following childbirth (see Ministry of

Health and Welfare, 2014). In addition to that, 5 days of paternal leave are also allotted for fathers (see Ministry of Health and Welfare, 2014).

Among the social policies mentioned above, parental leave and in-company child care facilities are major measures taken in order to support working parents. However, there are some doubts raised when it comes to the effectiveness of these policies in reality. Since the 1960s, during South Korea's economic boom, working mothers in particular have been a significant factor contributing to economic development. Since the 1990s, in order to assist such working women, the government has tried to address effective social policies to assist them in balancing their jobs and housework. The government also took some steps forward for gender equality and women's rights during this time (Sung, 2003).

Implementing policies for working women and observing the effectiveness of services and programs for women, however, are problematic. Confucian ideology has been deeply rooted in an emphasis on women's traditional roles, especially domestic roles for women in Korean society. Korea, in fact, has maintained a patriarchal system of rigid gender relations for more than 2 millenniums. Nowadays, Korean society does not follow Confucianism as much as it did in the past. There have been remarkable improvement opportunities for equality between men and women in society. However, working mothers still face many difficulties in paid employment and parental leave. First, compared with 5 days of paternal leave, 90 days of maternal leave implies that contemporary Korean society still asks more responsibility from childrearing women than men. Second, the amount of maternity pay is far below women's normal earnings, so working mothers are often hesitant to take advantage of maternity leave as this can cause financial strife for families. Third, only a few workplaces in the manufacturing industry allow parental leave to employees or offer the benefits only to full-time workers. Considering the fact that many working Korean women are only employed part-time, it is questionable whether or not all working women utilize the benefits for their well-being (Sung, 2003).

In order to help married women retain their jobs, some Korean companies have established in-company child care facilities for children between 2 months and 6 years old. The government provides a certain amount of compensation for workplaces that build nursery spaces within the building when the company has more than 300 female workers (Sung, 2003). However, in practice, only a few companies equip child care spaces in their buildings to support employed mothers (0.96%) (see Korea Institute of Child Care and Education, 2013). Since the regulation to build child care settings in the company is not compulsory, and it works only for big companies who hire many women, it is very doubtful a woman employed will be able to utilize these facilities (Sung, 2003).

Despite the noticeable problems that occurred when implementing policies and services for working parents, Korean society has been moving in a positive

(Continued)

(Continued)

direction. These changes especially benefit employed mothers who face hardships balancing work and child care. Another piece of child care legislation implemented in March 2013 was providing a certain amount of subsidies to parents who either raise children by themselves or who send their children ages between 0 and 5 years to child care or preschool regardless of family household income or social economic status. For example, a parent whose child is between 0 and 2 years old will receive an average of 340,000 Korean won ($311) per month for sending his or her child to a child care center. On the other hand, parents who take care of their child at home will receive an average of 150,000 Korean won ($137) every month if their child is between 0 and 3 years old. The significant change in child care subsidies compared to the past is that parents who took care of their children between ages 3 and 5 years old at home had not received any benefits from the government before; however, they will now receive 100,000 won ($91) every month until the children attend elementary school (see Ministry of Health and Welfare, 2013a). The intention of current child care policy is to lessen the economic burden of child care on working mothers, to help working mothers balance workload and childrearing, as well as to encourage an increase in birth rate.

References

Korea Institute of Child Care and Education. (2013). 유아교육. 보육주요통계 [Statistics for child care and education]. (May 31, 2011). Retrieved from www.kicce.re.kr/kor/pub lication/04_04.jsp?mode=view&idx=3468&startPage=0&listNo=87&code=etc04& search_item=&search_order=&order_list=10&list_scale=10&view_level=0

Ministry of Health & Welfare. (2013a). 영유아보육료 및 양육비 지원사업 [social services for child care subsidies and childrearing allowances]. Retrieved from www .mw.go.kr/front_new/sch/index.jsp?coll=ALL&query=%BA%B8%C0%B0%B7%E1%2C +%BE%E7%C0%B0%BC%F6%B4%E7+%C1%F6%BF%F8

Ministry of Health & Welfare. (2013b). *The First Basic Plan*. Retrieved from http:// english.mw.go.kr/front_eng/jc/sjc0108mn.jsp?PAR_MENU_ID=100313&MENU_ ID=1003130201

Ministry of Health & Welfare. (2013c). *The Second Basic Plan*. Retrieved from http:// english.mw.go.kr/front_eng/jc/sjc0108mn.jsp?PAR_MENU_ID=100313&MENU_ ID=1003130303

Ministry of Health & Welfare. (2014). 복지와 고용, 보건, 주거, 교육에 관련한 최 신 뉴스를 알려드립니다. Retrieved from www.bokjiro.go.kr/news/allNewsView .do?board_sid=308&data_sid=6293098

Organisation for Economic Co-operation and Development. (2013). Fertility. Retrieved from www.oecd.org/statistics/

Sung, S. (2003). Women reconciling paid and unpaid work in Confucian welfare state: The case of South Korea. *Social Policy & Administration, 37*(4), 342–360.

Source: Printed with permission of Hyejoon Park, PhD candidate, School of Social Work, University of Illinois, Urbana-Champagne.

Worldwide, UNICEF demonstrates that children in the Global North, do better in terms of infant mortality, access to health care, low teen pregnancy rates, and literacy than children in the United States. Social policy is powerful and where legislators pay attention to the CRC, children benefit. Children in the Global South continue to struggle. Where there are increases in literacy, for example, we can examine the areas in question and see the direct impact of changing policy and practice. In Kerala, in Southern India, there is attention to the schooling of girls, and the literacy rate has climbed.

Another serious challenge for the well-being of children is armed conflict. Not only are boys recruited and kidnapped to be soldiers, but almost half of the 300,000 children involved in wars are girls; they are abducted, raped, and often used as currency among fighters. These facts are contained in a report from Save the Children (Sengupta, 2005). In a powerful summary titled "Girl Soldiers: The Forgotten Victims of war" Kim Sengupta (2005) describes the fate of such girls:

> They are far more out of the reach of the international agencies than boy soldiers under 18, and are wary of joining rehabilitation schemes because of fear that it will expose what had happened to them and lead to further shunning by their home communities.

Countries affected by such civil unrest and exploitation of minors include Pakistan, Syria, Uganda, the Democratic Republic of Congo, and Colombia.

Amnesty International has also been focused on the abuse of children in their report "Hidden Scandal, Secret Shame Torture and Ill-Treatment of Children," especially in war torn regions; it lays out the framework of the CRC as it explores current realities and makes policy recommendations (Amnesty International, 2000). The book comes with its own warning: "Please note that readers may find some of the photographs and case histories contained in this report disturbing" (Amnesty International, 2000, p. 1). The report reviews torture during armed conflict and the plight of displaced children, torture at the hands of border guards and police, torture during detention including children held with adults (referred to earlier in terms of the death sentence), and corporal punishment of children by adults.

Despite stark and awful images, including a policeman wielding a baton to strike a child searching for food in Mumbai, there are also aspects of hopefulness: The "children of the peace community of San Jose de Apartado, Colombia" have declared themselves a peace community and their "Zona Neutral" is protected by posters of the CRC (Amnesty International, 2000, p. 3).

The report is powerful in terms of its juxtaposition of witness, report, and action. Recommendations from Amnesty International begin with a true implementation of the CRC and include specific emphasis on the rights of the child to be protected from institutional violence, for example, perpetrated by police forces in some countries.

Sixth Cluster of Articles: Education, Leisure, Play, and Culture

The CRC has highlighted the expectations we have for education—but many children are out of school for a variety of reasons. UNICEF (United Nations Children's Fund, 2014) reports that "in 2013, almost 30 million children were out of school due to armed conflict." The most recent Optional Protocol for the CRC refers to the requirement that children be protected from armed conflict.

In a video from the Swaminathan Research Foundation titled "Every Child a Scientist," there is vivid description of the movement in India to educate children about clean water and sustainable environments. Children are invited to identify the cycle of water and its relationship to health and well-being in their own communities. They are also encouraged to think of themselves as "scientists" who have the power to improve access to safe drinking water for their villages and families.

THINKING SUSTAINABLY

One of the most daunting elements about environmental degradation is that it seems beyond an individual to effect any real change. Yet we are reminded that the longest journey begins with a single step, and we are all asked to think of ways to live a more sustainable life.

The educational initiative in India to educate children about sustainability is one such way. Encouraging children to think of themselves as scientists is an empowering act that also underscores our own individual responsibility for taking care of our planet. What are some other ways to achieve this? Consider this question as it applies to individuals, families, schools, and communities. In what ways do you imagine thinking sustainably affects one's self-image?

Gender and School Attendance

There is a distinct gender disparity in who attends school. Girls are often kept at home for household chores and for every 100 boys not in primary school there are 117 girls not at primary school. The millennium goal (that by 2015 all children will have the opportunity to complete primary school) has meant more attention to this disparity, but there is much to do. As mentioned in the opening of this chapter, there are many innovative policies coming into place to encourage children to attend school. One is the effort to provide sanitary supplies for girls during their menses so that this natural and healthy aspect of their lives does not prevent access to education.

The United States has many of the resources girls need to attend school, including transport, immunizations, meals, and sanitary supplies, yet the United States struggles with retention and high school graduation. In a recent report for *USA Today*, Lynch (2008) suggests that "the USA could learn from South Korean Schools" (p. 1). It is reported that

> In South Korea 93% of all students graduate from high school on time. But in the United States, almost one-quarter of all students—more than 1.2 million individuals each year—fail to graduate. Once the world leader in secondary school education, the United States now ranks 18th among 36 nations examined by the Organisation for Economic Co-operation and Development.

Seventh Cluster of Articles: Special Protections and Measures of Implementation

This cluster of articles speaks to the rights of children in extraordinary situations: emergency situations such as war or becoming refugees, becoming involved in the juvenile justice system, or situations of exploitation. Fundamental rights such as being presumed innocent and the right to refrain from serving in a war until 15 years of age are included, but the rights to clear language regarding how to help children recover from abuses or how to rehabilitate if involved in crime are also included.

If children are to benefit from international policy, the notion of "special protection" has to be implemented in grassroots and practical ways. Earlier in the chapter we mentioned the movement to create a "child-friendly city" in Postoia, Italy. In the city of Ljubljana, there was a pilot project named *Child's Advocate—Voice of the Child* (Office of the Human Rights Ombudsman, 2007–2008). In the Nigerian village of Ogborodo, mothers and children are challenging and standing up to the oil giant Chevron in peaceful protest. An editorial in the *Japan Times* (2008) refers to the "responsibility to protect children" as the numbers of child abuse reports increase: "The number has been rising for 18 straight years" (*Japan Times*, 2008, p. 2).

Toward a Future of Well-Being for Children

At a 2012 conference of professional social workers, educators and students interested in global citizenship, the discussion turned from legislation and policy to their own commitments for practice (Link, 2012). The participants generated a wall of ideas about "actions for children going forward" and the list is inspiring:

Wall Writers for Children:

- I will write about Children's Rights in our local paper.
- I will research Child Sex Trafficking, no one knows.
- I will create opportunities for children to be happy—include clowns and Halloween and child-friendly places.
- I will challenge myself to become better informed.
- I will have more conversations with the kids who come to my agency with their parents.
- "I will continue to raise awareness regarding malaria across the globe, which takes the life of a child every 60 seconds."
- Children's issues are embedded in larger social problems such as war and poverty.
- I will teach children how to learn.
- I will break the silence of the trafficking of children throughout the world. We must end the SILENCE to end the VIOLENCE.
- We will challenge ourselves to learn more about child development.
- I will use technology innovation to create an APP to assist parents to foster and to develop child-friendly and safe environments.
- I will work to hold political candidates in the upcoming elections responsible to articulate specific ways they will work on children's issues.

- I will work every day to capture and to celebrate the spirit of the children in my community.
- I will share more of my values and heritage with grandchildren.
- I will continue to sign petitions to stop the death penalty, child sex trafficking, and encourage efforts to reduce poverty.
- I will help re-elect politicians supportive of an educational and social agenda.
- I will continue to work on and research arms trafficking from the United States and world war zones that so often end up in the hands of children.
- I will cocreate solutions with children in school.
- I will increase awareness in self and others about children's issues.
- I will teach my students about the CRC and raise awareness and commitment to specific action.
- I will lobby actively against the repeal of the Affordable Health Care Act.
- I will listen to the voices NOT heard.
- I will re-affirm the importance of play at every age.
- I will make others aware of the state of children's rights and the work we still have to do.
- I will focus on listening to children's views.
- I will be present and listen deeply to children.
- I will empathize, practice alternatives, and get involved at the macro-level.
- I will commit to understanding when a child says "no" and why
- I will provide dignity for institutionalized children.
- My continued action for children is to support the healthy development and flourishing of youth in my work.
- I will understand that "being with" is just as important as doing.
- My action for children, specifically girls, is to support them and to honor and appreciate their menses and thereby their bodies. When girls and women are empowered to appreciate their menses and their bodies, boys and men are also empowered and learn to respect and to appreciate the feminine energy.

Throughout the world there are innovative practices and good things happening in the lives of children. Amrita Patel, the courageous director of Operation Flood and managing director of the National Dairy Development Board in India, speaks in a similar way to the last wall writer. Patel tells the story of bringing milk to all children and profits to the mothers who are often in charge of the animal husbandry but at the mercy of middlemen negotiating the market trade. Patel speaks directly to the men in the audience, thanking them for their presence and their encouragement of the women in their lives and telling them how important men are in achieving change:

The values, attitudes and beliefs to which you give expression both in word and deed will undoubtedly have a far greater influence on your peers than most others in yours and related fields. We all know that the development of the dairy industry, and the development of nations, depends greatly on that half of the population often referred to as the weaker sex . . . by the respect you show to your women colleagues, students and farmers, you can make the crucial difference that matters. (Patel, 1998, p. 15)

Patel also asks men to imagine themselves "standing shoulder to shoulder" with women. While some men may be reluctant to give up their perceived power, sufficient men are now motivated to participate in events such as the groundbreaking Second Pan Commonwealth Veterinary Conference, where the role of women was center stage (Patel, 1998). Similarly, women are taking leadership roles worldwide:

Ellen Johnson, Sirlee, Prime Minister of Liberia

Aung San Suu Kyi, Democratic Party leader in Burma (Myanmar)

Hillary Clinton, U.S. Ambassador from 2008 to 2013

Melanne Vermeer, the U.S. Ambassador for Global Women's Issues

Quentin Bryce, Governor General, Australia

Angela Merkel, Chancellor of Germany

Marion Wright Edelman, Director Children's Defense Fund

Julia Gillard, Prime Minister of Australia

Joyce Banda, President of Malawi

Many of these women are holding these roles for the first time in history. Certainly there are many famous women in our collective past: Cleopatra, Queen Elizabeth I, Indira Gandhi (Prime Minister of India, assassinated), Mother Teresa, Harriet Tubman and many, many more, but they were in isolation in political systems dominated by men. Now, in the 21st century, more women are holding top leadership roles in their countries and regions, and consequently they have the capacity to reinforce each other's work in their concern for issues of poverty, women's pay, and the welfare of children throughout the world. Melanne Vermeer, the U.S. Ambassador for Global Women's Issues is one such woman in a new global role, well supported by top leaders such as Angela Merkel and Hillary Clinton. These women are "exemplifying what it means to stand up for women and girls" (Rolfes, 2013).

Spurred perhaps by the increased engagement of powerful women worldwide, some progress is seen in terms of girls' attendance at school and in programs to assist women and girls in receiving fair remuneration for their existing work. Similarly, there are communities that are dedicating themselves to eradicating child abuse and promoting their well-being within families that are resourceful in practicing peaceful discipline and age-appropriate communication (Southside Family Nurturing Center, n.d.). People working in child protection in the United States may not experience any downturn in their caseloads while the country emerges from the long recession (from 2008 to 2013). There are indicators, however, that physical abuse is not tolerated by the public; evidence of abuse is now challenged in schools and hospitals and has no place in the lives of young people in the 21st century.

Summary and Conclusion

Signs of progress are sources of energy but cannot be exaggerated. There is still much to be achieved in both policy and practice to ensure that children, indeed, have their rights and well-being honored. In the early days of the CRC, UNICEF stated the following:

> The Convention has produced a profound change that is already beginning to have substantive effects on the world's attitude towards its children. Once a country ratifies, it is obliged in law to undertake all appropriate measures to assist parents and other responsible parties in fulfilling their obligations to children. (United Nations Children's Fund, 1997, p. 10)

In the *Handbook of International Social Work* (Healy & Link, 2012) and an earlier book by Healy (2008), a distinction has been made between child labor, which is defined as "children working in conditions that are excessively abusive and exploitive" (quoted in Healy, 2008, p. 92), and child work, which is legitimate employment that helps support families and does not interfere with education. Furthermore, Kristen Ferguson (2012), points out that child employment cannot be eliminated entirely due to the economic pressures on families. It is counterproductive to suddenly remove opportunities for children to work if it plunges them into conditions of hunger and vulnerability. Instead, Ferguson argues for clear policies on hours that children may work, employment protections, and full access to education.

In 2004, the Children's World Congress on Child Labor was held in Italy. It "put children at the heart of the Congress advocating for the abolition of exploitive labour and national implementation of the CRC" (Leonard, 2004, p. 45). The views of children become a crucial way for adults to fully understand the impact that removing opportunities has on children's lives.

Finally, the challenge is now present that all social workers are party to the commitment to spread information about the CRC across all communities and to fulfill their professional obligation to implement the full intent of the convention. As stated in the last cluster of articles in the CRC:

> States Parties undertake to make the principles and provisions of the Convention widely known, by appropriate and active means, to adults and children alike. For the purpose of examining the progress made by States Parties in achieving the realization of the obligations undertaken in the present Convention, there shall be established a Committee on the Rights of the Child, which shall carry out the functions hereinafter provided. (United Nations Convention on the Rights of the Child, 1990)

As stated by Nelson Mandela (2000), the CRC is indeed a "luminous document," which if adequately implemented would lead all children to lives of dignity and fulfillment.

Critical Thinking Questions

1. What is the Convention on the Rights of the Child (CRC) about?

2. How is the CRC useful as a policy instrument to the practice of social work?

3. How do the millennium goals relate to children?

4. Why is there a different rate of participation in school for girls and boys?

5. What are some policies that might improve participation in school by girls?

6. What is meant by a child-friendly city?

7. In child protection work, there is frequent reference to the toleration of risk: What does this mean?

8. Why is the death by handgun rate so much lower in Canada than the United States?

9. What might be some of the "risk" and "protective" factors that are identified in order to assess the safety of a child at home?

10. Give an example of a policy toward children in a different country than your country of origin: How does it differ from your local policies?

11. What is the work of the Children's Ombudsman?

12. When we say there is a difference between punishment and discipline, what does that mean?

13. What aspects of the CRC are most useful to social work practice?

14. How does UNICEF serve children? Identify one policy that it is currently involved in developing.

15. What is meant by the distinction made between personal and institutionalized violence?

16. How do you distinguish child labor and child work?

17. Why are child protection workers often criticized by the general public despite the difficulty of their job?

References

Alvarez, L. (2012, April 18). No savings found in Florida welfare drug tests. *New York Times*, p. A14.

Amnesty International. (2000). *Hidden scandal, secret shame torture and ill-treatment of children*. London, England: Author.

Appelbaum, B. (2012, June 12). Family net worth drops to level of early '90s, Fed says. *New York Times*, p. 4.

Asha for Education. (2007, January). *Odanadi seva samsthe*. Retrieved from www.ashanet.org

Children's Defense Fund. (2008). *Protect children not guns*. Washington, DC: Author.

Children's Defense Fund. (2014). Retrieved from www.childrensdefense.org

Department of Health Services. (1997). *Minnesota family investment program* [Pamphlet]. St. Paul, MN: Author.

European Network of Ombudsman for Children. (2005, July 5). Submission to the Europe and Central Asia regional consultation conference, Ljubljana, Slovenia.

Ferguson, K. (2012). Children of the street. In L. Healy & R. Link (Eds.), *Handbook on International Social Work in 2012*. New York, NY: Oxford University Press.

Fraiberg, S. (1968). Parallel and divergent patterns in blind and sighted infants. *The Psychoanalytic Study of the Child, 23*, 264–300.

Garbarino, J. (1999). *Lost boys: Why our sons turn violent and how we can save them*. New York, NY: Free Press.

Handler, J. (1995). *The poverty of welfare reform*. New Haven: Yale.

Healy, L. (2008). *International social work: Professional action in an interdependent world*. New York, NY: Oxford University Press.

Healy, L., & Link, R. (Eds.). (2012). Handbook of international social work. New York, NY: Oxford University Press.

Helm, T. (2012, November 17). Benefit cap is immoral and divisive [Interview with Sarah Teather]. *The Observer* [UK]. Retrieved from www.guardian.co.uk/society/2012/nov/17/benefit-cap-immoral-sarah-teather

Jamaica Coalition on the Rights of the Child. (1995). *Children have rights too*. Kingston, Jamaica: Author.

Japan Times [Editorial]. (2008). *Japan Times*, p. 2.

Jebb, E. (1929). International social service. In *International Conference of Social Work: Proceedings, 1*.

Keller, J. (2012, March). *Internet protections for children*. Presentation to Executive Women International meeting, Des Moines, IA.

Leinen, N. (2013, Feb. 10). Human trafficking in Minnesota. *Twin Cities Daily Planet*, p. 1.

Leonard, M. (2004). Children's views on children's right to work: Reflections from Belfast childhood. In Lyons, K., Marion, K., & Carlsen, D., *International Perspectives on Social Work, 11*(1), 45–61. Basingstoke, England: MacMillan Palgrave.

Link, R. (2012, June 4). *Social work in a global context*. Presentation on children's rights, Augsburg College, Minnesota.

Lynch, D. J. (2008, November 24). USA could learn from South Korean schools. *USA Today*. Retrieved from www.usatoday.com

Mandela, N. (2000, May 6). *Building a Global Partnership for Children*. Speech presented at the Johannesburg conference on the Convention on the Rights of the Child, Johannesburg, South Africa.

Morten Wenstob, B. (2011). Norway's Ombudsman for children. In R. Link & C. Ramanathan, *Human behavior in a just world* (p. 63). New York, NY: Rowman & Littlefield.

Office for Civil Rights at the U.S. Department of Education. 2010. Retrieved from http://ocrdata.ed.gov

Office of the Human Rights Ombudsman. (2007–2008). *Child's Advocate—Voice of the Child*. Ljubljana Moste-Polje: Center for the Study of Democracy.

Patel, A. (1998, February 22). *Operation flood* [Anand 388 001]. Keynote address to the Second Pan Commonwealth Veterinary Conference, Bangalore, India.

Pope Francis understands economics better than most. (2013, November 27). *The Guardian*. Retrieved from www.theguardian.com

Rolfes, E. (2013, January 31). Hillary Clinton says farewell in final days as secretary of state. *PBS Newshour*. Retrieved from www.pbs.org/newshour/rundown/hillary-clinton-says-farewell-in-final-days-as-secretary-of-state/

Rotabi, K. (2012). International adoption. In L. Healy & R. Link (Eds.), *Handbook of international social work* (p. 81). New York, NY: Oxford University Press.

Saleebey, D. (1992). *The strengths perspective in social work practice*. New York, NY: Longman.

Scott J., & Ward H. (2007). *Safeguarding the lives of children*. Basingstoke, England: Mary Kingsley.

Segal, U. (2012). Work with immigrants and refugees. In L. Healy & R. Link (Eds.), *Handbook of international social work* (p. 73). New York, NY: Oxford University Press.

Sengupta, K. (2005, April 25). Girl soldiers: The forgotten victims of war. *Independent*, p. 4.

Southside Family Nurturing Center. (n.d.). Retrieved from www.ssfnc.org

Tanner, L. (2011, September 19). Child abuse rose during recession. *Associated Press*. Retrieved from www.chron.com

Taylor, C. A., Manganello, J. A., & Lee, S. J. (2010). Mothers' spanking of 3-year-old children and subsequent risk of children's aggressive behavior. *Pediatrics 125*(5), 1057–1065.

Tiong Tan, N. (2012). Cultural conflict and conflict resolution. In L. Healy & R. Link (Eds.), *Handbook of international social work* (pp. 128–136). New York, NY: Oxford University Press.

United Nations Children's Fund. (1997). *The state of the world's children*. New York: Author.

United Nations Children's Fund. (2011). *State of the world's children: Education*. New York, NY: Author.

United Nations Children's Fund. (2014). No "back to school" for 30 million children affected by conflict and crisis. Retrieved from www.unicefusa.org

United Nations Convention on the Rights of the Child. (1990, September 2). Office of the High Commission for Human Rights. Articles 42-43. Retrieved from www.ohchr.org

United Nations. Optional Protocol to the Convention on the Rights of the Child on the sale of children, child prostitution and child pornography. (2000, May). Retrieved from www.ohchr.org/EN/ProfessionalInterest/Pages/OPSCCRC.aspx

U.S. Department of Health and Human Services (DHHS). (2013). Child maltreatment 2012. Administration for Children and Families, Administration on Children, Youth and Families, Children's Bureau. Retrieved from http://www.acf.hhs.gov/programs/cb/research-data-technology/statistics-research/child-maltreatment

U.S. Department of Health and Human Services (DHHS). (2014). Office of the Assistant Secretary for Planning and Evaluation. 2014 poverty guidelines. Washington, DC: DHHS

Waldmeir, P. (2005, March 2). Top court abolishes U.S. death penalty for juveniles. *Financial Times*, p. 10.

World Health Organization. (2011). Western Pacific Region: Republic of Korea. Retrieved from www.wpro.who.int

Younge, R. (2012, April 16). America's deadly devotion to guns. *Guardian*, p. 1.

Sustainable Health Care Policies

Never clean the water until you get the pigs out of the creek.

—Traditional Iowa saying

Of all the forms of inequality, injustice in health care is the most shocking and inhumane.

—Dr. Martin Luther King, Jr. (1966)

In one sense, the United States has the best medical care in the world. For complicated procedures, people of means from all of over the world often travel to the United States' leading hospitals for treatment. Some of the most sophisticated and cutting-edge technology in modern medicine is found here. And yet, in contrast to other industrialized nations where health care is viewed as a service orientation, the U.S. health care system has the dual (and often conflicting) goals of providing a service *and* of making a profit for the health-related corporations. For this reason, the United States spends substantially more per capita on health care than does any other nation.

Because treatment is often more profitable to health care corporations than prevention, preventive medicine, until recently, was given lower priority. Crisis-oriented medicine receives the greater share of research funding, allocation of health care personnel, and building construction. American physicians may be the highest paid in the world, but their level of pay is declining, and it pales alongside the money that hospital CEOs get in 1 year, a figure that may reach into the millions. Major profits are made in private hospitals in affluent sections of large cities and by nursing homes and the drug industry.

In essence, health care in the United States is treated not as a right of citizenship but as a commodity, and services are rationed on the basis of a person's ability to pay (Chapin, 2007). The problems that spring from this simple fact are many. For individuals in need of care, such problems can include ever-rising costs, the influence of the pharmaceutical industry in setting the prices of medications, erosion or elimination of coverage, and the requirement by insurance companies to pay high deductibles before the insurance company covers the rest of the cost. But there are problems for the providers as well—for hospitals, clinics, treatment centers, and medical professionals who provide treatment to patients who are without the means to pay. With so many parties involved and so many different companies offering insurance, the system has grown more and more complicated over the years.

Health care policy is part of broad social policy, and like the social policies of a nation, it is reflective of the cultural values and the economic arrangements that are dominant. Kronenfeld (2009) spells out the central values on which the U.S. health care system is based. These are the right to choose a provider; protection of the private sector and an aversion to socialized models of care such as those that exist in other countries; a reliance on employers to provide health care insurance; a focus on treatment rather than prevention; and an emphasis on technology. These same values have shaped health care reform efforts, including the 2010 Affordable Care Act (ACA), passed under the Obama administration. One exception is the act's focus on prevention, an approach that is cost-effective in the long run. The ideological orientation of the United States toward capitalism and a belief in relying on state and local entities instead of the federal government drive the system. Why, then, one may ask, has public education been universally accepted by the general public and by politicians in a way that universal health care has not? To find the answers, we need to understand how the American system of health care evolved and how so many attempts to change it have failed.

This chapter begins with a history of health care reform in the United States. We will examine the paradox inherent in the way health care is provided: the fact that some of the best health care in the world is found here, yet so many seem to lack access to it. Inequities in the system along race and class lines as well as the disabled will be discussed, as will the related trend toward the corporatization of health care in the United States. We are in the midst of a major change in the way services are provided, and so we will look at the Affordable Care Act, discussing its passage and the basic provisions that are its underpinnings.

The final portion of the chapter looks at the state of health care worldwide and views U.S. health care in global perspective. Three boxed readings highlight this chapter: The first is a personal narrative by a woman who describes her experiences in providing health care for her mother before and after passage of the Affordable Care Act; the second provides a personal account of innovative and urgent work to save lives in Zambia through malaria prevention efforts; and the third takes us to Ghana to learn about some unique programming for people with physical disabilities.

History of U.S. Health Care Reform

Prior to the 20th century, the role of the federal government in health care was limited to the military. States began to set up public health programs in the early 1900s, and enacted notable health care reforms during the Progressive Era in response to the epidemics of cholera, malaria, and typhoid fever of the period. Local governments and private charities established public health centers where community residents received newly developed inoculations (Jansson, 2012).

The Expanding Federal Role

In response to the Great Depression, and as part of FDR's New Deal, the role of the federal government expanded in social policy in general, and health care was a part of that impulse toward reform. Major programs were developed to fund the building of hospitals, the training of health personnel, and research into diseases and other health concerns (Kronenfeld, 2009). Roosevelt sought to include coverage of health care costs as part of the Social Security Act (SSA) of 1935 for people over age 65 but was forced to back down due to opposition from the American Medical Association. Couched in the idea that a federal role in health care threatened "the doctor-patient relationship," opponents were to fight every proposal to expand health care, including Medicare and Medicaid for the next 50 years (Jansson, 2012, p. 167).

During the 1930s, the federal government did establish a principle of providing aid to the states for programs for public health and maternal and child health. Further, changes in the tax law enacted in 1943 provided that employees did not have to pay taxes on the money that went toward group health benefits.

Under the Johnson "Great Society" programs in the 1960s, many health care advances took place. Chief among them were Medicare and Medicaid. The workings of these policies were described in Chapter 5. Medicare, the larger of these two federal health care policies, is a social insurance program that covers all persons over age 65, as well as younger people with long-term disability such as kidney failure. It provided basic protection against the cost of hospital and certain posthospital services. Hospital services were provided up to 90 days during any episode and nursing home care was provided for up to 100 days. Another provision included a voluntary supplemental insurance program paid through a premium; it provided medical insurance to cover services such as X-rays and laboratory tests. Medicare was funded directly from the federal government, in contrast to Medicaid, which has been funded through grants to the states.

Medicaid, as we emphasized in Chapter 5, is a public assistance program designed to help the very poor regardless of age. Financing is shared with the states. Medicaid provides assistance in particular to both children and to aged and disabled persons. Government medical programs have displayed a strong institutional bias; hospitals and nursing homes receive far more money than home health or community services. However, because hospitals (under constraints from third-party payers) are discharging patients long before they are healed or well, home care is now more vital than ever to speed recovery.

An unintended result of Medicaid is that it has the means to limit physician payments while reimbursing hospitals fully. As a net result and because of all the paperwork involved, many doctors opted out of Medicaid. Preventive care was not provided, and poor sick people resorted to expensive emergency room use in public or private hospitals. Health care rates soared as hospitals shifted costs to third-party payers and to patients who paid cash. In recent times, cost containment strategies prevented such a recoupment of costs, so private hospitals dumped nonpaying patients onto public hospitals, sometimes with tragic results. Each state responded differently to the public's need for health care. The Clinton administration decided to do something about the lopsided provision of services.

The Clinton Health Care Initiative

It is interesting to go back to President Clinton's State of the Union Address (1994) to read his description of his (and his wife, Hillary's) fight to get a comprehensive health care bill passed:

> If you look at history, we see that for 60 years this country has tried to reform health care. President Roosevelt tried. President Truman tried. President Nixon tried. President Carter tried. Every time the special interests were powerful enough to defeat them but not this time. (p. 384)

Pointedly omitted from this list was any mention of Clinton's predecessor, Ronald Reagan. This is understandable because President Reagan had pushed for a reduction rather than an increase in federal health care expenditures, a reduction that even included public health services and research grants (Kronenfeld, 2009). Federal regulation of hospitals was increased under Reagan, and reimbursement rates were set in advance for each diagnosis.

As we know, the Clinton health care plan went down in defeat, doomed in part by a huge lobbying push and a barrage of negative commercials; these were financed by the Health Insurance Association of America. Sum total, over $100 million was spent to defeat the proposal. The ads confused the public, and, over time, the momentum for health care subsided. Clinton did pass the State Child Health Insurance Program (SCHIP), which was generously financed to fund health care for children. Apart from that, little progress was made in health care reform until President Obama was able, after a great deal of wheeling and dealing, to pass the Affordable Care Act.

Before we go into the specifics of this complicated act, we will look more closely at the role of corporations—the insurance and pharmaceutical companies—in health care today. The way health insurance works is that all members of a group, usually a work group, pay the same rate each month. Often the employer provides most of the coverage for the employee and his or her family. Let us say an individual requires surgery; the insurance company pays a certain percentage (say 80%), and the individual pays the rest. But many citizens don't work for large companies; they face not receiving the health care they need or of receiving the treatment at a cost that is exorbitant. A significant cause of the housing crisis was that individuals were unable to pay their mortgages due to indebtedness over medical bills that sometimes exceeded over $100,000. According to research published in the *American Journal of Public Health*, nearly 45,000 annual deaths are associated with lack of health insurance. That figure is about two and a half times higher than an earlier estimate from the Institute of Medicine (Wilper et al., 2009). The study, based on data from the Centers of Disease Control and Prevention (CDC), found that uninsured, working-age Americans have a 40% higher risk of death than their privately insured counterparts. Deaths associated with lack of health insurance now exceed those caused by many common killers, such as kidney disease.

Mizrahi and Gorin (2008), responding to earlier data on the high death rates linked to lack of health care, suggest the obvious solution to curb the morbidity and mortality rates is simple—expand the government-operated program, Medicare, to cover younger age groups, a plan that was endorsed by some representatives in Congress and by citizens' groups. Social workers, as these authors indicate, have been at the forefront of the campaign for universal health care. The power of special interest groups, unfortunately, has always stood in the way.

Obstacles to Change

Private insurance emerged during the Great Depression as a strategy to protect consumers from health care costs. Today, employers are the largest purchasers of private group insurance, and the second-largest payer of health care costs next to public payers. From 2000 to 2007, employer-based health plan premiums increased 87% while inflation was only 18%. This has caused many places of employment to use less costly plans, such as for-profit health maintenance organizations (HMOs). Under HMOs patients agree to receive all their care from one group of physicians that is paid a set fee per patient (Jimenez, 2010). By 2009, more than 80 million Americans were enrolled in an HMO, a form of managed care favored by universities and businesses in hopes of cutting costs (Karger & Stoesz, 2013). HMOs embody many of the contemporary criticisms of health care in the United States. Choice is limited: Employees are often forced to use primary care physicians instead of the specialists they desire to see; costs are spiraling higher while at the same time coverage is contracting. The 2007 Michael Moore film *Sicko* offered a biting commentary on America's health care system as it existed at that time; the focus was not on the uninsured but on the underinsured, focusing on the inadequate coverage people often receive from their insurance companies. The segments on a man who had to choose which finger to save as there was only enough coverage for one and the woman who was denied ambulance coverage because in her injured state she did not notify the company first, seem satirical but sadly were true.

Due to increasing health care costs, employers increasingly were limiting or eliminating the provision of health care for employees. A favorite strategy is to reduce the number of hours worked so workers become part-time workers, in which case employers are no longer required to provide health care. Outsourcing factories and work to foreign countries or increasingly using technological advances in computing and robotics are other strategies used by larger companies. Others hired workers from temp agencies who work for only limited periods of time. All these strategies continue to be used by companies, including some social service agencies, as cost-saving remedies in a society that relies on businesses rather than the government to pay for much of the nation's health care bills.

In *The Measure of a Nation*, Howard Friedman (2012), a health economist for the United Nations, compares the United States social welfare system with that of 13 peer competitor nations. If we are doing something wrong, as we are, he argues, we should look at others in our category and see what we can learn from them. Since our greatest failure arguably is our failure to provide for the health of all our people, Friedman devotes a great deal of attention in his study of the U.S. welfare state to the American system of health care. Friedman faults a system controlled by for-profit insurance companies and unregulated pharmaceutical companies and their political allies for the present state of affairs. Much of the overspending for health care is linked to drug costs, which are far higher than in other nations. Other governments—Canada, for example—negotiate the drug prices. The United States does not permit such negotiation. When the George W. Bush administration expanded Medicare to include coverage for prescription drugs, for example, the new law specifically prevented the U.S. government from negotiating the prices. Research based on recent federal data shows that between 2009 and 2013, drug companies spent more than $236 million to lobby Congress and the executive branch in the interests of increasing their profits in sales of their products to Medicare patients. In 2013, over $483 million was spent on health-related lobbying overall; the majority was on behalf of pharmaceutical companies and hospitals/nursing homes (Center for Responsible Politics, 2014).

Drug advertisements, which are forbidden in other countries, entice patients to urge their doctors to prescribe the expensive drugs they have seen on TV. Costs for marketing and advertising have diverted pharmaceutical profits away from research on cure and prevention. Many of the discoveries of effective medications now come not from the pharmaceutical companies but from university research centers.

At 17.6% of the gross domestic product, health spending in the United States is the highest in the world (Kane, 2012). The Netherlands is next at 12%, and most other industrialized nations spend around 9.5%. Present health care expenditures are unsustainable, yet there is no end in sight to the expenses. Given that there are more than seven lobbyists for every member of Congress working for various parts of the health care industry, the power is in the hands of the corporations. According to a cover story on medical costs in *Time* magazine, the health care industry has spent $5.36 billion on lobbying in Washington since 1998 (Brill, 2013). This figure includes the money spent by organizations representing nursing homes, hospitals, doctors, and health maintenance organizations as well as the pharmaceutical and health product industries. This amount is over three times what the military-industrial complex has spent on lobbying, according to Brill's estimation.

Health Disparities by Class and Race

One reason for the desperate need for reform of health care policy is the inequality in access to services. The death rates bear this out. According to the Commonwealth Fund's Commission (McCarthy, How, Schoen, Cantor, & Belloff, 2009), which compared health data across the states, potentially preventable deaths are considerably higher among blacks than among whites in every state. Among middle-aged African Americans and Native Americans, the death rates are much higher than for whites and Latinos (Jimenez, 2010). The differences within this age group are a reflection of disparities in levels of disease, access to health care, and quality of health care. The life expectancy of African American men on average, as Jimenez indicates, is 8.3 years shorter than that of white men. Black infants are over twice as likely to die as are white infants.

The statistics pertaining to health care on an Indian reservation are especially troubling. The YWCA (Young Women's Christian Association, 2010) of Missoula, Montana, lists the following facts from official sources:

- The Blackfeet Indian Reservation (2,371 square miles) compares with Missoula County (2,216 square miles) in size; however, the Blackfeet Reservation has a single hospital with 27 beds, while Missoula County has two hospitals with more than 350 beds.
- Federal funding per patient per year for Americans on average is $5,065; for federal prisoners it is $3,803; and for Indian Health Services it is $1,914.
- A serious toxic threat to Native Americans comes from governmental and commercial hazardous waste dumping of the rest of the nation's industrial products. (pp. 2–3)

In the United States, access to health care historically has been based on one's ability to pay. And income levels vary by race. Friedman (2012) summarizes the statistics: The median earnings for whites are about 45% higher than for Hispanics and nearly 30% higher than for African Americans. When broken down by gender, the gap between white and black men is about four times as large as the gap between white and black women.

The three-tier system that characterized American health care prior to 2014 provided protection for people who had health care insurance, usually through their work, services for older Americans through Medicare, and services for poor children and adults through Medicaid. Before the passage of the Affordable Care Act, people earning low incomes generally could not afford health care. Insurance rates for individuals with chronic health conditions were often exorbitantly high. Self-employed workers, similarly, often found insurance coverage prohibitively expensive.

At the time of the passage of the Affordable Care Act, 48 million Americans were without health insurance (Kaiser Family Foundation, 2012). Racial and ethnic minorities were especially at high risk of being uninsured. Following the recession of 2008, many people lost their employer-sponsored insurance after being laid off from work. Because hospital costs for patients without insurance can be astronomical, many families faced economic ruination. At the same time, hospitals were facing crises as increasing numbers of patients were failing to pay their bills. In the midst of this national crisis, the ACA was introduced to Congress.

The Affordable Care Act

Within the context of an urgent need for health care reform, President Obama set out to transform the system and to make this his signature achievement. Facing tremendous opposition from corporate interests and politicians tied in politically to the pharmaceutical companies and the insurance companies, the chances of success were slim. Each president before him who had tried to introduce universal health care had failed in turn.

Models to Consider

Had Obama been free to set up whichever kind of system he desired, he might have looked to other countries as models. He might have looked to France, where doctors frequently make house calls. The French health care system has long enjoyed the reputation of being one of the best in the world. It has become synonymous with universal health coverage and a generous supply of health services. This reputation comes in large part from success in meeting its goals of full coverage, access without waiting lists, and patient choice and satisfaction, according to an assessment provided by the European Observatory on Health Systems (Chevreul, Durand-Zaleski, Bahrami, Hernández-Quevedo, & Mladovsky, 2010). Citizens can pay into a voluntary complementary private insurance, which provides reimbursement for copayments required by the public system as well as coverage for medical goods and services that are not so well covered. A few shortcomings indicated by the study include some inefficiency in organization and lack of coordination between private and public provisions of care. A retiree who recently moved to France comments, "Until we qualified for the national health system I paid $29 for a doctor's visit with no insurance. Now we pay a small percentage of our income, which covers most of the cost of office visits, prescriptions, and hospitalizations" (Dawson, 2012, p. R8).

Obama might have looked to socialized medicine in Britain, where the doctors are employed directly by the state and operated by geographical primary care trusts. The National Health Service (NHS), according to the European Observatory on Health Systems assessment, provides preventive medicine, primary care, and hospital services to all residents. Around 12% of the population is covered by private medical insurance, which mainly provides access to acute elective care in the private sector. The quality of services is carefully monitored. Medical care has improved greatly under various Labour governments, and waiting times for most NHS hospital and primary care services have been substantially reduced since the late 1990s. National surveys of the public on their level of satisfaction with NHS indicate a satisfaction level of 77% regarding the health quality of hospital services. This compares with a 90% level of satisfaction in Sweden, 83% in France, and 79% in Germany. Austerity has come to the UK, however, due to a national economic crisis, and the risk is that there will be budget cuts to the services provided. Already cutbacks in doctors' pay and pensions are being enacted (Thomas, 2012).

Obama could have looked northward. The Canadian system is somewhat similar to the U.S.'s Medicare, a name that is shared by both countries. Reid (2010) in *The Healing of America: A Global Quest for Better, Cheaper, and Fairer Health Care*, examined health care systems all over the world, interviewing doctors, politicians, and patients. All seemed to be struggling with rising costs, but in all the countries he studied with universal health care, such as Canada, health care was seen as a right of citizenship. The Canadian system, which got its start in the 1940s in Saskatchewan, was so popular that this government-run, single-payer system became a model for all the provinces, and by 1961 everyone in Canada had free health care. This national health insurance program also became a model for the health care systems in Taiwan and South Korea, and, in 1965, it was adopted by the United States for citizens over age 65. As Reid summarizes his findings,

> Canada's universal health care system is still a source of universal pride. Beyond [the guarantee of health care] Canada has better statistics overall than the United States, a longer healthy life expectancy, and a lower rate of infant mortality. And it achieves all that for about half the cost of the U.S. system. (p. 128)

Drawbacks to the Canadian system are a shortage of medical professionals and an inability, as in the United States, to see a doctor the same day as the appointment is made.

When President Obama first came into office in 2008, he faced the following situation: The housing mortgage crisis was in full swing; the big banks were failing; and the stock market crumbled, affecting investors and retirees whose pensions depended on the strength of the markets. The part that was never made clear to the public was the extent that the lack of a sustainable health care policy played into the recession. The facts, which were revealed in Harvard research as summarized by Arnst (2009) in *Bloomberg Business Week,* showed that two-thirds of bankruptcies filed in 2007 were related to medical problems and health care costs. The large majority of these people who were forced into bankruptcy (78%) actually had medical insurance at the start of their illnesses, including 60.3% who had private coverage, not Medicare or Medicaid. But the coverage was inadequate, or people lost their insurance when they could no longer work because of illness. As we now know, the economic crash that came in 2008 stemmed from the housing crisis, generally blamed on the subprime mortgages the banks and other financial institutions had acquired. It's true that many of these people were overextended in their budgets. But when a health care crisis came, they could no longer meet their obligations. Personal troubles, therefore, created a public crisis of significant proportions. Given the facts as documented by these statistics, the passage of the ACA takes on added significance.

Strengthening the Safety Net

The reform bill was signed into law by President Barack Obama in March, 2010. Through this act, health care coverage would be extended to a projected 32 million previously uninsured Americans (World Health Organization, 2010). The ACA has brought about a number of improvements in the system, greatly expanding coverage and enacting some protections against some of the insurance companies' predatory practices. As we judge the merits of this act, we need to take into account the compromises that were necessary to gain congressional approval. In order to do so, the interests of the corporate medical and insurance company lobbying groups had to be accommodated. Business interests, therefore, gained precedence over the people's interest.

While far from embracing the model of universal single-payer health care advocated in this book and by many economists, the reform's easing of Medicaid eligibility thresholds and other improvements to the system are major advances in strengthening the safety net for people who were vulnerable to catastrophic loss in the face of failing health.

The ACA makes major changes to the organization and delivery of health care. Building on the existing public-private system for providing health insurance coverage, the act expands access to Medicaid significantly, strengthens employer-based coverage, and provides premium subsidies to make private insurance more affordable (Kaiser Family Foundation, 2012). For the first time, Americans will have guaranteed access to coverage at group rates outside of the employment setting, which is increasingly precarious in today's globalized world.

The Controversy Over the Individual Mandate

One controversial section of the Act One key provision was the individual mandate, which requires most Americans to maintain a minimal level of health insurance coverage, whether through government programs, the employer, or through a private company. The states were required to provide coverage by 2014 to adults with incomes up to 133% of the federal poverty level. Beginning in 2014, individuals who did not comply with the mandate were required to pay a fine to the Internal Revenue Service. The constitutionality of these mandates was challenged by over 20 states in lawsuits that were filed against the government in federal courts and eventually in the U.S. Supreme Court. In 2011, the U.S. Supreme Court ruled on the constitutionality of the two key mandates of the Affordable Care Act. The Supreme Court ruled that the federal mandate to require all citizens to acquire health care protection was constitutional but that the states could not be penalized if they failed to expand Medicaid funding.

The National Association of Social Workers (NASW) (2012), which had long been an outspoken advocate for health care reform, applauded the Supreme Court decision. The NASW statement mentioned that in the 2 years since the act was signed into law, reforms have already had a positive effect on the lives of people with chronic illnesses and millions of young adults who were previously uninsured. These young people could now be included under their parents' policies up to age 26. Another important change is that insurance companies can no longer exclude children and adults from coverage based on preexisting conditions, including cancer, autism, and mental health conditions such as depression.

Recent improvements in addition to Medicaid expansion as anticipated by NASW are the following: reduction in the costly use of emergency rooms as more people have access to medical clinics, better access to preventive care, prescription medication for older adults, and better coverage for mental and behavioral health needs in health care plans. Finally, the law addresses an increased need for medical social workers, aging specialists, and mental health practitioners to assist high need and high-cost communities.

A news release from the Department of Health and Human Services (DHHS) (2012) announced a new program, made possible by the Affordable Care Act, which will boost the number of social workers and psychologists who work with Americans in rural areas, military personnel, veterans, and their families. Through the Mental and Behavioral Health Education and Training grant program, 24 graduate social work and psychology schools and programs for 3-year grants will provide training in trauma and abuse, combat-related stress, substance abuse, and the needs of chronically ill people and their families.

Despite the positives, the Supreme Court decision allowing states to bow out of expanded Medicaid means that a cornerstone of the ACA, which was to provide practical universal coverage, will not be honored. As of 2014, 24 states have declined to accept the federal money for expansion of Medicaid in their states (Kaiser Family Foundation, 2014). In Texas, for example, the law was seen as an unwelcome federal intrusion into the affairs of the state (Pickert, 2013). This means that millions of poor people in the United States will still be denied coverage.

At the start of the sign-up period, there was much confusion over who was qualified or required to apply for health care insurance and how to do so. Fortunately, local hospitals and health clinics provided public education activities as well as individual guidance in helping people select plans to best meet their needs. The basic facts as explained to the public are the following:

- Only people without job-based health insurance who also don't qualify for Medicaid or Medicare are eligible for coverage.
- Health care exchanges are a key part of the ACA; information about the exchanges is available at www.health care.gov. and is organized by state.
- All the exchange plans offer basic services and preventive care, but the cheaper plans (bronze and silver) require high deductibles for treatment; the premium payments are higher for older enrollees.
- Federal subsidies are available for individuals and families who have relatively low to moderate incomes. (Pickert, 2013)

The following helpful definitions are provided at the health care website:

Premium: The amount that must be paid for your health insurance or plan. You and/or your employer usually pay it monthly, quarterly or yearly.

Deductible: The amount you owe for health care services your health insurance or plan covers before your health insurance or plan begins to pay. For example, if your deductible is $1,000, your plan won't pay anything until you've met your $1,000 deductible for covered health care services subject to the deductible. The deductible may not apply to all services. ("Health Plan Categories," 2014)

Also described on the health care website, are the basic plans offered in the marketplace. There are four health plan categories—Bronze, Silver, Gold, or Platinum. Differences are based on the percentage the plan pays of the average cost of providing essential health benefits to members ("Health Plan Categories," 2014). The percentages the plans will spend, on average, for medical care are 60% (Bronze), 70% (Silver), 80% (Gold), and 90% (Platinum). A person in excellent health anticipating no major medical expenses might choose the bronze plan to pay lower monthly premiums. Should a health problem arise, however, deductibles are quite high. An older person or one with a chronic health condition would do well to select the platinum plan and pay higher premiums to ensure more complete coverage. At the platinum level, the enrollee pays on average 10% of the total cost of the treatment up to the point that one's limit is reached. A key advantage of health care reform is that there are now limits on how much individuals have to pay. As of 2014, the maximum *out-of-pocket cost limit* for any individual marketplace plan is $6,350 for an individual plan and $12,700 for a family.

The ACA provides a safety net to families, and estimates are that 12 million more nonelderly people will have health insurance in 2014 than otherwise would have had it (Congressional Budget Office, 2014). Nevertheless, the ACA is still a work in progress. There are many challenges and potential pitfalls ahead. Compared to a single-payer plan such as Medicare and the Canadian health care system, the ACA does not provide universal health care. According to CBO estimates, around 31 million people will be without any health insurance in future years. Making up the uninsured group will be people who chose not to enroll, unauthorized immigrants, and those who live in states without expanded Medicaid. In the many states, including practically the entire South, Medicaid has not been expanded. In addition to physical health problems, the millions in these states who have mental health and addiction problems will receive little coverage.

A second major pitfall of the ACA has to do with the nation's dependence on private sector health insurers to provide coverage at reasonable rates. The for-profit companies thus have every incentive to keep the expenses high. The law also continues the reliance on employer-based coverage for individuals who have jobs. This coverage is less expensive and generally superior to coverage under the ACA but a major burden on businesses. For self-employed people, the ACA includes tax credits and subsidies to lower the expenses for some, but others will have to choose between higher premiums or plans with high deductibles before the medical coverage kicks in. Fortunately, the ACA provides great latitude for experimentation by the states (Caper, 2014). This means that some of the more progressive states are free to replace the insurance-based plan with a single-payer system.

State-Based Health Care Systems

As mentioned previously, individual states are free to set up their own health care systems, so, accordingly, programs vary and will continue to vary from state to state. According to the Commonwealth Fund's Scorecard on Health System Performance, Vermont emerges as the state with the most comprehensive health care, a single-payer plan similar to that offered in Canada. Unlike plans in other U.S. states, health insurance does not come from the employer but from the state (McElwee, 2013). It is anticipated that in Vermont savings will come from lower administrative expenses. Recently, however, due to funding problems, the future of this plan is uncertain.

In Hawaii, employers are required to insure workers who work more than 20 hours a week. Minnesota has a Health Rights program that extends coverage to all low-income residents based on a sliding scale. At the bottom of the Commonwealth Fund's scorecard, Mississippi had 20% of the population uninsured despite having some of the highest rates of hypertension, diabetes, obesity, and asthma. Because Mississippi did not choose to expand Medicaid under the ACA, the death rate of poor, uninsured people is expected to be high.

Massachusetts famously set up a plan in 2006 requiring every resident to obtain health care insurance coverage, with free insurance provided to low-income people. This is the plan on which President Obama modeled his proposed legislation. Now, after the passage of time, researchers have a rare opportunity to examine before and after effects of the introduction of an ACA-like plan. A relevant investigation was conducted by Sommers, Long, and Baicker (2014) and published in the *Annals of Internal Medicine*. This large-scale study compared the mortality rate in Massachusetts—the number of deaths per 100,000 people—from 2001 to 2010 with the rate found in a control group of similar counties in other states (Tavernise, 2014). Results showed that the death rate in Massachusetts fell by about 3% in the 4 years after health care reform went into effect, while there was no such decline in comparable counties. The decline was steepest in counties with the highest proportions of poor and uninsured people. The significance of these findings reveals that when people cannot afford health care, a significant number will die.

The election of a new Republican majority in Congress that convened January 2015 boasted a commitment to repealing or dismantling the health care law and brought major challenges to the viability of the ACA, primarily through threats related to funding. Of special relevance to the states was a legal challenge set to be resolved by the U.S. Supreme Court. The challenge concerned the legality of providing federal subsidies to the low- and mid-level income families that resided in the 36 states that did not set up their own exchanges. Without receiving subsidies many citizens would be unable to afford the premiums and therefore would be without health care. These individuals, many of whom lived in the southern states, had signed up for their health care benefits through a federal marketplace.

Read Box 8.1 for a case study from the state of Iowa. The author is a nontraditional student of social work who describes the difference that the passage of the ACA made in her life and that of her mother.

BOX 8.1   WHAT THE AFFORDABLE CARE ACT MEANS TO ME

Cynthia Kress

In 2013, I had a minimally invasive procedure done at Allen Hospital in Waterloo, Iowa. Though simple, it was expensive. I have United Health Care medical insurance, and like every other medical bill I have turned in to UHC, they paid it without dispute. My insurance is great. One week after my procedure, I received a thank you card from the doctor, staff, and hospital. While the card was very nice and professional, it made me angry as I compared the way that I was revered by the health care professionals at Allen Hospital to the way that my mother had been treated by the university hospital 2 years earlier.

My mother became ill with pancreatitis in 2011. At that time she had just opted to take an early retirement from her job as a licensed practical nurse, and she had no insurance. She was only 63 years old, and that is not old enough to qualify for Medicare or Medicaid. The staff at Allen Hospital was initially unable to care for my mother, as she was near death, so they sent her to the state university hospital in Iowa City. Mother was brought from the brink of death by a wonderful pancreatic specialist at Iowa City, but the road to recovery from pancreatitis is slow and extremely painful. Many relapses and readmissions ensued in the year after her initial hospitalization, each one terrifying and stressful for the entire family. My sister and I completed durable power of attorney papers regarding advanced directives for our mother and began to prepare ourselves for the worst. It was only after her doctor was confident that the treatment was working and that she was going to survive that he told us she had only been given about a 33% chance of living through it all. This was the event of my mother's lifetime. It was the most horrific and frightening thing she had ever experienced.

Despite our diligent efforts, my sisters and I were unable to sign Mother up for Medicare or Medicaid to pay for her illness. She slipped through every crack in the system. She was approved for a program called Iowa Cares, which is sponsored by the university hospital in Iowa City. Iowa Cares is medical coverage for indigent persons in Iowa who are ill, and local hospitals do not accept it. This brought Mother to Iowa City, 70 miles away from home, every time she was to be hospitalized with her chronic condition. We all took turns on our days off from school and work, driving the 70 miles to sit with our mother and oversee her care.

Our mother went from 140 pounds to a stark 97 pounds in a matter of months, due to the constant vomiting and diarrhea that pancreatitis caused her. She had to be fed through a feeding tube through her nose. The university hospital repeatedly discharged my mother, stating that she would be vomiting no matter where she was, so she might as well be at home. Every time they discharged her to my care, I would end up bringing her back, because I lack the skills required to care for a person on a feeding tube when complications arise. Each time she would return, the staff would become more irritated with her, and one resident doctor even accused her of removing her feeding tube on purpose so she could return to the hospital to be professionally cared for (the tube had been pulled out while she was sleeping, as it was tangled in her arms). It was a constant battle to get her the care that she needed. At one point, while arguing with a doctor about releasing our mother before she was well, my sister said that she was going to talk to a lawyer about their refusal to care for our mother. They reluctantly provided her the care that she needed after that, but she was always afraid that the doctors were going to "kick her out" again, and she wanted one of her family members to be with her all of the time to fight for her. She did not have the energy to fight for herself.

(Continued)

(Continued)

In March of 2014, I applied to be my mother's consumer directed attendant care provider, through a program called Elderly Waiver. After our battle with the health care system, I was unwilling to trust any institution to care for my mother, so instead of a nursing home, my mother moved in with me. The application process was simple, and the Affordable Care Act made the program more expansive to include people like my mother who fall through the cracks of our country's health care system. The response was immediate, and she was instantly approved for full Medicaid benefits that paid for a wheelchair, diapers, a life alert system in our home, all of her medical bills, and a decent rate of pay for the at home care. It was like I was dreaming; nothing was difficult anymore, and everything was as it should be. I no longer worry about what is going to happen if my mother becomes ill again. I no longer worry about how I will take care of my mother when she needs more intense nursing than I am able to perform. I feel secure and I know that there will be no more fighting for proper medical attention for my mother. She is never turned away from local hospitals or referred to the Iowa Cares program. My mother always receives prompt and professional care now for everything from eyeglasses to the nebulizer that she has gone without for several months because we could not afford to pay for it. I am confident that our medical system is being improved by the Affordable Care Act.

The Affordable Care Act helps people like my mother who desperately need medical care but have no insurance. People all over the United States have been fighting for proper medical attention for years, some of them going without, and even dying from lack of medical intervention. This is an inexcusable social injustice that most Americans are unaware of. I was unaware of it until it happened to my mother. Yes, there are some glitches, and I have read the stories about people actually losing their insurance because of the Affordable Care Act, and that is definitely inconvenient. However, I have witnessed the shambles that our nation's health care system was in before the Affordable Care Act was initiated, and it is without a doubt helping the people who it was designed to help, at this point.

Source: Published with permission of Cynthia Kress.

The road ahead to care for the millions of Americans who still lack coverage and to negotiate with insurance and pharmaceutical companies for better price control won't be easy. The decision to finance the bill partly with fees on employers who don't offer coverage for full-time workers may lead some companies to cut workers' hours to stay below the cutoff threshold.

Disability Policy

Before we begin this discussion, we need to consider the importance of language. The terms that we use to describe people—especially those oppressed in some way—can come to carry negative connotations, and advocates often work toward changing the terms. This at times can be dismissed as "political correctness," but that is a facile argument. For example, commonly used terms such as moron and idiot, clearly pejorative, were replaced by the label mental retardation. In turn "mentally challenged" was in wide use for a time and then "developmentally disabled." The term *handicap* fell out of favor.

For various health conditions, writers and others were advised not to say a person was "suffering from" AIDS, for example, but that the person was living with AIDS. For disabilities, in general, "person-first" language became widely adopted. Thus, one was cautioned not to refer to an individual as schizophrenic, but as a person with schizophrenia. The point was to stress the personhood of the individual before mentioning the disease. However, as Mackelprang (2008) indicates, many disability advocates increasingly are avoiding person-first language in favor of disability language, as a characteristic of diversity. Culturally, Deaf people, for example, emphasize their deafness as a defining and uniting trait. This use of disability-first language is especially common in Britain, where disability advocacy is strong. The use of language will continue to evolve over time.

Competing Views of Disability

There are two competing views of disability that often overlap with each other. British professor of disability policy Mark Priestley (2010) explains that the traditional view, within an individual model paradigm, was to assume that people with impairments would have difficulty fulfilling normal social roles. From this perspective, the most appropriate policy response was either to compensate them for their perceived loss or to provide less-valued social roles for them through segregated institutions. This had the net effect of socially excluding them from society. By contrast, the social interpretation of disability placed the focus on society's use of labels and the failure of society to accommodate the needs of all people. From this perspective, the most appropriate policy responses would be to assess disabling barriers in society's infrastructure to increase accessibility and also to work to change public attitudes. Universal access policies favor the use of automatic doors, curb cuts, wide doors, and adequate space to accommodate wheelchairs.

The impetus for the change toward a universal model, as Priestley (2010) indicates, came through the social movement in the 1970s. Within the residually based system of the United States, in contrast to European welfare models, the lack of universal safety net protection hindered strides in providing positive benefits for disabled people. Disability was acknowledged in the 1935 SSA, but Social Security Disability Insurance (SSDI) was not enacted until 1956 and was restricted to those whose impairments made gainful employment impossible for the rest of a person's life. The SSDI system was later expanded.

Significant disability policies, as delineated by Mackelprang (2008), that pertain to children are the following: The 1975 Education for All Handicapped Children Act mandated specialized education to meet children's needs and also encouraged main-streaming children with special needs in regular classrooms, the 1986 amendment to cover care from infant to childhood, and the 1997 Individuals with Disabilities Education Act that increased equity and accountability in education for children with disabilities.

The Americans with Disabilities Act

When Congress passed the Americans with Disabilities Act (ADA) in 1990, this was a breakthrough for persons with disabilities. The act

> prohibits private employers, state and local governments, employment agencies and labor unions from discriminating against qualified individuals with disabilities in job application procedures, hiring, firing, advancement, compensation, job training, and other terms, conditions, and privileges of employment. The ADA covers employers with 15 or more employees, including state and local governments. It also applies to employment agencies and to labor organizations. (Equal Employment Opportunity Commission, 2008)

The ADA has been amended several times and codified as Title 42, Chapter 126 (Equal Employment Opportunity Commission, 2008; 2011). Additional provisions were passed outlawing discrimination in public transportation, commercial facilities, and all levels of education. This act, which protects persons with a physical or mental impairment that substantially limits one or more major life activities, was a major civil rights measure. The passage came about after years of advocacy and highly publicized media events, including civil disobedience by persons with severe disabilities. The ADA Amendments Act of 2008 was designed to expand coverage in response to the U.S. Supreme Court's decisions that interpreted the ADA Act to refer only to certain classes of disability. With the amendments, Congress was embracing a social model of disability as well as a physical model, defining the problem of discriminatory behavior as stemming from larger society rather than from the impairment of the individual (Jimenez, 2010).

A major policy change that we can anticipate is an increase in home health care offerings in place of nursing care for people who could manage at home with skilled care services. But we are not there yet. An autobiographical essay by Barry Corbet (2007), published in the American Association of Retired Person's magazine reveals the response of a man confined in a nursing home following his injury in a helicopter crash. In his words,

> Nursing home residents are old, but it isn't age the gets them there. It's disabilities, the kind that make us unable to get in and out of bed or get dressed or go to the bathroom on our own. . . . Most people with longtime disabilities are terrified of nursing homes. (p. 62)

Disability rates in the population vary by race, ethnicity, and class. In an empirically based analysis of data from over 7,000 respondents of a health and retirement study, Song et al. (2007) found that the rates of disability among African Americans and Spanish-speaking Hispanics were almost twice that seen in whites. Interestingly, English-speaking Hispanics had disability rates similar to those of whites, perhaps, as the researchers speculated, because they experienced less stress linguistically and were of a higher socioeconomic status. Minorities, in general, had more coexisting medical conditions, while they often lacked health insurance to access treatment.

From a global perspective, disability, as Priestley (2010) suggests, is a poverty issue. Up to 80% of persons with disabilities in some countries are unemployed. Therefore disability, he further argues, should not be seen as linked to work and employment with only benefits being provided to working-age people when so many are older people in economically prosperous welfare states. Disability should be seen as a structural and relational problem of social exclusion; a major recent development is the shift toward a more holistic and rights-based approach to the inclusion of people with disabilities. See below for a photo from the Special Olympics Iowa event. Since 1968, Special Olympics Iowa has been serving the needs of children and adults with intellectual disabilities by providing sports training and competition in 23 Olympic-type sports. Social work student volunteers play active roles in working with the participants.

The connection between social exclusion and disability can be seen in the following personal story shared by Xia Wang (in private correspondence with van Wormer

Source: Photo permission by Kathy Irving, Director of Athletic Initiatives.

The Joy of Participating in Special Olympics. Special Olympics volunteer Bryan Coffey congratulates one of the contestants.

of September 21, 2013). When Wang arrived in the United States, she was astonished to see so many people with disabilities, unlike in China. Then she realized that families might be hiding their family members who are disabled as in the two examples known to her:

> When I was about nine years old, my friends and I who were living in the same apartment building all heard that a disabled boy was living in the same building with us, but none of us had met him. One day, I was playing with my friends in front of our apartment building. Suddenly, I felt somebody watching us. I stopped and saw a boy looking out of the window at me with a smile. That is the only time I saw him. I will never forget his smiling face.
>
> My second example is of my niece's cousin. This child is the only boy in his grandparents' big family. This family has a good reputation in the local city. Everyone spoiled the boy and they were proud of him. Unfortunately, when he was 12, he got sick with leukemia and became blind and learning disabled. They couldn't accept the fact that their only male child was disabled. They didn't talk about him in front of other people any more, even to my family. His parents are still open to taking him outside and are encouraging him to go to school, but the rest of the family doesn't view him in the same way. His grandparents didn't want him to show up at his cousin's wedding because they thought his appearance would bring bad luck and also shame on their family. Recently he has closed himself off in his room, doesn't talk to anyone, and refuses to go to school.
>
> *Source:* Printed with permission of Xia Wang.

Significantly, the government of China is making great strides in protecting the rights of people with disabilities. China was one of the first nations in the world to sign the UN Convention on the Rights of Persons with Disabilities, which was adopted by the United Nations in 2006 (Wang, 2009). We might conclude therefore that the social attitudes by the older generation are a legacy of the past.

In contrast to China, the United States has not ratified the International Disabilities Treaty. Recently the U.S. Senate failed by a narrow margin to get the necessary two-thirds vote for ratification. According to Secretary of State John Kerry (2013) ratification of this treaty would allow the United States to take an international role in protecting the rights of persons with disabilities and in ensuring that disabled Americans enjoy the same protections abroad as they do at home.

Global Perspectives on Health Policy

On a global scale the universal system of health care is rare. The opposite—specialized and residual care for the rich who can pay and emergency care for the poor—is the standard pattern. Much of the health care offered is curative rather than preventive and geared toward the young rather than the old; much of it is out of reach to the ordinary person. Yet good health is essential to human welfare and to sustained economic and social development (World Health Organization, 2010). Since 1995, The WHO has produced on a regular basis, usually every 2 years, a world health report. Each report has a central theme. The main purpose of these assessments of world health, according to the WHO (2010) website, is to provide policymakers, donor agencies, international organizations, and others with information to help them make appropriate health policy and funding decisions.

The World Health Report

It is interesting to revisit the first world health report, which was produced in 1995, and consider the accuracy of the predictions and the extent of improvement, if any, in the conditions we find today. This first report on the state of the world's health contained a note of optimism: conditions were improving; the infant mortality rate had fallen considerably, a rapid decline in population growth was projected, and immunization rates for children exceeded the target of 80% of the demand for vaccinations (World Health Organization, 1995). On the negative side, the report noted the widening disparities in health status between countries and among population groups within countries. Even within families, disparities in health care existed, and poor families tended to allocate health care and food on the basis of gender. The poor were further marginalized due to rapid urbanization, and the number of refugees and internally displaced persons increased exponentially. The report cited poverty as the primary underlying cause of disease and death worldwide. Many of the poor nations were experiencing a substantial death rate from the pandemic of AIDS, while the mortality rate from accidents and suicide for young adults was particularly high in industrialized countries.

The *World Health Report 1995* outlined three priorities for international action: to provide international funding and technical support for the poorest, most severely indebted countries such as in sub-Saharan Africa; to ensure that the poor, particularly families with young children and the elderly, had access to primary health care; and to improve the equity of access to health as public health policy, especially concerning women. The *World Health Report* was ambitious in its aims for the future and optimistic concerning expected results.

We can now consult recent health statistics and see if the optimism of almost 2 decades ago was justified. In some ways, life has improved for the world's people, with immunization rates continuing to climb and treatment for HIV/AIDS helping to reduce the death toll. But in other ways conditions related to health have grown dire, especially in the poor regions of the world. The prediction of rapid population decline certainly was not realized. In fact, the population that was 5.7 billion in 1995 was to rise to 7 billion, with the largest increase in the nations with the greatest food shortages and the least access to clean water.

Clean water, as we saw in Chapter 4, is essential to good health. According to the Water Project (2012), half of the world's hospital beds are filled with people suffering from a water-related disease. In fact, in poor countries in the world, about 80% of illnesses are linked to poor water and sanitation conditions. One out of every five deaths of persons under the age of 5 worldwide is due to a water-related disease.

The theme of the *World Health Report 2008* was the renewal of primary health care and the need for health systems to reduce class, ethnic, and racial inequalities in the delivery of health care treatment worldwide. The *World Health Report 2010* focuses on the topic of universal health care coverage and how countries can modify their financing systems to move toward this goal. The report provides an action agenda for countries at all stages of development and proposes ways that the international community can better support efforts in low-income countries to achieve universal coverage and improve population health outcomes.

The 2010 World Report spelled out experiences country by country and collectively. This research reveals three broad lessons to be considered when governments formulate health care policies. First, in every country a proportion of the population is too poor to qualify for health care through the payment of income taxes or insurance premiums. They will need to be subsidized from pooled funds, generally government revenues. Such assistance can take the form of direct access to government-financed services or through subsidies on their insurance premiums. Those countries whose entire populations have access to a set of services usually have relatively high levels of pooled funds—5% to 6% of gross domestic product (GDP). Second, contributions need to be compulsory. Otherwise, the rich and healthy will opt out leaving insufficient funding to cover the high-cost needs of the seriously ill. Insurance companies, if they are involved, will go out of business.

Third, the most important conclusion is that globally there is too much reliance on direct payments at the time of need as a source of domestic revenue for health. This method of collecting revenue for health care leaves many out and results in financial hardship for others.

A single pool is desirable to spread risks across the population. This is the conclusion of the 2010 World Report. The problem with multiple pools, each with their own administrations and information systems, according to this assessment, is that they are inefficient and lead to a division between relatively wealthy people, who will not want to cross-subsidize the costs of poorer, less healthy people, and the others who often receive less favorable treatment. Other problems are the high administrative costs and unnecessary duplication of services. Similar problems occur with the fragmentation of foreign aid. There are high administrative costs and unevenness of services as well as duplication of services. With more than 140 global health initiatives running in parallel, a tremendous strain is put on recipient countries and resources are wasted.

Malaria, a preventable and controllable disease, is the leading cause of death for African children under the age of 5. To learn about a successful program that provides a coordination of services in the control of malaria, read Box 8.2. This reading is assembled from e-mail writings from the journal of Jane Coleman. Coleman, a former Peace Corps volunteer in Togo and Zambia, was given a new short-term assignment to help coordinate a malaria-control project in Zambia. The work lasted from February to August 2012. To understand the importance of this project, we have obtained the following facts from the Bill and Melinda Gates Foundation (2011) website. This foundation is a major funding source for disease prevention in Africa. From the site we learn that a child dies of malaria every 45 seconds in sub-Saharan Africa and that most of the nearly 800,000 malaria deaths are children under the age of 5. The lost productivity in Africa caused by this disease is enormous. But thanks to the availability of new tools, more than 1 million African children have been saved. The distribution of long-lasting, insecticide-treated nets and artemisinin-based combination treatments

(ACTs)—along with prevention during pregnancy and indoor residual spraying—has made this recent progress possible. Against this backdrop, read the excerpts from the journal entries of Jane Coleman.

BOX 8.2 PEACE CORPS WORK IN ZAMBIA: MALARIA CONTROL

Jane Coleman

February 7, 2012

Sitting in a gypsy cab in traffic headed to JFK to fly to Dakar for "Stomp Out Malaria Boot Camp" . . . I was about to become one with the MOSQUITO.

The scale of the malaria problem was described to me as—"have you ever seen the eyes of a hippo just popping out of the water? . . . They look nice, sweet, and small . . . but once the hippo comes out of the water and you see the massive body—you know you are in trouble." . . . Well that is what the world is dealing with now regarding prevention, control and treatment . . . that darn small annoying bug has been buzzing around for thousands of years and causing one in five African kids to die.

- 50% of the world's population is at risk for malaria.
- 1 million people die every year from a disease that is preventable.
- Alexander the Great, Genghis Khan, Oliver Cromwell, Sir Francis Drake, David Livingstone's wife, and Dante all died from malaria.

Although there are clinical trials being rolled out for a vaccine, prophylactic drugs, bed nets, and indoor residual sprays, and great progress in malaria research, interventions, and funding . . . there is a lot to do!

I visited a district hospital and spoke with the doctor there that said in any given month, they have a request for 12,000 doses of malaria meds but usually only can distribute about 2,000 due to supply chain management, the "higher-ups," funding and stock out. . . . I then went to visit a warehouse that had 160,000 mosquito nets just sitting there (since last year) with no sign of their distribution anytime soon.

February 29

I have been a resident of Zambia for 3 weeks and despite the power outages, constant bargaining with cab drivers, fumbling over local language. . . . It is nice to be working and busy. So, what else is new. . . . I am up-country now—a little shy of the Tanzanian border—facilitating four malaria trainings with the President's Malaria Initiative (PMI) (established by George W. Bush) on a CDC

(Continued)

(Continued)

bed-net-longevity study, which we are rolling out right now to study the physical integrity and insecticide persistence of bed nets that were distributed by the Ministry of Health and paid for by the World Bank last year.

April 18, 2012

I spent the morning at Mansa General Hospital (a provincial hospital about an hour from the Congo border), a hospital that probably any American would run away from and a surgery room that would make even a plastic surgeon cringe; however, on that day, it was not. It was a place of peace and thankfulness to the 60 men, women, and children who had come in with cleft lips and palates, clubbed feet, burns covering their bodies, and a small baby that had skin flaking off her face and an eye that could no longer see the world around her.

Smile Train had arrived! An organization dedicated to helping people with deformities to be "treated or worked on" for free. I had the amazing opportunity to sit in the room with a Serbian doctor who has spent the last 20 years traveling around Zambia making dreams of smiling and dreams of walking finally come true. After so many years of being discriminated against and losing hope and faith, people sat next to other people with the same issues—realizing it was not just them, that they were not alone.

But just imagine traveling for almost 2 days to get to a hospital hoping to have surgery for something that has plagued you your whole life and with a single prick of blood—you find out you're positive for the malaria parasite and you can't get operated on, because there is not enough time to be treated, operated on, and put on the waiting list before the doctor has to pack up his tools and travel on.

I hate malaria.

May 15, 2012

The CDC and the United States Agency for International Development (USAID) team came to visit and worked with the government to determine where 24 million dollars should go to malaria control over the next year. . . . It is crazy to think about a group of people sitting in a room deciding that $10 million will go to indoor residual spraying, $8 million will go to long-lasting insecticide-treated bed nets, and another chunk of "change" will go to case management, intermittent prevention, and treatment for pregnant women. . . . We are talking about hundreds of thousands of lives and we haven't even begun to talk about purchasing all the commodities needed—Real Data Transport (RDT) and anti-malaria tests and treatment.

August 21, 2012

As the high noon sun beats down on the newly finished coffin and tears stream down people faces, I look around and tears swell up in my eyes. You can feel the deep sadness in the air, and knowing that this death could have been prevented if the right medical care was available makes the tears continue to roll down your face. A young mom in her 30s was in a car accident, and she went into the hospital to make sure everything was fine. Since she had no outer injuries, they said nothing was wrong and to go home. Days later, with severe internal bleeding and head swelling, the mom slipped into a coma and passed away.

What Zambians wear at funerals is different than in the United States; what Zambians say and do at the cemetery is different than in the United States; what prayers are said is different than in the United States, but one thing is the same, the verb "to mourn" means the exact same thing.

My time in Zambia is quickly coming to an end, and as I begin to wrap things up and pack up my curios I have collected, I stop to think about all the moms I have met in antenatal clinics, all the toothless old men that want to shake my hand as I pass, all the school kids walking along the dusty roads, and all of the people I have worked with on malaria control, and to the families that have lost loved ones due to a lack of health care and doctors available to properly treat a young woman in her 30s. So, here is my Tale. . . . Who knows where my life will go or what trajectory I will take, but may it be filled with smiling faces of children that have a doctor to care for them and communities that have resources to grow from.

Source: Jane Coleman, US Peace Corps, Lusaka, Zambia. Printed with permission of Jane Coleman.

Ebola

The 2014 outbreak of Ebola in West Africa first appeared in Guinea in March of 2014 and is the largest outbreak of the disease ever recorded, both in terms of geographic spread and number of people infected (Quince, 2014). As of November 2014, infections have been recorded in Guinea, Sierra Leone, Liberia, and Nigeria, with a reported 13,000 people affected and a death rate of just under 5,000 as of late 2014 (Sengupta, 2014). This disease, which is highly contagious and spreads through exposure to a sick person's body fluids, is not entirely new to the Global South. Ebola first emerged in 1976 in the Democratic Republic of the Congo, but after a number of outbreaks, it was contained. A vaccine should have been developed at that time, however, the big pharmaceutical companies were unwilling to invest in research on Ebola, since the profits were small (Quince, 2014). Today, in light of the present emergency, however, a frantic search is under way for a medical antidote, and a vaccine is being tested. In the meantime, an international effort to contain the deadly outbreak is centered on its source—Western Africa. But even though health care workers from all over the world are volunteering their time, there are still not enough doctors and nurses to run the treatment centers. And many of the African health workers have died.

Strategies to prevent the spread of the disease are the following: a restructuring of health care systems for centralized treatment and isolation of the sick; careful monitoring of travelers from the stricken countries to check for abnormally high body temperature (a symptom of Ebola); protection of health care workers from contamination through contact with a sick person's body fluids; and finally, the development of surveillance systems, so that we can identify and contain outbreaks as soon as they occur (Quince, 2014; Sengupta, 2014).

Displaced Persons and Refugees

The images are heartrending and difficult for citizens of northern lands to fathom: the vast migration of genocide's survivors from the Democratic Republic of Congo, Syria, and earlier in Darfur in western Sudan and Rwanda. Whatever the country, the images are the same: crying children huddled over dead parents, mass rape of women and the extermination of men, or a dump truck dropping dozens of bodies into a mass grave. Hardly a day goes by without a report of war, mass famine, or disaster, so much so, that the world spectators are getting almost inured to this kind of mass suffering.

Displaced people are those who have been uprooted within their own countries; *refugees* are people who have crossed national boundaries in search of refuge (Walter and Ahearn, 2008). However, in the literature the term *displaced* is often used to refer to people who have lost their place in general, as in *globally displaced* people. To clarify the distinction, this book will use the term, *internally displaced* persons.

The CDC (2011) draws on the 1951 United Nations Refugee Convention's definition of a *refugee* as someone who

> owing to a well-founded fear of being persecuted for reasons of race, religion, nationality, membership of a particular social group, or political opinion, is outside the country of his nationality, and is unable to or, owing to such fear, is unwilling to avail himself of the protection of that country.

Asylum seekers are those who have fled their countries and submitted a claim for refugee status.

Displacement and Disease

Each year, according to the CDC (2010), millions of people seek political asylum or become refugees in various parts of the world. Because most of them come from countries where infectious diseases (e.g., tuberculosis, hepatitis, malaria, various parasitic and emerging diseases) are prevalent, their health is a major concern to the host countries. These persons migrate mainly to the United States, Australia, and Canada. The state of Minnesota provides a unique specialty care program for refugees and immigrants—primarily Hmong, Cambodian, Vietnamese, Russian, Ukrainian, African, and Latin American. Diseases such as hepatitis B, tuberculosis, and parasitic diseases, as well as mental health problems are diagnosed and treated.

The mass migration of people amounts to over 42.5 million refugees, internally displaced persons, and asylum seekers, according to the United Nations High Commissioner for Refugees (UNHCR) (2012). The top ten countries of refugee origin in 2007 according to the CDC (2011) were Afghanistan, Iraq, Sudan, Somalia, the Democratic Republic of Congo, Burundi, Vietnam, Turkey, Angola, and Myanmar (Burma). There are many reasons for this—among them war, overpopulation, and government eviction. To these reasons we can add the powerful economic drives, the push of poverty, and the pull of opportunity, which is at the root of some of the largest movements of all. The pattern of this form of migration often splits up families and communities, but at the same time it leads to the transfer of large sums of money to the home country.

Relief Following Natural Disasters

Natural disasters are a major reason that people are uprooted in large numbers. Acute land hunger has pushed people onto uninhabitable regions such as flood plains and drought-prone areas; then when inevitable natural disaster strikes they are forced to evacuate for safety. Environmental degradation such as soil erosion and deforestation has caused mass population shifts, often from rural to urban areas. Similarly, millions have been forced to migrate as technological feats such as dam construction and urban and highway development have claimed the land. And yet, environmental refugees do not get the international help from nongovernmental or governmental organizations that are accorded to political refugees. However, these people are every bit as needy in their often urgent flights from their homelands. As political scientist Susan George (2010) informs us, millions of environmental refugees are "already virtually on our doorsteps" (p. 182). They will come when the water wells dry up as they are doing, when drought takes over the land, and when sea levels rise to the point that the residents are driven out, which are all the impacts of global warming. Bangladesh health workers were overwhelmed, according to George, when more than 50,000 people developed life-threatening diseases as a result of the massive floods of 2007. Such migrants, as George further indicates, are not recognized by any kind of international law.

Disasters, such as earthquakes or hurricanes, carry a substantial health burden for affected populations and compromise the capacity of local health services to address priority health care needs. (See Chapter 9 for a discussion of the mental health aspect of natural disasters.)

Among the most vulnerable people are refugees who are seriously disabled. Little attention has been paid until recently to the plight of these displaced women and children who have serious disabilities. Some were disabled at birth or as a result of childhood diseases such as polio; others have been injured in war, still others have lost limbs when they stepped on landmines. The Women's Refugee Commission (2010) has produced a first ever comprehensive report on refugees with disabilities. According to the report, an estimated 3.5 million refugees and internally displaced people live with disabilities in refugee camps and urban slums. These disabilities might be physical, mental, or sensory. The commission conducted field research in five countries—Ecuador, Jordan, Nepal, Thailand, and Yemen—to document existing services for displaced persons with disabilities and to identify gaps in services. The needs of this often-neglected group were great because of the inability of these refugees to procure food and other supplies for themselves.

Read Box 8.3 to learn of empowering work with women with disabilities in Ghana. See also the photo showing bicycles that are especially designed for women who had polio as children, as a unique means of transportation.

Source: Photo by Augustina Naami.

Accessible Transportation: Ghana. Their legs disabled from polio, these women of Ghana are highly mobile thanks to their special arm-powered bicycles.

BOX 8.3   WOMEN WITH DISABILITIES IN NORTHERN GHANA

Augustina Naami

Many persons with disabilities in Ghana struggle to provide for their basic needs due to their inability to meaningfully participate in mainstream society as a result of barriers related to attitudes, transportation, architecture, and lack of information, as well as the nonexistence of social welfare programs and services. The condition of women with disabilities is worsened as a result of the intersection of gender and disability. The majority of women with disabilities are excluded from education and employment opportunities, aggravating their conditions of poverty. To provide for their children and themselves, the majority engage in menial jobs while others, unfortunately, beg on the streets for survival. My passion to advocate for women with disabilities led me to work with Action on Disability and Development (ADD).

ADD is a British-based nonprofit organization, which seeks to build strong organizations of persons with disabilities as well as influence policy and practice in order to end the social exclusion and poverty among persons with disabilities in Africa and Asia. I worked as the Gender Programs Officer for ADD-Ghana for almost 3 years (November 2004 through October 2007) serving approximately 500 clients yearly. During that period, I worked with leaders of the organizations of persons with disabilities (Ghana Society of the Blind, Ghana National Association of the Deaf, Ghana Society of the Physically Disabled, and the Ghana Federation of the Disabled) to mainstream the issues and needs of women with disabilities in their programs and activities, and to increase their representation among the leadership of the organizations.

However, the greater part of my work centered on working with women with disabilities; empowering them to advocate for their human rights and their socioeconomic and political development, as well as advocating for the inclusion of their issues and needs in the programs and activities of both governmental and nongovernmental organizations. Many of the women I interacted with were single parents and unemployed. Despite the multiple challenges they encountered in the Ghanaian society, they persevered to succeed, thus, developing resilience. I assisted the women to develop funding proposals and raised funds for their small-scale income-generating activities. Access to funding was important for the women as the majority were single parents who were unemployed and had no regular source of income.

It is amazing how the women judiciously used the little money they received, from grants and microfinance, to establish small businesses and raise funds to feed and clothe their children, pay their children's school fees, and provide for their homes. For example, Ayi, a single mother of four who was blind, started a small trading enterprise with 6 Ghana Cedis (nearly $5 U.S.). She purchased sugar, bagged it in smaller bags, and sold them for 0.5 Ghana Peswas each (nearly 5 cents). With the profits accumulated, she expanded her business to sell matches, candies, and other goods. Ayi was very happy

(Continued)

(Continued)

that she could provide food for her children with the proceeds from her small entrepreneurial venture.

Other women started their businesses through their own funding initiatives; a credit venture where each woman contributes a small amount of money at every group meeting. The collection of money (also about $5) is given to one member at the end of each meeting. The process continues until every member receives their turn. The women were able to start their small businesses (e.g., food ingredients, detergents, household items) with the amount they received from the credit venture and provided for themselves and their children. The two funding strategies identified not only helped the women to generate their own incomes, they also provided opportunities for social participation and stronger social support networks.

These women gained visibility within the organizations of persons with disabilities. Their representation in the activities and programs of the organizations improved. As of December 2006, my annual report indicates that they held 19% of the leadership positions, such as president or vice president in the organizations. Also, these previously invisible and powerless women have now become active participants in other mainstream organizations in Ghana, including Orphans and Widows Ministries, Single Mothers Association, and Knights and Ladies of Marshall of the Catholic Church.

It was amazing working with these women, who were so determined to take care of themselves and their families. Their resilience and perseverance to succeed was encouraging and admirable, given the multiple barriers that exist in the Ghanaian society, which pose challenges to the effective participation of persons with disabilities in general in mainstream society. I was happy that I could impact their lives and was able to stand up for their rights and responsibilities. I feel fulfilled, because I was able to help women with disabilities take more control over their lives.

Source: Augustina Naami, MSW, PhD, Assistant Professor of Social Work, University of Northern Iowa. Printed with permission of Augustina Naami.

The U.S. in Global Perspective

According to the United Nation's Universal Declaration of Human Rights (1948),

Everyone has the right to a standard of living adequate for the health and well-being of himself and of his family, including food, clothing, housing, and medical care and necessary social services, and the right to security in the event of unemployment, sickness, disability, widowhood, old age or other lack of livelihood in circumstances beyond his control. (Article 25)

Because the United States played a role in drafting the treaty, even though this section of the UDHR was not ratified, and because this is clearly a key human right provided in international law, we can argue that health care should be recognized as a right rather than a privilege. A parallel would be the case of education. This is a right in Article 26 of the UDHR, but not under U.S. law. Yet American children attending school is clearly treated as a right, and, in fact, they must receive some sort of schooling. So health care could be regarded accordingly, as a right rather than a privilege. Most Americans (64%), according to a *CBS News* and *New York Times* poll, believe that the government has a responsibility to ensure universal health care (Toner & Elder, 2007). Today, all comparable nations have moved in this direction, with the exception of Greece, a nation that had an outstanding system of universal coverage until recently. When the Greek government looked as though it might default on loans due to a severe economic crisis, the European banks offered new loans at considerably higher interest rates. This rescue was offered on the condition that there would be huge cutbacks in social programs, especially health care (Durkin, 2012). Today, the health care system is there for the rich who can pay privately, while others get no treatment until their diseases have reached the near fatal stage. Greeks now say their health care has become privatized, such as in the United States.

A survey of the literature provides the following international rankings for health-related issues. Since the figures speak for themselves, we will simply list them here without comment at the close of this chapter. Compared to other nations and from lowest to highest, the United States ranks

- 48th for infant mortality rates (Central Intelligence Agency, 2012),
- 38th in life expectancy, which was 78 in 2010, compared to 83 for Japan and 79 for Cuba and Chile (World Bank, 2011),
- 48th for maternal mortality rates (Central Intelligence Agency, 2011),
- number one in small arms ownership, a fact that is related to the high homicide and suicide rate (Small Arms Survey, 2007),
- seventh for an obese and overweight population at 80.7% (World Health Organization Global Infobase, 2010), and
- has the highest per capita expenditures on health care in the world at $8,362 with only Norway close behind (World Bank, 2011).

THINKING SUSTAINABLY

A key component in the way health care has been set up in the United States is that it is considered a commodity rather than a right of citizenship. Even attempts at progressive measures such as the Affordable Care Act do not fundamentally reconsider this basic point. Yet the UDHR, which the United States helped to draft, asserts the opposite view: Health care is a human right.

Which view do you personally subscribe to? What are the arguments for each in terms of sustainability? What rights do you think you should be guaranteed in terms of your health care?

Summary and Conclusion

Societies that favor a social development approach direct economic policy efforts toward needy and vulnerable groups. Western European countries, for example, all offer universal health care as well as generous welfare programs and protections for persons with disabilities. Throughout the world, however, as we have seen in this chapter and Chapter 3, distorted development is widespread, with one segment of the population increasing its access to the resources at the expense of others.

The universal dilemma is whether the government should play a strong role, part benevolent and part coercive, in ensuring health care and housing for all or whether nations would do better focusing on economic investment and technological advancement in the belief that the market forces will ultimately take care of the needs of the people. How this issue is played out is seen in the global epidemic of maternal mortality, in the high death rate for female infants and children, in the increasing overpopulation in sub-Saharan Africa, and the unconscionable level of homelessness in the United States. (Homelessness is discussed in Chapter 9.)

In the United States, the issue of how to take care of people's needs has been resolved on the side of the market forces of profit-making constituencies who have a strong influence on public policy, the mass media, and maintenance of the status quo. Thus, in the only health care policy that could be approved by Congress, the interests of insurance companies, hospitals, and pharmaceutical companies all had to be taken into account. Still, the passage of the ACA was a triumph in its own right. Because of the need to regulate some of the corporate expenses, the act can be considered a work in progress. Yet its passage has laid the groundwork for greater economic security in an era of increasing employment uncertainty related to global economic forces beyond the control of any one nation. And few of those who opposed it, supposedly in the interest of capitalism, seemed to be aware of the facts revealed in Harvard research and reported in a business magazine (Arnst, 2009) that the economic recession, which was a real blow to capitalism, came about in large part because people, bankrupted by unmanageable medical costs, were forced to renege on mortgages in numbers large enough to place the U.S. banking system at risk of failure. The fact that the media did not link health care policy issues with the economic recession of 2008 is troubling in its own right.

Critical Thinking Questions

1. How does U.S. health care policy reflect general values of society? In what ways was the policy before 2010 in conflict with American values?

2. Is it true that the term *socialism* has negative connotations? Why or why not?

3. Review the various presidencies from Franklin Roosevelt to the present with regard to health care policy. What were some of the obstacles to providing needed care?

4. What are the major differences between Medicare and Medicaid? What are some of the drawbacks to means tested programs?

5. What is the corporate interest in health care policy? Why is health care so much more expensive in the United States than elsewhere?

6. What are some advantages and disadvantages of HMOs?

7. Give some examples of deaths associated with lack of health insurance.

8. Consider Martin Luther King, Jr.'s claim that injustice in health care is the most shocking form of inequality. What is the relevance of this statement today? Consider factors of race and class.

9. Discuss major changes in the ACA and whether any affect you personally or members of your family.

10. Compare the British and Canadian systems of health care. How are they similar and different?

11. Consider the claim made in this chapter that lack of adequate health care insurance played into the economic recession of 2008. Do you agree or disagree?

12. What are the two models of disability treatment? How was the ADA a major development?

13. What are some major conclusions of the World Health Reports from 1995 to 2010?

14. Would you like the job of a public health worker as described in Box 8.2?

15. How do the women of Ghana with disabilities cope with their impairments?

16. Comment on the UDHR's statement on health care. Is health care a right or a privilege?

References

Arnst, C. (2009, June 4). Study links medical costs and personal bankruptcy. *Bloomberg Business Week*. Retrieved from www.businessweek.com

Bill and Melinda Gates Foundation. (2011, October 18). Bill and Melinda Gates applaud progress against malaria while urging renewed effort [Press release]. Retrieved from www.gatesfoundation.org

Brill, S. (2013, February 20). Bitter pill: Why medical bills are killing us. *Time*, 19–21.

Caper, P. (2014, April 17). The business interests behind America's costly medical care. *Bangor Daily News*. Retrieved from www.bangordailynews.com

Center for Responsible Politics. (2014, April 28). Influence and lobbying: Health. Retrieved from www.opensecrets.org

Centers for Disease Control and Prevention. (2010, December 15). Immigrant and refugee health. Retrieved from www.nc.cdc.gov/eid/article/4/3/98-0323_article.htm

Centers for Disease Control and Prevention. (2011, Nov. 30). About refugees. Retrieved from www.cdc.gov/immigrantrefugeehealth/about-refugees.html

Central Intelligence Agency. (2011). The world factbook. Retrieved from www.cia.gov

Central Intelligence Agency. (2012). The world factbook. Retrieved from www.cia.gov

Chapin, R. (2007). *Social policy for effective practice: A strengths approach.* Boston, MA: McGraw-Hill.

Chevreul, K., Durand-Zaleski, I., Bahrami, S., Hernández-Quevedo, C., & Mladovsky, P. (2010). France: Health system review. *Health systems in transition, 12*(6), 1–291.

Clinton, W. (1994, January 25). State of the union address. In S. A. Warshaw, *Presidential profiles: The Clinton years* (pp. 378–385). New York, NY: Facts on File Library.

Congressional Budget Office. (2014, April). Updated estimates of the effects of insurance coverage provisions of the Affordable Care Act. U.S. Congress. Retrieved from cbo.gov/sites

Corbet, B. (2007, January/February). Embedded: Nursing home undercover. *AARP Magazine,* 80–91, 100.

Dawson, N. (2012, October 22). Moving to France. *Wall Street Journal,* p. R8.

Durkin, K. (2012, November 1). Greece wracked by health-care crisis. Workers World. Retrieved from www.workers.org

Equal Employment Opportunity Commission. (2008, September 9). Facts about the Americans with Disabilities Act. Retrieved from www.eeoc.gov

Equal Employment Opportunity Commission. (2011, March 25). Notice concerning the Americans with Disabilities Act. Retrieved from www.eeoc.gov/laws/statutes/adaaa_notice.cfm

Friedman, H. (2012). *The measure of a nation: How to regain America's competitive edge and boost our global standing.* New York, NY: Prometheus Books.

George, S. (2010). *Whose crisis, whose future: Towards a greener, fairer, richer world.* Cambridge, England: Polity Press.

Health plan categories. (2014). Glossary. Retrieved from www.healthcare.gov/glossary

Jansson, B. S. (2012). *The reluctant welfare state: Past, present, and future* (7th ed.). Belmont, CA: Brooks/Cole.

Jimenez, J. (2010). *Social policy and social change: Toward the creation of social and economic justice.* Thousand Oaks, CA: Sage.

Kaiser Family Foundation. (2012, October). The uninsured: A primer. The Kaiser Commission on Medicaid and the uninsured. Retrieved from www.kff.org

Kaiser Family Foundation. (2014, April 2). The coverage gap: Uninsured poor adults in states that do not expand Medicaid. Retrieved from www.kff.org/health-reform

Kane, J. (2012, October 22). Health costs: How the U.S. compares with other countries. PBS News Hour. Retrieved from www.pbs.com

Karger, H. J., & Stoesz, D. (2013). *American social welfare policy: A pluralist approach* (Brief edition). Boston, MA: Pearson.

Kerry, J. (2013, July 22). Disabled vets have earned access to the world. *USA Today,* p. 6A.

King M. L, Jr. (1966, March 25). [Presentation]. The Second National Convention of the Medical Committee for Human Rights, Chicago, IL.

Kronenfeld, J. J. (2009). Social policy and health care. In J. Midgley & M. Livermore (Eds.), *The handbook of social policy* (2nd ed., pp. 381–400). Thousand Oaks, CA: Sage.

Mackelprang, R. (2008). Disability. In T. Mizrahi & L. E. Davis (Eds.), *Encyclopedia of social work* (20th ed., pp. 36–43). New York, NY: Oxford University Press.

McCarthy, D., How, S. K., Schoen, C., Cantor, J. C., & Belloff, D. (2009, October). *Aiming higher: Results from a state scorecard on health system performance.* New York, NY: Commonwealth Fund.

McElwee, S. (2013, December 27). Can Vermont's single-payer system fix what ails American healthcare? *The Atlantic.* Retrieved from www.theatlantic.com

Mizrahi, T., & Gorin, S. H. (2008). Health care reform. In T. Mizrahi & L. E. Davis (Eds.), *Encyclopedia of social work* (20th ed., pp. 340–348). New York, NY: Oxford University Press.

National Association of Social Workers. (2012, September). NASW celebrates U.S. Supreme Court decision to uphold Affordable Care Act [Blog]. Retrieved from www.socialwork blog.org

National Council on Disability. (2012). Appendix D: Proposed ADA amendment. Retrieved from www.ncd.gov/publications/2012/Sep272012/ApxD

Pear, R. (2012, August 1). Many indigent refugees to lose federal assistance. *New York Times*, p. A23.

Pickert, K. (2013, October 14). The unfulfilled promise of Obamacare. *Time*, 28–32.

Priestley, M. (2010). Disability. In F. Castles, S. Leibried, J. Lewis, H. Obinger, & C. Pierson (Eds.), *The Oxford handbook of the welfare state* (pp. 406–419). New York, NY: Oxford University Press.

Quince, A. (2014, September 2). The history of plagues, pandemics and Ebola. ABC Radio National. Retrieved from www.abc.net.au

Reid, T. R. (2010). *The healing of America: A global quest for better, cheaper, and fairer health care*. London, England: Penguin Press.

Sengupta, S. (2014, November 12). U.N. seeks a more nimble response to Ebola in Africa. *New York Times*, p. A3.

Small Arms Survey. (2007). Small arms survey 2007. Retrieved. from www.smallarmssurvey .org

Sommers, B. D., Long, S. K., & Baicker, K. (2014). Changes in mortality after Massachusetts health care reform: A quasi-experimental study. *Annals of Internal Medicine, 160*(9), 584–593.

Song, J., Chang, J. H., Tirodkar, M., Chang R. W., Manhyeim, L. M., & Dunlop, D. D. (2007). Racial/ethnic differences in activities of daily living disability in older adults with arthritis: A longitudinal study. *Arthritis & Rheumatism, 57*, 1058–1066.

Tavernise, S. (2014, May 6). Mortality drop follows Massuchesetts health law. *New York Times*, p. A16.

Thomas, L. (2012, September 21). In Britain, austerity collides with pension system. *New York Times*, p. B1.

Toner, R., & Elder, J. (2007, March 7). Most support U.S. guarantee of health care. *New York Times*. Retrieved from www.nytimes.com

United Nations. (1948). *Universal declaration of human rights*. New York, NY: Author.

United Nations High Commissioner for Refugees. (2012). *Global trends report: 800,000 new refugees in 2011, highest this century*. Retrieved from www.unhcr.org

U.S. Department of Health and Human Services. (2012, September 25). *Health care law increases number of mental and behavioral health providers*. Washington, DC: Author.

Walter, J. A., & Ahearn, F. (2008). Displaced people. In T. Mizrahi & L. E. Davis (Eds.), *Encyclopedia of social work* (20th ed., pp. 73–76). New York, NY: Oxford University Press.

Wang, N. (2009, September 29). *Introductory statement of the meeting of the UN committee on the rights of persons with disabilities*. China disabled persons' federation. Retrieved from www.cdpf.org.cn

The Water Project. (2012). *Improving health in Africa begins with water*. Retrieved from http://thewaterproject.org/health.asp

Wilper, A. P., Woolhandler, S., Lasser, K. E., McCormick, D., Bor, D. H., & Himmelstein, D. U. (2009). Health insurance and mortality in U.S. adults. *American Journal of Public Health, 99*(12), 2289–2295.

Women's Refugee Commission. (2010, February 1). *Disabilities among refugees and conflict-affected populations*. Retrieved from www.womensrefugeecommission.org

World Bank. (2011). *Tables: Health expenditure per capita and life expectancy at birth*. Retrieved from www.data.worldbank.org

World Health Organization. (1995). *The world health report 1995: Bridging the gaps.* Bern, Switzerland: Author.

World Health Organization. (2008). *The world health report 2008: Primary health care.* Retrieved from www.who.int/whr

World Health Organization. (2010). *The world health report—health systems financing: The path to universal coverage.* Retrieved from www.who.int/whr

World Health Organization Global Infobase. (2011). *Stop the global epidemic of chronic disease.* Retrieved from https://apps.who.int

Young Women's Christian Association. (2010). *The broken contract of Indian health care.* Retrieved from www.ywcaofmissoula.org

Mental Health Care Policy

Jails and prisons—America's new mental hospitals.

—E. Fuller Torrey (1995)

ollowing a succession of horrendous shooting massacres—school children in Newton, Connecticut; movie theatergoers in Aurora, Colorado; a congresswoman at a rally in Tucson, Arizona; and shooting rampages throughout Santa Monica, California—the White House sponsored a National Conference on Mental Health. At the conference, President Obama called for a national conversation on mental health to speak about the stigma associated with mental illness and to bring mental illness out of the shadows. In his remarks, he stressed that most mentally ill people are not violent and that many violent people have no diagnosable mental problem. But mentally ill people are more likely to commit suicide, he said, and "when a condition goes untreated, it can lead to tragedy on a larger scale" (Somashekar, 2013).

This chapter begins by defining some key elements of mental health issues and some of the challenges it presents to society. We will then turn to a brief history of mental health policy in the United States. Following this overview of major historical events, we trace the development of current issues that concern us today. Many of these issues stem from flaws in the social welfare and health care systems. Homelessness of people with co-occurring disorders (having both a mental health and substance use disorder) is a major concern for our society and one that we emphasize in terms of its occurrence and treatment. Attention in this chapter is paid to severe mental illness, substance use disorders, posttraumatic stress disorder (PTSD) and policies pertaining to the treatment of these disorders. Because social workers, whatever their field of specialty, work with the victims of trauma on a regular basis, and because many of our social institutions actually exacerbate the psychological problems of people dealing with trauma, we devote special attention to situations associated with PTSD. The experiences of combat veterans, refugees escaping from war zones and other catastrophes, and trauma as a response to natural disasters are among the topics discussed. Additionally, we examine the fate of children who have survived wars in Africa and the Middle East where the psychological wounds inflicted upon the citizens are long lasting. To enhance the recovery of individuals suffering from PTSD or other forms of trauma, including mass events such as war and natural or industrial disasters, comprehensive treatment efforts are imperative. That such efforts must be trauma informed is a major argument of this chapter. Finally, we introduce a trauma-informed model within an ecosystems framework. This chapter contains one boxed reading, Box 9.1, which describes what one inclusive community arts program can mean to the family of a young man with severe autism.

Mental Health Issues: Definitions and Challenges

Mental illness poses a significant challenge to society, both in terms of the sheer number of people affected directly or indirectly by it and also by the breadth of the spectrum that mental illness can encompass. For our purposes, mental illness refers to any number of disorders that affect one's ability to think clearly and to behave rationally. The mental illness spectrum is vast, but the more common occurrences include depression, eating disorders, addiction, schizophrenia, and social anxiety disorders—including PTSD.

Discussing the full range of mental illness is far beyond the scope of this book. But two mental health concerns occur more frequently in the world of social work and social policy—schizophrenia and PTSD—so let us consider them in more detail.

Biological Aspects of Mental Disorders

Schizophrenia is a form of psychosis characterized by symptoms of disordered thoughts, hallucinations, delusions, and social withdrawal (American Psychiatric Association, 2013a). People with schizophrenia have been determined, through great advances in neuroimaging of the brain, to have a deficiency in gray matter in the frontal cortex and in the hippocampus, which controls memory and emotion. In children who show signs of schizophrenia, there is a progressive loss of gray matter that is correlated with the severity of the disease (Kolb & Whishaw, 2008).

Schizophrenia is thought to result from an excessive amount of the neurotransmitter dopamine. According to Meskanen et al. (2013), all presently available medications for psychosis are based on this principle, but given the serious side effects of these drugs, there is still a great, unmet medical need for further pharmacological research.

Schizophrenia can wreak havoc on the lives of individuals and their families and is generally considered to be the most serious and personally destructive of all of the major mental disorders (Ginsberg, Nackerud, & Larrison, 2004). Other mental disorders are associated with family dysfunction as well, for example, mood disorders that are unpredictable and disturbing to others, and conditions characterized by high anxiety and depression such as that resulting from severe trauma.

PTSD, which is caused by external experiences, also has a biological foundation like other mental disorders. In contrast to disorders such as schizophrenia in which the brain abnormality precedes the development of the disease, with PTSD, the mental disorder itself is associated with the changes in the brain's chemistry related to personal experience (Pittman & Delahanty, 2005). In this situation, extreme and horrific stress arising from one or more events is imprinted onto the mind and continuously reexperienced in the memory, to the extent that immediate and long-term alterations to brain chemistry take place. Ginsberg et al. (2004) cites functional magnetic resonance imaging (fMRI) studies that indicate that the size of the hippocampus (region of learning and memory) is reduced in trauma victims when compared to that of nontraumatized individuals.

The Diagnostic and Statistical Manual of Mental Disorders (5th ed.; *DSM-5*) (American Psychiatric Association, 2013b) identifies the following as situations often associated with trauma: exposure to actual or threatened death and serious injury or sexual violation. Five distinct patterns related to PTSD are the following: reexperiencing the event; avoidance of reminders of the event; negative cognitions and feelings, including self-blame or blocking off memories; arousal marked by aggressive or self-destructive behavior; and hypervigilance. The inclusion of self-blame as one of the criteria, which is new to this edition of the *DSM-5* was inspired by survey data on 200 Marines who had fought in Afghanistan; those who had PTSD reported that they were wrestling with moral conflict over what they had seen and done in the war (Zoroya, 2012). They were suffering from feelings of guilt, in other words, emotions not included earlier in the criteria for PTSD.

Trauma in childhood can be extremely damaging to child development. It is a recognized fact that violent adults often have a history of childhood psychological trauma and that traumatized children often have a problem with aggression as they grow up. Some of these individuals exhibit very real, physical alterations in a part of the brain called the orbitofrontal cortex. The connection has been demonstrated in very young rats who when exposed to extremely stressful situations were highly aggressive when grown (Márquez et al., 2013). According to a review of recent research in *Science Daily* ("Childhood Trauma," 2012), in individuals with a genetic predisposition, trauma causes long-term changes in DNA leading to a faulty regulation of the stress hormone system. This renders them less able to handle situations of stress in the future. We know from other research that many people who have suffered early life trauma turn to heavy use of alcohol and other drugs later in life. Environmental stress plays a role in the etiology of addiction and even in the development and exacerbation of mental disorders (van Wormer, 2011).

Given the recent high-profile cases of individuals with mental health problems who have committed mass shootings, a common question asked is "Aren't mentally ill people dangerous?" We might note from media accounts that many of the shooters were paranoid. Following each incident of a mass shooting (e.g., the 2013 rampage at the Navy yard), mental illness rather than easy access to guns is seen as the culprit. To evaluate such claims in addition to the notion promoted by the National Rifle Association (NRA), Bangalore and Messerli (2013) examined the correlation between gun ownership figures and gun violence mortality rates in 27 countries. Published in the *American Journal of Medicine*, their report found the prevalence of gun ownership (at 88.8 per 100 people) was the highest among both economically advantaged and disadvantaged nations. On one end of the spectrum, Japan had a gun ownership rate of .6% and a firearm-related death rate of .06 people per 100,000 compared to the 10.2 people per 100,000 in the United States, whereas the United Kingdom (.25 people per 100,000) had an extremely low rate of firearm-related deaths along with a very small gun ownership rate. Canada had a gun ownership rate of 30.8% and a firearm-related death rate of 2.44 people per 100,000. Clearly cultural factors come into play in these differences as well. Still, a significant positive correlation between guns per capita per country and the rate of firearm-related deaths was found across the board.

In any case, according to the National Institute of Mental Health (NIMH) (2009), people with schizophrenia are not usually violent, and most violent crimes are not committed by people with this illness. However, as NIMH indicates, some symptoms are associated with violence, such as delusions of persecution. Substance abuse might also increase the chance a person will become violent as might one's degree of suggestibility after exposure to provocative media accounts of mass shootings. Many of these accounts include murder-suicides.

Whether or not the individual with major mental problems becomes violent or attempts suicide, the stress on family members living with someone who is delusional and paranoid or chronically depressed is enormous. Exposure to a barrage of paranoid thoughts can be disturbing, and a close friend or relative's depression can be contagious. Although psychotropic medication can be extremely helpful for many disorders, as can psychological counseling, many who are in need of treatment do not receive it. According to a national survey of the general population conducted by Substance Abuse and Mental Health Services Association (SAMHSA) (2012b), among those reporting serious mental health disorders (5%), 61% received treatment. Cost was a major reason cited for failure to get the help needed. Keep in mind that this survey was taken before the passage of the Affordable Care Act (ACA) took effect with the promise of expanded treatment availability.

The Challenge of Unmet Treatment Needs

According to the National Alliance on Mental Illness (NAMI) (2012), four of the 10 leading causes of disability in the United States and other industrialized countries are mental disorders. Even though mental illness is widespread in the U.S. population, the main burden of illness is concentrated in a much smaller proportion—about 6%, or one in 17 Americans has a serious psychiatric illness. Included in this category are major depression, schizophrenia, bipolar disorder, panic disorder, and PTSD.

Psychoses, such as schizophrenia and bipolar disorder, are viewed as being caused by an underlying biological disturbance. PTSD is seen as resulting from a combination of personal biological vulnerability and exposure to environmental stresses of an extreme nature.

Despite the recognition of mental illness as a physical disease in the United States and many other countries, mental illness is criminalized. A recent article in the British journal *The Economist* describes the situation in Cook County Jail in Illinois, which could be considered the largest mental health institution in America ("Locked In," 2013). The expense to the county is enormous. On any given day, one building at the jail is home to over 2,000 people with diagnosed mental illnesses. Actual mental institutions are only for people determined to be a danger to themselves or others, and their stays are too short to provide sufficient medical treatment. When they, like the jail inmates, are released, they often end up on the streets.

Although the exact number of homeless people in America is unknown, we can turn to one-night surveys conducted each year by the U.S. Department of Housing and Urban Development (HUD). According to U.S. Department of Housing and Urban Development (2013), 610,042 people were homeless on a given night. Most (65%) were living in emergency shelters or transitional housing programs. About one in six of these were chronically homeless, a population that includes large numbers with mental health and addiction disorders.

Homeless people are often found on city streets, sleeping on park benches and in old cars. A study of people with serious mental illnesses seen by California's public mental health system found that 15% of these people were homeless at least once in a 1-year period (Folsom et al., 2005). Patients with schizophrenia or bipolar disorder are particularly vulnerable. An estimated 13% of the homeless population is thought to have serious mental disorders. For the single-adult homeless population the estimate is twice as high (National Coalition for the Homeless, 2009).

Historical Views of Mental Health and Illness

How did this situation of neglect for this vulnerable population come about? Historically, the medical view of mental disorders did not emerge until the 19th century (Jimenez et al., 2014). Before that time, people with mental disorders were thought to be possessed by the devil and were hidden from public view. In England, "lunatics" were either kept at home or boarded out in private asylums (Porter, 2002). In the 1700s, various acts were passed to require medical supervision in the private asylums. A large number of charitable asylums were opened up for the care of mentally ill people at this time. In Illinois in the 1880s, Dorothea Dix, a social reformer, worked to improve conditions for the treatment of mentally ill people (her efforts were described in Chapter 2). Although her advocacy brought national recognition to the plight of persons with mental illness, she failed to obtain the support from the federal government for which she had so strongly advocated.

New understandings of mental illness as a medical disease combined with urbanization led to the rise of treatment facilities in the form of public mental hospitals in every state. The impersonal quality of city life, characterized by overcrowding and people being uprooted from their homes, created a situation in which there was little tolerance for strange and abnormal behavior (DiNitto, 2011). This increased the numbers of people sent away to mental asylums. By the 1950s, half a million people were so confined (Human Rights Watch, 2003). Although the motives of reformers who had lobbied for this form of medical treatment in the first place were admirable, conditions deteriorated and insane asylums became places to dispose of the nation's problem people. Mental health treatment by the 1920s became outpatient treatment for people who could afford it; the others were largely forgotten and deprived of civil rights. Inmates were subjected to inhumane treatment, including electroconvulsive therapy, hydrotherapy in heated bathtubs, and, the most invasive of all—prefrontal brain surgery or lobotomies. Straitjackets were regularly used to restrain troublesome patients.

The Movement to Deinstitutionalize

Deinstitutionalization was made possible by the introduction in the 1950s of antipsychotic medication and by the creation of the Medicaid and Supplemental Security Income (SSI) programs in the 1960s that provided financial incentives for community care (SAMHSA, 2003). Several other forces converged in the 1960s and 1970s to reform the system. Personal stories, academic research from psychology and sociology, accounts in the popular media of people locked away forever in asylums, and the release of Hollywood films such as the 1975 award-winning *One Flew Over the Cuckoo's Nest* aroused the national consciousness to demand action.

The goal, which was attractive to progressives, was to set up community health care centers and halfway houses for the former members of mental institutions. However, when deinstitutionalization on a mass scale was realized and the patients were freed, they were left, for the most part, to their own devices. The federal funding did not materialize, however—not in sufficient amounts to provide protective care for the former patients. Without assistance, people with serious mental illnesses were among the first to be displaced when urban neighborhoods and single-room–occupancy hotels were gentrified in the 1980s (SAMHSA, 2003). The consequence of the deinstitutionalization movement of the 1970s, in short, is that large numbers of mentally ill Americans received no services at all, could not find affordable housing, and ended up homeless (Visser, 2011).

Many of the people on the streets had serious mental and substance use disorders. Transitional housing programs were offered on a limited and experimental basis to some homeless people with substance use problems. Program providers had the unrealistic expectation that these people would abstain from drinking if they were provided with a clean place to stay and given the treatment they needed. Total abstinence from alcohol and other drugs was strictly enforced. This model was not successful, however (Larimer et al., 2009). The majority of the residents began drinking again and ended up back on the streets.

An alternative program—Housing First—was tried experimentally in the 1990s in several U.S. cities such as New York, Minneapolis, and Seattle. Federal grants were available under the George W. Bush administration for these programs, which were controversial at the start but highly cost-effective in removing the most severely disturbed of the homeless populations from the streets and reducing the crime and incarceration rates.

Contemporary Developments in Treatment

Included in a bailout bill (a bill to bailout the troubled banks) passed by Congress and signed into law by President George W. Bush in 2008 was long-awaited legislation to provide addiction and mental health parity. Under the new law, insurance companies were required to treat addiction and mental health conditions in the same way as they treat other health conditions. Social workers had advocated for this improved coverage for some time, but this law applied only to larger employers (50 or more workers) that offered a health plan with benefits for mental health and substance abuse (Friedman, 2012). It did not mandate universal psychiatric benefits and applied only to people with good insurance coverage. The 2008 parity law was later strengthened through the addition of new rules requiring that copayments could not be less generous than those applied to most standard medical benefits ("Equal Coverage for the Mentally Ill," 2013).

Historically, Medicare had covered 80% of all outpatient care except for mental health care and substance abuse treatment, which was reimbursed at only a 50% rate (Humphreys, 2014). This fact rendered treatment for mental health disorders unafford-able for many. Now, since 2014, the ACA has extended the 2008 parity law to provide the same level of reimbursement as all other health care. For insurance companies, similarly, the more stringent requirements and lower benefit caps regularly applied to mental health care are now illegal. Keep in mind that the ACA had already helped families facing mental illness crises by allowing parents to keep their children on their insurance policies until the age of 26. Because substance use and psychiatric disorders generally develop in youths, this treatment expansion has been a major breakthrough for many.

Estimates from the U.S. Department of Health and Human Services are that under the ACA over 60 million more Americans will receive improved mental health insurance coverage who previously would not have so benefited (Wakefield, 2014). However, many of the uninsured, low-income people living in the states that have not chosen to expand Medicaid (11 of which are in the South) will still find themselves without adequate access to treatment.

THINKING SUSTAINABLY

The treatment of those who are mentally ill varies widely from country to country and tends to say a lot about the civility of society in question. In the United States, the emphasis on treating the mentally ill has undergone sweeping changes over the past hundred years, from massive institutionalization to a virtual 180 in mental health policy; millions of mentally ill people are attempting to fend for themselves in society, and too often end up in the criminal justice system.

What are some of the characteristics of sustainable mental health policy? What might be the long-term economic and societal benefits of promoting the mental health and well-being of new mothers and their children? What about work and school-based mental health initiatives? How might they contribute to the economic and social well-being of a population?

Social Aspects of Mental Illness

The Stigma of Mental Illness

Not only are homeless people stigmatized, but mental illness itself is a highly stigmatized disease. Rapp and Goscha (2012) see the use of labels for persons with psychiatric disabilities as relegating these people to a degraded social identity. Such identities are internalized with a detrimental effect on the person's self-efficacy. Another detrimental effect occurs with labeling whole groups and then designing treatments that are generic, one-size-fits-all, for example, social skills training that is the same for all the participants and geared toward the eradication of deficits rather than the building of strengths. Rapp and Goscha argue that people with psychiatric disabilities are both oppressed within society and by professionals as well. People who are labeled as mentally ill often find that "their space, time, energy, mobility, bonding, and identity are constantly being violated and assaulted" (p. 14).

This situation of mistreatment is not limited to the United States as the following narrative from an MSW student from Zimbabwe suggests.

> In my Zimbabwean experience, mental and substance abuse disorders seem to be a genetic issue, like in the United States, where a family can have two or more members with this dual disorder. However, there are some cultural differences. In Zimbabwe, people tend to think that such disorders are a result of witches who cast spells on others. They consider those who suffer from these spells as victims of witchcraft. Therefore, for social workers, cultural competence and a multidisciplinary approach would be instrumental in coming up with effective interventions. (personal communication, September 21, 2013)

And we heard the following from a student from China:

> In the early 1980s, physical disability was called *Feng Zi* meaning crazy, and mental disability was called *Can Fei* meaning "handicapped and useless." Nowadays, officially, people use *mental illness* and *disabled people* instead. But most people still regard disabled people as a useless group. (personal communication, September 21, 2013)

There are some powerful counterexamples, of course. Before turning to some of the other elements of mental illness that affect society and social work, let us learn of a positive community program that draws on the arts to integrate children with disabilities into performance efforts that are uniquely empowering. Box 9.1, written by the mother of one such child, describes such a community program in Bowling Green, Kentucky.

BOX 9.1   MY SON, NATHAN

Cindy Taulbee

The audience responded with a standing ovation. As the house lights came on, cast members mingled with the crowd. Glorying in the limelight, Nathan was delighted to sign autographs. What the audience did not know was that Nathan had been diagnosed with autism spectrum disorder at age 7.

Nathan was an easy baby to care for. He was content to lie on a quilt on the floor. He accepted being held but showed little interest in anyone other than me. During his first year, Nathan met his developmental goals by the end of each period. He was slow to sit up and to walk. He never crawled. He would roll where he wanted to go. The first alarm bell rang at his 15-month checkup. The doctor noted that Nathan was not talking or walking.

When I enrolled Nathan in preschool, at age 4, he was still not talking. I kept a list of words he had spoken. His words came one at a time and days apart. He was enrolled in preschool under the label of *developmental delay*. He had an individualized educational program and speech classes. Loud noises and high pitched sounds are painful to Nathan. At first, he was terrified by the school bell and fire alarm. Crying babies and shrill voices still give him a headache.

Nathan was 7 when he received the diagnosis of autism spectrum disorder. He began to speak three or four words at a time and often echoed words and phrases that he had heard on television. Nathan's first conversations were with a cartoon character in a computer game. Language has been his greatest challenge. Nathan took speech classes at school and at the local university. By the end of sixth grade, Nathan tested out of speech. He received the President's Education Award in recognition of outstanding academic achievement for making so much progress during his elementary school years.

A private therapist once told me, "People like Nathan tend to hit a plateau and not go any higher." The same counselor asked me where I was going to put Nathan after middle school since he would never be able to do high school work. The counselor was wrong. Nathan has finished 2 years of high school and is on track to receive a diploma. His teachers help him academically. Fitting in socially is hard for many teenagers, especially those with autism. Nathan's friends are the people he plays Xbox Live games with. He tried attending the local autism center but was not happy there. The other kids at the center were more severely affected by autism than Nathan. I was reminded of a line from *Rudolph the Red-Nosed Reindeer* where Yukon Cornelius says to Rudolph, "Even among misfits you are a misfit" (Roemer, Muller, & May, 1964).

Fortunately, Nathan has found a place where he does fit in. A prominent local attorney, Flora Templeton Stuart, started a program that is now called BG-On Stage. It began with classes in art and drama. Special needs kids and neurotypical kids were in classes together, and both groups benefited from the experience. Since then, BG-On Stage has begun doing plays. Nathan has been Peavy the gardener in *The Velveteen Rabbit*, a classmate in *The Hundred Dresses*, and is now rehearsing the role of pilot in *The Little Mermaid*. Nathan enjoys making friends with people of all age groups and learning how a stage production comes together. When asked what he likes most about the Art Education Task Force (AETF), Nathan said, "I have friends. It's good to be with people who have autism. It is also good to be with people who don't have autism and let them learn about autism. I want them to know that I can do things—big things!"

Source: Printed with permission of Cindy Taulbee.

Mental Illness and the Plight of the Chronically Homeless

Chronically homeless individuals make up about 18% of the total homeless population. These people generally have co-occurring disorders, which means their mental disorders are compounded by heavy substance use (National Alliance to End Homelessness, 2014b). These are the people who live under bridges and sleep on sidewalks in downtown areas of the city. Because they are arrested frequently for drunk and disorderly behavior and visit hospital emergency rooms on a regular basis, they are a great expense to cities. Their life expectancy is estimated at 42 to 52 years (Larimer et al., 2009).

To learn the racial/ethnic breakdown we can look to most recent survey of 25 cities by the U.S. Conference of Mayors, which took an inventory of the sheltered homeless population. This population is estimated to be 38.1% African American, 39.5% white, 8.9% Hispanic, 5% other (includes Native American and Asian people), and 7% multiple race (National Alliance to End Homelessness, 2014a). The majority of the homeless population is single; out of this group around two-thirds are male. Of people who are homeless in family groupings, 79% are female.

According to the National Coalition of the Homeless (2009), persons with severe mental illness represent about 26% of the total population of homeless people; these estimates come from surveys of all sheltered homeless persons and surveys from the general homeless population in selected cities. In addition, half of the mentally ill homeless population in the United States also has substance use disorders (SAMHSA,

Source: Photo by Rupert van Wormer.

Homelessness in a Big City. Homeless woman outside a bakery in Chinatown, San Francisco.

2003). While on the streets, many of the homeless people are drawn to use street drugs as a form of self-medication. This process can lead not only to addiction and crime to get money to sustain the habit but also to disease transmission from injection drug use. Having a combination of mental illness, substance abuse, and poor physical health makes it difficult for people to obtain employment or a stable housing situation. Still, institutionalization is not required in both cases. With appropriate supportive housing, formerly homeless people can live in the community and function quite well.

Victimization and Homelessness

People with psychiatric disabilities who are homeless are doubly stigmatized and oppressed. Whether they are in correctional facilities or on the streets, neglect and blame are the usual responses to the abnormal mind-set of mentally ill men and women. Homeless people often live in life-threatening circumstances. Their death toll is high from accidents, such as being run over by cars and trains, and from exposure to frigid temperatures. A person suffering from paranoia often will not sleep in shelters, much less seek medical help. Some shelters, in any case, will not admit people who are obviously psychotic or intoxicated.

Victimization relates to homelessness in a number of ways. First, people who have become homeless often have a background of personal trauma and victimization that might stem from early childhood. This background makes them highly susceptible to retraumatization. The association among childhood abuse, mental illness, and substance use is widely recognized, and researchers have found high rates of childhood physical and sexual abuse in adults who are homeless (SAMHSA, 2003).

Secondly, people who live on the streets or who are without a stable living situation are extremely vulnerable to physical attacks and other criminal harassment. Poverty, poor survival skills, and illegal activity place people with serious mental illnesses or co-occurring disorders in dangerous situations in which they are vulnerable to attack (SAMHSA, 2003). Some of the attacks involve rape of homeless women by other homeless people or assaults that take place in conjunction with turf battles or other disputes. But more often, the attacks come from the outside. A special report on hate crimes and violence against homeless people from the National Coalition for the Homeless (2012) documents a rise in violence that took place from 1999 to 2010. During this time, advocates and shelter workers around the country researched news reports of men, women, and even children being harassed, kicked, set on fire, beaten to death, and decapitated. There has been a sum total of 1,184 unprovoked acts of violence committed against homeless individuals at the hands of outsiders across the states. These acts have resulted in 312 fatalities. Most of the assailants could be characterized as thrill-seeking teenagers. The reported cases include teenage boys who punch, kick, shoot, or set afire people living on the streets and frequently kill them, simply for sport. To combat the violence, some states have passed a bill of rights concerning homeless people to give them more protection; others have passed hate crime laws to exact heavier punishments.

Finally, the criminal justice system itself perpetuates the victimization of homeless people. According to a report from SAMHSA (2003), about 1 million people with serious mental health problems are arrested each year, often for minor crimes related to their untreated diseases. Studies reveal that a person with a mental illness has a 64% greater chance of being arrested for committing the same offense as a person who does not have a mental illness. And following the enactment of "anti-homeless" legislation, including anti-begging, sleeping, and vagrancy ordinances, which is occurring in many of the country's largest cities, a person's contact with the criminal justice system may be even more likely than it was before.

Behind jail and prison walls, other inmates prey on those with behavior they see as bizarre and exploit those with developmental disabilities. The correctional officers resent dealing with them because they often act out in disturbing ways. Chemical spray, shackles, handcuffs, rough treatment, and solitary confinement are routine (Visser, 2011).

Mental Illness in the American Correctional System

According to the National Institute of Corrections, around 14% of men and 31% of women (taken together, 17% of those entering jail) meet the criteria for a serious mental illness (Osher, D'Amora, Plotkin, Jarrett, & Eggelston, 2012). These prevalence rates are at least three times higher than those found in the general population. Sixteen percent of state prison inmates are estimated to have a mental illness. Once confined within a correctional institution, people with mental health treatment needs often experience difficulty managing the stresses of living in close quarters with others and following orders. Accordingly, they incur disciplinary problems at high rates and often are placed in solitary confinement. They often end up serving longer sentences than inmates without mental disorders.

One major treatment innovation that is helpful to large numbers of men and women in trouble with the law is a new form of courtroom justice. We are talking about specialty courts as forms of diversion from prison. Included under this designation are mental health courts, drug courts, and more recently, veterans' courts. These diversion programs are designed to individualize correctional treatment for individuals whose offenses were committed in conjunction with a mental health problem, including addiction or disability. Specialty treatment courts represent the coordinated efforts of the judiciary, prosecution, defense attorneys, probation, law enforcement, mental health, social service,

Source: ©iStockphoto.com/wsmahar.

Jails and Prisons Are Today's Mental Asylums. It's questionable whether people with severe mental illness are better treated today than formerly.

and treatment communities to actively intervene and break the cycle of substance abuse, addiction, and crime. The programs are funded through federal grants (SAMHSA, 2012a).

Serious setbacks for the treatment industry followed the Great Recession of 2008. Deep cuts to state spending on services for children and adults with serious mental illness took place between 2009 and 2011. According to a report for the National Alliance on Mental Health, authored by Honberg, Diehl, Kimball, Gruttadaro, & Fitzpatrick (2011), the impact of these budget cuts led to significant reductions in both hospital and community services for vulnerable individuals. In some states, entire hospitals were closed; in others, community mental health programs were eliminated. The consequences have been particularly profound in those states that already had experienced major budget cuts. Nevada, for example, a state with a suicide rate and other mental problems that are among the nation's highest, cut mental health funding by 28% since 2009. Florida, another state near the bottom in per capita mental health spending, has come to rely on law enforcement and corrections as the first responders to people experiencing psychiatric crises who have not committed serious crimes. Taken to jail to be stabilized through medication, these people are then put back on the streets. Jail has become a revolving door for them.

Hope of improvement has come with the passage of the ACA. Medicaid and mental health treatment expansion mean that many more individuals will qualify for coverage. According to a recent article in *Health Affairs*, homeless adults should now have greater access to comprehensive mental health services than formerly (Tsai, Rosenbeck, Culhane, & Artiga, 2013). However, investment in case management services to enroll eligible people is essential for treatment needs to be met.

Social Programs for Better Mental Health

Members of the Social Welfare Action Alliance (SWAA), to which many social workers belong, are actively involved in the national convergence of training, education, and action on behalf of welfare rights and the prevention of homelessness. Their goal is to train 100,000 people across the country in sustained, nonviolent direct action to expose the injustices of the moment and demand change from those responsible (Johnson, 2012). SWAA members regularly organize rallies and teach-ins to focus on ways the United States was in violation of the UN Universal Declaration of Human Rights. The Kensington Welfare Rights Union (KWRU), which is affiliated with SWAA, makes a point of developing leadership from the ranks of the poor to provide housing for formerly homeless people. This organization uniquely links the Civil Rights Movement with international human rights; civil disobedience is a tactic that is used to house formerly homeless people in abandoned houses in the Kensington neighborhood of Philadelphia. Social workers and students who are involved in the movement see themselves as allies of the people rather than advocates. An internship program at the University of Iowa School of Social Work offers an immersion experience for social work students to learn about macro-level work from the KWRU in North Philadelphia (van Wormer, Kaplan, & Juby, 2012). The documentary film *Living Broke in Boom*

Times, available at New Day Films, provides commentary from key activists in the movement. For details on social work involvement in this social action project, see Chapter 12.

Supportive Housing Programs

Since the enactment of the McKinney Act in 1987, SAMHSA of the U.S. Department of Health and Human Services and HUD have funded innovative housing and service programs and research and demonstration projects to determine how best to serve people with serious mental illnesses and substance use disorders who are homeless (SAMHSA, 2003). Funding continues to be available today from various programs run by HUD, as well as from the Projects for Assistance in Transition from Homelessness. In 2009, the U.S. Congress passed the Homelessness Emergency Assistance Act with a focus on prevention, supportive housing, and aid for homeless families with children (National Alliance to End Homelessness, 2014a).

Even if homeless individuals with mental illnesses are provided with housing, they are unlikely to achieve residential stability and remain off the streets unless they have access to continued treatment and services. Housing First programs apply a harm reduction model to help residents make the changes they are willing to make, at their own pace. Intensive case management services are provided to enroll residents in welfare programs for financial aid, take care of their physical and medical needs, and provide mental health counseling (see Seattle's Downtown Emergency Services Center (DESC) website at www.desc.org for the most up-to-date research on harm reduction effectiveness with the chronically homeless population). As stated on this website, "Every year, DESC moves hundreds of homeless men and women off the streets and into supportive housing and serves over 7,000 of our community's most vulnerable individuals—particularly those disabled by serious mental and/or addictive illnesses."

Supportive housing has been shown to be highly successful in several ways. Thanks to the Housing First programming, between 2007 and 2013, chronic homelessness fell nationally by 19.3% (National Alliance to End Homelessness, 2014b). Permanent supportive housing and prevention have proven most cost-effective in the places where they have been directed at people with the most extensive service needs, people who were in and out of the local jails and hospital emergency rooms. For example, in Seattle, Washington, through DESC, new and neatly furnished apartments provide housing to homeless people with the most extensive substance use, mental health, and other chronic disease problems. According to a research study published in the *Journal of the American Medical Association*, which focused on a DESC apartment complex for alcoholic formerly homeless residents, the savings to the city amounted to nearly $30,000 per tenant per year in publicly funded services, while better housing and health outcomes were achieved for the individuals (Larimer et al., 2009). This program attracted controversial attention because the residents were allowed to drink in their rooms. An unexpected finding was that their drinking consumption decreased significantly, most likely because of the reduction of stress in their lives. Similar results were obtained in a study of chronically homeless people in New York City who were provided with permanent supportive housing. A 60% decrease in emergency shelter use for clients, as well as decreases in the use of public medical and mental health services and city jails and state prisons more than paid for the treatment and housing provided (National Alliance to End Homelessness, 2014b).

See Table 9.1 for a digest of essentials for treatment of homeless or housed persons with co-occurring disorders.

Table 9.1 Essential Service System Components

Evidence-Based and Promising Practices
Outreach and Engagement
• Meets immediate and basic needs for food, clothing, and shelter • Nonthreatening, flexible approach to engage and connect people to needed services
Housing With Appropriate Supports
• Includes a range of options from safe havens to transitional and permanent supportive housing • Combines affordable, independent housing with flexible, supportive services
Multidisciplinary Treatment Teams/Intensive Care Management
• Provides or arranges for an individual's clinical, housing, and other rehabilitation needs • Features low caseloads (10–15:1) and 24-hour service availability
Integrated Treatment for Co-Occurring Disorders
• Features coordinated clinical treatment of both mental illnesses and substance use disorders • Reduces alcohol and drug use, homelessness, and the severity of mental health problems
Motivational Interventions/Stages of Change
• Helps prepare individuals for active treatment and incorporates relapse prevention strategies • Must be matched to an individual's stage of recovery
Modified Therapeutic Communities
• View the community as the therapeutic method for recovery from substance use • Have been successfully adapted for people who are homeless and people with co-occurring disorders
Self-Help Programs
• Often include the 12-step method, with a focus on personal responsibility • May provide an important source of support for people who are homeless

(Continued)

Table 9.1 (Continued)

Involvement of Consumers and Recovering Persons

- Can serve as positive role models, help reduce stigma, and make good team members
- Should be actively involved in the planning and delivery of services

Prevention Services

- Reduce risk factors and enhances protective factors
- Include supportive services in housing, discharge planning, and additional support during transition periods

Primary Health Care

- Includes outreach and case management to provide access to a range of comprehensive health services

Mental Health and Substance Abuse Treatment

- Provides access to a full range of outpatient and inpatient services (e.g., counseling, detox, self-help/peer support)

Psychosocial Rehabilitation

- Helps individuals recover, function, and integrate or reintegrate into their communities

Income Support and Entitlement Assistance

- Outreach and case management to help people obtain, maintain, and manage their benefits

Employment, Education, and Training

- Requires assessment, case management, housing, supportive services, job training and placement, and follow-up

Services for Women

- Programs focus on women's specific needs (e.g., trauma, child care, parenting, ongoing domestic violence, etc.)

Low-Demand Services

- Help engage individuals who initially are unwilling or unable to engage in more formal treatment

Crisis Care

- Responds quickly with services needed to avoid hospitalization and homelessness

Family Self-Help/Advocacy
• Helps families cope with family members' illnesses and addictions to prevent homelessness
Cultural Competence
• Accepts differences, recognizes strengths, and respects choices through culturally adapted services
Criminal Justice System Initiatives
• Features diversion, treatment, and reentry strategies to help people remain in or reenter the community

Source: Adapted from Substance Abuse and Mental Health Services Administration (SAMHSA, 2003). Blueprint for Change: Ending chronic homelessness for persons with serious mental illnesses and co-occurring substance use disorders (DHHS Pub. No. SMA-04–3870). Rockville, MD: Center for Mental Health Services, 80–81.

Around 9% of the homeless population are veterans. According to the National Alliance to End Homelessness (2014b), veterans often become homeless due to war-related disabilities, including physical disability, mental anguish, and posttraumatic stress. Difficulties readjusting to civilian life can give rise to self-destructive behaviors, including addiction, abuse, and violence, which, coupled with these difficulties, can lead to homelessness.

Services for Veterans

The majority of mental health services are provided by social workers, whether in community mental health programs, substance abuse treatment facilities, hospitals, schools, or working with families, although a smaller percentage specializes in mental health diagnosis and treatment alone (Grohol, 2011). Today, clinical social workers are seeing returning veterans in large numbers, whether through the veteran's association (VA), where federal funding is expanding considerably, or in other areas of practice. The need is real. Smith College, which takes a psychoanalytical approach to trauma treatment, has been a leader in training mental health workers to address the psychological problems of returning combat veterans. The school was founded for this purpose in 1918 (Cole, 2008). According to research on returning soldiers from the Middle East, 15% to 17% met the criteria for depression, generalized anxiety disorder, or PTSD. A larger number reported they used alcohol more than intended (Sherman, 2008). Interpersonal conflicts are a major source of concern following soldier's deployment overseas.

PTSD is estimated to affect as many as one in five of the 2.6 million service members who have deployed to Iraq or Afghanistan (Dao, 2012b). The disorder, with symptoms that include flashbacks, sleeping disorders, irritability, and hypervigilance, often does not emerge for months or even years after a deployment. This and brain damage resulting from head injuries from explosions are associated with a risk of suicide.

Bell and Orcutt (2009) report preliminary research findings on a large sample of Vietnam veterans that show a striking correlation between war trauma and domestic partner violence following exposure to combat. The key aspect of posttraumatic stress disorder (PTSD) that emerged with a close correlation to aggression was the hyperarousal or hypervigilence response. Even when early childhood antisocial behavior was controlled, the relationship held. Alcohol problems that were related to the war experience were linked to the aggression as well. These veterans require mental health treatment for PTSD in addition to specialized domestic violence intervention programs.

The suicide rate among returning troops is significantly higher than that among people of the same age in the general population. In 2009, suicides in the military reached 285 of active-duty service members and 24 of reservists. As the services expanded suicide prevention programs, the numbers leveled off but in the first 6 months of 2012, 270 active-duty service members, half of them from the Army, committed suicide (Dao, 2012a). Over half used firearms. Although an important part of suicide prevention involves counseling individuals and their family members to remove guns from people, especially men, at high risk of suicide, a law endorsed by the National Rifle Association and passed by the Florida legislature prohibits doctors from providing this prevention advice. Mental health professionals and military commanders called for the law to be changed. A district court judge overturned the law as unconstitutional, but the state has appealed the decision (Lowes, 2013). Meanwhile, several other states are introducing similar legislation.

Substance Abuse Services

The toll that substance abuse takes on families, communities, and the criminal justice system is well documented. The total societal cost of illegal drug use is estimated at well over $100 billion. Nearly two-thirds of these costs (62%), according to a report by the National Institute of Corrections (NIC) by Osher et al. (2012), are associated with the enforcement of drug laws and the effects of illegal drug use on criminal behavior.

The impact of public policies and politics, as we have seen throughout this text, determines the availability of resources, the treatment methods employed, and the manner in which personal problems (for example, addiction-related behaviors) are defined. A public health approach, as studies show, is often far more effective for individuals and the society than a criminal justice approach for dealing with substance use and addiction. The damage inflicted upon society by the mass incarceration of drug users, in our opinion, far exceeds the damage caused by the drug use itself.

Similar to the situation concerning persons with severe mental health disorders, the correctional system is overflowing with inmates who got into trouble because of their substance use. The number of jail inmates with substance use disorders is even higher, in fact, than the number of those with mental disorders. National research based on self-report shows that in the year prior to their admission, 68% of jail inmates had symptoms consistent with alcohol and/or drug use disorders (Osher et al., 2012). The percentages were only somewhat lower for prisoners at the state and federal levels. Of women in state prison, 60% have been estimated to be dependent on or abusing drugs. Many of the inmates, especially in the federal system, were sentenced for their illicit drug use, but many others committed other crimes under the influence of intoxication. As Osher et al. (2012) argue, providing substance abuse treatment in community-based settings would be more cost-effective than that which is offered in incarcerated settings and it would have a deterrent effect on the commission of crime.

Elsewhere, other approaches have been applied with a greater degree of success. For example, in Britain and the Netherlands, many heroin addicts under medical supervision have been able to function successfully in their work and lead normal lives.

Aaron Pycroft (2010), senior lecturer in addiction studies at the University of Portsmouth, agreed to discuss harm reduction approaches in general, with a focus on the state of substance abuse treatment in the United Kingdom. He writes the following:

> Despite ongoing controversies concerning harm reduction approaches for illicit drug users, the international evidence continues to demonstrate their efficacy for reducing a range of drug related harms to individuals, their families and society. This evidence shows that a whole systems approach incorporating a range of interventions from needle exchange, to substitute prescribing and in combination with talking therapies is most effective. However a critical element that is often overlooked is the necessity of guaranteeing access to these services as a right of citizenship which is guaranteed constitutionally through legislation.
>
> In the United Kingdom, drug treatment has always been the remit of health services; the Rolleston Committee in 1926 recommended that general practitioners continue to prescribe heroin/cocaine for dependent users, which formed the basis of the so called "British System of Drug Control." In practice, following the Misuse of Drugs Act that was implemented in 1971 to sign into legislation the UN conventions on illicit drugs (one can consider the influence of America's war on drugs here), there was more involvement in drug treatment from the criminal justice system, and from then on methadone was the preferred treatment for heroin addiction. However, the values of the British social welfare system have always shaped the National Health Service (even the 1971 act allowed for the setting up of specialist treatment centers), which is why harm reduction has been relatively uncontentious in Britain in comparison with, say, the United States. The current coalition government in the United Kingdom is prioritizing "recovery" over "harm reduction," but most people in the substance misuse field recognize that that an either/or debate is sterile; harm reduction approaches can be an essential component of achieving recovery; and service user choice (as is the right of citizens) must be at the heart of this process (personal communication, July 17, 2013) (see Pycroft [2010] *Understanding and Working With Substance Misusers*).

Source: Published with permission of Aaron Pycroft.

In contrast to the more pragmatic policies in the United Kingdom, America's war on drugs and its zero tolerance policies can claim little success (van Wormer & Davis, 2012). Instead of harm reduction, standard U.S. policies have often had the effect of "harm induction" in that they have only made things worse, rarely better. We discussed the class and racial implications of America's war on drugs in Chapter 6.

There are many alternatives to current policies that would be more compassionate, have more support from scientific evidence, and actually address the problems related to addiction. The cost savings are substantial as well. According to a National Institute of Corrections report, a significant reduction in criminal justice costs occurs when appropriate treatment is provided (Osher et al., 2012). Research from Oklahoma, for example, found that sending 1,666 offenders to community-centered drug courts rather than prison saved the state $47 million over 4 years.

Treatment availability is essential to a reduction in illicit drug use. In Baltimore, for example, following a tripling of the funding for treatment in publicly supported clinics, the number of drug overdose deaths reportedly fell to the lowest level in 10 years (Brown, 2006). This approach was adopted in response to a drug epidemic that affected as many as one in six Baltimore residents. By 2011, Baltimore had residential and outpatient drug treatment slots to meet the needs of around 5,000 people and expanded methadone programs for many others. Even this was inadequate to meet the need, however, according to a *Baltimore Sun* editorial ("Rethinking Addiction," 2011) because underlying structural issues were not being addressed. The editors singled out the high rates of poverty, unemployment, homelessness, and the density of liquor stores as social factors that need to be addressed. Earlier drug policy experts at the University of Maryland-Baltimore and Baltimore's Abell Foundation in Baltimore recommended a more controversial approach to the drug epidemic in the city. This was the introduction of heroin maintenance programs as a strategy shown to reduce crime and to get people who were addicted to heroin into treatment (Brewington, 2009). Such an approach has been applied in Western Europe and British Columbia, Canada, but not in the United States.

Across the nation, unlike in Baltimore, where many of the same factors are present, treatment options are scarce. We learn from national statistics, that in 2012 the number of persons aged 12 or older needing treatment for a substance-related problem was 23.1 million (8.9% of persons aged 12 or older). Of these, 2.5 million received treatment at a specialty facility. Thus, 20.6 million persons (7.9% of the population aged 12 or older) needed treatment for an illicit drug or alcohol use problem but did not receive treatment at a specialty facility in the past year (SAMHSA, 2013). There were a number of reasons for not receiving treatment, but the primary one was lack of insurance.

With the advent of the ACA, this situation is expected to considerably improve. The ACA mandate that mental health and substance abuse treatment receives comparable insurance coverage to other medical services is evidence of a major paradigm shift by lawmakers. Increasingly, they are treating substance use disorders as a public health rather than a criminal justice problem. Accessibility to treatment, however, is still a concern for uninsured people who would qualify for Medicaid services under the ACA but who reside in states that have chosen not to expand their Medicaid programs.

Trauma and the Social Work Response

Trauma and Physical Displacement

The mental health care needs of these survivors of war or famine are great. Many of these needs preceded the survivor's flight itself and, in fact, precipitated the flight. The process of leaving to escape starvation, danger, and death is often fraught with additional traumatization. Treacherous sea and land voyages may compound the original misery. Insufficient food and water, a lack of medical care, inadequate housing, diseases, and injury—the physical and mental health implications are considerable (Hilleary, 2013; Mollica, 2006). Following such catastrophic events, many survivors experience trauma.

Women constitute three fourths of the world's refugees yet the literature on refugees tends to focus on three areas—protection within safe countries, practical concerns in resettlement, and policy reviews. This may be changing now through the advocacy of UN Women, an organization concerned with violence and food security for women internationally. Recently, it has raised alarm concerning the plight of Somali refugee women forced into exile and unsanitary living conditions in refugee camps in Kenya (UN Women, 2011). These women like all refugee women have become especially vulnerable to various forms of physical brutality and insecurity as well as to sexual intimidation and abuse. The pain that refugee women experience in transition from their home countries to host countries ranges from physical and psychological torture and trauma to horrendous stress associated with massive loss and acute cultural transition (Walter & Ahearn, 2008).

Men too suffer from the trauma of the displacement experience. They have often been injured, sometimes as conscripts in war, sometimes by landmines. Witnessing violence is traumatic for the onlooker as well as for the recipient. Children who have seen their parent or relative murdered—a frequent refugee experience—invariably suffer from trauma. Unresolved psychological problems may emerge many years later (Walter & Ahearn, 2008).

Nobel Peace Prize laureate and concentration camp survivor Elie Wiesel (1995) articulates the agony of being without a country in this excerpt from his memoirs:

> The refugee's time is measured in visas, his biography in stamps on his documents. Though he has done nothing illegal, he is sure he is being followed. He begs everyone's pardon: sorry for disturbing you, for bothering you, for breathing. How well I understood Socrates, who preferred death to exile. In the twentieth century, there is nothing romantic about the life of the exile, be he stateless person or political refugee. I know whereof I speak. I was stateless, and therefore defenseless. (p. 314)

Trauma Related to Natural Disasters and Accidents

Health-related crises and economic losses from natural disasters disproportionately affect developing countries—which account for more than 90% of natural disaster-related deaths—and predominantly affect the poor within those countries (Disease

Control Priorities Project, 2007). Floods bring lack of sanitation and a lack of housing; earthquakes such as the one that hit Haiti in 2010 left large sections of the population without adequate sanitation or shelter. And Hurricane Sandy, which struck New Jersey and New York in 2012, had a major impact on the most vulnerable people, tens of thousands of whom lost their housing. This disproportionate impact on the people with the least resources was reminiscent of the toll that Hurricane Katrina, which hit New Orleans in 2005, took on residents of the Ninth Ward and in St. Bernard Parish where many poor people lived as well. Of the approximately 1,500 people who died, the majority were living in low-income neighborhoods and were without personal transportation.

As described by social work graduate student Ardie Mohling (personal communication, September 15, 2008),

> On the sixth day (of living in the attic in the flooded-out house) a rescue boat arrived at the house and we were told to take only small and basic necessities. We were taken to the end of a bridge where we were informed that buses were going to arrive to bring us to a shelter in Texas. The buses that were promised never arrived and we were forced to spend the night on the bridge. On the bridge, there were families with members of all ages from infants to the elderly. The images that I saw were horrific and disheartening. Many of the

Source: ©iStockphoto.com/ParkerDeen.

Impact of Hurricane Katrina. Because of bad management, the death toll from Hurricane Katrina was one of the greatest ever.

families set up tent-like areas where their possessions were placed. There were a few portable toilets but they were filthy and loaded with mounds of fecal material, so individuals were forced to relieve themselves in an unoccupied area that was up the road. Food supplies were dropped from helicopters. My family and I eventually boarded a helicopter and we were given the assistance that we needed.

Source: Printed with permission of Ardie Mohling.

In light of all she had endured, Mohling stated that she never wished to go back to her native city and that she would find a new life elsewhere. The city had failed her. The inefficiency of the disaster relief effort following Hurricane Katrina is revealed in her narrative, which described desperate conditions facing residents in an African American neighborhood. The recovery efforts were not sustainable to preserving life then or in recovery efforts later. As noted by Pyles (2011), communities containing low income and vulnerable populations before a disaster often suffer a downward spiral afterward, and following recovery, the disparity between rich and poor communities is even more pronounced.

The human-generated form of disaster is especially regrettable, and there were many aspects of suffering caused by Hurricane Katrina that were the result of human error. The 1986 Chernobyl nuclear reactor explosion is a vivid symbol of human carelessness, which led to death, destruction, and the relocation of over 100,000 residents. And more recently, as was discussed in Chapter 4, was the 2011 Fukushima nuclear disaster that followed the tsunami, forcing 70,000 residents to flee from their homes. And still today, in the former Soviet Union, severe industrial pollution has led to massive internal migration to cleaner, healthier regions. Common to these latter two human-generated disasters is that they came about as a result of economic investment in the absence of any preparation for the possibility of accidents.

From a global perspective, a population's vulnerability to all types of disasters depends on demographic growth, the pace of urbanization, settlement in unsafe areas, environmental degradation, climate change, and unplanned development. Poverty also increases vulnerability due to lack of access to healthy and safe environments, poor education and risk awareness, and limited coping capacity. Individual vulnerabilities relate to capacity for resilience, mental health stability, and strong support systems. The psychological consequences of surviving when others die, of experiencing situations of extreme fear and even terror, and of trying to cope with loss in the midst of mass destruction can be long lasting.

Social Work in Disaster Response Efforts

The increase in the frequency and intensity of natural and technological disasters has rendered disaster practice one of the most salient areas of social work practice (Pyles, 2011). To alleviate traumatic stress in individuals and help people rebuild sustainable communities, intervention at the neighborhood level is imperative. Commenting in the aftermath of Hurricane Katrina, Loretta Pyles places an emphasis on social worker roles in helping such communities draw on their own strengths and assets. She also notes the need for massive economic supports and rebuilding efforts that failed to take place in New Orleans in the Ninth Ward; as a result, many residents could not return and community breakdown has occurred accordingly. Based on her survey of 11 individuals in two focus groups that she conducted in low-income African American neighborhoods in post-Katrina New Orleans, Pyles singles out the following aims as central to sustainable recovery: the development of community and social capital, housing construction and restoration, and a focus on safety concerns.

In the tradition of Jane Addams, many social workers and social work educators have offered their services to help provide immediate relief and psychological support to survivors of natural disasters and to help them navigate the system. In 2013, for example, a call was put out by the American Red Cross for social workers who have trained in disaster relief work to volunteer for deployment to Colorado following catastrophic flooding that decimated parts of the state.

Social worker Daisy Miller (2008) describes her volunteer work for the Family Assistance Foundation, which helps airline employees, customers, and family members of victims cope with the aftermath of an airplane crash. When an airplane disappeared in 2008 in the Andean mountains in Venezuela, family members waited anxiously for news. Miller, who was fluent in Spanish, worked to train and debrief airline employees as well as with community members of Mérida, Venezuela. As she informs us,

> Most of the one-on-one debriefing involved listening to their stories and helping them frame their experiences. Many were surprised and relieved to learn that the symptoms they were experiencing, such as nightmares, sleeplessness, difficulty concentrating, headaches, and feelings of guilt, were shared by others. They were also relieved to learn that these symptoms are almost universal, adaptive, and protective reactions to traumatic events. (p. 54)

In his book, *Healing Invisible Wounds*, Mollica (2006) discusses therapeutic strategies to help survivors, including frontline workers, such as medical personnel, cope with traumatic stress following the destruction of war or of a natural disaster. Society's neglect can have a serious impact on the fate of trauma survivors, as Mollica suggests, but efforts to help people heal in the aftermath of disaster can pave the way for hope and recovery. She describes an example of a therapy group that included doctors suffering from secondary trauma as a result of treating patient-survivors of Hurricane Katrina. Group members shared and analyzed their dreams that related to the tragedy. Mollica believes that we can teach about recovery to citizens by listening to the stories of survivors and helping them write down their memories and formulate recovery plans for themselves. We can ask people "What can we learn from your insights and knowledge?" And we can teach about recovery through national broadcasts. She cites the example of what she saw on public television in Peru that taught about recovery of citizens through the broadcasting of dramas based on the testimony of truth commissions. This was a part of the restorative justice process that took place in Peru following mass violence associated with political warfare and the mass raping of women by enemy forces.

Trauma Related to War

Of all the forces in society, warfare is clearly the least sustainable in terms of survival of people and the planet. War is unsustainable environmentally—tearing up the land, polluting the air and seas—and economically—redirecting a nation's resources toward killing machines. The legacy of war, if fought on one's home territory is likely to be mass traumatization affecting the citizens as well as former soldiers. The legacy of trauma coupled with hatred of the former enemy passes down through generations.

Research on societies in the aftermath of war in their countries reveals the extent of the problem. According to most studies, more than half of children exposed to war meet criteria for PTSD (Allwood, Bell-Dolan, & Husain, 2002).

We can look to Bosnia, which was ravaged by ethnic conflict: By the end of the war in 1995, more than 100,000 people had been killed and almost a million more injured and displaced (Hilleary, 2013). Twenty years after the start of the Balkan war, former soldiers are experiencing symptoms of PTSD and committing suicide in large numbers (Dzidic, 2012). Children who grew up in the war lost their childhoods; they witnessed people being killed and had to fight for survival. Today, serious juvenile delinquency and mass forms of hooliganism exist. In one of the most extensive studies of trauma in the aftermath of war, Allwood et al. (2002) found in a survey of 800 Bosnian children and their teachers during the 1994 siege of Sarajevo that 41% of the children had symptoms that would have qualified them for a PTSD diagnosis.

We can look eastward to the more recent wars in Afghanistan and Iraq. In Afghanistan, nearly 1 million youth are reported to be addicted to heroin, opium, or other drugs; in Iraq, many children take and sell drugs in order to cope with the aftereffects of wartime suffering (Hilleary, 2013). Girls may be kidnapped and forced into prostitution or take it up themselves.

In Cambodia, Richard Mollica (2006), the author of *Healing Invisible Wounds*, studied the psychological consequences of mass genocide and a horrendous reign of terror that took place in the 1970s. He compared the rates of depression in Cambodia with those of a neighboring country, Thailand, which was at peace. He found that the differences were striking: there were very high rates of depression and PTSD—almost 50% of the people living in Cambodia 25 years after the genocide. Rates of depression were very high, as well as rates of PTSD. Results from Thailand showed the rate of PTSD was only around 2%.

In the large majority of these situations, as in virtually all wars, rape of the enemy's women is an expected part of the process. In recent years, acts of rape committed during military hostilities have been recognized as war crimes, "crimes against humanity," prosecutable under international law. Historic precedents were set by the United Nations at the International Criminal Tribunals in Rwanda, as well as at the tribunal on behalf of the survivors of rape from former Yugoslavia (Farwell, 2004). Although we can expect continued international outcry against the wartime sexual degradation of women and prosecution under the new International Criminal Court, as long as men are trained to kill and dehumanize the enemy, wartime rape will continue.

When women started engaging in combat along with men, the fear was that if captured by the enemy, they would be raped. The fact that they would be so victimized by troops on their own side was not anticipated.

According to the facts revealed in a recent film, *The Invisible War*, a woman serving in Iraq or Afghanistan is more likely to be raped by a fellow service member than to be killed in the line of fire (Futures Without Violence, 2012). Estimates are that 20% of all active-duty female soldiers are sexually assaulted and an additional 20,000 male victims, as high as 1% of men in the military, are sexually assaulted by other men. As a result of the revelations provided in the film, the U.S. Department of Defense has announced new initiatives to prevent and respond to sexual assault in the armed forces. The initiatives are designed to create greater accountability of perpetrators, provide more supports to survivors, and establish more effective forms of prevention.

Sadly, the traumatic effects of war are by no means limited to adults. Children are increasingly vulnerable, not only due to displacement but also because children are deployed as soldiers. For example, during the current conflict in Syria, over 2 million children have been displaced inside the country, and 1 million more have fled as refugees. For over 4 years, the children of Syria have lived through shelling, endured trauma, missed school, fled their homes, and seen relatives die. To help these children survive, the United Nations Children's Fund (UNICEF) has conducted one of the largest relief efforts in history to aid the displaced children in Syria and the child refugees from Syria (Apitz, 2013). It will be years before the true extent of the psychological wounds of the survivors will be evident.

For children used as soldiers, the trauma might be even more pronounced. Many will live with the memories of having inflicted unspeakable atrocities, sometimes on their own parents and siblings. Many have been injected with drugs to induce greater aggression and reduce their inhibitions. Girls have been forced to serve as sex slaves. When the peace treaties are signed, the emergency humanitarian missions pull out. But these children's problems persist.

Traumatic Experiences of LGBT Youth

Gay and lesbian youth make up 40% of homeless youth. This figure comes from a recent eye-opening study from the Center for American Progress—*Seeking Shelter: The Experiences and Unmet Needs of LGBT Homeless Youth* (Cray, Miller, & Durso, 2013). According to the report, these youths typically have been rejected by their families after making their sexual orientation or gender identity known. Many have been kicked out of their homes; others have run away from the conflict. On the streets, there is little to equip them with survival as many have led sheltered, middle-class lives. Homeless gay youth are especially likely to engage in survival sex: an activity that increases their vulnerability to violence and disease (p. 15). They are at high risk of suicide, given their history of family rejection and harassment in schools. The shortcomings of juvenile justice and the child welfare/foster care systems make these institutions unequipped to handle the special needs of this population. For example, the system's emphasis on family reunification is often not helpful for youths whose families refuse to accept their identity, and foster care placements are not always LGBT friendly either. Such circumstances continue to drive these elevated rates of homelessness.

The report calls for an increase in LGBT cultural competency, particularly among health services staff; the development of interconnections with LGBT; focused community organizations; and amending The Runaway and Homeless Youth Act to include funding for specialized services to LGBT youth.

A recent issue of *Rolling Stone* magazine highlights this report with personal testimonials from young people who were cast out by their families and who ended up being victimized on the streets (Morris, 2014). This is a matter of life or death for these kids, according to the article. The rising number of homeless gay youth today, paradoxically, is a result of society's greater tolerance for the LGBT community, which is encouraging more youth to come out to their families. For those who come from strict, fundamentalist religious backgrounds, the result can be devastating.

An Ecosystems Framework for Trauma-Informed Care

Ecological approaches acknowledge that behavior does not occur in a vacuum but is affected by the larger culture and society, as well as the local community and its institutions. From this perspective, the mental health professional views each client as an individual with unique characteristics that, in interaction with the environment, may place him or her at risk for the development of a mental disorder or, conversely, may insulate him or her from unpleasant experiences. Central to the ecosystems approach is its perception of reality in terms of reciprocity or interactionism, the interaction between the person and his or her environment.

Similar to indigenous populations such as those in North America whose worldview is enriched by metaphors of wheels and concepts related to the reoccurring seasons, the ecosystems approach sees the person/environment configuration as circular. There is no cause and effect from this perspective. Related to the subject matter of this chapter, heavy alcohol and other drug use may be both the cause and effect of homelessness, as addictive habits may lead to the loss of home and family, and the ensuing stress of these losses increases the attraction of addictive substances. Heavy drinking and loss are mutually reinforcing. Similar interconnections can be found between PTSD symptoms and personal rejection, inasmuch as the rejection can intensify the power of the trauma.

Ecological approaches bring our attention to how cultural and psychological experiences shape human behavior. Each immigrant group has its own set of unique characteristics and hardships, including trauma, in many cases. Thus, the receiving environment and social service organizations have a crucial role to play in moving the new arrivals toward a position of further vulnerability or resilience.

Health management experts Bloom and Farragher (2013) in their book, *Restoring Sanctuary: A New Operating System for Trauma-Informed Systems of Care,* offer insights to enhance our understanding of social organizations as living systems. Their focus is on human service organizations, most of which serve people with mental health issues. The starting point for change, they contend, is for education of management and staff in how the organizational system works and how the moral/social environment of the agency filters through the system. When workplace stress is pronounced, for example, the whole atmosphere can become toxic to the extent that destructive processes parallel the very trauma-related processes that brought the clients to the agency to get help. A perceived lack of safety erodes trust at every level of the organization.

The mental health delivery system is malfunctioning in many ways, as Bloom and Farragher (2013) indicate. At the organizational level, many leaders and their staff have lost sight of the mission of their work and have become cynical and demoralized. Over time the leaders and the staff lost sight of the mission of their work and became demoralized. The end result in such situations is heightened authoritarianism by the managers and burnout for the staff. The result for providers is "a collective kind of trauma" (p. 21).

In *Restoring Sanctuary*, Bloom and Farragher (2013) tell us how a dysfunctional organization can be transformed into one that is trauma informed. Staff members must be reeducated into a whole new way of thinking to get beyond the negative labeling, overreliance on medication to control clients, and other forms of behavioral "management."

So what is trauma-informed care? According to the National Center for Trauma-Informed Care (2013), which is under the auspices of SAMHSA, when a human service program takes the step to become trauma informed, every part of its organization must be assessed and modified based on an awareness of the centrality of trauma in the mental health field. The focus of trauma-informed care is ecological and therefore can be understood within an ecosystems framework in that it is focused on interventions directed toward the organization or environment. Because consumers of mental health services are likely to be trauma survivors, the physical environment must generate a sense of safety and the social atmosphere should evoke a sense of peace and warmth. To achieve this end, service providers and the entire staff first require an understanding of the way in which trauma experiences shape survivors' responses to the services offered. Traumatized individuals, for example, might approach agency personnel with an aloof or sarcastic manner; his or her defenses are up. To establish trust with clients under these circumstances, staff members need to learn to avoid behaviors and practices that inadvertently might trigger a flashback to a traumatic event. Correctional systems such as juvenile residential facilities generally utilize practices of control that exacerbate juveniles' vulnerabilities and may lead to retraumatization. The end result is the opposite of the expectation.

Brian Sims (2013), senior medical advisor for the National Association of State Mental Health Program Directors, in his presentation on the neurobiology of trauma, differentiated between traditional treatment and trauma-informed care. Treatment centers and institutions that are trauma informed, he said, do not ask "What's wrong with you?" but rather ask "What happened to you?" The following are facts that he provided in his talk:

- Trauma-informed care, first and foremost, appreciates the high prevalence of trauma in clients.
- For individuals with severe mental illness, the rate of trauma is as high as 97%.
- Victims of trauma are found across all systems of care.
- The worst place to treat trauma is jail.
- The use of seclusion and restraints, as in juvenile institutions, is a trigger for retraumatization.
- Restraint produces a strong emotional response and further outbursts or a complete shutting down of feeling.

In his discussion of triggers for retraumatization, Sims listed loud noise a light suddenly coming on, touching, grabbing, and isolation as behaviors out for. The person who has experienced severe trauma experiences net changes that interfere with his or her reasoning ability. The symptoms can be improved with medication, but this is only a temporary solution. Treatment needs to get at the cause, which is the trauma itself. Non–trauma-informed care, as Sims further indicates, relies on overdiagnosis of symptoms and tough responses to behavior seen as deliberately provocative. Calming strategies are needed instead. Examples are going for a walk, quiet talking, working out, and lying down. In conclusion, Sims stated the following: "The needs of the individuals supersede the needs of the institution. Ask if HALT: Is the person Hungry, Angry, Lonely, Tired?"

As discussed in Chapter 6, historical trauma, the legacy of abuse and exploitation of minorities, including indigenous groups, should also be considered in designing programs in corrections and mental health agencies. Actions taken today, such as the temporary removal of children from an abusive situation, can increase the impact of present-day trauma for a family in the child welfare system. The reason is that such actions can serve as triggers of strong collective emotions among family members and by members of the community. Decision making by means of restorative justice practices, as institutionalized in the New Zealand child welfare system, can better establish trust and cooperation of concerned persons, as well as arriving at solutions that are practical and consistent with cultural norms and traditions (see van Wormer & Walker, 2012).

Summary and Conclusion

The criminalization of mental illness is a major theme of this chapter. Homelessness, incarceration, and victimization characterize the situation today for many persons with severe mental illness. The consequences of societal neglect in providing the care needed for people with psychiatric disabilities is harmful to the economy as well as to individual families in that states are forced to spend a large part of their revenue on the construction and maintenance of jails and prisons. These correctional facilities have become the new mental institutions for persons with serious mental disorders and problems with addiction.

The situation for people with chronic addiction problems parallels that of people with mental illness. In fact, they are often the same people who have co-occurring disorders, with each disorder feeding into the other in a cyclical fashion.

Harm reduction policies are essential to promote recovery for individuals and to get people off the streets into affordable and supportive housing. Fortunately, a number of American cities, like European cities, are instituting programs to provide the help and supervision that are needed. Housing First programming in conjunction with some other progressive initiatives in the forms of drug courts and mental health courts receive extensive, although still insufficient, federal funding. Public attitudes today favor treatment over punishment for people in trouble with the law due to their mental health and addiction problems.

Social workers and students of social work know from their professional training that addressing the needs of clients with co-occurring disorders often requires intervention at the policy level to make the environment more supportive and enabling. They are also aware that the clients generally come from backgrounds characterized by abuse and trauma, often from early childhood experiences. This means promoting and providing care that is trauma informed rather than trauma inducing.

The trauma to which most American clients have been exposed pales in contrast to some of the situations we have described in this chapter, situations that stem from war and other military conflict. The challenge in these nations is to save the children from such horrors as those faced by child soldiers and sex slaves who are forced to commit atrocities and other acts of savagery. A second challenge is to help give the survivors of this cruelty a life of purpose and meaning and to restore them to their communities. UNICEF and other funding sources are providing services, but the aid is far below the levels of what is needed.

There is much work to be done, in short, at home and abroad. Perhaps, as David Gil (2000) suggests, the incarceration of persons for offenses related to mental disorders may simply be a given in a competitive capitalist society with a weak social welfare system. Gil urges the social work profession to shift its focus from oppression and injustice to address the actual causes. The challenge, as Gil argues, must be to the "systemic sources in capitalist dynamics" (p. 85). Such a paradigm shift would be consistent with NASW's (2008) ethical mandate that we pursue social justice and resist oppression. Let us see how this goal pans out as we move on toward a discussion of policies related to old age.

Critical Thinking Questions

1. Recall the history of how prisons became the new mental institutions. How could this situation be corrected?

2. Consider the diagnosis of paranoid schizophrenia. How, in some cases, might individuals with this disorder become violent?

3. What does the evidence show about the connection between mental illness and violence overall?

4. Discuss the way the arts can help children diagnosed with autism. How did Nathan benefit (see Box 9.1) from the Kentucky theater program?

5. Consider the diagnoses of schizophrenia and PTSD. How are they alike and different?

6. Suggest policy changes to help prevent mass shootings, such as the ones that occurred in 2013 in the United States. What are some comparative international figures related to gun ownership?

7. Discuss the link between substance use and homelessness. How is this link considered to be cyclical?

8. Why do you think so many war veterans end up homeless? How can this be prevented?

9. How is Housing First a controversial but pragmatic program?

10. What are the treatment needs of people with addiction problems in the United States?

11. How do specialty courts work? Are there any in your area? If so, describe them.

12. Discuss the toll that war takes on soldiers and civilians when the fighting is on the home front. What is the nature of the trauma that is experienced by some?

13. What is the refugee crisis like currently? Relate today's crisis to the facts related to trauma that are presented in this chapter.

14. What are some things that can be done to rescue and help child soldiers after the fighting has stopped?

15. Based on your personal knowledge of organizations, how can the rules, regulations, and general treatment of people trigger their memories of past trauma? How can this organization become trauma informed?

References

Allwood, M., Bell-Dolan, D., & Husain. S. (2002). Children's trauma and adjustment reactions to violent and nonviolent war experiences. *Journal of the American Academy of Child and Adolescent Psychiatry, 41*(4), 450–457.

American Psychiatric Association. (2013a). *Diagnostic and statistical manual of mental disorders* (5th ed.). Arlington, VA: Author.

American Psychiatric Association. (2013b). Posttraumatic stress disorder. *Diagnostic and statistical manual of mental disorders.* Retrieved from www.dsm5.org

Apitz, A. (2013, April 3). Challenges in Syria remain enormous. United Nations Children's Fund. Retrieved from www.fieldnotes.unicefusa.org

Bangalore, S., & Messerli, F. H. (2013). Gun ownership and firearm-related deaths. *American Journal of Medicine, 126*(10), 873–876.

Bell, K. M., & Orcutt, H. (2009). Post-traumatic stress disorder and male-perpetrated intimate partner violence. *Journal of the American Medical Association, 302*, 562–564.

Bloom, S. L., & Farragher, B. (2013). *Restoring sanctuary: A new operating system for trauma-informed systems of care.* New York, NY: Oxford University Press.

Brewington, K. (2009, February 8). Foundation finds support for clinical heroin programs. *Baltimore Sun.* Retrieved from www.baltimoresun.com

Brown, D. (2006, June 9). Drug-related deaths hit 10-year low in Baltimore. *Washington Post,* p. A10.

Childhood trauma leaves mark on DNA of some victims. (2012, December 2). *Science Daily.* Retrieved from www.sciencedaily.com

Cole, K. (2008, Fall). Conference keynoter addresses treating veterans' mental health. *In depth: Perspectives in social work,* p. 3. Retrieved from www.smith.edu/ssw/docs/InDepth_08_Fall2008_web.pdf

Cray, A., Miller, K., & Durso, L. (2013, September). *Seeking shelter: The experiences and unmet needs of LGBT homeless youth*. Washington, DC: Center for American Progress. Retrieved from www.americanprogress.org

Dao, J. (2012a, October 8). As military suicides rise, the focus is on private weapons. *New York Times*, p. A13.

Dao, J. (2012b, July 13). Study calls for better assessment of PTSD programs. *New York Times*. Retrieved from www.atwar.blogs@newyorktimes

DiNitto, D. (2011). *Social welfare: Politics and public policy*. Boston, MA: Allyn & Bacon.

Disease Control Priorities Project. (2007, July). *Natural disasters: Coping with the health impact*. Retrieved from www.eird.org/isdr-biblio/PDF/Natural%20disasters%20coping.pdf

Downtown Emergency Services Center. (2009). What we do. Retrieved from www.desc.org/whatwedo.html

Dzidic, D. (2012, April 6). Bosnia still living with consequences of war. *Balkan Transitional Justice*. Retrieved from www.balkaninsight.com

Equal coverage for the mentally ill [Editorial]. (2013, November 9). *New York Times*, p. A18.

Farwell, N. (2004). War rape: New conceptualizations and responses. *Affilia, 19*(4), 389–403.

Folsom, D. P., Hawthorne, W., Lindamer, L., Gilmer, T., Bailey, A., Golshan, S., . . . Jeste, D. V. (2005). Prevalence and risk factors for homelessness and utilization of mental health services among 10,340 patients with serious mental illness in a large public mental health system. *American Journal of Psychiatry, 162*, 370–376.

Friedman, R. (2012, July 10). Good news for mental illness in health law. *New York Times*, p. D6.

Futures Without Violence. (2012, June 22). *Invisible war*: In theaters today. Retrieved from www.futureswithoutviolence.org

Gil, D. (2000). Challenging oppression and injustice. In M. O. Melia & K. K. Miley (Eds.), *Pathways to power: Readings in contextual social work practice* (pp. 35–54). Boston, MA: Allyn & Bacon.

Ginsberg, L., Nackerud, L., & Larrison, C. (2004). *Human biology for social workers: Development, ecology, genetics, and health*. Boston, MA: Allyn & Bacon.

Grohol, J. (2011). Mental health professionals: U.S. statistics. *Psych Central*. Retrieved from www.psychcentral.com

Hilleary, C. (2013, September 13). Syria's traumatized children: A national security concern? Voice of America. Retrieved from www.voanews.com

Honberg, R., Diehl, S., Kimball, A., Gruttadaro, D., & Fitzpatrick, M. (2011, March). *State mental health cuts: A national crisis*. National Alliance on Mental Illness. Retrieved from www.nami.org/budgetcuts

Human Rights Watch. (2003). *Ill-equipped: Prisons and offenders with mental illness*. New York, NY: Author.

Humphreys, K. (2014, January 21). We just had the best two months in the history of the U.S. mental-health policy. *Scope*. Retrieved from www.scopeblog.stanford.edu

Jimenez, J., Mayers Pasztor, E., & Chambers, R. M. (with Pearlman, C.). (2014). *Social policy and social change: Toward the creation of social and economic justice* (2nd ed.). Thousand Oaks, CA: Sage.

Johnson, D. (2012). You should know about the "99% Spring." Institute for America's Future. Retrieved from http://institute.ourfuture.org

Kolb, B., & Whishaw, I. (2008). *Fundamentals of human neuropsychology* (6th ed.). New York, NY: Worth.

Larimer, M., Daniel, K., Malone, D., Garner, M., Atkins, D., Burlingham, B., . . . Marlatt, A. (2009). Health care and public service use and costs before and after provision of housing for chronically homeless persons with severe alcohol problems. *Journal of the American Medical Association, 301*(13), 1349–1357.

Locked in: The costly criminalisation of the mentally ill. (2013, August 3). *The Economist*, 24–25.

Lowes, R. (2013, July 11). Physicians urged to ask elderly patients about guns. Retrieved from www.medscape.com

Márquez, C., Poirier, G., Cordero, M., Larsen, M., Groner, A., Marquis, J., . . . Sandi, C. (2013). Prepuberty stress leads to abnormal aggression, altered amygdala and orbitofrontal reactivity and increased prefrontal MAOA gene expression. *Translational Psychiatry, 3*(1), e216. doi:10.1038/tp.2012.144

Meskanen, K., Ekelund, H., Laitinen, J., Neuvonen, P. J., Haukka, J., Panula, P., & Ekelund, J. A. (2013). Randomized clinical trial of histamine 2 receptor antagonism in treatment-resistant schizophrenia. *Journal of Clinical Psychopharmacology 33*(4), 472–478.

Miller, D. (2008). Flight 518. *Social Work Today, 8*(4), 54–55.

Mollica, R. (2006). *Healing invisible wounds: Paths to hope and recovery in a violent world.* Nashville, TN: Vanderbilt University Press.

Morris, A. (2014, September 3). The forsaken: A rising number of homeless gay teens are being cast out by religious families. *Rolling Stone.* Retrieved from www.rollingstone.com

National Alliance on Mental Illness. (2012). Mental illness. Retrieved from www.nami.org/template.cfm?section=about_mental_illness

National Alliance to End Homelessness. (2014a). Frequently asked questions. Retrieved from www.endhomelessness.org

National Alliance to End Homelessness. (2014b). Snapshot of homelessness. Retrieved from www.endhomelessness.org

National Association of Social Workers. (2008). *Code of ethics.* Washington, DC: Author.

National Center for Trauma-Informed Care. (2013). *Trauma-informed care and treatment services.* Rockville, MD: Substance Abuse and Mental Health Services Administration.

National Coalition for the Homeless. (2009, July). *Who is homeless?* [Fact Sheet] National Coalition for the Homeless. Retrieved from www.nationalhomeless.org

National Coalition for the Homeless. (2012, January). Hate crimes and violence against people experiencing homelessness. National Coalition for the Homeless. Retrieved from www.nationalhomeless.org

National Institute of Mental Health. (2009). Schizophrenia. U.S. Department of Health and Human Services. Retrieved from www.nimh.nih.gov/health

Osher, F., D'Amora, D., Plotkin, M., Jarrett, N., & Eggleston, A. (2012). *Adults with behavioral health needs under correctional supervision: A shared framework for reducing recidivism and promoting recovery.* National Institute of Corrections. Retrieved from www.consensusproject.org

Pittman, R., & Delahanty, D. (2005). Conceptually driven pharmacologic approaches to acute trauma. *CNS Spectrums, 10*(2), 99–106.

Porter, R. (2002). *Madness: A brief history.* Oxford, England: Oxford University Press.

Pycroft, A. (2010). *Understanding and working with substance misusers.* London, England: Sage.

Pyles, L. (2011). Toward sustainable post-Katrina recovery: Lessons learned from African American neighborhoods. *Families in society, 2*(3), 344–349.

Rapp, C. A., & Goscha, R. (2012). *The strengths model: A recovery oriented approach to mental health services.* New York, NY: Oxford University Press.

Rethinking addiction: Expanding treatment isn't enough [Editorial]. (2011, July 16). *Baltimore Sun.* Retrieved from www.baltimoresun.com

Roemer, L. (Writer), Muller, R., & May, R. (Directors). (1964). *Rudolph the red-nosed reindeer* [Television broadcast]. In A. Rankin, Jr. (Producer). Toronto, Canada: Rankin/Bass.

Sherman, M. D. (2008). Trauma and the military family. *Social Work Today, 8*(1), 30–33.

Sims, B. (2013, April 26). *The neurobiology of trauma.* Presentation at a conference on trauma-informed care, Cedar Falls, IA, University of Northern Iowa.

Somashekar, S. (2013, June 3). Obama calls for national conversation about mental health. *Washington Post.* Retrieved from www.washingtonpost.com

Substance Abuse and Mental Health Services Administration. (2003). *Blueprint for change: Ending chronic homelessness for persons with serious mental illnesses and co-occurring substance use disorders* (SMA-04–3870). Rockville, MD: Center for Mental Health Services.

Substance Abuse and Mental Health Service Administration. (2012a, May 8). Grants to expand substance abuse treatment capacity in adult and family drug courts. Retrieved from www.samhsa.gov

Substance Abuse and Mental Health Services Administration. (2012b). *Results from the 2010 national survey on drug use and health: Mental health findings* (Series H-42, HHS Publication No. [SMA] 11–4667). Rockville, MD: Author.

Substance Abuse and Mental Health Services Administration. (2013). *Results from the 2012 national survey on drug use and health: Summary of national findings* (Series H-46, HHS Publication No. [SMA] 13–4795). Rockville, MD: Author.

Torrey, E. F. (1995). Jails and prisons: America's new mental hospitals. *American Journal of Public Health, 85*(12), 1611–1613.

Tsai, J., Rosenbeck, R., Culhane, D., & Artiga, S. (2013). Medicaid expansion: Chronically homeless adults will need targeted enrollment and access to a broad range of services. *Health Affairs, 32*(9), 1552–1559.

United Nations Women. (2011, April 3). *UN leaders raise alarm on plight of Somali refugee women and girls in Kenya.* Retrieved from www.unwomen.org

U.S. Department of Housing and Urban Development. (2013). *The 2013 annual homeless assessment report to Congress.* Washington, DC: Office of Community Planning and Development.

van Wormer, K. (2011). *Human behavior and the social environment, micro level.* New York, NY: Oxford University Press.

van Wormer, K., & Davis, D. R. (2012). *Addiction treatment: A strengths perspective.* Belmont, CA: Cengage.

van Wormer, K., Kaplan, L., & Juby, C. (2012). *Confronting oppression, restoring justice: From policy analysis to social action* (2nd ed.). Alexandria, VA: Council on Social Work Education.

van Wormer, K., & Walker, L. (Eds.). (2012). *Restorative justice today: Practical applications.* Thousand Oaks, CA: Sage.

Visser, S. (2011, September 29). Mentally ill inmates languish in local jails. Retrieved from www.correctionsone.com

Wakefield, M. K. (2014, July 31). HHS awards $54.6 million in Affordable Care Act funds to expand mental health services [Press Release]. Retrieved from www.hhs.gov

Walter, J. A., & Ahearn, F. L. (2008). Displaced people. In T. Mizrahi & L. E. Davis (Eds.), *Encyclopedia of Social Work* (20th ed., pp. 73–76). New York, NY: Oxford University Press.

Wiesel, E. (1995). *All rivers run to the sea.* New York, NY: Alfred A. Knopf.

Zoroya, G. (2012, February 29). Modern U.S. wars influence psychiatric thought. *USA Today,* p. 2A.

10

Sustainable Policy for Older Adults

Christina L. Erickson

It is not enough for a great nation merely to have added new years to life—our objective must also be to add new life to those years.

—John F. Kennedy (February 21, 1963)

Beautiful young people are acts of nature; beautiful old people are works of art.

—Unknown

Living out a long life, many years after working, was not a reality for people just a few generations ago. As human life expectancy rose, family and community supports for aging adults emerged. Throughout history, and still to this day, families have been the most sustainable support for our elder members all across the world. As countries develop, systems and policies to create a network for older adult care, beyond the scope of the family, emerge. Hence, policy development and implementation cannot focus on older adults alone, for sustainable policies are intergenerational policies, policies that use resources in ways that connect the generations rather than separate them (Generations United, 2012). In this chapter, we first look at the demographic changes in age across the globe and then examine the emergence of major older adult policy in the United States and select policy experiences from other countries. We then extend these policies through major older adult life experiences, including caregiving, ageism, and end-of-life care.

Aging Worldwide: An Overview

Aging-related global needs and responses are a relatively new experience for societies around the world, especially in such large numbers. The expansive nature of this "global graying" has not been seen before. For many years, developing nations around the world have been paying closer attention to the development of children and families (Takamura, 2007), and not until the past decade or so have they turned to consider the resources and challenges that a large aging population provides. The United Nations has identified some astounding figures in relation to older people across the globe. For example, the oldest old, those people 80 years and older, are the fastest growing population in the world (United Nations Department of Economic and Social Affairs, n.d.). A tripling of the aged population number in 50 years is expected, so that by 2050 the number of older persons in the world will exceed the number of younger persons for the first time in history. This growth in older adults is pervasive across the planet, and no reversal in this trend is expected (United Nations Department of Economic and Social Affairs, n.d.). As a whole, the number of older persons in developed countries has already surpassed the number of children, and this number is expected to double by 2050 (United Nations, 2013). The number of older people is growing around the world as life expectancy increases; simultaneously, the fertility rate is declining, leading to a demographic shift from a younger population to an aging population worldwide. Figure 10.1 highlights this demographic shift.

Figure 10.1   Percentage Change in the World's Population by Age: 2010–2050

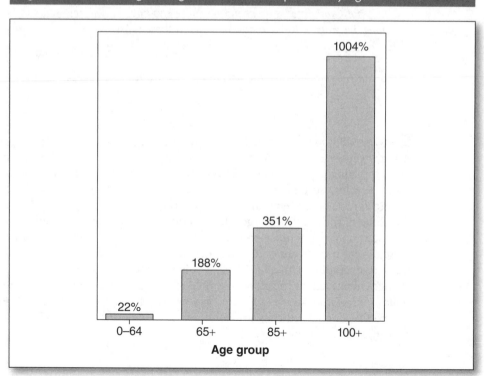

Source: United Nations, *World Population Prospects: The 2010 Revision.* Available at http://esa.un.org/unpd/wpp.

In response to the growth of older adults, the United Nations developed strategies for nations to implement to facilitate the creation of policy and programs that impact the well-being of older adult citizens in their countries (see Box 10.1). These Principles for Older Persons delineate five key areas that support the dignity and worth of older adults, matching a key social work value. The principles also provide a deeper exploration and definitions of universal values, definitions that can be translated into policy and practice in any country.

BOX 10.1   UNITED NATIONS PRINCIPLES FOR OLDER PERSONS

Independence

1. Older persons should have access to adequate food, water, shelter, clothing, and health care through the provision of income, family and community support, and self-help.

2. Older persons should have the opportunity to work or to have access to other income-generating opportunities.

3. Older persons should be able to participate in determining when and at what pace withdrawal from the labor force takes place.

4. Older persons should have access to appropriate educational and training programs.

5. Older persons should be able to live in environments that are safe and adaptable to personal preferences and changing capacities.

6. Older persons should be able to reside at home for as long as possible.

Participation

7. Older persons should remain integrated in society, participate actively in the formulation and implementation of policies that directly affect their well-being, and share their knowledge and skills with younger generations.

8. Older persons should be able to seek and develop opportunities for service to the community and to serve as volunteers in positions appropriate to their interests and capabilities.

9. Older persons should be able to form movements or associations of older persons.

Care

10. Older persons should benefit from family and community care and protection in accordance with each society's system of cultural values.

(Continued)

(Continued)

11. Older persons should have access to health care to help them to maintain or regain the optimum level of physical, mental, and emotional well-being and to prevent or delay the onset of illness.

12. Older persons should have access to social and legal services to enhance their autonomy, protection, and care.

13. Older persons should be able to utilize appropriate levels of institutional care providing protection, rehabilitation, and social and mental stimulation in a humane and secure environment.

14. Older persons should be able to enjoy human rights and fundamental freedoms when residing in any shelter, care or treatment facility, including full respect for their dignity, beliefs, needs, and privacy and for the right to make decisions about their care and the quality of their lives.

Self-Fulfillment

15. Older persons should be able to pursue opportunities for the full development of their potential.

16. Older persons should have access to the educational, cultural, spiritual, and recreational resources of society.

Dignity

17. Older persons should be able to live in dignity and security and be free of exploitation and physical or mental abuse.

18. Older persons should be treated fairly regardless of age, gender, racial or ethnic background, disability or other status, and be valued independently of their economic contribution.

Source: United Nations Principles for Older Persons (1993).

"Problematizing" Older Adults

The United States is not without challenges and opportunities as the country ages. Looking forward to mid-century, 2050, the U.S. Census Bureau (2008) suggests that the population will be older and more racially and ethnically diverse. By 2030, when all baby boomers will be over 65, nearly one in five members of the U.S. population will be 65 or older. By 2050, the number of older adults will more than double the number of older adults in 2008, with those over age 85 tripling in number. For example, there were 5.4 million adults age 85 and older in 2008, and that number is projected to reach 19 million by 2050. Simultaneously, the percentage of the population in the typical working ages, 18–64, will decline from 63% of the population to 57% of the population by 2050 (U.S. Census Bureau, 2008).

Unfortunately, the demographics showing our longer life expectancies are being met with "alarm" (Crampton, 2011). What could be accepted as good news is being reframed as a demographic disaster, as policymakers and care providers begin to worry about the rising care needs of older adults. This conversation of fear in regard to aging adult policy and practice calls for the enhanced participation of social work's ability to contextualize and define strengths within policy, community, and individual practice. Without this, the current conversations surrounding older adults are ageist and misleading, construing longer life expectancies as a population problem (Crampton, 2011). Recognition and incorporation of the United Nation's Principles of Older Person's by policymakers and organizations who implement policy can begin to shift this ageist attitude.

The Development of Programs for Older Americans

Benefits for older adults began in the United States with policies developed by individual states. By 1933, a few years before the Social Security Act, 30 states had enacted policy to provide state financed pensions for older adults. These first policy benefits for older adults often had age limits of 65, as well as residency requirements, support from family, and exhaustion of other resources (Day, 2009). These pension benefits were set at ages not much beyond the age of a typical life span. Policies in the United States were developed and implemented in times of youthful and growing populations and often growing economies (Crampton, 2011). Over time, all of the major policies for older adults have been amended to respond to the changing experiences and demographics of citizens.

OASI and OAAP

The Social Security Act, passed in 1935, offered Old Age and Survivors Insurance (OASI) providing pensions for those 65 and over, as well as their spouses. The financial viability of the program was planned through monies collected from taxes paid by employees and employers. Unfortunately, citizens outside of traditional employment sectors, for example farmers and domestic workers, were outside the sphere of these benefits (Day, 2009). An alternative was developed for poor elders who did not qualify for OASI—Old Age Assistance Program (OAAP). For these elders and their spouses, who had no savings and no work history, OAAP provided a small amount of money to help them carry out their lives (Day, 2009). Families continued to be the main source of support for older adults. As life expectancy grew, the United States began to consider other ways to support its older adult population. Awareness began in the 1950s, when it became clear that further development of support would be necessary.

The Older Americans Act

Developed in 1965, the Older Americans Act is the second piece of national legislation, after the Social Security Act, to address people growing older in the United States. The act provides a framework with deep linkages from national to local impact. Understanding policy for older adults cannot be undertaken without a review of these important policy elements.

Beginning elements of the Older Americans Act can be traced back to 1950 when the Federal Security Agency sponsored a National Conference on Aging (Rich & Baum, 1984). This was an early forerunner of the White House Conference on Aging that began in 1961, a catalyst of The Older Americans Act. The act set forth 10 objectives (see Box 10.2); many of them, even with slight modifications, are as valid today as they were back then (Baum & Rich, 1984).

BOX 10.2   OBJECTIVES OF THE OLDER AMERICANS ACT, 1965

1. An adequate income in retirement in accordance with the American standard of living

2. The best possible physical and mental health which science can make available and without regard to economic status

3. Suitable housing, independently selected, designed and located with reference to special needs and available at costs which older citizens can afford

4. Full restorative services for those who require institutional care

5. Opportunity for employment with no discriminatory personnel practices because of old age

6. Retirement in health, honor, and dignity—after years of contribution to the economy

7. Pursuit of meaningful activity within a wide range of civic, cultural, and recreational opportunities

8. Efficient community services, which provide social assistance in a coordinated manner and which are readily available when needed

9. Immediate benefit from proven research knowledge, which can sustain and improve health and happiness

10. Freedom, independence, and the free exercise of individual initiative in planning and managing their own lives

---

Source: Older Americans Act of 1965 (Public Law 89-73). Title I—Declaration of Objectives; Definitions. Section 101.

While these 10 ideals standardize what is hoped for among older adults in the United States, the full implementation of these objectives is still in pursuit, as the authority and economic capacity as well as structural racism and sexism, permeates the full implementation of these goals. Nonetheless, the Older Americans Act went beyond naming objectives and moved into instrumental change. It began by creating the Administration on Aging that provided grants to states for planning and services, as well as research and development for new programs for older adults. This is the basis of our older adult infrastructure in the United States and spawned a plethora of older adult policy and services across the country. Following the 1971 White House Conference on Aging, the 1973 amendments made to the Older Americans Act were momentous. One of the most significant changes was the addition of area agencies on aging (AAA), agencies developed to create a coordinated delivery of services to older adults at a local level. While not a provider of social services themselves, the AAAs were created to assess needs in local areas, coordinate ways to meet those needs with local resources and provide funding, develop contracts, and evaluate and monitor those services. These local agencies, still in operation today, provide an array of social services for older adults. Other additions to the Older Americans Act in 1973 included such things as access to library services, nutritional programs, and support of multi-purpose senior centers (Rich & Baum, 1984).

Contemporary AAAs focus on a range of services and civic engagement activities for older adults and touch nearly every community in the United States. Now a national network called the National Association of Area Agencies on Aging (n4a), they "allow older adults to choose the home and community-based services and living arrangements that suit them best, AAAs make it possible for older adults to remain in their homes and communities as long as possible" (National Association for Area Agencies on Aging, 2013). Current AAA programs address contemporary issues for older adults, expanding the reach of the organizations and touching on the 10 objectives first described for the OAAP back in 1965. AAAs address transportation, health screenings, food security, training and development for gerontological professionals, resources and referrals, and many other services in a network that is meant to evolve and respond to the changing needs and demographics of our nation's older adults.

Income Security for Older Adults

While it may seem that we can speak of older adults as a separate group, we are all potential older adults. We are discussing our future selves, our current elder loved ones, and the elders who live beside us in our communities. Provisions of social policy affect all of us, somewhere along our life span. One important facet of security for elders is economic. Income security for older adults can include a mix of pensions, Social Security, savings, and often continuing full- or part-time employment (Takamura, 2007). In the United States, Social Security is the most common source of income for older adults. Without Social Security, poverty rates for older adults would be far greater. In recent data, 41% to 58% of women over the age of 65 would have income levels at or below the poverty line without Social Security benefits. See Table 10.1 for a comparison of gender, age, and race and the effects on poverty rates.

Table 10.1   Poverty Rates With and Without Social Security, by Gender, Age, and Race/Ethnicity

		Men		Women	
		Aged 65–75	Aged 75+	Aged 65–75	Aged 75+
Overall	With Social Security	6%	7%	9%	13%
	Without Social Security	32%	48%	41%	58%
White, not Hispanic	With Social Security	4%	5%	7%	11%
	Without Social Security	30%	47%	39%	59%
Black, not Hispanic	With Social Security	11%	14%	17%	25%
	Without Social Security	40%	56%	49%	62%
Hispanic, any race	With Social Security	18%	16%	19%	21%
	Without Social Security	50%	29%	48%	59%

Source: Fischer and Hayes's (2013) calculations based on 2012 Current Population Survey Annual Social and Economic (ASEC) Survey. Earnings and income data are for the calendar year 2011.

Maintaining or growing a supportive economic system for older adult participation is a critical part of current economic policy work for countries around the globe. Around the world, older adults continue with paid and unpaid labor, in some capacity, as long as they are able (Wilson, 2000). While only paid work is measured, older adults also participate in uncounted labor. Roles such as caregiving and community involvement provide uncounted labor essential to the health and well-being of communities. The unpaid caregiving provided by older adults, often as they care for their grandchildren, partners, and friends, is often contributed by women and not counted in economic analyses. This clearly underestimates the important contributions of older adults in societal well-being. Government-provided economic systems, such as Social Security in the United States, are an important part of countries' economic stability and security for an aging population. These economic systems for older adults reduce poverty, secure retirement standards of living, and protect the most vulnerable of older adults from economic distress (Sowers & Rowe, 2007).

Amendments to OAAP

As mentioned earlier, the OAAP was an economic system developed to support elders who had never worked. This policy was amended in 1974 creating Supplemental Security Income (SSI) and replacing the OAAP program that was previously administered by states. This federally run version of assistance provides increased equity in financial distributions to poor elders as well as individuals who are blind or disabled (Gelfand, 2003). Many states supplement the federal amount offered to assure older adults the option to live independently.

Social Security in Context

Social Security is considered the most successful social policy ever created in the United States. The reasons for this are several. First and foremost, Social Security is universal; all older adults in the United States are eligible, no matter how much or how little one has earned. Second, there is no cap—benefits continue for a lifetime. It is also institutional; it prevents poverty among older adults. Poverty rates for older adults are low in relation to the rest of history, due to Social Security income benefits. The American Institute of Certified Public Accountants (2005, p. 14) provides the following information:

1. The reduction in poverty among the elderly is the major accomplishment of the current Social Security system. The poverty rate among the elderly in 2000 was approximately 10%, down from 35.2% in 1959. If Social Security benefits were not available and there were no other changes in the economy or government programs, the poverty rate among the elderly would be 48%.

2. Any reduction in the antipoverty element of Social Security is likely to put increased financial pressure on other government antipoverty programs.

3. Social Security provides more than half of the total income for almost 60% of beneficiaries. For almost 30%, it provides more than 90% of income.

4. In general, reform plans that move Social Security toward a defined contribution plan, particularly privatization plans, would reduce the system's features that redistribute income from high-income to low-income households.

Yet despite its universality and its strengths, the benefits of Social Security are not provided equally to all citizens. Institutionalized racism and sexism, pervasive along the life course, follows us into our old age as well and influences our Social Security benefits. While men received on average over $13,000 in Social Security income in 2011, women received just over $10,000. In every source of income for older adults in the United States, men earn more than women (Fischer & Hayes, 2013). Moreover, women are more reliant on Social Security, since they have lower levels of older adult income from other sources, such as pensions. As life expectancy rises, Social Security becomes even more important for the oldest old, as other forms of later-life income, such as savings, are reduced over time. Moreover, the cumulative effect of racism and sexism over many decades cannot be ignored. Lower earnings over one's lifetime translate into lower Social Security benefits in older adulthood. Simultaneously, these factors that affect the amount of Social Security benefits are the same factors that make Social Security such a necessity in later life. Women and people of color have a higher rate of dependency on Social Security income to meet their basic needs as shown in Table 10.2.

Table 10.2 Social Security as a Percentage of Total Income for Women and Men Aged 65 and Older, by Race/Ethnicity

	Women	Men
50% or More of Income from Social Security		
White, not Hispanic	51%	68%
Black, not Hispanic	59%	68%
Hispanic	61%	72%
80% or More of Income from Social Security		
White, not Hispanic	31%	50%
Black, not Hispanic	41%	53%
Hispanic	49%	61%
100% of Income from Social Security		
White, not Hispanic	15%	26%
Black, not Hispanic	30%	40%
Hispanic	37%	45%

Source: Fischer and Hayes's (2013) calculations based on 2012 Current Population Survey Annual Social and Economic Supplement (CPS ASEC) Survey. Earnings and income data are for the calendar year 2011.

Over the years, Social Security benefits have been modified to meet the needs of changing population demographics, and this is likely to continue. For example, young people joining the workforce today can expect to work at least until age 67 before receiving full Social Security benefits. In previous years full benefits were secured at age 65. Some mechanisms proposed to stabilize and make sustainable the Social Security program for older adults have raised controversy over the past several years. As a universal program, with some redistributive features, Social Security has been very successful at reducing poverty among older adults, and remains popular (Harrington Meyer, & Herd, 2007). Stabilization efforts should focus on maintaining the redistributive features to combat the effects of life experiences on individuals. One efficient and equitable solution to Social Security solvency is to raise the current tax cap to assure higher-income earners are paying in their fair share for Social Security benefits. Such a change would enhance equity, especially for women who often take time away from paying into Social Security tax to offset unpaid caregiving—reducing their Social Security benefit over their lifetimes.

A global look at income security for elders shows that more than 50% of the world's inhabitants lack access to social security benefits, and only 20% have adequate protection (Van Ginnekin, 2003). In many countries, as they debate the ability to create a sustainable income security system for old age, there is conflict over how much should be privately funded by individuals and how much should be publicly funded by the government and taxes (Takamura, 2007).

Prescription Drug Coverage

Older adults constitute the largest group of consumers of prescription drugs (Poisal & Murray, 2001). When Medicare was enacted, it was launched as an initiative to improve access to medical care for the aged (Aday, Fleming, & Andersen, 1984); however, medication was not a common intervention for illnesses experienced by older adults at that time. In recent years pharmaceuticals have played a more significant role in the control of chronic diseases experienced by the aging (Medicare Payment Advisory Commission, 2000). Over the decades since Medicare's enactment, prescription drug use among older adults has risen due to management of chronic conditions such as arthritis, hypertension, diabetes, and osteoporosis. The cost of medication has also risen, leaving older adults in a difficult position to purchase their needed medication (Gross, 2002).

In the over 30 years since Medicare was enacted, several unsuccessful efforts have been attempted in every decade to add prescription drug coverage to Medicare (Iglehart, 2001). Since 1966, more than 140 bills have been introduced to the U.S. Congress in support of prescription medication coverage for older adults (Moore & Lingle, 1987/1988). Like many federal policies, they first began as state policies. State-sponsored prescription drug coverage programs for older adults were implemented in 42 states by 2009 (National Conference of State Legislatures, 2014). The earliest programs began in 1975. In 2006, under the Bush administration, the first national prescription drug coverage program, Medicare Part D, was implemented as an addition to Medicare coverage. Critiqued by many, it left wide gaps in coverage, especially for older adults with a chronic medical condition with high prescription drug needs such as Parkinson's disease. It required individuals to choose from a complex array of prescription drug coverage providers and required a monthly fee, both barriers to participation. Partially in response to these gaps in older adult coverage, President Obama signed the Affordable Care Act (ACA) into law in 2010. One of the most important elements of the ACA for elders is the closing of the coverage gap for prescription medication by 2020. Prescription drug costs, only covered in part by Medicare, will be reduced significantly for older adults (Generations United, 2011). In addition to these benefits of the ACA, older adults will have increased access to preventative medical screening as well and more older adults will be eligible for long-term care help.

Older Adults in Society

As medical advancements have continually increased longevity of life, the role of older adults in the United States, as well as globally, evolves and increases in importance. Traditional and misguided notions about "putting folks out to pasture" are yielding to a more nuanced appreciation of the role that older adults play in a healthy society. Older adults continue to be fundamentally important contributors to society, and programs that contribute to their quality of life are not only a benefit to them but to society as a whole.

Caregiving

Informal help with living, such as assistance with cooking, shopping, or taking care of a home, is part of life for nearly all older adults everywhere in the world. These informal caregiving networks, provided by friends and family, are the main source of support for older adults. They are provided without cost to any government system and are the most sustainable way for a society to care for its older adults. These informal systems emerge out of the care and love of family and friends, often over decades of a relationship, and are given without intermediaries from nonprofits or the government, so resource expenditure is extremely low. The most sustainable policy development for older adults is to support the intergenerational networks of loved ones over the course of our human lives. These loved ones, especially intergenerational loved ones, become the backbone of caregiving for older adults who need it. In the United States, family caregivers provide 80% of all informal long-term care (Takamura, 2007). The Family Caregiver Alliance of the National Center of Caregiving has distilled research on caregiver outcomes. Through repeated studies, their findings have shown that caregivers tend to have stress, higher rates of depression, and other mental health problems, and in general they are in worse health than their counterparts who are not caregivers. The monetary value of this unpaid care is estimated to be over $300 billion annually (Family Caregiver Alliance, 2006). Unfortunately, support and recognition of caregivers in the United States continues to be minimal. Women are the main care laborers in the United States and often take time out from paid work activity to care for loved ones, which decreases their Social Security and other labor force retirement benefits. In Germany and France, where benefits are provided to informal caregivers, benefits include pay as well as some contributions to pensions (Takamura, 2007).

Families provide the majority of care for older persons globally. Programs and policies to support families in this endeavor are important, yet countries around the world are at varying stages of developing support programs to provide caregiving to family members (Hokenstad & Roberts, 2011). Mobility around the globe and the dispersal of families is a threat to the typical methods of family caregiving we have experienced over many years. Even in countries where access to family is available, there can be a tension between how much work should be placed on family and friends and how much should be taken care of by the government. In Box 10.3 we consider a case study from Norway regarding this tension.

BOX 10.3   CHALLENGES RELATED TO AN OLDER NORWEGIAN POPULATION

Bengt Morten Wenstøb

Norway has, since the Second World War, built up a welfare state, also known as the Scandinavian model, based upon universal rights and financed by taxes. Oil sales subsidize the welfare state when taxes aren't enough to finance it. Post 1940, politicians placed great effort on building Norwegian society. For many years after the Second World War, Norway had a social democratic government. There are two current perspectives on welfare for older people in Norway. The first and traditional belief is that the government should take care of elders. The other is to give more responsibility to the families. Family responsibility is more focused on nowadays, because recent immigrants and refugees to Norway bring this tradition to care for family elders. It is also a challenge in the Norwegian society, because few without Norwegian background would like to stay in institutions for older adults. There are fewer private institutions for older people in Norway, and the government normally pays the stay.

There are challenges for Norwegian elders in the near future. First, Norway has a large population of old people and a low birth rate. The oldest live longer and are healthier than in the past. This fact is critical for the Norwegian pension system, and the government has had to adapt the system. For example, now Norwegians must work more to get the same pension. The second is the medical system. If you are chronically ill in Norway, based upon a diagnosis, your medical bill is strongly subsidized. In the future, the government will evaluate what you have to pay and what should be subsidized. For several years now, there has been some discussion in parliament that not all diseases should be financed by the public sector. The third challenge is dental care. Surprisingly, dental care is not a part of the welfare state policy. Many think it should be. Therefore, some elders will have problems financing dental care. The fourth challenge is new technology. For many older persons it is important to feel secure in their home life and also when they are in institutions. One ethical dilemma is the parameters of new technology. For example, some elders have dementia and need to be monitored. A political discussion in the parliament is whether older persons with dementia should wear a GPS. If so, who should make the decision about wearing the GPS: the health personnel, the family or the person in question? The fifth challenge is the balance between the State and family. In the future, Norway will focus on what responsibilities older adults and their families should have in caring for older adults. Should families use institutional care and if so, how would they be paid? The second question is what roles should the professionals play? Norway needs cooperation between professionals and individuals to assure the health of the welfare state and the older adult citizens.

Source: Printed with permission of Bengt Morten Wenstøb, assistant professor, member of Norwegian Parliament and Standing Committee on Labour and Social Affairs.

Developing Sustainable Caregiving Policies

The network of caregiving supports is most helpful when it is broad. Caregiver stress occurs when caregiving responsibilities impede on the caregivers time with their work, family, or friends (Butterfield, Rocha, & Butterfield, 2010). Sustainable methods to combat this problem include expanding options for care—utilizing the existing connections of love and care present for families, combined with formal helping systems, such as nursing and personal assistance provided by paid workers, to assist when the informal networks of caregivers are absent. Options for this care include professional respite care, financial support to alleviate the economic stress, education and support for caregivers, and primary care interventions that attend to the caregiver (Family Caregiver Alliance, 2006). These kinds of formal systems, often provided through government programs or contracts, should be supported as the small costs they incur to support caregivers is far lower than costs for providing all of the care.

Developing successful and sustainable policies to support caregiving ideally will follow several guidelines. First, policies that provide for formal services with services provided by family members can reduce gaps and duplications. Second, family members can and should do the coordination and case management of some of these services. Combining professional care services for older adults, provided by nurses, doctors, social workers, geriatricians, and other professional helpers, can help individualize services for elders, while not replacing the successful work of families in caring for their older adult members. Attunement to the perception of need (Brubaker & Brubaker, 1995) and desire for help by the older adults and their families is crucial in determining formal support implementation for caregiving families. There is no one right way to determine the best use of public dollars to support the long-term care needs of older adults; evaluation of cost savings, along with quality of life and care are likely important components. Yet the evaluation should land with the elders themselves, determining their own satisfaction with their outcomes (Robert, 2003). Clearly, professional evaluations of what constitutes good care are not enough, as we acknowledge older adults' rights of participation in their own care.

In the end, caregiving itself may be a term in need of reform. Care partnerships, or the recognition of the long-term caring relationships family members provide to one another, are more attuned to the reality of life. Older adults continue to provide some care for their partners and children, even when they are often seen as the recipient of care. They may be holders of family stories, listeners and comforters to those around them, decision makers whose wisdom is sought after, and selfless contributors to the health and well-being of other family members. In most circumstances, the carepartnership that has developed over the years is adjusting, but some of the caregiving roles of the older adult continue—much as they have over the length of the relationship with the family members. The fears about demographic changes expressed earlier by policy analysts finds a strong basis in the idea that older adults are in *need* of caregiving and have little or no ability to *provide* caregiving. Social workers recognize and can highlight the ways in which interdependent caregiving is the realistic nature of these relationships. Being a contributor, and the desire to contribute to the well-being of one's loved ones does not end with the onset of old age; indeed, it might be magnified. Being referred to only as a recipient and no longer as

There is much planning to do as people approach old age and the possibility of facing disabling health conditions and perhaps moving to a smaller, more accessible place.

a contributor is a powerful recognition of our bias of older adulthood. Recognition of these enduring relationships through our word choice recognizes the sustainability and mutuality of these relationships.

Housing and Long-Term Care

Many older adults in the United States continue to live independently. In fact, the number of older adults living independently is rising in most countries, even in countries where intergenerational living has had strong cultural roots, such as Japan (World Health Organization, 2011). Older people may prefer to stay in their own homes, and the opportunity to age in place, with increased home ownership and community-based care, can make living independently a reality for older adults. In addition, in the U.S. a record 21.6 million adult children lived with at least one parent in 2012 (Pew Research, 2013). Bleak employment opportunities, expensive collegiate experiences, and lower marriage rates among young adults are some explanations, but digging deeper, there can be benefits to both parties. Others find that having adult children in the house is a benefit to the parent, as they have another person to watch over the home when they are gone, and the assurance and connections of family relations are paramount (Brenoff, 2013). Certainly, in cultures around the globe, living with and caring for elders is seen as a symbol of deep family ties. The same can certainly be true for families in developed countries as well.

Home-Based Versus Chronic-Care Facilities

For older adults experiencing chronic health needs, a continuum of care has been developing in the United States—from home-based services to long-term care. These chronic-care facilities include long-term care facilities, assisted living facilities, and adult day services as the main components. This range of care is meant to respond to the variety of care requirements and lifestyle needs of aging adults. For these programs, there are no national regulations, meaning that each state varies in the range and types of services offered (Alkema, Wilber, & Enguidanos, 2007). Social workers focus on self-determination as a main value in offering social work provision. This self-determination focuses on aging in place, meaning that older adults should be able to have services offered to them rather than having to move to receive medical or social care.

Offering diverse configurations is critical to meet the biopsychosocial needs of older adults.

Chronic care for elders, in a sense, began in the United States when poor houses were introduced. This early version of the long-term care facility provided shelter and food for older adults (along with other people of all ages) in need of care but without monetary or familial services to help care for them. It was only in the early 1980s that the Center for Medicaid Services began funding community based long-term care options (Robert, 2003). Prior to that, individuals in need of care had no place to turn but nursing homes where Medicaid was accepted. A focus on community-based long-term care options and on cost savings has focused attention on care in the community or home and has shaped research to address this perspective.

Over the past 30 years, a majority of long-term care spending has gone toward long-term care centers, and thus fewer resources are left over to support independent living in the community. For older adults who are near poor or do not qualify for Medicaid, additional services for independent living can be particularly scarce (Estes & Associates, 2001). Much of this is related to the intersection of social identities that can impact economic, health, and social standing as one moves through the life span. Many women and minority groups experience marginalization over the working years that impact their income status and the degree of services received as older adults. Their relatively lower-income results in lower savings and the lowest Social Security benefits, and the stress of life may be manifest in chronic health conditions and even disabilities.

Medicare will pay for intensive long-term care for older adults who need it but only under specific provisions. Short stays in a long-term care facility or rehabilitation center are covered by Medicare, but stays longer than 30 days require personal payment, often at very high rates. This means that long-term formal care is available only for the wealthiest or the most poor, leaving families in the middle concerned about the loss of family assets to pay for care. Connected with this loss of assets may be the hopes and dreams of older adults to pass along some resources to their children or other family and friends they care about. For middle-income and lower-income families, the loss of this hope can be hard for older adults to take, causing them to forgo long-term care as long as they can. Box 10.4 describes some of the changes occurring in China in regard to elder care.

BOX 10.4 SOCIAL CHANGES IN CHINA AND LONG-TERM CARE POLICY

楊嘉駿, *Max Yang, Social Worker*

The transformation of traditional values into modern values is appearing in China with the expansion of social and economic development (Banister & Hill, 2004). Filial piety is one of the values, which has been strongly influenced. The elder generation is composed of people who were born in the 1940s with strong traditional Chinese values; however, the younger generations have stronger modern values (Tsai, Chen, & Tsai, 2008). The different values regarding filial piety between two generations have influenced the expectations about ways of caring in contemporary Chinese families (Yeh, 1996). Meeting the needs of mature and young adults requires cooperation among the family and society, including understanding current perceptions of filial piety, improving the old age pension system, providing home-care elderly services, and establishing nursing homes, or long-term care facilities.

In current Chinese society, young adults may practice filial piety differently from the elder generation. As young adults prefer to move to more developed cities for work and income earning opportunities, which may be far away from their hometown, they have fewer opportunities to directly take care of their parents and to fulfill their filial piety duties. Younger Chinese may have other filial piety behaviors, such as sending money back to their parents, providing emotional support through the telephone, or finding a well-equipped nursing home for them (Tsai et al., 2008).

Understanding the newer displays of filial piety of young adults in China may help health care and social service professionals to nurture communication bridges between the different generations, facilitate family education programs, and to make better family policy. Currently in China, policies for the elderly are under serious consideration. The General Office of the State Council of China (2011) has published *The Social Endowment Service System Construction Planning From 2011 to 2015*. It emphasizes that by 2015, each city should set up a minimum of 30 nursing home service beds per thousand elderly and simultaneously rebuild 30% of nursing home services to meet national standards. The Civil Affairs Ministry of China (2000) also published *The City Planning Design Specifications* to emphasize that cities with a population of less than 60,000 should set up an elderly comprehensive welfare service center and one nursing home. Older adult social services and long-term community care services are moving toward full establishment in China.

Source: Printed with permission of Max Yang.

Elder Abuse

Elder abuse, according to the Administration on Aging, is "a term referring to any knowing, intentional, unintentional or negligent act by a caregiver or any other person that causes harm or a serious risk of harm to an older adult" (U.S. Department of Health and Human Services, n.d.). This definition encompasses a wide range of abuse, including physical, mental, emotional, sexual, and neglect/abandonment. This abuse can occur in homes as well as facilities.

With the onset of the rapidly aging population, there is potential for elder abuse to increase. There are cultural and economic factors that encourage elder abuse, identified by the World Health Organization (WHO) (2011). Factors to address include the following: depiction of older people as frail and dependent, erosion of familial intergenerational bonds, restructuring of basic support networks, systems of inheritance that impact power distribution, and migration of younger family members to other areas, limiting the elders' traditional familial care options.

No national system has been created in the United States to collect data on elder abuse, such as with other family violence issues such as child maltreatment and intimate partner violence (Butterfield, Rocha, & Butterfield, 2010). While all states do have adult protective service, there are not federal mandates guiding the construction of these departments, resulting in a great variety of systems making the collection of meaningful data difficult. This has complicated the process of forming a rigorous national policy as the lack of such data has led to debates about whether elder abuse is a social, legal, or health problem (Paveza & VandeWeerd, 2003). Adding to these issues are needs for comprehensive education in assessment and intervention for elder mistreatment (Paveza & VandeWeerd, 2003) along with evidence-based interventions. In 1992, the Older Americans Act was amended to include Programs for Prevention of Elder Abuse, Neglect, and Exploitation. It addresses violence against older persons and includes provisions for long-term care ombudsman programs and state legal assistance development (International Longevity Center, 2006).

Bereavement and End-of-Life Care

Grief and bereavement are part of a normal aging process. Aging increases the likelihood of loss of friends, parents, siblings, partners and facing the eventual death of oneself (Hansson, Hayslip, & Stroebe, 2007). Bereavement that has included a period of caregiving before the loss can be complex. For some, the relief of the role of caregiver is welcome, and others experience a loss of role and personal fulfillment that they are accustomed to (Hansson et al., 2007). Older adults receiving Medicare in the United States are eligible for Medicare hospice benefits when determined by a physician to have only 6 months to live. The elder agrees to sign a statement choosing hospice care instead of other Medicare-covered benefits for treatment, and care is provided by a Medicare-approved hospice program. Despite being a well-funded benefit, hospice use continues to be low. Fear of acknowledging a loved one's impending death along with a lack of awareness of the benefits are likely reasons. Box 10.5 tells the story of a typical American family seeking hospice assistance.

> ## BOX 10.5   HOSPICE CARE IN THE UNITED STATES
>
> Shirley's husband of 54 years, David, had been living with prostate cancer for 8 years. Both retired and in their mid-70s, Shirley and David had an active life with 5 children, many grandchildren, friends, and neighbors. They had a modest savings for their retirement but relied heavily on their Social Security benefits and Medicare. As David's cancer progressed and the caregiving of David became more involved, they decided to visit with a hospice nurse. The hospice nurse shared hospice philosophy: focus on living with purpose, comfort, and plan. Because of David's cancer diagnosis, the nurse was able to contact his physician and secure Medicare services to pay for David's in-home hospice care. This was a financial relief for David and Shirley because they had been paying for expensive medical supplies for David's health care, as well as high deductibles for copays.
>
> The hospice nurse, the spiritual director, and the hospice social worker began making regular visits to David and Shirley's home: providing care physically, spiritually, and emotionally. David and Shirley welcomed these visits for the emotional and tangible support they provided. The social worker would sometimes bring soup from a local café; the nurse brought necessary medical supplies; and the spiritual director spent time providing respite care so that Shirley could leave knowing David was not home alone.
>
> Three months after entering in-home hospice care, David died at home, where he had hoped to be upon his death, giving him a dignified and supported transition to the end of his life. Hospice was there for Shirley even after David's death. As a postgrief policy, hospice care does not end when the hospice patient dies but continues through the grieving process, up to 1 year. This helped Shirley transition to a life without her long-term partner.

Sustainable Policy for Older Adults: An Intergenerational Approach

The Natural Environment and Older Adults

The United States Environmental Protection Agency began its Aging Initiative in an effort to translate research findings into public health interventions for older adults, noting that even healthy older adults can experience negative impacts from environmental pollutants, especially those accumulated through a long life of exposure. Older adults with chronic health conditions are even more at risk (United States Environmental Protection Agency, 2011). One goal of the Aging Initiative is the development of a National Agenda for the Environment and the Aging with these critical components:

identify health hazards that affect older persons, examine a smart growth context for the impact of aging on the environment, and encourage civic involvement among older persons (United States Environmental Protection Agency, 2011).

In addition to environmental initiatives of the government sector, the Environmental Alliance for Senior Involvement (EASI) (www.easi.org) is a national nonprofit coalition of environmental, aging, and volunteer organizations. Established in 1991 in partnership between the U.S. Environmental Protection Agency and the American Association of Retired Persons, EASI's work increases opportunities for older adults to be active in protecting and improving their community environments. The environmental movement often frames the problem as one that affects youth, neglecting the interest and offerings of older adults in combating environmental problems. While young people are at risk of dealing with more significant environment troubles in the future, older adults are uniquely situated to understand environmental changes in a historical context and are committed to promoting the health of the environment because of the young people they love and care for. Bridging the generation's skills and passion for the environmental movement is likely an untapped potential in program implementation. Generations United has begun this work, putting forward a guide for communities to use in developing environmental programming. Policymakers as well as public and nonprofit agencies can utilize the guidelines provided in considering development of environmental programs in their community (Kaplan & Liu, 2004).

Source: Photo by Rupert van Wormer.

Raging Grannies at Peace Demonstration, Seattle. These older women draw on humor to protest issues of the day including militarism and environmental issues such as fracking.

Sustainable older adults' policies translated into practice are intergenerational. Intergenerational programs and activities are inherently more stable. Intergenerational programs create environments that are more diverse. Older adults pass on their skills and teachings to younger people; middle-aged adults benefit from engaging with both ends of the aging spectrum; and vibrancy is created in the synergy of age diversity. Sustainability is not about making policies and programs for older adults but about including their knowledge and perspective in the policymaking that impacts everyone. Older adults continue to be active in a wide array of issues impacting our community from an intergenerational perspective. One active group, the Raging Grannies, focus on several guiding principles that behoove people of all ages. According to their website (www.raginggrannies.com), the Raging Grannies strive to be nonviolent in all activities; court the press; shock with unladylike antics; use street theater, humor, satire, and props to get a message across; and act independently of any other organization. Raging Grannies value world peace, feminist values, social justice, and equal rights for all. Started in 1987 in British Columbia, the Raging Grannies continue to be active, demonstrating the commitment and contribution of older adults to the well-being of people of all ages, while simultaneously banishing the stigma of aging.

Ageism and Its Implications

Ageism is a discrimination embedded in United States institutions. Like racism and sexism, it can be found in the workplace, health care, language, the media, and nearly every other social experience. It is pervasive and not always visible. It can be described as

> the failure to hire or promote older persons, the absence of appropriate care of older persons in long-term care institutions, abusive language such as "crock," "gaffer," "old biddy," and "crone," ageism is apparent in direct personal responses toward older persons—insensitivity and impatience are not uncommon. Especially painful is the extent of various forms of abuse—physical, emotional, financial, even sexual. (International Longevity Center, 2006, p. 24)

Like all forms of discrimination, it is personally painful and outwardly corrosive to community life. With their comprehensive report, *Ageism in America*, which includes an action agenda for fighting ageism in health care, the workplace, the media, long-term care facilities, and other social institutions, the International Longevity Center (2006) created a comprehensive plan that will not only influence policy but also the ways in which policy will be implemented.

Ageism can thrive in any culture and society but can be most detrimental in areas that do not have comprehensive national health insurance and pension systems, in communities without educational options for older adults, and in places that lack health promotion and disease prevention (International Longevity Institute, 2006). It is important to identify the macro reasons for ageism because attributing physical and mental decline to old age, rather than a disease process, is detrimental to older adults and the perceptions people have about their own personal aging. There is a need to combat internalized ageism, which may lead to self-neglect and depression. As part of global efforts to address ageism, the WHO promotes positive images of aging. It begins with shifting the image of aging to one of contribution and ability. Box 10.6 describes one community initiative to do that.

BOX 10.6 AGING WITH GUSTO: AN ANTI-AGEISM INITIATIVE OF THE VITAL AGING NETWORK AND SAINT PAUL-RAMSEY COUNTY PUBLIC HEALTH, MINNESOTA, USA

We are ageist against our future selves.
Nancy Eustis, Vital Aging Network

Healthy cultures honor and respect their young and old.
Donald Gault, Saint Paul-Ramsey County Public Health Manager

Baby boomers are fighting not to get old. One way to stop ageism is to not adopt ageist attitudes toward each other and ourselves. The purpose of the Aging with Gusto initiative is to promote positive views of aging so all of us, as we age, feel valued and supported and can continue to make meaningful contributions to our families, friends, neighborhoods, and the larger world in which we live.

The Vital Aging Network (VAN) develops education and leadership development programs for people over age 50. Rather than serving older people, VAN views older people as change agents themselves. While planning a wellness initiative, its leaders realized that addressing ageism is one way to support wellness for older adults. They believe that in helping develop positive attitudes, older adults will be more able to take measures to improve and maintain their health.

The Aging with Gusto Initiative began with community conversations titled, "Aging with Gusto: Addressing Misconceptions, Fears and Biases as We Age." The following are the 4 guiding principles developed with this group:

1. Open minds open hearts

2. Being kind connects us

3. Everyone deserves respect

4. Environments matter

These conversations address such questions as the following: What does it mean to be old? How do you want to be treated as you age? How have you been treated differently because of your age? What individual steps to reduce ageism will you take in the community? With these conversations, the community begins to shift its perceptions of older adults. The following are goals of Aging with Gusto discussions:

1. Raise the consciousness about behaviors and practices that are based on misconceptions, misunderstandings, fears and biases based on stereotypes about people 50+.

2. Help people (including older adults themselves) use practices and behaviors that respect and value people who are 50 years and older.

3. Promote a new and more positive view of aging that values the contributions of people who are 50 years and older in our communities and culture.

The Vital Aging Network is a private and nonprofit organization. It found a complementary partner in the local Saint Paul-Ramsey County Public Health Department. The Vital Aging Network provides aging expertise and the Public Health Department provides outreach expertise as well as tangible benefits, such as printing, translation, and development planning. The first efforts of the initiative reached white, middle-class, and the young-old community members. Expanding their efforts, the partnership is now reaching older elders in retirement communities and reframing the Aging with Gusto initiative to fit three different local ethnic communities—Hmong, Somali, and Latino elders. A current priority is the development of an online community discussion guide, which will enable faith groups, community groups, and others to participate in community conversations about aging in any community.

While the initiative first focused on older adults themselves, this initiative is for everyone, old and young, from all social identities. It works to reclaim reverence for all community members, because healthy cultures honor and respect their young and old.

THINKING SUSTAINABLY

One of the most common misperceptions about care for older adults is that it is basically a short-term proposition. Not only have extended life expectancies changed that notion but also an increasing realization that policies regarding care of elder adults affects the entire family structure and can have greater and more far-reaching effects on more than just the elder in question.

What changes need to be made both in terms of our attitudes toward the elderly and our policies for caring for them, in your view? What are our collective obligations toward elder adults as a society, as well as our individual obligations within our own families? Explain how these changes will impact the goal of sustainability in all its forms.

Intergenerational Policy Assessment

Healthy, happy, and productive elders begin in youth. Isolating elders from policy decisions only serves to marginalize and continue the ageism that has evolved in the United States and some other parts of the world. Considering the macro- and micro-levels of policy implications, beginning with an intergenerational assessment, helps us view policy through the lens of the entire life span. Young people are our future older adults, and creating and implementing policies that include the entire life span assures us of an ever-growing attention to the needs of humans throughout their lives. Older adults are often portrayed and considered in policy planning and development as "unproductive and dependent" (Crampton, 2011). Social workers can begin to reframe these policy and practice conversations to recognize the strengths of older adults and the contributions they make to the communities in which they live.

The Intergenerational Legislation Impact Assessment (Generations United, 2012) is a tool to help us in our policy analysis. Inherently forward thinking, the assessment taps into the Native American belief that current decisions must be made with future generations in mind. Inherently sustainable, the assessment requires one to attend to the needs of the current generation without compromising the needs of future generations. With its attention to the fiscal impact of policy, it identifies potential pitfalls of division, those along monetary resources that can increase tensions among generations. The assessment ends with a clear use of the strengths perspective, recognizing the contributions of all generations, from birth to death, in the well-being of families and communities.

Social workers can use the Intergenerational Legislation Impact Assessment in broader ways too. Consider the implications of policies at an organization you may work in. The assessment has an inherent applicability to organizational decisions in communities as well, beyond that of legal policy legislation. Organizational policy, the mezzo-level of social work intervention and policy development, greatly impacts the utilization of services within communities and is often the starting point, the face, of social service offerings as well as lived policy experiences. The Intergenerational Legislation Impact Assessment, as seen in Box 10.7, can be utilized by social workers developing agency policies as well as government policies on all levels of social work practice.

BOX 10.7   INTERGENERATIONAL LEGISLATION IMPACT ASSESSMENT

Rating System

1. Harmful

2. Neutral

3. Helpful

4. Model intergenerational legislation

Intergenerational Principles

Make lifetime well-being for all the highest priority

1. Risks reducing lifetime well-being for one or more generations

2. Places no new risk toward lifetime well-being of one or more generations and offers no significant improvements toward lifetime well-being for one or more generations

3. Offers improvements in lifetime well-being for more than one generation without placing others generations at risk

4. Uses innovative or proven approaches to improve lifetime well-being for all generations

Consider the impact of every action on each generation.

1. Includes an assessment of economic, social, physical or psychological impact on generations or includes an assessment on one or more generations, which places at least one at risk

2. Includes an assessment of impact across the generations that demonstrates neutral returns

3. Includes an assessment of impact on one or more generations which demonstrates improvements for at least one generation without placing other generations at risk

4. Includes an assessment of both short-term and long-term impacts on each generation and demonstrates benefits for multiple ages

Unite rather than divide the generations for the greatest social and financial impact.

1. Pits one generation against another.

2. Neither pits generations against one another nor offers approaches to unite them.

3. Offers approach(es) to unite/promote connections across two or more generations.

4. Actively promotes innovative and proven strategies to unite two or more generations

(Continued)

(Continued)

Recognize and support every generation's ability to contribute to the well-being of their families and communities.

1. Fails to recognize or support the ability of some generations to contribute to their families and communities

2. Acknowledges but does not offer ways to engage or support each generation's ability to contribute to their families and communities

3. Acknowledges and provides opportunities for generations to contribute to their families and communities

4. Actively promotes innovative and proven strategies to support and engage every generation's ability to contribute to the well-being of their families and communities

Source: Published with permission of Alan King, Communications Specialist, Generations United.

Policy planning and implementation must be recognized as an ongoing process. As baby boomers age, having had fewer children than the generation before, the familial and community resources available for care must respond. Sustainable, efficient, and effective aging-care policy will need to be flexible to respond to these changing demographics. The best lens through which to view the beneficiaries of these policies is to recognize the older adult and his or her family as defined by the client. The important and dynamic sustainable interplay of private and public support for our aging members of society can vastly improve outcomes. As we analyze, develop, and support policies for older adults, we can consider not just at what age Social Security begins for citizens but also at what point support for family and friends and informal care networks enter into the public discourse. Finally, the successful longevity of current human life is not to be feared but celebrated and viewed as a positive aspect in life span development.

Drawing on the United Nations' Madrid International Plan on Action on Aging, the International Federation of Social Workers (IFSW, 2014) policy statement on older adults promotes and affirms the role of social workers in using these principles to help shape older adult policy around the globe (Hokenstad & Roberts, 2011). With an eye toward global development and advancement for older adults, the policy statement in Box 10.8 addresses needs such as safety, a pension system, and policy that can affect families in times of trauma, which may include a loss of family members, isolation, and frailty (Hokenstad & Roberts, 2011).

BOX 10.8 INTERNATIONAL POLICY ON AGING AND OLDER PERSONS

International Federation of Social Workers: Policy Position Statement

Social workers are in a unique position to create, implement, and advocate for policies, program, services, and research benefiting older adults. Recognizing that population aging profoundly affects all sectors of society, IFSW encourages the consideration of older adults in all policies and specifically supports the following policy principles that promote the well-being of all older adults:

- Participation of older adults in the design, implementation, and evaluation of aging program, policies, and research
- Respect for older adults' quality of life (physical, psychological, social, intellectual, and financial) and self-determination
- Support, protection, and strengthening of human rights for older adults, including elimination of physical, emotional, and sexual abuse, financial and material exploitation, neglect and self-neglect, abandonment, and implementation of human rights legislation and conventions
- Universal and equal access of older adults to affordable, comprehensive, and coordinated services in all sectors of society, regardless of race, ethnicity, gender, sexual orientation, gender identity or expression, religious or political belief or affiliation, migration background or civil status, physical, psychological, or cognitive ability, geographic location, or other diversity factors
- Elimination of socioeconomic and health disparities and discriminatory attitudes, practices, and policies that hinder older adults' participation in society
- Promotion of full societal integration of older adults—including people with physical, psychological, and cognitive disabilities, illnesses, and diseases, as well as intra- and international migrants—through lifelong learning, political participation, intergenerational relationships, cultural, social, and voluntary activities, and paid employment
- Safe, accessible housing for older adults in community and institutional settings and physical accessibility of public and widely used commercial spaces and services
- Introduction, preservation, and strengthening of public, private, and commercial pension systems that ensure adequate income to meet older adults' personal needs and the eradication of poverty among older adults, especially older women

(Continued)

(Continued)

- Health and mental health care, including promotion initiatives to prevent and ameliorate physical, psychological, and cognitive disability and disease, substance use disorders, and suicide among older adults; primary and acute care, including effective medications and sexual health care; rehabilitative services and assistive technology; psychotherapy and substance abuse treatment; palliative and hospice care; and specialized geriatric and gerontological health and mental health services
- Long-term services and supports—available in home, community, and facility settings, and including specialized services for older adults with Alzheimer's disease and other cognitive disorders—that maximize older adults' quality of life and facilitate ongoing participation in the community
- Labor market, economic, psychosocial, and respite support for family caregivers of all ages
- Specialized attention to the needs and contributions of older adults in emergencies such as natural disasters and humanitarian crises
- Promotion and expansion of gerontological, geriatric, and cultural competency, education, and training for all social workers and other health, mental health, and social service providers; recruitment and retention of gerontological and geriatric specialists; safe working environments, fair conditions, and just compensation for all workers in the field of aging
- Promotion and strengthening of the social work role in meeting the bio-psychosocial needs of older adults through practice, policy, research, and advocacy

The IFSW General Meeting in Salvador de Bahia, Brazil August 14, 2008, approved this Policy Statement.

Source: Published with permission of Rory Truell, IFSW Secretary-General.

Summary and Conclusion

The ever-increasing longevity of our life span represents a remarkable achievement, but the rhetoric of aging tends to focus more on the burden caused by older adults as opposed to the many contributions they can and do make to societal well-being. The developed portions of the world made the transition to larger numbers of older adults than children within two to three generations, but the developing world will make these leaps far more quickly (Frankenburg & Thomas, 2011). Focusing on policy initiatives that celebrate long life rather than problematize it and that consider intergenerational solutions will help us enjoy the benefits of old age and the value of older persons.

Critical Thinking Questions

1. Consider your own experiences in intergenerational environments. What about those experiences is different from being only with one's peers?

2. Who do you know that is dependent on a national benefit, such as Social Security or Medicare, for their income or medical security? Ask that person about the impact of Social Security or Medicare on their lives.

3. With a partner or in small groups, use the Intergenerational Legislation Impact Assessment as you analyze a local or national policy. Consider the implications and conclude with a recommendation and an evaluation of the policy.

4. Consider an older adult you know. Apply the United Nations Principles for Older Persons. Is there room for intervention to maximize this person's quality of life?

5. How is ageism displayed in your family? In your community?

6. Explore how internalized ageism might impact one's self-perception. What behaviors might occur because of this perception?

7. Have you ever had a conversation about death? Explore why this is a difficult topic to discuss when one is young, as an adult, and when one is old.

Resources

Ageless Alliance: www.agelessalliance.org
Alzheimer's Disease International: www.alz.co.uk
American Association of Retired Persons: www.aarp.org
Environmental Alliance for Senior Involvement: www.easi.org
Generations United: www.gu.org
HelpAge International: www.helpage.org
International Association of Gerontology and Geriatrics: www.iagg.com
International Federation of Ageing: www.ifa-fiv.org

References

Aday, L., Fleming, G. V., & Andersen, R. (1984). *Access to medical care in the U.S.: Who has it, who doesn't.* Chicago, IL: Pluribus Press.

Alkema, G. E., Wilber, K. H., & Enguidanos, S. M. (2007). Community- and facility-based care. In J. A. Blackburn & C. N. Dulmus (Eds.). *Handbook of gerontology: Evidenced-based approaches to theory, practice, and policy* (pp. 455–497). Hoboken, NJ: Wiley.

American Institute of Certified Public Accountants. (2005). *Understanding Social Security reform: The issues and alternatives* (2nd ed.). New York, NY: Author.

Banister, J., & Hill, K. (2004). Mortality in China 1964–2000. *Population Studies, 25*(1), 55–75.

Brenoff, A. (2013). Pew study: Why adult kids still live with their parents. *Huffington Post.* Retrieved from www.huffingtonpost.com/2013/08/01/living-with-parents_n_3690069 .html

Brubaker, E., & Brubaker, T. H. (1995). Critical policy issues. In G. C. Smith, S. S. Tobin, E. A. Robertson-Tchabo, & P. W. Power (Eds.). *Strengthening aging families: Diversity in practice and policy* (pp. 235–247). Thousand Oaks, CA: Sage.

Butterfield, A. K., Rocha, C. J., & Butterfield, W. H. (2010). *The dynamics of family policy: Analysis and advocacy.* Chicago, IL: Lyceum.

The Civil Affairs Ministry of China. (2000). The city planning design specifications. Retrieved from www.zzupb.gov.cn/data_news/2010/11/18/18FE448F-4449–4DCE-99DE-91520DB 860B0.shtml

Crampton, A. (2011). Population aging and social work practice with older adults: Demographic and policy challenges. *International Social Work, 54*(3), 313–329.

Day, P. J. (2009). *A new history of social welfare* (6th ed.). Boston, MA: Pearson.

Estes, C., & Associates. (2001). *Social policy & aging: A critical perspective.* Thousand Oaks, CA: Sage.

Family Caregiver Alliance. (2006). Caregiver health: A population at risk. Retrieved from www .caregiver.org/caregiver/jsp/content_node.jsp?nodeid=1822

Fischer, J., & Hayes, J. (2013). *The importance of Social Security in the incomes of older Americans: Differences by gender, age, race/ethnicity, and marital status* (Briefing Paper #D503). Washington, DC: Institute for Women's Policy Research.

Frankenburg, E., & Thomas, D. (2011). Global aging. In R. H. Binstock & L. K. George (Eds.), *Handbook of aging and the social sciences* (7th ed., pp. 73–89). London, England: Academic Press.

Gelfand, D. E. (2003). *Aging and ethnicity: Knowledge and services* (2nd ed.). New York, NY: Springer.

General Office of the State Council of China. (2011). The social endowment service system construction planning from 2011 to 2015. Retrieved from www.gov.cn

Generations United. (2011). *Health care benefits for children & older adults: The Affordable Care Act.* Washington, DC: Author.

Generations United. (2012). Impact assessment for intergenerational assessment. Retrieved from www.gu.org/OURWORK/PublicPolicy/PolicyImpact.aspx

Gross, D. (2002, March). *Medicare beneficiaries and prescription drugs: Costs and coverage.* AARP Issue Brief. Retrieved from http://research.aarp.org/health/dd77_rx.html

Hansson, R. O., Hayslip, B., & Stroebe, M. (2007). Grief and bereavement. In J. A. Blackburn & C. N. Dulmus (Eds.), *Handbook of gerontology: Evidence-based approaches to theory, practice, and policy* (pp. 367–394). Hoboken, NJ: Wiley.

Harrington Meyer, M., & Herd, P. (2007). *Market friendly or family friendly? The state and gender inequality in old age.* New York, NY: Russell Sage.

Hokenstad, M. C., & Roberts, A. R. (2011). International policy on ageing and older persons: Implications for social work practice. *International Social Work, 54,* 330–343.

Iglehart, J. K. (2001). Medicare and prescription drugs. *New England Journal of Medicine, 344*(13), 1010–1015.

International Federation of Social Workers. (2014). Ageing and older adults. Retrieved from http://ifsw.org/policies/ageing-and-older-adults/

International Longevity Center–Anti-Aging Task Force. (2006). *Ageism in America.* Retrieved from www.graypanthersmetrodetroit.org/Ageism_In_America_-_ILC_Book_2006.pdf

Kaplan, M., & Liu, N. (2004). *Generations united for environmental awareness and action.* Washington, DC: Generations United.

Medicare Payment Advisory Commission. (June, 2000). *Report to the congress: Selected Medicare issues.* Retrieved from www.medpac.gov/publications

Moore, T. S., & Lingle, E. W. (1987/1988). Economic issues of drug use in the elderly and access patterns. *Journal of Geriatric Drug Therapy, 2*(2–3), 11–20.

National Association for Area Agencies on Aging. (2013). About n4a. Retrieved from www.n4a.org/about-n4a/

National Conference of State Legislatures. (2014). NCSL health program state pharmaceutical assistance programs (subsidies and discounts for seniors, disabled, uninsured and others). Retrieved from www.ncsl.org/research/health/state-pharmaceutical-assistance-programs.aspx

Office of the United Nations High Commissioner for Human Rights. (1991). United Nations principles for older persons. Retrieved from www.ohchr.org/EN/ProfessionalInterest/Pages/OlderPersons.aspx

Paveza, G. J., & VandeWeerd, C. (2003). Elder mistreatment and the role of social work. In B. Berkman & L. Harootyan (Eds.), *Social work and health care in an aging society: Education, policy, practice and research* (pp. 245–268). New York, NY: Springer.

Pew Research. (2013). *A rising share of young adults live in their parents' home.* Retrieved from www.pewsocialtrends.org/2013/08/01/a-rising-share-of-young-adults-live-in-their-parents-home/

Poisal, J. A., & Murray, L. A. (2001). Growing differences between Medicare beneficiaries with and without drug coverage. *Health Affairs, 20*(2), 74–85.

Rich, B. M., & Baum, M. (1984). *The aging: A guide to public policy.* Pittsburgh, PA: University of Pittsburgh Press.

Robert, S. A. (2003). Home- and community-based long-term care policies and programs: The crucial role for social work practitioners and researchers. In B. Berkman & Harootyan, L. (Eds.), *Social work and health care in an aging society: Education, policy, practice and research* (pp. 351–376). New York, NY: Springer.

Sowers, K., & Rowe, W. S. (2007). Global aging. In J. A. Blackburn & C. N. Dulmus (Eds.), *Handbook of gerontology: Evidence-based approaches to theory, practice, and policy* (pp. 3–18). Hoboken, NJ: Wiley.

Takamura, J. (2007). Global challenges for an aging population. In J. A. Blackburn & C. N. Dulmus (Eds.), *Handbook of gerontology: Evidence-based approaches to theory, practice, and policy* (pp. 545–564). Hoboken, NJ: Wiley.

Tsai, H. H., Chen, M. H., & Tsai, Y. F. (2008). Perceptions of filial piety among Taiwanese university students. *Journal of Advanced Nursing, 63*(3), 284–290.

United Nations Department of Economic and Social Affairs, Population Division. (2013). World population ageing 2013. New York: United Nations. Retrieved from www.un.org

United Nations Department of Economic and Social Affairs, Population Division. (n.d.). World population ageing 1950–2050. Retrieved from www.un.org/esa/population/publications/worldageing19502050/

United Nations Principles for Older Persons. (1993). *Australian Journal on Ageing, 12*(13).

United States Environmental Protection Agency. (2011). Aging initiative: Basic information. Retrieved from www.epa.gov/aging/basicinformation.htm

U.S. Census Bureau. (2008). An older and more diverse nation by mid-century. Retrieved from www.census.gov/newsroom/releases/archives/population/cb08–123.html

U.S. Department of Health and Human Services, Administration for Community Living. (n.d.). Administration on aging: What is elder abuse? Retrieved from www.aoa.gov/AoA_programs/elder_rights/EA_prevention/whatisEA.aspx

Van Ginnekin, W. (2003). *Extending social security: Policies for developing countries.* International Labour Office: Geneva, Switzerland.

World Health Organization. (2011). *Global health and aging* (NIH Publication 11-7737). Washington, DC: Author.

World Health Organization, Media Centre. (2011). Elder Maltreatment [Fact Sheet]. Retrieved from www.who.int/mediacentre/factsheets/fs357/en/

Wilson, G. (2000). *Understanding old age: Critical and global perspectives.* London, England: Sage.

Yeh, K. H. (1996). The dilemmas and coping strategies of interactions between parents and children. *Academia Sinica Journal of Anthropology, 82,* 65–114.

▌▌ Human Rights

Guns are particularly lethal. . . . The US national map of suicide lights up in states with the highest gun ownership rates. . . . The literature suggests that having a gun in your home to protect your family is like bringing a time bomb into your house.

—Sabrina Tavernise (2013, p. 1)

Throughout this book, the essential issue of human rights has been a major theme. The reason is clear—populations whose rights have been violated (for example tribal groups oppressed by majority rule; women; children; religious minorities; refugees; people who are gay, lesbian, or transgender) by their society or by its representatives are populations at high risk of experiencing other abuses jeopardizing their general welfare. The interaction between human rights and social welfare is complicated, inextricable and ever present. Wronka (2012) writes that everyone needs to educate themselves thoroughly about human rights, because they protect everyone's well-being and welfare. He states that "human rights should be dragged into our lived awareness" (Wronka, 2012).

For those who are well fed and immunized with shelter and income, surrounded by the strength of others similarly well-off, human rights may seem abstract—an ideal, indistinct set of concepts. But for those who are suddenly plunged into war; caught up in violence; isolated on a border without identity papers; adjacent to a terrorist bomb; excluded due to disability, gender, or distinctive characteristic, the existence of codified human rights take on urgent and very real meaning.

This chapter alone is insufficient to address all facets of human rights, but it will raise some of the areas of progress and of challenge for the social work profession. We'll begin by looking at some of the most momentous threats to human rights, focusing on war and gun violence. We will discuss the importance of engaging the social worker and human service professional in seeing, understanding, and implementing the resources of the United Nations. These resources include the legal documents, international policy instruments, and laws passed in order to implement the Universal

Declaration of Human Rights (UDHR). In addition, we will consider the difficulties inherent in the concept of global government. Finally we will see how the application of the policy instruments put forth by the United Nations can impact human rights policy practice, both locally and globally.

Immediate Threats to Human Rights: War and Guns

The 20th century saw global citizens preoccupied with the devastation of the First World War, soon followed by the Second World War and serious regional wars throughout the world, including Vietnam, Korea, the Sudan, Iraq, Afghanistan, and the Balkans. At the same time, movements to promote numerous civil rights causes sprang up, from the women's suffrage movement, the eradication of Jim Crow laws, and the promotion of racial equality in the United States to the ending of apartheid in South Africa. The combination of forces that created these social movements (for example, with women's suffrage, it was a combination of the forces of industrialization, women's participation in the workforce, new freedoms with education, and progress with family planning that freed women to claim their vote) and the devastation caused by wars spurred the drafting and passage of international conventions and laws. These laws represent a new, collective human effort in the history of the world.

In the 21st century, there is a growing call for finding alternatives to war. The sanctions on Iran are holding at the time of writing, and it seems that the military Junta in Myanmar (Burma) has finally realized that economic and social isolation from the rest of the world is seriously damaging to their country's survival. The gun lobby in America is losing ground in the face of terrible massacres, plus tragic loss of life daily on the streets of cities such as Chicago and Los Angeles. There are windows of opportunity opening to continue the efforts to address torture and inhuman treatment of prisoners (Amnesty International, 2012). It is possible that the 21st century will be a time of implementation of the existing covenants and international policy instruments needed to achieve human rights.

Source: Photo permission by Charletta Sudduth and Annie Pearl Stevenson.

Charletta Sudduth, Coauthor of *The Maid Narratives*, With Her Mother, Annie Pearl Stevenson. Sudduth interviewed women who had survived Jim Crow hardships in Mississippi, including her mother.

Individual nations and their leaders are now being held accountable for a wide array of human rights violations, from collective social exclusion from resources to trafficking and torture. In a December 2012 ruling, the European Court of Human Rights "condemned CIA tactics under the Bush administration . . . a warning to President Obama that pressure for the United States and its partners to acknowledge and make amends for gross violations of international legal and human right standards is unlikely to subside" ("About Those Black Sites," 2013, p. A14).

The concern about gun violence is also unlikely to subside. In the aftermath of the awful massacre at Sandy Hook Elementary School in the United States in 2012, parents and news media were commenting on the utter defenselessness and powerlessness of the children who were murdered. Human vulnerability leapt into focus. This characteristic of powerlessness is one of the key elements defining human rights, spurring efforts to fully implement them in day-to-day life. National dialog followed the United States massacre in the wake of multiple funerals and a devastated school community, dialog that reached into the world of human rights and the right to be safe. Simultaneously, the world was receiving word of civil strife in Sudan and Mali, and images of children caught in war-torn areas came into focus (Gettlemen, 2012). Powerless children, parents, and teachers, involved in situations such as the Sandy Hook Elementary School shooting or in Timbuktu, Mali, trapped between violence and lost security, represent one of the emerging forces for the achievement of human rights worldwide.

The term *human rights,* represents both a concept and a reality. As a reality these rights are brought to life through covenants and legislation that refer to the ways in which a nation state and its representatives or region (e.g., the European Union or the European Court of Human Rights) of the world, treats its citizens and in particular responds to organized group grievances. Such grievances may be identified, expressed, and organized in a number of ways, for example, by nongovernment organizations and pressure groups or political parties and lobbyists at state, regional, and United Nations levels. Thus, police brutality and torture in any state are considered human rights violations, in contrast to a private assault such as a street mugging. The U.S. massacre at Sandy Hook demonstrates complex overlap, however, where a state action or inaction (in this instance to control access to handguns and semiautomatic weapons) leads to an individual action toward a community that is beyond private assault. The event and the public reaction concerning human vulnerability illustrates the long journey of recognition and implementation of human rights.

The Convention on the Rights of the Child, adopted by the United Nations in 1989, speaks to the right to be physically safe but has not been fully sanctioned by the United States for complex reasons. These reasons include the idea that an international entity, the United Nations, should not interfere in the policy of a nation, for example, in the question of whether someone under 18, legally a child, may be held on death row and dealt with in adult court. The immediate image, however, of rows of 6-year-old children being mowed down, allowed communities to come together to address the macro policy issue of gun violence. The images of children in war torn areas has yet to sufficiently motivate the world to eradicate war.

Many countries and states successfully control access to guns; the statistics for death by handgun are stunningly different when comparing the United States, Canada, Japan, Germany, and the United Kingdom, for example (see Table 11.1). This is the result of policy implementation, not an indicator of more peaceful people by nature. The contradiction that exists in the United States is that people carry guns to defend themselves only to have them turned on them (in the case of Sandy Hook, the shooter killed his mother, the owner of the guns). In a prescient headline, Tavernise (2013) summarizes her research: "With Guns, Killer and Victim Are Usually the Same" (Tavernise, 2013). The research Tavernise gathers indicates that

> nearly 20,000 of the 30,000 deaths from handguns in the US in 2010 were suicides. The national suicide rate has climbed by 12% since 2003, and suicide is the third leading cause of death for teenagers in the U.S. . . . and it is not just suicides . . . the literature suggests that having a gun in your home to protect your family is like bringing a time bomb into your house. (p. 1)

From the immediate micro-level and interpersonal exchange, the dialog in the United States reached out into the community, the country, and ultimately the macro-level of violence against people in multiple contexts and their human right for preservation of life.

Sometimes, human rights are seen as the preserve of macro- and high-level inter-action based in the work of the United Nations, as though elusive to the local human service or social work professional. Perhaps we need to see human rights as a core

Table 11.1   Death by Handguns

1986	
Canada	6
West Germany	17
Great Britain	4
United States	9,800
1993	
United States	38,077
Legal intervention[a]	259
2006	
United States	30,242
Legal intervention[a]	300

Source: National Safety Council, 1994 Accident Facts, Itasca, IL, Library of Congress Catalogue, Card #91-60648. *National Vital Statistics Reports, 54*(10), January 31, 2006. www.cdc.gov

a. Legal intervention: death as a result of action taken by law enforcement officers.

element in all policy practice. It is the social work practitioner's responsibility to be familiar with the language, concepts, resources and laws of human rights. It is both responsibility and opportunity; often, knowledge of specific human rights, including the right not to be discriminated against, provides a template for action in agencies. In discussion of the "new human rights," Clifford Bob (2009) identifies the areas of discrimination that persist, such as against people with disabilities or AIDS or who are gay, lesbian, bisexual, or transgendered.

Thus, by definition, while human rights are concerned with whole groups of people, they begin in every community. We can consider an indigenous group of people whose land and therefore livelihood is taken away, for example, by an oil company polluting and controlling land in the Niger Delta, the same land that was formerly fertile fishing grounds for villagers. The women of Ugborodo who organized themselves to infiltrate a terminal and demand fair access to employment and clean water are a brave example (Onishi, 2002). At the micro-level, or individual level, children may be sold or abducted into slave prostitution and doomed to lose their identity, their health, and their future. Parents may adopt a child through international adoption and be unaware that biological parents exist. Human rights are part of all of our lives, not separate and removed from reality, and the policies that surround them are resources for our ethical and responsive practice.

The United Nations and Universal Human Rights

The United Nations has existed only since 1945, but the impulse for this organization has been evolving for centuries, from the earliest notions of what it means to be human and how human life should be protected. It is crucial to note that humans have always struggled with good and evil, with the drive to love or to hate, and with peace over aggression. This struggle plays out through the narratives of culture, which include faith and ritual. The drafters at the United Nations included in their preamble the intent to "reaffirm" human rights, knowing they were not the first to grapple with such a vast and hopeful idea. Ball and Gready (2006) comment that "the absence of a single great narrative of human rights is a strength, allowing us all to participate, from diverse religions, cultures and philosophical traditions" (Ball & Gready, p. 12). Similarly Reichert (2007) states the following:

> The idea of human rights has a long history. John Locke espoused the concept of natural rights as the basis for life, liberty, and property, residing with individuals. . . . Rousseau supported the idea that individuals entered civil society and exchanged the right to life, liberty and equality for civil rights, which the government protected from violation on their behalf. (p. 19)

The United Nations was founded to bring global leaders together to expand these ideas of civil, social, and economic rights to a grand scale, where every person on Earth can benefit and find ways to avoid violence, degradation, war, and the awful loss and violence that follow. Box 11.1 offers a brief timeline that puts current practice into perspective.

BOX 11.1   RECENT HISTORY OF HUMAN RIGHTS

First Geneva Convention and Early Years

- 1863: The Red Cross was established, 16 countries came together in Geneva following the Battle of Solferino to express concern about the brutal impact of new weapons on humans.
- 1864: The International Peace Conference at The Hague adopted "A Convention for Peaceful Settlement of International Disputes."
- 1918: WWI Treaty of Versailles introduced the need for increased global collaboration.
- 1920: League of Nations was established, but the United States did not join because of concern for maintaining sovereignty.
- 1921 to 1931: The League drafted the first version of the declaration of human rights and brokered disputes successfully but was unable to control remilitarization of Europe in the 1930s, particularly Germany, under Nazi control, and Japan.

From the League to the United Nations

- 1942: Twenty-six nations ("allies") met in New York to pick up the work of the League and to draft the formal Declaration of Human Rights.
- 1945: In San Francisco, 50 nations signed the UN Charter; it was ratified by five permanent members known as the Security Council who collectively signed the peace accords in June 1945 (United States, United Kingdom, China, France, Russia).
- 1948: The Universal Declaration of Human Rights is approved by the United Nations, which was passed by the General Assembly, with eight abstentions but no dissenting vote.
- 1951: The Geneva Convention on the Status of Refugees is created and includes articles defining prisoners of war and their treatment; regrettably some countries, even in 2013, get around this international policy with new definitions of people who are excluded, such as "enemy noncombatants."
- 1950 to 1990: The Cold War undermined the United Nations, but the view of success depends on which country is asked.
- 1995: There is a resurgence of belief in the power of the UN in relation to women's rights and violence against women. The International Association of Schools of Social Work issues its resolution on the Human Rights of women at the UN World Conference of Women in Beijing, China (Link & Ramanathan, 2011, p. 173).

Structure of the United Nations

- Security Council 5 permanent + 10 member countries voted into terms: New York
- General Assembly: 191 countries: New York
- General Assembly Human Rights: Geneva
- International Court of Justice: The Hague (settles disputes including fishing rights between Iceland and Canada, sovereignty rights between Nicaragua and the United States) 15 judges, 9-year terms
- International Criminal Court tries individuals for crimes against humanity.

Secretariat

- Headed by secretary general and appointed by General Assembly
- Was Kofi Annan, now Ban Ki-Moon
- Five-year renewable term
- Extensive staff (6,900+), located in New York, The Hague, Nairobi, Kenya, and Geneva

Supporting Programs and Funds

- United Nations Children's Rights International Children's Emergency Fund (UNICEF), focus on children and poverty, State of the World's annual children reports
- United Nations Development Programme (UNDP) focus initially (1980s) on economic development
- 2012: UNDP focus is now on sustainable social and economic development.
- United Nations High Commissioner for Refugees (UNHCR) (Recently new High Commission for Human Rights in Afghanistan)

Specialized Agencies Cooperating and Linked With the United Nations

- International Labour Organization (ILO)
- Educational, Scientific & Cultural Organization (UNESCO)
- World Health Organization (WHO)
- World Bank
- International Monetary Fund (IMF)

Current View of the United Nations

- Depends on which country or region is asked
- Anti-UN bias in U.S. media

(Continued)

(Continued)

- General concern for reform
- Some terrible failures (Rwanda)
- Some major recognition of "global" issues by people and areas where the United Nations is making a significant difference; Simi Samar, rapporteur for northern Sudan, believes that "the UN is indispensable."

Following the Second World War, dialog between citizens and the leaders of nations included thinking that war was over. The firefighting mother of one of the authors of this book said, "We fought the Second World War to end wars." Similarly, in a discussion on the nature of future conflicts, Dower and Williams (2002b) suggest that the day will come when children will ask, What was war? They draw on the philosophy of Kant to explore the idea of the United Nations as a federation of all regions and states:

> A loose international confederation of such republics would enable, slowly and not without mishap and mistake, international disputes to be resolved peacefully to the extent that war would eventually become unthinkable. . . . Kant's plan was also partly a recognition that with increasing international travel, commerce and exploration, there was a need to accord strangers or foreigners respect—what he called the "cosmopolitan duty" of hospitality: foreigners should be treated with respect and their humanity recognized, even if they did not have to be made citizens or granted equal rights as existing full members of the community. (p. 3)

Tensions in the Concept and Interpretation of Human Rights

The theme of "cosmopolitan duty" among all peoples is a mission of the United Nations and an aspect of professional social work, with its core attention focused on the well-being of others. Such sense of duty abroad would create the environment where human rights would be fully accepted, but it has yet to arrive worldwide and is a source of tension. The perpetuation of war and inherent to it, the arms trade, is also a key obstacle to finding ways for people who are culturally different to live peacefully and with a sense of recognition of their common human condition, upheld by their governments in concert with global government.

Global government is currently represented by the ongoing efforts of the United Nations but is far from accepted as a reality; for example, the variety of responses to the expectation that countries contribute development aid according to their gross national product (GNP) clearly indicates how some powerful nations express their ambivalence about the United Nations' authority (Dower & Williams, 2002a, p. 3). The *common human condition* is assumed by the early documents of the United Nations and sows seeds of the relationships that would facilitate commitment to global government. It is defined by social workers as

> including the universal aspects of human existence such as the need for shelter, clean water, food safety, identity, civil rights, intimacy, and song, and the idea that we step back from judging people without access to resources and recognize that all of us are vulnerable as individuals and stronger when we work in community. (Link & Ramanathan, 2011, p. 28)

If there was a stronger sense of common humanity and empathy for living conditions and access to water and food, for example, it would be harder for people to become enemies and objectify one another to the point of killing. The central theme across all human rights is the devastation that follows in the path of military conflict and violence, when whole regions are caught up in warfare, and the damage to communities following massacres, abductions, or mass rape. The economic and structural forces that make up the machinery of war are a juggernaut that is hard to stop and these forces are the antithesis of recognition of common humanity. General Eisenhower warned after the Second World War that the machinery of war becomes unstoppable:

> We have been compelled to create a permanent armaments industry of vast proportions. . . . The total influence—economic, political, even spiritual—is felt in every city, every statehouse, every office of the federal government . . . In the councils of government, we must guard against the acquisition of unwarranted influence . . . by the military-industrial complex. (Barash, 2000, p. 100)

The redirection of a nation's wealth to war and guns has immediate consequences for tackling the infrastructure needs of education, communications, and health. It slows resources and services being directed to research into diseases that humans have the knowledge to overcome, such as polio and malaria and, increasingly, AIDS. The gun trade is also just that, a source of entrepreneurial creativity, albeit with a profit motive based on war and misery.

It is a paradox of human history that war itself led, in part, to the advancement of the worldwide concept of human rights. The application and full implementation of human rights remains patchy and a wider education of their complexity is a professional responsibility of social workers.

Certainly after the devastation of the Second World War, in addition to increased dialog, there was a new atmosphere of cooperation and optimism among nations. This is represented by the achievement of the most significant document of the early years of the United Nations, the United Nations Universal Declaration of Human Rights, which was passed by the General Assembly in 1948 with eight abstentions but no dissenting vote. It represents an imperfect yet powerful statement about the common goals of humankind, to establish standards of interpersonal behavior that protect everyone from harm. In the effort to address human needs prior to the First World War, Prime Minister Lloyd George in the United Kingdom shocked his sabre-rattling colleagues in 1911 by stating, "This budget is a war budget, to wage implacable war on poverty and all the wants that follow in its path" (Bruce, 1973, p. 146).

The Universal Declaration of Human Rights (UDHR)

The UDHR revisits and takes this war against poverty further by making concrete a new set of expectations of how we treat one another humanely. This declaration specifies the protection of the defenseless and the recognition of vulnerability of groups such as the imprisoned, the impoverished, and those who are subject to exploitation and torture. The UDHR spawned later conventions focusing on children and women who are powerless or oppressed and under the control of others. Ultimately the UDHR provides an appropriate organizing framework for social work practice in all fields, with the dignity of the individual, by virtue of being human, at its center.

The UDHR identifies economic, social, political, and civil rights as the following:

- Freedom from discrimination on the basis of birth, race, sex, religion
- Right to life, liberty, and security of person
- Freedom from slavery
- Freedom from torture and other cruel, inhuman, or degrading treatment or punishment
- Right to personhood and equality before the law
- Right to effective remedy for rights violations
- Freedom from arbitrary arrest, detention, or exile
- Freedom of movement and residence
- Right to privacy
- Right to leave any country and to return to one's own country
- Right to seek and to enjoy asylum from persecution

Source: Adapted from the U.N. Declaration of Human Rights (1948).

THINKING SUSTAINABLY

Accepting that we all share stewardship over the planet is a fundamental tenet of sustainable thinking. Some scoff at the idea that the earth is in the process of being damaged beyond repair by neglect and greed, yet the scientific evidence that there is significant climate change (a more accurate and more easily defensible claim than simple "global warming") seems undeniable.

Let's consider the four perspectives on human rights. How would the skeptic, the realist, the critical sojourner, and the world citizen each tend to view climate change? Which would be more likely to accept climate change as a reality that must be redressed? Which qualities held within those perspectives would be most useful in assessing and acting on the problem? Which qualities would be the most likely to hinder action?

Four Perspectives on Universal Human Rights

In a classroom of students studying global citizenship at Simpson College in Iowa, the work edited by Dower and Williams (2002a) assisted them in tracking their own

Source: Photo permission of the U.S. National Archives.

Eleanor Roosevelt Holding a Copy of the Universal Declaration, Written in Spanish. Appointed by President Harry Truman to serve as ambassador to the United Nations and elected to chair the Human Rights Commission, Eleanor Roosevelt played a major role in shaping the document that we have today.

approach to these complex global issues, such as what universal human rights mean to them (Simpson Colloquium, 2012). They chose the quote from a chapter author in Dower and Williams's (2002a) edited book that most represented them at the beginning of the class and again at the end 3 months later. Their ideas and quotes represent a spectrum that resonates with the general population of the United States as portrayed by the media reporting in 2013 on gun control and child trafficking, from skeptic, to realist, to critical sojourner, to world citizen.

The Skeptic

Skeptics are U.S. citizens who see their duties toward their country as paramount; they are skeptical of the idea of global citizenship, and to them "it is quite absurd to suppose that most people have duties towards others in distant parts of the world" (Dower, 2002, p. 37). Albeit a sharp rejection of efforts to work together in an interdependent world, this approach illustrates the tension between the idea of right and "duty." There are isolated communities in the world that may be out of touch with others (in central Australia or the Amazon) and therefore cannot be expected to experience a sense of connection or duty. However, as Dower (2002) states, "We have duties in principle towards all human beings, for example, not to undermine the bases of their well-being. We all have moral rights recognized by the international community" (p. 37).

The Realist

Realists acknowledge the hegemony of the nation state form of human organization since the Treaty of Westphalia in 1648. This momentous treaty brought "to an end the Thirty Years War. The Treaty helped end non-territorial claims to political authority, such as those of the Pope and the Holy Roman Emperor, thus establishing the territorial state as the highest form of political authority" (Dower & Williams, 2002a, p. xxvi). In effect, the Treaty of Westphalia drew the map of nation states in Europe that has largely endured. A reference to Westphalian beliefs or traditions reflects this acceptance of the political authority of a nation and government to its citizens, above all other authority. The existence of international law outdates these beliefs, but they persist and may be viewed as a tension slowing down progress to greater international collaboration.

For the most part, individual citizens find it impossible to achieve political or judicial results "without going through the mechanisms of their sovereign state" (Williams, 2002, p. 42). There is, however, an example, despite its messy unfolding, of a block of countries working together, which led one student to say, "I believe in supplemental citizenship such as enjoyed by 400 million people in the European Union." Thus, the realist acknowledges the forces of history that impede the advance of human rights and the work of the United Nations, while embracing the potential for change.

The Critical Sojourner

"All human beings are global citizens in virtue of rights and duties which we all have as human beings" (Dower, 2002, p. 40), but we have so far "failed to reach the United Nations target of donating 0.7 GNP to international development aid" (Williams, 2002, p. 47). "The view that we have a long way to go to be universal in our approach to human well-being acknowledges the realities but also engages everyone in this journey. Vandana Shiva (2002) in her book *Water Wars* combines scientific explanations of root systems and imported trees affecting the flow of rivers and flooded streams with the political explanation of what makes water so crucial in the next 50 years. Shiva expects her readers to engage in the journey of educating their communities and speaking on behalf of those without a basic human right: access to clean water.

The World Citizen

We are all world citizens and have need of each other; we are interdependent and continue to work on the institutions that will support the work of the United Nations, the WHO, and the International Criminal Court to achieve human rights and universal well-being. No dictator can now expect to evade accountability for their actions at the global level; they will be called to The Hague and the International Criminal Court.

This notion of being a world citizen—in effect, *stateless,* is a relatively recent phenomenon. Falk (2002) writes about the risk of being stateless: "Refugees are protected by the UN High Commissioner of Refugees, who can issue travel documents, which may or may not be widely recognized. Statelessness remains a status of severe deprivation, the very term implying the persistence of statism" (p. 8). Following the breaking apart of the former Yugoslavia for example, people were caught between countries and became shadows on the edge of society.

At the Olympic Games held in London in 2012, four athletes arrived without nationhood (three were from the former Netherlands Antilles, one from South Sudan) and appealed to the Olympic Committee for status as global athletes. Known as "the Independents," they rocked their way through the opening ceremonies and (with their own, Nike-designed gear) competed under the Olympic flag. In a way, these athletes hewed more closely to the Olympic ideal and sidestepped the political machinations of the various national Olympic committees.

It is broadly recognized that human rights are complex and their definition and implementation are evolving from broad aspirational policies to a realization of the dimensions and effects that their existence and implementation can create. For the skeptic, there is the clash of surrounding values and beliefs of any local community and the leap of faith that it takes to feel and to be more responsible for all human beings. However, as human rights are debated, it is also recognized that our local structure of organization through national boundaries is creating tension and confusion when the border becomes meaningless. The example identified above of stateless athletes petitioning the Olympic Committee is one illustration that has promoted a realization of the constraints of relying on national identity.

Despite shifting borders and changing nation states, individual countries continue to resist universal norms of human rights behavior. Abolition of the death penalty is an example. In January 2013, a British woman was convicted of drug trafficking in Thailand and sentenced to death. Immediately attention focused on the contradictions of a citizen of a country that has abolished the death penalty being caught, and found guilty, in one that still performs this human rights abuse. In the United States, it is a gradually spreading map of states that have abolished the death penalty that are influencing those that continue the practice.

From the human rights abuses committed at the national level, there are the wider scale horrors of war. The atrocities of the Holocaust stunned those emancipating the few survivors of concentration camps in the Second World War. These events led directly to the development of international human rights norms and actions designed to ensure that the Holocaust would never happen again. In truth, the human rights record of the Allies of World War II has come under scrutiny with the opening of war records. The world watched and essentially turned a blind eye to the genocidal massacre of 6 million Jews, a half-million Romany people, and tens of thousands of Communists, homosexuals, and others who were caught up in the terror. Some who were able to flee were denied refuge; no internationally based rescue missions were conducted. The Nuremburg war crimes trials that followed the war prosecuted leading Nazis under the new charge of crimes against humanity.

Although perhaps setting a dangerous precedent for victors judging losers, the Nuremburg trials marked an important moment in human rights history. From that point onward, human rights moved to the forefront in international discourse. Two years after the trials, marking a milestone in human relations, the General Assembly of the United Nations unanimously adopted the *Universal Declaration of Human Rights* (see Appendix A). As stated earlier, this remarkably progressive and concise document spells out in 30 brief articles, principles affirming the human dignity and equal rights of men and women to be protected under international law. These principles were later extended to children (see Chapter 7 of this book).

In an encouraging discourse concerning children imprisoned in adult jails, it is now the reality that nation states pay attention to implementing these policy instruments and risk internal and international criticism and sanctions if not. The United Kingdom recently was held in violation of the UN Convention on the Rights of the Child, Article 37, when it was proved that five children were detained in adult jails. The treaty states that every child who is locked up must be separated from adults, unless it is better for him or her to be with adults (Philby, 2013, p. 2).

This example of politicians being widely criticized for allowing children to be incarcerated with adults is an indication of progress in implementing international policy instruments. National dialog that gives recognition to the authority of the United Nations as a form of global government was missing for most of the last 50 years but has been gaining ground since the beginning of this century. Similarly, key decisions have been made at the European Court of Human Rights calling countries, including the United States, accountable for their treatment of suspected (but not proven) terrorists. According to a report from the *New York Times*, an Italian appeals court convicted a CIA station chief and two other Americans for kidnapping a radical cleric in Milan 10 years earlier and sending him to Egypt to be tortured ("About Those Black Sites," 2013). This decision means that 26 other Americans were found guilty as well; they were tried in absentia. In 2012, according to the *New York Times* article, a German citizen was mistaken for a terrorist and brutalized by a CIA team in Macedonia. The European Court of Human Rights has ruled that this treatment amounted to torture. According to the *New York Times* report, "Both judgments are important condemnations of CIA tactics and a warning to the U.S. and its partners to make amends for gross violations of international legal and human rights standards" ("About Those Black Sites," 2013, p. A14).

It is a key tension in the implementation of human rights that nation states still hold sway in the minds of citizens, but nations are becoming less viable in relation to issues that affect people of the world collectively, such as human rights, which cross all borders (as do issues involving water, air, acid rain, pollution, and germs).

Human rights is a concept that refers to the ways in which a state or region (e.g., the European Union) of the world treats its citizens. Thus, as stated earlier, institutionalized brutality and torture are considered human rights violations, in contrast to street muggings and private assault. The boundaries between state-sanctioned and private forms of violence, however, are not always clearly drawn, especially with regard to acts of war. It is another tension in the practice of human rights that some powerful countries, such as the United States, appear to have slowed their focus on international human rights violations, especially following the end of the Cold War against Communism and in the face of terrorist assaults such as 9/11. When the U.S. Patriot Act was passed, the introduction of the idea of *enemy noncombatants* entered the language and has since been part of the criticism of treatment of suspected terrorists, especially at places outside normal jurisdiction, such as Guantanamo Bay, and as identified in the critique above, Macedonia (Ramanathan & Ramanathan, 2011). More encouraging is the reality that well-respected nongovernmental organizations (NGOs) such as Amnesty International and Anti-Slavery International continue to inform the world of systematic abuses. Extensive documentation of abuses is provided at regular intervals and preserved in public sources of information. For a long time—45 years in fact—women's rights were not included in the panorama of human rights. Conceived as a largely cultural matter, violence against women and the denial of women's political and civil rights were not addressed. Then, in the Declaration of the 1993 World Conference on Human Rights, governments finally acknowledged that women's rights are human rights and should be protected as such (Amnesty International, 2012).

Three categories of rights are provided in the UNDHR: *economic and cultural rights; protection against discrimination* based on race, color, sex, language, religion, and political opinion; and *civil and political* rights against the arbitrary powers of the state. This chapter is particularly concerned with the latter category, the civil and political rights provided in the U.S. Constitution and in many other constitutions of governments of nation states, as well as the global government of the United Nations. Those articles of the UDHR concerned with economic, social, and cultural rights range from the positive rights of "rest, leisure, and reasonable limitation of working hours and periodic holidays with pay" (Article 24) to the more fundamental rights attacking lack of food, housing, health care, work and social security (Article 25).

The fact that these rights are included nowhere in the U.S. Constitution (but in many European constitutions) has hindered the American people in their claims to basic social and economic benefits. Wronka (2012) argues convincingly that human rights are central to social work curriculum and resources for advanced general practice. The articles of the policy instruments establishing human rights can serve as guiding principles for whole population (macro-level), at-risk (mezzo-level), clinical (micro-level), and research interventions. In the context of social work in the United States, Reichert (2007) urges the profession of social work to include these values, in addition to a peace and environmental platform in its National Association of Social Workers (NASW) Code of Ethics. At the global level, the expectation of the principles of social work established by the International Federation of Social Work (IFSW) and the International Association of Schools of Social Work (IASSW) is that human rights are at the core of the profession.

Moving Beyond the Universal Declaration of Human Rights

Despite the efforts made by the United Nations, there remains much work to be done. Let's take a look at some key areas where change is needed: Some of which are long standing; others that are more recently emerging:

Adoption

We often consider adoption from the micro perspective of couples in heart-wrenching and time-consuming efforts to find and adopt a child. This ignores a larger picture of agencies that become caught up in the socioeconomic factors that push families in poverty to give up their children under camouflaged circumstances. Rotabi (2012) has illustrated the macro issues of adoption vividly. She describes the trends that follow countries in disarray after natural disaster or the aftermath of war or stressful political and economic transitions, such as South Korea in the 1980s, Romania in the 1990s, and Colombia in the first decade of the 21st century (Rotabi, 2012). The UDHR did not specifically include the protocols for adoption, but it introduced the idea of the civil rights of each individual. This right directly led to the more specific directions of the international policy instrument passed later in 1989: the Convention on the Rights of the Child. The direct link to social work policy practice comes when an agency, such as the Seattle International Adoptions agency, claims lack of knowledge of the International Convention on Adoptions, and its staff members are arrested by the FBI for their lack of protocol according to international law (Shukovsky, 2003).

The Right to Identity

One of the successes of the UNDHR of 1948 was the way it identified concerns such as lost or lack of individual documentation, but one of the main challenges for the UNDHR was its dependence on nation states as the responsible parties for implementation. Dating back to the Treaty of Westphalia, which ended decades, if not centuries, of war in Europe, the notion of the rights of the nation state to design its laws of citizenship were established. In particular, border integrity and the control of human beings' identity has only recently prompted recognition of the uncertainty created for people caught between identities. The potential pitfalls of a person needing to rely upon their nation to establish their identity have become all too clear. If that nation is overcome or restructured as a result of independence or war (such as the restructuring of the Balkan States), their "universal right" is often denied at the new border. Similarly, for children brought to new countries illegally, they grow, are educated, learn the language, and become used to seeing themselves as "citizens" only to find themselves rejected and invited to voluntarily "deport and repatriate" themselves. The tension in the United States concerning the children and young adults of illegal immigrants has led to the Dream Act of 2012, which remains controversial and difficult for social workers to implement.

Documentation for refugee families is similarly complex and becomes a secondary infringement of human rights when a receiving country does not provide adequate legal support. In Box 11.2, the story is told of an Ethiopian refugee in the United States:

BOX 11.2 GROWING UP IN ETHIOPIA

Anonymous

I was born in Sudan but was raised in Ethiopia. It was difficult to live in such a harsh environment in Ethiopia. The reason my family and I lived in an Ethiopia refugee camp was because of the civil war that was going on in Sudan and that is still going on right now. As we settled in the refugee camp, people were moving from place to place because there were other tribes who were attacking us where we stayed. It made it too hard to get around everything including going to school, looking for food, water, clothing, and so on. People were dying from starvation and sickness, including children. Basically everything was so far away from where we lived. In order to get food, whether you bought it or went hunting, it was always dangerous both ways; either animals chased people and killed them or other tribes would stop you under the bushes and do whatever they pleased. If you were a woman, they would rape you or kidnap you and if you were man, or a young man, they would kill you. People were not allowed to leave or enter the camp, and I will never know the reason why the Ethiopian government does not let people leave or get out of the village.

During the 10 years I lived in Ethiopia, these were the major difficulties that I faced, including taking care of my brother and sister and dealing with sickness and shortage of food. As a 10-year-old taking on the role of woman, it wasn't just hard, it was also sad. Watching my parents go their separate ways to look for food was killing me so I had to do something. I found it very hard as a 10-year-old looking after my 7-year-old brother and my 3-year-old sister when I had no idea what I was doing. While my parents were gone, I learned how to be a caretaker for them. Sometime when either my brother or sister got sick it frustrated me, because I was not able to do anything about it, and there was no doctor in the village that could help. Walking to the hospital 3 hours from where we lived was frightening to me because sometimes you couldn't get help right away or for the whole day.

Shortage of food was another major problem I faced while I was in Ethiopia. This was the main reason why my parents were not home with us all the time because they had to find a way to take care of their children. When dealing with this kind of situation, I learned how to extend food for at least 1 day because whatever food my mom or dad brought with them did not last for long, and we have to keep some for the next day since we didn't know what was going to happen or where we were going to eat.

Coming to America it wasn't an easy process. My dad had to do a lot of paperwork with the UN people and sometimes people get denied after filling out the application for coming to America. My family and I waited a good 3 years just to process the application. My family and I came to the United States in 2004. Before we were back in Ethiopia, I thought that America was up in the sky, but when we came here it was just like where I came from except the buildings, the language, the culture, and their food were different. It was very hard for the whole family when we came here because we didn't speak the language or know anything about this country. The way people treated each other here is

(Continued)

(Continued)

different than how people treated each other back in Ethiopia. People can just walk into their neighbor's house and take anything they need and will watch your kids free without asking anything for return. I found the change very hard and struggled all through middle school and my sophomore year in high school. Kids at school started to pick on me because I didn't understand a thing they were saying. While I was in middle school, I had to be in the ESL (English as a second language) program to help me with my English and that's where I have been since. When I started school, the school people had to put me in seventh grade where I knew nothing about the American language. From seventh grade to ninth grade, I was still in the ESL program, just so I can learn English, which was very helpful for me. There was a sense of neglect of the differences I had from both American culture and language, which made it difficult for others to accept me. Fortunately, sometime my sophomore year, I found myself becoming more accepted because I found several things I had in common with some of the American students. I joined cross-country, basketball, and choir and that's when I started to understand the American culture, beliefs, values, and attitudes. Now living in America isn't as bad as I thought it would be. It is at least better than where I had lived before. Because I have freedom and the opportunity to go to school without worrying about what we will eat tomorrow and where I will find water for my children or my family to drink or to cook their food with.

Source: Anonymous (personal communication, May 4, 2012).

Due Process and the Criminal Justice System

Criminal justice is about social control of deviance through legal channels. It is also about protecting society at large from those who violate the most highly valued of society's norms. This protection, however, must be weighed against the rights of the individual accused of a crime. To learn of the criminal justice process, therefore, and of the laws that guide it, is to learn of the basics of power, privilege, and punishment both in a given society and also in our global society. We strive for a universal code of justice, where people are held responsible for their actions, no matter whether it is at a micro-level of physical violence or a macro-level of genocide. The key aspects of criminal justice—the crime, courts, and corrections—are part of the fabric of American society, indeed, of virtually any society. But within that commonality, there are significant differences in emphasis. Tiong Tan (2012) discussed the community conflict negotiation and "restorative justice" approach to justice in some parts of Asia at a meeting in Washington, DC (Tan, 2012). He demonstrates a contrast to the Western world's dominant approach to criminal behavior: retribution and punishment.

This tendency for the American criminal justice system to seemingly seek out revenge rather than rehabilitation is also inflected by one tragic but undeniable dimension in the United States—racism. We are talking here about racism embodied in the law and most certainly in the sanctions imposed by the law. The "ultimate sanction," the death penalty, is a human rights violation, and it is vastly and disproportionately wielded against people of color. Infused with ideology and emotion, the U.S. criminal justice labyrinth does not offer a picture of consistent attention to human rights but rather one marred by the public's seemingly insatiable appetite for revenge over rehabilitation.

Gender Discrimination

The Convention on the Elimination of All Forms of Discrimination against Women (CEDAW) has gained visibility in countries such as India and the United States. In early 2013, there were widespread protests throughout India because of the treatment of female victims of rape. The inherent bias of their legal system as well as statements made by male prosecutors implied the age-old suggestion that women are somehow at fault for being raped rather than holding the men accountable. This has spawned a nationwide movement to educate society as a whole and to protect Indian women. In the United States there are examples of local police being cited for lack of attention to CEDAW in their practices concerning women who are the victims of domestic abuse. Social workers have become educated in the articles of CEDAW and are now advocates. For example, at a human rights conference at the University of Connecticut in 2009, social workers and clients from Seattle presented the example of a family with a history of domestic assault being failed by the local law enforcement. A father, who had access to his children, took them to a fair and did not return. The mother, who had primary custody, became alarmed and called the police. Yet the police took several hours to respond and were reported to have looked for a lost dog before attending to this family—despite its record of abuse. Tragically, the father was found to have murdered his children; the mother has sought legal help to bring the articles of CEDAW to bear (*Human Rights in the USA*, 2009).

The Role of Social Work in Human Rights

The International Federation of Social Workers (IFSW) provides a strong endorsement of human rights as a framework for social work policy. Although the U.S. NASW (2008) does not yet include the term *human rights* in its code of ethics, the code, as Reichert (2007) indicates, bears a strong resemblance to important human rights documents, especially to the Universal Declaration of Human Rights. Reichert's reference is to Category 6 of the code of ethics, which urges social workers to engage in social and political action that seeks to ensure that all people have equal access to employment and resources, to expand opportunity for all people with special regard for those who are "disadvantaged, oppressed, and exploited" (National Association of Social Workers, 2008).

A human rights platform sees welfare aid for the poor as an entitlement, not a privilege; access to education and health care are both listed as human rights in the UDHR. The revised IFSW-IASSW Code of Ethics includes a strong endorsement of all the international human rights treaties, and the Global Agenda includes human rights as crucial to action in the profession. The agenda combined the work of the International Federation of Social Workers (IFSW), the International Association of Schools of Social Work (IASSW), and the International Council on Social Welfare (ICSW) and was agreed on at a conference in Hong Kong in March 2012 (International Federation of Social Workers, 2012). The agenda includes "a set of objectives to meet our joint aspirations for social justice and social development" in a context of human rights (IFSW, 2012).

In its manual of policy statements, the NASW (2012) has declared social work a human rights profession. In all fields of social work practice, according to this statement, whether with individuals, families, or communities, social work must be grounded in human rights. "The struggle for human rights remains a vital priority for the social work profession in the 21st century" according to the statement (p. 207). Under the guidelines of the Council of Social Work Education (CSWE) (2008), similarly, there is a clear endorsement for the inclusion of human rights in social work programs. The human rights focus of this chapter is in keeping with recommendations contained in the CSWE accreditation standards, which directs schools of social work to ensure that "studies on social and economic justice be grounded in an understanding of human and civil rights" (Educational Policy 2.1.5).

Catherine Hawkins (2009) argues that the inclusion of human rights documents and legal decisions arising from them are essential to social work education worldwide. Human rights laws provide a valuable theoretical and practical base for assisting social change. For Canadian social workers the perspective is clearly articulated that human rights are central. Because Canada was a signatory (unlike the United States) to the Covenant on Economic, Social and Political Rights, social workers in that country can use the document as a touchstone by which to examine social policy and to hold the government accountable: All the provinces in Canada, as well as the federal government, in fact have human rights legislation that is administered by a Human Rights Commission. For Canadian social workers, as Watkinson argues, human rights laws can be a valuable tool for advocacy and for social and economic justice within the era of globalization (Watkinson, 2001).

The struggle to fully implement a human rights perspective throughout the social work profession is not to be underestimated. Tensions discussed in this chapter have to be addressed and resolved. These tensions include the following:

- The paradox of the gun lobby and arms trade is that they are so beneficial to some in terms of entrepreneurial activity but at the same time devastating to human beings.
- Another paradox lies in the unresolved and outdated tension between the nation state as the imagined supreme form of organization juxtaposed with the

increasingly valuable work of the United Nations and regional collaborations. The Treaty of Westphalia is outdated It resolved the 30 Years' War in Europe in the 1600s; it drew the modern map of the West; it gave authority and territorial integrity to nation states. The treaty no longer affords a rational form of organization when global issues, particularly terrorism, viruses, global warming, threaten to undermine universal social and economic development when transnational companies are bigger than some small countries in their resources and are responsible to no one country (Moyers, 2006).

- A more elusive tension is that of "cosmopolitan duty," the term coined by Emmanuel Kant in the expectation that increased travel access to one another across the globe would increase a sense of fellowship and duty to everyone sharing the planet. Duty and right are two sides of the same coin. If we believe and feel a sense of recognition and duty with people who are culturally very different but share the ability to laugh in the same language, we are more likely to support the right to fair trial or to be protected from torture and wrongful arrest.

In his book on the new human rights, Bob (2009) concludes with a compelling discussion of the right to water. Ten years ago it would have been unthinkable for a hotel to charge $7 for a bottle of water in a guest room—more than for a glass of wine (e.g., at the Fairmont, Washington, DC; Renaissance Hotels worldwide.) Water has become an entrepreneurial commodity rather than a common right. In cities in India, the water in hotel fountains is cleaner than the water available for children to drink (Shiva, 2002). This is often the case in Mexico, where tourists enjoy ample water supplies in expensive hotels in Cancun and Cuernavaca, and families living in shanties on the edge of town have no household plumbing.

International media focus on the United Nations, the Criminal Court at The Hague, and the European Court, regarding international law and violations, is visibly increasing. The European Court's rulings on the CIA's use of torture, the work of Odanadi in India in documenting the vulnerability of children to be trafficked, the lack of documentation of international adoptions, and a long list of familiar events in people's everyday lives mean that human right's language is entering a broader imagination. Human rights, as Wronka (2012) firmly states, need to be dragged into "lived awareness," an action that in combination with witness, is an integral part of social work policy and practice (p. 445). Another cause for cautious optimism is the progress made amongst social workers worldwide. The Global Agenda for Social Work and Social Development demonstrates a high level of collaboration for social welfare. Finalized by three international professional groups, the IFSW, the IASSW, and the ICSW, it was launched at the United Nations on March 26, 2012. The global agenda includes four priority areas: promoting social and economic equality, promoting the dignity and worth of people, working toward environmental sustainability, and strengthening recognition of the importance of human relationships (Healy & Link, 2012). See Box 11.3 for a description by Lynne Healy of the Global Agenda for Social Work and Social Development.

BOX 11.3   A SOCIAL WORK PLAN FOR GLOBAL ACTION

Lynne M. Healy

In March 2012, the international social work organizations launched the Global Agenda for Social Work and Social Development at the 2012 Social Work Day at the United Nations. The agenda provides a blueprint for professional action on key global issues, encouraging efforts at all levels from local to national and global. The final plan resulted from several years of collaborative work by the International Association of Schools of Social Work, the International Council on Social Welfare, and the International Federation of Social Workers: the three major international bodies representing social work. Draft plans were circulated among the membership of the organizations and debated by leadership groups. At the formal launch, the agenda was presented to Helen Clark, chief administrator of the United Nations Development Program, as an indicator of the profession's intent to be more visible and active on the global scene.

The agenda commits the profession to acting across four major areas of focus:

- Promoting social and economic equality
- Promoting the dignity and worth of peoples
- Working toward environmental sustainability
- Strengthening recognition of the importance of human relationships

Priority issues and projects are identified within each area. Specific actions to promote social and economic equality include active support toward achieving the United Nations (UN) Millennium Development Goals (MDGs) and contributing to development of the UN's post-2015 Agenda—the priorities that will succeed the target date for the MDGs of 2015. At the more local level, the agenda identifies work to develop strong local communities and promotion of social work practice for local social development as priorities.

The profession's long-standing commitment to human rights is underscored in the second theme of promoting dignity and worth of peoples. The organizations will work at all levels toward universal implementation of human rights conventions; in countries where key treaties remained unratified, ratification campaigns are an important starting place. For the United States, efforts to pass the Convention on the Rights of the Child, the Convention on the Elimination of All Forms of Discrimination against Women, and the Convention on the Rights of Persons with Disabilities are imperative. In all countries, implementation can be strengthened. The profession will also advocate for a more explicit right to migrate and rights of all migrants to have access to services, step up efforts to eliminate human trafficking, promote peaceful resolution of conflicts, and strengthen social work practice in these areas.

In 2012, a major world meeting, Rio +20, was held to review progress made in the past 20 years to protect the environment and forge new commitments for sustainability. The Global Agenda commits social work to contribute to these efforts and to move sustainability to the forefront in its interventions. Increased emphasis on building capacity for disaster prevention, mitigation, and response is also identified as a priority area.

Finally, although the profession has always promoted human relationships as its cornerstone, the agenda encourages more work on social inclusion and cohesion, recommending that professionals embed "the importance of reducing social isolation" and enhancing social interaction in social work policies and practices, including education (International Association of Schools of Social Work, Institute for Clinical Social Work, & International Federation of Social Workers, p. 5).

The success of the Global Agenda will depend on efforts of social work and social development professionals at local and global levels. Awareness of the agenda and its purposes is a prerequisite. Local chapters of the social work organizations and schools of social work should lead in ensuring that current and future practitioners know about the agenda and how their efforts fit into the big picture. New curriculum and continuing education programs are also needed to build capacity on the themes of the agenda.

References

International Association of Schools of Social Work, Institute for Clinical Social Work, & International Federation of Social Workers. (2012). *The Global Agenda for Social Work and Social Development: Commitment to Action*. Retrieved from www.iassw-aiets.org

Source: Lynne Healy, Director of the Center for International Social Work Studies. Printed with permission of Lynne Healy.

This global agenda serves to unite and empower social workers. The policy instruments the agenda refers to affect all communities and influence all the interventions of social workers, sometimes without their realizing it and at other times with very deliberate use and solidarity across national borders. Illustrations related to human rights include working with children who are adopted by people in wealthier nations from countries with lower gross domestic product and the current demand that all countries abide by the Hague Convention on Adoptions (Rotabi, 2012). A current focus of policy is the movement of people across borders and the prevention of exploitation, including the sex trade and human trafficking.

Summary and Conclusion

In summary, human rights have been a long time unfolding and it would be disappointing for our social work leader, Jane Addams, speaking out for human rights in 1914 to see how slow the profession has been to adopt international policy instruments as frameworks and sources of support for action. However, a search of *Social Work Abstracts* (November 2012) produces 308 listings for *human rights*. This high number, which is three times the number of references provided in a search of 7 years ago, attests to the serious and growing interest by the profession in this subject area. A content analysis further indicates special concerns in regard to social welfare rights and minority issues.

Critical Thinking Questions

1. When you read and think about human rights, what are the key characteristics that define them?

2. What is meant by the term "institutionalized violence"?

3. In what ways are human rights reflective of the work of the United Nations?

4. Why has the United States been termed a reluctant partner with the United Nations?

5. What do social workers gain by studying human rights?

6. Explain the term *common human condition*.

7. The Universal Declaration of Human Rights is described as a momentous but imperfect document; can you explain this view?

8. To what extent does a social worker need to consider herself or himself a global citizen?

9. When do people lose their citizenship, and why are they considered to be vulnerable?

10. The IFSW provides a strong endorsement of human rights as a framework for social work policy; what does this mean?

11. Identify examples of human rights abuses and connect them to social work practice.

12. Nelson Mandela referred to the Convention on the Rights of the Child as a "luminous" document; give your own view of whether this is an accurate description.

13. In the 2013 murder of a prisoner of war in Afghanistan by a British soldier, the military court found the soldier guilty as charged and sentenced him to life in prison. There is an appeal and a public outcry saying "yes, but this is different from cold blooded murder" (Coghlan & Haynes, 2013, p. 1). Is it?

14. Human rights affect all our lives. What is your critical reflection of this idea?

15. Ways that the social work profession can "drag human rights into our lived awareness" (Wronka, 2012) include many aspects of practice; please identify three.

References

About those black sites [Editorial]. (2013, February 18). *New York Times*, p. A14.

Amnesty International. (2012). *State of the world annual report*. Retrieved from http://files.amnesty.org/air12/air_2012_full_en.pdf

Ball, O., & Gready, P. (2006). *The no-nonsense guide to human rights*. London, England: New Internationalist.

Barash, D. (2000). *Approaches to peace*. New York, NY: Oxford University Press.

Bob, C. (2009). *The international struggle for new human rights*, Philadelphia, PA: University of Philadelphia Press.

Bruce, M. (1973). *The rise of the welfare state*. London, England: Weidenfeld & Nicolson.

Coghlan, T., & Haynes, B. (2013, November 9). Clemency plea for battlefield murderer. *The Times*, p. 1.

Council on Social Work Education. (2008). *Educational policy and accreditation standards*. Retrieved from www.cswe.org

Dower, N. (2002). Global citizenship: Yes or no? In N. Dower & J. Williams (Eds.), *Global citizenship: A critical introduction* (pp. 30–40). New York, NY: Routledge.

Dower, N., & Williams, J. (2002a). *Global citizenship: A critical introduction*. New York, NY: Routledge.

Dower, N., & Williams, J. (2002b). Introduction. In N. Dower & J. Williams (Eds.), *Global citizenship: A critical introduction* (pp. 1–8). New York, NY: Routledge.

Falk, R. (2002). An emergent matrix of citizenship: Complex, uneven, and fluid. In N. Dower & J. Williams (Eds.), *Global citizenship: A critical introduction* (pp. 15–29). New York, NY: Routledge.

Gettlemen, J. (2012, July 1). Lost boys peril returns in Sudan: A new generation of refugees flees strife. *New York Times*, p. 1.

Hawkins, C. A. (2009). Global citizenship: A model for teaching universal human rights in social work education. *Critical Social Work, 10*(1), 116–131.

Healy, L. (2008). *International social work: Professional action in an interdependent world*. New York, NY: Oxford University Press.

Healy, L., & Link, R. J. (2012, June). *Global context: Local solutions* [Conference]. PowerPoint presented at Augsburg College, Minneapolis, MN.

Human rights in the USA. (2009, October 22–24). Conference at the University of Connecticut Law School, Hartford, CT.

International Federation of Social Workers. (2012, March 3). Statement of ethical principles. Retrieved from http://ifsw.org/policies/statement-of-ethical-principles/

Link, R. J., & Ramanathan, C. S. (2011). *Human behavior in a just world*. New York, NY: Roman & Littlefield.

Moyers, B. (2006). *Earth on edge* [Television broadcast]. New York, NY: Public Affairs Television Inc. and World Resources Institute.

National Association of Social Workers. (2008). *Code of ethics*. Washington, DC: Author.

National Association of Social Workers. (2012). International policy on human rights. In NASW, *Social work speaks: NASW policy statements, 2012–2014* (pp. 203–208). Washington, DC: Author.

Onishi, N. (2002, December 29). Nigeria's oil wealth flows out, not down. *New York Times*, p. 4.

Philby, C. (2013, January 28). Children detained in adult jails. *Independent* [UK], p. 2.

Ramanathan, C. S., & Ramanathan, R. (2011). Textbox 5.4: A case of the United States of America. In R. J. Link & C. S. Ramanathan, *Human behavior in a just world* (pp. 111–118). New York, NY: Roman & Littlefield.

Reichert, E. (2007). *Challenge in human rights: A social work perspective*. New York, NY: Columbia University Press.

Rotabi, K. (2012). International adoptions. In L. Healy & R. Link (Eds.), *Handbook of international social work* (pp. 81–87). New York, NY: Oxford University Press.

Shiva, V. (2002). *Water wars*. Cambridge, MA: South End Press.

Shukovsky, P. (2003, December 17). Feds claim adopted orphans had parents: U.S. agents break up local agency dealing in Cambodia. *Seattle Post-Intelligencer*, p. A1.

Simpson Colloquium. (2012). *Human rights and performance*. Indianola, IA: Simpson College. Retrieved from www.devweb.simpson.edu

Tan, T. N. (2012, November). *The East West divide in social work practice*. Plenary presentation to the Council on Social Work Education annual program meeting, Washington, DC.

Tavernise, S. (February 14, 2013). With guns, killer and victim are usually same. *New York Times*, p. 1.

Watkinson, A. M. (2001). Human rights laws: Advocacy tools for a global civil society. *Canadian Social Work Review, 18*(2), 267–286.

Williams, J. (2002). Good international citizenship. In N. Dower & J. Williams (Eds.), *Global citizenship: A critical introduction* (pp. 41–52). New York, NY: Routledge.

Wronka, J. (2012). Overview of human rights: The UN conventions and machinery. In L. Healy & R. Link (Eds.), *Handbook of international social work* (pp. 439–446). New York, NY: Oxford University Press.

12

Sustainability Policy Analysis and Policy Practice

Where there is no dream, the people perish.

—Proverbs 29:18, King James Version

There wasn't a social justice issue that lacked support from the social work profession.

—Elizabeth Clark (2012)

The National Association of Social Worker's (NASW) (2008) Code of Ethics urges social workers to "be aware of the impact of the political arena on practice and advocate for changes in policy and legislation to improve social conditions in order to meet human needs and promote social justice" (Standard 6.04a). Social workers are also enjoined to promote and facilitate evaluation and research "to contribute to the development of knowledge and for use in their professional practice" (see Standard 5.02b). Although the code of ethics fails to link the conducting of research to the goal of political advocacy, it seems clear that the acquisition of relevant knowledge is an indispensable prerequisite for the effective presentation of the case for needed policy change. This is what policy analysis is all about—preparation for shaping arguments on behalf of a proposed policy and arming oneself with rebuttal facts (and a healthy dose of enthusiasm that hopefully will be infectious) to counter any anticipated resistance. This chapter suggests that the best way for social workers to confront oppression in the social system and effect significant social policy change is through providing input into the shaping of public policy.

Defining Policy Analysis

The science of policy decision making or *policy analysis* concerns the who, what, where, when, and why of policy development, implementation, and revision. Engagement in the analysis of policy in this way is an exercise in critical thinking as we weigh existing standards of social welfare against a higher standard, such as that contained in the United Nations Universal Declaration of Human Rights (see Appendix A). This work requires a view of the reality of oppression as a limited situation that can be transformed.

Policy analysis to social work is the equivalent of learning scales for the pianist or basic leg movements for the dancer—techniques that later become automatic. This fundamentally intellectual exercise is an overture to the change effort, not an end in itself—although conducting research on a given policy can be highly educational (van Wormer, Kaplan, & Juby, 2013). Many graduate programs in social work and many undergraduate programs offer courses in policy analysis as a means of familiarizing students with the legislative process for human services advocacy. Central to such courses is a critical examination of the political, historical, and cultural context in which a particular policy was formulated and is now applied. The Social Work Dictionary defines *policy analysis* as the following:

> Systematic evaluations of a policy and the process by which it was formulated. . . . Three approaches to policy analysis are (1) the study of process (sociopolitical variables in the dynamics of policy formulation), (2) the study of product (the values and assumptions that inform policy choices), and (3) the study of performance (cost benefit outcomes of policy implementation). (Barker, 2014, p. 326)

Policy analysis is also employed by legislative bodies or lobbyists in order to determine whether to support or oppose a federal or state bill that has been introduced to Congress. The same strategy is also used as an advocacy tool by groups designed to advance social justice; the goal may be to support or oppose a given policy.

Progressive policy analysis, as conceptualized in this text, goes beyond mere formulation because it has a particular theoretical framework. It is a strategy for studying a particular policy and assessing the possibility of introducing progressive change toward a more just society. Such analysis involves assessment of the sustainability of current policies and of alternative approaches.

Progressive policy analysis begins with an assessment of the fundamental causes of social injustice. Such an assessment necessarily brings us into the realm of power arrangements and social and political imbalances in society. In this chapter, we will discuss the social welfare and criminal justice systems—systems badly in need of dramatic policy change.

How Are Social Policies Made?

There are two opposing explanations of how policies are made. The *pluralistic* position argues that decision making is relatively democratic as competing groups reach consensus on the issues. The power elite position views "the haves" as maintaining dominance over the "have-nots." Conflict characterizes the power elite position. There is some truth in both worldviews, of course. Some decisions such as funding for the defense industry over social welfare spending are clearly decisions driven by members of the "military-industrial complex." Other decisions, such as legislation for the rights of persons with disabilities, involve input from a number of different constituencies. Over the years, the political clout of major interest groups, from pharmaceutical companies to gun manufacturers to insurance companies, has grown increasingly pronounced. To what extent political campaign reform legislation, itself representing a compromise among opposing factions, will ever curb the "buying" of social policy legislation remains to be seen.

Often policy change is precipitated by some sort of national crisis. If we agree with Frances Fox Piven (2006) that ordinary people can be welcomed into the "councils of government" during times of turbulence when concessions might be made to them, we can speculate that a desired policy change has a heightened chance of success following a fear-inducing event such as a mass shooting. Recently, at Sandy Hook Elementary School in Connecticut, the horrific mass murder of 26 people, including 20 children, prompted outrage throughout the nation. The massacre, in which the 20-year-old killer used his mother's legally obtained weapons, including a semi-assault rifle that made the mass killings possible, ignited a firestorm of calls for stricter gun control laws. The shocking act may prove to be a tipping point in public opinion. And when public opinion becomes strong enough, the leaders often follow.

The Center for Media and Democracy describes the present state of affairs related to the availability of high power weapons in the United States in terms that echo the power elite position (Graves, 2012). Calls for gun control following school shootings have been thwarted in the past, as Graves points out, because of the power and wealth of the National Rifle Association (NRA) in alliance with the American Legislative Exchange Council (ALEC). ALEC is a right-wing organization that designs model legislation for the state legislatures to adopt in the interests of the big corporations. In this case, numerous bills to bar or impede laws that would help protect Americans from gun violence were drafted by the NRA and adopted by ALEC corporations and legislators as "models" for the rest of the country. In addition to the investment of large sums of money to the lobbying of legislators by the NRA and a media campaign to convince the public that gun ownership was a constitutional right, gun control laws in the United States uniquely have been stymied.

Sustainability and Policy

A major criticism of sustainability as a concept is that it is too vague to provide guidelines for policymakers (Baehler & Fiorino, 2011). When we examine the most commonly used definition of sustainability—that we meet our current needs without compromising the needs of future generations—we can understand the reason for the criticism. The concept of human needs, as Dover and Joseph (2008) point out, is well established in social work. It is included in the preamble to the social work code of ethics (NASW, 2008) and for the first time in the *Encyclopedia of Social Work* in the entry by Dover and Joseph (2008). The difficulty arises in determining what people's basic needs are, especially as they differ from society to society. Olson (2007) and Dover and Joseph (2008) emphasize the necessity of meeting one's physiological and safety needs; this they view as the foundation of economic justice.

For a list of the basic human needs, we can consult the United Nations (1948) Universal Declaration of Human Rights. Despite the fact that this document was written shortly after World War II, the needs are still relevant today. Teaching social work from a human rights perspective moves from a framework based on needs alone—the quest for what clients need to live productive lives—to a notion that to have one's needs met is an intrinsic right. A human rights focus provides a meaningful standard in that it directs our attention to systemic roots of social injustice. Moreover, a human rights focus provides us with a valuable theoretical basis for selecting the policies in need of change and in assisting in social change (Reichert, 2011). The starting point to contemplate meaningful social change is sustainable policy analysis to enhance social justice.

We view empowerment and self-determination as central to any effort by researchers and policymakers to effect meaningful social change. We often think of empowerment in psychological terms, as related to self-esteem and self-efficacy. But empowerment can also take a political form when an individual feels that he or she is part of the decision-making process, that one's voice is heard. And there is economic empowerment, which increases the choices one makes—what to buy and when to buy it. The removal of financial worries can enhance one's sense of power; collectively organizations such as NASW contribute to lobbying groups on issues of concern. The organization also hires lawyers to write legal briefs on behalf of progressive causes.

Membership in an activist organization can be empowering for participants, not only due to a favorable outcome but also through the process of networking for change. Even when the outcome is disappointing, the committee work, the taking on of leadership roles, and the progression through the planning stages—these can all be valuable learning experiences, and the networking can create alliances for future engagement in a different context.

In seeking to change the system, one learns what the stumbling blocks are and which barriers are too strong to break down. Organizers as well learn who in the community can be counted on, and which resources are helpful and which ones not. The strategies will vary depending on the type of change sought. The organizing goal may be the enhancement of existing services, for example, the addition of bilingual staff members, or more grandiosely, the goal may be the development of entirely new services. The setting up of needle exchanges in a high-risk community is an example of a realistic goal; effecting the passage of strict gun control laws may be a less practical, though desirable goal.

Working at the individual level, social workers impart new information and knowledge, teach problem-solving skills, and foster self-determination (Cummins, Byers, & Pedrick, 2011). See Box 12.1 for a personal description of empowering social work practice by one volunteer who placed an emphasis on client self-determination through her refusal to give up on a seemingly hopeless case. The principles learned in this personal narrative also relate to change efforts on a broader scale. Raising consciousness is a big part of moving people forward to take control over their own lives.

BOX 12.1 THE VALUE OF SELF-DETERMINATION IN HELPING PEOPLE CHANGE

When working as a crisis line volunteer for a local domestic violence agency in Chicago, I experienced the value of self-determination over and over again with the majority of my calls. One repeat caller in particular had a very devastating case and was difficult to work with due to her inability to find the strength to move forward. As stated in the van Wormer text, *Confronting Oppression, Restoring Justice*, "The fundamental value of self-determination is reified as practitioners entrust clients with rights and responsibilities to make decisions in each phase of the treatment process" (van Wormer, 2004, p. 137). This concept is most certainly present throughout the phases of the treatment processes. We all must remember this concept as we realize how immobilized our clients can become when stuck within one or more of these phases.

Before I received my first call from this survivor, I had heard tales from other crisis line volunteers and workers at the agency about how ridiculous this woman is and how she refuses to come in for treatment. Each time this caller called, I would routinely listen actively as I heard her over and over tell me the same story of all the ridiculous things her husband of 30-plus years forced her to do.

Eventually I began helping her recognize the power she had. Although there were nights when we'd discuss her leaving, just for the night, she'd call me on the crisis line to say, "I'm gone. Now what?!" The situation was difficult, as I had to be so careful not tell her what to do but to help her see her options within her situation. Through her gradual realization of the power she had no idea she possessed, she eventually went into the agency for counseling. This was well after over 2 years of indecision. The values of self-determination and empowerment played a key role in helping this client find her way.

Source: Emily Allaire, MSW, personal contribution submitted to the author as a class assignment on July 12, 2007. Printed by permission of Emily Allaire.

An Ecosystems Approach to Sustainable Policy Change

Moving from abstract ideas, such as empowerment, to concrete policy change that is sustainable is no easy task. Let's consider an ecosystems approach to construct a working definition of sustainability. Such an approach views the economy, environment, society, and political governance as four interconnected systems. Sustainability is described by Baehler and Fiorino (2011) as the task of sustaining each of these four systems over time and maintaining a balance among them. Although we are focusing on separate aspects of policy analysis (the economic, political, environmental, and so on) as a didactic exercise, we recognize that all the components are interlinked and that stress to any one of these systems would tend to reverberate throughout the whole. A government in a serious economic crisis, for example, is apt to overlook environmental issues to the extent that the land and waterways may be contaminated for short-term economic gains. Conversely, atmospheric and soil pollution can have serious consequences for the economic as well as physical health of the people. The actions that are taken depend to a large extent on the definition of the problem.

The problem/solution formulation from the social work point of view is not necessarily the problem formulation from the government's point of view or from the point of view of the power elites (van Wormer et al., 2013). Whereas social workers tend to view the problem from the standpoint of meeting the needs of the service users, many politicians tend to define the problem in terms of costs incurred in providing the services. Between success in reducing the welfare rolls and lowering the poverty rate, they would tend to favor statistics showing fewer people were receiving welfare benefits. Strengthening the safety net for all the people is not a top priority.

Keep in mind that the empowerment perspective of social work is premised on the belief that many of the societal social problems tend to come from class, educational, and political exclusion. In other words, the challenges to survival and fulfillment are seen to come from demographic rather than individual characteristics (Chapin, 2011; Lee & Hudson, 2011). The experts on the nature of the problem, from this perspective, are the people most directly affected by present and proposed policies, so their inclusion in any social change efforts is a clear necessity.

Often, politicians, who have ready access to the media, focus the attention of the public on a problem that may not really be solved by the means they suggest, such as illicit drug use or abortion or same-sex marriage, as a means of diverting attention away from issues that should be of major concern to everyone—for example, high poverty rates, unemployment, and lack of access to affordable health care and housing.

Sadly, the voices of the people who are the most affected by a proposed policy change are the least heard when important policy changes—such as plans to get homeless people off the city streets—are being considered. Many become apathetic. When the public becomes apathetic in the belief that individuals have no say, the policymakers can be expected to attend to the needs of those whom they see as their constituents. The ruling classes will only offer relief to the poor, according to a basic sociological principle espoused by Piven and Cloward (1971/1993) and Piven (2006), when they encounter mass discontent or rioting of the have-nots.

Social Workers as Change Agents

In light of the fact that they most directly deal with society's ills and seek to help people through inadequate social services, social workers often see themselves as change agents. The role of change agent, whether working within the system or without, can be quite frustrating. Sometimes it takes drastic measures, such as filing a lawsuit or "whistle-blowing," to bring about change in the organization. More often, united with their colleagues, they work to better meet the needs of their clients; for example, they hire bilingual members of staff or obtain more funding for the purposes of architectural improvements. Mullaly (2010) states that several schools of social work in Canada and Australia base their programs on a curriculum that includes discussion of resistance. He is not referring to client resistance but to the moral imperative of resistance to injustice and oppression. Critical self-reflection is an element in such programming used to help students recognize that we have all internalized parts of the dominant ideology, and we need to see how it constrains and limits our behavior. To prepare ourselves to work as an ally of oppressed groups, we need to critically examine our own experiences as both a member of an oppressed group and of an oppressor group (Bishop, 2002; Mullaly, 2010). Research of graduates of progressive Canadian programs, discussed by Mullaly (2010), provides examples of strategies of resistance that the graduates have used—for example, defense of the client practices, increasing the client's sense of power in the therapeutic relationship, and working with other staff members to initiate client-centered change.

A social worker from Iowa shares her thoughts as a change agent who has had over 20 years of experience:

> As I have become a "seasoned worker" I have found ways to manage the struggle to want to change things while managing a very large caseload by "working within the system to change the system." I have done this by drawing a parallel between system change and our work for client change. I measure change in small increments rather than an overnight total enlightenment. I use persistence and the "drip, drip, drip" approach to raise issues, awareness and highlight cognitive dissonance. I use words of respect and empowerment and look for the window of opportunity to create a change. I look for the domino effect that small change can bring throughout the system and then build on those changes. This is the way that my work has had an impact, albeit small, in the lives of my clients directly or indirectly through the agency's social policy or policy analysis on a grander scale, public awareness or agency committee work—as an advocate for change. (personal communication with Lori Eastwood, July 20, 2007)
>
> *Source:* Printed by permission of Lori Eastwood

The correspondent's reference to highlighting cognitive dissonance is a basic strategy used in motivational enhancement techniques to help move clients forward to motivate them for personal change—for example, to moderate their drinking habits. The therapist strives to direct their attention to the contradiction between their goals (e.g., of forming close relationships) and their behavior (turning people away through their bouts of intoxication). Hopefully, the client will feel some discomfort or dissolution and begin work to correct his or her problems. Motivational therapy has been highly successful in bringing about the desired behavioral change in individuals with substance use problems (see Miller & Rollnick, 2012). How about applying the same principle to political positions that people take? Most people, as we know, want to see themselves as good, unselfish human beings, Regarding small children, for example, even those who emphasize the importance of keeping taxes to a minimum will experience discomfort at the thought of children's needs not being met. To reconcile the conflict, they are apt to vote for taxes to fund such programs as educational improvements, free health care for infants and children, and welfare benefits for families that include children. As revealed in this example, the strategy of creating a situation of cognitive dissonance can be a useful one in convincing people to alter their behavior or political positions.

An especially effective way to bring about desirable change is to work toward progressive reform through lobbying or maybe writing op-ed articles in the local newspaper. Advocacy for social justice might take the form of work to increase funding for a women's shelter or to establish drug and mental health courts, working to have an anti-bullying bill passed in the state legislature, and grant-writing efforts to help keep people who suffer from drug addiction out of prison and get them into treatment programming instead.

Using Research to Influence Social Policy

Due to the thrust toward privatization (see Chapter 3) the hiring of social workers by state and federal agencies is expected to decline and the hiring of social workers by private nonprofit and for-profit agencies to increase. Third-party payers tend to stress the use of evidence-based practices in treatment and the micromanaging that comes from managed care. In other words, to ensure coverage of treatment, the effectiveness of a given intervention often must be documented, preferably in empirically based research that used a control group. It only makes sense to invest time and energy in treatments that are of demonstrable effectiveness, and this emphasis on outcomes is consistent with the reliance on science in modern society. Jane Addams herself was keen on science and believed that the place for social work education was not a specialized training school but the university (Soydan, 2012).

The risk of placing emphasis on evidence-based interventions is not in stressing the use of interventions that work but in the following factors: contradiction in the research findings, weakness in the methodology used, influence of third-party payers in favoring cost-effectiveness over other considerations, and the tendency to apply the treatments of provable success with certain groups in a one-size-fits-all manner.

Nevertheless, empirically based research is vital to the social work profession to show that our methods bring about the intended results. For advocates of more humane policies, for example, sentencing convicted felons with substance abuse problems to drug court instead of prison, evidence of cost-effectiveness of the program and of successful completion rates of participants is vital to make a convincing case with state legislators and funding institutes. Media accounts will publicize the statistics on program success; facts that may help persuade a reluctant public to support the community-based treatment. Advocacy of Housing First programs that provide housing to severely alcoholic homeless people, similarly, depends on positive results of outcomes research to ensure the programs' continuation. Policymakers must have the statistics at their fingertips when requests for initial funding and continued support are made. For all these reasons, including enhancement of the reputation of the field, the trend toward evidence-based research is one we can encourage.

Scientific Research and the Environment: A Case Study

Let us now look at the value of scientific research to further the goals of social justice. As applied to social justice, a thorough analysis of one social policy will reveal its relation to the whole, as well as its interconnectedness with other policies. This is in the tradition of teaching from the microcosm for in-depth understanding as described by Palmer (2007), which he contrasted with offering a bombardment of multiple facts in diverse situations. We can apply this strategy to one form of social justice that we discussed in Chapter 4—environmental justice. Environmental justice brings our attention to our respect for the earth and the earth's resources, a respect that is generally lacking when certain mining operations are employed.

Combining both the social work emphasis on social justice and the strategy of teaching from the microcosm, let us look at the recent conflict in the United States and Canada over hydraulic fracturing or "fracking." Fracking is a process in which large amounts of water, sand, and chemicals are injected deep underground to break apart rock and to free trapped natural gas. Though the process has been used for decades, recent technical advances have helped unlock vast stores of previously inaccessible natural gas, resulting in a fracking boom. Proponents of fracking correctly argue that the United States would be facing a serious energy crisis if the entire practice were banned and that the practice would reduce, or even eliminate our dependence on foreign oil. They claim that less reliance on coal for energy with its concomitant environmental damage would be a secondary benefit.

In the context of governance for sustainable development, environmental social scientists support policymakers through their traditional role of information provider by means of policy analysis (Runhaar, Dieperink, & Driessen, 2005). Most environmentalists, in consideration of the research, strongly oppose this form of mining of the earth as a means of obtaining energy. In western Wisconsin, the results are already apparent in of the loss of the farm fields and wooded hills that define the landscape as the land itself is ground up and shipped away to become toxic, radioactive waste somewhere else (Gerasimo, 2012). As some landowners become extremely rich overnight, their neighbors must endure heavy traffic, dust, air pollution, light pollution, and blight on the landscape caused by the mining. Environmentalists cite such scientific research as that conducted by hydrogeologist Tom Myers (2012). Myers (2012) predicts that chemicals introduced far below the earth in connection with fracturing eventually will move upward and affect the aquifers, the source of freshwater drinking supplies. Before more of this drilling takes place, Myers calls for more extensive research into the long-term consequences. The reason we have included this example is to show the importance of obtaining sufficient knowledge before the implementation of a policy thought to be cost-saving but that might take a toll on the environment and population that would far exceed the immediate gains. This is where sustainable policy analysis could come into play.

Researchers at the University of Michigan are working with government regulators, oil and gas industry representatives, and environmental groups to explore seven critical areas related to the use of hydraulic fracturing in Michigan: human health, the environment and ecology, economics, technology, public perception, law and policy, and geology/hydrodynamics. The 2-year study is to be conducted by experts who reportedly have no personal stake in the outcome of the study. The collaborative research will assess the pluses and minuses of this means of extraction of natural gas in terms of the sustainability factor. Because the economic and environmental interests in this process are vast and there are many stakeholders involved, hydraulic fracturing

Source: ©istockphoto.com/BanksPhotos.

Wisconsin Frac Sand Mine With Equipment. Fracking for oil provides short-term gains at the risk of damage to the earth's interior, including the water supply.

is a situation ripe for policy analysis. The key aspect of such research regarding influencing social policy is the dissemination of the results, most effectively through mass media sources. In any case, conducting the research to obtain the facts is the first important step toward making the case for change.

Lest we become too optimistic about the value of such research rigor for determining social policy as far as sustainability is concerned, we should heed the warning of Jansson (2009) that ideology often trumps scientific truths. Most policymakers, such as legislators, Jansson (2009) suggests, have scant knowledge of research methodology, statistics, or economics. This means that they are unlikely to read empirically based reports. Even worse, many are hostile to the findings of science as illustrated in their response to evidence concerning the causes of global warming. They have also turned a deaf ear, so to speak, to technical arguments concerning the lack of effectiveness of the death penalty in deterring crime or of gun control in preventing homicide or suicide.

Presenting Research Effectively

So what can be done? Jansson (2009) recommends that to avoid having their research relegated to the sidelines of policymaking, that policy analysts combine their technical skills with political ones and that they include important stakeholders in the process of information gathering from the start. The stakeholders would include the people with the greatest stake in the legislation or other policy changes being proposed, some of whom will try to block any efforts that might affect their vested interests in the status quo.

Legislators rely on lobbyists and advocates to provide them with fact sheets and personal testimonials concerning issues of the day. This saves time for them and enables them to make sound decisions on subjects they may not know enough about that will affect many people. Legislators can't be expected to be experts on every topic that comes up. This need for information creates an opportunity for advocates to simplify their research findings using bullet points and then to testify before members of Congress at public hearings and at lobby day when regular citizens meet with legislators to present their requests. Sometimes hearings are conducted at the legislature, and social workers then have an opportunity to testify and hand out prepared fact sheets.

In our state of Iowa, for example, legislators have been pleased to receive testimony from social work educators on issues ranging from opposition to a bill to reinstate the death penalty, to opposition to a fathers' rights proposal to make joint custody laws mandatory in divorce cases, to a plea to release more prisoners on parole at an earlier date.

The social work advocacy organization, Influencing State Policy, encourages university departments of social work to travel to the state capitals and meet with their state representatives on lobby day. This experience is invaluable in preparing student social workers for later advocacy and policymaking roles.

Progressive Policy Analysis for a Sustainable Future

Studies in the field of policy analysis are often based on only one operational criterion, for example, efficiency or cost-effectiveness, while ignoring criteria or values (Baehler & Fiorino, 2011). The method known as cost-benefit analysis often makes this mistake, overlooking the human factor in the obsession with numbers and graphs. Accordingly, the analysis does not always reflect social work or progressive values; the results may not even accurately measure sustainability. To gauge the actual impact of a given policy, a multidimensional approach is required.

As social work students or scholars, our interest is in policy analysis for effective social change in the interests of equity and social justice. From a progressive standpoint, engagement in the analysis of policy necessitates that we think critically regarding the existing standards of social welfare as weighed against the universals contained in the United Nations Universal Declaration of Human Rights (see Appendix A and Chapter 11). A human rights focus provides a meaningful standard in that it directs our attention to the systemic roots of social injustice. Such a focus, moreover, provides us with a valuable theoretical basis for assisting in social change (Reichert, 2011).

Progressive or radical policy analysis is described by David Gil (1998) as a didactic exercise that enables the student or scholar to examine the power arrangements in society and to gauge the possibility of significant change to help people better realize their basic needs. In order to do this, research needs to be conducted on the impact of a given policy that we wish to change with a special emphasis on the unintended as well as the intended consequences. In writing a policy proposal for change, Gil (1998) recommends that we include questions in the design concerning the effectiveness of similar policies to the ones proposed. Such a comparative examination of alternative policies that are all geared toward the same end can be persuasive in demonstrating the advantages of moving in a new direction.

Before we present the list of specific guidelines for sustainable policy analysis, we discuss each of the key components of sustainable analysis in terms of its contribution to the entire effort. We begin with an argument that knowledge of the historical development of a particular policy and of failed attempts to change it can be extremely helpful in revealing where the forces of resistance to the proposal are likely to come from, as well as the location of areas of support.

Historical Analysis

It is commonly said by literary writers and others that you can't understand the present without some knowledge of the past and that those who don't remember the past are condemned to repeat it. Historical knowledge is also helpful in knowing why certain customs are as they are, if they are to be changed. Take a worker at a human service organization, for example, or maybe a new director who wishes to transform the agency in some way to be more service-user friendly. The director will want to know how entrenched the present way of doing things is. Was there a time in the past when the community was more involved? How did the delivery of services work at that time, and how did they grow more bureaucratic (assuming this is the case)? Long-term residents of Waterloo, Iowa, will remember a time when substance abuse services were culturally specific, when the black community and counselors who lived in the community operated on a needs based and drop-in basis. But then bureaucratic dictates took over and local pride in the community treatment center was lost (see van Wormer & Davis, 2012). Another example from the same community involved a women's shelter that operated from a strong feminist-activist model that worked to raise the consciousness of the residents and authorities. When a politically prominent CEO was hired to run the agency, however, the entire staff at the shelter was overturned and a gender-neutral model prevailed. Ultimately, the shelter lost community support and state funding and was closed down and replaced by organizers who were aware of the history. Out of the local activism, Seeds of Hope, a social work, woman-centered organization evolved to more effectively provide the needed domestic violence services to battered women (see van Wormer & Besthorn, 2011).

An excellent illustration of how knowledge of history can help to generate progressive agency change is provided by Popple and Leighninger (2015). Their example concerns the situation when new staff members who have been trained in social work values and ethics see flaws in the system to which the senior staff are oblivious. Generally, suggestions by the newcomers are resented by those "who know best." Popple and Leighninger (2015) provide a true illustration of how new employees at a mental health agency were concerned about use of client Social Security numbers in the records. To find out if this practice was required as agency personnel insisted it was, the social workers went to the library and searched through old state mental health records related to legislation. On discovering there was no requirement for this client identification that could later be used against them in another capacity, the new staff members were able to convince the others to remove the request for the Social Security number from the intake forms.

These incidents illustrate the use of historical analysis in advocating for policy change at a social services agency. In striving to initiate change at the macro-level on behalf of children or adults in need of care, we can learn much from strategies that were applied and were effective or ineffective in the past so that history doesn't repeat itself. Historical analysis is concerned with the evaluation of success and failures of previous policies, many of which were well intended but failed to achieve the expected results. By the same token, the original Drug Abuse Resistance Education (DARE) program to discourage school children from experimenting with drugs was found to have more negative than positive results. The response of promoters of the program is interesting. As described by sociologist David Hanson (2002), when it became known that the prestigious *American Journal of Public Health* planned to publish a study indicating that DARE programming was counterproductive in preventing drug use, DARE supporters strongly objected and tried to prevent publication. Attacks were launched by leaders of DARE against numerous popular publications as well; the results were strenuously discounted, and the program continued in some schools while others wisely sought new approaches to prevention. In contrast to such emotional reactions, NASW supports evidence-based research to improve upon treatment offerings.

In shaping public policy, the left wing and right wing sometimes agree to the adopting of a new policy but for different reasons. Then when it becomes evident that the new laws or rules are ineffective or downright harmful, progressives have a difficult time turning back the clock. Just as No Child Left Behind was accepted in liberal circles as a way to promote education advances, deinstitutionalization of mental asylums was strongly supported by humanists as a way to grant treatment in the community rather than locking people away. And conservatives favored closing the mental institutions for cost-saving benefits and to reduce dependency on the state. The promised generous funding of community mental health services and halfway houses never materialized, and, as we know, behavior associated with mental illness became criminalized, and jails and prisons became the new mental institutions (see Human Rights Watch, 2003). From this example, we can learn that when legislative changes are made, especially those involving the closing down of programs, there must be guarantees of protection for the subjects of the change.

Popple and Leighninger (2015) consider the study of unintended consequences of a given policy as a type of research investigation that is commonly conducted by journalists who report on the research results for the public media. The topics necessarily are those often controversial programs in which the general public is interested. This approach is historic because the researcher must look at data over time to determine a program's effectiveness.

Much attention was paid in the 2012 presidential election to campaign claims that because the rich and super rich are apt to invest in companies providing jobs, the economy will prosper more by reducing the taxes on these people than through poverty prevention programs. Essentially this was a contemporary version of the "trickle-down theory" that was popular in the 1920s (see Chapter 2). The belief that the accumulation of vast wealth by big business will enrich the whole society fell out of favor during the Great Depression when it failed to work. Today, however, despite the unregulated banking systems and privatized health care system that resulted in the disastrous 2008 recession, this neoliberal ideology continues to be widespread. The fact that over time the distribution of the wealth has grown more lopsided with the widening gap between rich and poor and rewards going to the higher echelons in the society would seem to disprove the belief that wealth trickles down from top to bottom (Friedman, 2012).

Global Analysis

The impact of globalization, as discussed in Chapter 1, is felt in virtually every sphere of political and social life. It is seen in the blurring of trade and political barriers, in concern about wars that cross borders, in transnational crime (e.g., trafficking) and most strikingly in the communications revolution.

In policy planning, equal in importance to a historical analysis is a journey to foreign shores to view solutions to problems we all have in common. Thanks to the instantaneous access to information from abroad on a given issue, researchers increasingly are looking to how other countries are coping, for example, with national debt or more personal problems such as substance abuse. Harm reduction policies that have achieved success in substance abuse treatment programs in Europe are gradually making inroads in the United States while 12-step programming, so popular in the United States has been modeled in various places in Europe. There is so much we can learn of innovative practices and of possibilities that never would have been imagined without an international exchange of information. For this reason, we have included a global analysis in our policy analysis design. "Why reinvent the wheel?" as the common expression goes.

Advocates for strict gun control as a way to reduce murders, suicides, and mass shootings can search the Internet for research pertaining to a country that switched from open sales of weapons to a crackdown on gun ownership and look at the statistics. Australia is a case in point. Following a mass shooting of tourists that took place in 1996 that resulted in the deaths of 35 people, the conservative government instituted new policies (Oremus, 2012). A massive buyback of over 600,000 semiautomatic shotguns and rifles greatly reduced the numbers of these types of weapons in circulation. New gun laws were introduced to prohibit private sales, and gun buyers had to present a compelling reason to purchase a gun. The result was an end to mass shootings; homicides by firearm plunged 59% between 1995 and 2006, with no corresponding increase in non-firearm–related homicides, and suicides decreased by 65%. Although an analysis in the *Harvard Bulletin* emphasizes that the situations in Australia and the United States are not exactly comparable, the researchers conclude that the evidence cannot be ignored (Hemenway & Vriniotis, 2011).

Perhaps a better approach would be a study of suicide rather than homicide. A recent discussion of the use of firearms in suicide cases by Miller, Azrael, and Barber (2012) of the Harvard Injury Research Center reminds us of the following statistical facts: More people who die by suicide in the United States use a gun than all other methods combined; suicide is the second leading cause of death for Americans under age 40, exceeded only by motor vehicle crashes. The states with the highest rates of gun ownership have the highest suicide rates, and the U.S. rate for children's suicides in comparison to other industrialized nations is 11 times higher. Compared to other methods of committing suicide, attempts with a firearm are almost always fatal. The fact that nine out of 10 people who survive a suicide attempt do not go on to die by suicide later is a significant arguing point for the removal of lethal weapons from the home. Miller et al. conclude that the potential of suicide prevention is often not realized through the restriction of access to highly lethal devices. Most other industrially comparable nations, as we know, have strict gun control laws.

We are talking here of domestic policy as viewed from the global perspective. Some policy actions, as Healy (2008) suggests, have a direct transnational impact; laws and regulations pertaining to immigrants and foreign child adoptions are examples. Globalization has the potential to transport traditional social policy analysis into an ever-widening international arena, even to the extent, through information technology, of helping people to influence their own governments to consider human rights issues in foreign relations.

Contained in the Universal Declaration of Human Rights (United Nations, 1948) are principles germane to the alleviation of oppression and injustice. These principles provide a template for how the state should treat its citizens socially, culturally, and economically. A proposal for a county-funded, ethnic-sensitive substance abuse program, for example, is in keeping with Article 25, which endorses the right to medical care and necessary social services; Article 27, pertaining to participation in the cultural life of the community; and even with Article 16, which is directed toward protection of the family. A proposal to reduce school violence through anti-oppressive education can be guided by the principle found in Article 26, which states that education should be directed to the promotion of tolerance and to the furtherance of activities for the maintenance of peace. As backing for proposals that challenge economic or social oppression, one even finds an article of general tolerance.

There is a need, as Mullaly (2010) suggests, to develop a fully articulated alternative discourse to the free market deterministic position provided by the ruling elites. Social workers must counter the dominant social order "through the targeted use of facts" concerning the fallacies of global market economic theories. Another example of a counter discourse that has done much to arouse the consciousness of the world against the hegemony of male domination is the feminist movement.

Progressive policy analysis is enriched by a global feminist perspective, which may serve as a conceptual tool for understanding social problems such as gender inequality, poverty, and the sexual and economic exploitation of women as products of neoliberal economic globalization. In this sense, global feminism further extends social work's long standing person/environmental approach, which asserts that everything is connected—the personal to the political, the future to the past, the mind to the body, women to men, the community to the state, the poor to the rich.

Social workers as social activists sometimes become members of nongovernmental organizations (NGOs) such as Greenpeace, which engages in acts of civil disobedience to attract world attention to environmental damage committed by corporations, or Amnesty International, which focuses on freeing political prisoners and conducting research on government acts of commission or omission that threaten human life.

Economic Analysis

The economic sustainability perspective is concerned with long-term economic solvency of a nation and of its individual people. Consistent with the key social work value of social justice, this approach implies that proactive government policies are required to achieve economic development, which is both socially just and ecologically sound. William Roth (2011) effectively argues that the distribution of wealth has become so lopsided today that social justice is vanishing. Forces in the global economy, such as outsourcing, are having serious repercussions far and wide. From this standpoint, free market neoliberalism and economic globalization is associated with increasing inequality between and within nations. Increasing environmental destruction, the results of which fall most heavily on marginalized populations, is a consequence as well.

In order for social workers to fight against social inequalities and to create change in society for the good of all people, incorporation of a sustainability perspective in the design of social policies can challenge associated problems related to each trend—neoliberalism and globalization. Concerning neoliberalism, an economic sustainability approach can enable us to see neoliberalism's fixation on economic growth and individual responsibility that undermines global health. Moreover, such a pragmatic but ethically oriented perspective can support us in developing economy-conscious policies that lend sufficient consideration to existing structural constraints that perpetuate the oppression of marginalized citizens.

Kirst-Ashman (2010) considers both effectiveness and efficiency as important criteria in analyzing the viability of a policy under investigation. As a case example, she looks at the policy of requiring mandatory drug testing (urinalysis) for people receiving welfare benefits. From the effectiveness standpoint, researchers would want to look at the goals achieved by instituting such a policy. If the goal is to reduce drug use, there is no empirically based evidence that people with substance abuse problems and addiction would discontinue such usage under threat of drug testing. If the goal is to significantly reduce the numbers of people on the welfare rolls by eliminating those thought to be undeserving, research cited by Kirst-Ashman (2010) shows that only a tiny minority of the mostly single mothers who receive government assistance abuse drugs. But if the goal is to punish people and further stigmatize them for being poor (covert goals), then the policy would be successful. In any case, according to the stated goals, given the economic and social costs of initiating a drug testing policy, we can conclude it would not be effective. And as far as efficiency and the second criterion is concerned, drug testing is too expensive for a state to achieve any success in this regard. The Maryland legislature, as Kirst-Ashman (2010) notes, decided against such testing when policy analysis revealed that 1 year of such testing would cost the state over 1 million dollars.

Good policy analysis, as Popple and Leighninger (2015) suggest, almost always begins with solid description and historical analysis; is based on the best empirical data available; and then proceeds to focus on efficiency, effectiveness, and ethics. As well, good policy analysis is often comparative. In agreement with these authors, we now move to a model for policy analysis with an emphasis on sustainability from which students of social welfare and professionals in the field can evaluate policies of interest.

Cost-effectiveness criteria relates to efficiency as a criterion and is part of what Bruce Jansson (2009) calls a rational approach. This approach measures the net benefits to society when costs are compared to the social benefits, for example, a job training program for welfare recipients that compares the costs of the program against the estimated earnings from jobs and savings to tax payers for welfare benefits. Such quantitative measures, however, as Jansson (2009) indicates, are often static and fail to use a systems framework for a more holistic prediction of the estimated cost-effectiveness. When other factors are taken into account, such as mental health disabilities and poor social skills in individual cases, the homelessness of people removed from the welfare rolls who fail to get jobs, and the poor health of children living far below the poverty level, the conclusions about the effectiveness of the program may be very different. A system's framework directs analysts to examine the complex relationships among all the existing elements for a more accurate prediction of the likely outcomes of a certain policy.

Political Analysis

The *political analysis* aspect of policy analysis refers to power relations, laws, and political legislation affecting disadvantaged populations. One goal of this analysis is to prepare progressive social workers for the barriers they can expect to face. Straus, Richardson, and Haynes (2005) identify common barriers to the implementation of effective services. Among the political barriers they list are the following: disagreement over value of proposed services, organizational policies that prohibit the initiatives, traditionalism, authoritarianism, concerns about litigation, problems in applying the innovations, and/or client resistance. The economic barriers can be formidable as well.

What is the NASW position on the involvement of social workers in the political arena? In *Social Work Speaks*, under the entry "Electoral Politics," NASW (2012) states that it is imperative that social workers as professionals "become informed about and involved in all levels of politics" (p. 108). Although some members of the profession believe that social workers should take a nonpartisan approach to the issues, NASW (2012) contends that in order to influence policy outcomes, social workers must provide support to candidates who represent NASW values and issues.

See Box 12.2 for an outline that provides, in digest form, a list of questions that has been successfully used in a social work policy class by one of the authors for groups of social work students to follow in their joint written and oral presentations devoted to a policy issue of concern to the local community. Typical topics chosen were the following: the need to return low-risk prisoners to the community, an appeal for increased funding for domestic violence services, an initiative to support funding for the establishment of a mental health court in the county, and a proposal to restore citizenship status to ex-felons. The purpose of the exercise was to help prepare students for future advocacy roles. A secondary purpose was to promote awareness of the unsustainability of present programs, for example, the family breakup associated with mass incarcerations for crimes related to drug addiction.

BOX 12.2   GUIDELINES FOR SUSTAINABLE POLICY ANALYSIS

I.   Description of the Social Condition/Problem

A. What is the social condition that lacks sustainability to meet the future needs of people and therefore is in need of change?

B. What is the nature of dissatisfaction with the present condition? Is the situation one that is socially oppressive, or is it a question of economic or environmental unsustainability, for example?

C. What are the facts (from official and unofficial reports) concerning the social condition?

1. What does documentation through review of the literature show?

2. What do we know from official data, agency records, surveys, or interviews with key experts?

3. What are forecasts for future problems and expenses related to the problem?

D. To what extent is the social condition perceived by constituents as a social problem?

1. How is the problem defined by various factions in the society?

a. What value biases are implicit?
b. To what source is the problem attributed?

2. For whom is the situation in question a problem?

II.   Historical Analysis

A. What were the relevant social or environmental conditions like in the past?

B. How did the social condition (e.g., pollution of a local creek, need for affordable child care services, homelessness) come to be defined as a problem?

1. How was the definition of the problem affected by changing social values?

2. How was the problem dealt with historically?

C. Which influential groups were involved in supporting and opposing proposed remedies? Are the groups the same today?

D. What are the precedents for the ideas and values being used to correct the situation?

E. To what extent were the approaches to the problem effective or ineffective?

F. How did the manifest goals differ from the unstated or latent goals of potential solutions?

G. Comment on the lessons of history relevant to the present issue.

III.   Policy Formulation Overview

A. What are the goals (manifest and latent) of the proposed policy change?

B. Listen to the voices of the people: What can we learn from people's (clients') narratives about the need to strengthen resources?

C. What are the pros and cons of various ways of dealing with the problem?

  1. How does each of these competing policies meet the criteria of self-determination, empowerment, adequacy, feasibility, and efficiency?

  2. How is this proposal superior to other remedies?

D. To what extent can public opinion be mobilized in support of your proposed policy?

E. In general what do the research findings tell us about the problem?

F. What are anticipated barriers to policy change?

IV. The Global Context

A. What can we learn from other countries about similar policies or approaches to meet the same need?

B. Discuss international differences in funding sources and levels of support.

C. How is your proposed policy integrated within the cultural values of one or more other countries?

D. Could we advocate a similar policy for the United States given U.S. traditional values?

E. Relate the policy under consideration to the relevant section of the Universal Declaration of Human Rights.

V. Economic Analysis

A. How much will the proposed initiative cost?

  1. How does this expense compare with present or other proposed offerings?

  2. How will the proposed program be funded?

B. What will be the projected cost-savings (the benefits) to the state, county, or agency?

C. Which groups benefit financially from the social problem (e.g., landlords from housing shortages)?

D. Discuss the initiative in terms of its bearing on economic oppression.

E. If relevant, measure the economic benefits in terms of the impact on the physical environment.

  1. Is the policy consistent with environmental sustainability?

  2. If present conditions continue, what will be the impact on the livelihood of future generations?

F. If the initiative entails an economic benefit, is the benefit means tested?

VI. Political Analysis

A. Who are the major players involved in the policy innovation or policy to be changed (politicians, professionals, populations at risk)?

(Continued)

(Continued)

   B. Who are the major stakeholders who have vested interests in making/ resisting the proposed change?

      1. Assess the extent of opponents' political backing, clout, and media access.
      2. Assess the extent of the supporters' political backing, clout, and media access.

   C. What is the political context within which the policy initiative has been conceived? Is political/racial/gender oppression an issue of public concern?

   D. What are the major political arguments used by opponents against the proposal? Draw on research data to refute or acknowledge the truth of these arguments.

   E. What are the NASW Code of Ethics standards (2008) and NASW policy statements (see *Social Work Speaks* [NASW, 2012]) relevant to the policy?

   F. Describe any lobbying efforts, if any, and any relevant legislative bills introduced.

   G. Which profession (lawyers, psychologists, managed-care bureaucrats, etc.), if any, controls the territory? How does this influence affect the policy's acceptability?

   H. Gauge the likelihood of having the policy implemented and anticipate possible unintended (positive and negative) consequences of the initiative's enactment.

THINKING SUSTAINABLY

In this chapter, we have looked at the different lenses of analysis that are used to study social problems. Consider each of the four most prominent lenses:

   Historical

   Global

   Political

   Economic

What are the strengths and weaknesses of each lens as it pertains to the goal of pointing toward sustainable change? Which lenses seem to be the predominant lens through which U.S. society tends to view the following: health care, crime, and the environment? How do they relate to the Social Work code of ethics as discussed in the beginning of the chapter?

From Policy Analysis to Policy Practice

Social workers at the agency level often find themselves torn between their social care functions and their social control functions in working with clients. Workers in the human services field also may feel anger at the degrading social conditions experienced by their clients and at governments that cater to the wishes of the wealthy at the expense of the people. Mullaly (2010) sees such anger as a catalyst to attack injustice and oppression in the way that feminists have used the construction of anger to attack sexism and the patriarchy. Anger, we must recognize, has been a driving force behind many social movements; indeed mobilized anger at present conditions may be essential to the struggle for liberation. It also moves us from taking everyday injustices and challenges for granted to a position of readiness to work toward change. The point here is that unless there is some significant degree of dissatisfaction with the present state of affairs, it will be hard to mobilize people to advocate for policy change.

The skills required for policy practice are the same skills as those required for social work practice in general—good people skills and the possession of a probing, creative mind. Training in client advocacy can be immensely helpful in preparing social work students to stand up for their clients and to explain their needs to those in power positions to affect legislation that is potentially harmful. An article in *NASW News*, for example, provides numerous illustrations of how social work knowledge and know-how were influential in steering poorly thought-out punitive restrictions on welfare clients away from passage (Malai, 2012). Another illustration recounts how the about-to-be unemployed social workers of one social welfare office that was to be closed because of budget cuts conducted a food drive in the community and got a huge response of support. In the end, because of their efforts, the office is now in full operation. Social workers interviewed in the article attributed their success to their training for advocacy at the MSW level.

Although policy practitioners might favor one type of intervention over another, all types have a role to play in confronting societal injustice. Working within the system to change the system carries the least risks and the highest possibility of effectiveness in most situations. Being co-opted by the system, however, is always a risk; sometimes as the innovator compromises to move up within system, the compromises take a psychological toll. The role of conformist becomes a self-fulfilling prophecy. Barring that happenstance, the closer one can get to the source of the decision making, the better.

We talked about the importance of the definition of the problem and implications for policy analysis in the first portion of this chapter. We return to this discussion now. Regarding change efforts, as well, the way a problem is defined usually determines how it will be resolved (Dobelstein, 2003; Jimenez et al., 2014). Gun enthusiasts and manufacturers, for example, would see a problem with liberals trying to deprive individuals of their constitutional right to own handguns and high-powered weapons, which would leave them defenseless. Social workers might define the high male suicide rate committed through the use of handguns in the United States as a problem. The solution for the first group would be arming more Americans so that good people could defend themselves against the bad people. In fact, the head of the NRA made this very point in the organization's first news conference after the Newtown,

Connecticut massacre. "The only thing that stops a bad guy with a gun is a good guy with a gun," said the CEO Wayne LaPierre (2012). For the second group, the solution would be tight restrictions on handgun possession and instructions to members of the helping professions to discuss the risks of having guns in the homes of people at risk of suicide.

Examples of social problems as conceptualized by public officials and the corporate press are welfare fraud, Medicaid fraud, teen pregnancy, a high dropout rate from high school, underage drinking, and drug dealing. Examples of social problems as conceptualized by social workers and their clients are more likely to be the nonliving wage, industrial job loss due to global competition, absence of nationalized health care, unequal access to exemplary educational offerings, high infant mortality rates, marginalization of disabled persons, lack of available substance abuse treatment, punitive drug policies, lack of affordable housing, and so on.

The challenge to would-be policymakers begins here, in short, with the definition of the situation. Media reports can be immensely helpful in generating public awareness of the existence of a public health problem, such as the lack of availability of affordable substance abuse treatment, or the need for more foster care homes.

Grassroots Organizing

From *outside* the social welfare system at the grassroots level, typical activities that change agents might pursue range from waging informational campaigns through establishing radical listservs and websites on behalf of a particular cause or causes; to involvement in welfare rights' marches and other forms of direct action; to involvement in antiwar or anti-World Trade Organization demonstrations. From an international perspective, the work of NGOs is of vital importance in the protection of civil and minority rights. Armed only with access to the printing press, Internet, and media sources, NGOs such as Amnesty International have aroused the consciousness of the world. Many social workers, students of social work, and educators are members of such organizations, and we would be remiss to ignore their contributions to social reform. Such efforts by social workers to influence the development of social policies are known as *policy practice* (Barker, 2014).

We turn now to a description of one long-standing grassroots effort in which individuals have confronted (and continue to confront) oppression and unsustainable practices through mass organization. We present this description to document a unique effort that has involved hundreds of people over the years, many of them social workers and students of social work who have engaged in a confrontation of power elites on behalf of community residents. We are talking about the radical activist organization known as the Kensington Welfare Rights Union (KWRU). Founded in Philadelphia in 1991 in the economically impoverished Kensington neighborhood, the KWRU is a part of a larger mass movement to end poverty in the United States. KWRU is part of the Poor Peoples Economic Human Rights Campaign led by Cheri Honkala, which has received international publicity around the issue of housing for homeless people. The values and visions underpinning this mass movement are those contained in the UN Declaration of Human Rights (see Appendix A)—the right to economic and social security and to an adequate standard of living for health and well-being. Former social work educator and activist Mary Bricker-Jenkins (2004) chairs the Social Work Strategy Subcommittee of the education committee of this organization. Education, as Bricker-Jenkins (2004) states, is key to any successful social movement so everyone in the organization is expected to study.

An internship program at the University of Iowa, as described by a former participant Amanda Miller (2011), offers an immersion experience for social work students to learn about macro-level work from the KWRU in North Philadelphia. This experience, as Miller informs us, takes students out of their comfort zones as they stay in a church building in an area of dilapidated housing where people with drug and other problems roam the streets. Students learn firsthand from women what it's like to survive on welfare money and how resourceful they must be to get by on less than they, and their children, need to live.

The societal practice of leaving abandoned houses empty while homeless families live on the streets is clearly unsustainable. Health and sanitation issues are evident in those living conditions. KWRU networks with other volunteer organizations and social work students from various universities to fix up these houses to make them livable and then offers them to destitute families. Although this strategy of illegal occupancy operates outside the law, the authorities, fortunately, have looked the other way. Politically, the residents are encouraged to join the organization and to protest to end homelessness. The goal is to include them and other poor people and their allies in a mass movement to challenge the social system by demanding that their human rights be met.

The education and collective action that are integral to this poor people's campaign are also central to the sustainability paradigm. As participants in social action, social workers, like the people with whom they are aligned, move toward critical consciousness to understand the roots of oppression and to link their critical consciousness to effective sustainability actions toward the goal of social justice. Effective use of one's privilege as an ally to challenge oppression is an important factor in organizing for successful systemic change (Bishop, 2002; Sakamoto & Pitner, 2005).

Working Toward Legislative Change

Often out of the most dismal crisis or setback comes an opportunity that was unexpected. So it is with the trend known as *devolution*. Devolution is the word used for the turning over of many social work functions from the federal government to the states. State legislators have far fewer resources at their disposal than do members of the U.S. Congress, but today they are placed in the position of allocating scarce resources. Moreover, they live in the local community and answer to the people there; this means they are far more accessible to local influence than federal legislators. So it is, as Sherraden, Slosar, and Sherraden (2002) inform us, that the challenge of policy devolution opens the door for social workers, in collaboration with community leaders, to influence state policy. In each state, accordingly, the social worker lobby has gotten involved in writing letters, making friendly phone calls, and producing well-prepared fact sheets. Social workers, as Sherraden et al. (2002) point out, are the perfect liaisons between private troubles and political solutions, and between the populations at risk and the decision makers who can do so much to help or hurt them.

An article in *NASW News* describes activities of social work chapters in the Midwest in rallying on behalf of unions in the face of regressive legislation in Michigan, Ohio, Indiana, and Wisconsin (Malamud, 2011). Social workers in Wisconsin went to great lengths to quash the Republican-led plan to limit public employees' collective bargaining rights to wages. The social work chapter organized members to contact state representatives over proposed changes in health care benefits as well.

An excellent resource for learning the steps for influencing social policy is Influencing State Policy, the organization mentioned previously that links social work education programs and statewide lobbying efforts. The website at www.statepolicy.org defines the organization's purpose as to influence social policy for the benefit of social welfare and social work practice. The basic message is optimistic: Social workers today can have more influence than in the past. This is because of "the new federalism" or devolution—the continuing movement of more of the decision making from the central government to the states. As the social services budgets, decisions, and policies about social work clients' well-being increasingly are relegated to the states, the voices of the people at state and local levels can better be heard. Accordingly, the states are the focal point of change and reform. Social workers therefore are urged to enhance their credibility by making informed contributions to policy discourse in state capitals. And social work educators are encouraged to provide courses in state policymaking as a means of ensuring a long-term commitment of professional social workers in current and future decision making about vulnerable and disadvantaged persons. To learn more about legislative advocacy see www.statepolicy.org/About%20Us/Purpose.html.

Another excellent source, Haynes and Mickelson's (2010) *Affecting Change*, provides an excellent guide for navigating the political process. Their text offers a step-by-step guide to developing the necessary political action skills to engage in political advocacy, a central mission of social work practice.

It is crucial for practitioners in this field and social workers in this and related fields to engage in policy analysis to influence legislation through lobbying at the state and local levels for the strengthening and continuation of such funding. For up-to-date facts that should be of interest to policymakers seeking cost-effective alternatives to incarceration, visit "Making Drug Policy at the State Level" at www.drugstrategies.org/criticalchoices. Such programs offer extensive, long-term treatment at little cost to the offender; many opportunities exist for professionally trained counselors to find employment with such diversionary, community-based programs.

Harm Reduction and Restorative Justice

Harm reduction and restorative justice are two concepts that are rapidly becoming part of the social work lexicon. These concepts, in fact, are already well known to social workers throughout the English-speaking world and, increasingly, in the United States. The term *harm reduction* appeared for the first time in the 5th edition of *The Social Work Dictionary*. It is defined in the most recent edition as "a pragmatic, public health approach to reducing the negative consequences of some harmful behavior rather than eliminating or curing the problem (Barker, 2014, p. 189).

The aim of harm reduction is to reduce unhealthy practices as much as is feasible in the belief that taking small steps is better than nothing. To prevent the spread of

AIDS, for example, treatment priorities may prescribe moderate doses of the drug of choice or of a synthetic substitute; dirty needles may be exchanged free of charge for clean ones. This approach has been considered controversial in the United States, where moralism often wins out over pragmatism. Because the philosophy of harm reduction is consistent with the empowerment perspective of social work, however, we can expect that the profession will pay far more heed to its principles and practices in the near future. *Restorative justice* is a concept that still has a way to go in U.S. social work circles although it is widely known to correctional personnel. The fact that no definition was included in Barker's (2003) *Social Work Dictionary* is indicative of a lack of broad-based recognition of the importance of this concept to social work up to that time. Happily, a brief definition of this term is now included in the recent edition (as the editor, Robert Barker, promised in private correspondence with K. van Wormer in September 20, 2012).

Because so many in the profession work with persons who are ordered by courts into treatment as offenders, not to mention all the persons victimized by crime who come into treatment to work on issues of traumatization, it is fitting that the Center of Restorative Justice and Peacemaking at the University of Minnesota is housed in the department of social work. Social work practitioners often are trained through field placements for work in juvenile and adult correctional institutions and through coursework to provide counseling for personal issues and substance abuse treatment. Nevertheless, compared to other areas of social work practice, the clash between social work values and societal values is at its most pronounced here, in the correctional system. Whereas the general purpose of the criminal justice system is to punish offenders and deter others from law-breaking behavior by setting a harsh example, social work's mission, as we know, is to help people help themselves and to challenge social injustice (NASW, 2008). With its success in peacemaking, restorative justice strategies can effectively bridge the gap, forming a harmonious link between the criminal justice and social work fields.

Harm reduction and restorative justice are two examples of person-centered approaches, the former from health care, the latter from criminal justice, that closely resonate with social work values. Through heightened consciousness concerning these concepts, social workers, following the profession's commitment to social justice and political action, can make a difference in both small and major ways. The significance of the discussion of these approaches is its bearing on the social action component in social work. More work is necessary to confront the most onerous aspects of globalization, the oppression of socially excluded populations.

Social work educators Heidemann, Fertig, Jansson, and Kim (2011) got students directly involved in acquiring relevant knowledge to address the growing economic and social problems in California. After the students had selected a single target issue—the need for supportive or closely monitored housing for homeless people with mental disorders—the class articulated a rationale for engaging in policy advocacy. With the cooperation of the university, instructors were hired to teach relevant courses so that students would master the roles and skills they needed to influence the policy process. Each section of the course in the second year chose a homeless subpopulation, such as veterans, on which to focus their attention. In the end, after visiting homeless shelters to assess the needs, working with legislators, and generating public support, a

A Restorative Justice Session. Lorenn Walker facilitating a reentry circle for an individual in Tokyo, Japan, who is leaving prison. She is surrounded by personal supporters in the small inner circle. Participants from a restorative justice training workshop look on.

congresswoman agreed to convene a hearing on the matter and receive testimony from the students. Although Heidemann et al. (2011) did not refer to sustainability in their case history, we can assume that their statement of problem would have argued that the present system of mass homelessness was not sustainable. Then they might have drawn on local statistics to reveal the immense economic toll that homeless people were having on the community and the psychological/learning problems faced by children without appropriate housing.

The success of the class's research was realized in the politician's introduction of a bill in Congress to provide housing for children. In initiating legislative reform, a focus on children is appealing across political lines as is an emphasis on veterans. When the focus is on establishing housing for substance-addicted homeless people, an emphasis on alcohol problems is more palatable than an emphasis on heroin, cocaine, or meth addiction, which are highly stigmatized. As an example of effectiveness in using research to argue for supportive housing of the Housing First variety, see Apicello (2010) and Larimer et al. (2009). Housing First programs are controversial in that sobriety is not required at any point for the residents, despite their severe drinking problems. Empirical research such as that provided in the supportive housing research generally uses local statistics on the costs of incarceration and hospital care of chronically homeless populations compared to the costs of providing them with supportive housing. The cost savings as shown in such research is impressive. The fact that residents, as shown in the studies above, actually reduced their intake of alcohol over time further bolsters the case for effectiveness. In virtually all the litera-ture on supportive housing, the illicit drug addiction factor is underplayed, and the arguments center on economics (van Wormer & van Wormer, 2009). The cost-saving approach, perhaps sadly, has been found to be more persuasive than moral, humani-tarian arguments with city councils in making requests for funding of Housing First programs. This use of economic over moral arguments has also been found to work effectively for opponents of the death penalty who in California, for example, have resorted to using economic as opposed to value-laden arguments in seeking abolition (Cohen, 2012). Although Californians recently voted to retain the death penalty, its support significantly declined as surveys indicated, when the state's residents were informed of the facts concerning the huge expense to the state that the institutional-ization of the death penalty imposed.

Ethical Issues Relevant to Social Change Efforts

The core objective of policy practice according to Baehler and Fiorino (2011) is the study of the complementarity among the individual systems. We can consider, for example, the balance between the environment and economic considerations. Should we allow more pollution, resource development, or ecosystem damage in the interests of growth?—that is the perennial question. Because social work values promote enhancing the quality of life of people, which includes environmental concerns, individual social workers would be remiss not to work toward helping their constituents have a clean and healthy environment in which to live and raise their children.

The Sustainability Ethic

A *sustainability ethic* teaches us to reconsider our relationship with nature and each other, the crux of sustainability. The sustainability ethic states that nature is our teacher and our guide. Built on ecosystems understandings, this ethic connects all human and nonhuman life forms with the force that pulses through all life and views diversity as a key value principle that extends from the promotion of a healthy agri-culture with respect for the earth to the development of organizational policy. Diversity at this level means receiving input and ideas from a wide variety of people and carrying out policy in line with higher order values of social justice and harmony. Indeed, this would represent a paradigm shift. As described by Edwards and Orr (2005) in their groundbreaking *The Sustainability Revolution,* such a paradigm shift would center on the interdependencies of the three *E's*—ecology, economy, and equity. *Ecology* tells us to emphasize a long-term perspective and to acknowledge and respond in turn to our dependence on our life support systems. Looking at *economy,* Edwards and Orr stress healthy growth and cooperation; business enterprises are urged to mimic natural systems and work toward the good of the community. The *equity* component of the sustainability triangle views the well-being of individual and community as intertwined and interdependent. Edwards and Orr (2005) further emphasize education as a key component of the three E's as we weave our way into the sustainable path. *The Sustainability Revolution* describes tools created by task forces and working groups to implement long-term systematic approaches at regional, national, and international levels.

Relevant to the profession of social work, Allen Barsky's (2009) textbook on ethics and values discusses ways to incorporate values and ethics into the analysis of policies as well as into the promotion of policy change. Barsky (2009) lists the following principles as essential in the policy formation process: transparency or openness to the public of meetings concerning proposals of general interest, accountability to the people and responsiveness to their concerns, inclusiveness, and reasonableness of arguments for or against the proposals that are being considered. Consider Barsky's (2009) hypothetical case example concerning the distribution of a vaccine to the public when only a limited amount is available. Who will be given priority in receiving the vaccine?—that is the question. And how will the decision be made favoring certain groups over others? The starting point might be to have a public hearing so that all voices with a stake in the decision would be heard. Consensus would probably develop that the reasonable decision would be to target high-risk members of the society first—the oldest and the youngest residents—until more supplies became available. It would be unreasonable to favor the more important people over the others but might make sense to vaccinate health care workers who would be readily exposed to the germs and spread the virus to their patients. The principles represented in this example directly parallel those we consider daily related to the allocation of scarce resources. Social workers generally would advocate for disadvantaged and vulnerable groups to be protected. They would also be ethically bound to promote access to services on the basis of one's ability to pay. Sliding fee scales are thus commonly found at social service agencies.

Understanding ethics in this context means recognizing power imbalances built into the social system and actively working toward the promotion of change to redress the balance of power (Dalrymple & Burke, 2007). Empowering policy is built on understanding what life is like in the absence of choices and exclusion from the source of decision making. At the macro-level, as Dalrymple and Burke (2007) indicate, empowerment is seen as a process of increasing collective political power. One cannot really challenge oppression without challenging at least some aspects of the power structure, and therein lies the difficulty. Even though the pursuit of social transformation in the political system is the ultimate goal of anti-oppressive social work, David Gil (2002) emphasizes that pursuing short-range goals is not only necessary but is also ethically valid in order to alleviate the pain and suffering of oppressed people as soon as possible. In no way does the pursuit of short-range goals present an obstacle to the larger schemes that require lengthy processes involving "countercultural education" toward critical consciousness (p. 44). This process must be developed and sustained by social movements guided by transformation visions.

We cannot leave the topic of ethics without discussing the ethical dilemma of situations in which one's employers or supervisors support unethical practices. This to Barsky (2009) is one of the greatest challenges to advocates of social justice. He provides an example of an executive director siphoning off agency funds for his own personal use. The social worker is in a real ethical dilemma because his or her job may be at stake. The temptation is to rationalize the situation by telling oneself the following: The risks are too great; others will see him or her as a snitch; it'll be his or her word against the director's; or the director otherwise does a lot of good work. Unfortunately, the NASW Code of Ethics (2008) does not include whistle-blowing as an ethical strategy and therefore provides no guidance in situations such as these. One possible strategy that one of our authors used was to wait until a new job was pending and then to publicize the problems at the agency through writing an exposé in a widely circulated journal (this event took place at an alcoholism treatment center in Norway).

Some other ethical dilemmas also cannot be easily resolved. Consider the following challenging situation that presented itself to international social workers when a conference was held for 2013 in Kampala Uganda. "Opening new frontiers in social development" was the theme of the conference. The problem was that homosexuality has been outlawed in Uganda; the country's hostility toward gays and lesbians has been widely publicized. Letters shared with the global education (Globaled) listserv of Council of Social Work Education presented two opposing reactions to the dilemma. Several of the prospective attendees planned to boycott the conference in support of human rights. Lynne Healy (in a letter dated August 3, 2012) responded to the complaints with considerable tact:

> The question of whether the social work profession can best promote human rights by isolating colleagues in oppressive regimes or engaging with them has been with us for decades. It is certainly an issue that deserves more serious discussion and debate and on which I believe reasonable people can differ. I don't think there is a simple answer.

Drawing on Our Social Work Imagination

As spelled out by Mills (1959), the success of a productive idea depends on the following: the ability to connect private troubles and public issues, a multidisciplinary perspective, possession of a scientific understanding of the issue, and the use of imagination and creativity. These qualities that are the essence of social worker resourcefulness are referred to as *the social work imagination*. In Chapter 1, we introduced the term and discussed the resourcefulness required by this profession to help people find their way, made more urgent by the weakening of social service offerings.

An outstanding example of use of such collective and political imagination took place at Ramapo College in New Jersey. Here members of the social work department set out to develop a project related to community sustainability. This led to the development of City Green, a community-wide project that serves more than 2,000 school children per year in environmental education and the creation of community gardens in nearby urban areas (personal communication, August 17, 2013). Conferences for middle school children cover such educational topics as environmental injustice and the importance of sustainable living practices in the home and community.

Development of the social work imagination is enhanced by the development of skills for the critical analysis of modern social welfare policies and programs such as those described in this chapter. In the agency setting and in political advocacy for improvement in program offerings, social workers will need to use their best critical-thinking skills to ascertain whether specific policies and programs are harmful or beneficial to their clients. They face perhaps no greater challenge than in navigating the rough waters of resistance as they seek to apply the spirit of the NASW Code of Ethics (2008) in carrying out and shaping policies related to social problems for the benefit of people who are vulnerable, oppressed, and living in poverty.

Elizabeth Clark (2012), the executive director of NASW, editorialized at the close of the year about the accomplishments of social workers, both in their official capacity and also as concerned citizens. NASW, according to Clark, estimates that social workers in the United States helped 10 million people per day and performed inestimable hours of community service. Advocacy is what differentiates social work from other professions. "Our colleagues," she wrote, "were at every disaster, and we sent assistance to our Japanese counterparts when their country was devastated by earthquakes" (p. 3). She continues,

> In 2011, more than 21,000 letters were sent to Congress through the NASW advocacy listserv. Social workers stood shoulder-to-shoulder with unions in Michigan and Wisconsin, and with the Occupy Wall Street organizers across the country. We worked on women's rights, child fatalities, same-sex marriage, and "Don't Ask, Don't Tell." We voiced our concerns around affordable care and immigration, poverty, early childhood education, prisoner re-entry, and the need for more mental health services. (p. 3)

When situations look hopeless, as is often the case politically, the social work challenge is not to give up but to keep looking for other strategies and other avenues of approach. Through social work education with its focus on active listening skills, social justice values, and cultural sensitivity, social workers have the requisite training and background needed to work toward sustainable development. They are thus well placed to point the way toward the kinds of changes required as we aspire toward the realization of universal socioeconomic and environmental protections. Through using our social work imagination we can go beyond merely criticizing the current state of affairs in the social welfare system to offering fresh new ideas and discovering the means to implement them.

Summary and Conclusion

Policy analysis can be highly productive, and it can be an intensely bonding experience for students of social work in their shared enthusiasm toward a certain end. Whether the attempt to effect social change is successful or not depends to a large extent on the timing of the initiative and the cooperation of media avenues and local politicians. Whatever the outcome, the process is an excellent learning experience even if it just shows how entrenched are local attitudes or how stakeholders with sufficient clout can wreck even the most sensible proposals for a solution to the community's targeted problems. Only in knowing how the system works can effective change be generated.

Social workers can confront social and economic injustice one by one in their counseling and advocacy roles, or they can organize to confront injustice collectively. The profession today faces awesome challenges; many workers are torn between pressures to maintain high standards of efficiency in an environment of ever-diminished levels of external funding and a desire to take a public stand. Many will become disempowered by the seeming futility of much of their work; others will seize the opportunity to build on the current dissatisfaction with the growing gap in the distribution of resources (between rich and poor) to contemplate some kind of social action.

As a grassroots method, social action is communitarian, but its goals are larger than that; social action seeks outcomes that are tangible and controversial (Figueira-McDonough, 2007). Social action strives to make the invisible inequities in society visible for all to see.

This chapter presented a guiding outline for sustainability policy analysis that is progressive in its focus on critical thinking and global and environmental concerns. From a critical standpoint, progressive social work education challenges prevailing assumptions about poverty, homelessness, and unbridled faith in the market economy. Such teaching poses questions about the nature of the power structure, the rise of the corporation, and the true reason for the national debt. The sustainability ethic that was described in this chapter uses an ecosystems framework to raise questions about the long-term impact of present-day economic, social welfare, and environmental practices. The message for social work would-be change agents is to set goals for the long-term well-being of people and let nature be our teacher.

Critical Thinking Questions

1. How do standards from the NASW Code of Ethics relate to policy analysis?

2. What is your understanding of the role of policy analysis for social workers?

3. Contrast the pluralistic and power elite positions. What can we learn from each one?

4. Recall events of Sandy Hook Elementary School. What effect, if any, has it had on social policy?

5. Discuss Box 12.1 from the point of view of social work practice. Can you think of any similar cases regarding helping someone get motivated to change?

6. Should social workers be prepared for resistance in the sense of the meaning provided by Mullaly? Why or why not?

7. Review the facts on fracking from an environmental standpoint. What does the research tell us about the impact of this process?

8. What types of innovation can we learn about through global analysis?

9. How are measures of cost-effectiveness and efficiency important to policy analysis? Give an example.

10. What is the relevance of political analysis in preparing a policy proposal?

11. Can you give some examples historically of a time when a state of mass anger helped move people forward?

12. How can work toward legislative change be accomplished?

13. In what way are harm reduction and restorative justice important concepts for social work?

14. How does the sustainability ethic relate to social work ethics?

15. What are some ethical dilemmas facing social workers today and what they can do to resolve these issues?

References

Apicello, J. (2010). A paradigm shift in housing and homeless services: Applying the population and high-risk framework to preventing homelessness. *Open Health Services and Policy Journal, 3,* 41–52.

Baehler, K. J., & Fiorino, D. (2011, October). *Sustainability policy analysis: What is it? What can it do for us?* Paper presented at the 2nd International Conference on Government Performance Management and Leadership, Portland State University, Portland, OR.

Barker, R. (2003). *The social work dictionary* (5th ed.). Washington, DC: NASW Press.

Barker, R. (2014). *The social work dictionary* (6th ed.). Washington, DC: NASW Press.

Barsky, A. (2009). *Ethics and values in social work: An integrated approach for a comprehensive curriculum.* New York, NY: Oxford University Press.

Bishop, A. (2002). *Becoming an ally: Breaking the cycle of oppression.* Halifax, Nova Scotia: Fernwood.

Bricker-Jenkins, M. (2004). Legislative tactics in a movement strategy: The economic human rights-Pennsylvania campaign. *Meridians: Feminism, race, transnationalism, 4*(2), 108–113.

Chapin, R. K. (2011). *Social policy for effective practice: A strengths approach.* Oxon, England: Routledge.

Christian, J., & Thomas, S. S. (2009): Examining the intersections of race, gender, and mass imprisonment. *Journal of Ethnicity in Criminal Justice, 7*(1), 69–84.

Clark, E. J. (2012). From the director: Tough times bring out our best. *NASW News,* p. 3.

Cohen, A. (2012, October 26). Why California's death-penalty repeal is surging in the polls. *Atlantic.* Retrieved from www.theatlantic.com

Cummins, L. K., Byers, K. V., & Pedrick, L. (2011). *Policy practice for social workers: New strategies for a new era.* Boston, MA: Allyn & Bacon.

Dalrymple, J., & Burke, B. (2007). *Anti-oppressive practice: Social care and the law* (2nd ed.). Buckingham, England: Open University Press.

Dobelstein, A. (2003). *Social welfare: Policy and analysis.* Belmont, CA: Cengage.

Dover, M. A., & Joseph, B. H. R. (2008). Human needs: Overview. In T. Mizrahi & L. Davis (Eds.), *The encyclopedia of social work* (20th ed., pp. 398–406). New York, NY: Oxford University Press.

Edwards, A. R., & Orr, D. W. (2005). *The sustainability revolution: Portrait of a paradigm shift.* Gabriola Island, British Columbia: New Society.

Figueira-McDonough, J. (2007). *The welfare state and social work: Pursuing social justice.* Thousand Oaks, CA: Sage.

Friedman, H. S. (2012). *The measure of a nation: How to regain America's competitive edge and boost our global standing.* Amherst, NY: Prometheus Books.

Gerasimo, P. (2012, April 27). Mining companies invade Wisconsin for frac-sand. *EcoWatch, 12.* Retrieved from www.ecowatch.org

Gil, D. (1998). *Confronting injustice and oppression: Concepts and strategies for social workers.* New York, NY: Columbia University Press.

Gil, D. (2002). Challenging injustice and oppression. In M. O'Melia & K. K. Miley (Eds.), *Pathways to power: Readings in contextual social work practice* (pp. 35–54). Boston, MA: Allyn & Bacon.

Graves, L. (2012, December 15). Backgrounder: The history of the NRA/ALEC agenda. Center for Media and Democracy: The PR Watch. Retrieved from www.prwatch.org

Hanson, D. J. (2002). Drug abuse resistance education: The effectiveness of DARE. Retrieved from www.alcoholfacts.org/DARE.html

Haynes, K. S., & Mickelson, J. (2010). *Affecting change: Social workers in the political arena* (7th ed.). Upper Saddle River: Prentice Hall.

Healy, L. (2008). *International social work: Professional action in an interdependent world* (2nd ed.). New York, NY: Oxford University Press.

Heidemann, G., Fertig, R., Jansson, B., & Kim, H. (2011). Practicing policy, pursuing change, and promoting social justice: A policy instructional approach. *Journal of Social Work Education, 47*(1), 37–52.

Hemenway, D., & Vriniotis, M. (2011, Spring). The Australian gun buyback. Harvard Injury Control Research Center. *Harvard Bulletin, 4.* Retrieved from www.hsph.harvard.edu/hicrc

Human Rights Watch. (2003). *Ill-equipped: U.S. prisons and offenders with mental illness.* New York, NY: Author.

Jansson, B. (2009). Policy analysis. In J. Midgley & M. Livermore (Eds.), *The handbook of social policy* (2nd ed., pp. 51–65). Thousand Oaks, CA: Sage.

Jimenez, J., Mayers Pasztor, E., & Chambers, R. M. (with Pearlman, C.). (2014). *Social policy and social change: Toward the creation of social and economic justice* (2nd ed.). Thousand Oaks, CA: Sage.

Kirst-Ashman, K. K. (2010). *Introduction to social work and social welfare: Critical thinking perspectives* (3rd ed.). Belmont, CA: Brooks/Cole.

LaPierre, W. (2012, December 26). The NRA's latest spin: Need more "good guys with guns"? Center for Media and Democracy's PR Watch. Retrieved from www.prwatch.org

Larimer, M., Malone, D. K., Garner, M., Atkins, D., Burlingham, B., Lonczak, H., . . . Marlatt, A. (2009). Health care and public service use and costs before and after provision of housing for chronically homeless persons with severe alcohol problems. *Journal of the American Medical Association, 301*(13), 1349–1357.

Lee, J., & Hudson, R. (2011). Empowerment approach to social work practice. In F. Turner (Ed.), *Social work treatment: Interlocking theoretical approaches* (pp. 157–178). New York, NY: Oxford University Press.

Malai, R. (2012, June). Social workers use skills on the Hill. *NASW News*, p. 7.

Malamud, M. (2011, May). Social workers add voices to pro-union protests. *NASW News*, p. 5.

Miller, A. (2011). My immersion experience. In K. van Wormer & F. Besthorn, *Human behavior and the social environment, macro practice* (pp. 82–83). New York, NY: Oxford University Press.

Miller, M., Azrael, D., & Barber, C. (2012). Suicide mortality in the United States: The importance of attending to method in understanding population-level disparities in the burden of suicide. *Annual Review of Public Health, 33*, 393–408.

Miller, W. R., & Rollnick, S. (2012). *Motivational interviewing: Helping people change.* New York, NY: Guilford Press.

Mills, C. W. (1959). *The sociological imagination.* New York, NY: Oxford University Press.

Mullaly, B. (2010). *Challenging oppression and confronting privilege.* New York, NY: Oxford University Press.

Myers, T. (2012). Potential contaminant pathways from hydraulically fractured shale to aquifers. *Ground Water, 50*(6), 872–882.

National Association of Social Workers. (2008). *Code of ethics.* Washington, DC: Author.

National Association of Social Workers. (2012). Electoral politics (pp. 105–110). In *Social work speaks: NASW policy statements 2012–2014.* Washington, DC: Author.

Oremus, W. (2012, December 16). After a 1996 mass shooting, Australia enacted strict gun laws. *Slate Group.* Retrieved from www.slate.com

Olson, J. J. (2007). Social work's professional and social justice projects: Discourses in conflict. *Journal of Progressive Human Services, 18*(1), 45–69.

Palmer, P. (2007). *The courage to teach: Exploring the inner landscape of a teacher's life, 10th anniversary edition.* San Francisco, CA: Jossey-Bass.

Piven, F. F. (2006). *Challenging authority: How ordinary people change America.* Lanham, MD: Rowman & Littlefield.

Piven, F. F., & Cloward, R. A. (1971/1993). *Regulating the poor: The functions of public welfare.* New York, NY: Random House.

Popple, P. R., & Leighninger, L. (2015). *The policy-based profession: An introduction to social welfare policy analysis for social workers* (6th ed.). Upper Saddle River, NJ: Pearson.

Reichert, E. (2011). *Social work and human rights: A foundation for policy and practice* (2nd ed.). New York, NY: Columbia University Press.

Roth, W. (2011). Globalization: Its effects on the welfare state and social policy. In W. Roth & K. Briar-Lawson (Eds.), *Globalization, social justice, and the helping professions* (pp. 103–116). State University of New York Press.

Runhaar, H., Dieperink, C., & Driessen, P. (2005, June). *Policy analysis for sustainable development: Complexities and methodological responses.* Paper presented at the Workshop on Complexity and Policy Analysis, Cork, Ireland.

Sakamoto, I., & Pitner, R. (2005). Use of critical consciousness in anti-oppressive social work practice: Disentangling power dynamics at personal and structural levels. *British Journal of Social Work, 35*, 435–452.

Sherraden, M. S., Slosar, B., & Sherraden, M. (2002). Innovation in social policy: Collaborative policy advocacy. *Social Work, 47*(3), 209–221.

Soydan, H. (2012). Understanding social work in the history of ideas. *Research on Social Work Practice, 22*(5), 468–480.

Straus, S., Richardson, W., & Haynes, R. B. (2005). *Evidence-based medicine: How to practice and teach EBM* (3rd ed.). New York, NY: Churchill Livingston.

United Nations. (1948). *Universal declaration of human rights.* New York, NY: United Nations.

van Wormer, K. (2004). *Confronting oppression, restoring justice: From policy analysis to social action.* Alexandria, VA: Council of Social Work Education.

van Wormer, K., & Besthorn, F. (2011). *Human behavior and the social environment, macro practice.* New York, NY: Oxford University Press.

van Wormer, K., & Davis, D. R. (2012). *Addiction treatment: A strengths perspective.* Belmont, CA: Cengage.

van Wormer, K., Kaplan, L., & Juby, C. (2013). *Confronting oppression, restoring justice: From policy analysis to social action* (2nd ed.). Alexandria, LA: Council of Social Work Education.

van Wormer, R., & van Wormer, K. (2009). Non-abstinence-based supportive housing for persons with co-occurring disorders: A human rights perspective. *Journal of Progressive Human Services, 20*(2), 152–165.

Appendix A: Universal Declaration of Human Rights

Adopted and proclaimed by General Assembly resolution 217 A (III) of 10 December 1948

On December 10, 1948, the General Assembly of the United Nations adopted and proclaimed the Universal Declaration of Human Rights, the full text of which appears in the following pages. Following this historic act, the Assembly called upon all Member countries to publicize the text of the Declaration and "to cause it to be disseminated, displayed, read and expounded principally in schools and other educational institutions, without distinction based on the political status of countries or territories."

Preamble

Whereas recognition of the inherent dignity and of the equal and inalienable rights of all members of the human family is the foundation of freedom, justice and peace in the world,

Whereas disregard and contempt for human rights have resulted in barbarous acts which have outraged the conscience of mankind, and the advent of a world in which human beings shall enjoy freedom of speech and belief and freedom from fear and want has been proclaimed as the highest aspiration of the common people,

Whereas it is essential, if man is not to be compelled to have recourse, as a last resort, to rebellion against tyranny and oppression, that human rights should be protected by the rule of law,

Whereas it is essential to promote the development of friendly relations between nations,

Whereas the peoples of the United Nations have in the Charter reaffirmed their faith in fundamental human rights, in the dignity and worth of the human person and in the equal rights of men and women and have determined to promote social progress and better standards of life in larger freedom,

Whereas Member States have pledged themselves to achieve, in co-operation with the United Nations, the promotion of universal respect for and observance of human rights and fundamental freedoms,

Whereas a common understanding of these rights and freedoms is of the greatest importance for the full realization of this pledge,

Now, therefore THE GENERAL ASSEMBLY proclaims THIS UNIVERSAL DECLARATION OF HUMAN RIGHTS as a common standard of achievement for all peoples and all nations, to the end that every individual and every organ of society, keeping this Declaration constantly in mind, shall strive by teaching and education to promote respect for these rights and freedoms and by progressive measures, national and international, to secure their universal and effective recognition and observance, both among the peoples of Member States themselves and among the peoples of territories under their jurisdiction.

Article 1

All human beings are born free and equal in dignity and rights. They are endowed with reason and conscience and should act towards one another in a spirit of brotherhood.

Article 2

Everyone is entitled to all the rights and freedoms set forth in this Declaration, without distinction of any kind, such as race, colour, sex, language, religion, political or other opinion, national or social origin, property, birth or other status. Furthermore, no distinction shall be made on the basis of the political, jurisdictional or international status of the country or territory to which a person belongs, whether it be independent, trust, non-self-governing or under any other limitation of sovereignty.

Article 3

Everyone has the right to life, liberty and security of person.

Article 4

No one shall be held in slavery or servitude; slavery and the slave trade shall be prohibited in all their forms.

Article 5

No one shall be subjected to torture or to cruel, inhuman or degrading treatment or punishment.

Article 6

Everyone has the right to recognition everywhere as a person before the law.

Article 7

All are equal before the law and are entitled without any discrimination to equal protection of the law. All are entitled to equal protection against any discrimination in violation of this Declaration and against any incitement to such discrimination.

Article 8

Everyone has the right to an effective remedy by the competent national tribunals for acts violating the fundamental rights granted him by the constitution or by law.

Article 9

No one shall be subjected to arbitrary arrest, detention or exile.

Article 10

Everyone is entitled in full equality to a fair and public hearing by an independent and impartial tribunal, in the determination of his rights and obligations and of any criminal charge against him.

Article 11

(1) Everyone charged with a penal offence has the right to be presumed innocent until proved guilty according to law in a public trial at which he has had all the guarantees necessary for his defence.

(2) No one shall be held guilty of any penal offence on account of any act or omission which did not constitute a penal offence, under national or international law, at the time when it was committed. Nor shall a heavier penalty be imposed than the one that was applicable at the time the penal offence was committed.

Article 12

No one shall be subjected to arbitrary interference with his privacy, family, home or correspondence, nor to attacks upon his honour and reputation. Everyone has the right to the protection of the law against such interference or attacks.

Article 13

(1) Everyone has the right to freedom of movement and residence within the borders of each state.

(2) Everyone has the right to leave any country, including his own, and to return to his country.

Article 14

(1) Everyone has the right to seek and to enjoy in other countries asylum from persecution.

(2) This right may not be invoked in the case of prosecutions genuinely arising from non-political crimes or from acts contrary to the purposes and principles of the United Nations.

Article 15

(1) Everyone has the right to a nationality.

(2) No one shall be arbitrarily deprived of his nationality nor denied the right to change his nationality.

Article 16

(1) Men and women of full age, without any limitation due to race, nationality or religion, have the right to marry and to found a family. They are entitled to equal rights as to marriage, during marriage and at its dissolution.

(2) Marriage shall be entered into only with the free and full consent of the intending spouses.

(3) The family is the natural and fundamental group unit of society and is entitled to protection by society and the State.

Article 17

(1) Everyone has the right to own property alone as well as in association with others.

(2) No one shall be arbitrarily deprived of his property.

Article 18

Everyone has the right to freedom of thought, conscience and religion; this right includes freedom to change his religion or belief, and freedom, either alone or in community with others and in public or private, to manifest his religion or belief in teaching, practice, worship and observance.

Article 19

Everyone has the right to freedom of opinion and expression; this right includes freedom to hold opinions without interference and to seek, receive and impart information and ideas through any media and regardless of frontiers.

Article 20

(1) Everyone has the right to freedom of peaceful assembly and association.

(2) No one may be compelled to belong to an association.

Article 21

(1) Everyone has the right to take part in the government of his country, directly or through freely chosen representatives.

(2) Everyone has the right of equal access to public service in his country.

(3) The will of the people shall be the basis of the authority of government; this will shall be expressed in periodic and genuine elections which shall be by universal and equal suffrage and shall be held by secret vote or by equivalent free voting procedures.

Article 22

Everyone, as a member of society, has the right to social security and is entitled to realization, through national effort and international co-operation and in accordance with the organization and resources of each State, of the economic, social and cultural rights indispensable for his dignity and the free development of his personality.

Article 23

(1) Everyone has the right to work, to free choice of employment, to just and favourable conditions of work and to protection against unemployment.

(2) Everyone, without any discrimination, has the right to equal pay for equal work.

(3) Everyone who works has the right to just and favourable remuneration ensuring for himself and his family an existence worthy of human dignity, and supplemented, if necessary, by other means of social protection.

(4) Everyone has the right to form and to join trade unions for the protection of his interests.

Article 24

Everyone has the right to rest and leisure, including reasonable limitation of working hours and periodic holidays with pay.

Article 25

(1) Everyone has the right to a standard of living adequate for the health and well-being of himself and of his family, including food, clothing, housing and medical care and necessary social services, and the right to security in the event of unemployment, sickness, disability, widowhood, old age or other lack of livelihood in circumstances beyond his control.

(2) Motherhood and childhood are entitled to special care and assistance. All children, whether born in or out of wedlock, shall enjoy the same social protection.

Article 26

(1) Everyone has the right to education. Education shall be free, at least in the elementary and fundamental stages. Elementary education shall be compulsory. Technical and professional education shall be made generally available and higher education shall be equally accessible to all on the basis of merit.

(2) Education shall be directed to the full development of the human personality and to the strengthening of respect for human rights and fundamental freedoms. It shall promote understanding, tolerance and friendship among all nations, racial or religious groups, and shall further the activities of the United Nations for the maintenance of peace.

(3) Parents have a prior right to choose the kind of education that shall be given to their children.

Article 27

(1) Everyone has the right freely to participate in the cultural life of the community, to enjoy the arts and to share in scientific advancement and its benefits.

(2) Everyone has the right to the protection of the moral and material interests resulting from any scientific, literary or artistic production of which he is the author.

Article 28

Everyone is entitled to a social and international order in which the rights and freedoms set forth in this Declaration can be fully realized.

Article 29

(1) Everyone has duties to the community in which alone the free and full development of his personality is possible.

(2) In the exercise of his rights and freedoms, everyone shall be subject only to such limitations as are determined by law solely for the purpose of securing due recognition and respect for the rights and freedoms of others and of meeting the just requirements of morality, public order and the general welfare in a democratic society.

(3) These rights and freedoms may in no case be exercised contrary to the purposes and principles of the United Nations.

Article 30

Nothing in this Declaration may be interpreted as implying for any State, group or person any right to engage in any activity or to perform any act aimed at the destruction of any of the rights and freedoms set forth herein.

Source: United Nations, Resolution 217A (111). Passed by General Assembly, December 1948.

Appendix B: Relevant Internet Sites

Government Resources

Canadian Government Main Site: http://canada.gc.ca

Centers for Disease Control and Prevention: www.cdc.gov

National Institute of Drug Abuse: www.nida.nih.gov

National Institute of Mental Health: www.nimh.nih.gov

National Institutes of Health: www.nih.gov

Office of Violence Against Women, Department of Justice: www.doj.gov/ovw

Substance Abuse and Mental Health Services Administration: www.samhsa.gov

U.S. Bureau of Justice Statistics: www.bjs.gov

U.S. Census Bureau: www.census.gov

U.S. Department of Health and Human Services: www.os.dhhs.gov

Professional Advocacy

Ability, Disabilities Advocacy: www.ability.org.uk

Addiction Treatment Forum: www.atforum.com

Downtown Emergency Service Center (supportive housing): www.desc.org/index.html

Forum on Child and Family Statistics: www.childstats.gov

National Council on Aging: www.ncoa.org

Parents, Families and Friends for Lesbians and Gays: www.community.pflag.org

International Resources

Information for Practice from Around the World: http://blogs.nyu.edu/socialwork/ip

International Forum on Globalization: www.ifg.org

United Nations Children's Fund: www.unicef.org

United Nations Development Programme: www.undp.org

United Nations Enable: www.un.org/disabilities

Professional Links

Council on Social Work Education: www.cswe.org

Help Starts Here (by NASW): www.helpstartshere.org

Information for Practice: http://ifp.nyu.edu

International Association of Schools of Social Work: www.iassw.aiets.org

International Federation of Social Workers: www.ifsw.org

National Association of Social Workers: www.naswdc.org

Social Care Online: www.scie-socialcareonline.org.uk

Social Policy

Affordable Care Act: www.healthcare.gov

Center for Restorative Justice Peacemaking: www.ched.uma.edu/ssw/rjp

Child Welfare League: www.cwla.org

The Corporation: www.thecorporation.org

Disabled People's Association: www.dpa.org

Families Against Mandatory Minimums: www.famm.org

Family Violence Prevention Fund: http://endabuse.org

Hull House Museum (University of Illinois-Chicago): www.uic.edu/jaddams/hull

Influencing State Policy: www.statepolicy.org

Information on Labor and Inequality: www.robertreich.org

Institute for Women's Policy Research: www.iwpr.org

Moratorium Campaign Against the Death Penalty: www.MoratoriumCampaign.org

National Coalition Against Domestic Violence: www.ncadv.org

The Rape, Abuse and Incest National Network: www.rainn.org

Social Welfare Action Alliance: https://socialwelfareactionalliance.org

Violence Policy Center (gun control): www.vpc.org

War Resisters League: www.warresisters.org

World Health Organization: www.who.org

Human Rights

American Civil Liberties Union: www.aclu.org

Amnesty International: www.amnesty.org

Campaign for Equity-Restorative Justice: www.cerj.org

Child Welfare Information Gateway: www.childwelfare.gov/can

Disability Information: www.disabilityinfor.gov

Disabled People's International: www.dpi.org

Drug Policy Alliance Action Center: www.drugpolicy.org

Earth Policy Institute: www.earth-policy.org

Gay, Lesbian and Straight Education Network: www.glsen.org

Human Rights Watch: www.hrw.org

Minority Rights Group International: www.minorityrights.org

National Alliance on Mental Illness: www.nami.org

National Coalition Against Domestic Violence: www.ncadv.org

National Council of La Raza: www.nclr.org

National Gay and Lesbian Internet Task Force: www.ngltf.org

National Organization for Women: http://now.org

Office of Violence Against Women: www.ovw.usdoj.gov

Restorative Justice: www.restorativejustice.org

Restorative Justice Consortium: www.restorativejustice.org/uk

Signs of Homelessness: www.signsofhomelessness.org

Women's Human Rights: www.whrnet.org

The Environment

Alliance of Religions and Conservation: www.arcworld.org

Ecofeminism: www.ecofem.org

Ecological Social Work: www.ecosocialwork.org

Environmental Justice: www.epa.gov

Evangelical Environmental Movement: www.creationcare.org

Global Alliance for a Deep Ecology: www.ecosocialwork.org/index.html

Greenpeace: www.greenpeace.org

Indigenous Environmental Network: www.ienearth.org

Midwest High Speed Rail Association: www.midwesthsr.org

Sierra Club: www.sierraclub.org

Sustainable Communities Online: www.sustainable.org

Union of Concerned Scientists: www.ucsusa.org/global_warming

United Nations Environmental Programme: www.unep.org/greeneconomy

United States Environmental Protection Agency: www.epa.gov/environmentaljustice

United States High Speed Rail: www.ushsr.com

World Health Organization: www.who.int/en

Worldwatch Institute: Vision for a Sustainable World: www.worldwatch.org

World Wildlife Fund: www.worldwildlife.org

Index

About the Authors

Katherine S. van Wormer, MSSW, PhD, grew up in New Orleans, has a BA in English from the University of North Carolina, where she became active in the Civil Rights Movement and peace movement. She then moved to Northern Ireland and received a postgraduate degree in education from Queen's University. She taught English in Northern Ireland for 2 years and was active in the Irish Civil Rights Movement before returning to the United States to pursue graduate degrees in sociology and in social work much later on. As a social work practitioner, her specialty was alcoholism counseling, a specialization that provided her the opportunity to work for 2 years in Norway. Today, she is professor of social work at the University of Northern Iowa.

Since the 1990s, van Wormer has written around 20 books on various subjects related to various forms of social justice and oppression. Most relevant to the present text are the following: *Human Behavior and the Social Environment, Macro Level* (Oxford University Press, 2011, coauthored with Fred Besthorn); *Restorative Justice Today: Practical Applications* (2013, Sage, coedited with Lorenn Walker); *Confronting Oppression, Restoring Justice: From Policy Analysis to Social Action* (2012, CSWE Press, coauthored with Laura Kaplan & Cindy Juby); and *The Maid Narratives: Black Domestics and White Families in the Jim Crow South* (2012, LSU Press, coauthored with David W. Jackson III & Charletta Sudduth).

Dr. van Wormer's interest in policy and in the role of citizens in community organizing to accomplish social change is reflected in these writings as well as her community service work. On her university campus, she has been an active member of the University Committee on Sustainability and has worked unsuccessfully to integrate sustainability principles into the university core curriculum.

Rosemary J. Link, PhD, LISW, was born in St Albans, England, and gained her undergraduate honors degree in modern history and politics with sociology from the University of Southampton and her postgraduate diploma in applied social studies from the University of London. After 10 years as a school social worker then educational administrator, Dr. Link came to the University of Minnesota for her PhD in social work with a special interest in children's rights and social policy. Dr. Link served as a professor of social work and dean of graduate studies at Augsburg College, where she assisted in building the MA in leadership and gaining the accreditation of the

MSW and nursing programs. Rosemary is currently associate vice president for academic affairs at Simpson College, Iowa, where she is primarily responsible for building undergraduate and graduate programs for adult learners.

In addition to administration, Rosemary Link has chaired the Board of Southside Family Nurturing Center (www.ssfnc.org) for 6 years (2003–2009) and she has ongoing research interest in children's well-being and human rights. Dr. Link has served as external examiner to the University of the West Indies at Mona, Jamaica, and the University of Bharathair, Coimbatore. She has published numerous articles relating to child poverty, human rights, and social development and five books, including a study of child poverty together with Dr. Anthony Bibus, titled *When Children Pay* (CPAG, 2000); a textbook in human behavior together with coauthor Dr. Chathapuram Ramanathan, titled *All Our Futures* (Brooks/Cole, 1999); a curriculum design text together with Dr. Lynne Healy, titled *Models of International Curriculum in Social Work* (CSWE, 2005); a textbook in economic and social development *Human Behavior in a Just World* (Rowman & Littlefield, 2011) together with Dr Chathapuram Ramanathan; and coeditor of the *Handbook for International Social Work and Human Rights* (Oxford, 2012), which she coedited with Dr. Lynne Healy.

Dr. Link has taught on short programs in Slovenia, Mexico, India, and the United Kingdom. In 2005, Dr. Link received a State Department grant to serve as an educational ambassador in Slovenia, India, and Singapore. The project included working to set up exchanges for students of social work and human service and generating interactive video classrooms and curriculum with a global perspective. Dr. Link describes herself as an educational administrator, social worker, writer, and human rights advocate.

About the Contributors

Christina L. Erickson, MSW, PhD is an associate professor of social work and environmental studies at Augsburg College in Minneapolis, MN. After receiving her MSW, she practiced in community-based refugee services and in a medical neurology facility with older adults. She received her PhD at the University of Illinois at Chicago and has a special interest in how the natural environment and human experience interface. She has taught social work in China.

Suzanne McDevitt, MSW, PhD is an associate professor at Edinboro University of Pennsylvania, where she has taught since 2000. Previously she taught at the University of Northern Iowa, where was awarded the Regents Award for Faculty Excellence. Previously she served as manager of special projects at Allegheny County Children and Youth Services. Her current research focuses on food assistance and its impact on those who use it.